THOMAS COO

NORTH AMERICAN RAIL AND BUS GUIDE

SUMMER 1996 EDITION

Thomas Cook

CONTENTS

Published by Thomas Cook Publishing
The Thomas Cook Group Ltd
PO Box 227
Peterborough PE3 8BQ
United Kingdom

ISBN 0 906273 85 4

Front cover photograph reproduced by kind permission of Amtrak.
The publishers gratefully acknowledge the assistance of George Genge, Amtrak; Mme Bragdon, VIA Rail; Dave Atherton, Leisurail
Introductory pages edited by Kirk D. Schneider.
Original compilation by John Gage.
Timetable pages edited and compiled by Peter Tremlett and Peter Bass.
Maps by John Gage.
Managing editor: Stephen York
Cover design by Darwell Holland.
Typeset by Thomas Cook Publishing
Printed in Great Britain by Bell & Bain Ltd, Glasgow

IMPORTANT NOTE

New schedules for the current year are not released by some transport operators until early summer, after the press date of this publication. Where schedules have been released before the date of going to press, the timetables in this book are based on those schedules, which may be provisional in some cases. Timetables of operators whose summer schedules were not released at time of going to press are based on 1995 schedules amended wherever possible in accordance with latest information received. Even published schedules may change during the course of the summer period due to circumstances not foreseen at the time they were published or other operational reasons. *Readers are therefore strongly advised to reconfirm all transport timings locally with the operator concerned at the time of travel for each journey.*

INTRODUCTION

This is the third edition of the *Thomas Cook North American Rail & Bus Guide*. As before, it contains the most up-to-date timetables available for trains and long-distance buses in North America this summer, collected in one easy-reference volume for the benefit of independent travellers, with useful information and advice on tickets and passes, flights, public transport and sightseeing in major cities, and other travel details.

This year's edition has been enhanced by the inclusion of still more places in the Major Cities chapter. The chapters on Travelling North America by Rail, Travelling North America by Bus and Major Cities have been extensively revised this year by **Kirk D. Schneider**. Kirk Schneider has toured North America extensively by train and bus for over 15 years and is a professional transit marketing and planning consultant. He is the author of *California by Train, Bus and Ferry*.*

More and more people visit Canada and the USA each year. Hardly surprising really, as both these large and diverse countries contain thousands of places and attractions for the visitor to explore.

Fly-drive and coach tour holidays have become very popular in recent years, but with over 150 years experience in arranging holidays, we at Thomas Cook know that our customers are as diverse as the types of travel and holidays we arrange for them. We know that for many, much of the enjoyment of travel is meeting and mixing with the local population and getting the real 'feel' of the country, an experience frequently missed by those cocooned in their cars and coaches.

Contrary to popular myth, Canada and the USA have excellent public transport systems, which can be both an economical and enjoyable way to get around these countries. In most cities you will find a comprehensive urban transit system, many with a combination of buses, subways, trolleys (trams), suburban rail networks and rapid transit systems.

For longer-distance travel, there are the national railroad networks (Amtrak in the USA and VIA Rail in Canada). Both offer frequent services on major corridors such as Washington–New York–Boston and Los Angeles–San Diego, as well as long-distance trains operating once a day to several times a week. Buses, too, have nationwide networks such as Greyhound Lines of Canada, and Greyhound and Trailways in the USA, and also many smaller, more localised companies. Or, if you are pushed for time and don't mind missing a bit of the scenery, you can cover the longer distances by air.

The choice is yours. This guide incorporates the timetables of all the main North American long-distance rail and bus operators which are published every two months in the *Thomas Cook Overseas Timetable* (available on subscription or as single copies from Thomas Cook Publishing). With its comprehensive index and easy-to-use route maps, it helps you to find the services you need in order to plan your own itinerary and go where you want to go when you want to go.

To help you find your feet when you arrive, we've featured main gateway cities, with information about airports and connections to the downtown areas and other places of interest.

Rail and bus timetables can change, and furthermore there are some cases where the operators have not yet published their Summer '96 schedules. It's sensible to always follow the golden rule of travel by public transport, and check by phone with the operating company for latest timings before setting out on a particular trip. We give telephone numbers of the relevant transport operators in the footnotes of each timetable and in the Major Cities chapter.

Now for the crunch question. Surely it must work out more expensive to put together a trip like this, rather than buy an 'off the peg' package? The answer to this one is that by being in control yourself, your holiday can be as cheap or expensive as you care to make it. If you are on a tight budget, you can save on accommodation costs by travelling overnight (although this does require a bit of stamina after a while!). Instead of buying individual tickets for each sector of your trip, you can invest in one (or more) of the wide array of rail, bus and air passes available – this guide tells you about them and helps you to pick those best suited to your needs.

With careful planning, and this book as your guide, you can have the holiday you want, visiting the places you want to see, at a price you can afford. Bon voyage!

---

*(ISBN 1-879942-01-1), available in the UK from Rapid Transit Publications, 37 Wellesley Road, Ilford, Essex IG1 4JX, or by post at US$18.95 (inc. p & p, add US$6.00 for airmail) from California Transit Publications, PO Box 6427, Whittier CA 90609, USA; or e-mail the author at 76016.41@CompuServe.com.

TRAVELLING NORTH AMERICA BY RAIL

The various passes mentioned in this section can mostly be purchased only outside North America. They are available from official International Sales Agents; in the UK you can contact LEISURAIL, PO Box 113, Peterborough PE3 8HY, tel. (01733) 335913, or your local branch of Thomas Cook. Dollar prices (where shown) are converted into pounds sterling using exchange rates applicable at the time of booking.

USA – AMTRAK

Passes and fares

Amtrak rail passes

Amtrak rail passes are available to anyone who is permanently resident outside the United States. A variety of different options is available which covers the entire system and smaller geographical areas: the complete set of prices and options is given in the grid below. The passes are valid for travel in Coach Class; however, upgrades to Club Service, Custom Class or Sleeping Car service are available on payment of the appropriate supplement (see 'Accommodation', overleaf, for an explanation of these terms).

To use the pass, you must take it to an Amtrak ticket desk in the station, where you will be given a ticket for the journey of your choice. Most trains require advance reservations. It is important to make reservations as early as possible (preferably before arriving in the USA), especially for popular sleeping car accommodation. You must obtain a valid ticket before starting your journey (the pass itself is not actually a ticket – it merely entitles you to one). Without a valid ticket you will be charged the regular fare on the train and may have to pay a surcharge for being without a ticket.

The **National** pass covers the entire Amtrak network. The dividing line between the **East** and **West** passes is the Chicago–Memphis–New Orleans rail line, which is covered on either pass. Another option is the **Far West** pass, which covers an area to the west of an imaginary line stretching from Wolf Point to Denver and El Paso. The (new for 1996) **Northeast** pass covers the area from Montréal to Virginia as far west as Buffalo and Harrisburg. The **Coastal** Passes cover only the coastal routes between Seattle and San Diego (**Coastal West**), and from Montréal to Miami (**Coastal East**). The adult prices shown above are valid during the 1996 season. Peak period rates apply 17 June–21 August. Children aged 2–15 pay 50% of the adult price; children under 2 travel free.

Amtrak special domestic fares

Amtrak's **All-Aboard America** special domestic fares offer Coach Class travel with up to 3 stopovers in one, two or three zones (dividing lines between zones are Wolf Point–Denver–El Paso and Chicago–Memphis–New Orleans). Travel must be completed within 45 days from the start of your journey. The adult prices shown below are valid during the 1996 season. Peak period rates apply 14 June–18 August and 13 December–5 January 1997. Seniors aged 62 and over pay 85% of the adult price. Children aged

All-Aboard America fares

(Prices in US$)	Off-Peak	Peak
1 Zone	$198	$228
2 Zones	$258	$318
3 Zones	$318	$378

Amtrak USA rail passes

(Prices in US$)	Off-Peak		Peak	
	15 days	30 days	15 days	30 days
National Rail Pass	$245	$350	$355	$440
Northeast Rail Pass	$155	$195	$175	$205
East Rail Pass	$185	$240	$205	$265
West Rail Pass	$215	$290	$265	$330
Far West Rail Pass	$185	$235	$205	$265
Coastal Rail Passes	n/a	$205	n/a	$235

2–15 pay 50% of the adult price; children under 2 travel free.

International Gateway Fares

IGFs are special reduced fares for travel between certain cities, offered only to international travellers who make their reservations outside the USA. Some restrictions apply to use, e.g. Metroliners cannot be used in peak hours midweek. See grid below. (Note that if bought by themselves, these low fares would normally attract an extra booking fee: Leisurail, for instance, add a £15 fee to a booking which totals less than £300 in value.)

Other Amtrak offers

Amtrak's **Air–Rail Plan**, created in partnership with United Airlines, offers one-way Coach rail by Amtrak with up to three stopovers and one-way Coach Air by United Airlines and United Express, allowing for connections, but no stopovers. Travel must be completed within 180 days of the start of your journey. The adult prices shown in the grid below are valid during the 1996 season. Peak period rates apply 24 May– 14 September and 13 December–4 January 1997. Seniors 62 and over pay 85% of the adult price. Children aged 2–15 pay 50% of the adult price; children under 2 travel free.

Amtrak's **Auto–Train** is a unique service for those who want to travel by train from Washington DC to Florida – and take their cars along (some vehicle restrictions apply). The train travels between Lorton, Virginia (south of Washington) and Sanford, Florida (one-half hour from Walt Disney World). The train leaves each end point at 1530 and arrives at the other at 0900 the next day. Coach and First Class sleeping car accommodation is available. Only passengers with automobiles are permitted.

Accommodation

Two different types of rolling stock are to be found operating Amtrak's long-distance trains. The more modern, double-deck 'Superliners' were introduced back in 1979,

International Gateway Fares

(Prices in US$) **Route**	**Conventional trains**	**Metroliner trains**	**% saving on normal fares**
Boston–New York	$34	$N/A	– 47%
Boston–Philadelphia	$49	$59	38% 31%
Boston–Philadelphia/Washington	$49	$59	43% 44%
New York–Philadelphia	$25	$35	50% 48%
New York–Baltimore/BWI Airport	$40	$50	46% 49%
New York–Washington	$43	$55	48% 48%
Philadelphia–Baltimore/BWI Airport	$20	$25	44% 57%
Philadelphia–Washington	$24	$29	44% 61%

Amtrak Air–Rail Plan

(Prices in US$)	**Off-Peak**	**Peak**
Transcontinental (East Zone to West Zone)	$431	$492
Midwest-East (between Midwest and East Zones)	$309	$359
Midwest-West (between Midwest and West Zones)	$337	$409
Mountain-East (between Mountain and East Zones)	$420	$470
Mountain-West (between Mountain and West Zones)	$292	$376
Midwest-Mountain (between Midwest and Mountain Zones)	$259	$299
East Coast (within East Zone)	$309	$353
Midwest (within Midwest Zone)	$298	$331
West Coast (within West Zone)	$214	$248

and have proved to be exceptionally popular with the American public. Amtrak has recently received new Superliners, which are now in service; new Viewliner cars are beginning to replace the older 'Single Level' fleet.

In stations in New York, Chicago, Philadelphia and Washington DC, Amtrak's Metropolitan Lounges are available for use by Club service and sleeping car passengers. These private waiting lounges provide an oasis of calm in which to relax before commencing your journey.

Coach Class seating

Most coaches now have reclining seats, folding trays and personal reading lights. Long-distance trains have footrests as well. Coach passengers are entitled to use the dining and lounge cars. At least one WC is available in each car, situated at the end (or on the lower levels on the Superliners). **Metroliners** are premium all-reserved business-class trains, which feature all the facilities of Coach Class seating and in addition have footrests and legrests which fold out from under each seat.

Club Service

First Class Club Service (available on selected Northeast Corridor and Metroliner services) features reserved deluxe seating accommodation, hot towels and free newspapers. Complimentary meals and beverages (including a glass of wine) are served at your seat by an attendant. All First Class passengers are welcome in Amtrak's Metropolitan Lounges in Washington DC, New York and Philadelphia.

Custom Class

Custom Class Service (available on selected trains) offers reserved, deluxe seating, with a complimentary newspaper and non-alcoholic beverage available from the on-board café.

Roomette (single level)

A Roomette is a first-class enclosed compartment for use by one adult. An armchair by day converts to a single bed that folds out from the wall for night-time use. The room contains bathroom facilities (to use the WC at night the bed must be raised) and storage space for two average-sized suitcases.

Meals and complimentary tea or coffee are included. Room size: 2m x 1.1m.

Bedroom (single level)

Private first-class compartments designed for use by two adults (or one adult and two small children). Bedrooms have two fold-down beds, one above the other (access to the upper berth is by ladder), containing enclosed bathroom facilities which include a sink, mirror, and hanging space. Storage is available to accommodate two average-sized suitcases. Meals and complimentary tea or coffee are included. Room size: 2.3m x 1.6m.

Single Slumbercoach (single level)

Slumbercoach rooms are designed for budget-minded travellers who require sleeping car privacy and comfort. A single Slumbercoach provides one seat for daytime travel, with a bed which folds down from the wall for sleeping.

Bathroom facilities are included, as well as a mirror and reading lights. Storage space is minimal with room for two small suitcases only. Meals are *not* included. Room size 1.2m x 1.1m.

Double Slumbercoach (single level)

This enclosed room provides two single seats (facing each other) for daytime use, and two bunk beds which fold down from the wall. Facilities included as per single slumbercoach. Room size 1.8m x 1.1m.

Economy bedroom (Superliner)

Designed for use by one or two adults, and located on both upper and lower levels of the car. The room features two windowside reclining seats for daytime travel, which slide together to form the lower berth, and an upper berth which folds out of the wall. Other features include a large picture window, fold-down table, wardrobe, mirrors, and reading lights.

There are no WC or shower facilities within the room, but they can be found on the lower level of the car. The room can only accommodate two small overnight bags which will fit under the seats. Larger suitcases can be stored in a baggage area on the lower level. Meals and complimentary beverages are included. Room size 2m x 1.1m.

Deluxe bedroom (Superliner)

The largest accommodation on the Superliners, located on the upper level, and providing comfortable facilities for two adults. All have large picture windows, and by day a sofa and single armchair. At night a berth folds down out of the wall, and the sofa converts into a wider sleeping berth. The room also features WC facilities and a shower. Storage space is available for two average-sized suitcases. Meals and complimentary beverages are included. Room size 2m x 2.3m.

Family bedroom (Superliner)

There is one family bedroom in each carriage, extending the full width of the car, with windows on both sides. Each family bedroom will accommodate two adults and two children. The room contains a long sofa and two child seats for daytime use. These convert to an upper and lower berth for adults and two short berths for the children. Storage space is available for two to three suitcases. There are no WC facilities within the room, but they are located only a short distance away. Meals and complimentary tea and coffee are included. Room size 1.6m x 2.9m.

Special bedroom (Superliner)

There is one special bedroom in each Superliner sleeping car, designed to accommodate a disabled passenger and a travelling companion. There is ample space for access by a wheelchair throughout – including the WC.

The special bedroom is located on the lower level and extends the full width of the car. It contains two reclining seats which face each other during the day, with two single berths folding out of the wall for sleeping. Bathroom facilities are located at one end of the room, separated by a curtain. Also provided: fold-down tray, attendant call button, and storage space for two suitcases. Meals are included and will be brought to the room by the car attendant if required. Room size 2.9m x 2m.

Lounge cars

These cars have been designed especially for sightseeing, and have large picture windows which extend partly over the roof. They are often the social centre of the train,providing a meeting place for passengers. A video may be shown, or a local guide may provide commentary about the area you are passing through. Drinks may be purchased from the bar, most of which have a 'happy hour'.

Dining cars

A full meal service is available on all long-distance trains, and the quality can be of a very high standard, often featuring specialities of the region. Special dietary requirements can be catered for, although you are required to give 72 hours notice to Amtrak by telephoning (toll-free) 1-800-USA-RAIL when in the USA. These arrangements can only be made in the USA. Advance dinner reservations are normally taken so that the meal is ready to be served on your arrival in the dining car.

Other information

Reservations

Amtrak advise passengers to reserve all types

of accommodation as far in advance as possible, and provide a toll-free reservations number for use in the USA (1-800-USA-RAIL). Reservations are mandatory on certain services shown in this guide, and for all Club and sleeping car passengers.

Checked baggage

Passengers are allowed to check in up to 150lb of baggage free of charge, provided no single item exceeds 75lb. Special items such as surf boards, scuba equipment, musical instruments, etc., are normally subject to a $5 handling charge. Free assistance with baggage is provided at most major stations by Redcaps (porters), although most expect a tip.

Smoking

Cigars and pipes are prohibited at all times. Cigarettes may be smoked only in specially designated areas. Smoking accommodation is limited and passengers are requested to vacate the area if they do not wish to smoke in order to allow access to others. Smoking is generally prohibited altogether on trains whose total journey time is less than about 6 hours.

CANADA – VIA RAIL

Passes and fares

VIA Rail offers the system-wide **Canrailpass**, which as its name implies covers all of VIA's services. It entitles you to Economy Class travel, but you can upgrade to VIA 1 or to a sleeping car on payment of the appropriate supplement. The pass is valid for 12 days' actual travel within a period of 30 days (with option to purchase 3 extra days). Included with the Canrailpass is a 'HELLO! phone pass', worth $15 in long-distance calls, and also discounts at any of the 174 hotels in the Choice Hotels Canada chain and a 15% discount on Gray Line sightseeing tours. Special rates apply for seniors 60 and over and young adventurers between 2 and 24.

VIA Rail also offer a Canrailpass option in association with **Hertz Rent-a-car**. This includes 3 days' car hire in a mid-sized vehicle within the same 30-day period as the validity of the pass. This upgrade is only available to those over 25.

Passengers intending to use one of these passes should note that they are not valid for travel on certain specified dates within the Easter, Christmas, and New Year holiday periods.

If you are just intending to travel across Canada from east to west or vice versa, it may be cheaper to purchase a Canrailpass than the Economy Class single fares. For 1996 the high season is 15 May–15 October; low season is 6 January–14 May and 16 October–14 December.

Canrailpass		
(Prices in CA$)	Low Season	High Season
Adult	$365	$535
Youth/Senior	$329	$482
Extra days (maximum 3)		
Adult	$30	$47
Youth/Senior	$27	$42
Canrailpass plus Hertz		
Adult	$506	$706
Youth/Senior	$470	$653

Discounts can be obtained on regular Coach Class tickets by travelling off-peak, avoiding Fridays and Sundays; this can reduce ordinary fares by between 25% and 40%. These discounts may require purchase 5–7 days in advance.

Accommodation

Economy Class

Economy Class offers reclining seats, and folding trays, with WC facilities located at the end of the car. It provides a good basic standard of accommodation, with plenty of legroom and panoramic window views. There are normally four seats per row (two either side of the centre aisle).

VIA 1 Class

VIA 1 is only available within the Québec City–Windsor corridor. This first-class service provides wider, more comfortable reclining seats and full at-seat meal service with complimentary alcoholic beverages. VIA 1 Panorama Lounges are also available at stations in Toronto, Montréal, and Ottawa.

Silver and Blue Class

This first-class accommodation is available on the route of the Toronto–Vancouver *Canadian*, a train which has recently been restored to its original sleek 1950s style, and conveys a unique atmosphere of train travel during that era. The Park Car provides spectacular views from the observation dome; below this are the Bullet Lounge and Mural

Lounge, where passengers can relax in comfortable armchairs.

Easterly Class
This is the name for first-class accommodation on the route of the Montréal–Halifax *Ocean* and Montréal–Gaspe *Chaleur*, which convey a unique atmosphere as casual and cosy as a 'B & B' in the country. The Park Car provides spectacular views from the observation dome; below this are the Bullet Lounge and Mural Lounge, where passengers can relax in comfortable armchairs.

Single bedroom
A one-person room which affords individual privacy. A seat for day travel is converted into a sleeping berth for the night, and basic bathroom facilities are also provided. A shower is situated at the end of the car, and towels, shampoo, soap, etc., are provided.

Double bedroom
This accommodation is more spacious than the single bedroom and is designed for two adults. Seating is again converted into a berth for the night, as well as a bed which folds out from the wall. Basic WC facilities are inside the room; a shower is located at the end of the car. The same toiletries are provided as in the single bedroom.

Double berths
During the day a section is two couch-style seats facing each other, and at night they convert to an upper and lower berth, with a heavy-duty curtain screen for privacy. A section can be purchased separately as an upper or lower berth for one person. A WC is available at the end of each car.

Skyline cars
There's a warm, friendly mood in the Skyline Lounge – for games and socialising over a drink. Steps lead up to the Skyline Dome for 360 degree views of the passing countryside. Guests can purchase meals in the Skyline Café (on the *Canadian* only), or from the take-out counter and bar to enjoy at their seats.

Dining cars
On the *Canadian*, Silver and Blue Class includes meals in the spectacular art-deco dining car for breakfast, lunch or any of the 3 evening sittings – 'Sunset', 'Twilight' or 'Moonlight' service. Cocktails, a choice of fine wines, domestic and imported, arrive from the curved 50s style steward's bar. A new menu is presented at every meal – soups and salads, cold plates and superb hot entrees, wonderful breads and desserts. The *Ocean*'s dining car features hearty, home-style meals.

Other information

Reservations
Many of VIA's principal services are heavily patronised; reservations are recommended for coach class travel, and are essential for VIA 1 and sleeping car passengers. These should be made as far in advance as possible by phoning 1-800-561-8630 (toll free), or from outside Canada + 1 416 366 8411. Or in the UK contact LEISURAIL, directly (tel. 01733 335913) or through any Thomas Cook branch.

Checked baggage
If you are travelling with heavy luggage and will not need access to it during your journey, you may use the checked baggage facility available at most stations. You may check up to 45kg per adult without any charge. You must, however, check baggage at least 30 minutes before the scheduled departure of the train. VIA Rail employees may refuse to lift any single article in excess of 34kg.

Smoking
VIA Rail does not permit smoking on any of its trains travelling wholly within the Québec City–Windsor corridor or in any dining car. Smoking is permitted on long-distance trains in specified areas of the coach or lounge cars, and within fully-enclosed sleeping car accommodation. Smoking is banned at most stations.

Special trains

Two scenic train services offer the equivalent of a luxury cruise through the Canadian Rockies and some of the world's most spectacular scenery can be viewed from comfortable observation cars. **The Skeena** is a new VIA Rail service which makes a two-day journey through the Canadian Rockies from Jasper to Prince Rupert; passengers spend the overnight in a hotel in Prince George. The famous **Rocky Mountaineer**, privately operated, also spends two days traversing the Rockies along a variety of routes between Vancouver, Calgary, via Banff, Kamloops and Jasper. LEISURAIL are UK agents for both services and can provide full details and fares.

TRAVELLING NORTH AMERICA BY BUS

GENERAL INFORMATION

The various passes mentioned in this section can mostly be purchased only outside North America. They are available from official international sales agents; in the UK you can contact LEISURAIL, PO Box 113, Peterbrough PE3 8HY, tel. (01733) 335913, or your local branch of Thomas Cook. Prices of passes shown here in dollars will be converted into pounds sterling using exchange rates applicable at the time of booking.

Generally, reservations are not required, and you simply turn up, preferably about half an hour before the bus leaves. Many long-distance journeys involve a change (or several changes) of vehicle en route. From New York to Los Angeles for example, the bus you board in New York, although signed 'Los Angeles', will not go through all the way. Bear this in mind and make sure your luggage gets transferred onto the same bus as you at change points.

All passes are for use by the purchaser only and tickets are not transferable. You may be asked to show identification such as a passport or driving licence. A pass allows you to stop off anywhere just as often or as long as you wish, provided travel is completed within the time limit. Initially, the pass must be presented to a terminal, station ticket agent, or driver, who will validate it when he/she issues your first ticket.

There are hundreds of bus operators in North America, but many are quite small, local companies serving a relatively compact area. Obviously vehicle types vary according to the operator, but with the vast majority of fleets, buses are comfortable and are equipped with modern conveniences, which enable you to travel round the clock. Rest stops are still made every few hours, to stretch your legs, and meal stops are scheduled as near as possible to normal dining times.

PASSES

USA – Greyhound Lines

An **Ameripass** entitles you to travel over Greyhound's entire route system in the United States plus the routes of over 50 connecting bus lines. It's also valid on Greyhound routes from Seattle to Vancouver and Boston/New York to Montréal, and on Greyhound Lines of Canada between Buffalo or Detroit to Toronto. Prices are as shown in the grid below; a 4-day ticket costing £65 is valid only from Monday to Thursday. Prices are slightly higher if purchased in the USA.

The **Go Hostelling USA Double Deal Travel Pass** is a combination of the Ameripasses and vouchers exchangable for a night's accommodation (in a shared room) at any one of more than 130 hostels coast-to-coast belonging to Hostelling International (the International Youth Hostelling Federation). Go Hostelling USA Pass includes: your Ameripass; your first hostel reservation; hostel vouchers (valid for an extended period of three times the length of your bus pass); tourism pack and more. HI membership is not included. Prices in brackets in the grid below are for the HI package and Greyhound Pass combined during high season, July–September. Subtract £10–£20 for low season rates.

Greyhound Ameripass	
4 days	£65
5 days	£80
7 days	£105
15 days	£145 (£320)
30 days	£195 (£540)
60 days	£325

Greyhound Lines of Canada

The **Canada Pass** permits unlimited travel on all scheduled services of Greyhound Lines of Canada operating west of Toronto/Ottawa plus Voyageur Colonial's routes in Ontario and Québec, Brewsters between Banff and Jasper, Saskatchewan Transportation between Alsask and Saskatoon, Adirondack Trailways from New York to Toronto, VIA Rail Canada between Ottawa or Toronto to Montréal and Greyhound Lines Inc. between New York and Montréal and between Seattle and Vancouver. Prices are shown on the next page.

The **Canada Pass Plus** allows travel on the above routes plus those of Orleans Express (Montréal–Québec City–Rivière du Loup), Acadian Lines (Amherst–Halifax) and SMT Lines (Rivière du Loup–Fredericton–Moncton –Amherst, Rivière du Loup–Fredericton–St John–Moncton–Amherst (ferry)–Charlottetown). No daily extensions or child reductions

Greyhound Canada passes		
	Canada	Canada Plus
7 days	£99	n/a
15 days	£135	£165
30 days	£175	£225
60 days	£230	£290
Go Canada Budget Travel Pass		
15 days	£315	£345
30 days	£470	£520
Domestic Canada Pass		
7 days		CA$199
15 days		CA$259
30 days		CA$349
60 days		CA$449

are available on the Canada Passes.

The **Go Canada Budget Travel Pass** is a combination of the Canada Passes and vouchers exchangable for a night's accommodation (in a shared room) at any one of more than 70 hostels from coast-to-coast belonging to Hostelling International (the International Youth Hostelling Federation). A Go Canada Budget Travel Pass includes: your Canada Pass; your first hostel reservation; hostel vouchers (valid for an extended period of time three times the length of your bus pass); souvenir T-shirt; phone-card; tourism pack and more. HI membership is not included.

Greyhound Lines of Canada also has a **Domestic Canada Pass** which can be purchased in Canada. It must be purchased 7 days in advance of travel and is valid for travel on Greyhound Lines of Canada routes and Saskatchewan Transportation between Alsask and Saskatoon and Greyhound Lines between Vancouver and Seattle/SeaTac Airport, Washington.

FLIGHTS AND AIR PASSES

In this section we aim to provide some practical information on air travel both to and from North America, and within the countries themselves. Crossing the Atlantic affords some of the cheapest air fares in the world, on a cost-per-kilometre basis. Due to the number of carriers available on these routes, competition is fierce, and prices low, which can only be good news for consumers. Practically all travel agents now offer competitive fares, but it can still pay to shop around and obtain quotes. If you book with an ABTA bonded agent, you will at least receive compensation should the carrier or agent fail. Thomas Cook or any other good travel agent should be able to assist you in making the best choice.

FLYING THE ATLANTIC

Before deciding which airline to opt for, we would advise you to work out the itinerary for your holiday in advance. This will then dictate the most suitable type of ticket for you. For example, if you intend to start and finish your holiday in New York, and do not intend to use any internal US flights during your stay, then the cheapest possible return ticket to New York would be the best for you. You may, though, decide to fly into New York, travel by train to San Francisco, and then return to the UK from there, in which case you would require an 'open-jaw' ticket. This enables you to fly into one destination and return from another, although you must specify which cities at the time of booking. Another itinerary may consist of flying to and returning from the same city, but combining internal airline flights with rail or bus travel within the USA. One of the most cost-effective ways to do this is to buy a series of air coupons before you go, which allows you to travel on your chosen carrier's domestic network; however, many carriers require you to fly the Atlantic with them in order to qualify for these coupons at lower cost rates. Travel agents are more likely to view you seriously as a potential client if you present a detailed (but flexible) itinerary than if you just wander in and ask about the cheapest ticket. When planning your itinerary, bear in mind that flights are generally cheaper mid-week than at weekends.

The airlines flying the Atlantic fall into three basic categories: US, British and Others. Some of the cheapest point-to-point fares are with international carriers who fly from their own country to the USA and Canada via London. The US and Canadian carriers view their transatlantic routes as showpieces and often place their most highly trained crews and best equipment on them. Whilst their main aim is undoubtedly to attract the business-class passenger, they still aim to provide an above average level of service and comfort to all clients.

At the end of the day, the carrier which will suit you best is often a matter of personal preference. If your transatlantic flight is to be followed immediately by a connecting domestic flight, it's worthwhile considering using the same airline for both, as apart from the possible financial advantages, the transfer from one to the other will almost certainly be smoother and probably within the same terminal.

Whichever airline you fly, you may wish to consider joining its frequent flyer club. Even if you only intend to make one transatlantic trip, your accumulated points stay valid for a long time (often indefinitely). Normally it takes only two roundtrip transatlantic journeys before you qualify for an award. Even if you don't plan to return to the USA, you may change your mind at a later stage and regret not having joined. The other major advantage is that members of frequent flyer clubs don't get 'bumped' in the event of the flight being 'full'.

Being 'bumped' is trade slang for 'denied boarding' (due to overbooking), and the practice is becoming more common. Officially, the 'error' is invariably the fault of the ubiquitous computer; in reality the widespread practice of overbooking by a certain percentage is quite deliberate, and is calculated on the average number of 'no-shows' for that flight. The airlines cannot really be blamed for protecting themselves against those who are too inconsiderate to cancel unwanted reservations, but this is of little comfort to you if you arrive holding a valid ticket and have a reservation, but are denied boarding. One compensating factor is that US airlines often award worthwhile cash sums to passengers willing to give up their seats in this situation. A mini-auction may take place, whereby the airline starts by offering compensation of $50 to any passenger willing to give up their seat, and some people come forward. If there are still too many people wanting to fly, they increase the compensation to $100, and so on. If you are not in a rush to travel it may be worth your while to take advantage of this. You get a guaranteed seat on the next available flight, and if this involves an overnight wait, hotel accommodation will be provided for you.

DOMESTIC AIRLINES

Internal flights in North America are cheap by world standards. As well as the major carriers, smaller airlines have appeared; these usually offer basic services (i.e. cheap flights without meals or any other frills). Good examples of these include Kiwi, Reno and Valuejet. They offer excellent value-for-money point-to-point fares. Two larger domestic carriers of this kind, offering greater route networks, are Southwest and America West.

Flying in America is quite informal; you generally just turn up at the airport and get on the next flight heading where you want to go, like using a bus or a train. You don't have to book in advance using a travel agent, as the airlines have competitive 'walk-up' fares (some of the smaller 'value' carriers actually charge extra to those booking by telephone). With the smaller carriers you may not even receive a boarding pass, let alone a seat number. You just turn up at the aircraft and sit wherever there is a spare seat.

Airports in America can be very confusing. The terminal you need will generally depend on the carrier used, but can also be influenced by your destination and whether you are arriving or departing, so always check in advance from which terminal your flight is leaving. New York's JFK, for instance, has no fewer than nine separate terminal buildings. A United flight may arrive at one terminal and a connecting United flight may leave from another.

If you are planning to take several internal flights and are using a system of airpass coupons, do check that the cities you wish to visit are included on the carrier's domestic route network. This particularly applies to some smaller towns. Sometimes the major carriers have a separate 'feeder' airline, which normally employs small propellor-driven aircraft between major 'hubs' and local airports within the catchment area. Examples are Continental Airlines (who use Continental Express) and American Airlines (American Eagle). You may find that each area only has one feeder service carrier. Even the major carriers don't serve everywhere, so when you buy an airline's airpass coupons, make sure that the airline (or its subsidiary) actually flies where you want to go.

MAJOR CITIES

In this chapter we present a selection of North America's most-visited cities, with details of their public transit facilities and their terminals for longer-distance travel by air, rail and bus. Major sightseeing locations are listed, with details of access by public transport. The lists are not exhaustive and most cities have many more worthwhile sights than we have space for; always call at the Visitor Center or its equivalent to review all the possibilities.

Where no area code is quoted in phone numbers, use the code given for the relevant city when calling from outside the area. In **emergencies**, the number for police, ambulance or fire service is simply **911** in all cities.

For the boundaries and differences in hours of th day of the time zones quoted, see the map on p. 64.

All dollar amounts in this chapter are US$ unless CA$ (Canadian dollars) are specified.

ATLANTA

Area code 404
Time zone: Eastern Time

From humble beginnings as the terminus of the first Western & Atlantic Railroad line, and consequently (if not very imaginatively) originally named 'Terminus', Atlanta quickly grew to become the social, cultural and economic capital of the South. Despite destruction in 1864 during the Civil War, Atlanta has retained this position, acquiring fame along the way as the birthplace and home of worldwide household names as diverse as they are famous, including Gone With the Wind (based here), Martin Luther King Jr. (born here), Coca Cola (invented here) and Cable News Network (CNN) (headquarters here). In 1996, Atlanta will add another string to its bow, as host of the XXIII Summer Olympiad. Welcome South Visitors Center located on the street level of Atlanta Gift Mart (200 Spring St at International Blvd, 224-2000 – MARTA North Rail Line to Peachtree Center).

Getting around

CENTRE: The Metropolitan Atlanta Rapid Transit Authority (MARTA) operates a modern 62 km rapid rail system (still being extended – three new stations: Buckhead, Medical Center and Dunwoody will open in June 1996) comprising two lines (the North-South line and the East-West line) which intersect at Five Points in downtown Atlanta, and a comprehensive network of 150 bus routes throughout the City and surrounding area. A flat one-way fare system ($1.50, or 10 bulk tokens – from RideStores only – $15) applies, with free transfers (which must be obtained at the start of the journey) for bus-to-bus, bus-to-rail and rail-to-bus.

SURROUNDING AREAS: The MARTA network operates throughout Fulton and DeKalb counties, resulting in a coverage approximately corresponding to the area contained within the I-285 ring road. On journeys which extend beyond the boundaries of the above counties, the flat-fare is $2.25. To the north-east, **Greenville** is reached by Amtrak trains and by Greyhound Lines buses (both services continue to Charlotte, Washington and New York; bus services call additionally at Richmond); to the east, **Augusta** and **Columbia** are served by Southeastern Stages buses; in the south-eastern quadrant **Macon** and **Savannah** are reached by Greyhound Lines/Georgia Trailways buses, and **Jacksonville** by Greyhound Lines; to the south **Tallahassee** by C & H Bus Lines and Greyhound Lines; to the south-west and west, **Columbus** and **Montgomery** are reached by Greyhound Lines (services continue to Mobile and New Orleans, and to Jackson, Shreveport and Dallas), and **Birmingham** by Amtrak (service continues to New Orleans) and by Greyhound Lines (services continue to Jackson, Shreveport and Dallas, and to Memphis). To the north-west, **Chattanooga** and **Nashville** can be accessed by Greyhound Lines.

Main transport centres

Hartsfield Atlanta International Airport (ATL) – 14 km S (MARTA South Rail Line to Airport): One of the world's busiest airports and major domestic and international hub. One terminal serves all airlines. **Atlanta Amtrak/ Brookwood Station** (5 km north of Downtown on Peachtree Street – MARTA North Rail Line to Arts Center, then MARTA bus 23): For all Amtrak services. **Metro Atlanta Transport Center** (Greyhound-Trailways Bus Terminal) (81 International Boulevard – MARTA North Rail Line to Peachtree Center, or MARTA bus 13). Serves C & H Bus Lines, Greyhound Lines, Southeastern Stages.

Sightseeing by public transport

CENTRE: **Buckhead Village**, Peachtree, Roswell & Paces Ferry Rds, 266-9209 (MARTA North Rail Line to Buckhead – opens June 1996). Atlanta's premier shopping, dining and entertainment district. **Martin Luther**

King Jr Historic District (MARTA Rail Lines to Five Points then MARTA bus 3). Includes Martin Luther King Jr. Center for Nonviolent Social Change (449 Auburn Ave, NE, 524-1956) Self-guided tour includes Dr King's grave, birth home and Ebenezer Baptist Church. **Peachtree Center**, 225 Peachtree St NE, 654-1255) (MARTA North Rail Line to Peachtree Center). Over 80 shops and restaurants in close proximity to all major downtown hotels. **Scitrek – the Science and Technology Museum of Atlanta**, 395 Piedmont Ave, 522-5500 (MARTA North Rail Line to Civic Center then walk two blocks east on Ralph McGill Blvd, left on Piedmont). More than 100 interactive exhibits. **Underground Atlanta**, Peachtree at Alabama St, 523-2311 – MARTA Rail Lines to Five Points) Six-block urban subterranean marketplace featuring over 100 specialty shops, restaurants, and entertainment. **World of Coca-Cola**, 55 Martin Luther King, Jr, Dr., 676-5151 (MARTA Rail Lines to Five Points). The story of Coca-Cola – past, present and future. **Woodruff Arts Center**, 1280 Peachtree St, NE, 733-4200 (MARTA North Rail Line to Arts Center then covered walkway) The finest visual and performing arts in the southeast, including the High Museum of Art (733-4400).

SURROUNDING AREAS: **Six Flags over Georgia**, 7561 Six Flags Rd, SW at I-20, West Mableton, 948-4378 (MARTA West Rail Line to Hightower then MARTA bus 201). Family theme park, open daily during the summer. **Stone Mountain**, Hwy. 78, 770-498-5600 (MARTA East Rail Line to Avondale then MARTA bus 120). The world's largest exposed mass of granite, with recreational activities.

Useful telephone numbers

Amtrak 1-800-872-7245
Atlanta Visitors Bureau 521-6600
C & H Bus Lines (912) 746-6441
Georgia Trailways (912) 743-8489
Greyhound Lines (800) 231-2222
Hartsfield Atlanta Int'l. Airport 530-6600
MARTA 848-4711
Metro Atlanta Transport Center 584-1728
Southeastern Stages 874-2741
Thomas Cook Foreign Exchange: Hartsfield Airport 761-6331; 245 Peachtree Center 681-9700

BALTIMORE

Area code 410
Time zone: Eastern Time

Baltimore was named for Charles Calvert, the fifth Lord Baltimore. He was a descendent of the Lords Baltimore who founded Maryland. For a brief time during the American Revolution, Baltimore served as the nation's capital. During the War of 1812, Francis Scott Key penned the words to the American National Anthem as he watched the battle at Ft McHenry at the entrance of Baltimore Harbor. Today, the Inner Harbor is one of the top visitor attractions on the east coast with attractions including the National Aquarium, Maritime Museum and historic vessels. Visitor Center located on the west shore of the Inner Harbor.

Getting around

CENTRE: The Mass Transit Administration (MTA) of the Maryland Department of Transportation operates the Baltimore Metro subway (closed Sundays), the Central Light Rail Line and a comprehensive network of 60 local bus routes. A flat one-way fare system ($1.35, or 10 tokens – $13) applies, with a $0.35 surcharge for Express buses. Transfers (which must be obtained at the start of the journey) for bus-to-bus, bus-to-rail and rail-to-bus cost an additional $0.10. All-day passes, valid for unlimited travel on the MTA system, are available for $3 on buses, at Metro station attendants' booths and from light rail ticket machines.

SURROUNDING AREAS: The MTA network operates throughout Baltimore County, resulting in a coverage approximately corresponding to the area contained within the I-695 ring road. Commuter Bus fares from Baltimore to outlying areas are $1.35 plus zone charges ranging from $1 in zone 1 to $2.50 in zone 4. The Maryland Rail Commuter Service (MARC) operates a 300 km system between Washington DC, Baltimore and **Perryville, Maryland** as well as between Washington DC and **Martinsburg, West Virginia**. MARC Penn Line service operates from Baltimore Penn Station (Amtrak) to **BWI Airport** and Washington DC and to Perryville. To the north east, **Wilmington** and **Philadelphia** are on Amtrak's North East Corridor (service continues to Newark, New York and Boston). MARC commuter trains serve **Aberdeen**. To the east, **Annapolis, Lewes** (for Cape May – Lewes Ferry service to Cape May), **Rehoboth Beach** and **Ocean City** can be accessed by Carolina Trailways buses. To the south and west, **BWI Airport** and **Washington DC** are served by Amtrak (services continue to Atlanta and New Orleans, Charleston, Jacksonville and Miami and to Charleston (WV), Cincinnati and Chicago), and by Greyhound Lines buses (services continue to Atlanta).

Main transport centres

Baltimore-Washington International Airport (BWI),16 km S (Amtrak /MARC Penn Line to BWI Airport Station and then shuttle bus every 20 minutes to the Airport terminal; alternatively BWI Airport Shuttle service from Inner Harbor hotels). A popular alternative to Washington DC airports for domestic and international flights. One terminal serves all airlines. **Baltimore Penn Station**, 1 km N (1515 N Charles St – MTA bus 3, 11, 61, 63, 64). For all Amtrak and MARC Penn Line services. **Baltimore Camden Station**, Howard and Conway Sts (MTA Central Light Rail Line to Camden Yards). For all MARC Camden Line service. **BWI Airport Station**, 16 km S (MD Rte. 70 and Amtrak Way). For selected Amtrak services and MARC Penn Line services. Shuttle bus to Airport Terminal operates every 20 mins. **Greyhound Bus Terminal**, 210 W Fayette St (MTA Metro or Central Light Rail Line to Lexington Market and then walk south to Fayette St). Serves Carolina Trailways and Greyhound Lines. **Baltimore Travel Plaza**, 5 km E (5625 O'Donnell St (MTA bus 20 east on Baltimore St) Serves Capitol Trailways of Penn., Carolina Trailways and Peter Pan Trailways.

Sightseeing by public transport

Baltimore Inner Harbor, Pratt and Light Sts, 244-1030 (Light Rail/MARC to Camden Yards, Metro to Charles Center). Baltimore's Inner Harbor is a national treasure. The waterfront promenade features world-class attractions, shopping and dining. Includes Maritime Museum (Pier 3, 396-3854), Harborplace and The Gallery (332-4191), Maryland Science Center (601 Light St, 685-5225), National Aquarium (501 E Pratt St, 576-3810), Top of the World (World Trade Center, 27th Floor, 401 E. Pratt St, 837-4515) with Observation Deck and museum, and US Frigate *Constellation* (Pier 1, 539-1797), America's oldest warship, commissioned by the US Navy and launched from Baltimore in 1797. Water Taxi (563-3901) serves 35 Inner Harbor attractions, Museum of Industry and Fell's Point from 15 landings. All Day Pass $3.50.

Baltimore Streetcar Museum, 1901 Falls Rd, 547-0264 (Light Rail to North Ave). Ride authentic Baltimore streetcars and learn the history of the city's street railway system. **B&O Railway Museum**, Pratt St at Poppleton, 752-2490 (MTA bus 31) The birthplace of American railroading, including the roundhouse, oldest railroad station in Western Hemisphere. **Fell's Point**, Broadway S of Eastern Ave (MTA bus 10 and Water Taxi from Inner Harbor). One of Baltimore's oldest neighbourhoods. Features Broadway Public Market, antique shops, restaurants and historic pubs.

Fort McHenery National Monument, East Fort Ave, 962-4290 (MTA bus 1). Star-shaped fort where, in 1814, America's successful defence against the British Navy inspired Francis Scott Key to write *The Star-Spangled Banner*. **Lexington Market**, 400–600 blocks of Lexington Street between Eutaw and Greene (Light Rail/Metro to Lexington Market). World-famous 1782 market featuring 140 food stalls, including some that serve Maryland's famous Crab Cakes. **Oriole Park at Camden Yards** (Camden Yards Light Rail/MARC). Baltimore's brand-new old-fashioned baseball park. **Babe Ruth Museum**, 216 Emory St, 727-1539, is the birthplace of the baseball legend.

Useful telephone numbers

Amtrak 1-800-872-7245
Baltimore Area Convention/Visitors Association 659-7300
Baltimore Area Visitors Center 837-4636
Baltimore Travel Plaza 633-7146
BWI Airport 859-7100
Capitol Trailways of Penn. (717) 233-7673
Carolina Trailways (919) 833-3601
Greyhound Bus Terminal 752-1393
Greyhound Lines 1-800-231-2222
MARC 1-800-325-7245
MTA 539-5000
Peter Pan Trailways (413) 781-2900

BOSTON

Area code 617
Time zone: Eastern Time

A large port on the New England seaboard Founded in 1630 and famous for its association with the early Pilgrims, Boston is one of the oldest cities in the USA, with a deep sense of history. Due to its early beginnings, the historical centre is quite compact by American standards, and much of the central area can be explored on foot. Visitor Centres located at Boston Common and Faneuil Hall Marketplace.

Getting around

CENTRE: Massachusetts Bay Transportation Authority (MBTA) (popularly referred to as the 'T') operates a comprehensive bus and subway network (consisting of the Red, Green, Orange and Blue Lines) which covers the whole area. All four lines intersect in downtown Boston. Free transfers between lines at the following stations: Park Street – Red and Green Lines (with underground walkway to the Orange Line at Downtown Crossing). Transfer to the Blue Line by taking the Green Line to Government Center. Downtown Crossing – Red and Orange Lines (with underground walkway to Green Line at Park St). Government Center – Blue and Green Lines. State – Blue and Orange Lines. Haymarket and North Station – Green and Orange Lines. Fares range from $0.85 to $1.70 (zone system); system-wide passes are available at $5 (1-day), 9 (3-days) or 18 (7-days). These also offer discounts on popular attractions. Obtainable from Greater Boston Convention & Visitors Bureau Information Center at Boston Common (145 Tremont St – MBTA Green/Red Lines to Park St, or Orange/Red Lines to Downtown Crossing); details of other sales outlets and information on routes and schedules available on (617) 222-3200.

SURROUNDING AREAS: MBTA commuter rail services cover many of the suburbs and a number of towns in Eastern Massachusetts. **Plymouth** and the **Cape Cod** area are served by Plymouth and Brockton Street Railway buses to **North Plymouth**, **Hyannis** (for The Steamship Authority ferries to **Nantucket**) and **Provincetown**, and by Bonanza Bus Lines to **Wood's Hole** (for The Steamship Authority ferries to **Martha's Vineyard**). In the Rhode Island area, **Providence** can be reached by MBTA, by Amtrak (services continue to New London and along the coast via New Haven and Stamford to New York and beyond) and by Bonanza Bus Lines (service also to Newport). In Central and Western Massachusetts,

Worcester and **Springfield** are served by Amtrak (services continue to Albany, Buffalo and Chicago), Greyhound Lines (services continue to Albany, Buffalo and Cleveland) and by Peter Pan Trailways Bus Lines (services continue to Albany). Worcester can also be reached by MBTA. **Fitchburg** is served by MBTA and Vermont Transit buses.

In Northern Massachusetts, **Lowell**, **Lawrence**, **Haverhill**, **Ipswich** and **Rockport** are all on the MBTA commuter rail network. In New Hampshire, Vermont and Maine, **Manchester** and **Concord** are served by Vermont Transit (services continue to White River Junction, Barre, Montpelier, Burlington and Montreal) and Concord Trailways (services continue to Littleton (for Mt Washington Cog Railway), Laconia, Conway and Berlin). **Portsmouth** is served by C&J Trailways (service continues to Dover and Kennebunkport), and by Concord Trailways and Greyhound Lines (services continue to Portland and Bangor).

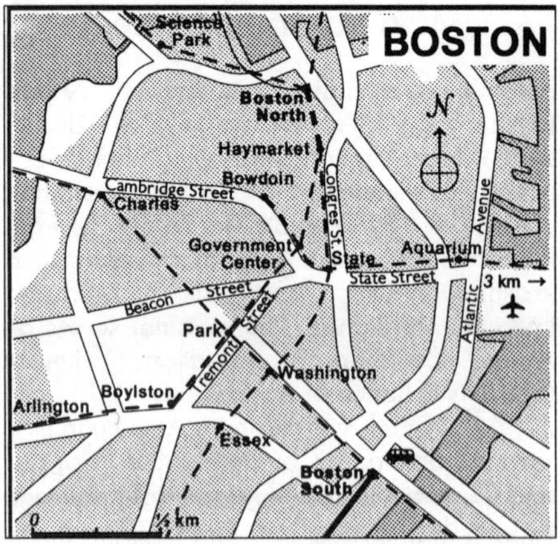

Main transport centres

Logan International Airport (BOS), 3 km E (MBTA Blue Line to Airport, then free Massport shuttle bus 22 to Terminals A and B, or 33 to Terminals C, D and E; alternatively by Airport Water Shuttle ferry from Rowes Wharf to Logan Airport Dock, then free Massport shuttle bus). Within the airport, free Massport shuttle bus 11 connects all five terminals. Major gateway for many international flights; also domestic flights to most US cities. **South Station**, Atlantic and Summer St (MBTA Red Line to South Station). The Amtrak terminus in Boston, and boarding point for North East Corridor trains to New York, Philadelphia and Washington, and for services to Springfield, Albany and Chicago. MBTA commuter rail services on the Attleboro/Stoughton, Fairmont, Framingham, Franklin and Needham lines also leave from here.

North Station, 126 Causeway St (MBTA Green/Orange Lines to North Station). MBTA terminus for commuter rail services on the Fitchburg, Reading/Haverhill, Lowell, and Rockport/Ipswich lines. **Back Bay Station**, 145 Dartmouth St (MBTA Orange Line to Back Bay Station). Amtrak services from/to South Station pick up and set down here but cannot be used for local journeys between South and Back Bay or vice versa. MBTA services from/to South Station also call here; these *can* be used for local journeys. See under 'South Station' for details of Amtrak/MBTA services. **South Station Transportation Center**, Upper level, Summer St and Atlantic (MBTA Red Line/Commuter Rail to South Station). For services of Bonanza Bus Lines Lines, C & J Trailways, Concord Trailways, Greyhound Lines, Peter Pan Trailways, Plymouth & Brockton and Vermont Transit Lines . **Rowes Wharf**, Atlantic Avenue (MBTA Blue Line to

Aquarium). For Airport Water Shuttle ferry to Logan Airport, and also for MBTA commuter boats to Hingham.

Sightseeing by public transport

CENTRE: **Boston Common**, Tremont and Park Sts (MBTA Green/Red Lines to Park St, or Orange/Red Lines to Downtown Crossing). The oldest public park in the USA. Visitor Information Booth (150 Tremont St) is the starting point for the Freedom Trail – 5 km self-guided walking tour of 16 historic sites from the Colonial and Revolutionary Era. **Boston Tea Party Ship and Museum**, Congress St Bridge, 338-1773 (MBTA Red Line/Commuter Rail to South Station). Relive history as Paul Revere and Sam Savage throw tea chests over board. **Children's Museum**, 300 Congress St, 426-8855 (MBTA Red Line/Commuter Rail to South Station) Interactive exhibits encourage imagination and curiosity. Adjacent **Computer Museum** (426-2800) features a giant Walk-Through Computer, vintage computers, robots and more than 150 hands-on exhibits.

Faneuil Hall Marketplace/Quincy Market, Congress St (MBTA Green Line to Government Center, or Blue/Orange Lines to State). Three 19th-century buildings with over 125 shops and restaurants situated on Boston's waterfront. **John F. Kennedy Library and Museum**, Columbia Point, Dorchester, 929-4523 (MBTA Red Line to JFK/UMass then shuttle bus every 20 mins to library) Extensive collection on the life and times of the nation's 35th President. **John Hancock Building Observatory**, 200 Clarendon St, Copley Sq., 247-1977 (MBTA Green Line to Copley, or Orange Line/Commuter Rail to Back Bay Station). Observation deck located on 60th floor of New England's tallest building. **Museum of Fine Arts**, 465 Huntington Ave, 267-9300 (MBTA Green Line E to Museum). Comprehensive collections offer a survey of the world's finest art. **Museum of Science**, Science Park, 723-2500 (MBTA Green Line to Science Park) Over 400 interactive participatory exhibits and Omni theatre. **New England Aquarium**, Central Wharf, 973-5200 (MBTA Blue Line to Aquarium). Four-storey Giant Ocean Tank contains sharks, giant turtles and tropical marine life.

USS Constitution and Museum, Old Navy Yard, Charlestown (MBTA Green/Orange Lines to Haymarket then MBTA buses 92, 93). Known as 'Old Ironsides' and launched in Boston in 1797, the oldest commissioned warship afloat in the world. Adjacent **Bunker Hill Pavilion** (241-7575) has a multi-media presentation on the Battle of Bunker Hill.

SURROUNDING AREAS: **Cambridge** (MBTA Red Line to Harvard). The area around Harvard Square is a lively mix of shops, bookstores and cafés popular with Harvard University and MIT students. Cambridge Discovery's Information Booth (497-1630) is next to the subway entrance. **Harvard University** has several museums, including the Busch-Reisinger Fogg and Sackler art museums, the Semitic Museum and the Harvard University Museums of Natural History. **Concord** (MBTA Fitchburg Commuter Rail Line from North Station). The site of the American Revolution's second battle and Thoreau's Walden Pond. The Old North Bridge and Concord Museum are 20 mins walk from the train station (leaving the station, turn right on Thoreau St, then left of Sudbury St to town centre). Walden Pond is 30 mins walk from the station (leaving the station, turn right on Thoreau St to its end, then right on Walden St; after crossing Route 2, take any of the trails right to the pond or continue straight on Walden St to a small beach).

Gloucester and **Rockport** (MBTA Rockport Commuter Rail Line from North Station). Located on Cape Ann, Massachusetts' scenic North Shore. The ancient fishing village of Gloucester is a 1 km walk down Washington St from the station. Virtually everything in Rockport, including the Bearskin Neck Artist's Colony, is within walking distance of the station. **Lexington** (MBTA Red Line to Alewife then MBTA bus 62-Bedford or 76-Hascom Field to Lexington Center, Mon –Sat). The Battle Green, where the first shots of the American Revolution were fired, Munroe Taverrn, Hancock House and Old Belfry are all within a short walk of the town centre. The Buckman Tavern and Museum of Our National Heritage are located a few bus stops before the town centre.

Lowell (MBTA Lowell Commuter Rail Line from North Station to Lowell then LRTA Downtown Shuttle Bus every 15 mins, Mon–Fri and every 30 mins Sat; electric tram links many of the historic sites). The birthplace of the American industrial revolution. Lowell National Historic Park (246 Market St, 508-970-5000) features the Boott Cotton Mills Museum, a re-created 1920s weave room with 88 operating power looms. The National Park Service also offers a 8 km canal voyage (reservations required) through the old textile mills and power plants.

Salem (MBTA Rockport/Ipswich Commuter Rail Lines from North Station). The site of the witch trials of the 1690s features the Salem Witch Museum, the House of Seven Gables, Pickering Wharf and the Salem Maritime

Historic Site. All are within 15 mins walk of the train station.

Useful telephone numbers

Airport Water Shuttle 330-8680
Amtrak 1-800-872-7245
Bonanza Bus Lines (401) 331-7500
Boston Visitor Information Center 536-4100
C&J Trailways (603) 742-5111
Concord Trailways (603) 228-3300
Connecticut Dept. of Econ. Dev. (203) 258-4200
Greyhound Lines 1-800-231-2222
Logan International Airport 567-1830
Massachusetts Travel & Tourism 727-3201
Massport 800-23-LOGAN
MBTA 222-3200
New Hampshire Vacation Travel (603) 271-2343
Peter Pan Bus Lines (413) 781-2900
Plymouth & Brockton Street Railway 746-0378
Rhode Island Tourism (401) 277-2601
The Steamship Authority (508) 540-2022
Thomas Cook Foreign Exchange: 160 Franklin St, 695-0269
Traveler's Aid Society 542-7286
Vermont Transit (802) 862-9761

CHICAGO

Area code 312
Time zone: Central Time'

The Heart of the Midwest' and 'The City on the Lake' are two descriptions often applied to Chicago. As the largest city in the Midwest and with a 29-mile frontage (much of it with parks and beaches) on Lake Michigan, these descriptions are well deserved (as is, at times, that other well-known attribute – 'The Windy City'). Chicago is also the home of the busiest airport in the USA and of the tallest skyscrapers in the world. Finding your way around is relatively easy due to the numerical grid system of streets which originates at the intersection of State and Madison Streets. Visitor Information Centres are located at the Cultural Center (Michigan and Randolph Sts.–across from Randolph St Station) and the Old Water Tower (N Michigan Ave and Chicago St)

Getting around

CENTRE: Chicago Transit Authority (CTA) operate the Rapid Transit System, called the 'L' (short for elevated), although trains also run in subways. The Each line now has a colour name: Blue (O'Hare–Congress–Douglas – board in the Dearborn Street subway); Red (Howard–Dan Ryan – board in the State Street subway); Purple (Evanston Shuttle and Express – board on the Loop elevated); Orange (Midway – board on the Loop elevated); Brown (Ravenswood – board on the Loop elevated); Green (Lake–Englewood–Jackson Park – board on the Loop elevated); and Yellow (Skokie Swift – board at Howard). Trains make all stops (the former skip-stop services have been discontinued-with the exception of the Purple Line Express, which makes limited stops between Howard and Chicago Ave). CTA also operate buses (routes 1 to 204) which cover the whole of the downtown area and the inner suburbs. Flat fares, currently $1.50, apply, add $0.30 for transfers (valid 2 hours) and express surcharge (certain bus routes and also on Purple Line Express train from Howard to Belmont). The basic bus fare may be paid to the driver or purchased in advance as tokens, 10 for $13.50, from banks, currency exchanges and from certain food stores. Transfers, which must be purchased when starting the trip, are required to change between buses and from bus to trains and vice versa Changing entirely between trains is done without charge. Pace operate suburban buses (Routes 208 and above); CTA monthly passes and transfers are valid on these services (except route 835).

Metropolitan Rail (METRA) operates commuter trains from various downtown stations to the suburbs and beyond, and to locations in northwestern Indiana. From METRA stations (NorthWestern, Union and La Salle St) to **Museums** (Art Institute of Chicago, Museum of Contemporary Photography, Field Museum of Natural History, Adler Planetarium and Shedd Aquarium) use CTA bus 130 – Grant Park Treasures (service weekends and holidays, mid-May to Labour Day; every 15 mins 0935 (1035 Sundays, holidays) to 1800).

SURROUNDING AREAS: In Northwestern Indiana, **Hammond**, **Gary** and **Michigan City** are served by METRA in association with the Northern Indiana Commuter Transportation District ('The South Shore Line') trains (service continues to South Bend); bus services are provided by American Trailways, by Greyhound Lines (services continue to Grand Rapids, Indianapolis and Cincinnati), by Indian Trails (service continues to Kalamazoo, Flint and Bay City), and by Southeastern Trailways (services continue to Indianapolis and Cincinnati). In Northern Illinois, **Kankakee** is served by Amtrak and Greyhound Lines (both services continue to Champaign, Memphis and New Orleans); **Joliet** is served by METRA, by Amtrak (service continues to St Louis, Kansas City, Albuquerque and Los

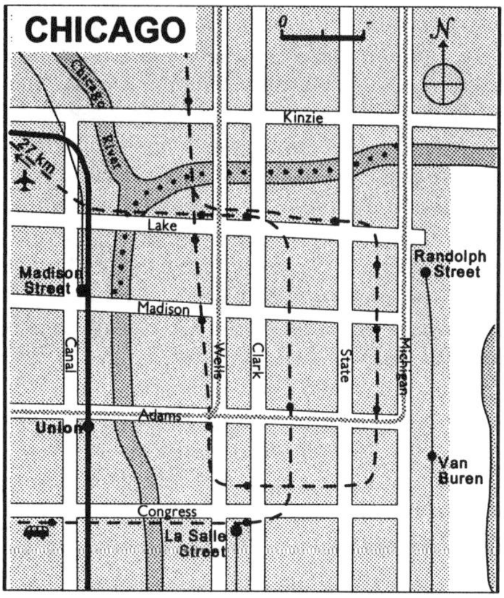

Angeles) and by Greyhound Lines (service continues to Bloomington, Springfield and St Louis); **Peoria** is served by Amtrak Thruway Bus and Illinois Valley Coaches; **Aurora** is served by METRA and by Greyhound Lines (service continues to Moline, Davenport, Cedar Rapids, Des Moines, Omaha, Denver and Salt Lake City); **Geneva, Harvard** and **Fox Lake** are served by METRA, **Elgin** is served by METRA and by Greyhound Lines (service continues to Rockford, Beloit and Madison); and **Rockford** by Amtrak Thruway Bus (service continues to Beloit, Janesville and Madison). In Wisconsin, **Kenosha** is served by METRA; **Milwaukee** by Amtrak (service continues to La Crosse, Minneapolis-St Paul, Fargo and Seattle), and by Greyhound Lines.

Main transport centres

O'Hare Inernational Airport (ORD), 28 km NW (CTA Blue Line to O'Hare 24 hours per day; alternatively Continental Air Transport Airport Express Bus 0600-2200). Major gateway for many international flights; also domestic flights to many US cities. The four terminals are numbered 1, 2, 3 and 5. **Midway Airport** (MDW), 15 km SW (CTA Orange Line to Midway; alternatively Continental Air Transport Airport Express Bus). Domestic flights to major US cities. **Union Station**, Canal St between Adams and Jackson Blvd (CTA buses 1, 60, 125, 130, 151, 156, 157). Amtrak's main station in Chicago and with 50 or so arrivals/departures per day, the hub of the Amtrak system. METRA Commuter Rail services to Fox Lake, Elgin, Antioch and Aurora, plus a few Mon-Fri evening peak journeys to Orland Park and Joliet also depart from here. **La Salle Street Station**, 434 S La Salle St (Blue Line to La Salle/Congress; Brown, Orange and Purple Lines to La Salle/Van Buren, one block away). METRA Commuter Rail services to Joliet. **Northwestern Station**, Madison and Canal Sts (CTA buses 23, 56, 125, 130, 157). METRA Commuter Rail services to Kenosha, Harvard and Geneva. **Randolph Street Station**, Michigan Ave between S Water and Randolph St (CTA buses 3, 6, 56, 60, 151, 157; Brown, Green, Orange and Purple lines to Randolph/Wabash, one block away). METRA Commuter Rail services to University Park, and NICD 'South Shore Line'. **Greyhound Bus Terminal**, 630 West Harrison Street (CTA bus 60; Blue Line to Clinton/Congress, one block away). For services of American Trailways, Burlington Trailways, Greyhound Lines, Illinois Valley Coaches, Indian Trails and Southeastern Trailways.

Sightseeing by public transport

CENTRE: **Art Institute of Chicago**, Michigan Ave at Adams St, 443-3600 (CTA Blue/Red Lines to Jackson; Brown/Green/Orange/Purple Lines to Adams and CTA buses 1, 3, 6, 60, 130, 151) One of the world's leading museums with one of the largest collections of French Impressionist masterpieces. Free on Tuesdays. **Chicago Architecture Foundation Tours**, 224 S Michigan Ave, 922-3432, are offered year-round. **Chicago Mercantile Exchange Tours**, 30 S Wacker Dr., 2 blocks east of Northwestern, Union METRA stations, 930-8249 (CTA Brown/Orange/Green Lines to Quincy then walk 2 blocks W on Adams to Wacker Dr.). Witness the exciting pace of the International Money Market. Open weekdays only. **Grant Park** (CTA bus 146 S on State; also bus 130, Sat–Sun and holdiays only) from Northwestern, Union stations). Attractions include **The Adler Planetarium** (1300 S Lake Shore Dr., 922-7827), with exhibits on astronomy, space exploration, telescopes and navigation; **Field Museum of Natural History** (Roosevelt Rd at Lake Shore Dr., 922-9410), with exhibits and displays of more than 15 million artifacts and specimens, and **Shedd Aquarium** (1200 Lake Shore Dr., 939-2438), the world's largest indoor aquarium, containing more than 6,000 freshwater and marine animals. **Lincoln Park** (CTA bus 151 N on State; also serves Union METRA) is home to the Lincoln Park Zoo (2200 N Cannon Dr., 742-7695), with more than 2,000 exotic and endangered species. The wonders of nature bloom year-round at Lincoln Park Conservancy (2400 N Stockton Dr., 294-4770), a botanical garden featuring exotic plants from all over the world. The nearby **Chicago Historical Society**, Clark St at North Ave, 642-4600, features an impressive collection of exhibits centered on Chicago and Illinois. **Museum of Science and Industry**, 57th St at Lake Shore Dr., 684-1414 (CTA bus 6 S on State St). Over 2,000 exhibits encompassing 75 fields. Highlights include a full-scale coal mine replica, WWII German U-boat, *Apollo 8* spacecraft and simulated space shuttle ride. **Navy Pier**, 600 E. Grand Ave, 595-7437 (CTA buses 29 N on State, 56 E on Washington). Historic landmark features a 150-foot ferris wheel, 1,500-seat Skyline Stage, an IMAX theatre, cruise boats and a variety of unique shops and restaurants. The adjacent **Chicago Children's Museum** (527-1000) features unique interactive exhibits. Located here are the North Pier Festival Market (435 E. Illinois St, 836-4300), with waterfront shops, restaurants and outdoor cafés on the Chicago River; the **Bicycle Museum of America** (222-0500), holding over 50,000 items related to the bicycle; and the Chicago Academy of Sciences (435 E. Illinois St, 871-2668), Chicago's first science museum. **North Michigan Ave** (CTA buses 11, 15, 145, 146, 151 N on State). The 'Magnificent Mile' features outstanding shopping venues which include Chicago Place (Saks Fifth Avenue), Water Tower Place (Marshall Field's and Lord & Taylor) and Bloomingdales (900 N Michigan Ave)..

Other attractions include **Here's Chicago**, 163 E. Pearson St, 467-7114, a sound and sight show that includes exhibits on the Chicago fire and more; **John Hancock Tower Observatory**, 875 N Michigan Ave, 751-3681, where a 40-second elevator ride takes you to the 94th floor for a panoramic view; the **Old Water Tower**, Chicago and N Michigan Aves, 744-2400, a famous Chicago landmark; **Oak Street**, with fine boutiques and beaches; and **Rush Street**, featuring some of Chicago's hottest nightlife. **Sears Tower**, 233 S Wacker Dr., across the Chicago River from Union Station, 875-9696 (CTA Brown/Orange/Purple Lines to Quincy and CTA buses 1, 60, 130, 151). The world's tallest building features an elevator to the 103rd floor Skydeck Observatory. includes the 'Chicago Experience,' a multi-media presentation.

SURROUNDING AREAS: **Geneva**, 58 km W (METRA Commuter Rail from Northwestern to Geneva). More than 200 landmark buildings, antique shops, restaurants, sidewalk cafés and Fox River walking paths are just a short walk from the train station. **St Charles**, 5 km (PACE bus 801 from Geneva METRA station), features old-fashioned Main St antique shopping, restaurants and Paddlewheel Riverboat cruises on the Fox River. **Oak Park**, 16 km W (CTA Green Line to Harlem; METRA Commuter Rail from NORTHWESTERN to Oak Park). The turn-of-the-century suburb of Oak Park has been preserved as a national historic district. The **Frank Lloyd Wright Prairie Scoll of Architecture Historic District** (913 Chicago Ave, 708-848-1976) features 13 Wright-designed buildings. Frank Lloyd Wright Home and Studio (951 Chicago Ave, 708-848-1976) was the architect's residence and workplace for the first 20 years of his career. The Visitor Center (158 N Forest Ave, one block N of the station) has walking tour maps, guidebooks and free brochures.

Useful telephone numbers

American Trailways (317) 635-4000
Amtrak 1-800-872-7245
Chicago Convention & Tourism Bureau 567-8500
Chicago Office of Tourism 744-2400
Continental Air Transport 454-7800
Chicago Transit Authority (CTA) 836-7000
Greyhound Lines 1-800-231-2222
Illinois Bureau of Tourism 1-800-223-0121
Illinois Valley Coaches (309) 674-5138
Indian Trails (517) 725-5105
METRA Commuter Rail 322-6777
Midway Airport 767-0500
NICD ('The South Shore Line') 1-800-356-2079
O'Hare Airport 686-2200
Pace Suburban Buses 836-7000
Southeastern Trailways (317) 635-8671
Thomas Cook Foreign Exchange: 100 E Walton, 649 0288
Traveler's Aid (O'Hare) 686-7562

DALLAS

Area code 214
Time zone: Central Time

Tennessee lawyer John Neely Bryan settled Dallas in 1841 when he established a trading post on the banks of the Trinity River. Bryan envisaged the new settlement becoming a hub of activity with steamboats carrying goods upriver from the Gulf of Mexico. Today, Dallas is the eighth largest city in the USA and is the business capital of the rapidly growing Southwest – with the third largest concentration of corporate headquarters and high-technology companies in the country. The city boasts more shops per shopper than any other city in the USA and more restaurants per capita than New York City. Like most southwestern US cities, Dallas sprawls for many kilometres in every direction, but fortunately, most important visitor attractions are located near the downtown area and are easily accessible by the Dallas Area Rapid Transit (DART) network of light rail trains (beginning in June 1996) and buses. Visitor Centres are located downtown at 1303 Commerce St and at West End Marketplace (open 7 days a week).

Getting around

CENTRE: Dallas Area Rapid Transit (DART) operates a 32 km light rail system including lines in West and South Oak Cliff (opens June '96), a 1.6 km downtown transitway mall, a 5.6 km subway under North Central Expressway, and service as far north as Park Lane (opens Dec. '96). The system features 21 passenger stations, including an underground stop below the landmark, 42-storey Cityplace Tower (opens 1998), north of the downtown area. In addition, a comprehensive network of over 140 bus routes operates throughout the city and surrounding area. Local Service is offered on Routes 1-155 and 301-530. Premium (Express) Service is offered on Routes 200 to 283. A flat one-way fare system ($1 for Local or $2 for Premium Express) applies, with free transfers (which must be obtained at the start of the journey) for bus-to-bus, bus-to-rail and rail-to-bus. The validity time of transfers is 90 minutes. With the introduction of light rail service in 1996 bus routes will be modified to serve new rail stations and transit centres. A commuter rail line to the Medical/Market Centre and the suburban South Irving Transit Centre will open in late 1996 with future extension to Dallas/Ft Worth International Airport.

Of particular interest to visitors are the two downtown shuttle bus systems: Dallasites and Hop-A-Bus. Dallasites is a circulator designed for downtown visitors and office workers serving Union Station, eight major hotels, West End, McKinney Avenue Streetcar, Arts District, City Centre District and the Convention Center every 30 minutes 1100–2300 Mon–Sat From 1100 to 1700 Dallasites also serves the Farmer's Market and Old City Park, replaced by service to Deep Ellum from 1700 to 1100. The fare is $1. One-day $3 and three-day $6 Dallasites passes are available through hotel concierges or DART's Retail Sales Centre located downtown at Elm & Ervay Sts. (open Mon – Fri 0700–1800). Hop-A-Bus is a downtown shuttle operating every 10 min. from 6:30 a.m. to 6:30 p.m. Mon – Fri on a route serving Union Station, the Reunion Arena, City Centre District and the Arts District.

SURROUNDING AREAS: DART operates throughout a 1,120 sq. km area with major suburban transit centres located in **Red Bird** (Southwest Dallas), **Richardson**, **South Irving**, **West Plano**, **North Carrollton** and **Garland**. To the north, **Oklahoma City** and **Tulsa** are served by Greyhound Lines (service continues to Springfield, St Louis and Chicago); to the east, **Texarkana** and **Little Rock** are served by Amtrak trains and Greyhound Lines buses (service continues to Memphis); in the south-eastern quadrant **Houston**, **Shreveport** (additionally served by Kerrville Bus Co.), **Jackson** and **Birmingham** are served by Greyhound lines; to the south-west **Austin** and **San Antonio** are served by Amtrak trains and Greyhound Lines buses (both services continue to El Paso, Tucson, Phoenix, Los Angeles and San Diego); **San Angelo** is served by Kerrville Bus Co.; and **Waco** by Central Texas Trailways; to the west, **Ft Worth**, **Abilene** and **El Paso** are served by Greyhound Lines; to the north-west **Lubbock** is served by TNM&O Coaches (services continue to Carlsbad, El Paso, Albuquerque and Santa Fe); Amarillo and Denver are served by Greyhound Lines/TNM&O Coaches.

Main transport centres

Dallas/Ft Worth International Airport (DFW), 28 km NW (574-3197). Bus, limo and taxi services are available at all terminals. Taxi service is available at the upper-level kerbside. All other ground transportation, including hotel shuttles, is reached from the lower level. Ground transportation information is provided in the baggage claim area of each terminal. Ground Transportation information, 574-5878. Major gateway for international and national flights, with four terminals. **Love Field** (DAL), 14 km NW, Cedar Springs at Mockingbird Lane, 670-6073 (DART bus 39 to downtown). Domestic flights to major US cities. **Union Station**, 400 Houston Street, 746-6600 (DART to Union Station – opens June '96 – Dallasites and Hop-A-Bus). Renovated 1916 railroad station includes restaurants and a visitor center. For all Amtrak and commuter rail (beginning late 1996) services. **Greyhound Terminal**, 205 S Lamar St, 655-7082 (DART to Union Station – opens June '96 – Dallasites and Hop-A-Bus). Serves Arrow Trailways of Texas, Central Texas Trailways, Greyhound Lines, Kerrville Bus Co., TNM&O Coaches.

Sightseeing by public transport

CENTRE: **Arts District** (DART Pearl Street Station – opens Dec. '96 – Dallasites, Hop-A-Bus and McKinney Ave Streetcar). Includes the Dallas Museum of Art (1717 N Harwood

St, 922-1200), Arts District Theater, and I. M. Pei-designed Meyerson Symphony Center (Pearl & Flora Sts., 670-3600). **Deep Ellum**, Elm & Crowdus Sts., 445-333) (Dallasites, 1100–1700 only). Warehouse area located just east of downtown features eclectic shops, live entertainment and restaurants. **Fair Park**, 1300 Robert B. Cullum Blvd, 670-8400 (DART buses 60, 64, 18, 50 on Commerce St). 277 acre National Landmark hosts the State Fair of Texas and seven museums including the Age of Steam Railroad Museum (421-8754), featuring the world's largest diesel locomotive. **McKinney Avenue Streetcar**, McKinney Ave, 855-5627 (DART St Paul Street Station – opens Dec. '96 – Dallasites and Hop-A-Bus). Historic tram line connecting the Arts District with McKinney Avenue. Operates Sun–Thurs. 1000–2200, Fri–Sat 1000– 1200. Board on St Paul St, adjacent to the Dallas Museum of Art. **Old City Park**, 1717 Gano St, 421-5141 (Dallasites, 1100–1700 only). 13-acre architectural and cultural museum village of original buildings depicting North Texas life 1840–1910. **Reunion Tower**, 300 Reunion Blvd, 651-1234 (DART Union Station – opens June '96 – Dallasites and Hop-A-Bus). 50-storey tower with observation deck and restaurant. Pedestrian tunnel to Union Station. **Sixth Floor Museum**, 411 Elm St, 653-6666 (DART West End Station – opens June '96 – Dallasites and Hop-A-Bus). Examines the life, death and legacy of President John F. Kennedy. Located on the Sixth Floor of the former Texas Book Depository. **West End Historic District**, 1801 N Lamar St, 720-7107 (Hotline 720-7717) (DART West End Station – opens June '96 – Dallasites and Hop-A-Bus). More than 100 shops, restaurants and nightclubs in restored warehouses. **Main Street/Pegasus Plaza**, (DART Akard Street Station – opens Dec. '96 – Dallasites and Hop-A-Bus). The heart of downtown Dallas and home to the legendary Neiman Marcus department store, located at Main & Ervay Sts, 741-6911. Many shops and restaurants are located along a network of underground walkways (closed evenings and weekends). Pegasus Plaza is the scene for special events, 746-6679.

Useful telephone numbers

Amtrak 1-800-872-7245
Arrow Trailways of Texas (817) 526-0545
Central Texas Trailways (817) 754-0531
Dallas Area Rapid Transit (DART) 979-1111
Dallas Convention and Visitors Bureau 746-6677
Dallas-Ft Worth Int'l. Airport 574-3197
Dallas Love Field Airport 670-6073
Greyhound Lines 1-800-231-2222
Kerrville Bus Company 263-0294
McKinney Avenue Streetcar 855-5267
TNM&O Coaches (806) 763-5389
Thomas Cook Foreign Exchange: at Dallas-Ft Worth Intn'l Airport (4 branches); Prestonwood Town Center 991-6688; and 2911 Turtle Creek Blvd 559 3564

DENVER

Area code 303
Time zone: Mountain Time

Known as the 'Mile High City', a reference to its altitude of 1613 metres, Denver is situated almost half-way between the Mississippi and the West Coast, at the foot of the Eastern edge of the Rocky Mountains. Originally a gold and silver prospectors' camp and subsequently a pioneer town, Denver prospered due to natural mineral and oil deposits. Tourism has become an important industry In recent years; the nearby ski resorts are as popular in summer as they are in winter. The heart of the city is 16th Street Mall, a 1.5 km pedestrian promenade. Visitor Centre located downtown at 225 W Colfax, across from Civic Center Park.

Getting around

CENTRE: The Regional Transportation District (RTD) operates a light rail service (route 101) through the downtown area, a free shuttle bus along 16th Street Mall between Market Street Station and Civic Center Station, and a comprehensive network of buses comprising local routes (often numbered, but not always, to reflect the street/avenue number primarily served), limited stop routes (numbered with 'Ltd' suffix), express routes (numbered with 'X' suffix), regional routes (single lettered), and airport 'SkyRide' routes (double lettered) throughout Denver and its suburbs.

RTD's 'Cultural Connection Trolley' serves all major downtown attractions as well as the Botanic Gardens, Museum of Natural History and Zoo every 30 mins 0930–1800 daily Memorial Day–Labor Day. Fares for light-rail, local and 'Ltd' services are $1 at peaks (0600–0900 and 1600–1800) and $0.50 at other times; transfers are free. Fare range for SkyRide airport services is $4–$8, depending on distance. Fares of $1.50 for Express services and $2.50 for Regional services apply irrespective of time or distance. All-day pass $3, valid on Trolley, light rail and local bus service ($1 credit on Express, Regional and skyRide routes), available at RTD Market

Street, Civic Center and Boulder stations as well as Ticket Bus (16th St Mall and Curtis) and Denver Visitor's Bureau (225 W Colfax).

SURROUNDING AREAS: Most suburbs are served from the downtown area by RTD regional routes; for some of the north-western suburbs it is necessary to change in **Boulder** (reached from downtown by hourly daily service on route B, with some additional Mon-Fri journeys on routes H and S). The plains to the east are relatively unpopulated, with only occasional small prairie towns. The nearest places of any size in this direction are 8–12 hours away by rail or bus. **Omaha** can be reached by Amtrak train or by Greyhound Lines bus (both services continue to Chicago); **Kansas City** by Greyhound Lines (service continues to St Louis).

To the south-east and south, **Lamar** is reached by TNM&O coaches (service continues to Amarillo and Dallas), as are **Colorado Springs** and **Pueblo** (services continue to Amarillo and to Albuquerque). To the west, **Vail, Glenwood Springs, Rifle, Granby** and **Grand Junction** are reached by Greyhound Lines and by Amtrak; both services continue to Salt Lake City (Amtrak also to San Francisco). To the north, **Cheyenne** and **Laramie** are reached by Amtrak (service continues to Ogden, Portland and Seattle); Cheyenne is also served by Greyhound Lines and TNM&O coaches.

Main transport centres

Denver International Airport (DIA), 36 km NE (RTD SkyRide bus AF hourly to/from Market Street Station, Downtown Denver/Greyhound Bus Center; journey about 45 mins, fare $6). Gateway mainly for domestic flights, but many international destinations can be reached by changing to connecting flights at major hubs. One terminal serves all airlines. **Union Station**, Wynkoop/17th Streets (RTD bus 20; within walking distance of Market Street Station). Departure point for all Amtrak services and Denver Rio Grande and Western Railroad Ski Train. **Denver/ Greyhound Bus Center**, 1055 19th Street (RTD SkyRide bus AF; within walking distance of many downtown bus routes and 18th/Stout and 18th/California light rail stations). For services of Greyhound Lines, Powder River Trailways and TNM&O Coaches. **Market Street Station**, Market/16th Streets (RTD buses 1, 2, 12, 16th St Mall Shuttle; within walking distance of many other downtown bus routes and of Union Station). Interchange point for a number of RTD express and regional bus services, including routes B to Boulder, and SkyRide route AF). **Civic Center Station**, Broadway/ 16th Ave (RTD bus 0, 2, 5, 6, 7, 8, 10, 12, 15, 16, 16th St Mall Shuttle): Interchange for a number of RTD express and regional bus services. **Boulder Station**, 14th and Walnut (RTD Boulder Local buses 200-208; SkyRide AB): Interchange for a number of RTD express and regional bus services, including routes B to Denver, G to Golden, M to Longmont and N to Nederland.

Sightseeing by public transport

CENTRE: **Black American West Museum**, 3091 California St, 292-2956 (RTD Light Rail to 30th and Downing). Exhibits on the contributions of African-Americans in the American West. **Colorado State Capitol**, Broadway at Colfax, 866-2604 (RTD 16th St shuttle to Civic Center Station). Features a gold dome and panoramic view of Denver and the Rockies. **Denver Art Museum**, 14th and Bannock St, 640-2793 (RTD 16th St shuttle to Civic Center Station; walk 1 block S to 14th St). More than 40,000 works of art, including an extensive Native American collection. Next door, the **Byers-Evans House Museum** (1310 Bannock St, 620-4933) includes interactive video programs and exhibits in the Denver History Museum. **Denver Botanic Gardens**, 1005 York St, 331-4000 (RTD bus 10 on 17th St). Outdoor gardens of native and exotic plants and award-winning Tropical Conservancy.

Denver Museum of Natural History, 2001 Colorado Blvd, 322-7009 (RTD buses 20, 32 on 17th St). Also in Central Park is the **Denver Zoo** (E 23rd between York St and Colorado Blvd, 331-4110). **Elitch Gardens** (595-4386 – RTD bus 10 on 15th St). More than 23 major thrill rides. Adjacent **Forney Transportation Museum** (1416 Platte St, 433-3643) features a large collection of classic automobiles, 'Big Boy' steam locomotive and more. **Museum of Western Art**, 1727 Tremont Pl., 296-1880 (RTD 16th St Shuttle to Tremont). Premier collection of classic Western art. **United States Mint**, W Colfax at Cherokee St, 844-3582 (RTD 16th St Shuttle to Court Pl.; walk 2½ blocks SW). More than 40 million coins are produced each workday. Free tours Mon-Fri.

SURROUNDING AREAS: **Boulder**, 48 km NW (RTD Regional Express bus 'B' from Market Street Station). University town located at the edge of the Rocky Mountains. The brick-paved Pearl Street Mall, lined with historic buildings, features a variety of shops, restaurants and entertainment. **Golden** (RTD bus 16 on 15th St) Historic Golden's attractions include free tours of the Coors Brewing Company (13th and Ford St, 277-2337), the world's largest single brewing facility and Dar Pioneer Museum (911 10th St, 278-7151) with artifacts from early American and pioneer history to 1930. **Colorado Railroad Museum**, 17155 W 44th Ave, 279-4591 (RTD bus 16 to Golden then buses 17, 44Ltd). Highlights Colorado's colourful railroad history. Features more than 50 historic locomotives and carriages. **Central City**, 46 km W (ACE Express bus every 2 hrs 0730-1930 from Holiday Inn, 15th and Glenarm Sts.). Historic gold mining town features gold panning, a colourful 'Old West' Main Street and limited-stakes gambling at 14 authentically restored casinos.

Useful telephone numbers

Amtrak 1-800-USA-RAIL
Denver & Rio Grande Railroad 595-2230
Denver/Greyhound Bus Terminal 293-6541
Denver Visitors Bureau 892-1112
Greyhound Lines 1-800-231-2222
Powder River Trailways (307) 682-0960
Regional Transport. District (RTD) 299-6000
Thomas Cook Foreign Exchange: 1580 Court Place, 571 0808
TNM&O Coaches (806) 763-5389

HOUSTON

Area code 713
Time zone: Central Time

Although Houston is 80 km inland, it is the third-largest port in the USA, thanks to its connection to the sea by a ship canal. For a city with such an outdoor-lifestyle climate, it is, perhaps, ironic that probably the best known view of Houston is an indoor one, in the Lyndon B. Johnson Space Center, some 30 km out of town. This is the location of NASA headquarters – 'Mission Control' to the manned space exploration programme, which, coinciding with early global satellite communication in the 1960s, became famous worldwide. The Downtown Tunnel System, a six-mile system of skywalks and underground pedestrian tunnels connects 55 buildings and hotels and more than 100 restaurants. Visitor Center located at 810 Congress St at Milam.

Getting around

CENTRE: METRO operates a comprehensive network of buses throughout the metropolitan area. Local and limited-stop ('Ltd') services are numbered 1–99, with a flat fare of $1; Express services 100–199, flat fare $1.50; Park & Ride services 200–299, fare $2–4 (depending on length of route). In off-peak times/directions, 'Local' fares are charged on Express and Park & Ride services. Texas Special shuttles operate four routes (Red, White, Blue and Silver) throughout the downtown area every 5 mins (weekdays only) for $0.25.

SURROUNDING AREAS: METRO operations extend well into the suburbs. To the south, **Galveston** is served by Texas Bus Lines. To the south-west, **Victoria** and **Corpus Christi** are reached by Greyhound Lines and Valley Transit buses (services continue to Laredo and Brownsville). In the west, **San Antonio** is reached by Amtrak trains (service continues to Del Rio, El Paso, Phoenix and Los Angeles), and by Greyhound Lines (service continues to El Paso in conjunction with Kerrville Bus Co.), and **Austin** by Arrow Trailways of Texas (service continues to Abilene) and by Kerrville Bus Co. To the north, **Waco** and **Dallas** are reached by Greyhound Lines and **Dallas** also by Amtrak Thruway Bus (service continues by train to Little Rock, St Louis and Chicago). In the north-east, **Shreveport** is reached by Kerrville Bus Co. (service continues to Texarkana). To the east, **Beaumont** and **Lake Charles** are reached by Amtrak (service continues to New Orleans and Jacksonville), and by Greyhound Lines (service continues to Lafayette, Baton Rouge and New Orleans).

Main transport centres

Houston Intercontinental Airport (IAH, 32 km. N. To/from Terminal C and downtown by METRO bus 102 on Travis St (weekdays only); alternatively by Airport Express shuttle to/from downtown hotels every 30 mins, 0715–2315. Major international gateway, with four terminals. **Houston Hobby Airport** (HOU), 16 km. SE (from downtown by METRO buses 50, 88 or 143; from Texas Medical Center by METRO bus 73). Domestic flights to many US cities. One terminal serves all airlines. **Amtrak Station**, 902 Washington Ave (METRO bus 36 or 85 after 1900). For all Amtrak services. **Greyhound Bus Center**, 2121 Main Street (METRO buses 1, 2, 3, 8, 15, 25, 65, 78). For services of Arrow Trailways of Texas, Greyhound Lines, Kerrville Bus Co., Texas Bus Lines and Valley Transit.

Sightseeing by public transport

CENTRE: **Astrodome**, 8100 Kirby Dr., 799-9595M (METRO bus 15 on Main St). The world's first domed stadium. Home to Houston Astros baseball and Oilers football. **Bayou Bend Collection and Gardens**, One Westcott, 639-7750 (METRO bus 17,70 on Travis, or 84 on Lamar). One of the finest collections of American decorative arts (paintings, furniture, ceramics, and silver) in the nation.

The blocks around **Old Market Square**,

bounded by Milam, Travis, Congress and Preston Sts (METRO downtown buses; Texas Special Blue Route). Houston's original business district, contain a number of historic buildings, taverns and restaurants. **Houston Arboretum and Nature Center**, 4501 Woodway, (713) 681-8433 (METRO bus 17 on Travis St, or 84 on Lamar). Over 60 species of indigenous Southwestern plant life, and small animals. **Houston Museum of Natural Science**, 1 Hermann Circle Dr., in Hermann Park, 639-4629). Includdes a world-class gem and mineral collection and the Cockrell Butterfly Center, 2,000 live butterflies in a tropical rainforest setting.

NASA Johnson Space Center, 40 km S, 1601 NASA Rd 1, 244-2100 (METRO bus 246 every 50 mins 0744–1442). Space Center Houston, the new visitors' center for NASA's Johnson Space Center, features hands-on exhibits and behind-the-scenes tours. Mercury, Gemini, and Apollo spacecraft are on display. **Sam Houston Historical Park**, 100 Bagby, 655-1912 (METRO bus 48 on Lamar; also Texas Special Red Route). Features eight historic structures dating from 1823 to 1905. The Museum of Texas History, which is also on the grounds, offers changing exhibits. **Six Flags Astroworld**, 9001 Kirby Dr., 799-1234 (METRO bus 18 W on Walker & Main). More than 100 rides, and attractions, including the Texas Cyclone, rated one of the world's best roller coasters.

SURROUNDING AREAS: **Galveston**, 80 km SE (Texas Bus Lines). A Victorian-era seaside town with many historic buildings. The Strand downtown, once the 'Wall Street of the Southwest', has gaslights, upmarket shops, restaurants and galleries. Trolleys ($2, or $4 for a narrated tour) link all the points of interest every 30 mins 1000–2100.

Useful telephone numbers

Airport Express 523-5694
Amtrak 224-1577
Arrow Trailways of Texas (817) 526-0545
Greyhound Bus Center 759-6581
Houston Chamber of Commerce 658-2404
Houston Hobby Airport 643-4597
Houston Intercontinental Airport 230-3100
Houston Visitors Bureau 523-5050
Kerrville Bus Co. (210) 257-7451
METRO 635-4000
Sierra Stage Coaches 947-2877
Texas Bus Lines 523-5694
Thomas cook Foreign Exchange: 2015-A West Gray, 521-2665; 10777 Westheimer, 782 8091
Valley Transit (512) 423-4710

LAS VEGAS

Area code 702
Time zone: Pacific Time

The most spectacular way to arrive in 'The Entertainment Capital of the World' is by air, at night, when the plethora of tungsten, fluorescent and neon combine to form a huge beacon of welcome in this unlikeliest of locations. It can also be seen from afar, if not quite as spectacularly, if you are arriving by rail or road. It may seem odd that this city of casinos, slot machines and entertainment palaces should have sprung up in the middle of nowhere, in the Mojave Desert. It was the legalisation in 1931 of gambling in Nevada (and equally the non-legalisation of gambling in California) which created the Las Vegas of today; a glance at a map will reveal the proximity of the Nevada/California State Line. Visitor Centre located at 3150 Paradise Rd, near the Convention Center.

Getting around

CENTRE: The two main areas of interest to visitors are the downtown area, and Las Vegas Boulevard (southwards from downtown), which contains most of the casinos and big-name entertainments and is invariably known as 'The Strip'. The city has an efficient public transport system, with buses throughout the area provided by Citizens Area Transit (CAT), and also the Strip Trolley which plies the length of The Strip. On CAT buses there is a flat fare of $1 ($1.50 on routes 301 and 303) and onward transfers – must be obtained on boarding first bus and are valid 1 hour – are free. Services numbered in the 100s operate north-south routes, the 200s east-west routes, and the 300s serve The Strip. Bus 301 runs the length of The Strip, every 10–15 mins, 24 hrs daily from downtown to Vacation Village. The Strip Trolley ($1.20) operates every 20 mins 0930-0200 daily, serving hotel entrances.

SURROUNDING AREAS: These are few, due to Las Vegas' isolated location. **Henderson** and **Boulder City** can be reached from downtown by CAT bus 107; Henderson is also accessible from Vacation Village by CAT bus 212 and 217. SURROUNDING AREAS: In the north-east, **Caliente** is served by Amtrak (service continues to Milford and Salt Lake City), and **Cedar City** by Greyhound Lines (services continue to Provo and Salt Lake City, and to Denver. To the south-east (all services continue to Phoenix), **Needles** is served by K-T Services, and **Kingman** by Greyhound Lines and by K-T Services. In the south-west, **Barstow** is reached by Amtrak and by Greyhound Lines (both services continue to Los Angeles). In the north-west, **Death Valley** and **Scotty's Castle** are reached by (charter only) services of Gray Line of Southern Nevada, and **Beatty** and **Tonopah** by K-T Services (service continues to Reno).

Main transport centres

McCarran International Airport (LAS), 10 km. S (CAT bus 109 to/from downtown; 108 to/from The Strip). Gateway mainly for domestic flights, but many international destinations can be reached by changing to connecting flights at major hubs. Amtrak STATION (Plaza Hotel, 1 S Main St) (CAT bus 205, 207; within walking distance of Greyhound Terminal and Downtown Transportation Center): For all Amtrak services. **Greyhound Terminal**, 200 S Main Street (CAT bus 205, 207; within walking distance of Amtrak Station and Downtown Transportation Center). For services of Greyhound Lines and K-T Services. **Downtown Transportation Center**, Stewart and Casino Center (within walking distance of Amtrak Station and Greyhound Terminal). For all CAT routes serving central downtown area, including 107 (Henderson and Boulder City), 109 (Airport), 205, 207 (Amtrak Station and Greyhound Terminal), 301 (Strip and Vacation Village), and 401 (Downtown Circulator). **Vacation Village**, Las Vegas Boulevard South). Interchange point for a number of CAT services at the southern end of The Strip.

Sightseeing by public transport

CENTRE: **Fremont Street**, Main and Fremont Streets, 678-5600 (CAT Downtown Transportation Center). 'Glitter Gulch' has been transformed into the Fremont Street Experience, where 2.1 million lights come to life nightly along with 540,000 watts of sound and music. **Las Vegas Boulevard Strip** (CAT bus 301; Strip Trolley). The famous 5.5 km Las Vegas Strip is lined with some of the world's and most luxurious resort hotels, each with its own 24-hour casino. Other attractions include: **Grand Slam Canyon at Circus Circus** (2880 Las Vegas Blvd South, 794-3939) a theme park based on the Grand Canyon; **Guinness World of Records** (2780 Las Vegas Blvd South, 792-3766); **Imperial Palace Antique Auto Collection** (3535 Las Vegas Blvd South, 731-3311) featuring over 200 antique, classic and special interest automobiles; **Luxor** (3900 Las Vegas Blvd South, 795-8118) a Pyramid-shaped hotel and casino where you can take a ride on a re-creation of the Nile; **MGM Grand Adventures** (3799 Las Vegas Blvd South, 891-1111) including the Deep Earth Exploration and Haunted Mine; **Treasure Island** (3300 S Las Vegas Blvd South, 894-7111), where Pirates battle the British Navy in Buccaneer Bay on the hour 1600–2200 nightly; and **Virtual World** (3053 Las Vegas Blvd South, 369-3583) where you can navigate the 'virtual reality' of your choice. **Liberace Museum**, 1775 E. Tropicana Ave, 798-5595 (CAT bus 201). A collection of some of Liberace's famous wardrobe, custom automobiles, and the world's largest rhinestone. **UNLV Museum of Natural History**, 4505 S Maryland Pkwy, 895-3381 (CAT bus 108, 109, 201, 203, 213). Live desert reptiles, mammals and insects.

SURROUNDING AREAS: **Clark County Heritage Museum**, 1830 S Boulder Hwy, Henderson, 455-7955 (CAT bus 107, then bus 116). Restored historic structures and ghost towns. **Hoover Dam and Lake Mead** (Gray Line Tour). Hoover Dam holds back the Colorado River to form one of the world's largest man-made lakes, with over 880 km of shoreline.

Useful telephone numbers

Amtrak 1-800-USA-RAIL
Citizens Area Transit (CAT) 228-7433
Gray Lines of Southern Nevada 384-1234
Greyhound Lines 1-800-231-2222
Greyhound Terminal 384-8009
K-T Services 644-2233
Las Vegas Visitors Center 892-7575
McCarran International Airport 261-5743
State of Nevada Information 486-7234
Strip Trolley 382-1404

LOS ANGELES

Area code 213
Time zone: Pacific Time

With an urban area of over 100 kilometres from east to west and some 70 km from north to south, Greater Los Angeles is huge. Not a city easily explored on foot. In fact, many Angelenos, as the locals are called, wouldn't dream of exploring anywhere on foot, in their city of boulevards and freeways dedicated to King Automobile. In recent years, however, the situation has begun to change. A slow, creeping paralysis, where commuter journeys by car can take up to 2 hours (and one then has the problem of finding somewhere to park it) has forced Angelenos into looking afresh at ways of getting around their city. The new Metro rail system is, making it easier to get around the city by public transport. Visitor Centres located downtown (685 S Figueroa St between Wilshire Blvd and 7th St – MTA Metro Red Line to 7th St/Metro Center) and The Janes House (6541 Hollywood Blvd – MTA buses 1, 420, 429).

Getting around

CENTRE: Los Angeles County Metropolitan Transportation Authority (MTA) operate a comprehensive bus and metro real system. The 35-km Blue Line Metro runs from 7th St Metro Center to Long Beach, an hour's journey away; the first 7 km of the Red Line currently operates from Union Station to Westlake/MacArthur (an extension to Wilshire/Western opens July 1996; extensions to Hollywood/Vine, North Hollywood/Universal Studios and a Blue Line extension to Pasadena are under construction). The two lines connect at 7th St Metro Center. The 32 km Green Line operates from El Segundo (near Los Angeles International Airport) to Norwalk, connecting with the Blue Line at Imperial/Wilmington. Bus lines numbered below 100 are local services covering the downtown area. Flat fares, currently $1.35, or 10 tokens for $9 (available at Union Station Gateway Transit Center and other locations) apply on the Metro Red, Blue and Green lines, local and limited-stop buses. Forward transfers, valid for 2 hrs, are $0.25 per use. Transfers between rail lines are free. Angel's Flight once again connects downtown (MTA Red Line Pershing Square Station) with Bunker Hill. A fare of $0.25 is payable at the top.

SURROUNDING AREAS: Metrolink operate commuter rail services Mon-Fri northwest to **Oxnard/Ventura** (also Amtrak and Greyhound services, continuing to **Santa Barbara** and **San Luis Obispo**, San Jose, Oakland, San Francisco, Portland and Seattle), **Lancaster**, **Oceanside** (also by Amtrak) and **Riverside** suburbs and Mon–Sat to **San Bernardino** (which is also served daily by Amtrak and Greyhound – both services continue to Barstow, Las Vegas, Salt Lake City, Flagstaff, Albuquerque and Chicago). MTA buses cover the suburbs with bus lines numbered 100 and above, which are arranged as follows: the 100s are local East–West services, the 200s local North-South services, the 300s are limited stop, the 400s and 500s are express services and the 600s are special event services. Downtown Los Angeles is also served by Antelope Valley Transit Authority Foothill Transit, Gardena Municipal Bus Lines, Montebello Bus Lines, LADOT Commuter Express, Orange County Transportation Authority, Santa Clarita Transit, Santa Monica Municipal Bus Lines and Torrance Transit. In inland California, **Bakersfield** (for Amtrak trains to Fresno, Merced, Stockton and Oakland) is served by Amtrak thruway buses which connect with the trains at Bakersfield, and by Greyhound Lines (services continue to Fresno, Merced, Stockton, Oakland, San Francisco and Sacramento). **Mojave** is served by Greyhound Lines (service continues to Bishop and Reno). **San Diego** can be reached by Amtrak.

Main transport centres

Los Angeles International Airport (LAX), 24 km SW (MTA bus 439 from Union Station Gateway Transit Center). Within the airport a free LAX Shuttle service operates between the nine terminals and to the MTA Green Line). Often referred to by its international designator code of LAX. Major gateway of many international and domestic flights.

Union Station, 800 North Alameda St (MTA Metro Red Line to Union Station): All Amtrak trains depart from here; also the pick-up point for Amtrak thruway buses to Bakersfield. All Metrolink trains also call here (service Mon-Fri only). Adjacent **Gateway Transit Plaza** is served by MTA buses 33, 40, 42, 55, 60, 333, 434, 436, 439, 442, 444, 445, 446, 447; DASH Route 'D' and Metrolink shuttles; Orange County and Santa Clarita commuter express buses. Several other MTA local and express buses stop on Cesar Chavez Dr. on the north side of the station or the Busway stop located south of the station (also served by Foothill Transit); Santa Monica Municipal Bus Lines, DASH Shuttle Route B and Torrance Transit stop on Alameda St in front of Union Station.

Greyhound Bus Terminal, 1716 East 7th St

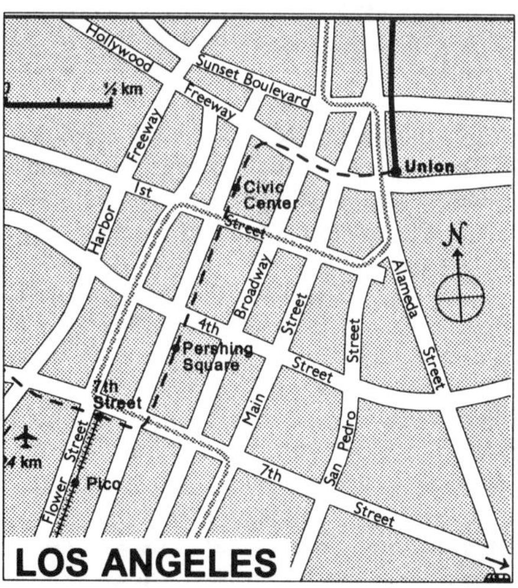

(MTA buses 60, 470, 471). For services of Greyhound Lines.

Sightseeing by public transport

CENTRE: **El Pueblo de Los Angeles State Historic Park**, 845 N Alameda St, across from Union Station, 628-1274 (MTA Metro Red Line to Union Station, or DASH Route 'B'). Features 27 historical buildings, including Avila Adobe, situated around the Plaza where Los Angeles began. **Olvera Street** features Mexican-style stalls, food vendors and restaurants. **Exposition Park**, 700 State Dr., near University of Southern California, 744-7400 (MTA buses 442, 444, 445, 446, 447; or MTA Metro Red/Blue Lines to 7th St/Metro Center, then DASH Route 'C' every 15 mins 0600–1900 Mon–Fri and every 30 mins 1000–1700). Home of the California Museum of Science and Industry (700 State Dr., 744-7400), Museum of Natural History, Memorial Coliseum (home of the 1932 and 1984 Olympic Games), Rose Garden and Sports Arena. **Grand Central Public Market**, 317 S Broadway, 624-2378 (MTA Metro Red Line to Pershing Square, or DASH Route 'D'). LA's largest open-air food market since 1917. The 1893 historic landmark Bradbury Building (304 S Broadway, 626-1893) is located across the street. **Museum of Contemporary Art (MOCA)**, 250 S Grand Ave, 626-6222 (Metro Red Line to Pershing Square then Angel's Flight, or DASH Route 'B'). Located on Bunker Hill (at the top of Angel's Flight). Exhibits include paintings, sculpture, photography and environmental works. Across the street is the **Wells Fargo History Museum** (333 S Grand Ave, 253-7166).

Hollywood, Hollywood Blvd from La Brea to Vine St, 689-8822 (MTA bus 1, 420, 429 on Broadway). Follow the stars along the 'Walk of Fame' or step into their shoes at Mann's Chinese Theater. **Hancock Park Museums**, Wilshire Blvd and Curson Ave (Metro Red Line to Wilshire/Western then MTA buses 20, 21, 22, 320, 322 – these buses also continue to Beverly Hills/Rodeo Drive, UCLA/Westwood Village and Santa Monica). Home of the **George C. Page Museum of La Brea Discoveries** (5801 Wilshire Blvd, 936-2230), featuring prehistoric fossils from the adjacent La Brea Tar Pits, the world's richest source of Ice Age mammal and bird fossils, and the **Los Angeles Couty Museum of Art** (5905 Wilshire Blvd, 857-6111), one of the largest art museums in the country. **Little Tokyo**, 1st and San Pedro St, 626-3067 (MTA Metro Red Line to Civic Center then DASH Route 'A'). Highlights include Japanese-American National Museum, and the Japanese Village and Plaza. **Southwest Museum**, 234 Museum Dr., 221-2164 (MTA bus 83 on Spring St). Extensive collection of Native-American art, and artifacts from the Southwest, Great Plains and Northwest Coast. **Universal Studios Hollywood**, 100 Universal City Plaza, (818) 508-9600–MTA Red Line to Civic Center then MTA buses 420, 424, 425 on Broadway). A behind-the-scenes look at the world's largest motion picture studio. City Walk features shops, restaurants, nightclubs, 18-screen cinema and street performers.

SURROUNDING AREAS: **Disneyland**, 57 km S, 1313 S Harbor Blvd, Anaheim, (714) 999-4565 (MTA Metro Red/Blue Lines to 7th St/Metro Center or Green Line to I-605/I-105-Norwalk and then MTA bus 460; alternatively Amtrak to Fullerton and then OCTA bus 43, or Airport Bus every 30–60 mins 0600–2300 from Los Angeles International Airport). Walt Disney's Magic Kingdom features over 60 world-famous rides and attractions in 8 theme lands. **Knotts Berry Farm**, 40 km S, 8039 Beach Blvd, Buena Park, (714) 220-5200 (MTA Metro Red/Blue Lines to 7th St/Metro Center or Green Line to I-605/I-105-Norwalk and then MTA bus 460). America's original Old West theme park features rides, shows, shopping and restaurants including Knott's famous Chicken Dinner Restaurant. **Long Beach**, 35 km SW (Metro Blue Line, then Long Beach Transit Mall and then Runabout shuttle bus). Downtown Long Beach features the *Queen Mary* (1126 Queens Hwy, (310) 435-3511; Runabout shuttle bus 'C'), the world's largest passenger ship. Passenger ferry service to **Catalina Island** (42 km) also departs from here.

Mission San Juan Capistrano, 58 km S, Ortega Hwy and Camino Capistrano, San Juan Capistrano, (714) 248-2048 (Amtrak/Metrolink to San Juan Capistrano). Old Mission located across the street) Founded in 1776, the 'Mission of the Swallows' is the site of one of the top 10 archaeological digs in North America. Chapel, museum and gardens. Pedestrian-friendly San Juan Capistrano also features a variety of shops and restaurants, including one in the train station.

Old Town Pasadena,14 km E, Colorado Blvd and Fair Oaks, Pasadena (MTA Metro Red Line to Union Station then MTA buses 401, 402 on Spring St, or 483 on Busway; alternatively Airport Bus from Los Angeles International Airport). Historic buildings and alleyways housing popular shops, restaurants and night spots. **Santa Barbara**, 165 km N (Amtrak and Greyhound Lines) One of California's most attractive beach towns.

Attractions include East and West beaches, Stearns Wharf and State Street.

Santa Monica, 16 km W, Third St from Wilshire Blvd to Colorado Ave (MTA Metro Red Line to Union Station then MTA buses 33, 333, 439 or Santa Monica bus 10 (Express) on Alameda St; alternatively Red Line to Wilshire/Western then MTA buses 20, 22, 320, 322). Features the 1909 Santa Monica Pier (complete with antique carousel and other rides) and Third Street Promenade-a lively pedestrian mall.

Useful telephone numbers

Amtrak 1-800-USA-RAIL
Anaheim/Orange County Visitor Bureau (714) 999 8999
California Office of Tourism 1-800-862 2543
Catalina Cruises. 253-9800
Catalina Express. (310) 519-1212
Greater Los Angeles Visitor Cent. 689-8822
Greyhound Lines 1-800-231-2222
Greyhound Terminal 629-8401
Los Angeles International Airport (310) 646 5252
Metrolink 808-LINK
MTA 626-4455
Thomas Cook Foreign Exchange: Seventh Marketplace, 735 S Figueroa St, 623-8584.

MIAMI

Area code 305
Time zone: Eastern Time

A large city, port and resort on Florida's East Coast at the southern end of the 100-km conurbation which stretches from West Palm Beach to South Miami. The warm Florida climate attracts not only many holidaymakers, but also a number of former residents of northern US cities who have made Miami their home; as a result the Miami area is one of the fastest-growing in the USA.

Getting around

CENTRE: Metro-Dade Transit operate a comprehensive rail and bus network throughout Dade County, which embraces the whole of Metropolitan Miami. A 33-km elevated rapid transit metro connects the north-west and south-west suburbs via the downtown area; in the downtown area itself, the elevated 3-km `people mover' connects with the metro at the Government Center and Bricknell stations. These three constituents are referred to as Metrobus, Metrorail and Metromover respectively. A flat-fare system operates, currently $1.25 for Metrorail or Metrobus; $1.50 for Express Metrobus and $0.25 from Metromover/Shuttle Bus with a transfer arrangement of $US 0.25 (transfers must be purchased at the start of the first journey) for changing from bus to bus, bus to rail or vice versa, or $1 for Metromover to Metrorail (Metrorail to Metromover is free).

SURROUNDING AREAS: Metro-Date Transit buses and trains serve the inner suburbs. Buses reach **Miami Beach** and **Key Biscayne** by causeways; these services employ route letters rather than the more usual numbers found elsewhere in Miami. Tri-Rail commuter trains connect Miami International Airport with the northern Dade, Broward and Palm Beach county suburbs; the downtown area can be reached by changing to Metrorail at Tri-Rail Station. Zone fares apply, ranging from $2 to $5.50. Transfers from Tri-Rail to Metrorail and Metrobus (within 0.5 km of Tri-Rail station) are free. Transfers from Metrorail/Metrobus to Tri-Rail are $0.25. Present rail transfer at ticket booth and receive a $1.50 discount off the price of a Tri-Rail ticket. Southward from Miami via **Homestead**, the remarkable trip along the causeways and bridges of the Florida Keys all the way to **Key West** is made by Greyhound Lines. To the west, the Everglades are crossed by Greyhound Lines en route to **Fort Myers** (service continues to St Petersburg and Tampa). To the north, Fort Lauderdale and West Palm Beach are served by Tri-Rail and by Amtrak (services continue to Orlando, Jacksonville, Richmond, Washington and beyond), and by Greyhound Lines (services continue to Orlando, Tallahassee, New Orleans, Jacksonville, Richmond and New York).

Main transport centres

Miamia International Airport (MIA), 10 km W. Metrobus 7 from downtown (board on SW 1st St, across from Downtown Bus Terminal; alternatively Metrorail from downtown to Tri-Rail Station, then Tri-Rail (infrequent service) to Miami Airport Station, then Tri-Rail shuttle bus to the Airport). Major international and domestic gateway. One terminal serves all flights. **Miami Amtrak Station**, 8303 NW 37th Ave (Metrorail to TriRail Station – one block; Bus L to Amtrak Station). Amtrak's most southerly station, about 12 km from downtown Miami. **Miami Airport Tri-Rail Station**, 1200 SE 11th Ave, Hialeah) The southern terminus of TriRail. The station is actually some 15 blocks from the airport; TriRail operate a free shuttle bus between the station and the airport. **Greyhound Bus Terminal**, 700 Biscayne Blvd, Bayside Marketplace. Downtown location;

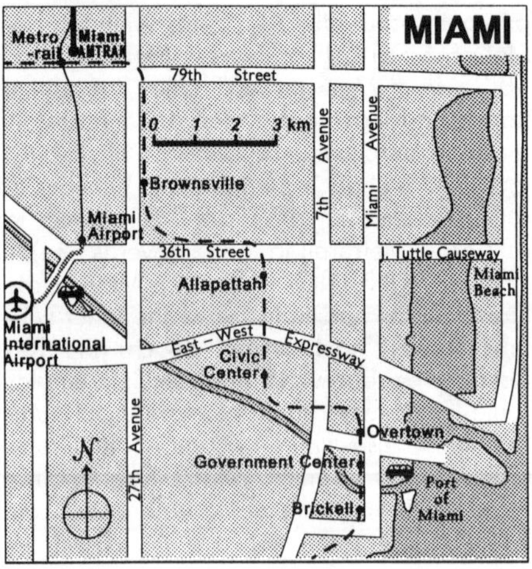

open daily 0630–1800 only (Metromover to College/Bayside, 2 blocks). Serves Greyhound Lines. **Greyhound Bus Terminal**, 4111 NW 27th St, Miami West. 10 km from downtown Miami; open 24 hours (Metrobus 7 from downtown – board on SW 1st St, across from Downtown Bus Terminal; TriRail ShuttleBus). Serves Greyhound Lines. **Metro-Dade Downtown Bus Terminal**, SW 1st St and 1st Ave (Metrobus 2, 3, 9, 110; 16, 21, C, K, S, T; within walking distance of many other downtown bus routes and Metrorail/Metromover Government Center Station).

Sightseeing by public transport

CENTRE: **Art Deco District and Miami Beach**, Ocean Drive. from 6th to 23rd Sts, 672-2014 (Metrobus C, K from Downtown Bus Terminal). More than 1,000 buildings designed in the Art Deco style. Ocean Drive is lined with revamped hotels and cafés. **Bayside Maret Place**, 401 Biscayne Blvd, 577-3344 (Metromover to College/Bayside and Metrobus 3, 16, 48, 95, C, S). Downtown marketplace features shops and restaurants reflecting the diversity of the city. Sightseeing boats and gondola rides. **Coconut Grove** (Metrobus 48 from downtown, or from Douglas Rd Metrorail). Former bohemian community now features fashionable shops, galleries, restaurants and clubs. **Coral Gables**, SW 22nd St at Douglas Rd (Metrobus 24 from downtown, or from Vizcaya Metrorail). The 'Miracle Mile' is dominated by department stores and specialty shops. **Key Biscane** (Metrorail to Brickell then Metrobus B-Key Biscayne). Attractions include Crandon Park Beach (Crandon Blvd), one of the finest in Miami. Farther out, covering the southern extremity of Key Biscayne, is **Cape Florida State Park**, a wooded area with beach, sand dunes and Cape Florida Lighthouse, built in the 1820s. **Little Havana**, SW Eighth St (Metrobus 8 from downtown, or from Brickell Metrorail). Many Cuban shops and restaurants line 'Calle Ocho.' **Metro-Dade Cultural Center/Center for Fine Arts**, 101 W Flagler St, 375-1492 (Metrorail/Metromover to Government Center). Presents 12–15 new exhibitions each year. Houses the Historical Museum of South Florida, with exhibits on Florida's past. **Miami Seaquarium**, 4400 Rickenbacker Causeway, 361-5705 (Metrorail to Brickell then Metrobus B-Key Biscayne). South Florida's largest marine attraction. **Miami MetroZoo**, 12400 SW 152nd St, 251-0400 (MetroRail to Dadeland North then Zoo Bus every 60 mins). Exotic animals in natural habitats. Across the street is the **Gold Coast Railroad Museum** (12450 SW 152nd St, 253-0063) with historic carriages, steam and diesel locomotives. **Miami Museum of Science and Space Transit Planetarium**, 3280 S Miami Ave, 854-4247 (Metrorail to Vizcaya). Over 140 hands-on exhibits and Planetarium with 19 metre dome. Across the street is the **Vizcaya Museum and Gardens** (3251 S Miami Ave, 250-9133), containing an eclectic art collection, antique furnishings, formal gardens and fountains.

SURROUNDING AREAS: **Bahamas**: Discovery Sea Tours (Pier 12, Port of Miami, located adjacent to Bayside Marketplace) offers day cruises to Freeport on Grand Bahama Island. **Key West** (Greyhound) The southernmost of a 160 km chain of islands that runs to within 144 km of Cuba, Key West is known for its laid-back lifestyle.

Useful telephone numbers

Amtrak 1-800-USA-RAIL
Discovery Sea Tours 1-800-866-8687
Florida Division of Tourism (904) 487-1462
Greyhound Lines (Miami Bayside) 374-6160
Greyhound Lines (Miami West) 871-1810
Miami International Airport 876-7000
Metro-Dade Transit 638-6700
Thomas Cook Foreign Exchange: 155 SE Third Ave, 381-9252
TriRail 1-800-TRI-RAIL

MONTRÉAL

Area code 514
Time zone: Eastern Time

Set on a series of islands in the midst of the St Lawrence River, Montréal is the second-largest French-speaking city in the world. It has a cosmopolitan flavour, with a unique culture and ambience ranging from French village to glittering metropolis. The Downtown/Centre-Ville area is where you can discover some of the city's most beautiful buildings, outstanding museums and the major shopping district: Ste Catherine, Sherbrooke, Crescent and Saint-Denis streets, Saint-Laurent Blvd, and the 29 km of passageways in the Underground City. Infotouriste Centre is located at 1001 Dorchester Square (Peel Metro).

Getting around

CENTRE: The Société de transport de la Communauté urbaine de Montréal (mercifully abbreviated to STCUM) operates a 4-line metro system (Line 1 – green, Line 2 – orange, Line 4 – yellow and Line 5 – blue; there is no line 3), which serves mainly the downtown area and inner suburbs, and a comprehensive network of buses which covers the whole of Metropolitan Montréal. A flat-fare timed-ticket system (which allows free transfer to other lines/routes up to the expiry time) applies on the metro and buses; normal cash (espèces) fare (*tarif régulier*) CA$1.85; a 6-ticket strip (*lisière de 6 tickets*) costs CA$7.75. Alternatively a Tourist Card (*La Carte Touristique*) for unlimited travel throughout the metro and bus network is available from Infotouriste (address above) and other outlets (call STCUM for details) for CA$5 for one day or CA$12 for three consecutive days. STCUM also operates two commuter rail services which serve the western and northwestern suburbs.

SURROUNDING AREAS: To the north and west across the Rivière-des-Prairies (Montréal North Shore), urban transport is provided by Société de transport de Laval (STL). STCUM commuter rail services reach **Dorval**, **Île-Perrot**, **Dorion**, **Hudson** and **Rigaud** in the west, and stations in **Western Laval** en route to **Deux-Montagnes** (Autoroute 640) in the north-west.

To the south and east across the St Lawrence (Montréal South Shore), urban transport is provided by Société de transport de la Rive-Sud de Montréal (STRSM). Yellow Line 4 of the STCUM metro crosses the St Lawrence to connect with STRSM buses at Longueuil. To the south-west, **Cornwall** is served by VIA Rail and by Voyageur Colonial buses (both services continue to Kingston, Belleville, Oshawa and Toronto). To the west, **Ottawa** can be reached by VIA Rail and by Voyageur Colonial. To the north west, **St Jérome** and **Ste Agathe** are served by Autobus Auger N-O (service continues to Mont Laurier, Grand Remous, Val d'Or and Noranda-Rouyn). To the north east, **Shawinigan** is reached by VIA Rail (services continue to Chambord and Jonquière, and to La Tuque, Senneterre and Cochrane); **Trois Rivières** by Orléans Express buses (service continues to Québec) and **St Hyacinthe** and **Drummondville** by VIA Rail (services continue to Québec, and to Lévis, Rivière du Loup, Mont Joli, Gaspé, Moncton, Amherst, Truro and Halifax). To the east, **Sherbrooke** is served by Autobus Auger Estrie and Autobus Bernier Lemay. To the south east, **Newport** is served by Autobus Viens. To the south, **Burlington, VT** is served by Amtrak thruway buses to St Albans (connecting train service continues to Burlington, Springfield, New York and Washington), and by Greyhound Lines; and **Plattsburg, NY** by Amtrak and by Greyhound Lines (both services continue to Saratoga Springs, Albany and New York).

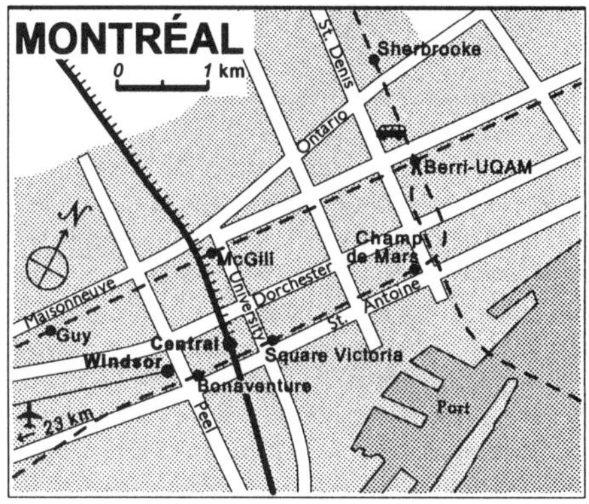

Main transport centres

Montréal International Airport (Mirabel) (YMX) (Aeroplus bus from Central Station and from the Voyageur bus terminal; Aeroplus also operate a service 0900–2320 between Mirabel and Dorval airports). Main gateway for international flights other than to the USA. One terminal serves all airlines. **Montréal International Airport (Dorval)** (YUL) (Autocar Connaisseur/Gray Line bus). For flights within Canada and to USA. **Central Station**, 895 rue de la Gauchetière Ouest (STCUM Orange Line 2 Métro to Bonaventure). All VIA Rail and Amtrak services leave from here; also STCUM trains on the Deux-Montagnes line. **Windsor Station**, Peel and de la Gauchetière (STCUM Orange Line 2 Métro to Bonaventure). For STCUM trains on the Rigaud Line. **Voyageur Bus Terminal**, 505 de Maisonneuve Blvd East) (STCUM Métro Green Line 1, Orange Line 2 or Yellow Line 4 to Berri-UQAM). For services of Greyhound Lines and Voyageur Colonial.

Sightseeing by public transport

CENTRE: **Château Ramezay Museum**, 280 Notre-Dame St East, 861-3708 (STCUM Métro Green Line 1 to Champ-de-Mars). One of the French regime's most beautiful legacies, built in 1705 for Claude de Ramezay, Governor of Montréal. Features a major collection of items relating to the history of Montréal and Québec.

Îles Notre-Dame (STCUM Yellow Line 4 to Île-Sainte-Helene). Popular for its floral park and a host of other activities, including a casino. Adjacent St Helen's Island features **La Biosphere** (283-5000), a learning and observation centre focusing on the St Lawrence River/Great Lakes ecosystem. At the east end of the island is **La Ronde** (872-6222), the largest amusement park in Québec. **Mount Royal Park**, 844-4928 (STCUM Orange Line 2 to Mont-Royal and bus 11). Designed by Frederick Law Olmstead, who also designed New York's Central Park. Outstanding views of the city and surrounding area from the Chalet and Lookout. **Montréal Botanical Garden**, 4101 rue Sherbrooke Est, 872-1400 (STCUM Green Line 1 to Pie-IX). One of the largest in the world, with thirty outdoor gardens, ten exhibition greenhouses and insectarium.

Notre-Dame Basilica, 116 Notre-Dame West, 842-2925 (STCUM Orange Line 2 to Place-d'Armes). A masterpiece of neo-Gothic architecture, highlighted by two towers and outstanding woodwork. The organ, built in 1887, is one of the largest in the world.

Old Montréal (STCUM Orange Line 2 to Square Victoria, Place-d'Armes or Champ-de-Mars). One of North America's most remarkable architectural locations, featuring many historic squares, churches and buildings. One of the liveliest spots is **Place Jacques Cartier** (Champ-de-Mars Métro), a public market since 1804. The **Old Port of Montréal** is among the largest redeveloped old ports in the world. The 2.5 km waterfront is the site of many exhibitions and sight-seeing cruises. **Olympic Park**, rue Sherbrooke and Blvd Pie-IX (STCUM Green Line 1 to Pie-IX/Viau). Attractions include the **Biodome** (868-3000), a unique museum of the environment, featuring the ecosystems of North America.

St Joseph's Oratory, 3800 Queen Mary Rd, 733-8211 (STCUM Blue Line 5 to Côte-des-Neiges). One of North America's leading pilgrimage destinations, topped by a copper dome surpassed in size only by St Peter's in Rome. **Sun Life Building**, 1155 Metcalfe (STCUM Green Line 1 to Pee.l) This impressive 1918 building, highlighted by colonnades, once held the distinction of being the largest building in the British Empire.

SURROUNDING AREAS: **Québec City**, 272 km NE (VIA Rail and Orleans Express). The only walled city in North America. A strong French-European influence (over 90 percent of the population speaks French) and unique appearance have made Québec City a popular tourist destination. Points of interest include: the Citadel, with its enormous walls overlooking the city; the Promenade des Gouveneurs, following the cliffside with expansive views of the St Lawrence River; Notre-Dame Basilica, one of the oldest churches in North America, and Place Royal in the lower town – the birthplace of the city.

Useful telephone numbers

Amtrak 1-800-426-8725
Autobus Auger Estrie 691-1654
Autobus Auger N-O 691-1654
Autobus Bernier Lemay 546-2490
Autobus Viens 293-3129
Autocar Connoisseur/Gray Line 934-1222
Dorval Airport 633-3105
Greater Montréal Tourism Bureau 873-2015
Greyhound Lines 842-2281
Orléans Express 847-4020
STCUM 288-6287
Thomas Cook Foreign Exchange: 625 René-Levesque Blvd, 397-4029; Thomas Cook Travel: Cavendish Mall, 484 1090.
Tourisme Québec 873-2015
VIA Rail 871-1331
Voyageur Bus Terminal 843-4231

NEW ORLEANS

Area code 504
Time zone: Central Time

Located on the Mississippi River near the Gulf of Mexico, New Orleans was founded by Jean Baptiste Le Moyne in 1718 and named for the Duc d'Orléans, regent of France. The city was laid out along the lines of a medieval French town, with a central square on the river. After purchase by the USA in 1803, New Orleans was known as the 'Paris of America.' Today New Orleans is a busy international port and its reputation for fine food, entertainment and music, make it one of the most visited cities in the USA. The city's historic French Quarter draws visitors from around the world, especially during the annual Carnival (Mardi Gras), held the ten days leading up to 'Fat Tuesday' (the day before Ash Wednesday and Lent). Visitor Centre located at 529 St Anne St, on Jackson Square in the French Quarter.

Getting around

CENTRE: The Regional Transit Authority (RTA) operates buses and historic trams (streetcars) throughout the City and to Kenner. The following routes are the most used by visitors: 2 – Riverfront Streetcar; 11 – Magazine Line ; 42 – Canal Line; 3 – Vieux Carré Line ; 12 – St Charles Streetcar, the world's oldest continuously operating street railway; and 48 – Esplanade Line. A flat one-way fare system ($1 for RTA buses and the St Charles Streetcar, or $1.25 for the Riverfront Streetcar) is in effect. Transfers are an additional $0.10. The RTA VisiTour Pass (1 Day $4, or 3 Day $8), valid on all RTA bus and streetcar routes except those in Kenner, is available through information counters at hotels and retail centres.

SURROUNDING AREAS: The RTA network extends to **Algiers** (served by Free Canal Street Ferry) and **Kenner**. **Jefferson Parish** and **New Orleans International Airport** are reached by Westside Transit (West Jefferson) and by Louisiana Transit (East Jefferson) buses; **St Bernard Parish** is served by St Bernard Urban Rapid Transit; there are no transfer privileges with RTA. To the north, **Hammond** is reached by Amtrak trains and by Greyhound Lines buses (services continue to Jackson, Memphis and Chicago); **Bogalusa** is reached by Greyhound Lines, to the north east, **Slidell** is served by Amtrak trains and by Greyhound Lines buses (services continue to Meridian, Birmingham, Atlanta and New York); **Biloxi** and **Mobile** are reached by Amtrak trains and by Colonial Trailways and Greyhound Lines buses (services continue to Montgomery, Birmingham and Atlanta, and to Tallahassee, Jacksonville and Miami); in the south-west quadrant **Houma** and **Morgan City** are reached by Greyhound Lines buses; to the west **Lafayette** is reached by Amtrak trains and Greyhound Lines buses (services continue to Lake Charles, Beaumont, Houston, Dallas, San Antonio, El Paso and Los Angeles); to the north-west, **Baton Rouge** is reached by Amtrak thruway bus and by Greyhound Lines (service continues to Alexandria and Shreveport).

Main transport centres

New Orleans International Airport (MSY), 16 km NW. Airport Shuttle, $10, every 10–15 mins to downtown hotels – ring 2 hrs prior to pick-up for service from downtown hotels to the airport. Alternatively by Louisiana Transit Airport Express bus ($1.20) every 15–30 mins 0600–1830 weekdays and every 20–40 mins 0630–1800 weekends from stop located at Tulane and Elk Place, 1 block from Canal St. Served by all major domestic and international carriers to Latin America and the Caribbean. **Union Passenger Terminal–Transportation Center**, 1001 Loyola Ave (RTA Canal Line bus to Rampart then bus 17). Serves Amtrak, Colonial Trailways and Greyhound Lines.

Sightseeing by public transport

CENTRE: **Canal Street Pier**, foot of Canal St (RTA Riverfront Streetcar) Free ferry to **Old Algiers National Historic District**, offering spectacular views of the New Orleans skyline and riverfront. The Pier is also the departure point for the Riverboat to the Audubon Zoo Here is the **Aquarium of the Americas**, 861-2537, a world-class museum of sea life, with over 8,000 fish, birds and reptiles indigenous to North, Central and South America and surrounding bodies of water. **Audubon Park**, St Charles Ave (RTA Magazine Line, or St Charles Streetcar; then free shuttle to zoo; alternatively by the *John James Audubon* from Aquarium of the Americas). Home of the **Audubon Zoological Gardens** (6500 Magazine St, 861-2537), one of the top zoos in the country, with over 1,500 animals. **Confederate Museum**, 929 Camp St, 523-4522 (Magazine Line). Civil War memorabilia, including flags, paintings, uniforms, weapons and personal effects of great Southern leaders. Adjacent to the museum is **Lee Circle**, erected in 1884, honouring the Confederacy's famous general.

French Market, 1008 N Peters St (RTA Riverfront Streetcar and Vieux Carré Line). The oldest public marketplace in America, featuring an assortment of shops and eateries along the waterfront from Jackson Square to the Old Mint. **French Quarter**, from Canal St to Esplanade (RTA Vieux Carré Line). The oldest section of the city, often called Vieux Carré (old square). Home to the Mardi Gras. Attractions include Burbon St, site of many of the city's most famous clubs and restaurants; Preservation Hall (726 St Peter St), the place to hear 'real' New Orleans Jazz; Royal St, with a variety of shops, and the Historic New Orleans Collection (533 Royal St, 523-4662), of paintings, documents and artifacts about New Orleans and Louisiana. **Garden District**, Magazine Ave (RTA Magazine Line). Historic 'American' quarter of the city, with elegant mansions, antique shops, galleries and restaurants. **Jackson Brewery**, 620 Decatur St (RTA Riverfront Streetcar and Vieux Carré Line). 1891 brewhouse now features over 75 shops, restaurants and entertainment. Departure point for the steamboat *Natchez* (586-8777), offering twice daily harbour cruises. **Jackson**

Square, between Decatur, Chartres, St Peter and St Anne Sts (RTA Riverfront Streetcar and Vieux Carré Line). Formerly known as the Place d'Armes, the French Quarter's Historic Square is surrounded by entertainment as street jugglers, musicians and artists perform. Across the Square stands the **St Louis Cathedral** (525-9585), the oldest in America, still used for daily worship. Also located on the square are the **Pontalba Apartments**, the oldest in America, still serving as residences, offices, shops and restaurants. The restored **1850 House** (523 St Ann St) displays the ostentatious tastes of a well-to-do Creole family. **The Old US Mint**, 400 Esplanade Ave (Riverfront Streetcar) houses Jazz and Carnival exhibits. **River Cruises**, 27 Poydras St Wharf, 529-4567 (RTA Riverfront Streetcar). The Riverboat *Cajun Queen* offers 3 daily 1½ hr. Plantation/Harbor Cruises departing from the Aquarium of the Americas. Paddlewheeler *Creole Queen* offers 2 daily 2½ hr Plantation/Battlefield cruises and nightly dinner/jazz cruises departing from the Canal St Dock at Riverwalk. **Riverbend**, St Charles Ave at Carrollton (St Charles Streetcar). A collection of cottages and 19th-century buildings featuring shops and restaurants. **Riverwalk**, Foot of Poydras St (RTA Riverfront Streetcar). Former riverfront warehouse district transformed into a specialty marketplace with more than 140 shops, restaurants and the Flamingo Casino. The International Cruise Ship Terminal is the departure point for cruises to Mexico, the Caribbean and Central America.

SURROUNDING AREAS: **Delta Quenn Stemboat Company**, Robin St Wharf, 586-0631. The last two overnight paddlewheel steamboats in the United States, the *Delta Queen* and *Mississippi Queen*, offer deluxe 3–12 night cruises up the Mississippi, including stops at antebellum plantations and historic towns such as Natchez and Vicksburg, Mississippi from February to December. Gray Line Tours (587-0861) operate City, Swamp and Bayou and Plantation tours. Tours depart from ticket office located at Toulouse St and the River (next to Jackson Brewery), in the French Quarter.

Useful telephone numbers

Amtrak 1-800-872-7245
Delta Queen Steamboat Company 586-0631
Greyhound Lines 1-800-231-2222
Louisiana Tourism 568-5661
Louisiana Transit 737-9611
New Orleans International Airport 464-0831
New Orleans Metropolitan Convention and Visitors Bureau 566-5005
Regional Transit Authority (RTA) 242-2600
Riverboat John James Audubon 586-8777
St Bernard Urban Rapid Transit 277-1907
Steamboat Natchez 586-8777
Westside Transit 367-7433

NEW YORK

Area code 212
Time zone: Eastern Time

New York, New York. The Big Apple. Broadway. Yellow cabs. Steaming hydrants. 'Walk/Don't Walk' signs. Everything you've seen on the movies, but for real. And with one of the most comprehensive public transport systems in the world, it's very easy to get around. The Metropolitan Transit Authority (MTA) is the coordinating body for the main transport agencies which operate in and around New York: New York City Transit Authority (TA) (subway system, buses in New York City, and Staten Island Rapid Transit); Long Island Rail Road (LIRR) (trains from New York City to Long Island destinations); Metro-North Commuter Railroad (trains from New York City on the Hudson, Harlem and New Haven lines, and from Hoboken on the Port Jervis and Pascack Valley lines); MTA Long Island Bus (buses linking western Long Island with LIRR stations and with the subway). Travel Information Centres located at Pennsylvania Station (upper level, near Amtrak), Grand Central Terminal (main concourse, near MetLife), Port Authority Bus Terminal (near 8th Ave and 40 St entrance), Times Square (42 St and 7th Ave) and World Trade Center (Building 2, near observation deck entrance).

Getting around

CENTRE: Comprised of the boroughs of Bronx, Brooklyn, Manhattan, Queens and Staten Island. All are served by TA buses, which carry a prefix (Bx, B, M, Q, S) in front of the route number according to the borough they primarily serve. Staten Island has its own self-contained TA Rapid Transit; the other 4 boroughs are all served by TA subway. The subway system is one of the most intensive in the world, with 25 lines, each designated either by a number or letter. However, most lines are operated as part of a larger group, and run on group tracks in Manhattan, only separating into branches at the outer ends of the lines, so it's not as complicated as it seems. Various patterns of service operate, with local, skip-stop, express, peak-hour or night-only services. Subway maps are available free of charge at token booths (or you can write for a copy to:

Customer Information, 130 Livingston St, Brooklyn, NY 11201). In Manhattan, platform signs for 'Uptown' refer to northbound trains and 'Downtown' to southbound trains. A flat-fare system (currently $1.50) operates on both the subway and the buses. For the subway this must be exchanged for a token at the token booth on entry to the system, or a 'Ten Pak' can be purchased. The fare can also be paid by using MetroCard, an automated fare card which can be bought in whole-dollar amounts from $5 to $80 at subway station booths, or a $15 card at above-ground newsstands, delis, pharmacies and other stores. The card can be used on all TA buses and in over 150 subway stations (by mid-1997 MetroCard will be able to be used at all 468 subway stations). You can transfer to another subway line at designated stations without extra charge. Buses accept either tokens or coins (exact change only); free transfers to intersecting bus routes are permitted (ask the driver for a transfer ticket when you board the first bus), but are only valid for 1 hour and for onward (not return) journeys.

SURROUNDING AREAS: In New Jersey, **Newark**, for New Jersey Transit (NJ Transit) rail and bus services to southern and western New Jersey suburbs, is served by Port Authority Trans-Hudson Corporation (PATH), NJ Transit and Amtrak trains (only certain Amtrak trains may be used for local journeys from New York to Newark or vice versa; see timetables for details), and by Greyhound Lines buses; **Jersey City** and **Hoboken**, for NJ Transit rail and bus services to central and western New Jersey

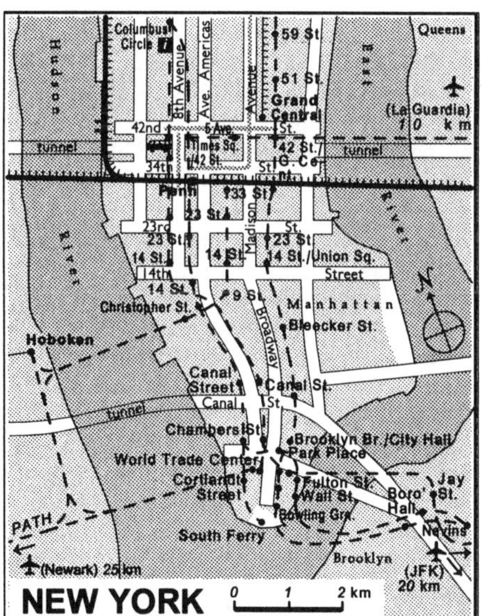

(Not all subway lines or stations are shown)

suburbs – also Metro-North/NJ Transit trains on the Port Jervis and Pascack Valley lines – is served by PATH. In New York State, the northern suburbs of New York city are served by Metro-North trains; the eastern suburbs by LIRR trains and by MTA Long Islandbuses. Southwards along the coast, **Atlantic City** can be reached by Greyhound Lines and NJ Transit trains (from Philadelphia) and buses. In Pennsylvania, **Philadelphia** is served by Amtrak (services continue to Baltimore, Washington, Charlotte, Atlanta, New Orleans, Jacksonville, Tampa and Miami and to Harrisburg, Pittsburgh and Chicago) **Bethlehem** and **Allentown** by Trans-Bridge Lines, and **Scranton** by Greyhound Lines (services continue to Binghamton, Rochester and Buffalo) and Martz Trailways (services continue to Wilkes-Barre). For destinations in upstate New York, **Albany**, **Syracuse**, **Rochester** and **Buffalo** are all reached by Amtrak (services continue to Cleveland, Toledo and Chicago, to Niagara Falls and Toronto, and to Plattsburgh and Montréal), by Greyhound Lines (services continue to Cleveland, and to Plattsburg and Montréal) and by Adirondack Trailways. In Connecticut and Massachusetts, **Danbury** and **Waterbury** are both reached by branches of Metro-North; **Hartford** and **Springfield** by Amtrak and by Greyhound Lines; **Stamford**, **Bridgeport** and **New Haven** by Metro-North and by Amtrak (service continues to New London, Providence and Boston).

Main transport centres

John F. Kennedy International Airport (JFK), 24 km in Queens (from Manhattan, direct service to all airport terminals from Pennsylvania Station, Grand Central Terminal/ Park Ave or Port Authority Bus Terminal by Carey Airport Express; alternatively by TA Subway 'A' to Howard Beach, then by free shuttle bus from Manhattan bound platform to all airport terminals. Within the Airport, free Port Authority Airline Connection bus serves all terminals 24 hrs. a day. Direct connection from/to La Guardia Airport by Carey Transportation bus; from/to Newark Airport by Princeton Airporter bus): Major gateway for international and domestic flights, with nine terminals. **La Guardia Airport** (LGA), 13 km NE in Queens. From Manhattan, direct service to all airport terminals from Pennsylvania Station, Grand Central Terminal/Park Ave or Port Authority Bus Terminal by Carey Airport Express; alternatively by TA subway line E, F, G or R to Roosevelt Avenue/Jackson Heights, then by Triboro Coach bus Q33, or by TA subway line 7 to 74th St–Jackson Heights then by

Trioboro Coach bus Q33. Alternatively by Delta Water Shuttle ferry from Wall Street Pier or East 34th Street to Marine Terminal. Within the airport, free Port Authority Airline Connection bus serves all terminals. Direct connection from/to JFK Airport by Carey Transportation bus; no direct connection from/to Newark Airport – use directions above and transfer in Manhattan. Gateway mainly for US domestic flights, but also some international destinations in Canada and Central America. Four terminals. **Newark International Airport** (EWR), 28 km SW in Newark NJ. From Manhattan direct service from Port Authority Bus Terminal by NJ Transit Express Bus 300, or from One World Trade Center or from Grand Central and Penn Stations by Olympia Trails. Alternatively by PATH, NJ Transit or Amtrak train to Newark Penn Station, then by NJ Transit Airlink Bus 302 which calls at all airport terminals. Within the airport a free Airline Connection Bus operates between Terminals A, B and C, 24 hours per day, every 10 mins Direct connection from/to John F. Kennedy Airport by Princeton Airporter bus; no direct connection from/to La Guardia Airport – use directions above and transfer in Manhattan. Major gateway for domestic and international flights, with three terminals. **Pennsylvania Station**, 7th and 8th Ave at W 32nd St, Midtown Manhattan (Subways 1, 2, 3, 9, A, C, E to Penn Station, or B, D, F, N, Q, R to 34th St; within walking distance of Port Authority Bus Station). Usually abbreviated to 'Penn', Pennsylvania is the arrival/ departure point for all Amtrak services, and also for Manhattan services of NJ Transit and LIRR. **Grand Central Terminal**, Park Ave at 42nd St, Midtown Manhattan (Subways 4, 5, 6, 7, S to Grand Central). Rather less 'Grand' these days than in its heyday (a $175 million rehabilitation is scheduled to begin in 1996), Grand Central Terminal is now confined to handling the commuter services of Metro-North on the Hudson, Harlem and New Haven lines to the northern New York suburbs and to Connecticut. **33rd Street PATH Station**, (Midtown Manhattan. Subways B, D, F, N, Q, R to 34th St offer nearby access. Subway stations 33rd St on subways 4, 5, 6, and 34th St on 1, 2, 3, 9 are a good walk away (34th St on A, C, E is further still) but all these are connected to 33rd Street PATH station by TA bus M34. Midtown Manhattan terminus (trains also call at 23rd, 14th, 9th and Christopher Streets) for PATH trains to Hoboken and Jersey City. **World Trade Center**, Battery Park City-Lower Manhattan (Subway E to World Trade Center; 1, 9 and N, R to Cortlandt Street; 2, 3 to Park Place): Lower Manhattan terminus for PATH trains to Hoboken, Jersey City and Newark. **Flatbush Avenue**, downtown Brooklyn (Subways 2, 3, 4, 5, D, Q to Atlantic Ave ; B, M, N, R to Pacific St): Main western terminus for LIRR trains to various Long Island destinations. **Jamaica**, Queens (LIRR from Penn; subways E, J, Z). The 'Clapham Junction' of the LIRR system (all lines except Flushing call here) and probably the best place to head for if your Long Island destination does not have a direct or convenient service from Penn. **Hoboken**, NJ (PATH train from 33rd St; PATH train or Port Imperial Ferry from World Trade Center/Battery Park). For PATH trains to Jersey City and Newark; NJ Transit trains to various destinations throughout New Jersey; NJ Transit/Metro-North trains on the Port Jervis and Pascack Valley lines to destinations in New Jersey and New York State. **Port Authority Bus Terminal**, 42nd St at 8th Ave, Midtown Manhattan (Subways A, C, E to 42nd St; 1, 2, 3, 7, 9, N, R, S to Times Square; within walking distance of Penn Station). Main bus station in New York, serving Adirondack Trailways, Bonanza Bus Lines, Capitol Trailways, Carey Transportation, Greyhound Lines, Hudson Transit-Short Line, International Bus Services, Martz Trailways, NJ Transit, Short Line, Susquehanna Trailways, Trans-Bridge Bus Lines. **George Washington Bridge Bus Station**, Upper Manhattan (Subway A to 175th St; 1, 9 to 181st St). Serves NJ Transit; also commuter buses to Upstate New York counties.

Sightseeing by public transport

CENTRE: **American Museum of History**, Central Park West at 79 St, 769-5100 (Subways B, C to 81 St). Over 34 million artifacts document the history of the earth, animals and man. **Central Park**, 59 St to 110 St between 5th Ave and Central Park West, 794-6564 (Subways N, R to 5th Ave; A, D, 1, 9 to 59 St; B, C to stops between 59 St and Cathedral Pkwy; 4, 5 to 59 St or 86 St; 6 to stops between 59 St and 110 St). 840-acre park designed by Frederick Law Olmstead. Includes zoo, carousel, tennis courts, ice-skating rinks, rowing lake and the 'Great Lawn.' **Ellis Island**, Liberty Island, New York Harbor, 363-3200 or 269-5755 for ferry information (Subways 1, 9 to South Ferry – ride in first five cars; N, R to Whitehall St-South Ferry). Entry point for over 11 million immigrants from 1892 to 1954. **Empire State Building**, 5th Ave at 34 St, 736-3100 (Subways B, D, F, N, Q, R to 34 St-Herald Sq.; 6 to 33rd St). The tallest building in the world for 40 years after it was built in 1931. 86th floor observation deck offers 80 km view. **Guggenheim Museum**, 1071 5th Ave, 423-3500 (Subways: 4, 5, 6 to 86 St). Frank Lloyd Wright-designed landmark features a permanent collection of Impressionist, Post-Impressionist, Modern and Contemporary masterpieces. **Lincoln Center**, Broadway and Amsterdam Ave at 65th St, 875-5350 (Subways: 1, 9 to 66th St–Lincoln Center). Includes the Vivian Beaumont Theater, Alice Tully Hall, Avery Fisher Hall, Metropolitan Opera House and the New York State Theater. **Metropolitan Museum of Art**, 5th Ave at 82nd St, 535-7710 (Subways 4, 5, 6 to 86 St). More than 3 million works of art including hundreds of world-famous masterpieces. **Museum of Modern Art**, 11 W 53rd St, 708-9480 (Subways B, D, Q to 50 St-Rockefeller Center; E, F to 5th Ave). A wide range of paintings, sculpture, drawings, prints and other works from the 1880s to the present. **New York Stock Exchange**, 20 Broad St at Wall St, 656-5167 (Subways 2, 3, 4, 5 to Wall St; 1, 9 to Rector St; J, M, Z to Broad St). **Rockefeller Center**, 6th Ave at 50th St, 698-2950 or 664-4000 for NBC Studios Tour (Subways B, D, F, Q to 50 St-Rockefeller Center; E to 5th Ave ; N, R to 49 St; 1, 9 to 50 St; 6 to 51 St). Nineteen-building complex includes the GE Building, NBC studios, an ice-skating rink and floral display. **St Patrick's Cathedral**, 5th Ave and 50th St, 753-2261 (Subways 6 to 51 St; 1, 9 to 50 St; B, D, F, Q to 50 St-Rockefeller Center; E to 5th Ave ; N, R to 49 St). English Gothic-style cathedral is the seat of New York City's Catholic Archdiocese. **South Street Seaport**, South and Fulton Sts. at Pier 16, 732-7678 (Subways 2, 3, 4, 5, J, M, Z to Fulton St; A, C to Broadway-Nassau). Features a museum and walking tours of ships and buildings. **Staten Island Ferry**, Battery Park, South Ferry, (718) 727-2508 (Subways 1, 9 to South Ferry (ride in first five cars); N, R to Whitehall St). A 50-cent round-trip offers magnificent views of the Manhattan skyline and New York harbour. **Statue of Liberty**, Liberty Island, New York Harbor, 363-3200 or 269-5755 for ferry information (Subways 1, 9 to South Ferry – ride in first five cars – N, R to Whitehall St). A national landmark in New York harbour for over 100 years. Viewing decks are located at the feet and crown. Ferry departures every 60 mins 0900–1600. **United Nations**, 1st Ave at 45 St (Subways 4, 5, 6, 7 to 42 St-Grand Central). Free tickets to the General Assembly and Councils are available on a first-come, first-serve basis just before the 1030 and 1530 meetings.

Useful telephone numbers

Adirondack Trailways 1-800-858-8555
Amtrak 1-800-872-7245
Bonanza Bus Lines 1-800-556-3815
Capitol Trailways 1-800-858-8555
Carey Transportation (718) 632-0500
Delta Water Shuttle 1-800-54-FERRY
Green Bus Lines (718) 995-4700
Greyhound Lines 1-800-231-2222
Jamaica Bus (718) 526-0800
John F. Kennedy Airport (718) 244-4444
La Guardia Airport (718) 476-5000
Long Island Rail Road (718) 217-LIRR
Martz Trailways 1-800-858-8555
Metro-North Commuter Railroad 532-4900
Newark Airport (201) 961-6000
New Jersey Transit (201) 762-5100
New York Convention & Visitors Bureau 484-1200
New York City Transit Authority (718) 330-1234
Olympia Trails 964-6233
PATH 1-800-234-7284
Princeton Airporter (609) 587-6600
Queens Surface (718) 445-3100
Short Line (201) 529-3666
Staten Island Ferry (718) 390-5253
Staten Island Rapid Transit (718) 447-8601
Susquehanna Trailways 1-800-858-8555
Trans-Bridge Bus Lines (610) 868-6001
Triboro Coach (718) 335-1000
Thomas Cook Foreign Exchange: At 29 and 1590 Broadway, 317 and 511Madison Ave (phone 757-6915); JFK (Intn'l Arrivals Building, phone (718) 656-8444)

ORLANDO

Area code 407
Time zone: Eastern Time

Situated in sunny Central Florida, Orlando is the home of Walt Disney World. To many people the two are synonymous, but splendid though it is, there is far more to Orlando than Disneyworld; even before Mickey Mouse, Donald Duck, Goofy et al arrived in 1971, Orlando already had several theme parks as part of its quest to become Fun Capital of the World, and today boasts so many attractions that it would need a stay of several weeks to do justice to them all. Visitor Information Centre located in the Mercado Mediterranean Shopping Village on International Drive.

Getting around

CENTRE: LYNX operate a network of buses throughout the Orlando and its suburbs. A flat-fare (currently $0.75) system is in operation; a transfer ($0.10) must be purchased to change from one bus to another. This transfer is free if using a book of 10 ($7) or 20 ($12) tickets.

SURROUNDING AREAS: The LYNX bus network operates throughout Orange county. **Sanford** is reached by LYNX bus 39, which visits the northern suburbs en route; **Kissimmee** is served by LYNX bus 4 and 18. **Daytona Beach** is reached by Greyhound Lines buses (service continues to Jacksonville); **Cocoa** (for Cape Canaveral and Port Canaveral), **Melbourne** and **Fort Pierce** (service continues to West Palm Beach, Fort Lauderdale and Miami); **Kissimmee** and **Sebring** by Amtrak (service continues to Okeechobee, West Palm Beach, Fort Lauderdale and Miami); **Lakeland** and **Tampa** (for Clearwater and St Petersburg) by Amtrak and by by Greyhound Lines; **Ocala** by Greyhound Lines (service continues to Gainesville, Tallahassee, Pensacola, Mobile and New Orleans).

Main transport centres

Orlando International Airport (MCO), 10 km SE (LYNX bus 11 from/to Downtown Bus Station, or bus 42 from/to International Drive). Airline arrivals and departures are designated by groups of gates rather than terminals. **Amtrak Station**, 1400 Sligh Blvd, about 2 km south of downtown area (LYNX bus 34, weekdays only, from Downtown Bus Station, or LYNX buses 7, 11, 18, 40 to Orange Ave and Columbia, then walk 2 blocks west). For all Amtrak services. **Greyhound Bus Station**, 555 N Magruder Blvd, about 3 km west of downtown area (LYNX Bus 25 from Downtown Bus Station, no Sunday service, or LYNX Bus 28, 29 from Downtown Bus Station to Colonial Dr. and John Young Pkwy, then walk 2 blocks south). Serves Greyhound Lines. **LYNX Downtown Bus Station**, between Central Blvd and Pine Street. For LYNX local services.

Sightseeing by public transport

CENTRE: **Church Street Station**, 129 West Church St, 422-2434 (LYNX to Downtown Bus Station). Downtown Orlando's nighttime dining, shopping and entertainment centre. Five showrooms feature rock, jazz, country and dance music for one admission. Exchange Shopping Emporium features three storeys of specialty shops. **Orange County Historical Museum**, 810 East Rollins St, 897-6350 (LYNX bus 1, 39 from Downtown Bus Station, no Sunday service). Explore Central Florida's past, from prehistoric to pioneer times. Includes 1926 firehouse with antique fire trucks. The adjacent **Orlando Science Center** (896-7151) features hands-on science fun for all ages. Includes WaterWorks, NatureWorks, John Young Planetarium, Tunnel of Discovery and Weather Central. **Sea World of Florida**, 351-3600 (LYNX bus 8 from Downtown Bus Station, or bus 42 from Orlando International Airport/ International Dr.). The world's most popular marine life park. **Universal Studios Florida** (LYNX bus 40 from Downtown Bus Station, no Sunday service). The No. 1 movie studio theme park in the world. **Walt Disney World** (LYNX bus 50 from Downtown Bus Station and then monorail from Transportation Ticket Center to the Magic Kingdom and EPCOT Center, or shuttle bus to Disney-MGM Studios and other attractions).

Useful telephone numbers

Amtrak 1-800-USA-RAIL
Florida Division of Tourism (904) 487-1462
Greyhound Lines 1-800-231-2222
LYNX 841-8240
Orlando International Airport 825-2001
Orlando Visitors Bureau 363-5800
Thomas Cook Foreign Exchange: 55 West Church St, 839-1700

PHILADELPHIA

Area code 215
Time zone: Eastern Time

Located almost halfway between New York and Washington, Philadelphia is sometimes overlooked by overseas visitors. Yet this fifth-largest city and one-time capital of the USA has much to offer, both historically and culturally. One of the oldest US cities, the historic area situated near the waterfront of the Delaware River is relatively compact and is easily explored on foot. The downtown area is known as Center City Philadelphia. Visitor Centre located at 16th St and John F. Kennedy Blvd across from Suburban Station).

Getting around

CENTRE: The Southeastern Pennsylvania Transportation Authority (SEPTA) operates a comprehensive system of surface routes (bus, tram and trackless trolley routes) throughout the city, plus two subway lines (the Broad Street and the Market–Frankford Line), subway-surface lines (tram routes that operate underground in Center City Philadelphia), and a suburban rail network (Regional Rail Lines). Transfers between Market-Frankford Line, Broad Street Line and Subway-Surface Lines are free, using designated passageways at the City Hall-15th Street, 13th Street-

Juniper Street and 39th St (Amtrak) stations. A flat fare (currently $1.50 – exact fare only) applies on most City Transit routes; reduced-rate tokens (currently $1.05 purchased in groups of 2, 5 and 10) and DayPass (currently $5 from the Visitor Centre at 16th and JFK Blvd), good for unlimited riding on all city transit vehicles plus a one-way trip on the Regional Rail Airport Line, are available. Of special interest to visitors is SEPTA's Visitor Route 76 (travels from the Society Hill/South Street area along Market Street and the Benjamin Franklin Parkway to the Philadelphia Museum of Art and the Zoo located in Fairmont Park every 15 mins 0900–1830 and Wednesdays to 1900); SEPTA's Welcome Line historic trolley loop ($0.50), operating via 11th and 12th Sts, between Noble and Bainbridge Sts, incorporates a mix of historic landmarks, shopping areas and cultural attractions (continues to the Philadelphia Zoo on weekends).

The Phlash Downtown Visitor Loop ($1.50 or Phlashpass for $3) also connects tourist attractions, restaurants, hotels and shopping areas. The Port Authority Transit Corporation of Pennsylvania and New Jersey (PATCO) operates a the Hi-Speed suburban line which calls at several Center City stations and can be used between them.

SURROUNDING AREAS: SEPTA commuter rail services (Regional Rail Lines) operate to suburbs and nearby towns in Pennsylvania and also to **Wilmington** in Delaware and to **Trenton** in New Jersey. The PATCO Hi-Speed Line crosses the Delaware River to serve the southeastern suburbs in New Jersey, including **Camden** (for connecting New Jersey Transit (NJ Transit) bus services to other destinations in Southern New Jersey), **Collingswood** and **Lindenwold**.

Within Pennsylvania, **Lancaster** and **Harrisburg** are served by Amtrak, and by Greyhound Lines buses (services continue to Pittsburgh, Cleveland and Chicago); **Pottstown** and **Reading** by Capitol Trailways buses, and **Allentown** and **Bethlehem** by Carl R. Bieber Tourways buses.

In New Jersey, **Trenton** is reached by Amtrak (service continues to Princeton, Newark, New York and Boston) and by SEPTA trains *(connecting* **NJ Transit** trains to Princeton, Newark and New York, and buses to various destinations in Central New Jersey); **Atlantic City** by NJ Transit trains and by Greyhound Lines.

In Delaware, **Wilmington** is reached by Amtrak (services continue to Baltimore, Washington, Richmond, Charleston, Jacksonville, Tampa and Miami, to Atlanta and New Orleans, and to Cincinnati, Indianapolis and Chicago), and by SEPTA trains.

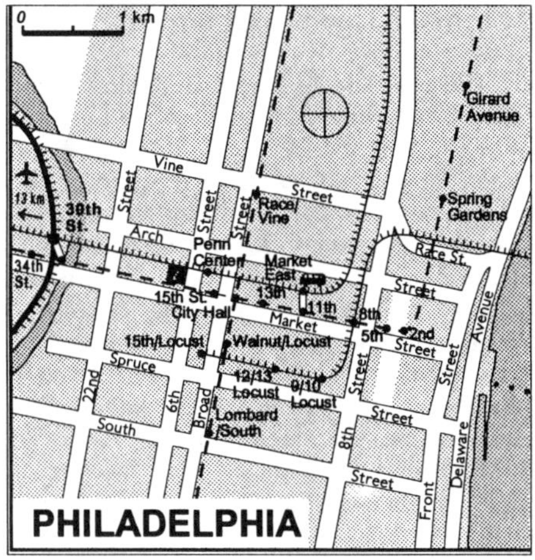

Main transport centres

Philadelphia International Airport (PHL), 12 km SW (SEPTA Airport Rail Line R1 from 30th Street, Penn and Market East Stations to Terminals B, C, D and E). Within the airport a free shuttle bus operates every 10–15 mins between the terminals and to parking areas. Gateway for a number of international and domestic flights, with five terminals. **30th Street Station**, 30th and Market Streets (Market–Frankford Subway or Subway-Surface Line to 30th St). All Amtrak services leave from here, as do all the Regional Rail lines of SEPTA and NJ Transit trains to Atlantic City. **Suburban Station**, 1617 John F. Kennedy Blvd (Market–Frankford Subway or Subway-Surface Line to 15th St; Broad Street Subway to City Hall). Alternative departure point for all SEPTA Regional Rail lines. **Market East Station** (Market–Frankford Subway to 11th Street). Alternative departure point for all SEPTA Regional Rail lines. **Market Street Station** (Market–Frankford Subway to 8th St). For PATCO trains to Camden and Lindenwold. These can also be boarded at 15-16th St or 12-13th St (both a couple of blocks from Walnut/Locust on the Broad Street Subway) or from 9-10th St. **Greyhound Terminal**, 1001 Filbert Street (Regional Rail lines to Market East; Market–Frankford Subway to 11th St). For services of Carl R. Bieber Tourways, Carolina Trailways, Greyhound Lines, Martz Trailways, NJ Transit, and Susquehanna Trailways buses. **Peter Pan Trailways Bus Terminal**, 55 N 11th St (Regional Rail lines to Market East; Market–Frankford Subway to 11th St). For services of Capitol Trailways and Peter Pan Trailways.

Sightseeing by public transport

CENTRE: **City Hall**, Broad and Market Sts, 686-9074 (SEPTA Market–Frankford Subway or Subway-Surface Line to 15th St; Broad Street Subway to City Hall). The largest and most elaborate City Hall in the country. **Museum of American Art**, Broad and Cherry Sts, 972-7600 (SEPTA Market–Frankford Subway or Subway-Surface Line to 15th St; Broad Street Subway to City Hall). America's first art museum – a National Historic Landmark with historic and contemporary masterpieces. **Fairmont Park** (SEPTA bus 76 on Market St in Center City). The largest landscaped city park in the world. Attractions include the **Philadelphia Museum of Art** (26th St and Benjamin Franklin Pkwy, 763-8100), founded in 1867, presenting both fine and applied arts from Asia, Europe and America. The **Philadelphia Zoo** (3400 W Girard Ave, 243-1100) is also located in the park.

Independence National Historic Park, 3rd and Chestnut Sts, 597-8974 (SEPTA Market–Frankford Subway to 5th St, SEPTA bus 76, or Phlash Visitor Loop). America's most historic square mile. The park's many historic landmarks include **Independence Hall** (Chestnut between 5th and 6th Sts), where the Declaration of Independence was adopted and the US constitution was written; the **Liberty Bell Pavilion** (Market St between 5th and 6th Sts), featuring the nation's most well-known symbol of liberty; **Congress Hall**, where the US Senate and House of Representatives met from 1790 to 1800; **Carpenters Hall**, where the First Continental Congress met in 1774; and **Franklin Court** (Market St between 3rd and 4th), featuring a print shop and a museum.

Parkway Museums (SEPTA bus 76 on Market St in Center City; or Phlash Visitor Loop). Includes the **Academy of Natural Sciences Museum** (19th St and Benjamin Franklin Pkwy, 299-1000); **Franklin Institute Science Museum** (20th St and Benjamin Franklin Pkwy, 448-1200); **Please Touch Museum** (210 N 21st St, 963-0667), the first museum in the country designed for children under eight years of age; and the **Rodin Museum** (22nd St and Benjamin Franklin Pkwy, 763-8100), featuring the largest collection of Rodin sculptures and drawing outside Paris. **Penn's Landing**, East Columbus Blvd between Market and South Sts, 923-8181 (SEPTA Market–Frankford Subway to 5th St, SEPTA bus 76, or Phlash Visitor Loop). Waterfront area features historic ships, marina, and restaurants. Adjacent **Independence Seaport Museum** (Columbus Blvd and Walnut St, 925-5439) features America's maritime heritage through hands-on exhibits. **The Gallery at Market East**, 9th and Market Streets, 625-4962 (PATCO Hi-Speed Line/SEPTA Market–Frankford Subway to 8th/Market, SEPTA bus 76, or Phlash Visitor Loop). The nation's largest enclosed urban shopping mall.

SURROUNDING AREAS: **Atlantic City** (NJ Transit trains from 30th St Station). Try your luck at one of the many hotel/casinos located along the famous boardwalk. **Pennsylvania Dutch Country** (Amtrak from 30th St Station). Trains pass through the rolling hills and picturesque farms of Lancaster County's Amish country. **Valley Forge National Historic Park**, N Gulph Rd and Rte 23, Valley Forge, (610) 783-1077 (SEPTA bus 125 from Suburban Station). Scene of the winter encampment of 1777– 78. Self-guided tours from the Visitor Centre feature reconstructed soldier's huts, the National Memorial Arch and Washington's Headquarters.

Useful telephone numbers

Amtrak 1-800-USA-RAIL
Capitol Trailways 1-800-237-8747
Greyhound Bus Terminal 931-4001
PATCO 922-4600
Philadelphia International Airport 937-6800
SEPTA 580-7800
Thomas Cook Foreign Exchange: 1800 John F. Kennedy Blvd, 563-5544
Visitor Information 636-1666 or 1-800-537-7676

PORTLAND, OREGON

Area code: 503
Time zone: Pacific Time

Portland was nearly named 'Boston' but the flip of a penny resulted in the city being named after Portland, Maine. Located near the end of the Oregon trail, this once notorious 19th-century port town is now consistently rated one of the most liveable cities in the country. Over the past two decades, 'The City of Roses' has been hailed as a national model for urban planning and superior quality of life with close access to the outdoor wonders of the great Pacific Northwest. Portland is a city of parks, outdoor artwork, sidewalk vendors, coffee-houses, microbreweries, bridges and book-stores, where city blocks half the size of those in other towns provide a pedestrian-friendly city centre. Urban growth boundaries have protected the surrounded countryside, a short distance from the city's core. Downtown Visitor Information Centre located at Two World Trade Center, SW Front and Salmon St.

Getting around

CENTRE: The Tri-County Metropolitan Transportation District (Tri-Met) operate a modern light rail system (still being extended) and a comprehensive network of bus routes throughout the City and surrounding area. The 24 km MAX (Metropolitan Area Express) light rail travels east from downtown to suburban Gresham. Vintage Trolley operates on the MAX line between downtown and Lloyd Center, weekends Mar.–Dec. and weekdays June–Dec. Nearly all of Tri-Met's 87 bus routes serve the Downtown Portland Transit Mall, located along SW Fifth and Sixth Aves, intersecting with MAX at Morrison and Yamhill Streets, near Pioneer Courthouse Square. All Tri-Met buses and MAX are free within the 300-block downtown 'Fareless Square,' bordered on the west and south by the I-405, on the north by Hoyt St and on the east by the Willamette River. Basic cash fare outside Fareless Square for buses and MAX is $1, or 10 tickets for $9 (available from ticket machines at MAX stations, on the transit mall, or at the Tri-Met office behind the waterfall at Pioneer Courthouse Square) for up to two zones; $1.30, or 10 tickets for $12 for all three zones. Free transfers, available from drivers, are good on any bus or MAX until expiry. Use MAX tickets to transfer free between MAX and any bus. A validated ticket or bus transfer is proof of payment, so keep it with you. Day Passes, good for unlimited riding on all Tri-Met buses and MAX, are available for $3.25 from ticket machines, bus drivers and Tri-Met's Customer Assistance Office, located in Pioneer Courthouse Square, on SW Sixth between Morrison and Yamhill Streets. Of special interest to visitors is Tri-Met's bus 63 serving downtown (intersecting with the Transit Mall at Main and Salmon Sts), Lloyd Center and cultural attractions including OMSI and Washington Park/Metro Zoo.

SURROUNDING AREAS: The Tri-Met network serves over 960 sq km throughout Clackamas, Multnomah and Washington counties, and across the Columbia River to Vancouver, WA (not to be confused with the Canadian city further north)Clark County Transit (C-Tran) operate within Vancouver, WA . and to the Portland Transit Mall and the Gateway MAX station. **Vancouver, WA** is also reached by Amtrak trains (services continue to Longview, Olympia, Tacoma and Seattle and Vancouver BC, and to Spokane, Minneapolis-St Paul and Chicago) and by Greyhound Lines and Northwestern Trailways buses; to the east, **Hood River** is reached by Amtrak trains (service continues to Boise, Salt Lake City, Denver and Chicago) and Greyhound Lines buses; to the south east, **Bend** is reached by C-A-C Transportation and Greyhound Lines buses; to the south **Salem, Albany, Eugene** and **Klamath Falls** are reached by Amtrak trains (service continues to Sacramento, Oakland/San Francisco and Los Angeles) and by Greyhound Lines buses (service continues to Grants Pass, Medford, Sacramento, Oakland/San Francisco); to the south-west and west, **Newport** and **Coos Bay** are reached by Greyhound Lines (services continue to Crescent City, Eureka/Arcata and San Francisco); to the north west **Astoria** and **Seaside** are reached by Pierce-Pacific bus.

Main transport centres

Portland International Airport (PDX), 14 km NE (Tri-Met bus 12 from Transit Mall; alternatively by Raz Airport Express bus ($7) every 30 mins, 0500–0000, to/from major downtown hotels). Served by major domestic airlines. Direct flights to/from New York. One terminal serves all airlines. **Union Station,** 800 NW 6th Ave (Tri-Met bus 14, 31, 32, 33, 35, 54, 56, 57, 58, 59, 60, 88, 89, 96 on Transit Mall). For all Amtrak, C-A-C Transportation and Northwestern Trailways services. **Greyhound Terminal**, 550 NW 6th Ave (Tri-Met bus 14, 31, 32, 33, 35, 54, 56, 57, 58, 59, 60, 88, 89, 96 on Transit Mall). Serves Greyhound Lines and Pierce Pacific Stages.

Sightseeing by public transport

CENTRE: **American Advertising Museum,** 524 NE Grand Ave, 230-1090 (Tri-Met bus 63 on Transit Mall) highlighting the power and influence of the nation's advertising industry. **Children's Museum**, 3037 SW 2nd Ave, 823-2227 (Tri-Met buses 1, 12, 40, 41, 43, 45 from Transit Mall). Hands-on fun for children from 6 months to 10 years. **Cowboys Then and Now Museum** (729 NE Oregon St (Tri-Met MAX, Vintage Trolley to 7th Ave). The evolution of the American cowboy and cattle industry. **End of the Oregon Trail Interpretive Center**, 1726 Washington St, Oregon City, 657-9336 (Tri-Met buses 32, 33, 34, 35, 79 on Transit Mall; 8 block walk from Oregon City Transit Center). Experience the living history of the people who settled the great American West. **Nob Hill/Northwest Portland,** NW 21st and 23rd Aves (Tri-Met bus 15 on Washington, or 17 on Transit Mall). Restored Victorian and Georgian mansions house more than 200 unique shops, galleries and cafés that draw customers from around the city. **Oregon**

History Center, 1200 SW Park Ave, 221-1741 (Tri-Met MAX to Pioneer Square). Explores the state's past and future through permanent and changing exhibits. **Oregon Maritime Center and Museum**, 113 SW Front, 224-7724 (Tri-Met MAX to Oak St). Explores Portland's rich maritime history. Includes the historic steam Sternwheeler *Portland*. **Oregon Museum of Science and Industry** (OMSI), 1945 SE Water Ave, 797-4000 (Tri-Met bus 63 on Transit Mall). Six exhibit halls filled with hands-on activities; Murdock Sky Theatre, offering astronomy and laser-light shows; the submarine USS *Blueback;* and OMNIMAX Theatre.

Pioneer Courthouse Square, bordered by SW Broadway and Sixth Ave, and Morrison and Yamhill Sts, 223-1613 (Tri-Met MAX to Pioneer Square). Portland's outdoor 'living room,' located in the heart of downtown. Features whimsical sculpture, waterfall and at noon the 7.5 metre-tall 'Weather Machine' predicts whether the day will bring rain, sun or storms. Surrounded by the city's best shopping at The Galleria, Nike Town and Pioneer Place. **Portland Art Museum**, 1219 SW Park Ave, 226-2811 (Tri-Met MAX to Galleria/10th Ave). Exhibits span 35 centuries of Asian, European and American art. Renowned collection of Native American art. The museum's Northwest Film Center presents film programs five nights a week and is host to the acclaimed Portland International Film Festival.

Portland Saturday Market, located under the west end of the Burnside Bridge to the Fire Museum between Front and First Aves, 222-6072 (Tri-Met MAX to Skidmore Fountain). Arts and crafts from over 250 vendors, international food stalls and entertainment.; open Sat. and Sun, Mar. to Christmas Eve. **Washington Park** (Tri-Met bus 63 on Transit Mall). Located in the West Hills with the best views of the city and an ideal site for picnics. Includes the city's most popular visitor attraction, the **International Rose Test Garden** (400 SW Kingston Ave, 823-3636), with more than 7,000 roses. Other attractions include the **Japanese Garden** (611 SW Kingston Ave, 223-1321); **Metro Washington Park Zoo** (4001 SW Canyon Rd, 226-1561); and **World Forestry Center** (4033 SW Canyon Rd, 228-1367).

SURROUNDING AREAS: **Ashland**, 465 km S (Greyhound Lines). Home of the Oregon Shakespeare Festival (late Feb.–Oct.), featuring world-renowned performances of Shakespeare, classical and contemporary dramas in three theatres, including the outdoor Elizabethan Stage. Beautiful Lithia Park, many smaller theatres, shops and restaurants surround the compact city centre. **Columbia Gorge–Hood River**, 100 km E (Amtrak and Greyhound Lines). Hood River is known as the 'Windsurfing Capital of the World.' The city is also terminus of the Mount Hood Railroad (110 Railroad Ave, 541-386-3556), a vintage 1910 railroad linking the Columbia River with Mount Hood.

Eugene, 177 km S (Amtrak and Greyhound Lines). A pleasant university town, known for starting the jogging craze along its many kilometres of Willamette River Greenway trails. Attractions include the Fifth Street Public Market, and Hult Center for the Performing Arts. **North Coast**, 150 km NW (Pierce Pacific Stages). Located on the Oregon Coast's northernmost tip, the historic hillside town of **Astoria** features restored Victorian homes, the Columbia River Maritime Museum and the Astoria Column, featuring magnificent views. **Seaside** offers a 3.2 km Oceanfront Promenade and deep-sea wonders at the Seaside Aquarium.

Useful telephone numbers

Amtrak 1-800-872-7245
Greyhound Lines 1-800-231-2222
Metropolitan Airport Shuttle 331-2335
Northwestern Trailways (509) 838-4029
Oregon Tourism 238-7433
Pierce Pacific Stages 692-4437
Portland Int'l. Airport 231-5000
Portland Oregon Visitors Association 275-9750
RAZ Transportation 246-3301
Tri-Met 238-7433
Thomas Cook Foreign Exchange: Pioneer Courthouse Sq., 222-2665

ST LOUIS

Area code 314
Time zone: Central Time

Located on the Mississippi River, St Louis is known as the 'Gateway To The West'. Founded in 1764 by the French fur trader Pierre Laclede and named after Louis IX of France, the city was annexed to the USA in 1804 as part of the Louisiana Purchase. St Louis played an important role in the westward expansion of the United States. Lewis and Clark set off on their expeditions from here and many traders, adventurers and settlers passed through the city on their way west. Steamboats called here on their way up and down the Mississippi and railroads helped to stimulate trade between the Southwest and the East, making St Louis a major transportation crossroads, a role that it enjoys to this day. The decline of industrialism took its toll, and the downtown hit a low point in the 1970s, but the years since have seen considerable improvement with the successful redevelopment of the riverfront including the magnificent Gateway Arch and Laclede's Landing. Visitor Center located at 308 Washington Ave, near the riverfront and also at the Convention Center.

Getting around

CENTRE: The Bi-State Development Agency (Bi-State) operate a modern light rail system (MetroLink) and a comprehensive network of 139 bus routes throughout the City and surrounding area. The 28 km MetroLink light rail travels from Lambert-St Louis International Airport to downtown (via a short underground segment) and across the Mississippi River to East St Louis, Illinois. An integrated flat-fare system ($1 exact cash, or $8 for a 10-ride ticket valid for ten rides plus transfer on bus/rail service) is in effect. A transfer ($0.10) is required when it is necessary to change vehicles to complete your trip (from bus to bus, from bus to MetroLink or MetroLink to bus). Transfers are valid for two hours while traveling in the same general direction away from your point of origin. Transfers are not valid for a return trip on the issuing line. It is not necessary to use a transfer with any pass. Day Passes, valid for one day ($3) or three days ($7) are good for unlimited riding on all Bi-State buses and MetroLink. Bi-State weekly passes ($11) are valid the week of issue on all Bi-State buses and MetroLink. One-ride and multi-ride tickets, and one-day and three-day passes are available at the ticket vending machines at all MetroLink stations. Valid proof of payment can be a valid MetroLink ticket, a ten-ride ticket, a daily, monthly or weekly pass or bus transfer. Travel on MetroLink is free within MetroLink Ride Free Zone, from Union Station to Laclede's Landing weekdays 1000-1500.

SURROUNDING AREAS: The Bi-State network serves suburbs out to the I-270 loop road and beyond including **Clayton** and **St Charles**, Missouri, and **Belleville**, **Granite City** and **Madison County**, Illinois. To the north, **Hannibal** and **Quincy** are reached by Burlington Trailways buses (service continues to Cedar Rapids); to the north east, **Springfield** and **Chicago** are reached by Amtrak trains and Greyhound Lines buses; **Effingham**, **Terre Haute** and **Indianapolis** are reached by Greyhound Lines (service continues to Columbus and Pittsburgh; to the south east **Mt Vernon**, **Evansville** and **Nashville** are reached by Greyhound Lines buses, as is **Cape Girardeau** (service continues to Memphis); to the south-west, **Poplar Bluff** and **Little Rock** are reached by Amtrak (service continues to Dallas, San Antonio, Phoenix and Los Angeles) and by Greyhound Lines (service continues to Houston); **Springfield** and **Joplin** are reached by Greyhound Lines (service continues to Tulsa, Oklahoma City, Amarillo, Albuquerque, Flagstaff for Grand Canyon National Park and Los Angeles); to the west **Kirkwood** and **Jefferson City** are reached by Amtrak (service continues to Kansas City, Albuquerque, Flagstaff for Grand Canyon National Park and Los Angeles), and **Columbia** by Greyhound Lines (service continues to Kansas City, Denver, Salt Lake City and San Francisco).

Main transport centres

Lambert-St Louis International Airport (STL), 16 km NW (Bi-State MetroLink to Airport Main Station). Major hub for domestic flights to most US cities, with two terminals. **Amtrak Station**, 550 S 16th St (Bi-State MetroLink to Union Station; walk 2 blocks east on Clark to 16th). A 'temporary' depot, opened in 1978, in a somewhat unsavoury neighbourhood. For all Amtrak services. **Kirkwood Amtrak Station**, Argonne and Kirkwood Rds, Kirkwood (Bi-State MetroLink to Airport Main Terminal; then Bi-State bus 49). Suburban station for Amtrak Chicago–Kansas City services. **Greyhound Bus Terminal**, 1450 N 13th St (Bi-State bus 30 on 9th St). For Greyhound Lines and Burlington Trailways.

Sightseeing by public transport

CENTRE: **Busch Brewery**, Broadway and Pestalozzi, 577-2626 (Bi-State bus 40 south on Broadway). Produces Budweiser and Michelob beers; free tours. **Casino Queen Riverboat**, 200 S Front St, East St Louis, IL, 618-874-5000) (Bi-State MetroLink to East Riverfront). Gambling and entertainment. **Central West End District**, Lindell Blvd (Bi-State bus 93 on Washington, or Bi-State MetroLink to Central West End; then 'Shuttle Bug'). Trendy shops, bars and turn-of-the-century mansions line the leafy streets. The Cathedral of St Louis (4431 Lindell Blvd, 533-2824) houses the world's largest collection of mosaics. **Forest Park** (Bi-State MetroLink to Forest Park; then 'Shuttle Bug'). Larger than New York's Central Park. Take 'Shuttle Bug' shuttle bus from MetroLink to attractions including the St Louis Art Museum (721-0067); the beautiful grounds of the St Louis Zoological Park (781-0900); the History Museum, with thematic collections tracing the city's past including river life and

African-American music; and the St Louis Science Center (622-5500). **Gateway Arch**, 11 N 4th St, 425-4465 (Bi-State MetroLink to Laclede's Landing). A 189-metre stainless steel monument overlooking the St Louis waterfront, honours westward expansion. Small trams take visitors to the top. Beneath the arch the **Museum of Westward Expansion** recounts the story of the Lewis and Clark Expedition which set off from St Louis in 1804 to explore the Missouri River and routes to the Pacific Ocean. **Laclede's Landing**, 2nd St between Eads and Martin Luther King Bridges (Bi-State MetroLink to Laclede's Landing). 1850s Riverfront Historic District, featuring antique stores, restaurants and nightclubs. **Missouri Botanical Garden**, 4344 Shaw Blvd, 577-5100 (Bi-State MetroLink to Central West End; then Bi-State bus 13). Highlights include the Climatron, a two-level geodesic greenhouse that re-creates a tropical environment. **National Bowling hall of Fame and Museum**, 111 Stadium Plaza, 231-6340) (Bi-State MetroLink to Busch Stadium). Traces the history of bowling from ancient Egypt to the present. **Old Court House Museum**, 11 N 4th St at Market, 425-4465 (Bi-State MetroLink to 8th and Pine). Two restored courtrooms which were the site of the Dred Scott trial. **St Louis Union Station**, 1820 Market St, 421-6655 (Bi-State MetroLink to Union Station). Built in 1884 and closed as a railway station in 1979, Union Station features a grand waiting room (now a hotel lobby) and 69 metre clock tower.

SURROUNDING AREAS: **Hannibal**, 145 km N (Burlington Trailways). The boyhood home of Samuel Langhorne Clemens, better known as Mark Twain, whose books were influenced by his experiences growing up here. Attractions include the restored Mark Twain Boyhood Home; the Mark Twain Museum; and the law office of Twain's father. The route from St Louis to Hannibal is one of the most scenic along the Mississippi. **St Charles**, 40 km NW (Bi-State MetroLink to North Hanley, then Bi-State buses 34, 134, weekdays only). Riverfront town with three historic districts. The **Katy Trail**, following the Missouri River for 80 km along an abandoned railway, is popular for cycling (rentals available on the riverfront) and strolling.

Useful telephone numbers

Amtrak 1-800-872-7245
Bi-State Transit 231-2345
Burlington Trailways (319) 753-2864
Greyhound Lines 1-800-231-2222
Lambert-St Louis Int'l. Airport 426-8000
Missouri Tourism Information 869-7100
St Louis Convention and Visitors Commission 421-1023

SAN DIEGO

Area code 619
Time zone: Pacific Time

Birthplace of California, San Diego is the second-largest city in the state and sixth-largest in the USA. Yet unlike Los Angeles, 190 km to the north, it doesn't have the feel of a large city. The downtown area is relatively compact, the airport is only 5 km from the centre, and it has a laid-back feel to it, perhaps due in part to its proximity to Mexico, only some 30 km to the south (if you intend to visit Mexico, non-US citizens need a multiple-entry visa as well as a passport). The climate is ideal year-round, the beaches are superb, there's plenty of history. International Visitors Information Centre located at 11 Horton Plaza (First Ave and 'F' St). Visitor information is also available in the Amtrak/Santa Fe Depot.

Getting around

CENTRE: Metropolitan Transit System (MTS). MTS operates the San Diego Trolley light rail system which comprises three lines (North, East and South), all of which serve the downtown area (known in San Diego as Centre City), 'Coaster' commuter rail, San Diego Transit (SDT) and suburban buses. Flat-fare arrangements (currently $1.50) apply on local buses; the Trolley fare ($1–$1.75 depending on distance travelled) must be purchased from vending machines at stations before boarding. Transfers between vehicles, and between one mode of transport and another are available at a small supplement. Day Tripper passes (one day $5 or four-day $15, available at the San Diego Transit Store, 102 Broadway) allow unlimited access to all Metropolitan Transit Systems buses, the trolley and San Diego Bay Ferry.

SURROUNDING AREAS: All suburbs are served by the MTS network of local and express buses (express service numbers end in '0', so they are easily identified). The San Diego Trolley line north to Old Town Transit Centre will open in June, 1996. Northwards along the coast, **Oceanside** is reached by Amtrak and Coaster commuter trains and by Greyhound Lines buses (Amtrak and Greyhound services continue to Santa Barbara, San Luis Obispo, San Jose, Oakland, San Francisco, Sacramento, Portland and Seattle). To the east, **Calexico** (for buses across the border to Mexicali, from where onward bus and rail services further into

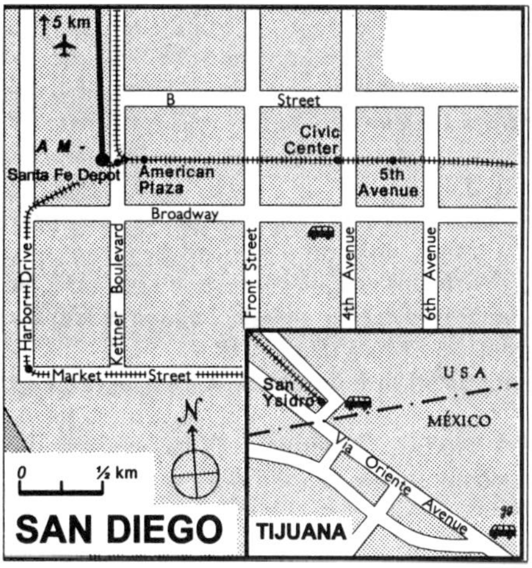

Mexico are available) is served by Greyhound Lines buses (service continues to Yuma, Phoenix and El Paso). To the south, **San Ysidro** trolley station is only 100 metres from the frontier; **Tijuana**, a short distanmce away (see below) offers onward bus services further into Mexico.

Main transport centres

San Diego International Airport (SAN), otherwise known as Lindbergh Field, 5km NW (SDT Bus 2 from/to Broadway). Gateway for a number of domestic and international flights. Two terminals serve all airlines. **Amtrak Station**, 1050 Kettner Blvd at Broadway (Trolley to Santa Fe Depot). For all Amtrak and Coaster services. **Greyhound Bus Station**, 120 W Broadway (Trolley to Civic Center). All Greyhound Lines services.

Sightseeing by public transport

CENTRE: **Balboa Park, Museums**, 1549 El Prado Blvd, 239-0512 (SDT bus 7 from/to Broadway). Includes the San Diego Zoo (see below), museums, art galleries, theatres and sports facilities all within easy walking distance of each other. Highlights include: San Diego Aerospace Museum (234-8291); San Diego Automotive Museum (231-2886) ; San Diego Hall of Champions Sports Museum (234-2544); San Diego Model Railroad Museum (696-0199); San Diego Museum of Art (232-7931); the San Diego Museum of Man (239-2001); Museum of Photographic Arts (239-5262); Museum of San Diego History (232-6203); Natural History Museum (232-3821); and the Reuben H. Fleet Space Theater and Science Center (238-1233). **Coronado Ferry/Harbour Tours**, Broadway Pier at Embarcadero, 234-1111 (Trolley to Santa Fe Depot). The Coronado Ferry ($2) carries pedestrians and bicycles to the Ferry Landing Marketplace. San Diego Harbour Excursion offers 1- and 2-hour narrated harbour tours, dinner/dance cruises and whale-watching trips. **Gaslamp Quarter**, 4th & Island Aves, 233-5227 (Trolley to Gaslamp/Convention Center). The Gaslamp Quarter National Historic District features Victorian-era buildings housing shops, restaurants, clubs and theatres. **Horton Plaza**, 324 Horton Plaza at Broadway, 239-8180. (Trolley to Civic Center). Architecturally unique downtown shopping centre.

La Jolla, pronounced 'La Hoya' (SDT bus 34 from/to Broadway). Prospect Street offers chic specialty shops and restaurants. Nearby is the **Stephen Birch Aquarium Museum** (2300 Expedition Way, 543-3474), the public education centre fro the world-renowned Scripps Institute of Oceanography. More than 1,500 fish and interactive oceanographic museum. **Old Town**, 4002 Wallace St, 220-5422 (Coaster/Trolley to Old Town Transit Centre). Old Town San Diego State Historic Park features original 19th-century adobe buildings, shops and restaurants.

San Diego beaches include: Ocean Beach, Cable St & Narragansett Ave (SDT bus 35 from/to Broadway), featuring 660 metre lighted fishing pier; Mission Beach, Mission Blvd and West Mission Bay Dr. (SDT bus 34 on Broadway), home of Belmont Park and its 'Giant Dipper' roller-coaster; Pacific Beach, Mission Blvd & Garnet Ave (SDT bus 9,30,34 on Broadway), featuring a pier and boardwalk. **San Diego Maritime Museum**, 1306 N Harbor Dr., 234-9153 (trolley to County Center/Little Italy, or SDT bus 2 from/to Broadway). Historic ships include the 1863 sailing ship *Star of India*, 1898 ferryboat *Berkeley* and 1904 steam yacht *Medea*.

San Diego Zoo, 2000 Zoo Drive, Balboa Park, 234-3153 (SDT bus 7 on Broadway). World-famous zoo and botanical garden features 3,400 animals of 900 species. Bus tour and Skyfari aerial tram. **Sea World**, 1720 S Shores Rd, 226-3901 (SDT bus 9 from/to Broadway). Marine park features more than 20 exhibits and shows. **Seaport Village**–W Harbor Dr. & Kettner Blvd, 235-4014 (trolley to Seaport Village, or SDT bus 7 from/to Broadway). Waterfront shopping, dining and entertainment complex features 6 km of walkways and boardwalk with harbor views.

SURROUNDING AREAS: Northern San Diego County is home to many beautiful beaches. Among those accessible by train are **Carlsbad State Beach**, Carlsbad Blvd from Elm St to Tamarack Ave, Carlsbad, 729-8947 (Coaster to Carlsbad) and **Moonlight State**

Beach, 4th & 'C' Sts, Encinitas, 729-8947 (Coaster to Encinitas) and **Solana Beach County Park** (Amtrak/Coaster to Solana Beach). All are within walking distance of the train station, shops and restaurants.

You can visit Mexico for the day in **Tijuana**, just 30 km from San Diego. (trolley to San Ysidro/International Border, then walk 100 metres, across pedestrian bridge into Mexico). Note the information at trhe beginning of this section regarding passports and visas.

Useful telephone numbers

Amtrak 1-800-USA-RAIL
Greyhound Lines 1-800-231-2222
Metropolitan Transit System (MTS) 233-3004
Oceanside Chamber of Commerce 721-1101
San Diego Visitors Bureau 236-1212
San Ysidro Chamber of Commerce 428-1281
Thomas Cook Foreign Exchange: 177 Horton Plaza, 235-0900; University Towne Center, La Jolla, 457-0841

SAN FRANCISCO

Area code 415
Time zone: Pacific Time

A city full of character, with its famous Golden Gate Bridge and its cable cars. Surrounded on three sides by water, San Francisco has a temperate climate, which is probably just as well if you intend to do much exploring on foot, as parts of the city are incredibly hilly. So much so, in fact, that motorists must, by law, turn their wheels into the kerb when parking on hills. Fortunately for non-motorists and non-mountaineers, there is an excellent public transport system. It was the hills that spawned San Francisco's best known form of public transport – the cable car network. This reached its heyday in the 1880s and early 1890s, when 8 companies provided cable car service on 22 lines, although not all of these were operating at the same time. The system was gradually allowed to fall into disrepair by the 1960s and 1970s. Nowadays, after a restoration programme in the early 1980s, 3 cable car lines remain, with about 18 km of track.

Getting around

CENTRE: San Francisco Municipal Railway (usually abbreviated to MUNI) operates a 5-line Metro (light-rail) system which connects the downtown area (where it runs underground) with the western and southwestern parts of the city. This is supplemented throughout the city by a comprehensive network of buses, and additionally in the downtown area by the cable cars, which, although now a also tourist attraction, are still used by some members of the local population for the purpose for which they were originally intended – as a means of public transport. The Metro lines are identified by letter (J, K, L, M, N), buses by route numbers and the cable cars by the streets on which the line operates. Muni also operates the F surface line, using historic streetcars, serving Market St between downtown and the Castro (to be extended to Fisherman's Wharf). A flat-fare system applies (currently $1 for metro and buses, $2 for cable cars) with free transfers given when fare is paid – valid for two more rides in any direction within the 90 minute to two hour time limit. No transfers issued or accepted for cable car service. Various duration passes ('MUNI passports') are available, starting at $6 for a one-day passport; these are valid on all MUNI scheduled services including Cable Cars. The Bay Area Rapid Transit (BART) system has 8 stations in San Francisco and many more in the suburbs (see below); fares depend on distance travelled.

SURROUNDING AREAS: To the north, **Sausalito** and **Larkspur** are reached by Golden Gate Transit ferries and buses; **Tiburon** by Red & White Fleet ferries; **Mill Valley** by Golden Gate Transit buses which also serve **San Raphael** together with Greyhound Lines. Across the Bay, **Richmond**, **El Cerrito**, **Berkeley**, **Oakland**, **Hayward** and **Fremont** are all reached by BART trains and by Alameda-Contra Costa Transit District (AC Transit) buses. To the south, **Daly City** is the western terminus of BART and is also served by MUNI

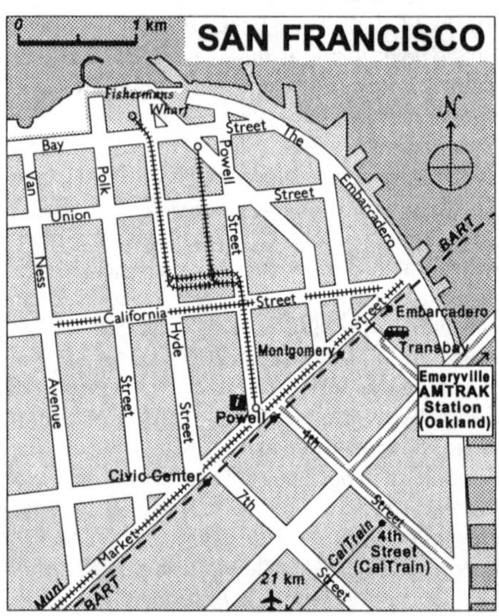

and San Mateo County Transit District (SamTrans) buses; **Pacifica** by SamTrans buses; **South San Francisco**, **San Bruno**, **Burlingame**, **San Mateo**, **San Carlos** and **Redwood City** by CalTrain and by SamTrans buses; **Menlo Park** and **Palo Alto** by CalTrain and by SamTrans and Santa Clara County Transportation Agency (TA) buses; **Mountain View** by CalTrain and Santa Clara County Transportation Agency (TA) buses. To the north, **Petaluma** and **Santa Rosa** are served by Golden Gate Transit and Greyhound Lines buses (service continues to Ukiah, Willits, Eureka and Portland); **Napa** is reached by Greyhound Lines, as is **Vallejo** (services continue to Redding, Eugene and Portland, and to Sacramento and Reno); **Sacramento** by Amtrak (services continue to Redding, Eugene, Portland and Seattle, and to Reno, and Salt Lake City).

To the east, **Concord** is served by BART; **Stockton** by Amtrak (service continues to Merced *(for* Amtrak Thruway buses to Yosemite National Park), Fresno and Bakersfield). To the south, **Santa Cruz** and **Monterey** are reached by Greyhound Lines and Amtrak Thruway buses from San Jose; **Salinas** by Amtrak and by Greyhound Lines (both services continue to San Luis Obispo, Santa Barbara and Los Angeles); **San Jose** by CalTrain, by Amtrak and Greyhound Lines (both services continue to Salinas, San Luis Obispo, Santa Barbara and Los Angeles) and by Santa Clara County Transportation Authority buses from Fremont BART station.

Main transport centres

San Francisco International Airport (SFO), 19 km S. Direct service from downtown San Francisco, Transbay Terminal, by Samtrans bus 7F (express – carries passengers *without* luggage only); Samtrans bus 7B (local – calls additionally at 7th/Mission); BART train to Colma, then by Samtrans bus 3X (every 20–40 mins, no Sunday evening service). Alternatively by SFO Airporter (0500–2300, every 15–30 mins) serving major downtown hotels. Within the airport a free shuttle bus connects all three terminals, 0530–0100 every 5 mins. Major gateway for both international and domestic flights. **Amtrak Station**, Ferry Building, 31 Embarcadero, Suite 140, at foot of Market St (MUNI buses 2, 6, 7, 9, 14, 21, 31, 71; 2 blocks from BART/MUNI Metro Embarcadero Station). For shuttle bus to all Amtrak services calling at Emeryville/ Oakland, which serves as San Francisco's main-line station. **Caltrain Depot**, (4th and Townsend Streets (MUNI buses 15, 30, 32, 42, 45, 76). For CalTrain services to the southern suburbs, San Mateo, Redwood City, Palo Alto and San Jose (for Amtrak services to Salinas, San Luis Obispo, Santa Barbara and Los Angeles). **Ferry Terminal**, Embarcadero and Market St (MUNI buses 2, 6, 7, 9, 14, 21, 31, 71; 2 blocks from BART/MUNI Metro Embarcadero Station). For Amtrak shuttle bus to trains calling at Emeryville/ Oakland, Golden Gate Transit ferries to Larkspur and Sausalito, and Red & White ferries to Tiburon, Alameda-Oakland Ferry and Vallejo Ferry. **Transbay Terminal**, First and Mission Sts (MUNI buses 5, 12, 14, 15, 38, 42, 76, and F – Market historic streetcar – one block from BART/MUNI Metro Embarcadero Station). For Golden Gate Transit buses to northern suburbs, SamTrans buses to southern suburbs and Greyhound Lines buses to all destinations.

Sightseeing by public transport

CENTRE: **Cable cars** (673-6864). One of the nation's moving historical landmarks. The Powell–Hyde and Powell–Mason lines (BART/MUNI Metro to Powell) serve Fisherman's Wharf. The California St line (BART/MUNI Metro to Embarcadero) is the least crowded and operates to Van Ness Ave The **Cable Car Barn and Museum**, 1201 Mason St, 474-1887 (BART/MUNI Metro to Embarcadero then MUNI bus 1, or Powell Cable Cars). Features cable drive machinery at work. **Chinatown**, Grant Ave and Stockton St from Bush to Broadway (BART/MUNI Metro to Montgomery then MUNI buses 15, 30, 45, or California Cable Car). The largest Chinese quarter outside Asia. **Fisherman's Wharf**, Jefferson St from Hyde to Powell St (BART/MUNI Metro to Montgomery then MUNI bus 15 or 30, or BART/MUNI Metro to Embarcadero then MUNI bus 32, or Powell Cable Cars). Open markets and food stalls selling sea food and San Francisco's sourdough French bread. Includes **Pier 39** (981-7437), with tourist-oriented shops, restaurants, bay cruises and passenger ferry services. Red & White Fleet (546-2700) operate city tours, bay cruises and passenger ferry service to Alcatraz, Angel Island State Park, Muir Woods Redwoods and Napa Valley from Piers 41 and 43½. Nearby are **The Cannery** (2801 Leavenworth St) and **Ghirardelli Square** (900 North Point St), for more shopping and eating. The **Maritime Museum** (Jefferson and Hyde Sts, 929-0202) features the world's largest historic ship collection. **Golden Gate Bridge**, Hwy 1/101 at Doyle Dr. (Golden Gate Transit buses 10, 20, 30, 50, 80, 90, or MUNI bus 76 from Transbay Terminal). Completed in 1937, a great achievement in art and engineering. Pedestrians and bicycles cross free. **Golden Gate Park**, John F. Kennedy Dr., 666-7200 (MUNI Metro N-Judah train to 9th Ave then 1 block north to park and museums). Features the **Asian Art Museum** (668-8921) and the museums of the **California Academy of Sciences**. **North Beach**, Columbus from Broadway to Union St (BART/MUNI Metro to Montgomery then MUNI buses 15, 30, 45, or Powell–Mason Cable Car). San Francisco's finest cabarets, jazz clubs, coffee houses, bistros, restaurants and Italian delis. **Union Square**, located between 4th, Geary, Powell and Post Sts, 781-7880 (BART/MUNI Metro to Powell). The heart of downtown San Francisco shopping and hotels.

SURROUNDING AREAS: **Monterey**, 195 km S (Amtrak to San Jose then Amtrak Thruway Bus or Greyhound Lines). Birthplace of the California Republic, with a compact downtown, easy to explore on foot. Rent a bike, walk or take Monterey-Salinas Transit bus 1 or 15, or Wave Shuttle (summer only) to Cannery Row (408-373-4812) and the Monterey Bay Aquarium (408-648-4888). **Sacramento**, 140 km NE (Amtrak or Greyhound Lines) is California's state capital, located on the banks of the Sacramento River. Just steps from the Sacramento Amtrak station is the California State Railroad Museum (916-552-5252). The adjacent Old Sacramento State Historic Park features the Discovery Museum and the largest concentration of historic Gold-Rush era buildings in California. Also of interest is the magnificent, domed California State Capitol (916-324-0333) – Regional Transit buses 30, 31, 32 from Amtrak. **Yosemite National Park**, 345 km SE. Hotel and camping reservations 209-372-0264. Amtrak to Merced, then Yosemite Amtrak Thruway/VIA Bus. Yosemite Transportation System (YTS) operates free shuttle buses throughout the park.

Useful telephone numbers

AC Transit (510) 839-2931
Alameda-Oakland Ferry (510) 522-3300
Amtrak 1-800-872-7245
BART (415) 992-2278
CalTrain 1-800-660-4287; (415) 508-6200
Golden Gate Transit 923-2000
Gray Line 558-9400
Greyhound Lines 1-800-231-2222
Red & White Fleet Ferries 1-800-229-2784; (415) 546-2628
SamTrans 1-800-660-4287; 508-6200
San Francisco Intn'l Airport 876-2421
San Francisco Municipal Railway 673-6864
San Francisco Visitors Bureau 391-2000
Santa Clara County Transportation Agency (408) 321-2300;
SFO Airporter 673-2432
Thomas Cook Foreign Exchange: Pier 39, 362-6271; 75 Geary St, 362-3452
Traveler's Aid Society (415) 255-2252
Yosemite VIA Bus (209) 722-0366; 1-800-369-7275

SEATTLE

Area code 206
Time zone: Pacific Time

Located between Puget Sound and Lake Washington, and with a number of smaller lakes dotted around the city, Seattle at first gives the impression that it is surrounded by water. This impression becomes a three-dimensional one if it happens to be raining (a not infrequent phenomenon). However, the climate results in Seattle being one of the greenest cities in the USA (it is known as 'The Emerald City'), and due to this and the beautiful surroundings, it is also considered one of the most 'livable' cities in the country (despite the rainfall). The nearby Cascade Mountain range crowned by the snow-capped 4392m. Mt Rainier (pronounced 'R'neer' in these parts) is visible on clear days. Visitor Center located at Washington State Convention and Trade Center, 800 Convention Place, Galleria Level.

Getting around

CENTRE: King County Metro operate bus and trolleybus services throughout Seattle and King County on over 180 routes, and the Waterfront Streetcar. A number of bus routes run through the 2 km Metro Tunnel in the downtown area during the day on weekdays (0500–1900) and Saturdays (1000–1800), reverting to surface operation in the evenings and on Sundays and holidays. Although operated by buses rather than trains, the tunnel functions in just the same way as the more conventional subway/metro arrangement, with stations at intervals along 3rd Avenue and Pine Street.

The Waterfront Streetcar operates every 20 mins daily (except Thanksgiving, Christmas and New Year's Day) from the International District to attractions including Pioneer Square, Waterfront Park, Pike Place Market and the Seattle Aquarium. A 2-zone fare structure is in operation; journeys entirely within Seattle city limits counting as one zone, and those which cross these limits counting as two zones. The time of your journey can also affect the fare; trips made during the weekday morning or evening rush hours (0600– 0900,

1500–1800) are charged peak fares ($1.10 for one zone, $1.60 for two zones); off-peak fares ($0.85 for one zone, $1.10 for two zones) apply at other times.

Fares are payable as you enter the bus when travelling to downtown Seattle. When leaving downtown, pay when you get off the bus. Transfers, valid for 90 minutes, can be used from one bus to another, and between buses and the Waterfront Streetcar. An All Day Pass ($1.70) is available from transit drivers Saturdays, Sundays and holidays only.

There is a 'Ride Free' area in the central downtown district, where no fare is required for journeys made entirely within the Area between 0600 and 1900; outside these times normal fares apply. The Waterfront Streetcar is *not* included within this area. The 1.9km Seattle Center Monorail links Westlake Center (5th and Pine Sts–Metro Tunnel to Westlake) with Seattle Center and the Space Needle. The monorail is not part of the Metro system and requires a separate fare ($0.90).

SURROUNDING AREAS: Metro bus services extend well into the suburbs within the western half of King County. To the south, **Tacoma** is served by Pierce Transit; to the north, **Everett** is served by Community Transit and by Everett Transit within the city. To the west, Washington State Ferries serve **Bainbridge Island**, **Bremerton** and **Vashon Island**.

In the north, **Anacortes** (for Washington State Ferries service to **Sidney**) is reached by Gray Line of Seattle buses (service continues on the ferry to Sidney and then to Victoria). **Bellingham** (for Alaska Marine Highway ferry services) is served by Amtrak and by Greyhound Linesbuses en route to **Vancouver BC**, which is reached direct by Amtrak, Quick Shuttle and by Trailways Northwest.

In the east, **Spokane** is reached via **Wenatchee** by Amtrak trains (service continues to Minneapolis and Chicago) and by Greyhound Lines, and via **Ellensburg** by Amtrak thruway bus, Greyhound Lines (service continues to Minneapolis), and by Northwestern Trailways (service continues to Billings). In the south-east, **Richland** and **Yakima** are served by Bassett Transit and by Greyhound Lines (services continue to Walla Walla).

To the south, **Vancouver, WA** and **Portland** can be reached by Amtrak (services continue to Oakland and Los Angeles, and to Denver), and by Greyhound Lines. In the north-west, **Victoria** can be accessed by Victoria Clipper passenger ferry (year-round) and by Victoria Line car/passenger ferry (between 16 May and 15 October).

Main transport centres

Seattle-Tacoma International Airport (SEA). Gray Line Airport Express bus ($7.50) 0500–0000 every 20 mins to downtown Seattle (Greyhound Bus Terminal) or Metro bus 194 (Express), 174 (Local service) or 184 (Local night service) to a number of downtown locations; there are also direct services to/from Vancouver BC provided by Greyhound Lines and Quick Shuttle. Within the airport, free shuttle connects all three terminals and parking area. Colloquially known as 'Sea-Tac', this is a major gateway for a large number of international and domestic flights.

King Street Station, 303 South Jackson St (Metro buses 7, 14, 15, 18, 21, 22, 36, 56, Metro Tunnel to International District, or Waterfront Streetcar). For All Amtrak and Trailways services. **Greyhound Bus Terminal**, Eighth Ave and Stewart Street (no direct local bus, but Metro buses 10, 12, 14, 74, 302, 305 pass nearby; within walking distance of Metro Tunnel Convention Place Station). Serves Gray Line of Seattle and Greyhound Lines. **Washington State Ferries**, Colman Dock, Pier 52 (Metro buses 15, 18, 302, 305, or Waterfront Streetcar). For Washington State Ferry services.

Sightseeing by public transport

CENTRE: **International District**, 5th and S Jackson St (Metro buses 7, 14, 36, Metro Tunnel to International District, or Waterfront Streetcar). The third largest **Chinatown** in the USA, with many shops, ethnic restaurants, Wing Luke Museum, and Uwajimaya, a large Asian grocery and department store. **Kingdome**, 201 S King St, 296-3100 (Metro buses 7, 14, 15, 18, 21, 22, 36, 56, Metro Tunnel to International District, or Waterfront Streetcar). Indoor stadium home to Seattle Mariners baseball, Seahawks football, concerts and other special events.

Museum of History and Industry, 2700 24th Ave, 324-1125 (Metro bus 43 east on on Pike St). Features the colourful history of Seattle and the Pacific Northwest; exhibits include Seattle's first cable car. **Museum of Flight**, 9404 E Marginal Way South, 764-5720 (Metro bus 174 south on 2nd Ave). The history of flight from Da Vinci to the space age. Glassed-in Great Gallery features historic aircraft.

Pioneer Square, 1st and 2nd Aves. from Columbia to King Sts, (Metro buses 15, 18, 21, 22, 56 on 1st Ave, Metro Tunnel to Pioneer Square, or Waterfront Streetcar). Six-block restored historic district, site of the original Skid Road, where loggers once 'skidded' timber from the road into Elliott Bay. Attractions include the **Klondike Gold Rush National Historic Park** (117 S Main St), commemorating Seattle's leading role as a staging area for the 1890s Gold Rush; the historic, tongue-in-cheek **Underground Tour** (610 First Ave, 682-4646); and many shops, galleries and restaurants.

Seattle Art Museum, 100 University St, 654-3100 (Metro buses 15, 18, 20, 21, 22, 54, 55, 56 to 1st and Union Sts, Metro Tunnel to University Street, or Waterfront Streetcar). Collections include Asian, African, Native American and Modern art.

Seattle Center, 305 Harrison, 684-7200 (Metro buses 1, 2, 3, 4, 6, 15, 16, 18, or Monorail). Built for the 1962 World's Fair. Hosts the city's symphony, ballet, opera and theatres. The focal point is the **Space Needle** (443-2111), featuring an observation deck with 360-degree views of the region, two revolving restaurants and coffee shop. Other attractions include the Chuildren's Museum (298-2521); Fun Forest Amusement Park (728-1585); the Pacific Science Center (443-2001), featuring virtual reality, robotic dinosaurs, planetarium and laser shows; and the Seattle Center Monorail, operating 1.9 km from Westlake Center downtown.

SURROUNDING AREAS: **Bainbridge Island**, 15 km W (Washington State Ferry). Quaint shops, galleries, and restaurants are all located within a short hike of the ferry terminal.

Tillicum Village and Tours, Blake Island, 443-1439 (Tillicum Village and Tours from Pier 55-56). Native-American Longhouse and Cultural Center operated in conjunction with Washington State Parks.

Useful telephone numbers

Amtrak 800-872-7245
Bassett Transit (509) 943-6847
Gray Line Airport Express 626-6088
Gray Line of Seattle 624-5077
Greyhound Lines 1-800-231-2222
Metro 553-3000
Northwestern Trailways (509) 838-4029
Quick Shuttle 244-3744
Seattle Visitor Center 461-5840
Seattle-Tacoma Int'l Airport 431-4444
Thomas Cook Foreign Exchange: three locations at the airport, 248-0401; also at 906 and 928 Third Ave, 623-3937
Trailways Northwest 875-1307
Victoria Clipper 448-5000
Victoria Line 625-1880
Washington State Ferries 464-6400

TORONTO

Area code 416
Time zone: Eastern Time

Named Toronto ('place of meeting') by the Huron Indians, this largest city in Canada is located on the northwest shore of Lake Ontario, a situation which tempers the severity of the Canadian winter and results in one of the mildest climates in the country. Fast-growing Toronto has become one of the most ethnically diverse cities of the world, a fact borne out by the bewildering choice of cuisine among the 5,000-or-so restaurants. The fabulous view from the CN Tower, whether by day or by night, will reveal Toronto as a gleaming, modern city. Rather less obvious from this vantage point are the pockets of Toronto's 200-year history, nestling among – and dwarfed by – the surrounding skyscrapers. Although a large city, much of downtown Toronto can be explored on foot, both on the surface and in the world's largest subterranean complex (with more than 1,000 shops) located under the Financial District. The city has an efficient public transport system, with a network of subways, buses, and trams (streetcars) and a suburban rail system. Tourism Toronto Visitor Centre is at Queen's Quay Terminal at Harbourfront Centre. Ontario Ministry of Tourism and Recreation's Travel Centre is located in the Eaton Centre, 220 Yonge St, Level One.

Getting around

CENTRE: Comprises the municipalities of Toronto, Etobicoke, Scarborough, York, North York and East York. Throughout the six municipalities the Toronto Transit Commission (TTC) operates a comprehensive bus and tram (streetcar) network and two subway lines, plus the Scarborough Rapid Transit and the Harbourfront LRT. A flat-fare system, currently CA$2 exact cash, or 10 tickets or tokens for CA$15 from subway station collectors and TTC ticket agents, applies within the Metropolitan Area; special fares may be charged on routes which run beyond Metro's boundaries. Transfers are free but must be obtained when you pay your fare. Day Pass (CA$6 from subway station collectors and TTC ticket agents), good for one person, allows unlimited travel on any one day on all regular TTC routes within Metro after 0930 weekdays and all day Saturdays, or up to six persons, maximum two adults, on any one Sunday or Holiday. Government of Ontario (GO) operate suburban rail and bus services designed primarily to serve communities beyond the Metropolitan Area, but some of these may be used for journeys within it. The GO Lakeshore Line operates a frequent all-day service from Oakville in the west to Pickering in the east; the other GO rail lines and extended Lakeshore services to Hamilton and Oshawa operate mainly in weekday peak hours only and are replaced by buses outside these periods. Zone fares (minimum fare CA$2.30) apply, with fares increasing with distance. Tickets must be purchased from vending machines before boarding.

SURROUNDING AREAS: To the west, **Mississauga** is served by GO buses and trains, and by Mississauga Transit buses; **Oakville**, **Burlington**, **Hamilton** and **Milton**, are all reached by GO buses and trains, as are **Aldershot** (the VIA Rail station and major transit centre serving Burlington and Hamilton), **Brampton** and Georgetown (all additionally served by VIA Rail) and **Guelph** (also served by VIA Rail and by Gray Coach Lines).

To the north, **Bradford**, **Barrie**, **Richmond Hill** and **Stouffville** are reached by GO buses and trains, as is **Markham**, which is also served by Markham Transit. To the east, GO buses and trains serve **Guildwood** (additionally served by VIA Rail), **Pickering**, **Whitby** and **Oshawa** (additionally served by VIA Rail).

To the south around the Lake, **St Catharines** and **Niagara Falls** can be reached by VIA Rail (service continues to Buffalo and New York) and by Greyhound Lines of Canada and Trentway-Wager buses (services continue to Buffalo). To the west, **Woodstock** and **London** are reached by VIA Rail (services continue to Windsor and to Sarnia), and by Greyhound Lines of Canada (service continues to Chatham, Windsor and Detroit); **Kitchener** by Greyhound Lines of Canada and Trentway-Wager buses and by VIA Rail (service continues to Stratford (for **Sherwood Transportation** buses to Goderich) and to London and Windsor).

To the north, **Owen Sound** is served by Greyhound Lines of Canadaand by Penetang Midland Coach Lines; **Washago** by VIA Rail (service continues to Parry Sound, Sudbury, Capreol, Sioux Lookout, Winnipeg, Saskatoon, Edmonton and Vancouver) and by Ontario Northland buses and trains (both services continue to North Bay; rail goes onward to Cochrane). To the east, **Peterborough** is served by Greyhound Lines of Canada buses (services continue to Pembroke, and to Havelock and Ottawa); **Belleville** by VIA Rail (services continue to Kingston, Ottawa, Cornwall and Montréal) and by Greyhound Lines of Canada (service continues to Ottawa) and Voyageur Colonial buses (service continues to Kingston, Ottawa, Cornwall and Montréal).

Main transport centres

Toronto (Lester B. Pearson) International Airport (YYZ) .To/from Metro Toronto Coach Terminal (stops on corner of Bay and Edward Street) or Union Station (stops at Royal York – connected by understreet tunnel) and all three terminals by Pacific Western Airport Express every 20 mins 0625–0045 – one-way fare CA$11.45. Alternatively, by TTC (Yonge–Spadina Subway to Lawrence West; then 85A Airport bus. Within the airport a free shuttle bus connects all three terminals). Major gateway for international and national flights. **Union Station**, (65 W Front St) (Yonge–Spadina Subway to Union Station): Main station of Toronto; departure point for all VIA Rail and Ontario Northland rail services, and hub of the GO Rail System. The TTC Harbourfront LRT also leaves from here, and GO buses which replace trains depart from outside the station in Front Street. Pacific Western Airport Express buses stop at Royal York – connected by understreet tunnel. **Metro Toronto Coach Terminal** (610 Bay Street) (Yonge–Spadina Subway to Dundas or St Patrick – 1–2 blocks; across street from Penetang Midland Terminal). Serves Can Ar Coach Service,Greyhound Lines of Canada, Ontario Northland buses, Penetang Midland Coach Lines, Trentway-Wager, Voyageur Colonial. Hamilton GO bus and Pacific

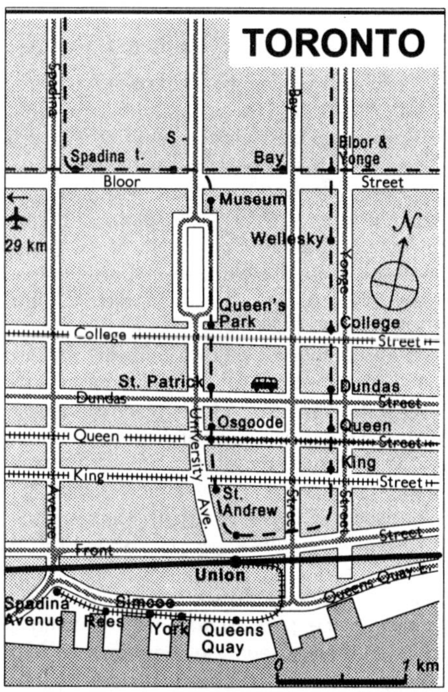

Western Airport Express buses do not come into the terminal, but stop nearby at the corner of Elizabeth and Edward Sts. **Kipling** (Bloor–Danforth Subway to Kipling): Transfer point from subway to GO trains on the Milton Line. **Islington** (Bloor–Danforth Subway to Islington). For connections with Mississauga Transit services, and Pacific Western Airport Express bus to Lester B. Pearson Airport. **Lawrence West** (Yonge–Spadina Subway to Lawrence West). For TTC bus 58A to Lester B. Pearson Airport. **Yorkdale** (Yonge–Spadina Subway to Yorkdale). For Milton, Georgetown, Brampton, Newmarket, Barrie, Sutton and Oshawa GO Bus services, and Pacific Western Airport Express bus to Lester B. Pearson Airport. **York Mills** (Yonge–Spadina Subway to York Mills). For Milton, Georgetown, Brampton and Oshawa GO Bus services, and Pacific Western Airport Express bus to Lester B. Pearson Airport. **York Region Terminal** (Yonge–Spadina Subway to Finch). For North Yonge, Newmarket and Bayview GO Bus services, and connections with Brampton Transit, Markham Transit and Vaughan Transit services. **Kennedy** (Bloor–Danforth Subway to Kennedy). Transfer point from subway to TTC Scarborough Rapid Transit. **Scarborough Centre** (Bloor–Danforth Subway to Kennedy; then Scarborough RT to Scarborough Centre). For Stouffville-Uxbridge and Oshawa GO Bus services, and Pacific Western Airport Express bus to Lester B. Pearson Airport.

Sightseeing by public transport

CENTRE: **Art Gallery of Ontario**, 17 Dundas St W., 979-6648 (Yonge–Spadina Subway to St Patrick; walk 3½ blocks west on Dundas St). One of the largest and finest art museums in North America. **Bata Shoe Museum**, 327 Bloor St W, 979-7799 (Bloor–Danforth or Yonge–Spadina Subway to St George). Footwear from all cultures-from ancient times to the present. **Black Creek Pioneer Village**, 1000 Murray Ross Pkwy, Downsview, 905-736-1733 (Bloor–Danforth Subway to Jane; then 35B Jane bus). One of the largest living-history centres in Canada. Authentic mid-19th century village with over 40 fully-restored homes and shops staffed by interpreters in period costume. **Canada's Wonderland**, 9580 Jane St, Maple, 905-832-7000 (Yonge–Spadina Subway to York Mills or Yorkdale; special GO Transit bus operates from both locations). Canada's largest theme park, attractions including 8 roller-coasters. Open May-September. **Casa Loma**, 1 Austin Terrace, 923-1171 (Bloor–Danforth or Yonge–Spadina Subway to Spadina, then Davenport 127 bus north to Walmer. Walk 1 block north to Austin Terrace). Features unique architecture, furnished rooms, secret passages, towers and 240 metre tunnel connecting the mansion to luxurious stables. **Chinatown**, Dundas St W from Bay to Spadina Sts (Yonge–Spadina Subway to St Patrick). **CN Tower**, 301 Front St W, 360-8500 (Yonge–Spadina Subway to Union; walk west 2½ blocks). The world's tallest free standing structure at 553 metres. Attractions include Eco-Deck, a state-of-the-art interactive environmental exhibit, glass floor, Space Deck and Motion Simulator Theatre. **Eaton Centre**, Younge at Dundas, 598-2322 (Yonge–Spadina Subway to Dundas). Three-level shopping galleria features Eaton's flagship department store. **Fort York**, 100 Garrison Rd, 392-6907 (Bloor–Danforth Subway to Bathurst; then Bathurst 511 streetcar south). Early 19th-century fort recreates the drama of the War of 1812. **Harbourfront Centre**, 410 Queens Quay W., 973-3000 (Yonge–Spadina Subway to Union; then Harbourfront 604 streetcar). 37-hectare complex includes Canada's largest permanent Antique Market (390 Queens Quay W., 260-2626). **MC Michael Canadian Art Collection**, 10365 Islington Ave, Kleinburg, 905-893-1121 (Penetang Midland Coach Lines from Metro Toronto Coach Terminal, call museum for fare and schedule information). **Metro Toronto Zoo**, 361-A Old Finch Ave, Scarborough, 392-5900 (Bloor– Danforth Subway to Kennedy; then Scarborough 86A bus; for weekend service telephone 393-4636). One of the world's best zoos, featuring over 5,000 native and exotic animals. **Ontario Parliament Buildings**, Legislative Building, ½ block north of College St and University Ave, 325-7500 (Yonge–Spadina Subway to Queen's Park; then walk north on Queen's Park Crescent). Includes Legislative Chamber and Legislative Assembly (free passes required) and museum. Free tours year-round. **Ontario Place**, 955 Lake Shore Blvd W., 314-9811 (Yonge–Spadina Subway to Union, then 121 Front/Esplanade bus direct to park; or Bloor–Danforth Subway to Ossington, then 63 Ossington bus). Entertainment complex located on Lake Ontario Waterfront. **Ontario Science Centre**, 770 Don Mills Rd, North York, 429-4100 (Bloor–Danforth Subway to Pape; then any 25 Don Mills bus north). Interactive exhibits feature the wonders of science and technology. **Royal Ontario Museum**, 100 Queens Park, 586-8000 (Yonge–Spadina Subway to

Museum). Exhibits include Ancient Egypt and dinosaur galleries, working paleontology lab, Bat Cave and Chinese Tomb. **The Beaches**, Queen St East from Woodbine to Victoria Park Ave, 698-9053 (Yonge–Spadina Subway to Osgoode or Queen; then Queen 501 streetcar). Toronto's original cottage country, located on the shore of Lake Ontario. **Toronto Islands** (Yonge–Spadina Subway to Union; then Harbourfront 604 streetcar to Bay/Queens Quay and walk south to the ferry docks). Miles of sandy beaches, lagoons, parks and picnic grounds, hiking and cycling trails.

SURROUNDING AREAS: **Georgian Bay Islands National Park**, 210 km N (Penetang-Midland Coach Lines). Located in southern Georgian Bay (part of Lake Huron). 30,000-island bus-boat tours operate May–late Oct. **Niagara Falls** (Greyhound Lines of Canada, Trentway-Wager and VIA Rail). One of the natural wonders of the world. The 49-metre falls are beautiful at any time of year. Attractions include *Maid of the Mist* boat tours, a Spanish Aerocar trip over the whirlpool gorge, and Skylon observation tower. **Niagara on the Lake**, 125 km (Charterways bus, 905-688-9600). Historic town, a significant site during the War of 1812 between England and the USA, is now home of the renowned Shaw Festival (468-2172), featuring works by Bernard Shaw and other well-known playwrights. **Stratford**, 158 km SW (VIA Rail from Union Station). Home of the largest repertory theatre company in North America. The Stratford Festival features works by Shakespeare, musicals and works by both new and well-known playwrights in three theatres. Stratford also features fine shopping, dining and picnicking on the banks of the Avon.

Useful telephone numbers

Brampton Transit (905) 874-2999
GO Transit 869-3200
Greyhound Lines of Canada 367-8747
Markham Transit (905) 475-4888
Metro Toronto Coach Terminal 393-7911
Mississauga Transit (905) 279-5800
Ontario Ministry of Tourism 314-0944
Ontario Northland (705) 472-4500
Pacific Western Airport Express (905) 564-3232
Penetang Midland Coach Lines 236-7625
Richmond Hill Transit (905) 884-4636
Toronto International Airport (905) 676-3506
Thomas Cook: Branches, both foreign exchange and travel agency, throughout the city and suburbs. All services at 10 King St E, 366-1961
Toronto Transit Commission (TTC) 393 4636
Tourism Toronto 203-2500
Trentway-Wagar 593-2565
Vaughan Transit (905) 832-8527
VIA Rail 366-8411
Voyageur Colonial (514) 843-4231

VANCOUVER

Area code 604
Time zone: Pacific Time

Located in the southwestern corner of British Columbia, about 40 km from the US border, Vancouver is set in breathtaking natural surroundings between the mountains and the sea. A modern yet interesting city, it is also an ideal base for exploring the surrounding area, both the mountainous hinterland and the many islands, including the large Vancouver Island across the Strait of Georgia. Although Vancouver is an extensive city, it has a comprehensive regional transit system which makes getting about easy. Vancouver Tourist InfoCentre located on the Plaza Level of Waterfront Centre, Burrard and Cordova Sts.

Getting around

CENTRE: The Vancouver Regional Transit System of BC Transit operate a network of buses and trolleys, plus the SkyTrain Rapid Transit (underground in the downtown area and elevated in the suburbs) and the SeaBus ferry to North Vancouver. Most buses stop on, or near, the downtown Granville Street Mall, located between Hastings and Georgia Streets. A zonal fare system applies during Mon–Fri peak hours; outside these times a flat-fare system is in operation. Fares are currently CA$1.50 for travel within one zone, CA$2.25 for two zones and CA$3 for three zones; off-peak CA$1.50 for any distance. Transfers are free, but must be obtained when you board the first vehicle. A day pass is available (currently CA$4.50). Fares, transfers and passes are valid on all methods of transport and for interchange between them.

SURROUNDING AREAS: North across the Burrard Inlet, **Horseshoe Bay** (for BC Ferries to Nanaimo, Bowen Island and Langdale) and **West Vancouver** are served by BC Transit buses, as is **North Vancouver**, which is reached additionally by BC Transit SeaBus. In the east, **Burnaby** and **Port Moody** can be reached by BC Transit buses and by West Coast Express commuter trains (services continue to Mission). In the south east, BC Transit SkyTrain and buses serve **New Westminster** and **Surrey**; the bus services also extend to

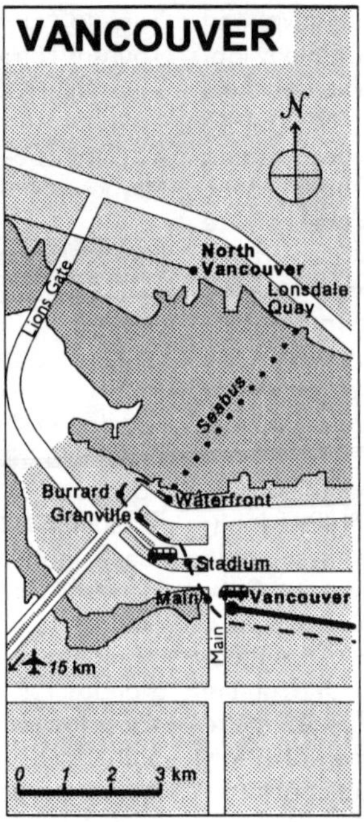

Langley, **White Rock** and **Delta**. In the south, **Richmond**, **Ladner** and **Tsawwassen** (for BC Ferries to Swartz Bay, Nanaimo and the southern Gulf Islands) are all reached by BC Transit buses. Northwards along the coast, **Powell River** is reached by Maverick Coach Lines; inland, **Squamish** and **Whistler** by BC Rail (service continues to Lilooet, Williams Lake, Quesnel and Prince George) and by Maverick Coach Lines (service continues to Pemberton). To the east, **Port Coquitlam** (also served by BC Transit) and **Chilliwack** are served by VIA Rail (service continues to Kamloops, Jasper, Edmonton, Saskatoon, Winnipeg and Toronto), and **Hope** is served by Greyhound Lines of Canada (services continue to Kamloops, Revelstoke, Lake Louise and Calgary, and to Penticton and Kelowna). To the south, **Bellingham** and **Seattle** are reached by Amtrak, Greyhound Lines, Quick Shuttle and Trailways Northwest (Seattle only). To the south and west across the Strait of Georgia, **Victoria** can be reached by BC Ferries Tsawwassen–Swartz Bay service (BC Transit provide bus connections between ferry terminals and downtown areas), or direct by Pacific Coach Linesbus-ferry service. The southern **Gulf Islands** are served by BC Ferries from Tsawwassen. **Nanaimo** can be reached by BC Ferries services from Tsawwassen and Horseshoe Bay, or direct by Maverick Coach Lines bus-ferry service.

On Vancouver Island, service between **Victoria**, **Nanaimo** and **Courtenay** is operated by VIA Rail and by Island Coach Lines buses; services continue to Port Alberni, Tofino (for Pacific Rim National Park) and Port Hardy (for BC Ferries to/from Prince Rupert).

Main transport centres

Vancouver International Airport (YVR). Direct service from/to Level II and downtown Vancouver every 15 mins by Charter Bus Lines – alternate journeys serve different areas of downtown – service to Pacific Central Station and Bus Terminal every 30 mins; one-way fare CA$9. Alternatively, BC Transit trolleybus 20 to Granville/70th Ave then bus 100 to airport (if coming from the airport, bus 100 to Granville/70th Ave then bus 20 to downtown.) Major international and domestic gateway. **Pacific Central Station** (SkyTrain to Science World-Main Street; buses 3, 8,19). Western terminus of the VIA Rail system and departure point for all Amtrak and VIA Rail services. Adjacent bus terminal serves Greyhound Lines of Canada, Maverick Coach Lines, Pacific Coach Lines, Quick Shuttle, Trailways Northwest and Vancouver Airporter. **North Vancouver Station** (special BC Transit bus from Stadium SkyTrain Station, which also picks up along Georgia, or from North Vancouver SeaBus Terminal). Departure point for all BC Rail trains. **Seabus Terminal–Waterfront Station** (SkyTrain or bus 1 or 50 to Waterfront). For BC Transit SeaBus ferry to North Vancouver (Lonsdale Quay) and West Coast Express commuter trains to Mission. **Horseshoe Bay** (BC Transit bus 250 or 257 or Maverick Coach Lines from Georgia). For BC Ferries to Nanaimo, Bowen Island and Langdale. **Tsawwassen** (direct by Pacific Coach Lines from Cambie, or by BC Transit bus 601 from Howe to Ladner Exchange, then BC Transit bus 404 – summer only – or 640). For BC Ferries to Swartz Bay, Nanaimo and the southern Gulf Islands.

Sightseeing by public transport

CENTRE: **Bloedel Conservatory–Queen Elizabeth Park**, Cambie at 33rd Ave, 872-5513 (BC Transit bus 15 on Burrard). Vancouver's only 'garden under glass' features a magnificent display of plants and birds from around the world. Excellent city views from the surrounding park. **Capilano Suspension Bridge**, 3735 Capilano Rd, North Vancouver, 985-7474 (BC Transit SeaBus to Lonsdale Quay then BC Transit bus 236). The longest (150 m) and highest (80 m) suspended footbridge in the world, located above the Capilano River canyon. **Chinatown**, Pender St between Carrall and Main Sts (BC Transit bus 19 or 22 east on Pender). North America's second largest Chinatown features many shops, restaurants and Dr Sun Yat-Sen Classical Chinese gardens (578 Carral St, 689-7133). **Gastown**, Water St between Richards and Carrall Sts (BC Transit SkyTrain to Waterfront, or BC Transit bus 50 north on Granville Mall, or bus 1 north on Burrard). The oldest part of the city, with many Victorian-era buildings. Home of the famous steam clock, Blood Alley, shops and restaurants. **Granville Island**, Cartwright, Duranleau and Johnson Sts, under Granville Bridge, 666-5784 (BC Transit bus 50 south on Granville Mall). Popular shopping complex features many special events. **Grouse Mountain**, 6400 Nancy Greene Way, North Vancouver, 984-0661 (BC Transit SeaBus to Lonsdale Quay then BC Transit bus 236). Aerial tramway featuring panoramic vistas. Mountain-top attractions include multimedia presentation, logging shows, chairlift rides, walking and hiking trails and restaurant. **The Lookout! at Harbour Centre**, 555 West Hastings St, 689-0421 (BC Transit SkyTrain to Waterfront). Glass-enclosed elevator to the top of Harbour Centre Tower for 360 degree view of Vancouver and the Lower Mainland. **Playland**, Exhibition Park, Hastings at Cassiar, 255-5161 (BC Transit buses 14, 16 north on Granville Mall). Home of Canada's largest roller-coaster. **Royal Hudson**, 1311 W 1st St, North Vancouver, 984-5246 (BC Transit Royal Hudson Special bus on Georgia). The Royal Hudson offers steam train excursions between North Vancouver and Squamish. Operates Wed–Sun, mid-June to Sept. **Stanley Park**, Stanley Park Loop, 681-1141 (BC Transit bus 19 west on Pender then bus 52 from Stanley Park Loop Apr. – Oct. weekends). One of the world's great urban parks. Attractions include 8.8 km seawall walk, forest, beaches, rose gardens, children's farmyard, miniature railway. **UBC Museum of Anthropology**, 6393 W Marine Dr., U.BC Campus, 822-3825 (BC Transit bus 4, 10 south on Granville Mall). Stunning displays of Northwest Coast Native American art and artifacts. **Vancouver Aquarium**, 268-9900 (BC Transit bus 19 west on Pender then bus 52 from Stanley Park Loop Apr.–Oct. weekends) Features marine life of the North Pacific Coast and Canada's Arctic including Beluga whales. **Vancouver Museum**, 1100 Chestnut St, Vanier Park, 736-4431 (BC Transit bus 22 south on Burrard; Granville Island Ferry). Canada's largest civic museum. Adjacent **H. R. MacMillan Planetarium** (738-7827) features astronomy and space science programs and laser-light shows. The nearby **Vancouver Maritime Museum** (1905 Ogden Ave, 257-8300) highlights the maritime heritage of BC and Vancouver and a one-of-a-kind hands-on Children's Maritime Discovery Centre.

SURROUNDING AREAS: **Victoria**, 110 km SW (Victoria Clipper/Victoria Line ferry, also by BC Ferries from Vancouver). British Columbia's capital city, named after England's longest-reigning monarch, still retains a regal quality. The inner harbour is home to the Empress Hotel (721 Government St, 604-384-8111), Victoria's elegant, turn-of-the-century hotel serving high tea every afternoon, the Royal British Columbia Museum (675 Belleville St, 604-387-3701) , the 1897 Parliament Buildings (501 Belleville St). The world-famous **Butchart Gardens** (800 Benvenuto Ave, Brentwood Bay BC, 652-5256) are accessible by city bus (BC Transit bus 75 on Douglas St) and Gray Line Tours.

Whistler, 120 km N (BC Rail, Maverick Coach Lines). One of the top ski resorts in North America, but offers year-round recreational facilities. BC Rail provides an excellent schedule for both day trippers and overnight visitors.

Useful telephone numbers

BC Ferries 669-1211
BC Rail 984-5246
BC Transit (Vancouver) 521-0400
BC Transit (Victoria) 382-6161
Discover British Columbia 663-6000
Greyhound Lines of Canada 662-3222
Island Coach Lines 385-4411
Maverick Coach Lines 662-8051
Pacific Coach Lines 662-8074
Quick Shuttle 244-3744
Thomas Cook: Many foreign exchange and travel branches in Vancouver, including at Eaton's, Pacific Centre, 701 Granville St, : 687-0055
Tourism Assoc. Southwestern BC 739-9011
Tourism Victoria 953-2033
Trailways Northwest 875-1307
Vancouver Airporter Bus 244-9888
Vancouver Bus Terminal 662-7575
Vancouver International Airport 276-6060
Vancouver Travel Info Centre 683-2000
VIA Rail 669 3050
West Coast Express 689-3641
West Vancouver Transit 985-8691

WASHINGTON DC

Area code 202
Time zone: Eastern Time

The overwhelming impression of Washington DC for most first-time visitors is one of space. Although it contains some of the largest buildings in the country, including, of course, the White House, the Capitol and the vast Pentagon, these are separated by wide avenues and parklands which keeps everything in perspective. One result of this spaciousness is that it is easy to underestimate distances; 'a few blocks' may not sound very far, but it does rather depend on the size of the blocks. However, it is relatively easy to find your way around, as Washington is laid out on a grid pattern. Streets which run north–south are numbered, and streets which run east–west are lettered; the numbers/letters rise as you progress away from the Capitol, which is the hub of the system. This principle applies equally to the house or building numbering system and can result in up to four apparently identical addresses, so it's important to identify in which quadrant (NW, NE, SW, SE) the required address is situated. Streets which run diagonally are all 'avenues' and are named after states. Getting around is also aided by Washington's excellent Metro system. Visitor Center located at 1450 Pennsylvania Ave NW, across from the White House.

Getting around

CENTRE: The Washington Metropolitan Area Transit Authority (WMATA) operates a comprehensive network of subways (Metrorail) and buses (Metrobus) throughout the District of Columbia and into neighbouring states. The collective name of the system is 'Metro'. The Metrorail network is modern (the first section was opened in 1976) and now comprises 5 lines (Red, Orange, Blue, Green and Yellow); the system is still being expanded. Metrorail stations are easily identified by a brown column with a large 'M' at the top; underneath this is a stripe (or stripes) in the colour(s) of the line(s) serving the station. Fares vary according to the distance travelled and the time of day; they are higher in the peak periods (0530–0930 and 1500–2000 Mon–Fri) than at other times. A farecard must be purchased on arrival at the station; this electronically records the amount paid. The farecard must be inserted into a gate on both entry and exit; the fare for the journey will be automatically deducted as you exit. If there is any remaining credit when you leave the system, the farecard will be returned to you; otherwise the machine retains it, and, in the event of an insufficient amount on the farecard to meet the cost of the journey just made, you will be instructed to go the 'Addfare' machine to pay the shortfall. If you intend to continue your journey by Metrobus, you should obtain a transfer on entering the Metrorail system. This must be presented to the driver on boarding the bus, together with any additional transfer fees. Metrobus services run throughout DC; bus schedules are co-ordinated with those of Metrorail. A flat-fare system (currently $1.10) applies for journeys wholly within DC; supplements apply during peak periods and for journeys which cross into Maryland or Virginia. Transfers to another Metrobus service are free and are valid 2 hours; however, transfers are *not* available from Metrobus to Metrorail.

SURROUNDING AREAS: WMATA Metro services extend into the suburbs; additionally the northwestern, northern and northeastern suburbs are served by Maryland Department of Transportation (MARC) trains; the northwestern and northern suburbs also have their own bus network provided by Montgomery County Transit, operating under the name of Ride On. Some southern and southwestern suburbs can be reached by Virginia Railway Express. Buses are provided throughout the southern, southwestern and western suburbs by Fairfax Connector, and individual transit systems in Alexandria by DASH and in Fairfax City by CUE. To the south, **Fredericksburg** is reached by Virginia Railway Express and by Amtrak (not all Amtrak services can be used for journeys between Washington and Fredericksburg – see timetables); **Richmond** by Amtrak (services continue to Charleston, Jacksonville and Miami, and also to Williamsburg and Newport News with Thruway Bus connection to Virginia Beach), and by Greyhound Lines buses. To the south west, **Manassas** is reached by Virginia Railway Express and by Amtrak; **Culpeper** and **Charlottesville** are both served by Amtrak (services continue to Atlanta and New Orleans, and to Charleston (WV), Cincinnati and Chicago); Charlottesville is also served by Greyhound Lines (services continue to Roanoke and Nashville). To the north west, **Brunswick** and **Martinsburg** are reached by MARC and by Amtrak trains (service continues to Pittsburgh, Cleveland and Chicago), and **Hagerstown** by Greyhound Lines (service continues to Pittsburgh, Cleveland and Chicago). To the north-east, **Baltimore**, **Wilmington** and **Philadelphia** are all on Amtrak's North East Corridor (service continues to Newark, New York and Boston); and by Greyhound and Peter Pan Trailways buses. **Baltimore** can also be reached by MARC and by Capitol Trailways buses (service continues to Harrisburg and Syracuse). To the east, **Annapolis**, **Lewes** (for **Cape May** by Lewes Ferry service), **Rehoboth Beach** and **Ocean City** can be accessed by Carolina Trailways buses.

Main transport centres

Washington Dulles International Airport (IAD), 42 km W. From the downtown Washington Air Terminal (16th and K Streets NW) to the Main Airport Terminal every 30–60 mins 0615–2115 by the Washington

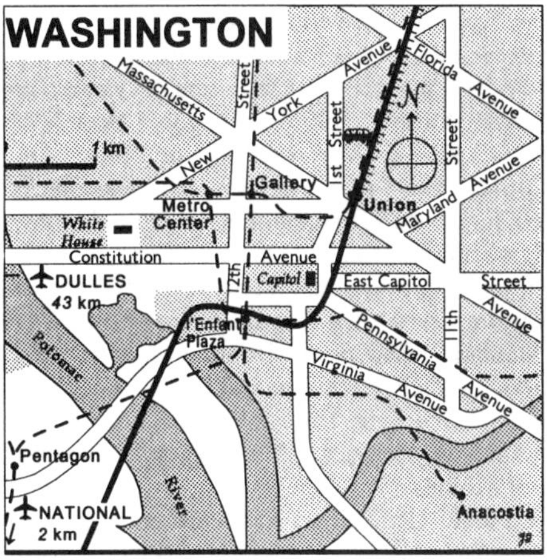

Flyer Bus (operated by the Metropolitan Washington Airports Authority). Alternatively, by WMATA Metrorail Orange Line to West Falls Church, then every 15–30 mins 0630–2300 by Washington Flyer to the Main Airport Terminal. Washington Flyer also operate an inter-airport service between Dulles Airport (Main Terminal) and National Airport (both terminals) every 1–2 hrs, 0500–2300. Within Dulles Airport the Midfield and Main terminals are connected by a courtesy Mobile Lounge service which operates as required. Major gateway for international flights, two terminals. **Washington National Airport** (DCA), 7 km S. From the downtown Washington Air Terminal (16th and K Streets NW) every 30–60 mins, 0605–2235, to both airport terminals by Washington Flyer. Alternatively by WMATA Metrorail Blue and Yellow Lines to National Airport. The Metrorail station is located opposite the Main Terminal and is within walking distance of all terminals, or a courtesy shuttle bus is available.See above for connections to Dulles International. Within the airport, courtesy shuttle buses run frequently between both terminals and the Metrorail station. Major hub for domestic flights, with connections to most US cities. **Baltimore-Washington International Airport** (BWI), 48 km NE (MARC or Amtrak train to BWI Airport Station, then by free shuttle bus). See Baltimore section, p 17. **Union Station**, 50 Massachusetts Ave NE (WMATA Metrorail Red Line to Union Station). Restored to its former glory, and now also a major shopping centre, Union Station is *the* rail station of Washington. All Amtrak, MARC, and Virginia Railway Express services arrive and depart here. **Greyhound Terminal**, 1st and L Sts (WMATA Metrorail Red Line to Union Station, then 1 km walk). For services of Carolina Trailways and Greyhound Lines. **Peter Pan Trailways Terminal**, 1st and L Sts (WMATA Metrorail Red Line to Union Station, then 1 km walk). For services of Capitol Trailways and Peter Pan Trailways.

Sightseeing by public transport

CENTRE: **Arlington National Cemetery** (WMATA Metrorail Blue Line to Arlington Cemetery). America's largest national burial ground includes the grave of President John F. Kennedy. The changing of the guard at the Tomb of the Unknown Soldier takes place every hour in winter and every half-hour in summer. **Dupont Circle**, Connecticut Ave and 'P' St NW (WMATA Metrorail Red Line to Dupont Circle). Lively neighbourhood with all types of bookstores, unique shops and restaurants. Many of the city's 150 foreign embassies are found nearby along Massachusetts Ave NW. Historic **Georgetown**, 'M' St and Wisconsin Ave NW (WMATA Metrorail Blue and Orange Lines to Foggy Bottom-GWU; then Metrobus) was a colonial port and later a strategic point on the Underground Railroad. **Jefferson Memorial**, Tidal Basin, south end of 15th St NW, 426-6841 (WMATA Metrorail Blue or Orange Lines to Smithsonian). Large bronze statue of America's third president stands beneath a rotunda inscribed with passages from the Declaration of Independence. **Lincoln Memorial**, West Potomac Park at 23rd St NW, 426-6841 (WMATA Metrorail Blue or Orange Lines to Foggy Bottom-GWU). Grand memorial, overlooking the Reflecting Pool, was patterned after a classic Greek temple. Inside a marble statue of the 16th president is surrounded by inscriptions from his Gettysburg Address. **National Gallery of Art**, 4th St and Constitution Ave NW, 842-6353 (WMATA Metrorail Green or Yellow Lines to Archives-Navy Memorial, or Red Line to Judiciary Sq.). Permanent collection of American and European art and changing exhibitions of art from around the world. **National Archives**, 7th St and Pennsylvania Ave NW, 501-5200 (WMATA Metrorail Green or Yellow Lines to Archives-Navy Memorial). Houses more than three billion records and documents, including the Declaration of Independence, Constitution and Bill of Rights. **National Museum of American Art**, 8th and 'G' Sts NW, 357-2840 (WMATA Metrorail Green, Red and Yellow Lines to Gallery Place-Chinatown). Part of the Smithsonian Institution. **National Zoo**, 3000 Connecticut Ave NW, 673-4800) (WMATA Metrorail Red Line to Woodley Park-Zoo) Part of the Smithsonian Institution.

More than 5,000 animals, exotic birds and reptiles. **Smithsonian Institution Museums**, The Mall between 7th and 14th Sts (WMATA Metrorail Blue or Orange Lines to Smithsonian). Includes 14 museums. Major attractions include The **Visitor Information Center** (1000 Jefferson Dr. SW, 357-2700), known as The Castle, which houses the crypt of founder James Smithson, two orientation theatres and scale models of Washington's monumental core; **Art and Industries Building** (900 Jefferson Dr. SW, 357-2700), with exhibits from the 1876 US Centennial Exposition in Philadelphia; **Freer Gallery of Art** (12th S and Jefferson Dr. SW, 357-4880); **Hirschhorn Museum and Sculpture Garden** (7th St and Independence Ave SW, 357-2700); **National Air and Space Museum** (6th St and Independence Ave SW, 357-2700), the world's most visited museum, with aviation and space technology treasures that include the Wright Brothers' 1903 flyer, Lindbergh's *Spirit of St Louis* and the *Apollo 11* command module; **National Museum of American History** (14th St and Constitution Ave NW, 357-2700), whose wealth of Americana includes the flag that inspired *The Star Spangled Banner*; **National Museum of Natural History** (10th St and Constitution Ave NW, 357-1650), the world's largest natural history museum, featuring the 45.5-carat Hope Diamond.

Supreme Court of the United States, 1st St and Maryland Ave NE, 479-3030 (WMATA Metrorail Blue and Orange Lines to Capitol South, or Red Line to Union Station). When in session, the court meets Mon–Wed 1000–1500. Limited gallery seating on a first-come, first-serve basis. **United States Capitol**, east end of the Mall on Capitol Hill, 225-6827 (WMATA Metrorail Blue and Orange Lines to Capitol South). Includes United States Senate and House of Representatives, the Rotunda, the Statuary Hall and the original Supreme Court Chamber. Guided tours daily 0900–1545. **Vietnam Veterans Memorial**, Constitution Ave and Henry Bacon Dr. NW, 634-1568 (WMATA Metrorail Blue and Orange Lines to Foggy Bottom-GWU). Modern V-shaped memorial of black granite inscribed with the names of 58,192 people killed or missing in action in the Vietnam War.

Washington Monument, 15th St and Constitution Ave NW, 426-6841 (WMATA Metrorail Blue and Orange Lines to Smithsonian). One of the tallest masonry structures in the world. Dedicated in 1885 to the memory of the first US President. Free elevator to the top for spectacular view. **The White House**, 1600 Pennsylvania Ave NW, 456-2322 (WMATA Metrorail Blue and Orange Lines to Farragut West). The official residence of the President of the United States. Free guided tours Tues–Sat, 1000– 1200 (tickets required during summer). White House Visitors Center, US Department of Commerce Building, 1450 Pennsylvania Ave NW, 523-3847 (WMATA Metrorail Blue and Orange Lines to Federal Triangle), offers free, timed tickets for touring the White House and historical exhibits.

SURROUNDING AREAS: **Alexandria**, 14 km S (WMATA Metrorail Blue and Yellow Lines to King St or Braddock Rd, then Alexandria DASH bus). Founded in 1749 as a tobacco seaport. Old Town is home to historic homes, a waterfront museum, shops, galleries and restaurants along King Street. **Colonial Williamsburg** (Amtrak to Williamsburg) The former capital of colonial Virginia has been preserved as it was during the 18th-century. Outstanding collection of historic structures, gardens and tree-shaded streets. Artisans demonstrate historic crafts dressed in colonial attire.

Useful telephone numbers

Amtrak (800) 872-7245
Baltimore-Washington Airport (410) 859-7032
Capitol Trailways (717) 233-7673
Carolina Trailways 682-1889
DASH (703) 370-3274
Fairfax Connector (703) 339-7200
Greyhound Lines (800) 231-2222
MARC 1-800-325-7245
Maryland Tourist Development (301) 333-6611
Montgomery County Transit (Ride On) (301) 217-7433
Peter Pan Trailways 371-2111
Thomas Cook Foreign Exchange: 1800 'K' St NW, 872-1233; 1818 'H' St NW, 458-4342
Virginia Division of Tourism (804) 786-2051
Virginia Railway Express (703) 497-7777
Washington DC Visitors Assoc. 789-7000
Washington Dulles Intl. Airport (703) 661-2700
Washington National Airport (703) 685-8000
WMATA (Metrobus/Metrorail) 637-7000

GENERAL TRAVEL INFORMATION

UNITED STATES OF AMERICA

Documentation: Passports: are required by all except persons carrying valid Alien Registration Card. Visas are not required by citizens of Canada or citizens of the UK and most other Western European countries, and New Zealand, who are travelling on an unexpired national or EC passport for business, pleasure or transit purposes only, for a stay in the USA for a maximum of 90 days and who hold valid non-refundable return tickets together with a completed form I-94W issued by a participating carrier (if arriving overland from Canada or Mexico, form I-94W must be obtained from the immigration authorities at the point of entry). The foregoing also applies to British Passports issued by the Falkland Islands and Dependencies, Guernsey and Dependencies, Jersey, and the Isle of Man (but not to British Dependent Territories). UK subjects resident in Bermuda or Canada who hold valid UK passports and, in the case of Canada, have the status of 'landed immigrants', and UK citizens who hold unexpired full British Passports and whose National Status is shown in their passport as 'British Citizen' (passports showing status 'British Subject' must be endorsed 'Holder has the right of abode in the United Kingdom' to qualify). Travellers with certain serious communicable illnesses, criminal racords, previous deportations from the USA and other problems must apply for a restricted visa; attempts by these travellers to enter on the visa-free arrangement will be refused. Travellers not falling into the above categories should consult their travel agent or local US Embassy.

Public holidays: Jan. 1; July 4; Nov. 11; Dec. 25; also Martin Luther King's Birthday (third Mon. in Jan.), Washington's Birthday (third Mon. in Feb.), Memorial Day (last Mon. in May), Labor Day (first Mon. in Sept.), Columbus Day (second Mon. in Oct.), and Thanksgiving Day (fourth Thurs. in Nov.); these apply to all states and territories. A large number of additional holidays are observed in various states and cities, especially Lincoln's Birthday, which is widely observed in the North and largely ignored in the South.

Currency: 100 Cents = 1 US Dollar (US$)

Post boxes are blue.

Time zones: see map on p. 64.

Electricity: 110–120v 60Hz AC.

Phone calls abroad: Dial 011 (Mainland), via operator (Alaska and Hawaii). Call boxes are blue. 5-, 10- and 25-cent coins accepted.

CANADA

Documentation: Passports are required by all except nationals of France (residing in and entering from St Pierre & Miquelon) and USA, and residents of Greenland entering from Greenland. Visas are not required by nationals of the UK and most Western European countries, Australia, New Zealand and most other Commonwealth countries, or of the USA. All visitors must hold onward or return tickets. If in doubt, consult your travel agent or nearest Canadian Embassy or High Commission.

Public holidays: National: Jan. 1; July 1; Nov. 11; Dec. 25, 26; also Good Friday, Easter Monday, Victoria Day (penultimate Mon. in May), Labour Day (first Mon. in Sept.) and Thanksgiving (second Mon. in Oct.). Additional regional holidays: Alberta – Heritage Day*. British Columbia – British Columbia Day*. Manitoba, New Brunswick, North West Territories, Ontario, Saskatchewan – Civic Holiday*. Newfoundland – St Patrick's Day (Mon. prior to Mar. 18), St George's Day (nearest Mon. to Apr. 24), Discovery Day (Mon. prior to July 5), Orangeman's Day (4 prior to July 16). Québec – June 24. Yukon – Discovery Day (Mon. prior to Aug. 22).
(* – First Mon. in Aug.)

Currency: 100 Cents = 1 Canadian Dollar (CA$).

Postage abroad: Postcard or airmail letter to USA (up to 30g) 43; elsewhere (up to 20g) 74. Post boxes are red.

Time zones: see map on p. 64.

Electricity: 110v 60Hz AC.

Phone calls abroad: Dial 011. Call boxes (internal calls and calls to USA only – colour varies with province/territory accept 5-, 10- and 25-cent coins.

BBC WORLD SERVICE

BBC World Service broadcasts to North America at 1100–1745 and 2100–0730 on the following frequencies: 15260 15220 15205 15070 12095 11820 11775 9915 9740 9640 9590 9515 6175 5975 and 5965 kHz.

HOW TO USE THE TIMETABLES

1. To find the service required, refer either to the index of place names on pp. 139–142 or to the index map of the area concerned (see p. 2 for page numbers of these maps). **All index and map references are to table numbers, not page numbers.** On the maps, the numbers of the tables appear along the lines to which they refer. Rail services are denoted by a thick (main railway) or thin (secondary railway) solid black line with table numbers in **bold** type, bus services by a grey line and table numbers in grey, and shipping services by a dotted black line and table numbers in normal type. See the 'Key to maps and town plans' on page 57.
2. All timings are given in the twenty-four hour clock format. The hours are numbered consecutively from 1 to 24, starting from midnight. A train or bus arriving or departing at 1.10 p.m. is shown as 1310; at 5.15 p.m. as 1715; at 9.30 p.m. as 2130, and so on. The figures '2400' indicate a service arriving at midnight, but a departure at that hour is shown as '0000'. Arrivals and departures at any time between midnight and 1.00 a.m. are expressed by '0001' to '0059'.
3. One list of places serves, in many of the tables, for both directions. In these cases the times on the left of the names are to be read downwards, but those on the right must be read upwards, from bottom to top. Most tables have small arrows above the place names or by the times to indicate in which direction the times should be read.
4. Places on branch lines or routes are printed slightly to the right as compared to those of the primary line/route and those of connecting lines/routes appear in italics. When a table number (e.g.

Specimen Timetable

TOWNS: For each table we have selected the towns to be shown and the omission of a town does not automatically mean that the town is not served by the services shown. The main towns are shown in **bold**. Towns with more than one station/terminus have the relevant station after their names. Towns whose station serves other places of note have these places shown in brackets and *italics*. Indented towns are served by branch routes. Towns in *italics* only have services connecting with the main service shown. Full service will be shown in the table indicated (**9999**) in **bold**.

Symbols and letters against town names are explained in the footnotes. Times shown against town names are normally departure times (d., a. = arrival time); certain services may arrive at stations some time before the departure times shown.

Information shown above the list of towns refers to all services in the table.

HEADINGS: Each table has a heading showing the table number, the main service covered, the type of transport used (symbols page 57) and the operator code(s) (in *italics*) – see footnote.

FARES: Fares are given from the fares basepoint in the table (shown as 0 or 0.00). This is normally the first town in the table, but can occasionally be the last, or even at a mid-point, in which cases the fares should be read upwards or in both directions from the basepoint. The fares are for basic accommodation in the class shown (see introduction at the beginning of each country's entry), are shown in local currencies whenever possible and are generally one-way fares. In a few cases, round-trip fares are shown (indicated by RT). Fares are for direct services and usually do not include stopovers. Readers are reminded that these fares are for guidance only; in some cases different operators on the same route have different fare scales – in these cases we have shown the highest fares we have received for the class.

KILOMETRES: Kilometres are normally shown from the first town in the table (shown as *0*) and are via the most direct route.

Table 0000 BLACKADDER – TIGER VALE ### *MT SSS*

	MT		*MT*			*MT*		*MT*
$	**26**		**100**			**101**		**4XL**
2 cl.	12		12		**Summer Service Only**	12		123
			◆	km	↓ ↑	◆		alt⑥
0.00	0730	....	1220A	*0*	d. **Blackadder** Central..a.	1000B	....	1200
7.50	1115	....	|	*5*	d. Fox Woods...........d.	|	....	|
10.25	▬	....	|	*28*	d. Shepherd①........d.	|	....	1030
13.55	*SSS*	....	|	*45*	d. Blue Bay①.........d.	|	....	0915b
23.45	12	....	2358A	*40*	a. **Goshawk** Union....d.	2130A	....	0620
	1536	....	0002B	*40*	d. **Goshawk** Union....a.	1930A	....	0600
30.00	1625s	....	|	*52*	*d.* **Aardvark** *(Aardwolf)*.d.	|	....	0430
40.00	1700	....	0230B	*58*	a. **Tiger Vale** West ...d.	1700A	....	....
					a. Gorgon Swamp **9999** *d.*	*1500a*	....	....

100/101– 1, 2 cl, 1, 2 cl and ✕, Blackadder - Tiger Vale and v.v.
①– Daily service (hourly) Shepherd - Blue Bay and v.v. Journey 3 hours *(SSS)*.
a– ⑥ only.
b– Does not stop on ⑦.
MT– Municipal Transport.
SSS– Special Services Ltd.

FOOTNOTES: Footnotes explain non-standard letters and symbols used in the tables and **should always be referred to.**

Standard footnotes (e.g. '**s**' in this example) are shown on page 61 and are not repeated in individual tables; always therefore check page 61 if a symbol or letter does not have an explanation in the footnotes to a table.

SERVICES AND TIMES: Each service is headed by the operator code (in tables with more than one operator) in *italics* and the train or service number (where known) in **bold**. Other symbols indicate accommodation and dining facilities available and days of running (see page 57). Fuller details of services indicated with black diamonds ◆ can be found in the footnotes (listed by train/service number). Non-standard symbols and letters are explained in the footnotes. Times are shown in the 24-hour clock system throughout the book (see page 59, and also the conversion table below) and are normally in local times (see the COUNTRY FACTS AND FIGURES section).

Where two services are shown in the same column and are separated by a thick black line ▬ the services are totally independent of one another and no through facility is available.

Times in *italics* are connecting services; passengers must change en route.

Condensed bold CAPITAL letters against service times indicate duration of travel: **A** = First day, **B** = Second day etc.

Services operate daily unless otherwise qualified by a number or letter in a circle (see page 57). These symbols may be further combined, for example: alt ⑥ = Operates on alternate Saturdays; Ex ⑤ = Daily except Fridays; ①–④ = Daily Mondays to Thursdays.

Symbols in the tables are explained in the footnotes or on page 57.

In tables with a central list of town names, times should be read **down** on the left and **up** on the right, as indicated by the small arrows above the departure and arrival columns.

101) is added, see that table for full details of the service on the connecting line or route, including train or trip numbers. Table numbers appearing against other place names indicate another table covering the same journey.

5. In rail tables, the classes of accommodation are usually printed at the head of each train thus: C, P, S, 1, etc. These classes are described on pp. 4–9 This heading denotes the accommodation available in the class concerned; more details of special accommodation and through cars is shown by footnotes. The classes shown may not apply to the trains over connecting lines, for which see the tables indicated.
6. Various categories of sleeping accommodation are available on Via Rail and Amtrak services; see pp. 4–9.
7. Other indications at the head of the train columns refer to the train category and the train number; supplements are charged for travel on certain trains and in superior accommodation. These categories are explained at the head of the first table of the country concerned.
8. A list of the standard symbols used to denote days of running, sleeping and restaurant cars, etc., appears on page 57. All other notes (for example those giving dates of running for seasonal trains) are explained in the table itself. All services run daily unless otherwise stated.
9. All timings throughout the timetables are given in local time unless otherwise stated. Both Canada and the USA have a number of time zones; furthermore, most (but not all) states and territories adopt Daylight Saving Time throughout the summer months. Time zone boundaries are shown on the map on page 64.
10. The services shown are liable to alteration, and we recommend that you compare these tables with the local tables at the stations before commencing each journey.

Symbols used in the timetables

Railway	++++	Daily except Saturdays	⑧
Bus	🚌	Mondays	①
Taxi	🚕	Tuesdays	②
Ferry/Ship	⛴	Wednesdays	③
Tram	🚋	Thursdays	④
Mountain railway	🚞	Fridays	⑤
Cablecar	🚡	Saturdays	⑥
Through car	🚃	Sundays	⑦
Sleeping car	🛏	Saturdays, Sundays and holidays	©
Couchettes	━	Sundays and holidays	†
Restaurant car	✕	Calls by request	r
Buffet car	⊗	Calls to set down only	s
Light Refreshment	🍷	Calls to take up only	u
Observation car	🚃OB	Train/bus does not stop	|
Dome-car	D	Runs when required	¶
Car-carrier	🚗	No fixed schedules	◐
Air-conditioned	‡	Service temporarily suspended	Σ
Railcar	🚃	Subject to confirmation	▲
Reservation obligatory	R	Information not available at press date	⁘
Some, or all, of the services shown in this table offer special facilities for the carriage of disabled passengers	♿	Supplement payable	⊡
		Alternate days only	●
		International bus journey	♣
Frontier point	▦	See footnote (by number)	◆
Daily except Sundays and holidays	⚒	See footnote	P,Q,b,◇, etc.
Mondays to Fridays only, except holidays	Ⓐ	Train or bus number	1, 103, 81EE

Symbols used in the timetable maps and in the town plans in 'Major Cities'

━━━	Main railway	∿∿∿	Bus route	🚡	Cablecar
┷┷┷	(electrified)	· · · · ·	Ship/ferry service	🚞	Mountain railway
───	Secondary railway	— · —	Frontier	🚌	Bus station
┴┴┴	(electrified)	●	Station (main line)	○	Town/city
╫╫╫	Tramway	•	Station (local/metro)	i	Information point
- - - -	Metro	⊂⊃	Station (interchange)		

NORTH AMERICA: PRINCIPAL ROUTES AND TIME ZONES

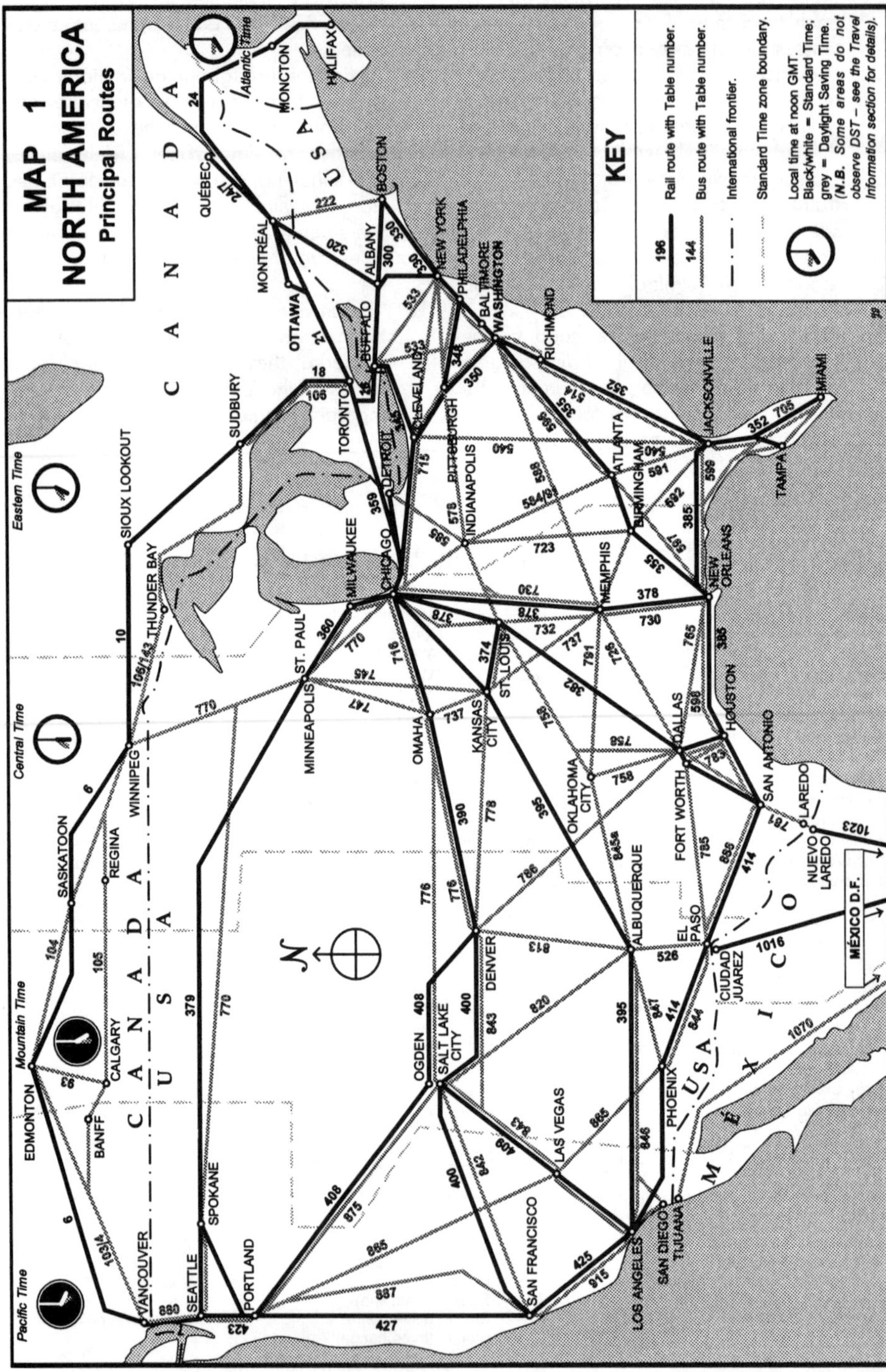

CANADA

See MAPS 2 and 3 (p. 68, 77) *9922385 sq. km.* Capital: Ottawa

il services in Canada are operated mainly by VIA RAIL. A basic one-class structure is provided, with a standard fare allowing travel in ordinary seats. A range of 'additional' commodation is provided (parlour [club] cars on certain day trains, sleeping accommodation on overnight and long-distance trains, plus 'Silver&Blue' class on the NADIAN), for which supplementary charges are payable. In this timetable, trains conveying coaches will be shown as C class, whilst those offering club cars (VIA 1 Service, ich includes complimentary meals) will be shown as P. Sleeping cars will be shown as S. Children of 2 but under 12 years pay half the basic fare but full accommodation arges; children of 12 and over must pay full fare. One child, under 2 years, not occupying a separate seat or unit of accommodation, may travel free with each passenger of 18 ars or over. Excellent bus services operate throughout the country, except in the far North; many services are fully air-conditioned and most of the operators have through oking arrangements allowing tickets to be purchased in advance.

able 3 VANCOUVER ISLAND #### *VIA*

A $; cl.		199 C‡◆ ⚒	199 C‡◆ †		km	396 1.435m ↓ ↑			198 C‡◆ ⚒	198 C‡◆ †
.00	....	0815	1200	....	*0*	d.**Victoria**............a.	....	....	1745	2140
.26	....	1100	1435	....	*117*	d.Nanaimo............d.	....	....	1522	1917
.31	....	1250	1625	....	*225*	a.**Courtenay**.........d.	....	....	1315	1715

8/9– MALAHAT. ⚒–Daily except Sundays and holidays. †–Sundays and holidays. ‡–Air-conditioned.
–VIA Rail. ☎Winnipeg 204 949 1830. Fax 514 393 1519.

Table 7 VANCOUVER - SEATTLE #### *NRPC*

US $ C cl.				761 C‡[R] ◆⊗	km	396 1.435m. ↓ ↑	760 C‡[R] ◆⊗			
24.00	....	....	....	1800	*0*	d.**Vancouver**........a.	1140	....	....	....
	....	....	....	1927	*93*	d.Bellingham ....d.	0952	....	....	....
13.00	....	....	....	2042	*198*	d.Everett..............d.	0834	....	....	....
0.00	....	....	....	2155	*251*	a.**Seattle** King Street.d.	0745	....	....	....

760/1– MOUNT BAKER INTERNATIONAL. At a date to be announced, this train may be replaced by an extension of the COAST STARLIGHT.
[R]– Reservation obligatory. ⊗–Buffet car. ‡–Air-conditioned.
NRPC–AMTRAK. ☎Los Angeles 213 624 0171. Fax 202 906 3865.

able 4 PRINCE GEORGE - VANCOUVER #### *BCR*

A $; cl.			2 🚃 C‡ ◆🍷 ②③⑤⑦	2 🚃 C‡[R] ◆▼✕ ①④⑥	km	396 1.435m. ↓ ↑		1 🚃 C‡ ◆🍷 ①②④⑥	1 🚃 C‡[R] ◆▼✕ ③⑤⑦	
.00	....	....	....	0700	*0*	d.**Prince George** BCR a.	....	....	2030	....
.00	....	....	....	0850	*125*	d.Quesnel.............d.	....	....	1841	....
.00	....	....	....	1035	*239*	d.Williams Lake....d.	....	....	1700	....
.00	....	....	....	1205	*327*	d.Exeter Ω............d.	....	....	1526	....
.00	....	....	....	1340r	*400*	d.Clinton..............d.	....	....	1407r	....
	....	....	....	1354r	*417*	d.Kelly Lake ....d.	....	....	1354r	....
.00	....	....	1520	1520	*491*	d.Lillooet..............d.	....	1235	1250	....
.00	....	....	1632r	1632r	*546*	d.D'Arcy ....d.	....	1116r	1116r	....
.00	....	....	1727	1727	*592*	d.Pemberton.........d.	....	1018	1018	....
.00	....	....	1810r	1810r	*623*	d.Whistler.............d.	....	0934r	0934r	....
.00	⊠	....	1915	1915	*680*	d.Squamish..........d.	⊠	0822	0822	....
.00	⊠	....	2045	2045	*744*	a.**North Vancouver** d.	⊠	0700	0700	....

–CARIBOO. r–Calls by request. ①–Mondays. ②–Tuesdays. ③–Wednesdays. ④–ursdays. ⑤–Fridays. ⑥–Saturdays. ⑦–Sundays. ♿–Facilities for the disabled. 🚃–f-propelled train/railcar. [R]–Reservation obligatory. ⊠–ROYAL HUDSON steam train (♿) rates daily ex①② North Vancouver-Squamish and v.v. from early June to mid Sept. 🍷–Light eshments. ✕–Dining car. ▼–✕ and 🍷 service is available to holders of reserved seats, charges are included in the fares. ‡–Air-conditioned. Ω–For 100 Mile House. *BCR*–BC . ☎Vancouver 604 984 5246. Fax 604 984 5505.

able 6 PRINCE RUPERT - WINNIPEG #### *GCRT VIA*

A $; cl.	*GCRT* Lux S‡✕[R] ◆■ 1	*GCRT* Lux S‡✕[R] ◆■ 7	*VIA* 2 S‡C‡ [R]◆ ①④⑥	*VIA* 6 C‡ [R]◆ ③⑤⑦	km	396 1.435m. ↓ ↑	*GCRT* Lux S‡✕[R] ◆■ 1	*GCRT* Lux S‡✕[R] ◆■ 7	*VIA* 5 C‡ [R]◆ ③⑤⑦	*VIA* 1 S‡C‡ [R]◆ ③⑤⑦
.95	....	....	....	0800	*0*	d.**Prince Rupert**...a.	....	....	2000	....
.11	....	....	....	1013	*95*	d.Terrace (*Kitimat*)d.	....	....	1742	....
.76	....	....	....	1240	*181*	d.New Hazelton....d.	....	....	1514	....
.48	....	....	....	1408	*227*	d.Smithers............d.	....	....	1357	....
.66	....	....	....	1740r	*373*	d.Fort Fraser........d.	....	....	1014r	....
.54	....	....	....	0800c	*467*	d.**Prince George** VIA d.	....	....	0745t	....
.17	0730	0730	2000	|	*÷846*	d. **Vancouver** .....a.	1700	1700	|	0830
.10	|	|	2055	|	*÷818*	d. Port Coquitlam d.	|	|	|	0725
.82	|	|	2230	|	*÷755*	d. Chilliwack........d.	|	|	|	0524
.47	|	|	2313r	|	*÷675*	d. Hope...............d.	|	|	|	0436r
.14	b	b	0506	|	*÷438*	d. Kamloops North .d.	b	b	|	2305
.11	|	|	1047r	|	*÷80*	d. Valemount.......d.	|	|	|	1625r
.41	1700	|	1455	1615	*721*	d.Jasper...............d.	0900	|	1300	1530
	....	1700	|	....		a. Banff...............d.	....	0800	....	|
	....	1930a	|	....		a. **Calgary**.........d.	....	0630a	....	|
.50	....	....	1712	....	*991*	d.Edson................d.	....	....	....	1156
.75	....	....	2035	....	*1099*	d.**Edmonton**.........d.	....	....	....	0855
.70	....	....	2257	....	*1302*	d.Wainwright.........d.	....	....	....	0557
.44	....	....	0120	....	*1528*	d.Biggar................d.	....	....	....	0334
.81	....	....	0300	....	*1618*	d.**Saskatoon**.........d.	....	....	....	0215
.18	....	....	0406	....	*1718*	d.Watrous..............d.	....	....	....	0050
.71	....	....	0630	....	*1926*	d.Melville...............d.	....	....	....	2247
.03	....	....	1013	....	*2070*	d.Brandon North...d.	....	....	....	2052
.26	....	....	1119	....	*2288*	d.Portage la Prairie d.	....	....	....	1933
.00	....	....	1235	....	*2378*	a.**Winnipeg**..........d.	....	....	....	1835

–CANADIAN–🛏‡, 🚃, D and ✕ Toronto(**1/2**)-Vancouver and v.v. [R] Ψ. **5/6**–EENA–D, 🚃 and ✕. a–June 4-Sept. 19 only. b–Compulsory overnight hotel stop. Arr. 2010. Passengers stya overnight in hotel, continuing next day. r–Calls by request. rr. 1915. Passengers stya overnight in hotel, continuing next day. ①–Mondays. ②–sdays. ③–Wednesdays. ④–Thursdays. ⑤–Fridays. ⑥–Saturdays. ⑦–Sundays. Dome lounge car. 🛏–Sleeping car. 🚃–Seating car. [R]–Reservation obligatory. Restaurant car. ‡–Air-conditioned. ÷–Km ex Jasper. Ψ–The 🛏, lounge, D and er facilities on this train are of a higher quality than generally provided, and are known as ver&Blue' class. Ø–Information not available at press date. ■–ROCKY UNTAINEER. 1–About every 4/5 days June 4-Sept. 19. 7–About every 4/5 days 16-Oct. 4. *GCRT*–Rocky Mountaineer Railtours. ☎Vancouver 604 984 3315. Fax 604 2883. *VIA*–VIA Rail. ☎Winnipeg 204 949 1830. Fax 514 393 1519.

able 11 THE PAS - LYNN LAKE #### *VIA*

A $ cl.		291 C ①③⑤			km	495 1.435m. ↓ ↑		290 C ②④⑥		
.00	....	1100	....	....	*0*	d.**The Pas**............a.	....	1735	....	....
.19	....	1235	....	....	*89*	d.Cranberry Portage a.	....	1604	....	....
.33	....	1300r	....	....	*115*	d.Optic Lake.........d.	....	1524r	....	....
.75	....	1355	....	....	*157*	d.Sherridon...........d.	....	1439	....	....
.78	....	2115	....	....	*389*	a.**Lynn Lake**........d.	....	0730	....	....

alls by request. ①–Mondays. ②–Tuesdays. ③–Wednesdays. ④–Thursdays. ⑤–ays. ⑥–Saturdays. *VIA*–VIA Rail. ☎Winnipeg 204 949 1830. Fax 514 393 1519.

Table 8 WINNIPEG - CHURCHILL #### *VIA*

CA $ C cl.		295 C ①	295 C ⑦	693 S‡C‡ [R]◆ ②④⑦	km	396 1.435m. ↓ ↑		692 S‡C‡ [R]◆ ②④⑥	294 C ⑥	294 C ③
0.00	....	....	....	2200	*0*	d.**Winnipeg**..........a.	....	0730	....	....
19.26	....	....	....	2301	*88*	d.Portage la Prairie .d.	....	0629	....	....
49.22	....	....	....	0155	*283*	d.Dauphin.............d.	....	0341	....	....
73.83	....	....	....	0425	*484*	d.Canora ....d.	....	2305	....	....
81.32	....	....	....	0557r	*586*	d.Reserve.............d.	....	2123r	....	....
86.67	....	....	....	0640	*635*	d.**Hudson Bay**.....d.	....	2039	....	....
105.93	....	....	....	0920	*777*	a. The Pas.........d.	....	1955	....	....
	....	....	....	1000		d. The Pas.........a.	....	1915	....	....
127.33	....	....	....	1303r	*949*	d.Ponton...............d.	....	1604r	....	....
133.75	....	....	0830	1359	*997*	d.Wabowden ....d.	....	1516	1605	....
143.38	....	....	1010	1514	*1074*	d.Thicket Portage .d.	....	1359	1433	....
146.59	....	....	|	1830	*1135*	d.Thompson ....d.	....	1210	|	....
166.92	....	1000	1500	2359	*1302*	d.Gillam φ ....d.	....	0555	1000	1635
192.60	....	1735	....	0730	*1597*	a.**Churchill** ....d.	....	2200	....	0900

692/93– HUDSON BAY–🛏‡, 🚃 and ✕.
r– Calls by request. ①–Mondays. ②–Tuesdays. ③–Wednesdays.
④– Thursdays. ⑥–Saturdays. ⑦–Sundays. [R]–Reservation obligatory.
🛏– Sleeping car. 🚃–Seating car. ✕–Restaurant car. ‡–Air-conditioned.
φ– Nelson River.
VIA– VIA Rail. ☎Winnipeg 204 949 1830. Fax 514 393 1519.

Table 10 WINNIPEG - CAPREOL #### *VIA*

CA $ C cl	2 S‡C‡ [R]◆ ①③⑥				km	496 1.435m. ↓ ↑			1 S‡C‡ [R]◆ ②④⑥	
0.00	1335	....	....	....	*0*	d.**Winnipeg**..........a.	....	....	1735	....
33.00	1611	....	....	....	*183*	d.Minaki................d.	....	....	1452	....
36.00	1641	....	....	....	*217*	d.Redditt...............d.	....	....	1430	....
38.00	1658r	....	....	....	*223*	d.Farlane..............d.	....	....	1414r	....
49.00	1807	....	....	....	*290*	d.Red Lake Road .d.	....	....	1300	....
65.00	2003	....	....	....	*405*	d.Sioux Lookout ...d.	....	....	1110	....
79.00	2122	....	....	....	*465*	d.Savant Lake ......d.	....	....	0934	....
95.00	0010	....	....	....	*629*	d.Armstrong..........d.	....	....	0855	....
117.00	0226	....	....	....	*809*	d.Nakina...............d.	....	....	0626	....
139.00	0555	....	....	....	*1020*	d.Hornepayne.......d.	....	....	0340	....
145.00	0651	....	....	....	*1083*	d.Oba...................d.	....	....	0209	....
161.00	0919	....	....	....	*1258*	d.Foleyet..............d.	....	....	2355	....
184.00	1315	....	....	....	*1498*	a.**Capreol**.............d.	....	....	2015	....
221.00	2100	....	....	....	*1958*	a.*Toronto*.............d.	....	....	1245	....

1/2– CANADIAN–🛏‡, 🚃, D and ✕ Toronto(**1/2**)-Vancouver and v.v. Ψ.
r– Calls by request. ①–Mondays. ②–Tuesdays. ③–Wednesdays.
④– Thursdays. ⑥–Saturdays. D–Dome car. 🛏–Sleeping car.
🚃 – Seating car. [R]–Reservation obligatory. ✕–Restaurant car. ‡–Air-conditioned.
Ψ– The 🛏, lounge, D and other facilities on this train are of a higher quality than generally provided, and are known as 'Silver&Blue' class.
VIA– VIA Rail. ☎Winnipeg 204 949 1830. Fax 514 393 1519.

Table 12 HEARST - SAULT STE. MARIE #### *ACR*

CA $ C cl.	ST C‡ ST	2 C‡ Q ①⑥⑦	4 C‡ T ✕	2 C‡ P ex②	km	396 1.435m. ↓ ↑	3 C‡ T ✕	ST C‡ ST	1 C‡ Q ⑤⑥⑦	1 C‡ P ex①
76.65	....	0800	....	0845	*0*	d.**Hearst**..............a.	....	....	1805	1845
63.45	....	0930	....	1013	*82*	d.Oba...................d.	....	....	1630	1712
56.45	....	1015	....	1037	*126*	d.Mosher..............d.	....	....	1552	1658
50.50	....	1041	....	1129	*162*	d.Franz.................d.	....	....	1514	1554
42.75	....	1150	....	1225	*211*	d.Hawk Junction...d.	....	....	1425	1520
31.35	....	1300	....	1350	*282*	d.Eton ....d.	....	....	1256	1350
29.55	1210	1310	1330	1410	*292*	d.Canyon..............d.	1130	1145	1242	1330
0.00	1610	1645	1700	1750	*475*	a.**Sault Ste. Marie**d.	0800	0800	0900	0940

P– May 13-Oct. 9: 🚃 Sault(**1/2**)-Hearst and v.v.; conveys on ③-⑦: ⊗ Sault(**1/2**)-Eton and v.v.
Q– Oct. 10-May 12: 🚃 Sault(**1/2**)-Hearst and v.v.; conveys on ⑥⑦ Dec. 31-Feb 29: ⊗ Sault(**1/2**)-Eton and v.v.
T– June 5-Oct. 9.
①– Mondays. ②–Tuesdays. ③–Wednesdays.
⑤– Fridays. ⑥–Saturdays.
⑦– Sundays. 🚃–Seating car. ⊗–Buffet car. ✕–Restaurant car.
‡– Air-conditioned.
ST– SNOWTRAIN TOUR.
ACR– Algoma Central Railway. ☎Sault Ste. Marie 705 254 4331. Telex 067 77146.

CANADA

Table 13 WHITE RIVER - SUDBURY #### *VIA*

CA $ C cl.			186		km	396 1.435m.	185			
			🚃 C‡◆ ③⑤⑦			↓ ↑	🚃 C‡◆ ②④⑥			
0.00	....	....	0930	....	*0*	d.**White River** ......a.	1800	....	....	....
16.05	....	....	1105	....	*49*	d.Franz.................d.	1635	....	....	....
29.96	....	....	1400	....	*130*	d.Chapleau...........d.	1430	....	....	....
67.41	....	....	1900	....	*301*	a.**Sudbury** ....d.	0940	....	....	....

186/7– LAKE SUPERIOR.
②– Tuesdays.
③– Wednesdays.
④– Thursdays.
⑤– Fridays.
⑥– Saturdays.
⑦– Sundays.
🚃– Self-propelled train/railcar.
‡– Air-conditioned.
VIA– VIA Rail. ☎Winnipeg 204 949 1830. Fax 514 393 1519.

Table 14 SEPT ÎLES - SCHEFFERVILLE #### *QNSL*

CA $ C cl.	🚃 C **S** ④		🚃 C **P** ②	🚃 C **P** ①	km	496 1.435m. ↓ ↑	🚃 C **S** ⑤	🚃 C **P** ③	🚃 C **P** ②⑤	
0.00	0900	....	1900	0900	*0*	d.**Sept Îles** ....a.	2015	1900	1730	....
α41.99	1830	....	0630	1830	*361*	a.Ross Bay Junctiond.	1230	1300	1130	....
α48.83	1930	....	0730	1930	*420*	a. Labrador City ..d.	|	1200	1030	....
α66.89	2015	....	....	....	*576*	a.**Schefferville**.....d.	0900	....	....	....

P– 🚗, 🚃 C cl. and 🍷.
S– 🚗, 🚃 C cl. and 🍷 Sept Îles-Schefferville and v.v.; 🚃 C cl. and 🚗 Sept Îles-Labrador City and v.v. ①–Mondays. ②–Tuesdays. ③–Wednesdays. ④–Thursdays. ⑤–Fridays.
🚃– Self propelled train/railcar. 🚗–🚃conveyed by this train. α–Tickets cannot be bought at stations; they must be purchased in advance from *Vacances Inter* in Sept Îles.
QNSL– Québec, North Shore and Labrador Railway. ☎Sept Iles 418 968 7495. Fax 418 968 7498.

Table 15 TIMMINS/COCHRANE #### O

CA $ C cl.	423		421	121	km	496 1.435m.	122	622		62
	C‡ ®R ✕		C‡ ①③⑤ ⊗	C‡ ®◆ Ⓑ		↓ ↑	C‡ ®◆ Ⓑ	C‡ ②④⑥ ⊗		C‡ ®R ✕
0.00	....	....	....	1200	*367*	d.*Toronto*..............a.	1835	....	....	....
62.86	....	....	....	1650	*0*	d.**North Bay** ON ..a.	1350	....	....	....
93.06	....	....	....	1855	*146*	d.Cobalt.................d.	1145	....	....	....
93.06	....	....	....	1910	*161*	d.New Liskeard ....d.	1130	....	....	....
103.15	....	....	....	1945	*205*	d.Englehart...........d.	1100	....	....	....
108.12	....	....	....	2020	*255*	d.Swastika............d.	1020	....	....	....
123.26	....	....	*0930*a	2100	*330*	d.Matheson ....d.	0940	....	....	....
128.61	....	....	*0840*a	*2200*a	*417*	a. **Timmins**.........d.	*0840*a	*1555*a	....	....
131.29	0830	....	1040	2150	*386*	d.**Cochrane**..........d.	0850	1430	....	212
♧77.04	1250	....	1615	|	*685*	a. Moosonee.....d.	|	0900	....	171
147.39	....	....	....	*0030*a	*594*	a.Kapuskasing......d.	*0640*a	....	....	....
147.39	....	....	....	*0140*a	*695*	a.Hearst ....d.	*0530*a	....	....	....

121/2– NORTHLANDER–🚃 and ⊗ Toronto(**121/2**)-Cochrane and v.v.
R– POLAR BEAR EXPRESS-Daily ex ⑤ June 24-Sept. 4.
a– Connection by 🚌.
Ⓑ– Daily except Saturdays.
①– Mondays.
②– Tuesdays.
③– Wednesdays.
④– Thursdays.
⑤– Fridays.
⑥– Saturdays.
♧– RT fare ex Cochrane.
®– Reservation obligatory.
🚃– Seating car.
✕– Restaurant car.
⊗– Buffet car.
‡– Air-conditioned.
ON– Ontario Northland. ☎North Bay 472 4500. Fax 705 476 5598.

Table 16 TORONTO - LONDON - WINDSOR/BUFFALO #### *GO NRPC VIA*

CA $ C cl.	396 1.435m.	km		*VIA* 85			*VIA* 71	*VIA* 97		*VIA* 685		*VIA* 73	*VIA* 75	*VIA* 689	*GO* 973	*VIA* 81	*VIA* 77	*GO* 977	*GO* 925	*VIA* 95			*VIA* 89	*VIA* 79	
	↓			C‡ ◆ ⚒			C‡ ◆	C‡ ◆		C‡ ◆ †		C‡ ◆	P‡C‡ ◆ ⊗	P‡C‡ ◆ †🍷	C‡ Ⓐ	P‡C‡◆ ⊗ ex④⑥†	P‡C‡ ◆ ④†⊗	C‡ Ⓐ	C‡ Ⓐ	🚃 C‡ ◆			C‡ ◆ ⚒🍷	P‡C‡ ◆ ⊗	
0.00	**Toronto** Union ...d.	*0*	....	0750	....	....	0835	0930	....	1150	....	1230	1630	1625	1637	1715	1715	1719	1743	1745	....	....	1825	1900	....
10.70	Oakville ....d.	*34*	....	|	....	....	0857	0952	....	|	....	1252	1654	|	1706	|	|	1745	1820	1810	....	....	|	1924	....
⅄12.84	Aldershot.............d.	*56*	....	|	....	....	0911	1007	....	|	....	1307	|	|	1731	1748	1748	1810	1846	1824	....	....	|	1937	....
21.40	Brantford ....d.	*96*	....	a	....	....	0941	|	....	a	....	1338	1735	a	|	1816	1816	|	|	|	....	....	a	2007	....
26.45	Woodstock ....d.	*139*	....	|	....	....	1006	|	....	|	....	1405	|	|	|	1842	1842	|	|	|	....	....	|	2033	....
39.59	London................d.	*185*	....	1100	....	....	1055	|	....	1450	....	1445	1839	1922	|	1917	1927	|	|	|	....	....	2125	2120	....
53.50	**Sarnia** 🛃 ....a.	*280*	....	1205	....	....	|	|	....	1552	....	|	|	2040	|	....	|	|	|	|	....	....	2246	|	....
51.36	Chatham ....d.	*290*	....	....	....	....	1157	|	....	....	....	1547	1940	....	|	....	2033	|	|	|	....	....	....	2221	....
66.34	**Windsor** ....a.	*360*	....	....	....	....	1242	|	....	....	....	1637	2028	....	|	....	2114	|	|	|	....	....	....	2303	....
6.60	Hamilton CN ..d.	*63*	....	....	....	....	....	|	....	....	....	....	....	....	1744	....	....	1823	1859	|	....	....	....	....	....
19.00	St. Catharines ..d.	*114*	....	....	....	....	....	1059	....	....	....	....	....	....	....	....	....	....	....	1914	....	....	....	....	....
21.40	**N. Falls** *Canada* 🛃d.	*133*	....	....	....	....	....	1130	....	....	....	....	....	....	....	....	....	....	....	1941	....	....	....	....	....
△19.00	N. Falls *USA* 🛃...d.	*153*	....	....	....	....	....	1300	....	....	....	....	....	....	....	....	....	....	....	....	....	....	....	....	....
△20.00	**Buffalo** Depew a.	*192*	....	....	....	....	....	1350	....	....	....	....	....	....	....	....	....	....	....	....	....	....	....	....	....
△96.00	*New York*.........a.	*879*	....	....	....	....	....	2135	....	....	....	....	....	....	....	....	....	....	....	....	....	....	....	....	....

396	*GO* 960	*GO* 962	*GO* 964	*VIA* 90	*VIA* 80	*VIA* 92	*VIA* 70			*VIA* 84	*VIA* 670		*VIA* 72		*VIA* 74					*VIA* 76	*NRPC* 63		*VIA* 78	*VIA* 88	
↓	C‡ Ⓐ	C‡ Ⓐ	C‡ Ⓐ	🚃 C‡◆ Ⓐ	P‡C‡ ◆Ⓐ ⊗	🚃 C‡◆ Ⓒ	P‡C‡ ◆⚒⊗			C‡ ◆ 🍷	P‡C‡ ◆† ⊗		P‡C‡ ◆⚒ ⊗		P‡C‡◆ ①⑤†					C‡ ◆	C‡ ◆		C‡ ◆	C‡ ◆	
New York..............d.	....	....	....				....	....	....			....		....	....	....	....	....	....	....	0720	....	....	....	....
Buffalo Depew ......d.	....	....	....	....	....	....	....	....	....	....	....	....	....	....	....	....	....	....	....	....	1456	....	....	....	....
Niagara Falls *USA* 🛃 .d.	....	....	....	....	....	....	....	....	....	....	....	....	....	....	....	....	....	....	....	....	1600	....	....	....	....
N. Falls *Canada* 🛃 .d.	....	....	....	0635	....	0740	....	....	....	....	....	....	....	....	....	....	....	....	....	....	1715	....	....	....	....
St. Catharines........d.	....	....	....	0657	....	0802	....	....	....	....	....	....	....	....	....	....	....	....	....	....	1737	....	....	....	....
Hamilton CN ....d.	0621	0641	0701	|	....	|	....	....	....	....	....	....	....	....	....	....	....	....	....	....	|	....	....	....	....
Windsor ....d.	|	|	|	|	....	|	0600	....	....	....	0705	....	0930	....	1115	....	....	....	....	1440	|	....	1805	....	....
Chatham ....d.	|	|	|	|	....	|	0646	....	....	....	0752	....	1011	....	1157	....	....	....	....	1527	|	....	1851	....	....
Sarnia 🛃 ....d.	|	|	|	|	....	|	|	....	....	0635	|	....	|	....	|	....	....	....	....	|	|	....	|	1855	....
London.....................d.	|	|	|	|	0645	|	0755	....	....	0750	0859	....	1114	....	1258	....	....	....	....	1630	|	....	1955	2000	....
Woodstock ....d.	|	|	|	|	0711	|	0827	....	....	|	0929	....	1140	....	|	....	....	....	....	|	|	....	2028	|	....
Brantford ....d.	|	|	|	|	0737	|	0854	....	....	a	0957	....	1206	....	1348	....	....	....	....	1719	|	....	2055	a	....
Aldershot..................d.	0634	0654	0714	0747	|	0853	0929	....	....	|	1032	....	1241	....	|	....	....	....	....	1754	1830	....	2131	|	....
Oakville ....d.	0700	0720	0740	0801	|	0907	0944	....	....	|	1046	....	1255	....	1433	....	....	....	....	1808	1845	....	2146	|	....
Toronto Union ....a.	0727	0743	0803	0823	0832	0931	1012	....	....	1035	1111	....	1322	....	1500	....	....	....	....	1833	1914	....	2214	2251	....

63– MAPLE LEAF–🚃 and ⊗ New York(**63**)-Niagara Falls(**98**)-Toronto.
70– TRILLIUM.
71– TRILLIUM–🚃 and ⊗ (🚃 and 🍷 on ⑥).
72– POINT PELÉE.
73– POINT PELÉE–🚃 and ⊗(🚃 and 🍷 on ⑥).
74– ST. CLAIR.
75– ERIE.
76– ERIE–🚃 and ⊗(🚃 and 🍷 on ⑥)
77– ST. CLAIR.
78– MOHAWK–🚃 and ⊗(🚃 and 🍷 on ⑥).
79– MOHAWK.
80/81– FOREST CITY.
84– HURON.
85– INTERNATIONAL–🚃 and ⊗ Toronto(**85**)-Sarnia(**365**)-Chicago.
88– INTERNATIONAL–🚃 and ⊗ Chicago(**364**)-Sarnia(**88**)-Toronto.
89– HURON.
90/92/95– GENERAL BROCK.
97– MAPLE LEAF–🚃 and ⊗ Toronto(**97**)-Niagara Falls(**64**)-New York.
670– TRILLIUM.
685– INTERNATIONAL–🚃 and ⊗ Toronto(**685**)-Sarnia(**367**)-Chicago.
689– HURON.
a– Via Stratford.
Ⓐ– Mondays-Fridays only, except holidays.
Ⓒ– Saturdays, Sundays and holidays.
⚒– Daily except Sundays and holidays.

†– Sundays and holidays.
①– Mondays.
④– Thursdays.
⑤– Fridays.
⑥– Saturdays.
⊗– Buffet car.
🍷– Light refreshments.
🚃– Self propelled train/railcar.
🛏– Sleeping car.
🚃– Seating car.
⅄– *GO* fare is $5.45.
‡– Air-conditioned.
△– US $.
GO– Government of Ontario Transit. ☎Downsview 416 665 9211. Fax 416 665 9006.
NRPC–AMTRAK. ☎New York 736 4545. Fax 202 906 3865.
VIA– VIA Rail. ☎Toronto 366 8411. Fax 514 393 1519.

Table 17 TORONTO - GUELPH - LONDON #### *VIA*

A $ cl.	85	685	689	89	km	396 1.435m.	84		88	
	C‡	C‡	C‡	C‡			C‡		C‡	
	◆	◆	◆	◆			◆		◆	
	⚒	†	†	⚒		↓ ↑				
.00	0750	1150	1625	1825	*0*	d.**Toronto** Union ..a.	1035	....	2251	....
.77	0827	1223	1657	1857	*34*	d.Brampton ....d.	1006	....	2210	....
.77	0839	1235	1709	1909	*47*	d.Georgetown.......d.	0954	....	2200	....
.12	0903	1300	1734	1934	*79*	d.Guelph ....d.	0930	....	2136	....
.33	0934	1323	1755	1955	*101*	d.Kitchener...........d.	0906	....	2115	....
.75	1002	1352	1823	2023	*143*	d.Stratford ....d.	0837	....	2048	....
.59	1050	1445	1912	2115	*195*	a.**London**.............d.	0750	....	1955	....

89/689–HURON–▭ and 🍷 Sarnia(**84/89/689**)-Toronto and v.v.
88/685–see Table 16.
⚒– Daily except Sundays and holidays.
†– Sundays and holidays.
🍷– Light refreshments.
▭– Seating car.
‡– Air-conditioned.
VIA– VIA Rail. ☎Toronto 416 366 8411. Fax 514 393 1519.

Table 18 CAPREOL/NORTH BAY - TORONTO #### *ON VIA*

CA $ C cl.			*ON* 122	*VIA* 2	km	396 1.435m.			*ON* 121	*VIA* 1	
			C‡◆	S‡C‡Ⓓ					C‡◆	S‡C‡Ⓓ	
			⑤	◆②④⑦		↓ ↑			⑤	◆②④⑥	
63.13	....	....	....	1330	*460*	d.**Capreol**..............a.	....	....	....	2000	....
63.13	....	....	....	1401	*426*	d.Sudbury Junction d.	....	....	....	1920	....
41.73	....	....	....	1644	*257*	d.Parry Sound ......d.	....	....	....	1617	....
62.86	....	....	1400	|	*367*	d. **North Bay** ON a.	....	....	1640	|	....
43.65	....	....	1553	|	*235*	d. Huntsville ....d.	....	....	1447	|	....
35.73	....	....	1634	|	*180*	d. Gravenhurst ....d.	....	....	1402	|	....
33.17	....	....	1653	1825	*159*	d.Washago............d.	....	....	1343	1452	....
18.19	....	....	|	1841	*139*	d.Orillia.................d.	....	....	|	1436	....
17.12	....	....	|	1913	*101*	d.Barrie ....d.	....	....	|	1406	....
0.00	....	....	1835	2100	*0*	a.**Toronto** Union ..d.	....	....	1200	1245	....

1/2– CANADIAN–🛏, ▭, Ⓓ and ✕ Toronto(**1/2**)-Vancouver and v.v. Ⓡ Ψ.
121/2– NORTHLANDER–▭ and ⊗ Toronto(**121/2**)-Cochrane and v.v.
⑤– Daily except Saturdays. ②–Tuesdays. ④–Thursdays. ⑥–Saturdays.
⑦– Sundays. Ⓓ–Dome car. Ⓡ–Reservation obligatory. ✕–Restaurant car.
⊗– Buffet car. 🛏–Sleeping car. ▭–Seating car. ‡–Air-conditioned.
Ψ–The 🛏, lounge, Ⓓ and other facilities on this train are of a higher quality than generally provided, and are known as 'Silver&Blue' class. *ON*–Ontario Northland. ☎North Bay 472 4500. Fax 705 476 5598. *VIA*–VIA Rail. ☎Toronto 416 366 8411. Fax 514 393 1519.

Table 20 OTTAWA - MONTRÉAL #### *VIA*

A $ cl.	30	630	32	34	36	km	396 1.435m.	31	33	35	37
	P‡C‡	C‡	P‡C‡	C‡	C‡			C‡	C‡	P‡C‡	C‡
	◆	◆	◆	◆	◆			◆	◆	◆	◆
	①⊗	⑥⊗	⊗	⑤			↓ ↑	⚒		①⊗	
.74	0655	0800	1000	1440	1730	*0*	d.**Ottawa** Union............a.	0859	1239	1642	1947
.37	0745r	0858r	1054r	1532r	1824r	*87*	d.Alexandria ....d.	0804r	1143r	1549r	1854r
.67	0813r	0920r	1115r	1559c	|	*124*	d.Coteau ....d.	|	1122r	|	1825e
π	0838	0944	1139	1623	1915	*167*	d.Dorval π ....d.	0712	1057	1457	1802
.00	0858	1005	1159	1643	1934	*187*	a.**Montréal** Central π....d.	0655	1040	1440	1745

-VILLE MARIE. **31**–VILLE MARIE–▭ and ⊗ (▭ and 🍷 on ⑥). **32**–GATINEAU. **33**–GATINEAU–▭ and ⊗ (▭ and 🍷 on ⑦). **34**–VANIER–▭ and ⊗ (▭ and 🍷 ⑦). **35**–VANIER. **36**–LAURIER–▭ and ⊗ (▭ and 🍷 on ⑥). **37**–LAURIER–▭ and ⊗ (▭ and 🍷 on ⑥). **630**–VILLE MARIE. c–Calls on ⑤ only. Note s applies. e–Calls on ⑦ only. Note u applies. r–Calls by request. s–Calls to set down only. u–Calls to take up only. Ⓐ–Mondays to Fridays except holidays. ①–Daily except Saturdays. Ⓒ–Saturdays, Sundays and holidays. ⑤–Fridays. ⑥–Saturdays. ⑦–Sundays. ⊗–Buffet car. 🍷–Light refreshments. ‡–Air-conditioned. π–Local traffic not carried. *VIA*–VIA Rail. ☎Montréal 514 871 1331. Fax 514 393 1519.

Table 21 TORONTO - MONTRÉAL #### *GO VIA*

A $ cl.	396 1.435m.	km	*VIA* 52	*VIA* 40	*VIA* 56	*VIA* 42	*VIA* 60	*VIA* 44	*VIA* 64	*VIA* 66	*VIA* 46	*GO* 978	*VIA* 68
			P‡C‡	P‡C‡	P‡C‡	P‡C‡	P‡C‡	P‡C‡	P‡C‡	P‡C‡	P‡C‡	C‡	P‡C‡
			Ⓡ◆	Ⓡ◆	◆Ⓡ	◆Ⓡ	Ⓡ◆	◆Ⓡ⊗	Ⓡ◆	Ⓡ◆	Ⓡ◆	Ⓐ	◆Ⓡ
	↓		⚒⊗	⚒⊗	①⊗	⊗	⊗	ex②⑥	⚒⊗	①⊗	⊗		⊗
.00	**Toronto Union** Φ ..d.	*0*	0710	0900	1000	1100	1200	1500	1545	1700	1730	1733	1800
.60	Guildwood Φ ......d.	*20*	0726	0916	1015	1116	1218	1516	1601	|	1747	1757	1821
.05	Oshawa..............d.	*51*	0743	|	|	1133	1235	|	|	|	1807	1831	|
.31	Belleville.............d.	*182*	0845	|	|	1243	1346	1629	|	|	1916	....	|
.50	Kingston ....d.	*254*	0920	1104	1200	1320	1428	1706	1747	|	1956	....	2013
.85	Brockville............d.	*335*	1000	1147	1239	1404	1512	1746	|	|	2040	....	2056
.32	**Ottawa** Union ..a.	*446*	|	1312	|	1519	|	1905	|	|	2155	....	|
.55	Cornwall ....d.	*428*	1044	....	1323	....	1602	....	1905	|	....	....	2146
.81	Dorval Φ..............d.	*521*	1128	....	1409	....	1650	....	1951	2036	....	....	2231
.81	**Montréal** Central Φ .a.	*539*	1156	....	1441	....	1723	....	2021	2059	....	....	2256

6	*GO* 955	*VIA* 41	*VIA* 53	*VIA* 641	*VIA* 57	*VIA* 43	*VIA* 61	*VIA* 45	*VIA* 65	*VIA* 67	*VIA* 47	*VIA* 69	*VIA* 669
	C‡	P‡C‡	P‡C‡	P‡C‡	P‡C‡	P‡C‡	P‡C‡	P‡C‡	P‡C‡	P‡C‡	P‡C‡	P‡C‡	P‡C‡
	Ⓐ	◆Ⓡ	Ⓡ◆	Ⓡ◆	◆Ⓡ	◆Ⓡ	Ⓡ◆	◆Ⓡ⊗	Ⓡ◆	Ⓡ◆	Ⓡ◆	Ⓡ◆	Ⓡ◆
↓		Ⓐ⊗	⚒⊗	⑥⊗	⊗	⊗	①⊗	ex②⑥	⚒⊗	①⊗	⊗	⚒⊗	⊗†
ntréal Central Φ ..d.	....	....	0715	....	1000	....	1215	....	1545	1700	....	1800	1825
rval Φ..................d.	....	....	0733	....	1021	....	1233	....	1603	1718	....	1818	1843
rnwall ....d.	....	....	0816	....	1110	....	|	....	1648	|	....	1912	1933
ttawa Union ....d.	....	0600	|	0755	|	1135	|	1535	|	|	1740	|	|
ockville.................d.	....	0708	|	0905	1200	1252	|	1645	|	|	1855	2003	2022
gston ....d.	....	0747	0936	0943	1245	1335	1431	1725	1807	|	1935	2043	2102
lleville ....d.	....	0823	|	1018	1326	|	1503a	1801	|	|	2008b	2120	2138
hawa......................d.	0719	|	1109	1123	1442	|	|	1907	|	|	|	2232	2246
ildwood Φ ....d.	0753	0943	1126	1140	1500	1529	1620	1924	1953	|	2124	2248	2302
ronto Union Φ .....a.	0819	1010	1156	1207	1530	1555	1649	1951	2024	2059	2142	2310	2325

41–CAPITAL. **42/43**–LAKESHORE. **44/45**–RIDEAU. **46/47**–SIMCOE. **52/53**–YORK. **56/57**–LA SALLE. **60/61**–MERIDIAN. **64/65**–RENAISSANCE. **66/67**–METROPOLIS. **69**–BONAVENTURE. **641**–CAPITAL. **669**–BONAVENTURE. a–Calls on ⑦ only. b–Calls on ② only. Ⓐ–Mondays to Fridays except holidays. ①–Daily except Saturdays. ⚒–Daily except Sundays and holidays. †–Sundays and holidays. ②–Tuesdays. ⑥–Saturdays. ⑦–Sundays. Ⓡ–Reservation obligatory. ⊗–Buffet car. ‡–Air-conditioned. Φ–Local traffic Toronto-Guildwood and Montréal-Dorval or v.v. not carried on *VIA* trains. §–Fare by *GO* to Guildwood; *GO* fare to Oshawa: 5.35. *GO*–Government of Ontario Transit. ☎Toronto 630 33. Fax 416 665 9006. *VIA*–VIA Rail. ☎Toronto 416 366 8411. Fax 514 393 1519.

Table 22 MONTRÉAL - JONQUIÈRE/COCHRANE #### *VIA*

A $ cl.	601	603	607	605	605	km	396 1.435m.	600	604	602	606	606
	C‡	C‡	C‡	C‡	C‡			C‡	C‡	C‡	C‡	C‡
	◆	◆	◆	◆	◆			◆	◆	◆	◆	◆
	①③🍷	①③🍷	⑤🍷	⑤🍷	⑥		↓ ↑	②④🍷	②④🍷	⑦🍷	⑦	⑦🍷
.00	0830	0830	1015	1015	....	*0*	d.**Montréal** Central.......a.	1825	1825	2225	....	2225
.21	1107	1107	1252	1252	....	*156*	d.Shawinigan.................d.	1554	1554	1954	....	1954
.05	1210	1230	1355	1415	....	*203*	d.Hervey........................d.	1505	1505	1905	....	1905
.47	1307	|	1452	|	....	*237*	d.Rivière à Pierre ....d.	1346	|	1746	....	|
.00	1455	|	1640	|	....	*325*	d.Lac Édouard................d.	1210	|	1610	....	|
.81	1651	|	1836	|	....	*430*	d.Chambord ....d.	1005	|	1405	....	|
.95	1755	|	1940	|	....	*496*	a.**Jonquière**...................d.	0900	|	1300	....	|
.58	....	1350	....	1535	....	*283*	d. La Tuque ....d.	....	1309	....	....	1830
.54	....	1557r	....	1742r	....	*402*	d. Sanmaur ....d.	....	1059r	....	....	1459r
.37	....	1721	....	1906	....	*481*	d. Parent ....d.	....	0940	....	....	1340
.49	....	1820	....	2005	....	*547*	d. Clova ....d.	....	0822	....	....	1222
.14	....	2125	....	2230	0930	*703*	d. **Senneterre** ....d.	....	0615	....	0935	1015
9.40	....	2241	....	....	1046	*772*	d. Amos ....d.	....	0439	....	0819	....
6.23	....	2330	....	....	1136	*817*	d. Taschereau ....d.	....	0350	....	0730	....
9.03	....	....	....	....	1555	*999*	a. **Cochrane** ....d.	....	....	....	0315	....

0/1/2/7–SAGUENAY. **603-6**–ABITIBI. r–Calls on request. ①–Mondays. ②–Tuesdays. ③–Wednesdays. ④–Thursdays. ⑤–Fridays. ⑥–Saturdays. ⑦–Sundays. ▭–Seating car. 🍷–Light refreshments. ‡–Air-conditioned. *VIA*–VIA Rail. ☎Montréal 514 871 1331. Fax 514 393 1519.

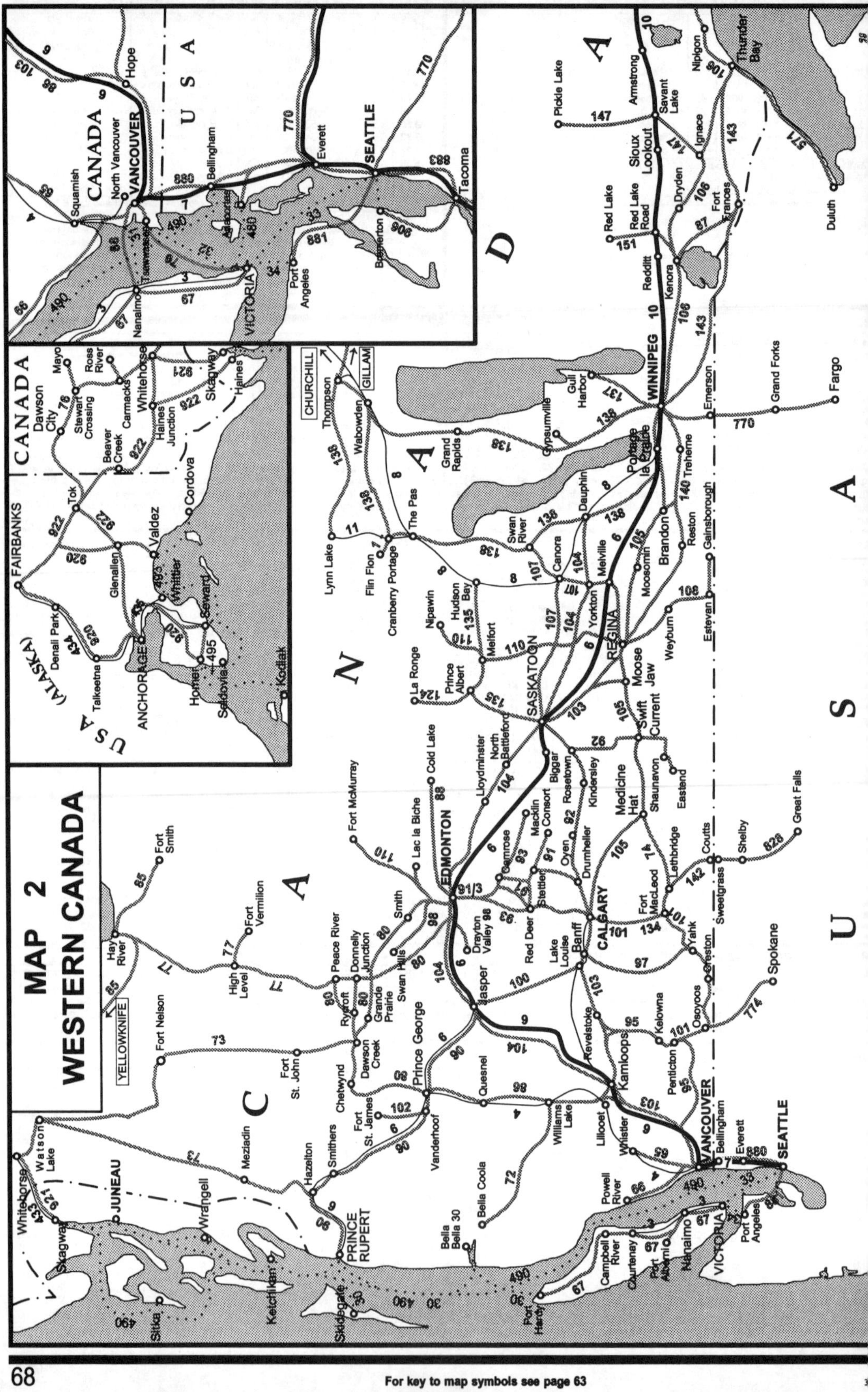

For key to map symbols see page 63

ıble 24 MARITIME PROVINCES

VIA

A $ cl.		14	16		km	396 1.435m.	17		15	
		S‡C‡	S‡C‡				S‡C‡		S‡C‡	
		Ⓡ◆	Ⓡ◆				Ⓡ◆		Ⓡ◆	
		ex②	③⑤⑦			↓ ↑	①④⑥		ex②	
.00	....	1900	1900	....	0	d.**Montréal** Central a.	0825	....	0825	....
	....	1915u	1915u	....	6	d.St. Lambert ......d.	0758s	....	0758s	....
.81	....	1947	1947	....	53	d.St. Hyacinthe.....d.	0726	....	0726	....
.65	....	2025	2025	....	101	d.Drummondville ..d.	0655	....	0655	....
.00	....	2153	2153	....	246	d.Charny ....d.	0525	....	0525	....
.00	....	2230	2230	....	259	d.Lévis ....d.	0505	....	0505	....
.98	....	2321	2321	....	317	d.Montmagny ....d.	0408	....	0408	....
.21	....	0034	0034	....	401	d.Rivière du Loup.d.	0251	....	0251	....
.91	....	0106	0106	....	487	d.Trois Pistoles ....d.	0157	....	0157	....
.02	....	0148	0148	....	549	d.Rimouski ....d.	0111	....	0111	....
.72	....	0233	0233	....	578	d.**Mont Joli** ....d.	0047	....	0047	....
.42	....	0432	0505	....	727	d.Matapédia ....d.	2247	....	2247	....
.19	....	|	0957	....	989	d. Percé ....d.	1704	....	|	....
.19	....	|	1110	....	1052	a. **Gaspé**..............d.	1550	....	|	....
.84	....	0645	....	....	748	d.Campbellton ......d.	....	....	2250	....
.93	....	0909	....	....	920	d.Newcastle..........d.	....	....	2015	....
.75	....	1050	....	....	906	a.}Moncton.........{d.	....	....	1842	....
	....	1110	....	....		d.} {a.	....	....	1822	....
.86	....	1221	....	....	983	d.Amherst.............d.	....	....	1717	....
.26	....	1400	....	....	1107	d.**Truro** ....d.	....	....	1538	....
.37	....	1530	....	....	1210	a.**Halifax** ....d.	....	....	1400	....

15– OCEAN–🛏‡, Ⓓ, 💺 and ✕.
17– CHALEUR–🛏‡, 💺 and ✕.
Calls to set down only. u–Calls to take up only. ①–Mondays. ②–Tuesdays. Wednesdays. ④–Thursdays. ⑤–Fridays. ⑥–Saturdays. ⑦–Sundays. Reservation obligatory. 🛏–Sleeping car. Ⓓ–Dome car.
💺– Seating car. ✕–Restaurant car. ‡–Air-conditioned.
– VIA Rail. ☎Montréal 514 871 1331. Fax 514 393 1519.

Table 27 MONTRÉAL - QUÉBEC

VIA

CA $	396 1.435m.	km	20	620	22	24		26		14
			P‡C‡	C‡	P‡C‡	P‡C‡		P‡C‡		S‡C‡
			◆	◆	◆	◆⊗		◆		◆✕
	↓		Ⓐ⊗	⑤🍸	⊗	ex①⑥		⊗		ex②
0.00	**Montréal** Central..d.	0	0705	0820	1320	1600	....	1800	....	1900
	St. Lambert ....d.	6	0717u	0832u	1332u	1612u	....	1812u	....	1915u
14.81	St. Hyacinthe.........d.	53	0743	0858	|	|	....	1838	....	1947
21.65	Drummondville .....d.	100	0812	0923	1421	1701	....	1903	....	2025
49.00	Charny ....d.	246	|	|	1533	|	....	|	....	2153
49.00	Ste. Foy ....a.	250	0927	1039	1543	1824	....	2029	....	....
49.00	**Québec** Palais .....a.	272	0957	1107	1612	1855	....	2103	....	....

396	15		21		23		25		27	
	S‡C‡		P‡C‡		P‡C‡		P‡C‡		P‡C‡	
	◆✕		◆		◆		◆⊗		◆	
↓	ex③		Ⓐ⊗		⊗		ex①		⊗	
Québec Palais ....d.	....	....	0630	....	0835	....	1330	....	1735	....
Ste. Foy ....d.	....	....	0649	....	0854	....	1349	....	1754	....
Charny ....d.	0525	....	|	....	0902	....	|	....	|	....
Drummondville ....d.	0655	....	0806	....	1024	....	1511	....	1916	....
St. Hyacinthe...............d.	0726	....	|	....	1050	....	|	....	1943	....
St. Lambert ....a.	0758s	....	0855s	....	1115s	....	1559s	....	2008s	....
Montréal Central........a.	0825	....	0923	....	1139	....	1625	....	2034	....

14/15–OCEAN–see Table **24**. **20/21**–CHAMPLAIN. **22/23**–CITADELLE. **24/25**–CHAUDIÈRE. **26/27**–FRONTENAC. **620**–CHAMPLAIN. **s**–Calls to set down only. u–Calls to take up only. Ⓐ–Monday to Fridays only, except holidays. ①–Mondays. ②–Tuesdays. ③–Wednesdays. ⑥–Saturdays. 🍸–Light refreshments. ⊗–Buffet car. ✕–Dining car. ‡–Air-conditioned.
VIA– VIA Rail. ☎Montréal 514 871 1331. Fax 514 393 1519.

ıble 29 396 TORONTO LOCAL SERVICES

🚎 🚌 *BRT GLC GO MAR MSS TRW TTC VTR*

(C cl. only, 1.435m. [⑤ 1.495m.]), 🚎 (1.435m.) and 🚌 services operate in the Toronto area as follows:

npton M *(GO)* (*34* km, CA $: 4.75). From Toronto Union: 1615Ⓐ, 1645Ⓐ, 1715Ⓐ, 1745Ⓐ, returning at 0643Ⓐ, 0708Ⓐ, 0733Ⓐ, 0758Ⓐ. Journey: 40 mins. Also (÷) *(GO)*: 1130Ⓐ, 1330Ⓐ, 1430Ⓐ, 1830Ⓐ, 1900Ⓐ, 1930Ⓐ, 2030Ⓐ, 2130Ⓐ, 2230Ⓐ, returning at 0935Ⓐ, 1022Ⓐ, 1322Ⓐ, 1820Ⓐ. Also (÷) *(GO)* from Yorkdale: 0025, 0125, 0555Ⓐ, 0630Ⓐ, 0655Ⓐ, 0725⚒, 0755Ⓐ, 0825⚒, 0855⚒, 0925 and frequent to 2255, 2325, returning at 0515Ⓐ, 0530Ⓐ, 0600⚒, 0630Ⓐ, 0700⚒, 0730 and frequent to 2200, 2230, 2330. Also (÷) *(BRT)* from Finch: 0520Ⓐ/0530⑥ and about every 30 mins. to 1900⑥/2200Ⓐ, returning at 0520Ⓐ/0530⑥ and about every 30 mins. to 1900⑥/2130Ⓐ.

York M *(TTC⑤)* (*4* km, CA $: 2.00). From Toronto Yonge/Bloor: 0605Ⓐ/0612⑥/0912† and frequent to 0154, returning from East York Greenwood Station at 0559Ⓐ/0602⑥/0902† and frequent to 0144. Journey: 20 mins.

icoke ÷ *(TTC)* (*6* km, CA $: 2.00). From Lawrence West: 0605Ⓐ/0620⑥/0930† and frequent to 0100①/0132⑦/0142②-⑥, returning at 0522Ⓐ/0523⑥/0833† and frequent to 0003①/0042⑦/0048②-⑥. Journey: 30 mins.

h M *(TTC⑤)* (*6* km, CA $: 2.00). From Toronto Union: 0604Ⓐ/0612⑥/0900† and frequent to 0144, returning at 0600⚒/0900† and frequent to 0115. Journey: 30 mins.

rgetown M *(GO)* (*47* km, CA $: 6.30). From Toronto Union: 1615Ⓐ, 1645Ⓐ, 1715Ⓐ, 1745Ⓐ, returning at 0629Ⓐ, 0654Ⓐ, 0719Ⓐ, 0744Ⓐ. Journey: 55 mins. Also (÷) from Toronto Union: 1130Ⓐ, 1430Ⓐ, 1830Ⓐ, 1900Ⓐ, 1930Ⓐ, *2030*Ⓐ, 2130Ⓐ, returning at 1000Ⓐ, 1300Ⓐ. Also from Yorkdale: *0555*Ⓐ, 0655Ⓐ, 0855⚒, *0925*⚒, 1155, *1225*⚒, 1455, *1525*⚒, 1555Ⓐ, 1625Ⓐ, 1655Ⓐ, 1725Ⓐ, 1755, *1830*Ⓐ, *2025*⑥, 2055⑥, *2325*, returning at 0600Ⓐ, 0630Ⓐ, 0700Ⓐ, *0700*⑥, 0730Ⓐ, 0800Ⓐ, 0900⚒, 0900†, *1100*⚒, 1200, 1400Ⓐ, *1400*⑥, 1500, *1700*⚒, 1800, *1900*Ⓐ, 2100⑥, *2100*⑥.

ph M *(GO)* (*79* km, CA $: 9.35). From Toronto Union: *1615*Ⓐ, *1715*Ⓐ, returning at *0535*Ⓐ, *0625*Ⓐ. Journey: 1¾ hours. Also (÷) *(GLC)* from Toronto at: 0700, 0830, 0930, 1130, 1400, 1530, 1615Ⓒ, 1630, 1700, 1730Ⓐ, 1800, 2100, 2330, returning at 0530Ⓐ, 0600Ⓐ, 0630Ⓐ, 0700Ⓐ, 0810ex⑦, 1010, 1210, 1340, 1610, 1710, 1810, 2015, 2240.

dwood M *(GO)* (*20* km, CA $: 3.60). From Toronto Union: 0013, 0613⚒, 0631Ⓐ, 0653Ⓐ, 0713⚒, 0813⚒, 0913, 1013, 1113, 1213, 1313, 1413, 1513, 1549Ⓐ, 1613, 1630Ⓐ, 1654Ⓐ, 1703Ⓐ, 1713, 1733Ⓐ, 1747Ⓐ, 1813, 1913, 2013, 2113, 2213, 2313, returning at 0611Ⓐ, 0631Ⓐ, 0651Ⓐ, 0711Ⓐ, 0713⑥, 0740Ⓐ, 0753Ⓐ, 0813⑥, 0823, 0833Ⓐ, 0912Ⓐ, 0913⑥, 1013, 1113, 1213, 1313, 1413, 1513, 1612Ⓐ, 1613Ⓒ, 1652Ⓐ, 1713Ⓒ, 1731Ⓐ, 1755Ⓐ, 1812Ⓐ, 1813Ⓒ, 1834Ⓐ, 1912Ⓐ, 1913Ⓒ, 2012Ⓐ, 2013Ⓒ, 2113, 2213, 2313. Journey: 30 mins.

gton M *(TTC⑤)* (*5* km, CA $: 2.00). From Toronto St George: 0555Ⓐ/0601⑥/0912† and frequent to 0154, returning at 0547Ⓐ/0550⑥/0850† and frequent to 0134. Journey: 25 mins.

e M *(TTC⑤)* (*3* km, CA $: 2.00). From Toronto St George: 0555Ⓐ/0601⑥/0912† and frequent to 0154, returning at 0557Ⓐ/0600⑥/0900† and frequent to 0144. Journey: 15 mins.

ington 🚋 (TTC) (*2* km, CA $: 2.00). From Toronto College: frequent service day and night, returning frequently, day and night. Journey: 10 mins.

ng M *(TTC⑤)* (*5* km, CA $: 2.00). From Toronto Yonge/Bloor: 0555Ⓐ/0601⑥/0902† and frequent to 0154, returning at 0547Ⓐ/0550⑥/0850† and frequent to 0144. Journey: 25 mins.

bton Mills ÷ *(TTC)* (*5* km, CA $: 2.00). From Royal York: 0515Ⓐ/0518⑥/0815† and frequent to 0040②-⑥/0045①⑦, returning at 0517Ⓐ/0558⑥/0825† and frequent to 0053⑦/0057①/0102②-⑥. Journey: 25 mins.

rence West M *(TTC⑤)* (*5* km, CA $: 2.00). From Toronto Union: 0604Ⓐ/0612⑥/0900† and frequent to 0140, returning at 0606⚒/0906† and frequent to 0121. Journey: 22 mins.

kham M *(GO)* (*9* km, CA $: ∅). From Toronto Union: 1720Ⓐ, 1803Ⓐ, 1945Ⓐ(÷)returning at 0642Ⓐ, 0726Ⓐ. Journey: 45 mins. Also ÷ *(MAR)* from Finch: 0600Ⓐ/0800⑥/0900† and frequent to 2345†/0115②-⑦, returning at 0545Ⓐ/0730⑥/0845† and frequent to 2245†/0030②-⑥/0130⑥⑦. Journey: 45 mins.

ico M *(GO)* (*3* km, CA $: ∅). From Toronto Union: 0013, 0623Ⓐ, 0643⚒, 0708Ⓐ, 0723Ⓐ, 0743⚒, 0843⚒, 0943 and hourly to 1543, 1617Ⓐ, 1643, 1725Ⓐ, 1743, 1802Ⓐ, 1826Ⓐ, 1843 and hourly to 2243, returning at 0615Ⓐ, 0637Ⓐ, 0656Ⓐ, 0737Ⓐ, 0754⑥, 0757Ⓐ, 0819Ⓐ, 0841Ⓐ, 0854⚒, 0954 and hourly to 1654, 1728Ⓐ, 1754Ⓒ, 1816Ⓐ, 1854 and hourly to 2354. Journey: 10 mins.

Mississauga ÷ *(MSS)* (*6* km, CA $: 1.40). From Islington: 0534Ⓐ/0623⑥/0855† and frequent to 0055①/0130⑦/0155②-⑥, returning at 0458Ⓐ/0545⑥/0810† and frequent to 0010①/0100⑦/0118②-⑥. Journey: 30 mins.

North York M *(TTC⑤)* (*7* km, CA $: 2.00). From Toronto Union: 0604Ⓐ/0612⑥/0900† and frequent to 0144, returning at 0603⚒/0903† and frequent to 0118. Journey: 35 mins.

Oakville M *(GO)* (*34* km, CA $: 4.40). From Toronto Union: 0013, 0623Ⓐ, 0643⚒, 0703Ⓐ, 0708Ⓐ, 0743⚒, 0843⚒, 0943, 1043, 1143, 1243, 1343, 1443, 1543, 1617Ⓐ, 1637Ⓐ, 1643, 1702Ⓐ, 1719Ⓐ, 1725Ⓐ, 1743, 1755Ⓐ, 1823Ⓐ, 1843, 1943, 2043, 2143, 2243, returning at 0610Ⓐ, 0630Ⓐ, 0700Ⓐ, 0710⑥, 0720Ⓐ, 0730⚒, 0740Ⓐ, 0750Ⓐ, 0815Ⓐ, 0830⚒, 0930, 1030, 1130, 1230, 1330, 1430, 1530, 1630, 1704Ⓐ, 1730Ⓒ, 1752Ⓐ, 1830, 1930, 2030, 2130, 2230, 2330. Journey: 30 mins.

Queen's Quay 🚋 *(TTC)* (*1* km, CA $: 2.00). From Toronto Union: 0600⚒/0900† and frequent to 2300, returning at 0620⚒/0920† and frequent to 2320. Journey: 5 mins.

Richmond Hill M *(GO)* (*34* km, CA $: 2.95). From Toronto Union: 1630Ⓐ, 1700Ⓐ, 1730Ⓐ, 1840Ⓐ, 1940(Ⓐ÷) returning at 0650Ⓐ, 0710Ⓐ, 0745Ⓐ, 0810Ⓐ. Journey: 40 mins. Also ÷ *(GO)* from Finch: 0520Ⓐ/0600Ⓒ and frequent to 0135, returning at 0530 and frequent to 0100.

Royal York M *(TTC⑤)* (*5* km, CA $: 2.00). From Toronto St George: 0555Ⓐ/0601⑥/0912† and frequent to 0154, returning at 0549Ⓐ/0552⑥/0852† and frequent to 0136. Journey: 25 mins.

Scarborough M *(GO)* (*4* km, CA $: ∅). From Toronto Union: 0013, 0613⚒, 0631Ⓐ, 0658Ⓐ, 0713⚒, 0813⚒, 0913, 1013, 1113, 1213, 1313, 1413, 1513, 1549Ⓐ, 1613, 1633Ⓐ, 1703Ⓐ, 1713, 1720Ⓐ, 1747Ⓐ, 1803Ⓐ, 1813, 1913, 2013, 2113, 2213, 2313, returning at 0621Ⓐ, 0641Ⓐ, 0701Ⓐ, 0711Ⓐ, 0722⑥, 0755Ⓐ, 0803Ⓐ, 0822⑥, 0833Ⓐ, 0843Ⓐ, 0921Ⓐ, 0922⑥, 1022, 1122, 1222, 1322, 1422, 1522, 1621Ⓐ, 1622Ⓒ, 1701Ⓐ, 1722Ⓒ, 1736Ⓐ, 1804Ⓐ, 1821Ⓐ, 1822Ⓒ, 1843Ⓐ, 1921Ⓐ, 1922Ⓒ, 2021Ⓐ, 2022Ⓒ, 2122, 2222, 2322. Journey: 20 mins.

Scarborough Centre M *(TTC)* (*3* km, CA $: 2.00). From Kennedy: 0600⚒/0912† and frequent to 0135, returning at 0547Ⓐ/0550⑥/0902† and frequent to 0120. Journey: 11 mins.

Stouffville M *(GO)* (*46* km, CA $: 4.90). From Toronto Union: 1720Ⓐ, 1803Ⓐ, 1945Ⓐ(÷), returning at 0628Ⓐ, 0712Ⓐ. Journey: 1 hour. Also ÷ *(TRW)* from Toronto at 1610Ⓐ, 1640Ⓐ, returning at 0620Ⓐ, 0650Ⓐ, and *GO* from Scarborough at 0810Ⓐ, 1025⑥, 1055Ⓐ, 1325Ⓒ, 1355Ⓐ, 1625Ⓒ, 1655Ⓐ, 1755Ⓐ, 1925Ⓒ, 2125Ⓐ, returning at 0702Ⓐ, 0927⑥, 0957Ⓐ, 1227Ⓒ, 1257Ⓐ, 1527Ⓒ, 1557Ⓐ, 1827Ⓒ, 2027Ⓐ.

Vaughan ÷ *(VTR)* (*3* km, CA $: ∅). From Finch: 0555Ⓐ/0715⑥ and frequent to 1900⑥/2230Ⓐ, returning at 0610Ⓐ/0730⑥ and frequent to 1915⑥/2245Ⓐ. Journey: 15 mins.

Weston ÷ *(TTC)* (*5* km, CA $: 2.00). From Keele: 0425Ⓐ/0510⑥/0630† and frequent to 0130①⑦/0230②-⑥, returning at 0449Ⓐ/0556⑥/0713† and frequent to 0209①/0214⑦/0307②-⑥. Journey: 25 mins.

Yorkdale M *(TTC⑤)* (*5* km, CA $: 2.00). From Toronto Union: 0604Ⓐ/0612⑥/0900† and frequent to 0140, returning at 0603⚒/0903† and frequent to 0118. Journey: 25 mins.

York Mills M *(TTC⑤)* (*6* km, CA $: 2.00). From Toronto Union: 0604Ⓐ/0613⑥/0906† and frequent to 0140, returning at 0607⚒/0907† and frequent to 0134. Journey: 30 mins.

y ####. Ⓐ–Mondays to Fridays only, except holidays. Ⓑ–Daily except Saturdays. Ⓒ–Saturdays, Sundays and holidays. ⚒–Daily except Sundays and holidays. †–Sundays and holidays only. 🚋–By . ÷–By 🚌. ∅–Information not available at press date.

BRT– Brampton Transit. ☎Brampton 905 874 2999.
GLC– Greyhound Lines of Canada. ☎Toronto 416 393 7911. Fax 416 465 4410.
GO– Government of Ontario Transit. ☎Toronto 630 3933. Fax 416 869 3525.
MAR– Markham Transit. ☎Markham 905 475 4888.
MSS– Mississauga Transit. ☎Mississauga 279 5800.
TRW– Trentway-Wagar Inc. ☎Peterborough 705 748 6411. Fax 705 748 2452.
TTC– Toronto Transit Commission. ☎Toronto 393 4636. Fax 416 393 2068.
VTR– City of Vaughan Transit. ☎Vaughan 832 8527.

ıble 30 PORT HARDY - PRINCE RUPERT

⛴ *BCF*

A $	496	km	W	V	X	ϒ	Λ	Y	Ψ	U
.00	Port Hardy (Bear Cove) .d.	0	....	1800	....	....	1800	0730	....	....
.00	Bella Bella Ⓜ ....d.	220	....	0100	....	....	0530	1300	....	....
.50	**Prince Rupert** ...{a.	480	....	1300	....	....	1730	2230	....	....
.00	{d.		1100	....	1400	1700	....	....	2100	2300
.75	Skidegate ✉ ....a.	630	1730	....	2030	2330	....	....	0600	0600

	☑	Ω	Π	ϑ	Z	ℵ	Ξ	Θ	C	ϱ
↓										
degate ✉ ....d.	....	....	....	0900	1100	....	2300	2300	0030	....
nce Rupert ....{a.	....	....	....	1500	1800	....	0630	0730a	0630	....
{d.	0730	1100	1100	....	....	1900	....	....	....	2200
la Bella Ⓜ ....d.	1700	2330	0230	....	....	0600	....	....	....	0600
t Hardy (BearCove)a.	2230	0800	0930	....	....	1230	....	....	....	1230

rr 0600 on May 30, June 1, 7, 15, 21, 29, July 5, 7, 11, 13, 17, 19, 21, 25, 27, Aug. 2, 4, 8, 10, 16, 18, 22, 24, 30, Sept. 3, 15, 21. C–Feb. 5. U–①⑦ Sept. 27-May 23 (also Dec. 21, not Feb. 4). V–④ Sept. 29-May 23, also May 1, 8, 22 (ex Oct. 14, Nov. 11, 25, Dec. 9). W–③⑤⑦ May 24-Sept. 24 (also ④ July 4-Aug. 29 and ⑥ July 6-Sept. 21). X–③ t. 27-Apr. 28 (ex Dec. 20). Y–● May 25-Sept. 24. Z–①② May 24-Sept. 24. ①–Mondays. ②–Tuesdays. ③–Wednesdays. ④–Thursdays. ⑤–Fridays. ⑥–Saturdays. ⑦–Sundays. ℵ–Dec. 22, Mar. 15, Apr. 30, May 7, 14, ϑ–Dec. 22. Θ–④⑤ May 24-Sept. 24, also ③ July 3-Aug. 28 and ⑥ July 6-Sept. 21. Ξ–④ Sept. 27-Apr. 28, also 7, not Dec. 21, Feb. 8). Λ–Oct. 14, Nov. 11, 25, Dec. 9, 20. ϒ–Feb. 4. ϱ–Dec, 19. Π–Oct. 27, Nov. 24, Jan. Ω–⑤ Sept. 29-May 23 (ex Oct. 27, Nov. 24, Dec. 22, Jan. 5, Mar. 15). ☑–● May 26-Sept. 25. ●–Alternate days. Ⓜ–McLoughlin Bay. Ψ–① May 24-Sept. 24.

– Local sailings operate Skidegate-Alliford Bay and v.v., from Skidegate at 0730, 0830, 1000, 1100, 1300, 1400, 1600, 1700, 1830, 1930, 2130, 2230, returning at 0700, 0800, 0850③, 0930ex③, 1030, 1230, 1330, 1540, 1630, 1730, 1900, 2100, 2200. Journey: 20 mins.

F– BC Ferries. ☎Victoria 604 386 3431. Fax 604 381 5452.

Table 30a 496 DISCOVERY COAST

⛴ *BCF*

Local ferries operate a summer only (generally late May to end September) service Port Hardy-Finn Bay or Namu-McLoughlin Bay-Shearwater-Klemtu or Ocean Falls (outbound only)-Bella Coola. *400* km. Fare: up to CA $: 94.00. Journey: 20-24 hours.

From Port Hardy: generally weekly to Klemtu at 2200, and 3 times weekly to Bella Coola at 2200, returning from Klemtu usually at 0300, from Bella Coola at 0630 or 2300.

BCF– BC Ferries. ☎Victoria 604 386 3431. Fax 604 381 5452.

Table 31 296 NANAIMO

⛴ *BCF*

⛴ service Nanaimo-Horseshoe Bay and v.v. *48* km. Journey: 1½ hours. Fare: CA $: 6.25.

From Nanaimo Departure Bay: 0545∇, 0600⊖, 0700, 0800Π, 0900, 1000⊖, 1030∇, 1100, 1145x, 1200=, 1300, 1500, 1600÷, 1630x, 1700, 1900, 2000*, 2100.

From Horseshoe Bay: 0700, 0800§, 0900, 1000Π, 1100, 1200⊖, 1245∇, 1300, 1400+, 1500, 1700, 1800=, 1845x, 1900, 2100, 2200*.

⛴ service Nanaimo-Tsawwassen and v.v. *55* km. Journey: 2 hours. Fare: CA $: 6.25.

From Nanaimo Departure Bay: 0515, 0745, 1015, 1245, 1515, 1745, 2015, 2245.

From Tsawwassen: 0515, 0745, 1015, 1245, 1515, 1745, 2015, 2245.

=– June 24-Sept. 10, also Nov. 10, 13, Dec. 22, 26-28.
*– June 24-Sept. 10.
+– Sept. 15, 17, 22, 24, 29, Oct. 1, 6, 9, Nov. 10, 13, Dec. 22, 26-28.
⊖– Dec. 23.
÷– June 24-Sept. 10, also Nov. 10, 13, Dec. 22, 26-28.
∇– Oct. 7.
x– Sept. 15, 17, 22, 24, 29, Oct. 1, 6, 9.
Π– June 24-Sept. 10, also Dec. 22, 26, 27.
§– Oct. 7 and Dec. 23.
BCF– BC Ferries. ☎Victoria 604 386 3431. Fax 604 381 5452.

Table 32 396 TSAWWASSEN — BCF

service Swartz Bay-Tsawwassen and v.v. *39* km. Journey: 1½ hours. Fare: CA $: 6.25.
From Swartz Bay: 0700, 0730∀, 0800ϑ, 0900, 1000Ξ, 1100, 1130∀, 1200Θ, 1300, 1400η, 1500, 1600α, 1700, 1800ψ, 1900, 1930∀, 2000δ, 2100, 2200δ, 2330∀.
From Tsawwassen: 0530∀, 0700, 0800ε, 0900, 0930∀, 1000ϕ, 1100, 1200γ, 1300, 1400♄, 1500, 1600φ, 1700, 1730∀, 1800α, 1900, 2000δ, 2100, 2130∀, 2200δ.

④-Thursdays. ⑤–Fridays. ⑦–Sundays. ∀–July 29-31, Aug. 1-11, 13-31. η–Jan. 1, May 27, 29, June 24-Sept. 10, Oct. 7, 9, Nov. 10, 13, Dec. 21-24, 26-29 and 31, also ④⑤⑦ Sept. 11-Oct. 10. ϑ–May 20-Sept. 10, ex⑦ Sept. 11-Oct. 10, Dec. 21-24 and 26-30. Ξ–Jan. 1, June 24-Sept. 10, Oct. 6, 7, 9, Dec. 21-24 and 26-31. Θ–Jan. 1-Oct. 10, Nov. 13, and Dec. 21-31, also ⑤⑦ Oct. 11-Dec. 20. α–Jan. 1-Sept. 30, Oct. 1-10, Nov. 13, Dec. 21-24, 26-29 and 31, also ⑤⑦ Oct. 11-Dec. 20. ψ–Jan. 1, May 27, 29, June 24-Sept. 10, Oct. 9, Nov. 10, 13, Dec. 21, 22, 24, 26-28 and 31, also ④⑤⑦ Sept. 11-Oct. 10. δ–June 24-Sept. 10. ε–June 24-Sept. 10, Oct. 6, 7, 9, Dec. 21-24 and 26-30. ϕ–May 20-Sept. 10, Dec. 21-30, also ex⑦ Sept. 11-Oct. 10. γ–Jan. 1, May 27, 29, June 24-Sept. 10, Oct. 7, 9, Nov. 10, 13, Dec. 21-29, 31, also ④⑤⑦ Sept. 11-Oct. 10. ♄–Jan. 1, May 20-Oct. 10, Nov. 13, Dec. 21-24 and 26-31, also ⑤⑦ Oct. 11-Dec. 20. φ–Jan. 1, May 27, 29, June 24-Sept. 10, Oct. 7, 9, Nov. 10, 13, Dec. 21, 22, 24, 26-29 and 31, also ④⑤⑦ Sept. 11-Oct. 10. *BCF*–BC Ferries. ☎Victoria 604 386 3431. Fax 604 381

Table 33 VICTORIA - SEATTLE — VL

CA $					km	396 ↓ May 16-Oct. 15 ↑				
	....	....	....	....	*0*	d.Vancouver ....a.	....	....	....	....
	....	....	....	....	*120*	a. Victoria .... d.	....	....	....	....
0.00	0730	....	....	....		d. Victoria .... a.	....	....	1730	....
27.00	1200	....	....	....	*250*	a.**Seattle** ....d.	....	....	1300	....

VL– Victoria Line. ☎Victoria 604 480 5555. Fax 604 480 5222.

Table 34 VICTORIA - PORT ANGELES — BBT

US $	396 ↓	km	U	R			T	Q		V
0.00	**Victoria**................d.	*0*	0620	1030	....	....	1500	1600	....	1930
6.50	**Port Angeles**.......a.	*40*	0755	1205	....	....	1635	1735	....	2105

396 ↓	P			V	Q		V			S
Port Angeles.............d.	0820	....	....	1245	1400	....	1715	....	....	2130
Victoria.....................a.	0955	....	....	1420	1535	....	1850	....	....	2305

P– Jan. 1-20; Feb. 5-Dec. 31. **Q**–Mar. 7-May 15; Oct. 12-Jan. 3.
R– Mar. 7-Jan. 3. **S**–June 2-Sept. 20.
T– Jan. 4-20; Feb. 5-Mar. 6; May 16-Oct. 11.
U– June 3-Sept. 21. **V**–May 16-Oct. 11.
BBT– Black Ball Transport Inc. ☎Bellevue 206 622 2222.

Table 35 396 NIAGARA FALLS ♿ — MM

Regular cruises to the foot of the falls, from both US and Canadian sides, May to end of October. Every 15 mins. Duration 30 mins. Fare: CA $: 8.65. Hooded raincoats provided.
From Niagara Falls *(USA)*: Spring/Autumn (Fall) 1000-1700Ⓐ/1800Ⓒ; Summer 0915-1930 (2000 in peak season).
From Niagara Falls *(Canada)*: Spring/Autumn (Fall) 0945-1645Ⓐ/1745Ⓒ; Summer 0900-1915 (1945 in peak season).

Ⓐ–Mondays to Fridays, except holidays. Ⓒ–Saturdays, Sundays and holidays. ♿–Facilities for the disabled. *MM*–Maid of the Mist Cruises. ☎Niagara Falls (Canada) 416 358 5781.

Table 36 396 PELEE ISLAND — PIT

service Pelee Island-Leamington/Kingsville and v.v. *25* km. Journey 1½ hours. Fare: CA $: 5.00.
From Leamington: 0900ψ, 0915Λ, 1215Λ, 1330Ω, 1600Π, 1615Λ, 1745Λ, 1800ψ, 2115Λ.
From Kingsville: 0845δ, 0900ε, 0915ϱ, 1215ϱ, 1330ϒ, 1415∀, 1600Ξ, 1615ϱ, 1745ϕ, 1800ε, 2115ϑ.
From Pelee Island (to Leamington): 0700ϰ, 1015Λ, 1130Ω, 1415Λ, 1600ϰ, 1930Λ, 2230Π.
From Pelee Island (to Kingsville): 0700ℵ, 1015ϱ, 1130ϒ, 1230∀, 1415ϱ, 1600ℵ, 1930ϑ, 2230Ξ.
service Pelee Island-Sandusky and v.v. *37* km. Journey 2 hours. Fare: CA $: 9.00.
From Pelee Island: 0530Θ, 1100η, 1800α.
From Sandusky: 0800η, 1330η, 2030γ.

②–Tuesdays. ③–Wednesdays. ④–Thursdays. ⑤–Fridays. ⑥–Saturdays. ⑦–Sundays. ϴ–March-June 22. η–June 23-Sept. 5. ∀–②③⑤⑥ Oct. 29-Nov. 12. ℵ–Aug. 1-mid December. ϰ–March-July 31. Λ–June 23-July 31. Ω–④⑤⑦ March-June 22. Π–⑥⑦ May 5-June 22. ϱ–Aug. 1-Sept. 5. ϒ–④⑤⑦ Sept. 6-Oct. 28. ϑ–Aug. 1-Sept. 5; also ④⑤ Oct. 29-Nov. 12. Ξ–⑥⑦ Sept. 6-24. Θ–④ June 23-Sept. 5. α–June 23-Sept. 5; also ⑥⑦ May 5-June 22 and Sept. 6-24. δ–Oct. 29-Nov. 12. ε–Sept. 6-Oct. 28 and Nov. 13-mid December. ϕ–Aug. 1-Sept. 5 and Oct. 29-Nov. 12. γ–⑥⑦ May 5-June 22 and Sept. 6-24; ⑤ June 23-Sept. 5.
PIT– Pelee Island Ferry (Owen Sound Transportation Co.). ☎Pelee Island 519 724 2115.

Table 37 396 WOLFE ISLAND — HT MTC

(MTC) service Kingston-Wolfe Island and v.v. *5* km. Journey: 25 mins. Free ferry.
Subject to alteration during ice conditions.
From Kingston: 0040, 0200, 0615, 0715, 0830, 0930, 1030**a**, 1100**b**, 1130**a**, 1230, 1400, 1500, 1600, 1700, 1800, 1900**a**, 1920**b**, 2000**a**, 2040**b**, 2100**a**, 2200, 2320.
From Wolfe Island: 0000, 0120, 0545, 0645, 0800, 0900, 1000**a**, 1015**b**, 1100**a**, 1145**b**, 1200**a**, 1315, 1430, 1530, 1630, 1730, 1830**a**, 1840**b**, 1930**a**, 2000**b**, 2030**a**, 2120**b**, 2130**a**, 2240.
(HT) service Cape Vincent-Wolfe Island and v.v. *11* km. Journey: 10 mins. Fare: CA $: 1.00.
May 5-Oct. 22 only.
From Cape Vincent: 0815, 0930, 1030, 1130, 1230, 1400, 1500, 1600, 1700, 1800, 1930**c**.
From Wolfe Island: 0800, 0915, 1015, 1115, 1215, 1315, 1445, 1545, 1645, 1740, 1900**c**.

a–May 1-Dec. 31. **b**–Jan. 1-Apr. 30. **c**–May 5-Sept. 30; ⑤⑥⑦ Oct. 1-22. ⑤–Fridays. ⑥–Saturdays. ⑦–Sundays.
HT– Home Transportation. ☎Wolfe Island 613 385 2262.
MTC– Ministry of Transportation & Communications. ☎Wolfe Island 613 548 7227.

Table 40 396 BARKLEY SOUND — AMT

Local service Port Alberni-Kildonan-Bamfield-Port Alberni. *Ø* km. Journey: 2 hours Kildonan, 4½ to Bamfield. Fare: CA $: 12.00-18.00.
From Port Alberni: 0800δ-Kildonan 1000δ-Bamfield 1330δ-Port Alberni 1730.
Additional sailings on ⑦ July 1-Labour Day from Port Alberni 0800-Bamfield 1100-Sechart 1230-Bamfield 1500-Port Alberni 1800.
Additional sailings ①③⑤ June 2-Sept. 22 from Port Alberni 0800-Sechart 1100-Ucluelet 1400-Sechart 1500-Port Alberni 1900.

①–Mondays. ②–Tuesdays. ③–Wednesdays. ④–Thursdays. ⑤–Fridays. ⑥–Saturdays. ⑦–Sundays. δ–②④⑥ (also ⑤ July 1-Labour Day). *Ø*–Information not available at press date.
AMT–Alberni Marine Transportation (1982) Inc. ☎Port Alberni 723 8313. Fax 604 723 8314.

Table 41 396 ST. LAWRENCE FERRIES — ST

service Lévis-Québec and v.v. *1* km. Journey: 10 mins. Fare: CA $: 1.25. ♿.
From Lévis: 0000, 0100, 0200, 0315, 0600, 0700 and every 30 mins. to 1100, 1145, 12 and every 30 mins. to 1800, 1900, 2000, 2100, 2200, 2300.
From Québec: 0030, 0130, 0230, 0345, 0630, 0730 and every 30 mins. to 1100, 1145, 12 and every 30 mins. to 1830, 1930, 2030, 2130, 2230, 2330.
service Montmagny-Île aux Grues and v.v. *4* km. Journey: 25 mins. Free ferry.
From Montmagny and Île aux Grues: Apr. 1-Nov. 30: 1-3 sailings daily (times variable)
service Tadoussac-Baie Ste. Catherine and v.v. *2* km. Journey: 8 mins. Free Ferry.
From Tadoussac and Baie Ste. Catherine: Every 20-40 mins. (hourly at night).
service Matane-Baie Comeau and v.v. *62* km. Journey: 2½ hours. Fare: CA $: 9.75.
From Matane: Apr. 1-June 8 and Sept. 9-Jan. 7: 0800⑥, 1400ex⑥⑦, 1500⑦; June 9-Sept. 1100①⑤, 1400⑥⑦, 1700ex⑥⑦, 1930⑦✖; Jan. 8-Mar.31: 0800⑥, 1400①⑤, 1500⑦.
From Baie Comeau: Apr. 1-June 8 and Sept. 9-Jan. 7: 1700ex⑦, 1800⑦; June 9-Sept. 1400①⑤, 1700⑥⑦, 2000ex⑥⑦, 2230⑦✖; Jan. 8-Mar. 31: 1700①⑤⑥, 1800⑦.
service Matane-Godbout and v.v. *55* km. Journey: 2½ hours. Fare: CA $: 9.75. ♿
From Matane: Apr. 1-June 8 and Sept. 9-Jan. 7: 0800ex⑥⑦, 0900⑦; June 9-Sept. 0530ex⑥⑦, 0800⑥⑦, 1100②③④, 1930⑥✖, 2300ex⑥⑦ℜ; Jan. 8-Mar. 31: 0800ex⑥⑦.
From Godbout: Apr. 1-June 8 and Sept. 9-Jan. 7: 1100ex⑥⑦, 1200⑦; June 9-Sept. 0200ex①⑦ℜ, 0800ex⑥⑦, 1100⑥⑦, 1400②③④, 2230⑥✖; Jan. 8-Mar. 31: 1100①⑤, 1700②③④

①–Mondays. ②–Tuesdays. ③–Wednesdays. ④–Thursdays. ⑤–Fridays. ⑥–Saturdays. ⑦–Sunda ♿–Facilities for the disabled. ℜ–July 6-Aug. 1. ✖–June 24-Aug. 13. *STQ*–Société des Traversiers Québec. ☎Baie Comeau 418 296 2593. Fax 418 438 2144.

Table 42 396 ST. LAWRENCE RIVER — SLC

4-night HERITAGE WATERWAY cruise from Kingston to Montréal and v.v. calling 1000 Islands Retreat, Brockville, Upper Canada Village and Côteau Landing downstrea Côte Ste. Catherines, Upper Canada Village, Brockville and Rockport upstream. *296* k Fares from US $: 930.
From Kingston: June 15, July 15, Aug. 26, Oct. 5.
From Montréal: June 19, July 19, Aug. 30, Oct. 9.
5-night CANADA'S CAPITAL cruise from Kingston to Ottawa and v.v. calling at 10 Islands Retreat, Upper Canada Village, Côteau Landing, Montréal and Montebe downstream; Montebello, Oka, Côte Ste. Catherines, Upper Canada Village and Brockv upstream. *Ø* km. Fares from US $: 1163.
From Kingston: June 5, 23, Aug 4, Sept. 3, 16.
From Ottawa: June 10, 28, Aug. 9, Sept. 8, 30.
6-night CANADIAN CONNECTION cruise from Kingston to Québec and v.v. calling 1000 Islands Retreat, Upper Canada Village, Côteau Landing, Montréal and Trois Riviè downstream; Québec City, Trois Rivières, Côte Ste. Catherines, Upper Canada Villa and Brockville upstream. *520* km. Fares from US $: 1395.
From Kingston: May 24, July 3, 23, Aug. 14, Sept. 13, Oct. 13.
From Québec: May 30, July 9, 29, Aug. 20, Sept. 19, Oct. 19.

Ø– Information not available at press date.
SLCL– St. Lawrence Cruise Lines Inc. ☎Kingston 613 549 8091. Fax 613 549 8410.

Table 43 RIMOUSKI - BLANC SABLON — L

CA $ ℑ		⊞	Ѡ		km	396 ↓ Apr. 4-Jan. 9 only ↑	⊞	Ѡ		
176.82	....	1600②	1600②	....	*0*	d.**Rimouski**..........a.	0645②	0415②	....	....
134.79	....	0830③	0830③	....	*215*	d.Sept Îles............d.	1915①	1645①	....	....
113.70	....	1815③	1745③	....	*353*	d.Port Menier ....d.	|	|	....	....
100.87	....	0245④	0215④	....	*385*	d.Havre St. Pierre d.	0100①	0345①	....	....
84.40	....	1345④	1415④	....	*506*	d.Natashquan.......d.	1515⑦	1645⑦	....	....
80.00	....	1745④	1915④	....	*548*	d.Kegaska ....d.	1100⑦	1230⑦	....	....
54.82	....	0545⑤	0800⑤	....	*695*	d.Harrington Harbour.d.	0115⑦	0245⑦	....	....
49.34	....	0915⑤	1130⑤	....	*727*	d.Tête à la Baleine d.	2145⑥	2315⑥	....	....
34.79	....	1815⑤	2030⑤	....	*902*	d.St. Augustin.......d.	1430⑥	1630⑥	....	....
0.00	....	0145⑥	0400⑤	....	*918*	a.**Blanc Sablon** ...d.	0600⑥	0800⑥	....	....

①–Mondays. ②–Tuesdays. ③–Wednesdays. ④–Thursdays. ⑤–Fridays. ⑥–Saturdays. ⑦–Sunda ℑ–Basic fare only (berth and meals extra). ⊞–Apr. 4-June 13 and Sept. 5-Jan. 9. Ѡ–June 14-Sept. 4. Relais Nordik Inc. ☎Blanc Sablon 418 723 8787. Fax 418 722 9307.

Table 44 396 HALIFAX - ST. PIERRE — AS

cargo/passenger service Halifax-St. Pierre and v.v. *400* km. Journey: 31 hours. Fa CA $: 116.00.

Summer service.

From Halifax: 1700②.
From St. Pierre: 2300⑦.

Winter service.

From Halifax and St. Pierre: Sailings every 10 days.

②–Tuesdays. ⑦–Sundays. *ASR*–Atlantic Searoute Limited for Armement Paturel-Dag – St Pierre Ro Ro Service. ☎Halifax 902 429 9201.

Table 45 695 BLANC SABLON - ST. BARBE — NC

service Blanc Sablon-St. Barbe and v.v. *31* km. Journey: 1½ hours. Fare: CA $: 8.
From Blanc Sablon: 0630✪, 0730♡, 0800♤, 0845◇, 1015♛, 1100❋, 1115☗, 1230 1315■, 1445♛, 1530♄, 1700♤.
From St. Barbe: 0630◇, 0845♖, 0900∽, 1000♡, 1015♤, 1100◇, 1230♛, 1315♄, 1330 1445♤, 1530■, 1700♛.

M–♛②④ May 1-June 30, ①②④ Sept. 1-Oct. 31. ①–Mondays. ②–Tuesdays. ③–Wednesdays. ④–Thursda ⑤–Fridays. ⑥–Saturdays. ⑦–Sundays. ♤–⑤ June 1-Oct. 2. ◇–②④⑥ July 1-Aug. 31, ⑥ June 1-30 Sept. 1-Oct. 2. ♡–Nov. 1-Dec. 24, Dec. 27-31, Jan. 2, 3. ♛–⑤⑦ May 1-31 and Oct. 3-31, ⑦ June 1-Oc ☗–②④ May 1-June 30. ∽–③ Sept. 1-Oct. 31. ■–②④⑥ July 1-Aug. 31. ♄–①③ July 1-Aug. 31. ♖–①②③ May 1-31, ①②③④ June 1-30, ①③ July 1-Aug. 31, ①②④ Sept. 1-Oct. 31. ❋–①③ July 1-Aug. 31, ①②④ Sept. 1- 31. ✪–①②③④⑤ May 1-31, ①②③④ June 1-30 and Sept. 1-Oct. 31, ①③ July 1-Aug. 31.
NCL– Northern Cruiser Ltd. ☎Blanc Sablon 418 461 2056.

Table 46 695 RIVIÈRE DU LOUP - ST. SIMÉON — TRL

service Rivière du Loup-St. Siméon and v.v. *26* km. Crossing: 65 mins. (5 hours on tr marked **d**). Fare: CA $: 9.10.

No service Jan. 3-Apr. 12.

From Rivière du Loup: 0700**a**, 0800**c**, 0900**f**, 1015**a**, 1045(**d**)**l**, 1115**l**, 1200**n**, 1315**p**, 134 1445**l**, 1515**f**, 1600**n**, 1615**l**, 1700**a**, 1800**l**, 2000**a**.
From St. Siméon: 0830**a**, 0930**x**, 0945**p**, 1030**f**, 1200**a**, 1300**l**, 1400**n**, 1500**b**, 1530**a**, 163 1645**f**, 1730**d**, 1830**a**, 1930**l**, 2115**a**.

a–July 9-Aug.13. **b**–June 3, 4, 10, 11, 17, 18, Sept. 10, 17, 24, Oct. 1, Dec. 10-Jan. 2. Apr. 13-July 8, Aug. 14-Oct. 29, Dec. 10-Jan. 2. **d**–Apr. 13, 15, 16, 18-30, May 1-18, 20, 23-31, June 1-22, Sept. 5-30, Oct. 1-5, 7, 8, 10-29. **f**–Oct. 30-Dec.9. **l**–June 3, 4, 10, 17, 18, Sept. 10, 17, 24, Oct. 1. **l**–Apr. 14, 17, May 19, 22, June 23-July 8, Aug. 14-Sept Oct. 6, 9. **n**–Apr.13, 15, 16, 18-30, May 1-18, 20, 21, 23-31, June 1, 2, 5-9, 12-16, 19- Sept. 5-9, 11-16, 18-23, 25-30, Oct. 2-5, 7, 8, 10-29. **p**–Dec. 10-Jan.2. **x**–Apr. 13-July Aug. 14-Oct. 29.
TRLS–Traverse Rivière du Loup-St. Siméon Ltée. ☎418 862 9545. Fax: 418 862 5382.

Ÿ–Light refreshments OB–Observation car D–Dome car

Table 47 396 PRINCE EDWARD ISLAND — MA

service Borden-Cape Tormentine and v.v. *14* km. Journey: 45-60 mins. Fare: CA $: 7.75.
om Borden: 7-20 sailings daily 0630-0200.
om Cape Tormentine: 7-20 sailings daily 0630-0200.

– Marine Atlantic/Marine Atlantique. North Sydney 902 794 5700. Fax 902 564 7480.

Table 48 396 TROIS PISTOLES - ESCOUMINS — TPE

service Trois Pistoles-Les Escoumins and v.v. *30* km. Journey: 1½ hours. Fare: CA $: 6.00.

May 1-Oct. 14 ⛍.

om Trois Pistoles and Les Escoumins: 1-3 sailings daily. Sailing times vary according to tides.

– Information not available at press date. ⛍–Season extended if necessary.
PE– Traverse Trois Pistoles-Les Escoumins. Trois Pistoles∅.

Table 49 SYDNEY - ARGENTIA — MA

CA $	P		Q		km	396 ↓June 16-Sept. 29↑				
	②⑤		②⑤					③⑥		
0.00	0800	....	1600	....	*0*	d.**North Sydney**...a.	....	2300	....	....
9.00	2200	....	0600	....	*426*	a.**Argentia** ....d.	....	0900	....	....

June 16–Sept. 9. **Q**–Sept. 10–Sept. 29. ②–Tuesdays. ③–Wednesdays. ⑤–days. ⑥–Saturdays. *MA*–Marine Atlantic/Marine Atlantique. North Sydney 902 794 00. Fax 902 564 7480.

Table 50 396 DEER ISLAND — ECF NBDOT

service *(NBDOT)* L'Etete-Deer Island and v.v. *10* km. Journey: 1 hour. Fare: free.
om L'Etete and Deer Island: 0700 and frequent (irregular in winter) to 2100 (2200 in June and July).
service *(ECF)* Deer Island-Eastport and v.v. *8* km. Journey: 25 mins. Fare: CA $: 2.00.
om Deer Island: µ 0900 and hourly to 1800 (1900 in July and August).
om Eastport: µ 0930 and hourly to 1830 (1930 in July and August).
service *(ECF)* Deer Island-Campobello and v.v. *12* km. Journey: 40 mins. Fare: CA $: 2.00.
om Deer Island: µ 0915, 1040, 1215, 1340, 1515, 1640, 1815ω.
om Campobello: µ 1000, 1130, 1300, 1430, 1600, 1730, 1900ω.

mid June-mid September only. ω–July 1-Aug. 31. ∅–Information not available at press te. *ECF*–East Coast Ferries. Deer Island ∅. *NBDOT*–New Brunswick Department Transportation. Fredericton 506 636 3922. Fax 506 636 3924.

Table 51 YARMOUTH - PORTLAND — PF

US $		P			km	396 ↓ ↑			Q	
0.00	....	1000	....	....	*0*	d.**Yarmouth** ....a.	....	....	0900	....
5.00	....	2000	....	....	*298*	a.**Portland** ....d.	....	....	2100	....

May 7-Oct. 25: daily **except** May 7, 11, 13, 15, 18, 20, 27; June 3, 10, 17; Sept. 9, 16, 23, ; Oct. 7, 14, 16, 19, 21, 23. **Q**–May 4-June 22 and Sept. 20-Oct. 22: daily **except** May 10, , 14, 17, 19, 26; June 2, 9, 16; Sept. 8, 15, 22, 29; Oct. 6, 13, 15, 18 , 20, 22, 25.

– US $75.00 June 19-Sept 22.
– Prince of Fundy Cruises. Portland 207 775 5616. Fax 207 773 76403. Tx 944446.

Table 52 YARMOUTH - BAR HARBOR — MA

CA $	Q		P	R	km	396 No service Mar. 1–Apr. 11 ↓ ↑	R	Q	S	P
	②④⑦		②④⑦					①③⑤	②④⑦	①③⑤
0.00	0800	....	1500	1630	*0*	d.**Yarmouth** ....a.	1500	1530	1530	0630
0.00	1330	....	2030	2130	*153*	a.**Bar Harbor** ....d.	0800	0800	0800	2300

Jan. 1-Feb. 29, Apr. 12-May 15 and Oct. 18-Dec. 31. **Q**–Sept. 14-Oct. 17. **R**–June 26-pt. 13. **S**–May 16-June 25. ①–Mondays. ②–Tuesdays. ③–Wednesdays. ④–ursdays. ⑤–Fridays. ⑦–Sundays. ♀–CA $ 45.00 June 1-Sept. 30.

– Marine Atlantic/Marine Atlantique. 902 794 5700. Fax 902 564 7480.

Table 53 396 GRAND MANAN — CT

service Black's Harbour-North Head and v.v. *38* km. Journey: 1½hours. Fare (round trip-payable at North Head only): CA $: 8.20.

Jan. 2-June 29, Sept. 5-Dec. 24 and Dec. 26-31.

om Black's Harbour: 0930, 1330, 1730, 2130⑥.
om North Head: 0730, 1130, 1530, 1930⑥.

June 30-Sept. 4.

om Black's Harbour: 0730⚒, 0930, 1130, 1330, 1530, 1730.
om North Head: 0730, 0930⚒, 1130, 1330, 1530, 1730.

–Daily except Sundays and holidays. ⑤–Fridays. ⑦–Sundays. ⑥–⑤⑦ Sept. 5-24.
– Coastal Transport. Grand Manan 506 636 3922.

Table 54 396 SAINT JOHN - DIGBY — MA

service Saint John-Digby and v.v. *69* km. Journey: 2½-3hrs. Fare: CA $: 15.00/20.00.

Jan. 1-June 20, Sept. 13-Oct. 8 and Oct. 13-Dec. 31.

om Saint John: 0001②-⑥, 1000.
om Digby: 0500②-⑥, 1430.

June 21-Sept. 12.

om Saint John: 0030⚒, 0930, 1645.
om Digby: 0500⚒, 1300, 2015.

Oct. 9-12.

om Saint John: 0001⑥, 0030①⑤, 1000, 1645①⑤.
om Digby: 0500⚒, 1300①⑤, 1430©, 2015①⑤.

–Mondays. ②–Tuesdays. ⑤–Fridays. ⑥–Saturdays. ⚒–Daily except Sundays and lidays. ©–Saturdays, Sundays and holidays. *MA*–Marine Atlantic/Marine Atlantique. Saint John 902 794 7500. Fax 902 564 7480.

Table 55 SYDNEY - PORT AUX BASQUES — MA

CA $	396 ↓	km	P	Q	R	S	γ	T		U
0.00	**North Sydney** d.	*0*	0100	0130	0900	1130	1330	1600	....	2330
7.75	**Port aux Basques** ..a.	*174*	0800	0830	1500	1830	2030	2300	....	0630

6 ↓	γ		ħ	S		R		γ		φ
rt aux Basques.....d.	0800	....	0900	1130	....	1600	....	2000	....	2330
rth Sydney............a.	1500	....	1600	1830	....	2300	....	0300	....	0630

④⑦ June 16-Sept. 30. **Q**–③⑥ June 16-Sept. 9. **R**–②④ June 6-15, ④⑦ June 16-Sept. 9, ②⑤ pt. 10-30, ③⑤⑦ Oct. 1-Nov. 16. **S**–Jan. 1-Feb. 18, Apr. 23-June 5 and Nov. 17-Dec. 24, ④⑤⑥⑦ b. 19-Apr. 22, ex②④ June 1-15, ① June 16-Sept. 9, ①④⑦ Sept. 10-30. **T**–②④ June 6-15, ③④⑥⑦ ne 16-Sept. 9, ③⑥ Sept. 10-30, ②④⑥ Oct. 1-Nov. 16. **U**–Jan. 1-June 15 and Nov. 17-Dec.31, ④⑦ June 16-Sept. 9, ex③⑥ Sept. 10-30, ex ②⑥ Oct. 1-Nov. 16. ①–Mondays. ②–Tuesdays. –Wednesdays. ④–Thursdays. ⑤–Fridays. ⑥–Saturdays. ⑦–Sundays. φ–Jan. 1-June and Nov. 17-Dec. 31, ex ②⑤ June 16-Sept. 30, ①②④⑥ Oct. 1-Nov. 16. ħ–②④ June 6-15, ③④⑥ ne 16-Sept. 9, ②③⑤⑥ Sept. 10-30, ②④⑥ Oct. 1-Nov. 16. γ–②⑤ June 16-Sept. 9. *MA*–Marine antic/Marine Atlantique. North Sydney 902 794 7500. Fax 902 564 7480.

Table 56 396 NEWFOUNDLAND SOUTH COAST — MA

service Terrenceville-English Harbour West-Harbour Breton-Gaultois-Ramea-Burgeo-Port aux Basques and v.v. *425* km. Fare: CA $: 0.125 per mile (minimum CA $ 5.70).
From Terrenceville to Port aux Basques: Jan. 5-Apr. 29 and Nov. 30-Dec. 17: 2100③⑥; May 2-June 17 and Sept. 10-Nov. 27: 0800①; Dec. 19-Jan. 4: 0900①③, 2100⑤;
to **Burgeo**: May 2-June 17 and Sept. 10-Nov. 27: 0800④; June 18-Sept. 9: 0800①④⑥.
From Port aux Basques to Terrenceville: Jan. 5-Apr. 29 and Nov. 30-Dec. 17: 0900②⑤; May 2-June 17 and Sept. 10-Nov. 27: 0800③; Dec. 19-Jan. 4: 0900①③⑤;
to **Harbour Breton**: May 2-June 17 and Sept. 10-Nov. 27: 0800⑥;
to **Hermitage**: June 18-Sept. 9: 0800①④⑥.
From Harbour Breton to Terrenceville: May 2-June 17 and Sept. 10-Nov. 27: 0800⑦.
From Burgeo to Port aux Basques: May 2-June 17 and Sept. 10-Nov. 27: 0800⑤;
to **Terrenceville**: June 18-Sept. 9: 0800②⑤⑦.
From Hermitage to Port aux Basques: June 18-Sept. 9: 0800②⑤⑦.

①–Mondays. ②–Tuesdays. ③–Wednesdays. ④–Thursdays. ⑤–Fridays. ⑥–Saturdays. ⑦–Sundays. *MA*–Marine Atlantic/Marine Atlantique. North Sydney 902 794 7500. Fax 902 564 7480.

Table 57 LABRADOR COAST — MA

CA $	①		④		km	396 Direct Service ↓ June 15-Sept. 7 ↑	②			⑥
0.00	1000A	....	1900A	....	*0*	d.**Lewisporte** ....a.	1300C	....	....	0030C
	|	....	1800B	....	*508*	d.Cartwright..........d.	1500B	....	....	|
	1930B	....	0600C	....	*821*	a.**Goose Bay** ....d.	2359A	....	....	1600A

stopping service Lewisporte-St. Anthony-Battle Harbour-Port Hope Simpson-Black Tickle-Spotted Islands-Domino-Indian Tickle-Cartwright-Rigolet-Goose Bay-Makkovik-Hopedale-Davis Inlet-Nain and v.v. ▣. *2133* km.

June 21-Nov. 14 only.

From Lewisporte: ∅.

①–Mondays. ②–Tuesdays. ④–Thursdays. ⑥–Saturdays. ∅–Information not available at press date. *MA*–Marine Atlantic/Marine Atlantique. 902 794 7500. Fax 902 561 7180.

Table 58 396 MADELEINE ISLANDS — CTMA

service Souris-Cap-aux-Meules and v.v. *70* km. Journey: 5 hours. Fare: CA $: 24.20.

Apr. 1-June 15 and Sept. 14-30.

From Souris: 1400ex①.
From Cap-aux-Meules: 0800ex①.

June 16-Sept. 13.

From Souris: 0200③, 1400ex②.
From Cap-aux-Meules: 0800ex②, 2000②.

Oct. 1-Nov. 30.

From Souris: 0800⑤, 1000②, 1400③⑥⑦.
From Cap-aux-Meules: 0800ex②⑤.

Dec. 1-Jan. 23.

From Souris: 0800②(Jan. only)④⑥, 1000②(Dec. only).
From Cap-aux-Meules: 0800①③⑤.

Cargo/passenger service Montréal-Cap-aux-Meules and v.v. *1200* km. Journey: 2 days. Fare: CA $: 302.00.

▲ Apr. 1-Jan. 9 ▲

From Montréal: ②.
From Cap-aux-Meules: 0800⑤.

①–Mondays. ②–Tuesdays. ③–Wednesdays. ④–Thursdays. ⑤–Fridays. ⑥–Saturdays. ⑦–Sundays. ▲–Subject to confirmation. *CTMA*–CTMA Traversier. Cap aux Meules 418 986 5101.

Table 59 FORTUNE - ST. PIERRE — ABF

CA $		X			km	396 ↓ ↑		X		
	②⑤⑦		②⑦	⑤			②⑤⑦		②⑦	⑤
27.00	....	1430	....	....	*37*	d.**Fortune**............a.	....	1355	....	....
8.00	0915	|	1745	1815	*15*	d.Miquelon............d.	0855	|	1725	1755
0.00	1010	1555	1840	1910	*0*	a.**St. Pierre** ....d.	0800	1330	1630	1700

X–①③⑤⑥ June 16-29 and Sept. 4-25; daily June 30-Sept. 3. ①–Mondays. ②–Tuesdays. ③–Wednesdays. ⑤–Fridays. ⑥–Saturdays. ⑦–Sundays.
ABF– Armement Borotra Frères. St. Pierre 412078.

Table 60 496 DARTMOUTH - HALIFAX — HMT

service Dartmouth-Halifax and v.v. *1* km. Journey: 15 mins. Fare: CA $: 1.10.
From Dartmouth: 0630⚒ and frequent to 2330⚒. (Also † June 1-Sept. 30 1200-1730).
From Halifax: 0645⚒ and frequent to 2345⚒. (Also † June 1-Sept. 30 1215-1745).

⚒– Daily except Sundays and holidays. †–Sundays and holidays only.
HMT– Halifax Metro Transit. Dartmouth 902 421 6600. Fax 902 421 6605. Tx 019 31557.

Table 64 TORONTO - NORTH BAY — ONT

CA $	799	711	731	783 ex⑦	km	496 ↓ ↑	738	722	742 ex⑦	790
0.00	0030	0930	1430	1900	*0*	d.**Toronto** ....a.	0750	1200	1730	2230
	0200	1105	1605	2030	*58*	d.Barrie ....d.	0620	1030	1600	2100
	0235	1145	1635	2105	*90*	d.Orillia.................d.	0535	0945	1515	2020
33.17	0255	1205	|	2120	*115*	d.Washago..........d.	0510	0925	|	1955
35.73	0310	1225	1710	2140	*180*	d.Gravenhurst ......d.	0450	0845	1425	1915
43.65	0410	1345	1815	2250	*235*	d.Huntsville...........d.	0330	0745	1340	1815
62.86	0545	1530	1945	0030	*367*	a.**North Bay**.........d.	0200	0600	1215	1630

ONT– Ontario Northland. North Bay 705 472 4500. Fax 705 495 4745.

Table 65 PEMBERTON — MCL

CA $	25	31		37	km	396 ↓ ↑	22	26	30	36
0.00	0800	1300	1500	1900	*0*	d.**Vancouver**........a.	1100	1605	1920	2145
6.75	0910	1415	|	2010	*65*	d.Squamish..........d.	0945	1445	1800	2035
13.00	1025	1530	1700	2130	*121*	d.Whistler.............d.	0830	1330	1645	1915
16.75	1110	1610	1735	2210	*152*	a.**Pemberton** ....d.	0730	1235	....	1835

MCL– Maverick Coach Lines. Vancouver 604 662 8051. Fax 604 255 5770.

Table 66 POWELL RIVER — MCL

CA $	1			5	km	496 ↓ ↑		4	6	
0.00	0830	....	....	1830	*0*	d.**Vancouver**........a.	....	1345	2145	....
	0930u	....	....	1925u	*10*	d.Horseshoe Bay..d.	....	1300s	2100s	....
15.90	1100	....	....	2100	*60*	d.Sechelt..............d.	....	1135	1930	....
24.75	1340	....	....	2340	*150*	a.**Powell River**.....d.	....	0845	1630	....

s– Calls to set down only. u–Calls to take up only.
MCL– Maverick Coach Lines. Vancouver 604 662 8051.

Table 67 VICTORIA - NANAIMO - CAMPBELL RIVER

🚌 ICL

CA $	4			6		8	10		12	14		km	496		5		7	9	11		13	15		17
								🅁					↓ ↑									🅁		
0.00	0620	....	....	0805	....	1145	1345	1645	1645	1915	....	0	d.**Victoria**....a.	0745	1010	....	1320	1730	....	....	1850	2055	....	2300
14.70	0820	....	....	1020	....	1415	1620	1845	1920	2105	....	124	a.Nanaimo....d.	0530	0745	....	1100	1510	....	....	1650	1915	....	2100
14.70	|	....	....	|	1100	|	|	....	....	|	2115	124	d. Nanaimo....a.	....	....	1015	|	1420	....	....	|	....	2015	|
25.20	|	....	....	|	1230	|	|	....	....	|	2240	211	a. Port Alberni....d.	....	....	0845	|	1250	....	....	|	....	1850	|
14.70	0900	....	....	1100	....	1500	1700a	....	....	2115	....	124	d.Nanaimo....a.	....	....	....	1010	....	1410	....	1605	....	....	2005
29.40	1055	....	....	1250	....	1650	1850a	....	....	2250	....	234	d.Courtenay....d.	....	....	....	0805	....	1205	....	1410	....	....	1805
33.60	1145	....	....	1345	....	1755	1945a	....	....	2345	....	280	a. **Campbell River**....d.	....	....	....	0715	....	1115	....	1315	....	....	1715
	1220	....	....	....	....	....	....	....	....	....	....		d. **Campbell River**....a.	....	....	....	....	....	....	....	1220	....	....	....
72.45	1600	....	....	....	....	....	....	....	....	....	....	360	a.Port Hardy....d.	....	....	....	....	....	....	....	0845	....	....	....

a– ⑤⑥⑦. ⑤–Fridays. ⑥–Saturdays. ⑦–Sundays. 🅁–⑤⑦ (also ① of holiday wekends). *ICL*–Island Coach Lines. ☎Victoria 604 388 5248.

Table 68 396 VANCOUVER LOCAL SERVICES

⛴ 🚌 *BCT CCS GLC MCL PFC SB VRTS WCX*

Local #### (C cl. only, 1.435m.) and 🚌 services operate in the Vancouver area as follows:

Abbotsford ⊸ *(CCS)* (*65* km, CA $: Ø). From Vancouver: 0745Ⓐ, 0900Ⓐ, 0930Ⓒ, 1030Ⓐ, 1135Ⓒ, 1330, 1530Ⓐ, 1540Ⓐ, 1630Ⓐ, 1640Ⓐ, 1650Ⓒ, 1730Ⓐ, 1800Ⓒ, 2130, 2245Ⓒ, 2300Ⓐ, returning at 0455Ⓐ, 0525Ⓐ, 0540Ⓐ, 0555Ⓐ, 0610Ⓐ, 0630Ⓐ, 0725Ⓒ, 0930, 1100Ⓒ, 1115Ⓐ, 1130Ⓐ, 1330Ⓐ, 1400Ⓒ, 1530Ⓐ, 1800, 2015Ⓒ, 2030Ⓐ. Journey: 1½ hours. Also by *GLC* from Vancouver at 0600, 1130, 1645, returning at1210, 1925, 1930.

Burnaby ⊸ *(VRTS service 120)* (*12* km, CA $: 1.50 [2.25 at peaks]). From Vancouver: 0625Ⓐ/0723⑥/0800† and frequent to 0006, returning from Burnaby Brentwood Exchange at 0550Ⓐ/0640⑥/0715† and frequent to 2327. Journey: 30 mins.

Chilliwack ⊸ *(CCS)* (*89* km, CA $: Ø). From Vancouver: 0900Ⓐ, 0930Ⓒ, 1030Ⓐ, 1135Ⓒ, 1330, 1540Ⓐ, 1630Ⓐ, 1640Ⓐ, 1650Ⓒ, 1730Ⓐ, 2130, 2245Ⓒ, 2300Ⓐ, returning at 0500Ⓐ, 0520Ⓐ, 0530Ⓐ, 0555Ⓐ, 0640Ⓒ, 0845, 1010Ⓒ, 1030Ⓐ, 1245Ⓐ, 1310Ⓒ, 1445Ⓐ, 1710, 1930Ⓒ, 1945Ⓐ. Journey: 2 hours. Also by *GLC* from Vancouver at 0550, 0600, 1130, 1630, 1645, returning at 1145, 1150, 1900.

Coquitlam ⊸ *(VRTS service151)* (*10* km, CA $: 1.50 [3.00 at peaks]). From Vancouver: 0715Ⓐ/0725Ⓐ/0816† and frequent (hourly on †) to 0018, returning at 0524Ⓐ/0556⑥/0700† and frequent (hourly on †) to 2300. Journey: 1¼ hours. Also ♂ *(WCX)* from Vancouver Waterfront at 1615Ⓐ, 1645Ⓐ, 1715Ⓐ, 1745Ⓐ, 1815Ⓐ, returning from Coquitlam Central at 0611Ⓐ, 0636Ⓐ, 0656Ⓐ, 0716Ⓐ, 0741Ⓐ. Journey: 35 mins.

Departure Bay ⊸ *(MCL)* (*56* km, CA $: Ø). From Vancouver: 0600, 0800, 1000, 1200, 1400, 1600●, 1800, 2000, returning at 0700, 0900, 1100, 1300, 1500, 1700, 1900●, 2100. Journey: 2½ hours.

Horseshoe Bay ⊸ *(VRTS)* (*10* km, CA $: 1.35 [2.75 at peaks]). From Vancouver: 0605⚒/0705† and about every 30 mins. to 2305†/0010②-⑦, returning at 0558Ⓐ/0703⑥/0803† and about every 30 mins. to 0005. Journey: 45 mins.

Ladner ⊸ *(VRTS service 601, also 602/6/8 at peaks)* (*17* km, CA $: 1.50 [3.00 at peak periods]). From Vancouver: 0633Ⓐ/0636⑥/0638† and about every 30 mins. to 1841, then about hourly to 0055, returning at 0545Ⓐ/0700Ⓒ and about every 30 mins. to 1919Ⓒ, 1924Ⓐ, then about hourly to 2324 . Journey: 45 mins.

Langley ⊸ *(GLC)* (*55* km, CA $: Ø). From Vancouver: 0550, 1130, 1630, returning at 1240, 2000. Journey: 1¼ hours.

Maple Ridge ⊸ *(GLC)* (*40* km, CA $: Ø). From Vancouver: 0600, 1645, returning at 1300, 2015. Journey: 1 hour.

Nanaimo ⊸ *(MCL)* (*66* km, CA $: 13.25). From Vancouver: 0600, 0800, 1000, 1200, 1400, 1600●, 1800, 2000, returning at 0630, 0830, 1030, 1230, 1430, 1630, 1830●, 2030. Journey: 3 hours.

New Westminster ♂ *(BCT)* (*20* km, CA $: 1.50 [2.25 at peaks]). From Vancouver Main Street: 0555Ⓐ/0655⑥/0855† and frequent to 0020†, 0120⚒, returning at 0520Ⓐ/0620⑥/0820† and frequent to 2345†, 0045⚒. Journey: 25 mins.

North Vancouver ⊸ *(VRTS service 240)* (*6* km, CA $: 1.50 [2.25 at peaks]). From Vancouver: 0622Ⓐ/0638⑥/0838† and frequent (every 30 mins. on Ⓒ) to 2303†/0033⚒, returning at 0546Ⓐ/0616⑥/0818† and frequent (every 30 mins. on Ⓒ) to 2248†/0018⚒. Journey: 40 mins. Also ⛴ *(SB)* from Vancouver Granville Waterfront: 0016ex†, 0046ex†, 0616⚒/0816† and every 15 mins. (every 30 mins. on †, early ⑥ and all evenings) to 2316, 2346⚒, returning from Lonsdale Quay at 0002ex†, 0032ex†, 0602 0802† and every 15 mins. (every 30 mins. on †, early ⑥ and all evenings) to 2302, 2332⚒. Journey: 12 mins.

Pitt Meadows ⊸ *(CCS)* (*35* km, CA $: Ø). From Vancouver: 1400Ⓒ, 1600Ⓐ, 1635Ⓐ, 1705Ⓐ, 1800Ⓒ, 1805Ⓐ, returning at 0610 0640Ⓐ, 0710Ⓐ, 1245Ⓒ. Journey: 1¼ hours. Also ♂ *(WCX)* from Vancouver Waterfront at 1615Ⓐ, 1645Ⓐ, 1715Ⓐ, 1745 1815Ⓐ, returning at 0558Ⓐ, 0623Ⓐ, 0643Ⓐ, 0703Ⓐ, 0728Ⓐ. Journey: 45 mins.

Port Coquitlam ⊸ *(VRTS service 151/152/160)* (*28* km, CA $: 1.50 (3.00 at peaks)). From Vancouver: 0617⚒/0745Ⓒ a frequent (about hourly on †) to 2230, returning at 0513⚒/0826† and frequent (about hourly on †) to 2200. Journey: 1 hour. A by *CCS* from Vancouver at 0900Ⓐ, 1300Ⓐ, 1400Ⓒ, 1600Ⓐ, 1635Ⓐ, 1705Ⓐ, 1800Ⓒ, 1805Ⓐ, returning at 0620Ⓐ, 065 0720Ⓐ, 1155Ⓐ, 1255Ⓒ, 1655Ⓒ. Journey: 1 hour. Also ♂ *(WCX)* from Vancouver Waterfront at 1615Ⓐ, 1645Ⓐ, 1715Ⓐ, 174 1815Ⓐ, returning at 0606Ⓐ, 0631Ⓐ, 0651Ⓐ, 0711Ⓐ, 0736Ⓐ. Journey: 40 mins.

Port Moody (St. Johns) ⊸ *(VRTS service 160)* (*23* km, CA $: 1.50 [2.25 at peaks]). From Vancouver: 0602Ⓐ/0736⑥/0806† a frequent (hourly on †) to 2306†/0004⚒, returning at 0510Ⓐ/0635⑥/0730† and frequent (about hourly on †) to 2250. Journey mins. Also ♂ *(WCX)* from Vancouver Waterfront at 1615Ⓐ, 1645Ⓐ, 1715Ⓐ, 1745Ⓐ, 1815Ⓐ, returning at 0619Ⓐ, 0644Ⓐ, 070 0724Ⓐ, 0749Ⓐ.

Richmond ⊸ *(VRTS service 401/3/6/7)* (*5* km, CA $: 1.50 [2.25 at peaks]). From Vancouver: 0610, 0631, 0651 and frequent 0105, returning at 0535Ⓐ/0625Ⓒand frequent to 0025. Journey: 35 mins.

Surrey ♂ *(BCT)* (*14* km, CA $: 1.25 [1.75 at peaks]). From Vancouver Main Street : 0555Ⓐ/0655⑥/0855†and frequent to 002 0120⚒, returning at 0505Ⓐ/0605⑥/0805† and frequent to 2340†/0040⚒. Journey: 32 mins

Tsawwassen ⊸ *(VRTS service 601 also 602/6/8 at peaks)* (*20* km, CA $: 1.50 [3.00 at peaks]). From Vancouver: *0633*Ⓐ, 063 *0638*†, 0703Ⓐ, 0731⑥, 0738† and about every 30 mins. to 2045 and hourly to 0055, returning at *0516*Ⓐ, 0649⑥, 0650†, 074 0754⑥, 0755† and about every 30 mins. to 2001 and hourly to 2301. Journey: 1 hour.

Victoria ⊸ *(PFC)* (*84* km, CA $: 20.75). From Vancouver: 0545, 0645∓, 0745, 0845∓. 0945, 1045∓, 1145, 1245∓, 13 1445∓, 1545, 1645∓, 1745, 1845∓, 1945. Journey: 3½ hours.

Vancouver International Airport ⊸*(VRTS service 100 connects the airport to Downtown Vancouver via service 20; change 70th Ave/Marpole Loop)* (CA$ 1.50[2.25 at peaks]) service 100 from Marpole 0534Ⓐ, 0604Ⓐ, 0630Ⓐ, 0633Ⓒ, then freque (every 30 mins. on Ⓒ) to 1842, 1943, 2042, 2143, 2242, 2352, returning at 0605Ⓐ, 0637Ⓐ, 0705Ⓐ, 0708⑥, 0717†, th frequent, (every 30 mins. on Ⓒ) to 1808⚒, 1817†,1839⚒, 1917, 2017, 2117, 2217, 2317, 0017. Service 20 from Marpole Lo 0541⚒, 0615†, then frequent to 0041 then every 30 mins. to 0241, returning at 0543†, 0550⚒, then frequent to 0316.

West Vancouver ⊸ *(VRTS)* (7 km, CA $: 1.25 [1.75 at peaks]). From Vancouver: 0605⚒/0705† and about every 30 mins. 2305†/0010②-⑦, returning at 0611Ⓐ/0717⑥/0818† and about every 30 mins. to 0018. Journey: 30 mins.

⊸– By 🚌. ♂–By ####. ⛴–By 🚢. ∓–July 1-Sept. 1.
●– Jan. 1-8 and June 15-Dec. 31. ②–Tuesdays. ⑥–Saturdays.
⑦– Sundays. ⚒–Daily except Sundays and holidays.
†– Sundays and holidays. Ⓐ–Mondays to Fridays, except holidays.
Ⓒ– Saturdays, Sundays and holidays.

Ø– Information not available at press date.
BCT– BC Transit (Skytrain). ☎Vancouver 604 264 5000.
CCS– Cascade Charter Service. ☎Sardis 604 795 7443. Fax 604 795 4433.
GLC– Greyhound Lines of Canada. ☎Vancouver 604 662 3222.
MCL– Maverick Coach Lines. ☎Vancouver 604 662 8051.
PFC– Pacific Coach Lines. ☎Vancouver 662 4275.
SB– SeaBus (Vancouver Regional Transit System). ☎Vancouver 604 264 5000.
VRTS– Vancouver Regional Transit System. ☎Vancouver 604 264 5000.
WCX– West Coast Express. ☎Vancouver 689 3641.

Table 70 396 VICTORIA LOCAL SERVICES

🚌 *PFC VRT*

Local 🚌 services operate in the Victoria area as follows:

Esquimalt *(VRT)* (*4* km, CA $: 1.25). From Victoria: 0002, 0600Ⓐ/0720⑥/0805† and frequent (about every 40 mins. on †) to 1922, 1942Ⓐ, 2002, 2042, 2122, 2202, 2242, 2322, returning at 0017, 0614Ⓐ/0703⑥/0823† and frequent (about every 40 mins on †) to 1903⑥, 1904Ⓐ, 1924Ⓐ, 1943⑥, 1944Ⓐ, 1948†, 2000Ⓐ, 2023, 2103, 2143, 2223, 2303, 2343. Journey: 15 mins.

Oak Bay *(VRT)* (*4* km, CA $: 1.25). From Victoria: 0615Ⓐ, 0628Ⓐ, 0639Ⓐ, 0658Ⓐ, 0701⑥, 0712Ⓐ, 0717⑥, 0727Ⓐ, 0733⑥, 0750⚒, 0802†, 0807⑥ and frequent to 2242, 2322, returning at 0626Ⓐ, 0646Ⓐ, 0654Ⓐ, 0700⑥, 0707Ⓐ, 0725⚒, 0733Ⓐ, 0734⑥, 0757Ⓐ, 0759⚒, 0808⑥, 0820†, 0822Ⓐ and frequent to 2300, 2340. Journey: 15 mins.

Saanich *(VRT)* (*8* km, CA $: 2.50). From Victoria: 0519Ⓐ, 0530⑥, 0554Ⓐ, 0624Ⓐ, 0659Ⓐ, 0700†, 0703⑥, 0759Ⓐ, 0800†, 0803⑥, 0856Ⓐ, 0900⑥, 0956Ⓐ, 1000⑥, 1056Ⓐ, 1100⑥, 1205Ⓐ, 1208⑥, 1301Ⓐ, 1308⑥, 1401Ⓐ, 1408⑥, 1501Ⓐ, 1505⑥, 1507†, 1555Ⓐ, 1605⑥, 1607†, 1625Ⓐ, 1655Ⓐ, 1705⑥, 1707†, 1740Ⓐ, 1805⑥, 1810Ⓐ, 1817†, 1917, 2017, 2117, 2217, 2300, 2330, returning at 0012, 0635Ⓐ, 0705Ⓐ, 0720⑥, 0745Ⓐ, 0759†, 0820⚒, 0859†, 0920⚒, 0959†, 1020⚒, 1059†, 1120⚒, 115 1220⚒, 1320†, 1332⑥, 1338Ⓐ, 1420†, 1432⑥, 1438Ⓐ, 1520†, 1532⑥, 1538Ⓐ, 1620†, 1632⑥, 1638Ⓐ, 1720†, 1732⑥, 173 1820†, 1832⑥, 1838Ⓐ, 1917, 2017, 2117, 2217, 2312. Journey: 1¼ hours.

Swartz Bay *(VRT)* (*14* km, CA $: 3.75). From Victoria: 0530⑥, 0545Ⓐ, 0641Ⓐ, 0642†, 0646⑥, 0742Ⓐ, 0746⑥, 0840Ⓐ, 084 0846⑥, 0940, 1040, 1138⚒, 1140†, 1237⑥, 1238Ⓐ, 1240†, 1338⚒, 1340†, 1438⚒, 1440†, 1538⚒, 1540†, 1600Ⓐ, 163 1638⑥, 1640†, 1700Ⓐ, 1715⚒, 1740, 1817†, 1840⚒, 1917, 2017, 2117, 2217, 2300, 2330, returning at 0549Ⓐ, 0619Ⓐ, 063 0647Ⓐ, 0654⑥, 0717Ⓐ, 0754⚒, 0755†, 0854Ⓐ, 0855†, 0954Ⓐ, 0955†, 1054Ⓐ, 1055†, 1154Ⓐ, 1155†, 1254Ⓐ, 1255†, 135 1355†, 1454Ⓐ, 1455†, 1554Ⓐ, 1555†, 1654Ⓐ, 1655†, 1755†, 1756Ⓐ, 1855, 1955, 2055, 2155. Journey: 1¼ hours.

Vancouver *(PFC)* (*84* km, CA $: 20.75). From Victoria: 0600, 0700η, 0800, 0900η, 1000, 1100η, 1200, 1300η, 1400, 1500η, 16 1700η, 1800, 1900η, 2000. Journey: 3½ hours.

η–July 1- Sept. 1. Ⓐ–Mondays to Fridays, except holidays. ⚒–Daily except Sundays and holidays. ⑥–Saturdays. †–Sundays and holidays.
PFC– Pacific Coach Lines. ☎Vancouver 662 7575.
VRT– Victoria Regional Transit System. ☎Victoria 382 6161.

Table 72 BELLA COOLA - WILLIAMS LAKE

🚌 *CPT*

CA $		②⑤			km	396 ↓ ↑		①④		
0.00	....	0900	....	....	0	d.**Bella Coola**....a.	....	1800	....	....
60.00	....	1700	....	....	484	a.**Williams Lake**..d.	....	0930	....	....

①– Mondays. ②–Tuesdays. ④–Thursdays. ⑤–Fridays.
CPT– Central Pacific Transit. ☎Williams Lake 604 392 5461.

Table 73 WHITEHORSE - DAWSON CREEK

🚌 *GLC RVL*

CA $	*GLC* 522	*GLC* 522	*RVL*	*GLC* 526	km	496	*GLC* 521	*GLC* 525		*RVL*
	②④⑥	③⑤⑦	●🅑	②④⑥		↓ ↑	ex⑦	②④⑥		●🅑
0.00	1300	....	Ø	....	0	d.**Whitehorse**....a.	....	0415	....	Ø
18.75	1530	....	|	....	182	d.Teslin....d.	....	0230	....	|
45.15	1900	....	Ø	....	451	d.Watson Lake....d.	....	2315	....	Ø
	|	....	Ø	....	644	d. Cassiar....d.	....	|	....	Ø
	|	....	Ø	....	825	d. Dease Lake....d.	....	|	....	Ø
	|	....	Ø	....	964	d. Iskut....d.	....	|	....	Ø
	|	....	Ø	....	1363	d. Meziadin ✂....d.	....	|	....	Ø
	|	....	Ø	....	1776	d. Terrace....d.	....	|	....	Ø
	|	....	Ø	....	2007	a. **Prince Rupert** d.	....	|	....	Ø
83.70	r	....	....	....	836	d.Summit Lake....d.	....	1700	....	....
98.40	0235	0250	....	0825	982	d.Fort Nelson....d.	1415	1500	....	....
137.75	....	0820	....	1330	1374	d.Fort St. John....d.	0855	....	....	....
145.35	....	0930	....	1440	1450	a.**Dawson Creek** .d.	0745	....	....	....

r–Calls on request. ✂–for Stewart. 🅑–Summer only. ②–Tuesdays. ③–Wednesdays. ④–Thursdays. ⑤–Fridays. ⑥–Saturdays. ⑦–Sundays. ●–Alternate days only. Ø–Information not available at press date. *GLC*–Greyhound Lines of Canada. ☎Dawson Creek 604 782 4275. *RVL*–Rival Highway Tours. ☎Whitehorse 403 667 7896.

Table 74 MEDICINE HAT - LETHBRIDGE

🚌 *GLC*

CA $	1184	1575	1152	1145	km	496 ↓ ↑	1151		1156	1141
17.85	0515	....	....	....	0	d.**Medicine Hat**....a.	....	....	....	2030
0.00	0735	0830	1400	2200	168	d.**Lethbridge**....d.	1000	....	1645	1800
5.40	....	0915	1445	2250	220	a.Fort MacLeod....d.	0920	....	1600	1640

GLC– Greyhound Lines of Canada. ☎Lethbridge 403 327 1551.

Table 76 DAWSON CITY

🚌 *MT NOR NWS*

CA $		*NOR* 202	*NWS*		km	396	*NWS*		*NOR* 205	
		P	②⑤			↓ ↑	②⑤		P	
0.00	....	0900	0930	....	0	d.**Whitehorse**....a.	2245	....	2315	....
24.61	....	1115	1150	....	180	d.Carmacks....d.	2030	....	2115	....
59.92	....	|	1545	....	408	a. Ross River....d.	1630	....	|	....
47.00	....	1320	....	....	345	a.Stewart Crossing..d.	....	....	1830	....
66.00	....	1600	....	....	560	a.**Dawson City**....d.	....	....	1600	....
CA $		P		P	km	590 *MT*		P	P	
0.00	....	1335	....	1905	0	d.Stewart Crossing..a.	....	1310	1800	....
15.00	....	1410	....	2030	60	a.**Mayo**....d.	....	1230	1730	....
CA $					km	389				
0.00	....	....	....	....	0	d.**Dawson City**....a.	....	....	....	....
25.00	....	....	....	....	130	d.Action Jackson ▬..d.	....	....	....	....
55.00	....	....	....	....	275	a.**Tok**....d.	....	....	....	....

P–③⑤ Jan. 1-May 31 and Sept. 1-Dec. 31; ①③⑤ June 1-Aug. 31. ①–Mondays. ②–Tuesdays. ③–Wednesdays. ⑤–Fridays. *MT*–Mayo Taxi. ☎Mayo 996 2240.
NOR– Norline Coaches (Yukon) Ltd. ☎Whitehorse 668 3355.
NWS– North West Stage Lines. ☎Whitehorse 403 668 7240.

Table 77 HAY RIVER - PEACE RIVER

🚌 *GLC NBS*

CA $	*GLC* 808	*NBS* 2			km	396		*NBS* 1	*GLC* 807	
	ex①	⚒				↓ ↑		⚒	ex⑦	
64.90	0820	....	....	....	0	d.**Hay River**....a.	....	....	1545	....
60.35	0850	....	....	....	45	d.Enterprise....d.	....	....	1515	....
39.15	1105	....	....	....	249	d.Meander River...d.	....	....	1300	....
31.90	1220a	1215	....	....	318	d.High Level....d.	....	1030	1215b	....
§10.70	|	1315	....	....	400	a. Fort Vermilion .d.	....	0900	|	....
0.00	1600	....	....	....	629	a.**Peace River**....d.	....	....	0745	....

a–Arr 1150. b–Arr 1130. §–Fare ex High Level. ①–Mondays. ⑦–Sundays. ⚒–Daily except Sundays and holidays. *GLC*–Greyhound Lines of Canada. ☎Calgary 403 265 91
NBS– Norline Bus Service. ☎La Crete 403 928 2996.

Table 78 TOFINO

🚌 *OSL*

CA $		Ⓐ			km	396 ↓ ↑	Ⓐ			
0.00	....	1000	1600	....	0	d.**Tofino**....a.	0940	....	1530	....
	....	1100	1645	....	50	d.Ucluelet....d.	0830	....	1410	....
	....	1230	1830	....	150	a.**Port Alberni**....d.	0700	....	1230	....

Ⓐ– Mondays to Fridays except holidays.
OSL– Orient Stage Lines Ltd. ☎Port Alberni 723 6924.

Table 80 EDMONTON - DAWSON CREEK ♿ GLC

CA $	509	703	401	N	117		103	101 ⑧	801		501	km	496 ↓ ↑	704	702 ex⑦	N	502	202	118	604		506		802
).00	....	....	0830	....	1130	....	1830	1915	2359	....	0001	0	d.**Edmonton** ....a.	....	0530	....	0530	1235	1255	1940	....	....	....	2245
6.35	....	....	│	....	│	....	│	2115	│	....	│	162	d. Athabasca ....d.	....	│	....	│	│	1055	│	....	....	....	│
1.75	....	....	│	....	│	....	│	s	│	....	│	239	d. Smith ....d.	....	│	....	│	│	│	│	....	....	....	│
5.95	....	....	│	....	1500	....	│	2315	0325	....	│	240	d. Slave Lake ....d.	....	0215	....	│	│	0940	│	....	....	....	│
).40	....	....	1115	....	│	....	2130	│	│	....	0215	140	d.Whitecourt ....d.	....	│	....	0330	0955	│	1720	....	....	....	2050
7.70	....	....	1315	1320	│	....	2330	│	│	....	0445	348	d.Valleyview ....d.	....	│	0055	0110	0730	│	1500	....	1815	....	1835
7.70	....	....	│	r	1730	....	│	s	0548	....	│	425	d.Donnelly Junction ....d.	....	2315	r	│	│	0657	│	....	│	....	1730
4.10	....	0730	│	1615	1835	....	│	0200	0645	....	│	491	a. **Peace River** ....d.	2130	2215	2200	│	│	0600	│	....	│	....	1630
4.10	....	0905	│	▬	....	....	│	....	....	....	│	577	d. Fairview ....d.	2010	▬	....	│	│	▬	│	....	│	....	....
4.10	....	1005	│	....	....	....	│	....	....	....	│	632	d. Rycroft ....d.	1930	....	....	│	│	....	│	....	│	....	....
4.10	....	1100	1450	**207**	....	....	0055	....	....	....	0610	462	d.Grande Prairie ....d.	1815	**510**	....	2345	0615	**208**	1335	....	1705	....	....
7.45	1020	....	1535	1605	....	....	....	....	....	....	0700	581	d.**Dawson Creek** ....d.	....	1555	....	2030	....	0535	1020	....	....	....	....
7.95	1150	....	....	1725	....	....	....	....	....	....	....	676	d.Chetwynd ....d.	....	1440	....	....	....	0420	....	....	....	....	....
7.10	1650	....	....	2225	....	....	....	....	....	....	....	998	a.**Prince George** ....d.	....	0915	....	....	....	2330	....	....	....	....	....

Calls by request. s–Calls to set down only. ①–Mondays. ⑦–Sundays. ⑧–Daily except Saturdays. ♿–Facilities for the disabled. *GLC*–Greyhound Lines of Canada. ☎Edmonton 3 421 4211.

Table 84 ELLIOT LAKE AJB

CA $		23	25	27	km	396 ↓ ↑	22		26	28
).00	....	0930	1500	2150	0	d.**Serpent River**...a.	0910	....	1436	2050
3.88	....	1000	1530	2210	32	a.**Elliot Lake**....d.	0845	....	1400	2030

B– A J Bus Lines Ltd. ☎Elliot Lake 705 848 3013.

Table 85 YELLOWKNIFE - HAY RIVER AFC

CA $			1▽ ⛴	1 ①-⑤	km	396 ↓ ↑	2 ①-⑤	2▽ ⛴		
4.20	....	....	0055	....	0	d.**Yellowknife** ....a.	....	2235	....	....
7.35	....	....	0220	....	73	d.Rae ....d.	....	2120	....	....
).71	....	....	0515	....	285	d.Fort Providence.d.	....	1830	....	....
6.42	....	....	0646	....	425	d.Enterprise....d.	....	1645	....	....
).00	....	....	0720	1615	470	d.**Hay River** ....d.	1445	1615	....	....
6.55	....	....	....	1930	752	a.Fort Smith ....d.	1100	....	....	....

–Service liable to disruption April-May and October-December due to icing conditions on ackenzie River. ⛴–Generally operates ②④⑥ when river is frozen, ①-⑤ when ferry is in eration. ①–Mondays. ②–Tuesdays. ④–Thursdays. ⑤–Fridays. ⑥–Saturdays.
C– Arctic Frontier Carriers. ☎Yellowknife 403 873 4437. Fax: 873 6423.

Table 86 PRINCE GEORGE - VANCOUVER ♿ GLC

CA $	1251		1253	1255	km	496 ↓ ↑	1252		1254	1256
).00	0800	....	1730	2300	0	d.**Prince George**..a.	2005	....	0550	0835
2.55	0940	....	1905	0035	125	d.Quesnel....d.	1835	....	0415	0705
4.90	1150	....	2110	0215	240	d.Williams Lake....d.	1700	....	0235	0525
1.75	1355	....	2315	0430	400	d.Clinton....d.	1405	....	0015	0310
5.95	1500	....	0000	0515	440	d.Cache Creek.....d.	1335	....	2345	0240
5.70	1745	....	s	0815	633	d.Hope ....d.	1000	....	2030	│
1.35	1840	....	0400	0855	698	d.Chilliwack ....d.	0900	....	1935	2215
7.80	s	....	s	s	787	a.New Westminster .d.	0800	....	1830	2110
7.80	1945	....	0555	1045	807	a.**Vancouver**....d.	0730	....	1800	2045

Calls to set down only. ♿–Facilities for the disabled. *GLC*–Greyhound Lines of nada. ☎Vancouver 604 662 3222.

Table 87 KENORA - FORT FRANCES XL

CA $	23 ex③				km	396 ↓ ↑			24 ex③	
).00	1030	....	....	....	0	d.**Kenora**....a.	....	....	1810	....
	1305	....	....	....	188	d.Emo ....d.	....	....	1545	....
	1335	....	....	....	224	a.**Fort Frances** ....d.	....	....	1515	....

Wednesdays. *XL*–Excel Coach Lines. ☎Kenora 807 468 6667.

Table 88 EDMONTON - COLD LAKE GLC

CA $		135 ex⑥⑦		139	km	496 ↓ ↑	138 ex⑥⑦		180 ⑥⑦	142 ex⑥⑦
).00	....	1130	....	1815	0	d.**Edmonton** ....a.	1130	....	1800	2230
2.60	....	1335	....	2000	110	d.Smoky Lake ....d.	0934	....	1604	2034
3.35	....	1455	....	2115	203	d.St. Paul ....d.	0815	....	1445	1915
3.65	....	1635	....	2320	330	a.**Cold Lake**....d.	0630	....	1300	1730

1125 on ①. ①–Mondays. ⑤–Fridays. ⑦–Sundays.
C– Greyhound Lines of Canada. ☎Edmonton 403 421 4211.

Table 90 PRINCE RUPERT GLC

CA $	1529 ①③⑤⑦	511	1531	209	km	496 ↓ ↑	512	1630 ①③⑤⑦	210	1632
0.00	....	....	2200	....	0	d.**Edmonton** ....a.	....	....	....	1130
39.90	....	....	0250	....	378	d.Jasper ....d.	....	....	....	0605
51.35	1115	....	│	....	458	d.Valemount ....d.	....	1040	....	0335
79.40	1455	2315	0615	0815	632	d.**Prince George**..d.	0615	0700	2150	0001
89.75	....	0035	....	0935	724	d.Vanderhoof....d.	0500	....	2035	....
	....	│	....	│	768	a. Fort St.James .d.	│	....	│	....
103.15	....	0235	....	1155	854	d.Burns Lake....d.	0305	....	1855	....
106.85	....	r	....	r	900	d.Broman Lake....d.	r	....	r	....
117.90	....	0500	....	1410	980	d.Smithers....d.	0115	....	1615	....
124.90	....	0540	....	1500	1068	d.New Hazelton....d.	0001	....	1500	....
138.75	....	0750	....	1705	1208	d.Terrace....d.	2225	....	1320	....
153.75	....	0940	....	1900	1362	a.**Prince Rupert**...d.	2015	....	1115	....

r– Calls by request.
GLC– Greyhound Lines of Canada. ☎Prince George 604 564 5454.

Table 91 EDMONTON - CONSORT FBL GLC

CA $		GLC 153 ①	GLC 153 ⑤	FBL 157	km	496 ↓ ↑	FBL 158 ex⑦	GLC 156 ①⑤	FBL 158 ⑦	
0.00	....	....	....	....	0	d.**Edmonton** ....a.	....	....	....	....
10.40	....	2000	2000	....	95	d.Camrose ....d.	....	0945	....	....
	....	│	│	2015	♦114	d.Red Deer....d.	0940	│	1400	....
22.85	....	2125	2125	2150	211	a. Stettler ....d.	0805	0810	1235	....
	....	2155	2155	2200		d. Stettler ....a.	0735	0755	1225	....
	....	│	│	0005	360	a.**Consort** ....d.	0600	│	1020	....
33.30	....	2310	2310	....	315	a. Drumheller ....d.	....	0645	....	....
	....	....	0155	....	502	a. Oyen ....d.	....	....	....	....

②–Tuesdays. ④–Thursdays. ⑦–Sundays. ♦–Km ex Stettler. *FBL*–Ferguson Bus Lines. ☎Edmonton 403 421 4211. *GLC*–Greyhound Lines of Canada. ☎Edmonton 403 421 4211.

Table 92 CALGARY - SASKATOON FBL GLC SAS

CA $	SAS 31/341 ex⑦	GLC 1164	FBL 1162 ②③	GLC 1166	km	496 ↓ ↑	FBL 1161 ③④	SAS 107	SAS 32/331	SAS 105
0.00	....	0745	1745	2305	0	d.**Calgary** ....a.	1150	2125b	....	0620b
16.69	....	0940	1955	0055	142	d.Drumheller....d.	0950	1930b	....	0435b
25.79	....	1040	2115	0155	220	d.Hanna ....d.	0845	1830b	....	0340b
	....	1155	2240	0312	328	d.Oyen ....d.	0715	1643b		0222b
	....	1235	▬	0335	362	a. Alsask ....d.	....	1615b	....	0200b
	....	1315a	....	0340a		d. Alsask ....a.	....	1610	....	0200
30.70	....	1400a	SAS	0425a	426	d.Kindersley ....d.	....	1515	....	0110
	0630c	│	312	│	△301	d. Eastend....a.	....	│	2330c	│
	0700c	│	⑦	│	△267	d. Shaunavon....a.	....	│	2300c	│
	0830	│	1655	│	△155	d. Swift Current...d.	....	│	2135	│
35.00	1035	1505a	1900	0520a	518	d.Rosetown ....d.	....	1415	1930	0005
41.90	1210	1630a	2035	0650a	634	a.**Saskatoon**....d.	....	1245	1800	2245

a–*SAS*. b-*GLC*. c–②④ only. ①–Mondays. ③–Wednesdays. ⑤–Fridays. ⑦–Sundays. △–Km ex Saskatoon. *FBL*–Ferguson Bus Lines. ☎Calgary 403 265 9111. *GLC*–Greyhound Lines of Canada. ☎ Calgary 403 265 9111. *SAS*–Saskatchewan Transportation Co. ☎Saskatoon 306 664 5700.

Table 93 EDMONTON - CALGARY ♿ GLC RA

CA $	496 ↓	km	GLC 1111	GLC 1117 ex⑦	RA 8 a	GLC 1195	GLC 1105	GLC 1189 Ⓡ	GLC 2001	GLC 1181⑥ Ⓡ①⑤⑥⑦	RA 10	GLC 1113	GLC 1107	GLC 1191 Ⓡ	GLC 1177	GLC 1185⑥ ⑤⑦Ⓡ	RA 12	GLC 1193 ⑤⑦Ⓡ	GLC 1179	GLC 1109 ①③⑤	GLC 1115 ②④⑥⑦	GLC 147/151 ①③⑤	RA 14	GLC 2003	GLC 1187
).00	**Edmonton** ....d.	0	0001	....	0800	0800	0930	1000	1100	1200	1215	1300	1300	1400	1500	1600	1630	1800	1800	1815	1815	1815	1800	1900	2015
∝	South Edmonton d.	5	0015	....	0810	0815	0945	1015	1115	1215	1225	1315	1315	1415	1515	1615	1640	1815	1815	1830	1830	1830	1810	1915	2030
9.85	Wetaskiwin ....d.	69	0120	....	│	│	1100	│	│	│	│	│	1515	│	│	│	│	│	│	1945	2035	│	│	│	│
2.95	Camrose ....d.	91	│	....	│	│	│	│	│	│	│	│	1440	│	│	│	│	│	│	│	2000	1955	│	│	│
2.15	Macklin ....a.	306	│	....	│	│	│	│	│	│	│	│	│	│	│	│	│	│	│	│	│	2355b	│	│	│
3.70	Red Deer ....d.	156	0240	0955	1000	0955	1230	│	1300	│	1415	1500	1710	│	1700	│	1830	│	2005	2110	2205	....	2000	2115	2215
1.00	**Calgary**....a.	303	0535	1235	1130	1155	....	1320	1445	1520	1545	1645	1955	1730	1840	1920	2000	2120	2145	....	....	....	2130	2255	2359

6 ↓	GLC 1112	GLC 1120	GLC 1118 ①③⑤⑦	RA 7 ⚒	GLC 146/8 ①③⑤	GLC 1114	GLC 1102 ②④⑥	RA 7 †	GLC 1194⑥ ①⑤⑥⑦Ⓡ	GLC 1188 Ⓡ	RA 9	GLC 1116	GLC 1106	GLC 1190 Ⓡ	GLC 150 ⑦	GLC 1178	GLC 1182⑥ ⑤⑦Ⓡ	RA 11	GLC 1108	GLC 1192 ⑤⑦Ⓡ	RA 13	GLC 1180	GLC 1110 ⑧	GLC 1196	GLC 1186 Ⓡ
lgary....d.	0030	0700	....	0800	....	0900	....	1000	1100	1200	1215	1300	1100	1400	....	1500	1600	1630	....	1800	1800	1800	1755	1900	2000
d Deer ....d.	0250	0840	0845	0945	....	1045	0845	1145	│	│	1400	1505	1400	│	....	1700	│	1800	1700	│	1945	1945	2050	2100	rs
acklin ....d.	│	│	│	│	0600a	│	│	│	│	│	│	│	│	│	1201	│	│	│	│	│	│	│	....	│	│
amrose ....d.	│	│	│	│	0950	│	1055	│	│	│	│	│	│	│	1605	│	│	│	1915	│	│	│	....	│	│
etaskiwin....d.	0425	│	1015	│	1025	│	1015	│	│	│	│	│	1525	│	1640	│	│	│	1835	│	│	│	....	│	│
uth Edmonton ....a.	0535	1030	1115	1120	1135	1230	1220	1320	1400	1500	1535	1640	1630	1715	1750	1850	1900	1945	2025	2105	2115	2120	....	2230	2310
monton ....a.	0550	1045	1130	1130	1150	1245	1250	1330	1415	1515	1545	1655	1705	1730	1805	1905	1915	2000	2050	2120	2130	2145	....	2245	2325

0545 on ⑤. b–2325 on ①③. ⚒–Daily except Sundays and holidays.
Calls by request. s–Calls to set down only. ∝–Local fares not available.
Runs on ① instead of ⑦ on holiday weekends. ①–Mondays. ⑤–Fridays.
Saturdays. ⑦–Sundays. †–Sundays and holidays. ⑧–Daily except Saturdays.
Saturdays, Sundays and holidays. Ⓡ–Reservation obligatory.

♿– Facilities for the disabled.
GLC– Greyhound Lines of Canada. ☎Calgary 403 265 9111.
RA– Red Arrow Deluxe Services. ☎Edmonton 403 468 6360.

Table 95 VANCOUVER - VERNON - KAMLOOPS

GLC

CA $	4	1258	1478	38	3012	34	32	1266	2	3008 ⑤	36	km	496 ↓ ↑	19	35	3009	1259	33	39	3017 ⑤	1681	21	1257	15
0.00	0115	....	....	0715	0730	1030	1230	....	....	1630	1800	*0*	d.**Vancouver**..........a.	....	1315	1430	....	1615	1935	2055	....	2235	....	053
	0140	....	....	0745	0800	1055	1255	....	....	|	1830	*20*	d.New Westminster......d.	....	s	s	....	s	s	|	....	s	....	s
	0205	....	....	|	*0725*	|	|	....	....	|	|	*55*	d.Langley..........d.	....	|	|	....	|	|	|	....	|	....	s
16.20	|	....	....	0925	0950	|	|	....	....	2020	2005	*174*	d.Hope..........d.	....	s	1215	....	|	s	1745	....	2020	....	s
29.40	0445	....	....	1120	|	|	1555	....	....	|	|	*282*	d.Merritt..........d.	....	|	|	....	s	1600	|	....	s	....	s
32.25	|	....	....	|	1210	|	|	....	....	2220	|	*308*	d.Princeton..........d.	....	|	1030	....	|	|	1545	....	|	....	|
39.10	|	....	....	|	1310	|	|	....	....	2310	|	*376*	d.Keremeos..........d.	....	|	0910	....	|	|	1430	....	|	....	|
41.75	|	0730	0920	|	1415	|	|	*1700*	*1700*	2350	|	*423*	d.Penticton..........d.	*0910*	|	0830	*1200*	|	|	1345	1415	|	2015	|
43.90	|	|	0940	|	1430	|	|	|	|	....	|	*410*	d. Okanagan Falls..d.	|	|	0755	|	|	|	....	1305	|	|	|
43.95	|	|	1030	|	1530	|	|	|	|	....	|	*454*	d. Osoyoos..........d.	|	|	0705	|	|	|	....	1220	|	|	|
48.95	|	|	1125	|	1610	|	|	|	|	....	|	*505*	a. Rock Creek..........d.	|	|	0615	|	|	|	....	1125	|	|	|
43.25	0745	0900	0800	1345	....	1550	1750	1835	1835	....	2340	*487*	d.Kelowna..........d.	0745	0800	....	1035	1045	1400	....	1530	1730	1900	234
46.10	0840	0955	....	1440	....	....	....	1930	1935	....	0020	*538*	d.Vernon..........d.	0650	....	....	0945	....	1245	....	....	1515	1805	203
46.10	|	|	....	1535	....	....	....	2035	2100	....	....	*583*	d. Salmon Arm..........d.	0540	....	....	|	....	....	....	....	|	|	192
46.10	|	1215	....	....	....	....	....	2225	|	....	....	*650*	d.**Kamloops**..........d.	|	....	....	0800	....	....	....	....	|	1615	....
46.10	|	1320	....	....	....	....	....	2330	|	....	....	*742*	a.Cache Creek..........d.	|	....	....	0515	....	....	....	....	|	1440	....
56.75	1105	....	....	....	....	....	....	....	2240	....	....	*685*	a. Revelstoke..........d.	0400	....	....	....	....	....	....	....	1255	....	....
92.00	1825	....	....	....	....	....	....	....	0525	....	....	*1105*	a. *Calgary*..........d.	2315	....	....	....	....	....	....	....	0730	....	....

s– Calls to set down only.
GLC– Greyhound Lines of Canada. ☎ Vancouver 604 662 3222.

Table 96 TORONTO - WINNIPEG - VANCOUVER ♿

GLC

SUMMARY TABLE

CA $												km	496 ↓ SUMMARY TABLE ↑											
0.00	....	0100A	....	....	....	....	1230A	....	1700A	....	....	*0*	d.**Toronto**..........a.	....	0550D	....	....	1515D	....	1745D	....	....	....	....
51.65	....	0600A	....	....	....	....	1800A	....	2215A	....	....	*397*	a. Sudbury..........d.	....	0050D	....	....	1000D	....	1245D	....	....	....	....
	....	0715A	....	....	....	....	1915A	....	2315A	....	....		d. Sudbury..........a.	....	2340C	....	....	0855D	....	1135D	....	....	....	....
139.00	....	0810B	....	....	....	....	1825B	....	2255B	....	....	*2137*	a. Winnipeg..........d.	....	2200B	....	....	0730C	....	1030C	....	....	....	....
	....	1000B	....	....	1300A	....	1900B	....	2345B	....	....		d. Winnipeg..........a.	....	2140B	....	....	0600B	....	0910C	....	....	....	173
187.00	....	1745B	....	....	2050A	....	0125C	....	0555C	....	....	*2721*	a. Regina..........d.	....	1210B	....	....	2100A	....	0035C	....	....	....	073
	....	1830B	....	....	2120A	....	0140C	....	0640C	....	....		d. Regina..........a.	....	1125B	r....	....	2005A	....	0015C	....	....	....	063
227.00	....	0530C	....	....	0710B	....	1145C	....	1740C	....	....	*3505*	a. Calgary..........d.	....	0030B	....	....	0830A	....	1400B	....	....	....	200
	....	0730C	....	....	....	....	1215C	....	1830C	....	....		d. Calgary..........a.	....	2220A	....	....	....	....	1030B	1040B	....	....	....
265.65	....	2015C	....	....	....	....	0125D	....	0745D	....	....	*4590*	a.**Vancouver**..........d.	....	0700A	....	....	....	....	1830A	2045A	....	....	....

A– 1st day. B–2nd day. C–3rd day. D–4th day. ♿–Facilities for the disabled. *GLC*–Greyhound Lines of Canada. ☎ Calgary 403 265 9111.

Table 97 CALGARY - BANFF - CRANBROOK

GLC

CA $				1155	km	396 ↓ ↑			1676	
0.00	....	....	....	1830	*0*	d.**Calgary**..........a.	....	....	1850	....
15.75	....	....	....	2035	*127*	d.Banff..........d.	....	....	1705	....
30.50	....	....	....	2230	*252*	d.Radium Hot Springs.d.	....	....	1450	....
43.82	....	....	....	0030	*381*	d.Kimberley..........d.	....	....	1235	....
47.08	....	....	....	0100	*408*	a.**Cranbrook**..........d.	....	....	1201	....

GLC– Greyhound Lines of Canada. ☎ Calgary 403 265 9111.

Table 98 EDMONTON - SWAN HILLS

GLC

CA $			123 ①④⑤⑦	127 ②③	km	396		128 ③④	126 ①②⑤⑥	
0.00	....	....	1830	1830	*0*	d.**Edmonton**..........a.	....	1040	1040	....
11.00	....	....	1950	1950	*90*	d.Westlock..........d.	....	0900	0900	....
	....	....	|	|	*138*	a. Drayton Valley d.	....	|	|	....
15.30	....	....	2030	2030	*131*	d.Barrhead..........d.	....	0830	0830	....
26.10	....	....	2145	....	*230*	a.**Swan Hills**..........d.	....	....	0715	....

①– Mondays. ②–Tuesdays. ③–Wednesdays. ④–Thursdays.
⑤– Fridays. ⑥–Saturdays. ⑦–Sundays.
GLC– Greyhound Lines of Canada. ☎ Edmonton 403 421 4211.

Table 100 COLUMBIA ICEFIELD

BRW

CA $		⛷			km	396 ↓ ↑			☞	✈
0.00	....	1130	1440	1655	*0*	d.**Calgary**..........a.	1100	1500	1830	2130a
30.00	....	1430	1715	1945	*127*	d.Banff..........a.	0805	1200	1545	1815
34.00	....	1600	....	2050	*187*	d.Lake Louise..........d.	0715	1115	....	1715
	....	1830	....	....	*262*	d.Columbia Icefield d.	....	....	....	1500
53.00	....	2020	....	....	*415*	a.**Jasper**..........d.	....	....	....	1250

a– June 1-Sept. 30. ⛷–May 31-Sept. 29. ☞–Apr. 8-Oct. 25. ✈–Apr. 13-Oct. 29.
BRW– Brewster's Transportation. ☎ Banff 403 762 6767.

Table 101 CALGARY - KELOWNA

GLC SB

CA $	1575	5003 ex①⑦	1375		km	496 ↓ GLC ↑		1476	1676	115
0.00	0630	....	2130	....	*0*	d.**Calgary**..........a.	....	0820	1850	194
20.40	0935	....	0005	....	*75*	d.Fort MacLeod....a.	....	0520	|	153
37.45	1250	....	0250	....	*340*	d.Fernie..........d.	....	0255	|	130
40.60	1310	....	0310r	....	*372*	d.Elko..........d.	....	r	|	123
45.65	1425	....	0430	....	*441*	d.Cranbrook..........d.	....	0140	1201c	114
52.35	1415	....	0415	....	*595*	d.Yahk..........d.	....	2320	0840	....
56.70	1505	....	0510	....	*645*	d.Creston..........d.	....	2250	0805	....
65.40	1700	....	0700	....	*730*	d.Salmo..........d.	....	2120	0645	....
69.70	1750	1200	0750	....	*770*	d.Nelson..........d.	....	2030	0520	....
	1800a	*1100b*	*0800a*	....	✪*37*	d. Trail..........a.	....	*2030a*	*0500a*	....
74.25	1840	1245	0835	....	*808*	d.Castlegar..........a.	....	1925	0420	....
74.25	2020	1425	1015	....	*899*	d.Grand Forks......d.	....	1805	0300	....
74.25	2055	1455	1050	....	*936*	d.Greenwood..........d.	....	1640	0211	....
74.25	2135	1530	1125	....	*968*	d.Rock Creek..........d.	....	1615	0145	....
74.25	|	|	|	....	*1019*	d.Osoyoos..........d.	....	|	|	....
74.25	|	|	|	....	*1065*	d.Okanagan Falls.d.	....	|	|	....
74.25	|	|	|	....	*1086*	a. Penticton..........d.	....	|	|	....
74.25	2320	1715	1315	....	*1149*	a.**Kelowna**..........d.	....	1415	0001	....

a– Connection by *SB*.
b– No service on ⑥. Note a applies.
c– Arr. 1040. r–Calls by request.
①– Mondays. ⑥–Saturdays. ⑦–Sundays. ✪–Km ex Castlegar.
GLC– Greyhound Lines of Canada. ☎ Calgary 403 265 9111.
SB– Dewdney Coach Lines Ltd. ☎ Trail 604 368 5555.

Table 102 FORT ST.JAMES

NB

CA $		①a		④b	km	396 ↓ ↑	②-⑤b	①a	⑤b	
0.00	....	0715	....	1600	*0*	d.**Prince George**..a.	1110	1210	2110	....
	....	0830	....	1720	*92*	d.Vanderhoof..........d.	0950	1050	1950	....
	....	0920	....	1815	*136*	a.**Fort St.James**..d.	0900	1000	1900	....

a– Runs on ② when ① is a holiday. b–Runs on ④ when ⑤ is a holiday.
①– Mondays. ②–Tuesdays. ④–Thursdays. ⑤–Fridays.
NBL- Northland Bus Lines. ☎ Victoria 604 388 5248.

Table 103 VANCOUVER - KAMLOOPS - CALGARY ♿

GLC

CA $	62 Ⓡ	38	22	2		6	64 Ⓡ	1256	4	20	1676	km	496 ↓ ↑	1		61 Ⓡ	21	63	15	1155	1253	11	19	9
0.00	0700	0715	1330	....	....	1830	2045	2045	0115	....	....	*0*	d.**Vancouver**..........a.	1645	....	2015	2235	0125	0530	....	0555	0745	....	125
4.00	0730	0745	1400	....	....	1900	2110	2110	0140	....	....	*20*	d.New Westminster......d.	s	....	s	s	s	s	....	s	s	....	s
5.15	0835	0850	1505	....	....	2005	|	2215	0245	....	....	*109*	d.Chilliwack..........d.	1455	....	s	2105s	s	s	....	0420	0510	....	112
16.20	0910	0925	1540	....	....	2035	|	|	|	....	....	*174*	d.Hope..........d.	1420	....	|	2020	|	s	....	s	s	....	s
29.40	|	|	1710	....	....	2210	|	|	|	....	....	*282*	d.Merritt..........d.	1235	....	|	s	|	s	....	s	s	....	092
38.60	1230	|	1900	....	....	2355	0125	0100	|	0745	....	*449*	d.Kamloops..........d.	1130	....	1600	|	2115	|	....	0125	0235	....	081
46.10	1405	1535	2035	2100	....	0115	|	....	|	0930	....	*554*	d.Salmon Arm..........d.	0925	....	1350	|	1915	1920	....	....	0055	0525	054
56.75	1550	....	....	2310	....	0245	0410	....	1110	1110	....	*665*	d.Revelstoke..........d.	0800	....	1225	1255	1740	....	....	....	2340	0400	....
72.10	1905	....	....	0215	....	0555	0735	....	1430	1430	....	*816*	d.Golden..........d.	....	....	1105	1125	1615	....	....	....	2230	0300	....
82.40	|	....	....	0320	....	0710	|	....	1545	1545	....	*898*	d.Lake Louise..........d.	....	....	|	1000	1445	....	....	....	2115	0135	....
90.10	2045	....	....	0410	....	0815	|	....	1640	1640	1705	*958*	d.Banff..........d.	....	....	0910	0915	1400	....	2020	....	2030	0050	....
92.00	2220	....	....	0525	....	1030	1040	....	1825	1825	1850	*1085*	a.**Calgary**..........d.	....	....	0730	0730	1215	....	1830	....	1830	2315	....

s– Calls to set down only.
Ⓡ– Reservation obligatory.
♿– Facilities for the disabled.
GLC– Greyhound Lines of Canada. ☎ Calgary 403 265 9111.

able 104 VANCOUVER - EDMONTON - WINNIPEG ♿

GLC SAS

CA $		SAS 8/801/2 ex⑦	GLC 1428	GLC 1632	GLC 76	GLC 1826 Ⓡ	SAS 803 ⑦	GLC 143 ②④⑦	GLC 1172 ⑧	GLC 72 Ⓡ	GLC 1628	km	496 ↓ ↑	GLC 1531	GLC 75 Ⓡ	GLC 71 Ⓡ	SAS 13 ①②⑤	GLC 1527	GLC 1723 ②④	GLC 144 ②④	GLC 1729	GLC 1171 ex⑦	GLC 1327	
0.00	....	....	1330	....	....	1830	....	....	....	0700	....	0	d.**Vancouver** a.	....	....	1230	....	2055	....	....	....	....	1010	....
4.00	....	....	1400	....	....	1900	....	....	....	0730	....	20	d.New Westminster d.	....	....	s	....	s	....	....	....	....	s	....
5.15	....	....	1505	....	....	2005	....	....	....	0835	....	109	d.Chilliwack d.	....	....	1105s	....	1915	....	....	....	....	0830	....
6.20	....	....	|	....	....	2040	....	....	....	|	....	174	d.Hope d.	....	....	s	....	|	....	....	....	....	0750	....
9.40	....	....	|	....	....	2210	....	....	....	1035	....		d.Merritt d.	....	....	|	....	1715	....	....	....	....	0620	....
8.60	....	....	1915	....	....	0005	....	....	....	1210	....	449	d.Kamloops d.	....	....	0815	....	1615	....	....	....	....	0520	....
2.85	....	....	2230	....	....	0310	....	....	....	1535	....		d.Blue River d.	....	....	0450	....	1250	....	....	....	....	0205	....
2.20	....	....	2335	0335	....	0415	....	....	....	1640	....		d.Valemount d.	....	....	|	....	1110	....	....	....	....	0045	....
0.55	....	....	0210	0605	....	0650	....	....	....	1915	....		d.Jasper d.	0245	....	0315	....	1040	....	....	....	....	0020	....
8.85	....	....	0320	0705	....	0750	....	....	....	2015	....		d.Hinton d.	0150	....	|	....	0935	....	....	....	....	2310	....
8.40	....	....	0415	0830	....	0915	....	....	....	2130	....		d.Edson d.	0030	....	|	....	0835	....	....	....	....	2210	....
5.50	....	....	0640	1130	....	1140	....	....	....	2345	....		a. **Edmonton** d.	2200	....	2300	....	0600	....	....	....	....	1930	....
	....	....	0800	....	1330	1330	....	1830	1830	....	0001		d. **Edmonton** a.	[redacted]	2245	[redacted]	....	0545	....	1030	1235	1255	1905	....
6.25	....	....	0915	....	1445	|	....	|	1945	....	0115		d.Vegreville d.	....	|	....	....	0425	....	|	|	1141	1750	....
0.75	....	....	|	....	|	1500	....	2030	|	....	|		d. Viking d.	....	|	....	....	|	....	0834	1105	|	|	....
2.95	....	....	1150	....	1655	|	....	|	2145	....	0325		d.Lloydminster d.	....	2000	....	....	0240	....	|	|	0940	1555	....
8.75	....	....	|	....	|	1620	....	2125	....	....	|		d. Wainwright d.	SAS	|	....	....	|	....	0745	0920	....	|	....
	....	....	|	....	|	|	....	[redacted]	....	....	|		a. Chauvin d.	7	|	....	....	|	....	[redacted]	|	....	|	....
29.10	....	0800	|	....	|	|	1230	....	....	....	|		d. Meadow Lake a.	2020	|	....	....	|	....	....	|	....	|	....
4.00	....	1015d	1340	....	1820	1830	1530	....	....	....	0505		d.North Battleford d.	1920	1805	....	1900	0035	....	....	0750	....	1340	....
4.00	....	1145c	1515	....	2000	2010	1700	....	....	....	0655		a. Saskatoon d.	1630	1630	....	1715	2300	....	....	0615	....	1201	....
	....	....	1700a	....	....	2100	[redacted]	....	....	....	0725		d. Saskatoon a.	....	....	....	....	2125	....	....	0545	....	1120b	....
8.00	....	....	1910a	....	....	|	....	GLC	....	....	0925		d.Dafoe d.	....	....	....	....	1930	....	GLC	|	....	0910	....
8.00	....	....	1950a	....	....	2320	GLC	**1830**	....	....	1005		d.Wynyard d.	....	....	....	....	1905	....	**1725**	0330	....	0845b	....
8.00	....	....	2140a	....	....	0105	**1832**	①③⑤	....	....	1240		d.Yorkton d.	....	....	....	....	1655	....	①③⑤⑦	0200	....	0645b	....
8.00	....	....	....	....	....	|	②④⑥	0816	....	....	1605		d.Dauphin d.	....	....	....	....	1441	....	2320	|	....	....	....
8.00	....	....	....	....	....	0345	0730	|	....	....	|		d. Russell d.	....	....	....	....	|	0000	|	0125	....	....	....
8.00	....	....	....	....	....	0520	0940	|	....	....	|		d. Minnedosa d.	....	....	....	....	|	2150	|	2325	....	....	....
8.00	....	....	....	....	....	|	1020	1030	....	....	1820		d.Neepawa d.	....	....	....	....	1235	2125	2125	|	....	....	....
8.00	....	....	....	....	....	0820	1125	1135	....	....	1935		d.Portage la Prairie d.	....	....	....	....	1045	1950	1950	2015	....	....	....
8.00	....	....	....	....	....	0945	1300	1300	....	....	2045		a.**Winnipeg** d.	....	....	....	....	0930	1830	1830	1900	....	....	....

-⑤. b–Ex ⑦. c–1205 on ①④, 1245 on ⑤. d–1110 on ⑤. s–Calls to set down only. ■–Fare ex Saskatoon. ①–Mondays. ②–Tuesdays. ③–Wednesdays. ④–Thursdays. ⑤–idays. ⑥–Saturdays. ⑦–Sundays. ⑧–Daily except Saturdays. Ⓡ–Reservation obligatory. ♿–Facilities for the disabled. *GLC*–Greyhound Lines of Canada. ☎Edmonton 403 421 11.

able 105 CALGARY - WINNIPEG

GLC SAS

$		GLC 12		SAS 36 ①③⑤ξ	GLC 56 ⑤⑦		SAS 361	GLC 2	SAS 78 ①③⑤⑦		GLC 64 Ⓡ	GLC 1826		GLC 10		km	496 ↓ ↑	SAS 551 Ⓐ			GLC 3		SAS 51 ①③⑤⑦	SAS 35 ①③⑤ξ	SAS 351 ②-⑤	GLC 55 ⑤⑦	GLC 5		GLC 1729	GLC 63 Ⓡ	GLC 11	
.00	....	0030	....	....	....	....	....	0830	....	....	1400	....	....	2000	....	0	d.**Calgary** a.	....	....	....	0530	....	....	....	....	....	0710	....	....	1145	1740	....
.30	....	0210	....	....	....	....	....	1040	....	....	|	....	....	2155	....		d.Bassano d.	....	....	....	0325	....	....	....	....	....	0510	....	....	0940	1535	....
.35	....	0240	....	....	....	....	....	1130	....	....	1610	....	....	2245	....		d.Brooks d.	....	....	....	0305	....	....	....	....	....	0440	....	....	0908	1505	....
.15	....	0430	....	....	....	....	....	1320	....	....	1800	....	....	0030	....	306	d.Medicine Hat d.	....	....	....	0150	....	....	....	....	....	0325	....	....	0745	1355	....
.10	....	0545	....	....	....	....	....	1430	....	....	1915	....	....	0145	....		d.Maple Creek d.	....	....	....	0015	....	....	....	....	....	0200	....	....	0605	1210	....
.50	....	0800	....	....	....	....	....	1650	....	....	2120	....	....	0340	....	533	d.Swift Current d.	....	....	....	2235	....	....	....	....	....	0035	....	....	0440	1030	....
.15	....	1025	....	1135	....	....	1605	1910	2045	....	2320	....	....	0535	....	713	d.Moose Jaw d.	0805	....	....	1940	....	1825	1825	1855	....	2210	....	....	s	0745	....
.30	....	1210	....	1230	....	....	1700	2100	2140	....	0035	....	....	0730	....	784	d.**Regina** d.	0700	....	....	1830	....	1730	1730	1800	....	2120	....	....	0140	0640	....
.85	....	1310	....	....	....	....	....	2135s	....	....	|	....	....	0830	....	853	d.Indian Head d.	....	....	....	1650	....	....	....	....	....	2000	....	....	|	0500	....
.60	....	1455	....	....	....	....	....	2330	....	....	|	....	....	1010	....		d.Whitewood d.	....	....	....	1530	....	....	....	....	....	1840	....	....	|	0356	....
.00	....	1530	....	....	....	....	....	0000	....	....	|	....	....	1045	....	1007	d.Moosomin d.	....	....	....	1440	....	....	....	....	....	1750	....	....	|	0324	....
.70	....	1725	....	....	....	....	....	0200	....	....	0455	....	....	1240	....	1163	d.Virden d.	....	....	....	1500	....	....	....	....	....	1800	....	....	2320	0340	....
.95	....	1855	....	....	1715	....	....	0315	....	....	0645	0645	....	1430	....	1252	d.Brandon d.	....	....	....	1345	....	....	....	....	1530	1610	....	2205	2215	0240	....
.50	....	2030	....	....	|	....	....	0425	....	....	|	0820	....	1555	....	1282	d.Portage la Prairie d.	....	....	....	1125	....	....	....	....	|	1425	....	2015	|	0055	....
.00	....	2140	....	....	1945	....	....	0600	....	....	0910	0945	....	1735	....	1368	a.**Winnipeg** d.	....	....	....	1000	....	....	....	....	1300	1300	....	1900	1900	2345	....

-Calls to set down only. ξ–Does not run on ① of holiday weekends. ①–Mondays. ③–Wednesdays. ⑤–Fridays. ⑦–Sundays. Ⓐ–Mondays to Fridays except holidays. ⑧–Daily cept Saturdays. Ⓡ–Reservation obligatory.
LC– Greyhound Lines of Canada. ☎Calgary 403 265 9111. *SAS*–Saskatchewan Transportation Co. ☎Saskatoon 306 664 5700.

able 106 TORONTO - WINNIPEG

GLC

CA $	3	1077 ⑦	47 ex③⑦	7	49 ③	45 ⑦		63 Ⓡ	1079 ex⑦		11	km	496 ↓ ↑		12	1080 ⑧	2 Ⓡ		64 Ⓡ	1082 ⑥	50	48 ex③	52 ③	
0.00	0100	....	....	....	....	....	....	1230	....	....	1700	0	d.**Toronto** a.	....	0550	....	1515	....	1745	....	....	....	....	....
3.65	0715	....	....	1315	....	....	....	1915	....	....	2315	397	d.Sudbury a.	....	2340	....	0855	....	1135	....	1645	....	....	....
2.65	0820	....	....	1420	....	....	....	2017	....	....	0015		d.Espanola d.	....	2230	....	0750	....	1023	....	1532	....	....	....
0.00	0912	....	....	1512	....	....	....	2107	....	....	s		d.Serpent River d.	....	2140	....	r	....	0928	....	1436	....	....	....
7.70	1245	....	....	1750	....	....	....	2355	....	....	0315	710	d.Sault Ste. Marie d.	....	1920	....	0440	....	0715	....	1215	....	....	....
6.25	1545	....	....	....	....	....	....	s	....	....	0605		d.Wawa d.	....	1550	....	0145	....	0340	....	....	....	....	....
8.25	1647	....	....	....	....	....	....	0400	....	....	0717	1038	d.White River d.	....	1407	....	0040	....	0240	....	....	....	....	....
8.25	1835	....	....	....	....	....	....	0505	....	....	0906		d.Marathon d.	....	1255	....	2320	....	|	....	....	....	....	....
8.25	2010	....	....	....	....	....	....	r	....	....	1035		d.Schreiber d.	....	1120	....	2145	....	|	....	....	....	....	....
9.00	2120	2120	....	....	....	....	....	s	1105	....	1155	1318	d.Nipigon d.	....	1010	2015	2035	....	2300	0000	....	....	....	....
9.00	0005	2250	....	....	....	....	....	1000	1235	....	1415	1427	d.Thunder Bay d.	....	0840	1845	1905	....	2135	2230	....	....	....	....
9.00	0140	....	....	....	....	....	....	1150	....	....	1605		d.Upsala d.	....	0545	....	1620	....	1900	....	....	....	....	....
9.00	0205	....	....	....	....	....	....	1205	....	....	1630		d.Ignace d.	....	0335	....	1355	....	1635	....	....	....	....	....
9.00	0330	....	0700	....	0700	1350	....	1350	....	....	1830	1790	d.Dryden d.	....	0225	....	1240	....	1525	....	....	2315	2345	....
9.00	0530	....	0850	....	0850	1535	....	1535	....	....	2025	1926	d.Kenora d.	....	0035	....	1025	....	1315	....	....	2130	2200	....
9.00	0810	....	1115	....	1205	1805	....	1825	....	....	2255	2137	a.**Winnipeg** d.	....	2200	....	0730	....	1030	....	....	1830	1830	....

Calls by request. s–Calls to set down only. ③–Wednesdays. ⑥–Saturdays. ⑦–Sundays. ⑧–Daily except Saturdays. Ⓡ–Reservation obligatory. *GLC*–Greyhound Lines of anada. ☎Winnipeg 204 783 8840.

able 107 SASKATOON - YORKTON

SAS

CA $	62 ex⑦	94	6 ①③⑤	72 ⚒	km	396 ↓ ↑	5 ①③⑤	71 ⚒	95	61
7.55	0715	....	1715	1645	0	d.**Saskatoon** a.	1210	1155	....	2130
	|	....	1853	|		d. Watrous d.	1035	|	....	|
8.10	0840	....	|	1830	112	d.Humboldt d.	|	1010	....	2005
	0930	....	|	1930		d.Watson d.	|	0930	....	1930
	1010	....	|	2015		d.Wadena d.	|	0830	....	1830
	|	....	1937	|		d. Nokomis d.	0950	|	....	|
	|	....	2030	|		d. Raymore d.	0905	|	....	|
1.05	|	0845	|	|	⁓243	d. **Regina** a.	|	|	2115	|
8.65	|	1035	2238	|	⁓93	d. Melville d.	0650	|	1920	|
5.25	|	1145	....	|	⁓49	d. Yorkton d.	....	|	1845	|
0.00	1120	1235	....	2135a	296	d.Canora d.	....	0710a	1740	1715
5.25	1205	|	....	|	339	a.**Yorkton** d.	....	|	|	1630
	....	|	....	2245		a.Norquay d.	....	0600	|	....
3.20	....	1445	....	....	431	a. Swan River d.	....	....	1530	....

- ①③⑤ only ⁓–Km ex Canora. ①–Mondays. ③–Wednesdays.
- Fridays. ⑦–Sundays. ⚒–Daily except Sundays and holidays.
AS– Saskatchewan Transportation Co. ☎Saskatoon 306 664 5700.

Table 108 REGINA - GAINSBOROUGH

SAS

CA $	902	90 ④⑤	92 ①②③⑦		km	396 ↓ ↑	93 ①②③④	91 ⑤⑥	903 ⑥⑦	904 Ⓐ
0.00	1135	1730	1730	....	0	d.**Regina** a.	1205	1205	1715	2115
10.90	1310	1730	1930	....	117	d.Weyburn d.	1030	1030	1545	1945
18.20	1415	2055	2040	....	204	d.Estevan d.	0915	0915	1435	1830
28.35	....	2245	....	....	323	a.**Gainsborough** d.	....	0710	....	....

①–Mondays. ②–Tuesdays. ③–Wednesdays. ④–Thursdays. ⑤–Fridays. ⑥–Saturdays. ⑦–Sundays. Ⓐ–Mondays to Fridays except holidays. *SAS*–Saskatchewan Transportation Co. ☎Regina 306 787 3346.

Table 109 MATAGAMI

ANO

CA $	1		3 ⑧	5	km	396 ↓ ↑	2	4 ⑧		6
0.00	0630	....	1530	2245	0	d.**Val d'Or** a.	0920	2345	....	0040
	0725	....	1705	2340	70	d.Amos d.	0800	2250	....	2345
	....	....	1945	....	284	a.**Matagami** d.	....	2030	....	....

⑧– Daily except Saturdays.
ANO– Autobus Norouest Inc. ☎Rouyn Noranda 842 2281.

Table 110 EDMONTON - FORT McMURRAY ♿

Bus GLC RA

CA $	GLC 181 ex⑦Ⓡ	GLC 133 Ⓡ⑦	GLC 251 ex⑦	RA 18 ⑤		GLC 105 Ⓡ	RA 20		GLC 129	GLC 253 Ⓑ		km	496 ↓ ↑		GLC 250 ex⑦	GLC 130	RA 19		GLC 106 Ⓡ			RA 17 ④⑤	GLC 252 Ⓑ	GLC 134 Ⓡ
0.00	0015	0730	....	1030	....	1300	1730	....	1800	....	....	0	d.**Edmonton** ....a.	....	....	1210	1530	....	1700	....	....	2230	....	2245
9.95	|	|	....	|	....	|	|	....	1910	....	....		d.Thorhild ....d.	....	....	1110	|	....	|	....	....	|	....	|
17.20	|	0905	....	1215	....	|	1915	....	2005	....	....		d.Boyle ....d.	....	....	1015	1345	....	|	....	....	2045	....	|
16.80	0155	|	....	|	....	1450	|	....	|	....	....		d. Athabasca ....d.	....	....	|	|	....	1500	....	....	|	....	2100
20.65	|	0925	1000	1235	....	1525	1935	....	2045	2030	....		d.Grassland ....d.	....	0930	0955	1325	....	1425	....	....	2025	2015	2025
26.40	|	|	1035	|	....	|	|	....	|	2105	....		a. Lac la Biche ....d.	....	0855	|	|	....	|	....	....	|	1940	|
26.20	|	1010	....	|	....	1620	|	....	2115	....	....		d.Wandering River ....d.	....	....	0910	|	....	1355	....	....	|	....	1955
37.25	0515	1230	....	1330	....	1830	2230	....	2335	....	....	440	a.**Fort McMurray** ....d.	....	....	0700	1030	....	1130	....	....	1730	....	1730

④– Thursdays. ⑤–Fridays. ⑦–Sundays. Ⓡ–Reservation obligatory.
♿– Facilities for the disabled.
GLC– Greyhound Lines of Canada. ☎Edmonton 403 421 4211.
RA– Red Arrow Deluxe Services. ☎Edmonton 403 468 6360.

Table 113 TORONTO - DETROIT ♿

Bus GLC

CA $	2111 Ⓡ	89/93/97 Ⓡ	2109	367 Ⓡ	2163	2113/5 Ⓡ	2135	357/9 Ⓡ	2125 ⑤⑦	2145	2141 ①⑤⑥	km	396 ↓ ↑	362	2136	92/88 Ⓡ	2164	366 Ⓡ	2134/52 Ⓡ	2122	2124	370/2 Ⓡ	2108	90 ⑤⑦
0.00	0830	1030d	0900	1230	1330	1430	1600	1830	2030	2330	0100	0	d.**Toronto** ....a.	0630	1015	1050e	1615	1305	1545f	1750	2045	2050	2350	2305
	|	|	0940	|	|	|	|	|	|	|	|		d. Mississauga ....d.	|	|	|	|	|	|	|	|	|	|	|
	|	|	|	|	|	|	1700	|	2100	|	|		d. Oakville ....d.	|	|	|	1525	|	|	|	|	|	s	|
7.25	|	|	1050	|	1450	|	1810	|	2120	0020	|		d.Hamilton ....d.	s	|	|	1425	|	|	|	|	|	2250	|
13.90	|	|	1130	|	1525	|	1845	|	2155	0055	|		d.Brantford ....d.	s	|	|	1350	|	|	|	|	|	2215	|
17.25	|	|	1210	|	1615	|	1935	|	|	s	|		d.Woodstock ....d.	|	0740	|	1305	|	|	|	1810	|	2145	|
21.75	1115	1250	1330	1515	1715	1730	2035	2110	2310	0210	0315		d.**London** ....d.	0355	0700	0830	1200	1030	1330	1530	1730	1830	2100	2045
39.00	|	....	|	|	....	|	....	|	....	....	|		a. Port Huron 🛃 ....d.	|	....	....	|	|	....	|	....	|	|	|
32.30	1245	....	1515	|	....	1905	....	2240	....	....	|		d.Chatham ....d.	|	....	....	1010	|	....	1325	....	|	1855	|
35.25	1310	....	1540	|	....	|	....	|	....	....	|		d.Tilbury ....d.	|	....	....	0945	|	....	|	....	|	|	|
40.35	1400	....	1720	1730	....	2010	....	2340	....	....	0545		a.Windsor 🛃 ....d.	0135	....	....	0805	0800	....	1220	....	1600	1800	1800
46.75	1430	....	....	1800	....	2040	....	0010	....	....	0615		a.**Detroit** ....d.	0110	....	....	0730	0730	....	1145	....	1535	1730	1730

d– Additional departures at 1630 and 2030. e–Additional departure at 1530. f–Additional departure at 1730. s–Calls to set down only. ①–Mondays. ⑤–Fridays.
⑥– Saturdays. ⑦–Sundays. Ⓡ–Reservation obligatory.
GLC– Greyhound Lines of Canada. ☎Toronto 416 393 7911.

Table 114 LONDON - WINDSOR

Bus GLC

CA $			2109		km	396 ↓ ↑	2164			
0.00	....	....	1330	....	0	d.**London** ....a.	1150	....	....	....
12.00	....	....	1515	....		d.Chatham ....d.	1010	....	....	....
14.75	....	....	1540	....		d.Tilbury ....d.	0945	....	....	....
17.85	....	....	1618	....		d.Leamington ....d.	0905	....	....	....
18.80	....	....	1636	....		d.Kingsville ....d.	0845	....	....	....
19.70	....	....	1720	....		a.**Windsor** ....d.	0805	....	....	....

GLC– Greyhound Lines of Canada. ☎Toronto 416 393 7911.

Table 115 QUÉBEC - DOLBEAU

Bus FOU

CA $					km	396 ↓ ↑				
0.00	....	1010	1410	1910	0	d.**Québec** ....a.	1215	....	1645	2045
	....	1240	1640	2140		d.Hébertville ....d.	0940	....	1400	1810
	....	1250	1650	2150		d. Alma ....d.	0930	....	1350	1800
	....	....	1735	2235		a.Chambord ....d.	0842	....	....	1712
	....	....	1905	0005		a.**Dolbeau** ....d.	0700	....	....	1530

FOU– Autocars Fournier. ☎Québec 688 1222.

Table 120 396 MONTRÉAL LOCAL SERVICES

╪╪╪ Bus STCUM STL

Local ╪╪╪ (C cl. only, 1.435m.) and (bus) services operate in the Montréal area as follows:

Anjou N *(STCUM)* (Ø km, CA $: Ø). From Honoré Beaugrand: 0500Ⓒ/0510Ⓐ and frequent to 0100ex⑦/0130⑦, returning at 0440Ⓐ/0530Ⓒ and frequent to 0130ex⑦/0200⑦. Journey: 15 mins.

Beaconsfield ♁ *(STCUM)* (Ø km, CA $: Ø). From Montréal Windsor: 0715Ⓐ, 0747Ⓐ, 1000Ⓐ, 1200⑥, 1220Ⓐ, 1330†, 1500⑥, 1538Ⓐ, 1640Ⓐ, 1700⚒, 1715†, 1718Ⓐ, 1725Ⓐ, 1745Ⓐ, 1830Ⓐ, 2000Ⓐ, 2100†, 2207Ⓐ, 2310⑥, returning at 0625Ⓐ, 0657Ⓐ, 0715Ⓐ, 0729Ⓐ, 0742Ⓐ, 0804Ⓐ, 0825Ⓐ, 0842Ⓐ, 0918⑥, 1126Ⓐ, 1243†, 1318⑥, 1449Ⓐ, 1618⑥, 1628†, 1727Ⓐ, 1754Ⓐ, 1843⑥, 2013†, 2123Ⓐ. Journey: 35 mins.

Côte Vertu ♁ *(STCUM)* (Ø km, CA $: Ø). From Montréal Berri UQAM: 0540 and frequent to 0048①/0049ex①⑦/0121⑦, returning at 0530 and frequent to 0030ex⑦/0101⑦. Journey: 30 mins.

Deux Montagnes ♁ *(STCUM)* (Ø km, CA $: Ø). From Montréal Central: 0030, 0710Ⓐ, 0745Ⓐ, 0800Ⓐ, 0855⚒, 0930Ⓐ, 1030⑥, 1130⚒, 1230Ⓐ, 1330⚒, 1430⑥, 1545⚒, 1645Ⓐ, 1720⚒, 1750⑥, 1810Ⓐ, 1830⚒, 1900Ⓐ, 1940Ⓐ, 2015⚒, 2115Ⓐ, 2215, 2315Ⓐ, returning at 0550Ⓐ, 0630Ⓐ, 0645⚒, 0700Ⓐ, 0740Ⓐ, 0800, 0944Ⓐ, 1044⚒, 1144Ⓐ, 1244, 1344Ⓐ, 1444⚒, 1538Ⓐ, 1640, 1805Ⓐ, 1835Ⓐ, 1925⚒, 2030⑥, 2130⚒, 2230Ⓐ, 2330. Journey: 40 mins.

Dorion ♁ *(STCUM)* (Ø km, CA $: Ø). From Montréal Windsor: 0715Ⓐ, 1000Ⓐ, 1200⑥, 1220Ⓐ, 1330†, 1500⑥, 1538Ⓐ, 1700⚒, 1715†, 1718Ⓐ, 1725Ⓐ, 1745Ⓐ, 1830Ⓐ, 2000Ⓐ, 2100†, 2207Ⓐ, 2310⑥, returning at 0606Ⓐ, 0639Ⓐ, 0653Ⓐ, 0722Ⓐ, 0742Ⓐ, 0824Ⓐ, 0901⑥, 1106Ⓐ, 1226†, 1301⑥, 1431Ⓐ, 1601⑥, 1611†, 1736Ⓐ, 1826⑥, 1956†, 2105Ⓐ. Journey: 1 hour.

Dorval ♁ *(STCUM)* (20 km, CA $: Ø). From Montréal Windsor: 0715Ⓐ, 0747Ⓐ, 1000Ⓐ, 1200⑥, 1220Ⓐ, 1330†, 1500⑥, 1538Ⓐ, 1640Ⓐ, 1700⚒, 1715†, 1718Ⓐ, 1725Ⓐ, 1745Ⓐ, 1830Ⓐ, 2000Ⓐ, 2100†, 2207Ⓐ, 2310⑥, returning at 0639Ⓐ, 0713Ⓐ, 0732Ⓐ, 0746Ⓐ, 0801Ⓐ, 0821Ⓐ, 0840Ⓐ, 0852Ⓐ, 0931⑥, 1141Ⓐ, 1256†, 1331⑥, 1502Ⓐ, 1631⑥, 1641†, 1738Ⓐ, 1806Ⓐ, 1856⑥, 2026†, 2135Ⓐ. Journey: 20 mins.

Hampstead N *(STCUM)* (Ø km, CA $: Ø). From Montréal: 0520Ⓐ/0530⑥/0600† and frequent to 0030ex⑦/0100⑦, returning at 0549Ⓐ/0600⑥/0630† and frequent to 0109ex⑦/0140⑦. Journey: 20 mins.

Lachenaie N *(STCUM)* (Ø km, CA $: Ø). From Montréal: Ø, returning at Ø. Journey: Ø.

Lasalle N *(STCUM)* (Ø km, CA $: Ø). From Angrignon: 0513Ⓐ/0530⑥/0555† and frequent to 0130ex⑦/0150⑦, returning at 0500Ⓐ/0515⑥/0540† and frequent to 0115ex⑦/0133⑦. Journey: 12 mins.

Laval N *(STVL)* (Ø km, CA $: Ø). From Montréal: Ø, returning at Ø. Journey: Ø.

Mascouche N *(STCUM)* (Ø km, CA $: Ø). From Montréal: Ø, returning at Ø. Journey: Ø.

Montréal Nord N *(STCUM)* (Ø km, CA $: Ø). From Cadillac: 0425Ⓐ/0428Ⓒ and frequent to 0125ex⑦/0155⑦, returning at 0458Ⓐ/0501Ⓒ and frequent to 0050, 0120⑦. Journey: Ø.

Outremont ♁ *(STCUM)* (Ø km, CA $: Ø). From Snowdon: 0530 and frequent to 2301, returning at 0545 and frequent to 2325. Journey: 10 mins.

Pointe aux Trembles N *(STCUM)* (Ø km, CA $: Ø). From Montréal: Ø, returning at Ø. Journey: Ø.

Repentigny N *(STCUM)* (Ø km, CA $: Ø). From Montréal: Ø, returning at Ø. Journey: Ø.

Rigaud ♁ *(STCUM)* (Ø km, CA $: Ø). From Montréal Windsor: 1718Ⓐ, returning at 0649Ⓐ. Journey: 1¼ hours.

St. Léonard N *(STCUM)* (Ø km, CA $: Ø). From Crémazie: 0456Ⓐ/0457⑥/0528† and frequent to 0125①/0130②-⑥/0208⑦, returning at 0440Ⓐ/0444⑥/0450† and frequent to 0053①/0058②-⑥/0136⑦. Journey: 25 mins.

Terrebonne N *(STCUM)* (Ø km, CA $: Ø). From Montréal: Ø, returning at Ø. Journey: Ø.

Val Royal ♁ *(STCUM)* (Ø km, CA $: Ø). From Montréal Central: 0015, 0440Ⓐ, 0515Ⓐ, 0545⑥, 0550Ⓐ, 0620Ⓐ, 0700⚒, 0730 0745Ⓐ, 0825Ⓐ, 0847Ⓐ, 0915⑥, 0945Ⓐ, 1045†, 1115⑥, 1145Ⓐ, 1345Ⓐ, 1445Ⓐ, 1545⚒, 1630Ⓐ, 1640Ⓐ, 1705Ⓐ, 1715†, 1720 1730⑥, 1735Ⓐ, 1750Ⓐ, 1815Ⓐ, 1830⚒, 1945Ⓐ, 2115Ⓐ, 2130Ⓒ, 2215Ⓐ, returning at 0139, 0610Ⓐ, 0650Ⓐ, 0701Ⓐ, 070 0724Ⓐ, 0740Ⓐ, 0751Ⓐ, 0805Ⓐ, 0821Ⓐ, 0824⑥, 0830Ⓐ, 0854†, 0855Ⓐ, 1009Ⓐ, 1039⑥, 1109Ⓐ, 1209†, 1239⑥, 1309Ⓐ, 150 1609Ⓐ, 1704⚒, 1715Ⓐ, 1745Ⓐ, 1810Ⓐ, 1839⑥, 1854⑥, 1900Ⓐ, 1919Ⓐ, 1954⑥, 2004Ⓐ, 2109Ⓐ, 2239Ⓐ, 2254Ⓒ, 233 Journey: 20 mins.

♁–By ╪╪╪. N–By (bus). Ø–Information not available at press date. ①–Mondays. ②–Tuesdays. ⑥–Saturdays. ⑦–Sundays. ⚒–Daily except Sundays and holidays. †– Sundays and holidays.
Ⓐ– Mondays to Fridays except holidays.
Ⓑ– Daily except Saturdays.
Ⓒ– Saturdays, Sundays and holidays.
STCUM–Société de Transport de la Communauté urbaine de Montréal. ☎Montréal 288 6287.
STVL– Société de Transport de la Ville de Laval. ☎Laval 688 65

Table 124 PRINCE ALBERT - LA RONGE

Bus SAS

CA $		224 ②④⑤⑦		73 ◊	km	396 ↓ ↑	74 ◊ex⑦		742 ◊⑦	
0.00	....	1630	....	1700	0	d.**Prince Albert** ....a.	1145	1330	1620	....
8.90	....	|	....	1910		d.Waskesiu ....d.	0935	|	1450	....
25.10	....	|	....	2015		a.**La Ronge** ....d.	0830	|	1345	....
	....	1840	....	....		d.Caribou Creek ....d.	....	1145	....	....
	....	2145	....	....		a.Creighton ....d.	....	0830	....	....

②– Tuesdays. ④–Thursdays.
⑤– Fridays. ⑦–Sundays.
◊– SUMMER SERVICE into WASKESIU effective May 9-Sept. 11.
SAS– Saskatchewan Transportation Co. ☎Saskatoon 306 664 5700.

Table 125 REGINA - NIPAWIN

Bus SAS

CA $	11 ex①	47	431 ⑦	43 Ⓑ	km	396 ↓ ↑	44 ex①⑦	441 ①	48	12
0.00	....	0845	1645	1645	0	d.**Regina** ....a.	1201	1201	2215	....
	....	1045	1845	1845		d.Dafoe ....d.	1005	1005	2015	....
	....	1115	1930	1930		d.Watson ....d.	0935	0935	1945	....
	1040	|	|	|		d. **Prince Albert** .a.	|	|	|	1945
	1230	1230	2100	2100		d.Melfort ....d.	0805	0805	1815	1805
	1305	|	2135	*2135*		d.Tisdale ....d.	|	0715	|	1730
	1350	|	2215	*2215*		a.**Nipawin** ....d.	|	0635	|	1645
	....	|	2245	*2245*		a.Carrot River ....d.	|	0600	|	....
	....	1345	....	2210		a.Prince Albert ....d.	0640	....	1645	....

①– Mondays.
⑦– Sundays.
Ⓑ– Daily except Saturdays.
SAS– Saskatchewan Transportation Co. ☎Regina 306 787 3346.

╪╪╪╪–Rail (bus)–Bus (ship)–Ship

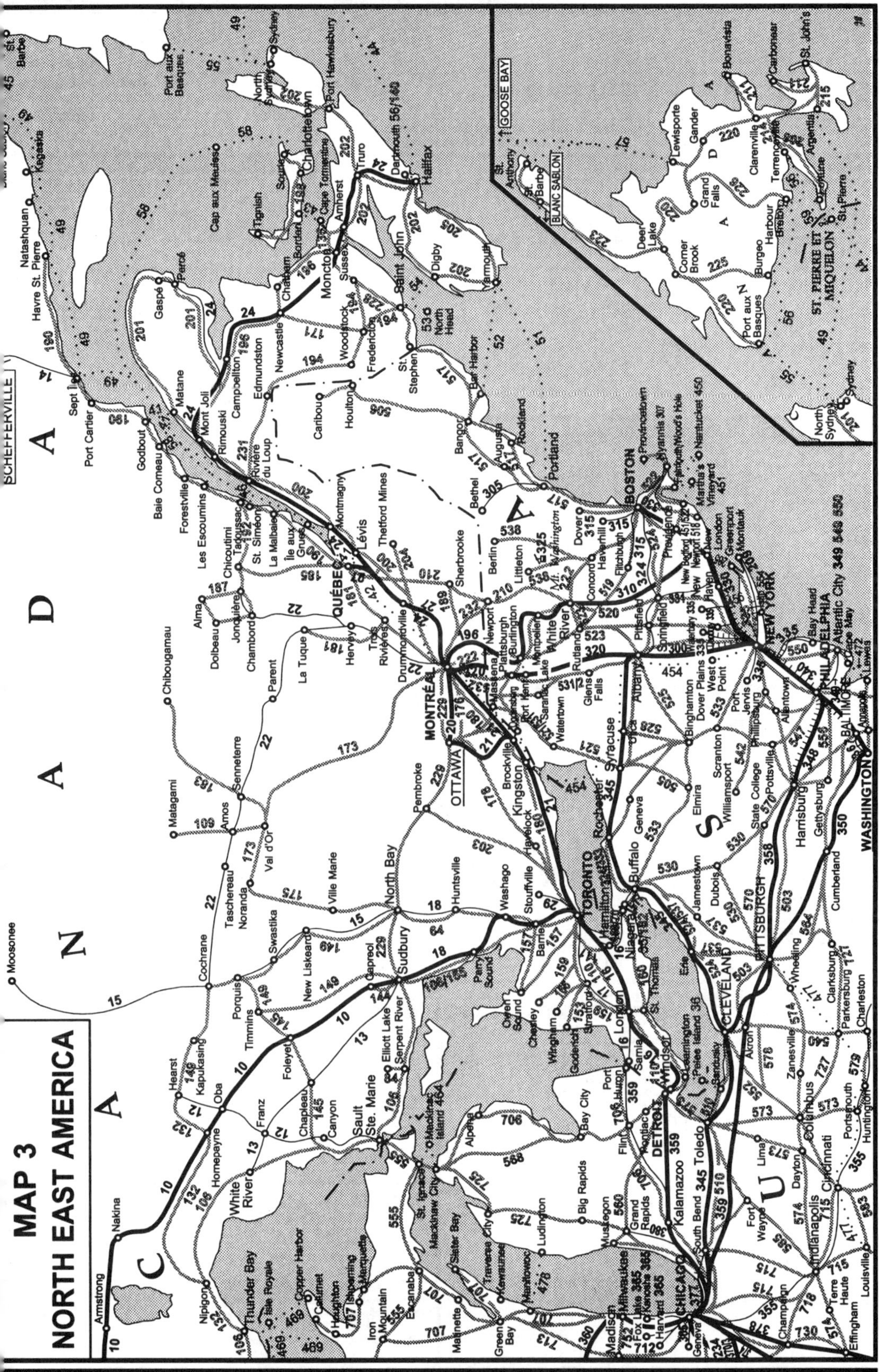
MAP 3
NORTH EAST AMERICA
C A N A D A
U S A
GOOSE BAY
BLANC SABLON
SCHEFFERVILLE
ST. PIERRE ET MIQUELON
MONTRÉAL
QUÉBEC
OTTAWA
TORONTO
BOSTON
NEW YORK
PHILADELPHIA
BALTIMORE
WASHINGTON
PITTSBURGH
CLEVELAND
DETROIT
CHICAGO
Halifax
Saint John
Moncton
Charlottetown
Sydney
Thunder Bay
Sudbury
North Bay
Cochrane
Moosonee
Sault Ste. Marie
Windsor
London
Hamilton
Niagara
Buffalo
Rochester
Syracuse
Albany
Kingston
Gaspé
Sept Îles
Rimouski
Trois Rivières
Sherbrooke
Portland
Bangor
Harrisburg
Toledo
Milwaukee
Indianapolis
Cincinnati
Columbus

Table 130 396 OTTAWA LOCAL SERVICES — OCRT STO

Local bus services operate in the Ottawa area as follows:
Britannia Bay *(OCRT)* (Ø km, CA $: Ø). From Ottawa: Ø, returning at Ø. Journey: Ø.
Carlington *(OCRT)* (Ø km, CA $: Ø). From Ottawa: Ø, returning at Ø. Journey: Ø.
Cyrville *(OCRT)* (Ø km, CA $: Ø). From Ottawa: Ø, returning at Ø. Journey: Ø.
Elwood *(OCRT)* (Ø km, CA $: Ø). From Ottawa: Ø, returning at Ø. Journey: Ø.
Gatineau *(STO)* (Ø km, CA $: Ø). From Ottawa: Ø, returning at Ø. Journey: Ø.
Hawthorne *(OCRT)* (Ø km, CA $: Ø). From Ottawa: Ø, returning at Ø. Journey: Ø.
Hull *(OCRT STO)* (Ø km, CA $: Ø). From Ottawa: 0500⚒/0900† and frequent to 2200, returning at 0530⚒/0930† and frequent to 2300. Journey: 15 mins.
New Edinburgh *(OCRT)* (Ø km, CA $: Ø). From Ottawa: Ø, returning at Ø. Journey: Ø.
Overbrook *(OCRT)* (Ø km, CA $: Ø). From Ottawa: Ø, returning at Ø. Journey: Ø.
Pointe Gatineau *(STO)* (Ø km, CA $: Ø). From Ottawa: Ø, returning at Ø. Journey: Ø.
Rockcliffe *(OCRT)* (Ø km, CA $: Ø). From Ottawa: Ø, returning at Ø. Journey: Ø.
Tetreau *(OCRT STO)* (Ø km,. CA $: Ø). From Ottawa: Ø, returning at Ø. Journey: Ø.
Vanier *(OCRT)* (Ø km, CA $: Ø). From Ottawa: Ø, returning at Ø. Journey: Ø.
Westboro *(OCRT)* (Ø km, CA $: Ø). From Ottawa: 0500⚒/0800† and frequent to 0030, returning at 0445⚒/0830† and frequent to 2350. Journey: 12 mins.

Ø–Information not available at press date. ⚒–Daily except Sundays and holidays. †–Sundays and holidays.
OCRT–OC TRANSPO – Ottawa Carleton Regional Transit Authority. ☎Ottawa 613 741 6440.
STO– Société de Transport de l'Ouatais. ☎Hull ❖.

Table 132 HEARST - THUNDER BAY — GLC

CA $	1079	1075		1077	km	496			1080	1082
	ex④⑦	④		⑦		↓ ↑			Ⓑ	⑥
0.00	0600	0600	....	1615	*0*	d.**Hearst**..............a.	....	....	0120	0505
3.35	r	0625	....	1640		d.Calstock ....d.	....	....	s	s
4.95	0645r	0645	....	1700r	Ø	d.Hornepayne.......d.	....	....	0035r	0420r
22.20	0820	0820	....	1835	Ø	d.Longlac ....d.	....	....	2300	0245
26.40	0850	0850	....	1905	Ø	d.Geraldton ....d.	....	....	2230	0215
34.00	1005	1005	....	2020	Ø	d.Beardmore ....d.	....	....	2130	0115
43.50	1105	1105	....	2120	Ø	d.Nipigon ....d.	....	....	2015	0015
54.70	1235	1235	....	2250	Ø	a.**ThunderBay** (PA)..d.	....	....	1845	2230

r– Calls by request.
s– Calls to set down only.
Ø– Information not available at press date.
④– Thursdays. ⑥–Saturdays. ⑦–Sundays.
Ⓑ– Daily except Saturdays.
GLC– Greyhound Lines of Canada. ☎Thunder Bay 807 345 2194.

Table 135 SASKATOON - HUDSON BAY — SAS

CA $	29	63	65	3	km	396	64	66	4	30
			⑤⑦a			↓ ↑		⑤		
0.00	0830	1400	1800	1800	*0*	d.**Saskatoon**........a.	1135	1540	1550	1950
3.25	r	r	|	1823	*30*	d.Warman ....d.	1112	|	r	r
13.20	0937	|	|	1920	*147*	d.Duck Lake ....d.	1015	|	1443	1843
13.20	1020	1550	1940	2005	*160*	a.**Prince Albert**....d.	0930	1400	1400	1800
	....	....	....	*2200*c		a.Nipawin ....d.	*0700*d	....	....	....
CA $	**83**	**9011**	**9012**	**9/901**	**km**	**296**	**82**	**10/101**	**1012**	**1011**
	②	①②③⑤	④	①-⑤			②	②-⑥	④	①②③
34.95		....	....	1745	*0*	d. **Saskatoon**......a.	....	1025b	....	....
22.95	1845	....	1845	|	*31*	d.**Prince Albert**....a.	0925	|	1015	....
14.45	2100	....	2100	2100	*112*	d.Melfort...............d.	0815	0815	0815	....
11.05	2130	2135	2135	2135	*151*	d.Tisdale ....d.	0730	0715	0730	0720
	....	|	|	2245		a.Carrot River.......d.	....	0600	|	|
0.00	....	2335	2310	....	*266*	a.**Hudson Bay**.....d.	....		0550	0525

a– Runs on ⑤① of holiday weekends. b–1115 on ②④. c–④⑤⑥ only. d–③④⑤ on
①– Mondays. ②–Tuesdays. ③–Wednesdays. ④–Thursdays.
⑤– Fridays. ⑥–Saturdays.
SAS– Saskatchewan Transportation Co. ☎Saskatoon 306 664 5700.

Table 134 CALGARY - LETHBRIDGE ♿ — GLC

CA $	496 ↓	km	1158	1198	1151	1157	1156	1141	1145	1375
			②④	ex②④						
0.00	**Calgary**................d.	*0*	....	....	0630	0700	....	1400	1845	2130
20.40	Fort MacLeod.......d.	*167*	0645	0645	0920	|	1600	1640	|	2345
26.00	**Lethbridge** ....a.	*219*	0730	0730	1000	0945	1645	1720	2200	....

496 ↓		1476	1198	1158	1575	1150	1152	1156		1145
			ex②④	②④						
Lethbridge ....d.	....	....	0745	0745	0830	1100	1400	1700	....	2200
Fort MacLeod.............d.	....	0545	|	|	0915	|	1445	|	....	2250
Calgary.....................a.	....	0820	1050	1055	....	1345	1735	1945	....	....

②– Tuesdays.
④– Thursdays.
♿– Facilities for the disabled.
GLC– Greyhound Lines of Canada. ☎Calgary 403 265 9111.

Table 137 WINNIPEG - RIVERTON — GG

CA $			025	025	km	396		026		026
			Ⓐ	†		↓ ↑		Ⓐ		†
0.00	....	....	1800	2030	*0*	d.**Winnipeg**..........a.	....	1000	....	1940
2.25	....	....	1840	2110	*33*	d.Selkirk ....d.	....	0920	....	1900
Ø	....	....	1900	2125		d.Petersfield ....d.	....	0900	....	1835
9.15	....	....	1920	2145		a.Winnipeg Beach d.	....	0830	....	1810
12.10	....	....	1945	2200	*89*	a.Gimli...................d.	....	0810	....	1750
17.10	....	....	2030	2230	*129*	a.**Riverton** ....d.	....	0720	....	1700

Ⓐ– Mondays to Fridays except holidays.
†– Sundays and holidays. Ø–Information not available at press date.
GG– Grey Goose Bus Lines. ☎Winnipeg 204 786 8891.

Table 138 WINNIPEG - THOMPSON — GG

CA $	041	083	031	035	105	037	099		047	043	045	km	496	100	046	044	048	038	032	106	036	038	084	042
			Ⓑ		②③④⑤	Ⓐ	Ⓑ						↓ ↑	Ⓑ				exⒶⒸ	Ⓑ	③④⑤⑦		†		
0.00	0900	....	1030	1201	1700	1830	2000	....	....	2200	....	*0*	d.**Winnipeg**.................a.	0705	....	0705	....	1215	1625	1815	2040	2020	....	2200
28.20	1445	....	|	|	2250	|	|	....	....	0315	....	*448*	d.Grand Rapids............d.	|	....	0135	....	|	|	1235	|	|	....	1615
5.25	|	....	1145	1310	|	|	|	....	....	|	....	*88*	d. Portage la Prairie ....d.	|	....	|	....	|	1515	|	1930	|	....	|
20.00	|	....	1535	1645	|	2315	|	....	....	|	....	*328*	d. Dauphin ....d.	|	....	|	....	0745	1145	|	1610	1610	....	|
30.85	|	....	1740	1855	|	0055	|	....	....	|	....	*505*	d. Swan River ....d.	|	....	|	....	0600	0915	|	1350	1345	....	|
43.95	|	....	....	2130	|	....	0535	....	....	|	....	*744*	d. The Pas ....d.	2340	....	|	....	....	....	|	1105	....	....	|
50.65	|	....	....	2255	|	....	0645	....	....	|	....	*864*	d. Cranberry Portage ..d.	2230	....	|	....	....	....	|	0935	....	....	|
52.30	|	....	....	2330	|	....	0720	....	2145	|	....	*895*	a. Flin Flon ....d.	2200	....	|	1035	....	....	|	0900	....	....	|
58.85	1645	....	....	....	0050	....	....	....	0040	0510	....	╤*650*	d.Ponton.......................d.	....	....	2345	0750	....	....	|	|	....	....	1415
58.85	1720	....	....	....	0120	....	....	....	r	0545	....	╤*710*	d.Wabowden ....d.	....	....	2315	0710	....	....	1010	|	....	....	1345
58.85	1840	1930	....	....	0230	....	....	....	0225	0700	0815	╤*820*	d.**Thompson**................d.	....	2100	2200	0600	....	....	0900	0630	....	1130	....
Ⓡ19.85	....	|	....	....	....	....	....	....	....	....	1315	╤*1190*	a.Lynn Lake ....d.	....	1600	....	....	....	....	....	....	....	|	....
Ⓡ20.25	....	2315	....	....	....	....	....	....	....	....	....	╤*1365*	a. Gillam....................d.	....	....	....	....	....	....	....	....	....	0730	....

a– 30 mins. later on ⑥. r–Calls by request.
╤– Via Grand Rapids.
Ⓡ– Fare ex Thompson. ①–Mondays. ②–Tuesdays. ③–Wednesdays.
④– Thursdays. ⑤–Fridays. ⑦–Sundays.
Ⓐ– Mondatys to Fridays except holidays.
Ⓑ– Daily except Saturdays. Ⓒ–Saturdays, Sundays and holidays.
†– Sundays and holidays.
GG– Grey Goose Bus Lines. ☎Winnipeg 204 786 8891.

Table 140 WINNIPEG - REGINA — GLC

CA $			3021	3041	km	496	3042	3022		3020
			ex⑦	ex⑥⑦		↓ ↑	ex①⑦	ex①⑦		⑦
0.00	....	....	1745	....	*0*	d.**Winnipeg**..........a.	....	1220	....	1815
12.85	....	....	2005	....	*132*	d.Treherne ....d.	....	1020	....	1615
19.20	....	....	2200	2220		d. Brandon ....d.	0800	0815	....	1415
21.50	....	....	....	2300	*259*	d.Souris................d.	0720	....	....	....
27.05	....	....	....	2345	*328*	d.Reston...............d.	0630	....	....	....
	....	....	....	....	*375*	d.Redvers.............d.	....	....	....	....
	....	....	....	....	*486*	d.Stoughton..........d.	....	....	....	....
	....	....	....	....		d.Fillmore ....d.	....	....	....	....
	....	....	....	....	*626*	a.**Regina**..............d.	....	....	....	....

①– Mondays. ⑤–Fridays. ⑦–Sundays.
GLC–Greyhound Lines of Canada. ☎Winnipeg 204 783 8840.

Table 143 WINNIPEG - THUNDER BAY — GG

CA $	053		055	051	km	396	052	056	054	052
			♣	♣			♣	♣		♣
	①③⑤					↓ ↑	†		①③⑤	⚒
0.00	....	....	1000	1800	*0*	d.**Winnipeg**..........a.	1510	1840	....	1225
Ø	....	....	|	|	*260*	d.Baudette 🛃.......d.	|	|	....	|
23.90	0730	....	1540	2330	*372*	d.Fort Frances......d.	1000	1320	2200	0715
Ø	1040	....	1845	....	Ø	d.Atikokan ....d.	....	1220	2105	....
39.00	|	....	s	....	*722*	a.**Thunder Bay** S.⪢ d.	....	s	|	....
39.00	1325	....	2125	....	*724*	a.**Thunder Bay** N.Ø d.	....	0930	1800	....

s– Calls to set down only. Ø–Port Arthur. ⪢–Fort William.
♣– International bus service. ①–Mondays. ③–Wednesdays. ⑤–Fridays.
Ø– Information not available at press date. ⚒–Daily except Sundays and holidays
†– Sundays and holidays. *GG*–Grey Goose Bus Lines. ☎Winnipeg 204 786 8891

Table 142 LETHBRIDGE - SWEETGRASS — GLC

CA $		1151			km	396		1152		
		♣				↓ ↑		♣		
0.00	....	1000	....	....	*0*	d.**Lethbridge**........a.	....	1330	....	....
13.65	....	1120	....	....	*109*	d.Coutts 🛃...........d.	....	1210	....	....
	....	1125	....	....	*111*	a.**Sweetgrass** ......d.	....	*1115*	....	....

♣– International bus service.
GLC– Greyhound Lines of Canada. ☎Lethbridge 403 327 1551.

Table 144 396 CAPREOL - SUDBURY — NWB

Bus service Capreol-Sudbury and v.v. *35* km. Journey: 1 hour. Fare: CA $: 3.55.
From Capreol: 0700Ⓐ, 0750⚒, 1000⚒, 1100†, 1230⚒, 1530⚒, 1615†, 1645⚒, 1730⚒, 1930⚒, 2225④⑤.
From Sudbury: 0800Ⓐ, 0850⚒, 1115⚒, 1200†, 1430⚒, 1640⚒, 1715†, 1735⚒, 1830⚒, 2135⚒, 2330④⑤.

④– Thursdays. ⑤–Fridays.
Ⓐ– Mondays to Fridays except holidays.
⚒– Daily except Sundays and holidays.
†– Sundays and holidays.
NWB– Northway Bus Lines. ☎Capreol 705 858 1320.

Table 145 TIMMINS - SAULT STE MARIE

CA $					km	396 ↓ ↑				
0.00	....	....	....	....	0	d.**Timmins**..........a.	....	....	....	....
Ø	....	....	....	....	113	d.Foleyet..............d.	....	....	....	....
Ø	....	....	....	....	209	d.Chapleau............d.	....	....	....	....
Ø	....	....	....	....	338	d.Hawk Junction...d.	....	....	....	....
Ø	....	....	....	....	344	d.Wawa.................d.	....	....	....	....
Ø	....	....	....	....	573	a.**Sault Ste. Marie**.d.	....	....	....	....

Ø– Information not available at press date.

Table 147 PICKLE LAKE

LL

CA $					km	396 ↓ ↑				
0.00	....	Ø	....	....	0	d.**Ignace**...............a.	....	Ø	....	....
Ø	....	Ø	....	....	Ø	d.Valora.................d.	....	Ø	....	....
Ø	....	Ø	....	....	Ø	d.Savant Lake......d.	....	Ø	....	....
Ø	....	Ø	....	....	Ø	d.Central Patricia..d.	....	Ø	....	....
Ø	....	Ø	....	....	Ø	a.**Pickle Lake**......d.	....	Ø	....	....

Ø– Information not available at press date. *LL*–L&L Transportation. ☎Ignace ❖.

Table 149 TORONTO - HEARST

ON

CA $	1	47	3	11	km	396 ↓ ↑	12	4	46	2
0.00	*0030*	....	*0930*	*1230*		d.*Toronto* **57**.........a.	*1900*	*2230*	....	*0745*
26.00	0600	....	1600	|	0	d.**North Bay**.........a.	|	1545	....	0140
	|	....	|	1830		d. Sudbury ....a.	1255	|	....	|
39.00	0750	....	1750	|	146	d.Cobalt................d.	|	1355	....	2350
39.00	0815	....	1815	|	161	d.New Liskeard ....d.	|	1330	....	2325
43.00	0910	....	1910	|	205	d.Englehart...........d.	|	1235	....	2230
Ø	0950	....	1950	|	251	d.Kirkland Lake ....d.	|	1155	....	2150
46.00	1005	....	2005	|	255	d.Swastika............d.	|	1140	....	2135
53.00	1100	1100	2100	|	363	d.Matheson ....d.	|	1045	2040	2040
57.00	1215	|	|	2230	417	d.**Timmins** ....d.	0845	|	|	1940
Ø	*1135*	1135	2140	....	344	d. Iroquois Falls ..d.	....	1005	1950	|
58.00	*1215*	1215	2300	....	386	a. **Cochrane** ....d.	....	0930	1915	|
69.00	1420	....	0030	....	594	a.Kapuskasing......d.	....	0640	....	1725
≤48.75	1530	....	0140	....	695	a.Hearst ....d.	....	0530	....	1615

≤– Fare ex North Bay.
Ø– Information not available at press date.
ON– Ontario Northland. ☎North Bay 705 472 4500.

Table 150 SASKATOON - REGINA

SAS

CA $	52 Ⓐ		521 Ⓒ	56 ①③⑤	36 ①③⑤	54		2	78 ①③⑤⑦			km	396 ↓ ↑	77 Ⓐ	771 Ⓒ	551 Ⓐ	55 ①③⑤			53		1	51 ①③⑤⑦	
0.00	0800	....	0800	0800	....	1330	....	1730	1730	....	....	0	d.**Saskatoon**..............a.	1035	1120	....	1135	....	....	1630	....	2035	2140	....
20.50	|	....	|	1050	1135	|	....	|	2045	....	....	233	d.Moose Jaw...............d.	|	|	0805	0840	....	....	|	....	|	1835	....
23.20	1105	....	1120	....	1230	1635	....	2035	2140	....	....	306	a.**Regina**.....................d.	0730	0800	0700	....	....	....	1330	....	1730	1730	....

①– Mondays. ③–Wednesdays. ⑤–Fridays.
⑦– Sundays. Ⓐ–Mondays to Fridays except holidays. Ⓒ–Saturdays, Sundays and holidays.
SAS– Saskatchewan Transportation Co. ☎Regina 306 787 3346.

Table 151 RED LAKE

XL

CA $		3			km	396 ↓ ↑			4	
0.00	....	1030	....	....	0	d.**Kenora**.............a.	....	....	1800	....
Ø	....	1140	....	....	95	d.Vermilion Bay....d.	....	....	1650	....
Ø	....	|	....	....	Ø	d.Red Lake Road .d.	....	....	|	....
Ø	....	1305	....	....	198	d.Ear Falls............d.	....	....	1530	....
Ø	....	1400	....	....	270	a.**Red Lake**..........d.	....	....	1430	....

Ø– Information not available at press date.
XL– Excel Coach Lines. ☎Kenora 807 468 6667.

Table 153 396 GODERICH

SWD CHHO

service Goderich-Stratford and v.v. 72 km. Journey: 1¼ hours. Fare: CA $: 7.30.
From Goderich: 0750⚒, 1700a. **From Stratford**: 1900.
service Goderich-London and v.v. Ø km. Journey: 1¾ hours. Fare: CA $: Ø.
From Goderich: 0850⑤b, 1920⑤b. **From London**: 0700⑤b, 1730⑤b.

a– Runs on † (ex on ⑦ of holiday weekend).
b– Runs on ④ when ⑤ is a holiday.
④– Thursdays. ⑤–Fridays. ⑦–Sundays.
⚒– Daily except Sundays and holidays. †–Sundays and holidays.
Ø– Information not available at press date.
CHHO–Cha-Co Trails. ☎Chatham 519 681 2861.
SWD– Sherwood Transportation. ☎Goderich 519 524 2092.

Table 155 SUDBURY - PARRY SOUND - TORONTO

GLC ON

CA $		ON 16			GLC 2 Ⓡ	GLC 64 Ⓡ	ON 32			ON 40	GLC 12	km	396 ↓ ↑	GLC 3		ON 21	GLC 63 Ⓡ	ON 23		GLC 11 Ⓡ	ON 49			
0.00	....	0730	....	....	1000	1245	1315	....	....	1730	0050	0	d.**Sudbury** ....a.	0600	....	1245	1800	1815	....	2215	2315	....	....	....
	....	0900	....	....	|	|	1445	....	....	1900	|		d.Pointe au Baril...........d.	|	....	1110	|	1640	....	|	2140	....	....	....
16.25	....	0930	....	....	|	|	1515	....	....	1930	|	165	d.Parry Sound.............d.	|	....	1015	|	1545	....	|	2045	....	....	....
29.55	....	1145	....	....	|	|	1730	....	....	2145	|	302	d.Barrie ....d.	|	....	0835	|	1405	....	|	1835	....	....	....
34.50	....	1315	....	....	1515	1745	1900	....	....	2315	0550	397	a.**Toronto** ....d.	0100	....	0700	1230	1230	....	1700	1700	....	....	....

Ⓡ– Reservation obligatory.
GLC– Greyhound Lines of Canada. ☎Toronto 416 393 7911.
ON– Ontario Northland. ☎North Bay 705 472 4500.

Table 157 OWEN SOUND - TORONTO

GLC PMCL

CA $	PMCL 23O ⚒	PMCL 1O	GLC 5639 ①③⑤	GLC 5503 ②④⑥	PMCL 9C ⚒	GLC 5641 ⑦	PMCL 5O ⚒	PMCL 11SC ⑦	PMCL 19C ⑧	GLC 5515 ①③⑤⑦	GLC 5637 ②④⑤⑥	km	396 ↓ ↑
0.00	....	0815	0830	0830	1015	1230	1515	1515	1645	1800	1800	0	d.**Toronto** ....a.
9.85	....	0950	|	|	1150	|	1700	1645	|	|	|	98	d.Barrie ....a.
	....	|	|	1015	|	|	|	|	|	1940	|		d. Guelph....................d.
16.00	0540	1115	|	|	1315	|	1825	1800	2035	|	|	173	d.Collingwood...............d.
9.20	|	|	1000	|	....	1400	|	....	....	|	1930	73	d. Orangeville..............d.
11.90	|	|	1024	|	....	1424	|	....	....	|	1954	96	d. Shelburne ....d.
20.15	0640	1220	1145	1240	....	1545	1930	....	....	2205	2115	≮194	a.**Owen Sound**............d.

396 ↓ ↑	PMCL 20C Ⓒ	PMCL 40 ⚒	GLC 5622 ②④⑥	GLC 5502 ①③⑤	PMCL 12C ⑤	GLC 5642 ⑤	PMCL 12C ⚒	PMCL 8O ⚒	GLC 5652 ①③⑤⑦	GLC 5502 ②④⑥⑦	PMCL 36FO ⑤
d.**Toronto** ....a.	0810	1100	1055	1130	1435	1525	1630	1950	2035	2130	2340
d.Barrie ....a.	|	0920	|	|	|	|	1500	1820	|	|	2210
d. Guelph....................d.	|	|	|	1010	|	|	|	|	|	2015	|
d.Collingwood...............d.	0445	0800	|	|	1050	|	1330	1655	|	|	2055
d. Orangeville..............d.	....	|	0920	|		1350	....	|	1900	|	|
d. Shelburne ....d.	....	|	0851	|		1321	....	|	1836	|	|
a.**Owen Sound**............d.	....	0700	0730	0730		1200	....	1545	1715	1715	1940

①– Mondays. ②–Tuesdays. ③–Wednesdays. ④–Thursdays. ⑤–Fridays.
⑥– Saturdays. ⑦–Sundays. ⑧–Daily except Saturdays.
Ⓒ– Saturdays, Sundays and holidays. ⚒–Daily except Sundays and holidays.
≮– Km via Collingwood.
GLC– Greyhound Lines of Canada. ☎Toronto 416 393 7911.
PMCL–Penetang Midland Coach Lines. ☎Midland 705 526 0161.

Table 159 TORONTO - GUELPH - LONDON ♿

CHHO CRY GLC

CA $	2K	4K ⑤a	6K	8K	km	396 CHHO ↓ ↑	1K	3K ⑤a	9K	11K
0.00	....	....	....	....	0	d.**Toronto** ≥........a.	....	....	....	....
13.75	....	....	....	....	80	d.Guelph ≥..........d.	....	....	....	....
13.75	1205	1500	1805	1930	100	d.Kitchener ≥ ......d.	1015	1250	1720	1920
	1230	|	1830	|		d.New Hamburg ...d.	0945	1220	1650	1850
	1240	|	1840	|		d.Shakespeare .....d.	0935	1210	1640	1840
15.05	1255	1605	1855	|	140	d.Stratford ....d.	0920	1155	1625	1825
	1315	|	1915	|		d.St. Marys............d.	0900	1135	1605	1805
16.50	1405	1705	2005	2100	195	a.**London**.............d.	0815	1050	1520	1720

≥– service *(GLC)* Toronto-Kitchener and v.v. Journey: 2 hours. From Toronto: , 0630ex⑥⑦, 0730ex⑦, 0830, 0930, 1130, 1400, 1530, 1615Ⓐ, 1615⚒, 1645Ⓐ, 1700, 1730, 1830, 1900⑥⑦, 1945, 2030, 2330, returning at 0550Ⓐ, 0610Ⓐ, 0630Ⓐ, 0700Ⓐ, 0730ex⑦, 0900, 0930ex⑦, 1030, 1130, 1230⑥, 1300, 1430, 1530, 1640, 1730, 1800⑥⑦, 1930, 2200.

CA $		2A ①	4A ⑤	6A	km	695 CRY ↓ ↑	1A	5A †	7A ⑤	9A ①
0.00	....	1300	1300	1825	0	d.**Kitchener**..........a.	1010	1710	1750	1750
	....	1410	1410	1935		d.Listowel ....d.	0855	1555	1650	1650
	....	....	s	1955		d.Harriston ....d.	0830	1530	1625	....
	....	....	1515	2040		d.Hanover ....d.	0745	1445	1545	....
	....	....	....	2055		a.**Chesley** ....d.	0720	1425	....	....

a– Will run on ④ when ⑤ is a holiday. s–Calls to set down only.
①– Mondays. ④–Thursdays. ⑤–Fridays. ⑥–Saturdays. ⑦–Sundays.
Ⓐ– Mondays to Fridays except holidays. ⚒–Daily except Sundays and holidays.
†– Sundays and holidays.
CHHO–Cha-Co Trails. ☎Chatham 519 681 2861.
CRY– Cherrey Bus Lines Inc. ☎Drayton 519 681 3395.
GLC– Greyhound Lines of Canada. ☎Toronto 416 393 7911.

CANADA

Table 160 BUFFALO - LONDON

GLC TWW

US $		GLC♣ 2103 ⑤	TWW 602A	TWW 202A	km	296 ↓ ↑	TWW 201B	TWW 201C	TWW 603B	GLC♣ 2104 ⑤
0.00	....	1420	....	....	0	d.**Buffalo**............a.	....	....	....	2015
6.00	....	1530	....	....	40	d.Niagara Falls *USA* ▆ .d.	....	....	....	1920
	....	│	0930	1700		d. **Toronto**..........a.	0840	1005	1600	│
	....	│	1100	1835		d. St. Catharines .d.	0645	0835	1430	│
6.00	....	1630	1120	│	47	d.N. Falls *Canada* ▆ ..d.	│	│	1400	1520
6.40	....	1700	1150	1855	68	d.Welland.............d.	0615	0805	1325	1449
	....	│	1205	1915		a. Port Colborne d.	0550	0740	1300	│
18.90	....	1957	....	....	258	d.St. Thomas ★...d.	....	....	....	1135
26.00	....	2030	....	....		a.**London** ★........d.	....	....	....	1100

★– Local service (*GBA*) St Thomas-London and v.v. from St Thomas 1220⚒, 1450⚒, 1640⚒ from London 1130⚒, 1400⚒, 1600⚒ . Journey time 40 mins.
♣– International bus service.
⑤– Fridays. ⚒–Daily except Sundays and holidays.
GBA– Grey-Bruce Airbus ☎Port Elgin 519 389 4433.
GLC– Greyhound Lines of Canada. ☎London 519 434 3245.
TWW– Trentway-Wagar Inc. ☎Peterborough 705 748 6411.

Table 162 695 NIAGARA FALLS

GLC NF TWW

🚌 service (*GLC*) links Niagara Falls (*Canada*) with Buffalo, St. Catharines and Toronto. See Table **168**.
🚌 service (*TWW*) links Niagara Falls (*Canada*) with Buffalo, St. Catharines, Hamilton (Table **170**) and Kitchener (6-7 daily).
🚌 service (*NF*) links Niagara Falls (*USA*) with Buffalo. See Table **577**.
GLC– Greyhound Lines of Canada. ☎Toronto 416 393 7911.
NF– Niagara Frontier Transit Metro. ☎Buffalo 285 9319.
TWW– Trentway-Wagar Inc. ☎Peterborough 705 748 6411.

Table 166 WINGHAM - STRATFORD

CRY

CA $	1 ①④⑤	3 ②③	5 †		km	396 ↓ ↑		6 †	4 ②③	2 ①④⑤
	0810	....	1510	....		d.**Wingham**..........a.	....	2015	....	2020
	0850	....	1550	....		d.Listowel............d.	....	1935	....	1940
	0900	0900	1600	....		d.Tralee................d.	....	1925	1930	1930
	0915	0915	1615	....		d.Milverton...........d.	....	1910	1915	1915
0.00	0940	0940	1640	....	0	a.**Stratford**...........d.	....	1835	1835	1835

①–Mondays. ②–Tuesdays. ③–Wednesdays. ④–Thursdays. ⑤–Fridays. †–Sundays and holidays. *CRY*–Cherrey Bus Lines Inc. ☎Drayton 519 681 3395.

Table 168 TORONTO - BUFFALO

GLC TWW

CA $	2015 ♣	302 ♣	1035	1031 ♣		1043		2061 ♣	1059	2079 ♣	2081 ♣			2083	1091	km	296 ↓ GLC ↑	1006 ♣	1004 Ⓐ	1014 Ⓒ	2016 ♣	2020 ♣	305 ♣		1040	1048 ♣	1054		2060 ♣		1078 ♣	2064 ♣
0.00	0700	0800	1030	1130	....	1430	....	1630	1730	1930	1945	....	....	2045	2330	0	d.**Toronto**.............a.	0640	0850	0950	0905	1100	1400	....	1530	1745	1905	....	2050	....	2315	0100
	│	│	│	│	....	1455	....	│	│	│	│	....	....	│	│		d.Mississauga........d.	│	│	│	│	│	│	....	│	s	│	....	s	....	│	│
	│	│	1120	│	....	1525	....	1725	1825	│	│	....	....	│	│	44	d.Burlington...........d.	│	│	│	│	1015	1315	....	│	1650	1820	....	s	....	│	│
	│	│	1150	│	....	1555	....	1800	1900	s	│	....	....	│	s		d.Grimsby..............d.	│	0720	0820	│	0945	s	....	│	1620	│	....	1930	....	│	│
12.20	│	0945	1215	│	....	1620	....	1825	1925	2100	│	....	....	│	0050	107	d.St. Catharines ⊗ .. d.	│	0700	0800	│	0925	1225	....	1400	1600	1730	....	1910	....	2145	│
13.55	│	1010	1235	1305	....	1640	....	1850	1945	2125	│	....	....	│	0110	120	d.Niagara Falls Canada ⊗▆ d.	s	0635	0735	s	0900	1200	....	1335	1535	1705	....	1845	....	2120	│
16.00	0915	1115	....	1405	....	....	....	1950	....	2215	2200	....	....	2300	0210	153	a.**Buffalo** ⊗ ....d.	0355	....	....	0620	0745	1045	....	....	1420	....	....	1730	....	2020	2245

CA $		610A ♣		601AA ♣	601A		611A ♣	613A	603A ♣	604A ♣	607A ♣	608A ♣	612A ♣⑤⑦	605A ♣	609A	km	296 ↓ TWW ↑	613B ♣	610B Ⓐ	611B	615B ♣	601B ♣	616B ♣	612B	602B ♣	614B	604B ♣		606B ♣	608B ♣	605B ♣	609B ♣
0.00	....	0530	....	0715	0745	....	1015	1145	1330	1630	1745	1945	2000	2045	2359	0	d.**Toronto**.............a.	0630	0730	0905	0930	1015	1045	1135	1420	1830	2000	....	2200	2345	0050	0150
	....	│	....	│	│	....	│	│	s	s	s	s	│	│	s		d.Grimsby..............d.	│	0605	0750	│	│	│	1035	│	1720	│	....	│	│	2340	0040
12.20	....	│	....	│	s	....	│	│	1500	1815	1920	2110	│	│	0120	107	d.St. Catharines ⊗ .. d.	│	0545	0730	0810	│	0925	1005	1300	1700	1840	....	│	│	2320	0020
13.55	....	│	....	0845	0930	....	1145	1330	1530	1840	2000	2145	│	│	0145	120	d.Niagara Falls Canada ⊗▆ d.	│	0520	0705	0745	│	0900	0945	1235	1630	1815	....	2015	2200	2300	2359
16.00	....	0750	....	0945	....	....	1245	....	1630	1940	2100	2245	2215	2300	....	153	a.**Buffalo** ⊗ ....d.	0400	....	....	0645	0740	0740	....	1130	....	1700	....	1900	2100	2145	2245

s– Calls to set down only. ⑤–Fridays. ⑦–Sundays.
Ⓐ– Mondays to Fridays except holidays. Ⓒ–Saturdays, Sundays and holidays.
♣– International bus service.
⊗– Intermediate traffic not carried between St. Catharines and Buffalo.
GLC– Greyhound Lines of Canada. ☎Toronto 416 393 7911.
TWW– Trentway-Wagar Inc. ☎Peterborough 705 748 6411.

Table 170 HAMILTON - BUFFALO

TWW

CA $	110A †	100A Ⓐ	101A ♣	102A ♣		103A	104A ♣	105A ♣	108A ⑤	106A	107A ♣	km	396 ↓ ↑	107B Ⓐ	100B ⚒♣	101B	102B ♣	103B	104B	105B ♣	111B ⑤	109B †	106B ♣	
0.00	0015	0630	0815a	1010	....	1230	1400	1615	1730	1815	2010	0	d.**Hamilton**...................a.	0815	1020	1135	1405	1615	1800	1950	2025	2055	0030	....
6.20	0110	0745	0930	1115	....	1350	1500	1735	1820	1935	2125	59	d.St. Catharines ....d.	0655	0905	1040	1300	1500	1645	1855	1930	1955	2325	....
8.50	0130	0810	0955	1145	....	1415	1530	1840	1845	2000	2145	72	d.Niagara Falls *Canada* ▆ .d.	0625	0840	1010	1235	1430	1615	1830	1900	1930	2300	....
12.35		....	....	1245	....	....	1630	1940	....	2100	2245	105	a.**Buffalo**.......................d.	....	0740	....	1130	....	....	1700	....	....	....	....

a– ⚒ only. ♣–International bus service. Ⓐ–Mondays to Fridays except holidays. *TWW*– Trentway-Wagar Inc. ☎Peterborough 705 748 6411.
⚒– Daily except Sundays and holidays.
†– Sundays and holidays. ⑤–Fridays.

Table 171 FREDERICTON - NEWCASTLE

SMT

CA $		30			km	296 ↓ ↑			33	
0.00	....	1150	....	....	0	d.**Fredericton** ......a.	....	....	1745	....
	....	1245	....	....		d.Boiestown..........d.	....	....	1650	....
	....	1305	....	....		d.Doaktown...........d.	....	....	1630	....
	....	1405	....	....	175	a.**Newcastle**.........d.	....	....	1530	....

SMT– SMT (Eastern) Ltd. ☎Moncton 506 859 5105.

Table 175 NORANDA - NORTH BAY

ANO

CA $		1			km	396 ↓ ↑			4	
0.00	....	0825	....	....	0	d.**Noranda** Rouyn a.	....	....	2030	....
15.65	....	1020	....	....	138	d.Ville Marie ....d.	....	....	1840	....
31.00	....	1235	....	....	302	a.**North Bay**..........d.	....	....	1600	....

ANO– Autobus Norouest Inc. ☎Rouyn Noranda 762 0735.

Table 173 NORANDA - MONTRÉAL

ALA AMA

CA $	AMA 8/1	AMA 8/3	AMA 8/7	ALA 44/2/4 ⚒	km	396 ↓ ↑	AMA 8/2	AMA 8/4	ALA 44/15/19 ex⑤⑦	AMA 8/8
0.00	0730	1300	2200	....	0	d.**Noranda** Rouyn a.	1705	2255	....	0800
11.65	0930	1509	2355	....	108	d.Val d'Or.............d.	1535	2125	....	0630
34.65	1300	1830	0320	....	365	d.Grand Remous..d.	1215	1800	....	0310
38.15	1325	1855	0345	0805a	401	d.Mont Laurier......d.	1100	1655	2140	0150
51.05	│	2035s	0530s	1030	540	d.Ste. Agathe ....d.	0900	1510	1915	0030
55.40	│	2050s	0600s	1125	585	d.St. Jérome.........d.	0820	│	1820	│
60.95	1615	2205	0700	1215	644	a.**Montréal**..........d.	0730	1400	1730	2315

a– 0825 on ⑥. ⚒–Daily except Sundays and holidays.
⑤– Fridays. ⑥–Saturdays. ⑦–Sundays.
ALA– Autobus Laurentides Ltée. ☎Boisbriand 514 435 8899.
AMA– Autobus Maheux Ltée. ☎Rouyn Noranda 819 762 2200.

Table 176 MONTRÉAL - OTTAWA

VCL

CA $	102	29	220	33	km	396 ↓ ↑	28	223	32	107
0.00	0820	0815	....	1810	0	d.**Montréal**...........a.	1215	....	2210	2215
	│	0939	....	1934		d.Lachute...............d.	1048	....	2042	│
16.00	1020	1020	1720	2015	104	d.Hawkesbury ......d.	1020	1335	2015	2015
	│	1212	│	2207		a.Hull....................d.	0816	│	1811	│
29.85	1220	1230	1715	2225	215	a.**Ottawa**..............d.	0800	1225	1755	1815

VCL– Voyageur Colonial Ltd. ☎Montréal 514 842 2281.

Table 178 OTTAWA - TORONTO

GLC

CA $	6117	6201	6121 ex⑦	6203	6205	6107 ⑤⑦	6209	6329	6211	6213 ⑤⑦a	6115	km	296 ↓ ↑	6118	6120	6124 ⚒	6204	6206	6108 ⑤⑦	6210	6212	6116	6220 ⑤⑦a	6216
0.00	0030	0700	0845	0930	1130	1215	1430	....	1630	1800	1745	0	d.**Ottawa**.......................a.	0550	....	1550	1435	1625	1855	1935	2135	2335	2335	0155
	│	│	1255	│	│	1600	│	....	│	│	2120	245	d.Havelock ....d.	│	....	1135	│	│	│	│	│	2026	│	│
37.55	0410	│	1350	│	│	1650	│	1750	│	│	2210	286	d.Peterborough.............d.	0205	1055	1055	│	│	1505	│	│	1945	│	│
46.95	0610	1205	1600	1440	1625	1905	1925	1945	2140	2310	2345	428	a.**Toronto** ....d.	0020	0810	....	0930	1130	1245	1430	1630	1715	1830	2100

a- runs on ① instead of ⑦ on holiday weekend.
⚒- Daily except Sundays and holidays.
⑤- Fridays. ⑦-Sundays.
GLC- Greyhound Lines of Canada. ☎Toronto 416 393 7911.

Table 180 MONTRÉAL - TORONTO

GLC VCL

CA $	VCL 602/169	VCL 602/179	VCL 502/265 P	VCL 502/239	VCL 502/267 P	VCL 502/245	VCL 502/269 P	VCL 502/251	VCL 502/257 ⑤⑦	VCL 502/253	VCL 502/263	km	396 ↓ ↑	VCL 602/170	VCL 502/266 P	GLC 6172	VCL 502/242	VCL 502/268 P	VCL 502/234	VCL 502/270 P	VCL 502/250	VCL 502/256 ⑤⑦	VCL 502/252	VCL 502/264
0.00	....	0715	0830	0830	1030	1030	1400	1400	1600	1730	0005	0	d.**Montréal** ....a.	1520	1530	....	1555	1830	1845	2025	2120	2230	0055	0655
17.00	....	0930	|	1005	|	1205	|	1535	|	1905	0120	130	d.Cornwall ....d.	1305	|	....	1415	|	1705	|	1940	|	2315	0515
	....	1100	|	|	|	|	|	|	|	|	|	Ø	d.Prescott ....d.	1115	|	....	|	|	|	|	|	|	|	|
	....	1124	|	|	|	|	|	|	|	|	|	226	d.Brockville ....d.	1020	|	....	|	|	1615s	|	1850bs	|	2225s	|
33.90	0820	1330	|	1225	|	1430	|	1800	|	2135	0340	308	d.Kingston ....d.	0855	|	1230d	1235	|	1525	|	1800	|	2135	0335s
	1000c	1530c	|	|	|	|	|	|	|	2220s	|	388	d.Belleville ....d.	....	|	1049d	|	|	|	|	|	|	|	|
	1145c	1720c	|	|	|	|	|	|	|	|	|		d.Port Hope ....d.	....	|	0855	|	|	|	|	|	|	|	|
56.00	1355c	1840c	1500	1530	1700	1735	2030	2105	2230	0050	0655	587	a.**Toronto** ....d.	....	0900	0645	0900	1200	1200	1415	1415	1600	1800	0015

P– June 30-Sept. 8 and Dec. 22-Jan. 3. a–⑤⑦ only. b–⑤ only. c–*GLC*. d–*VCL*. date. *GLC*–Greyhound Lines of Canada. ☎Toronto 416 393 7911.
s–Calls to set down only. ⑤–Fridays. ⑦–Sundays. Ø–Information not available at press *VCL*– Voyageur Colonial Ltd. ☎Montréal 514 843 4231.

Table 181 MONTRÉAL - QUÉBEC

OEX

CA $	35	169	201	41/51	15 ⑦	41/233		41/251	248/171 ⑦	41/235	41/11	km	396 ↓ ↑	41/30 ex⑦	30	41/202	41/52	41/230	41/204	40	41/234	248/166	50	41/236
0.00	....	0555	0730	1000	....	1300	....	1530	1740	1900	2200	0	d.**Montréal** ∧ ....a.	0835	....	1200	1425	....	1805	....	2005	2145	....	2225
18.00	0545	|	1010	1155	1215	1500	....	1735	|	2045	2355	150	d.Trois Rivières ....d.	0630	1000	1015	1230	1219	1620	1725	1735	|	2015	2040
	0640	|	|	....	1310	|	....	|	|	....	....		d.Shawinigan ....d.	....	0910	....	....	|	....	1635	|	|	1925	|
	0830	|	|	....	1500	|	....	|	|	....	....		a.La Tuque ....d.	....	0915	....	....	|	....	....	|	|	1730	|
	....	|	1128	....	....	|	....	1853	|	....	....		d.Portneuf ....d.	....	....	....	....	1102	....	....	|	|	....	1917
32.00	....	0945	1244	....	....	1650	....	2009	2105	....	....	270	a.**Québec** ∧ ....d.	....	....	....	....	0945	....	....	1530	1800	....	1800

⑦– Sundays. ∧–Additional (non-stop, journey 3 hours) trips from Montréal: 0100⑤⑥⑦, 0600 and hourly to 2100, 2300; from Québec: 0600ex⑦, 0700 and hourly to 2100, 2300.
OEX– Orleans Express Inc. ☎Montréal 514 847 4020.

Table 183 CHIBOUGAMAU

MES

CA $			2J		km	396 ↓ ↑		1J		
0.00	....	....	0920	....	0	d.**Chibougamau** ..a.	....	2205	....	....
39.05	....	....	1420	....	348	d.Senneterre ....d.	....	1700	....	....
44.85	....	....	1520	....	420	a.**Val d'Or** ....d.	....	1605	....	....

MES– Autobus Messier Chibougamau Inc. ☎Chateauguay 514 691 1654.

Table 185 QUÉBEC - JONQUIÈRE

ICR

CA $	1	5/7	11	15	km	396 ↓ ↑	2	4/6	10	16/18/20 ◇
0.00	1030	1415	1815	2330	0	d.**Québec** ....a.	0910	1210	1610	2210
22.45	1245	1630	2030	0145	203	d.Laterrière ....d.	0650	0950	1350	1950
22.45	1300	1645	2045	0200	219	a.Chicoutimi ....d.	0635	0935	1335	1935
22.45	1320	1705	2105	0220	230	a.Arvida ....d.	0610	0910	1310	1910
22.45	1330	1715	2115	0230	237	a.**Jonquière** ....d.	0600	0900	1300	1900

⑤– Fridays. ⑦–Sundays. ◇–1 hour earlier on ⑤⑦.
ICR– Intercar. Tel.: Jonquière 418 547 2167.

Table 187 DOLBEAU/ALMA

AJ AL

CA $	AJ 251 ex⑦	AL 100 ex⑦	AL 102		AJ 253 ⑥⑦		AL 104	AJ 104 P	AJ 255 Ⓐ			km	396 ↓ ↑		AL 101 ex⑦			AL 103	AJ 254 ex⑦	AJ 105 Q	AL 105	AJ 256		
0.00	0730	0810	1210	....	1235	....	1710	....	1715	....	....	0	d.**Chicoutimi** ....a.	....	1030	....	....	1450	1510	....	1930	2020	....	....
Ø	0745	0820	1220	....	1250	....	1720	....	1730	....	....	Ø	d.Arvida ....d.	....	1015	....	....	1435	1455	....	1915	2005	....	....
Ø	0800	0835	1235	....	1305	....	1735	....	1745	....	....	Ø	d.Jonquière ....d.	....	1005	....	....	1425	1445	....	1905	1955	....	....
Ø	|	0915	1315	....	|	....	1815	1825	|	....	....	Ø	d. Alma ....d.	....	0925	....	....	1345	|	1815	1825	|	....	....
	0830	....	....	....	1340	....	....	|	1820	....	....		d.Hébertville ....d.	....	....	....	....	....	1410	|	....	1920	....	....
8.55	0910	....	....	....	1420	....	....	|	1900	....	....	Ø	d.Chambord ....d.	....	....	....	....	....	1330	|	....	1850	....	....
16.55	1055	....	....	....	1600	....	....	1940	2045	....	....	Ø	a.**Dolbeau** ....d.	....	....	....	....	....	1200	1700	....	1710	....	....

P– ⑤ Sept. 1-Apr. 30. Q–⑦ Sept. 1-Apr. 30. Ⓐ–Mondays to Fridays except holidays. ⑤–Fridays. ⑥–Saturdays. ⑦–Sundays. Ø–Information not available at press date.
AJ– Autocars Jasmin. ☎Jonquière 547 2167. *AL*–Autobus Laterrière. ☎Chicoutimi 549 2463.

Table 189 396 MONTRÉAL - SHERBROOKE

AQC NOL

service Montréal-Sherbrooke and v.v. *159* km. Journey: 2½-3 hours. Fare: CA $: 16.95.

From Montréal: *AQC* **47** at 0615Ⓐ, 0700①, 0800ex①, 0900①, 0905⑥, 1045, 1300, 1305⑤⑥⑦, 1500, 1600⑤⑦, 1615④, 1700②③⑤⑦, 1730①④⑥, 1800, 1900⑤⑦, 2000, 2130⑤⑦, 2300; *NOL* at 0945⑥, 1500⑦, 1610①-④, 1710⑤.

From Sherbrooke: *AQC* **47** at 0600Ⓐ, 0800, 0845, 1000, 1130, 1255⑤-⑦, 1300, 1500, 1600⑤⑦, 1615④, 1700⑧, 1730⑥⑦, 1800, 1900⑦, 2000, 2230⑦; *NOL* at 0800①-④, 1200⑦, 1750⑤⑦.

Ⓐ–Mondays to Fridays except holidays. ⑧–Daily except Saturdays. ①–Mondays. ②–Tuesdays. ③–Wednesdays. ④–Thursdays. ⑤–Fridays. ⑥–Saturdays. ⑦–Sundays. *AQC*–Autobus Auger Estrie Inc. ☎Chateauguay 514 691 1654. *NOL*–Voyages Nolisés. Tel.: Acton Vale 514 546 2490.

Table 190 QUÉBEC - SEPT ÎLES

ICR LIT

CA $	396 ↓	km	LIT Ⓐ	ICR	LIT ⚒	LIT †	ICR ⑤	ICR ex⑤	ICR ⑤	ICR
0.00	**Québec** ....d.	0	....	0915	....	....	1245	1500	1640	1815
14.60	La Malbaie ....d.	144	....	1155	....	....	1440	1655	1835	2040
17.75	St. Siméon ....d.	178	....	1225	....	....	....	....	....	2105
23.15	Tadoussac ....d.	217	....	1320	....	....	....	....	....	2155
	Les Escoumins ....d.	259	....	1355	....	....	....	....	....	2230
32.95	Forestville ....d.	315	....	1450	....	....	....	....	....	2315
46.60	**Baie Comeau** ....d.	418	....	1615	1630	1710	....	....	....	0025
⊖5.50	Godbout ....d.	467	....	....	1740	1815	....	....	....	....
⊖17.25	Port Cartier ....d.	579	....	....	1915	2000	....	....	....	....
⊖22.55	**Sept Îles** ....d.	634	1630	....	2010	2050	....	....	....	....
	Magpie ....d.		1815	....	....	....	....	....	....	....
⊖39.80	Mingan ....d.	814	1850	....	....	....	....	....	....	....
⊖44.10	Havre St. Pierre ...a.	849	1915	....	....	....	....	....	....	....

395 ↓	ICR ex⑦	ICR	LIT	ICR	ICR ⑦	LIT Ⓐ				
Havre St. Pierre ....d.	....	....	....	....	....	0900	....	....	....	....
Mingan ....d.	....	....	....	....	....	0925	....	....	....	....
Magpie	....	....	....	....	....	1000	....	....	....	....
Sept Îles ....d.	....	....	0800	....	....	1145	....	....	....	....
Port Cartier ....d.	....	....	0845	....	....	....	....	....	....	....
Godbout ....d.	....	....	1040	....	....	....	....	....	....	....
Baie Comeau ....d.	....	0800	1150	1200	....	....	....	....	....	....
Forestville ....d.	....	0930	....	1330	....	....	....	....	....	....
Les Escoumins ....d.	....	1010	....	1410	....	....	....	....	....	....
Tadoussac ....d.	....	1045	....	1445	....	....	....	....	....	....
St. Siméon ....d.	....	1135	....	1535	....	....	....	....	....	....
La Malbaie ....d.	0740	1245	....	1630	1830	....	....	....	....	....
Québec ....a.	0950	1445	....	1825	2025	....	....	....	....	....

Ⓐ–Mondays to Fridays except holidays. ⚒–Daily except Sundays and holidays. †–Sundays and holidays. ⑤–Fridays. ⑦–Sundays. ⊖–Fare ex Baie Comeau. *ICR*–Intercar. Tel.: Jonquière 418 547 2167.

Table 192 396 CHICOUTIMI - TADOUSSAC

ATT

service Chicoutimi-Tadoussac and v.v. *140* km. Journey 1¾ hours. Fare CA $: ❖.
From Chicoutimi: 1120. **From Tadoussac**: 1520.

❖–Information not available at press date. *ATT*–Autobus Tremblay & Tremblay. Tel.: Chicoutimi 549 2463.

Table 194 MONCTON - EDMUNDSTON

SMT

CA $	30	32			km	396 ↓ ↑		31		33
0.00	0930	1825	....	....	0	d.**Saint John** ....a.	....	1250	....	1935
	1040	1935	....	....		d.Oromocto ....d.	....	1140	....	1825
9.75	1100	1955	....	....	108	a.**Fredericton** ....d.	....	1120	....	1805

CA $		23		25	km	296 ↓ ↑	20	24		
0.00	....	1155	....	1750	0	d.**Moncton** ....a.	1340	2000	....	....
7.00	....	1305	....	|	76	d.Sussex ....d.	1235	|	....	....
16.75	....	1505	....	2015	194	d.**Fredericton** ....d.	1105	1800	....	....
26.25	....	1630	....	2140	300	d.Woodstock ....d.	0925	|	....	....
28.00	....	1825	....	|	423	d.Grand Falls ....d.	0735	|	....	....
32.00	....	1915	....	2350	487	a.**Edmundston** ....d.	0645	1430	....	....

SMT– SMT (Eastern) Ltd. ☎Moncton 506 859 5105.

Table 196 CAMPBELLTON - MONCTON

SMT

CA $	30	41			km	396 ↓ ↑			40	33
0.00	....	1130	....	....	0	d.**Campbellton** ....a.	....	....	1800	....
❖	....	1330	....	....	❖	d.Bathurst ....d.	....	....	1615	....
16.75	1415	|	....	....	182	d. Newcastle ....a.	....	....	|	1530
17.25	1435	1505	....	....	188	d.Chatham ....d.	....	....	1505	1505
25.00	....	1700	....	....	346	a.**Moncton** ....d.	....	....	1230	....

❖– Information not available at press date.
SMT– SMT (Eastern) Ltd. Tel.: Moncton 506 859 5105.

Table 198 PRINCE EDWARD ISLAND

ITR

CA $			ex③⑦	Y	km	396 ↓ ↑	P ex③⑦	W ex③⑦	Y	
14.40	....	....	....	1425	104	d. New Glasgow ....a.	....	....	1400	....
7.00	0730	....	....	|	80	d. Souris ....a.	....	....	|	1935
0.00	0845	....	1600	1730	0	d.**Charlottetown** ....d.	1015	1115	1045	1800
8.15	....	....	1720	....	71	d.Summerside ....d.	0905	1005	....	....
12.00	....	....	1900	....	153	a.**Tignish** ....d.	0700	0800	....	....

P–May 29-Oct. 28. W–Oct. 30-May 26. Y–May 29-Oct. 9. ③–Wednesdays. ⑦–Sundays. *ITR*–Island Transit. Tel.: Charlottetown 902 368 5100.

Table 200 MONTRÉAL - RIMOUSKI 🚌 OEX

CA $	3L	227L	31	11	223L	33L	133L	15L	221	37L	64/243	km	396 ↓ ↑	150M	160	132M	224M	36M	66	136M	154M	166 ⑤⑦	34	64/130
0.00	....	0930	....	....	1400	....	....	1700a	1800	....	2230	0	d.**Montréal** ....d.	....	....	....	1625	....	....	2035	....	....	....	0610
	1130	|	1300	....	|	1600	1745	2015	|	0100	|		d. **Québec** ....a.	1025	1025	1335	|	1835	1730	|	2240	2315	0315	|
28.10	1215	1215	|	....	1645	1645	|	2100	|	0140	s	259	d.Lévis ....a.	|	0940	|	1335	1750	|	1750	|	2230	|	|
32.15	1305	1330	|	....	1810	1735	|	2150	|	0225	|	314	d.Montmagny ....a.	|	0855	|	1220	1705	|	1625	|	2150	|	0210
49.00	1510	1500	1525	1525	1930	1940	2015	2355	2330	0350	0345	449	d.Rivière du Loup ....d.	0800	0650	1100	1100	1500	1505	1505	2015	2005	0050	0050
❖	....	|	|	1601	....	....	2046	....	0006	s	|	❖	d.Trois Pistoles ....d.	0721	....	1015	....	1421	|	|	1926	....	....	0013
52.05	....	1620	1645	1655	....	....	2140	....	0055	0510	0505	559	a.**Rimouski** ....d.	0630	....	0930	....	1325	1335	1335	1830	....	....	2325

a- Ⓐ only. s–Calls to set down only. Ⓐ–Mondays to Fridays except holidays. ⑤–Fridays. ⑦–Sundays. *OEX*–Orléans Express Inc. Tel.: Montréal 514 847 4000.

Table 201 RIMOUSKI - GASPÉ 🚌 OEX

CA $	143M	39M			131M	111		127		133M ④⑤		km	396 ↓ ↑			70L	66		166 ⑤⑦	34			230	236L
0.00	0600	0615	....	....	1700	1730	....	1730	....	2215	....	0	d.**Rimouski** ....a.	....	....	1235	1255	....	1750	2255	....	....	2255	0045
	0633	0646	....	....	1738	|	....	1807	....	2246	....	32	d.Mont Joli ....d.	....	....	sr	1223	....	1715	2223	....	....	2225	0015
	0743	|	....	....	|	|	....	1915	....	....	....	94	d. Matane ....d.	....	....	|	|	....	....	|	....	....	2125	2315
	0857	|	....	....	|	|	....	2029	....	....	....	182	a. Ste. Anne des Monts d.	....	....	|	|	....	....	|	....	....	2005	2155
	|	0903	....	....	1937	|	....	....	....	....	....	192	d.Matapédia ....d.	....	....	|	1009	....	....	2006	....	....	|	....
	|	1032	....	....	2025	|	....	....	....	....	....	213	a.**Campbellton** ....d.	....	....	|	1047	....	....	2044	....	....	|	....
	|	1105	....	....	2120	2125	....	....	....	....	....		d.Carleton ....d.	....	....	0925	0850	....	....	1845	....	....	|	....
	|	1425	....	....	....	0040	....	....	....	....	....	471	a.Percé ....d.	....	....	0535	....	....	....	1445	....	....	|	....
	1255	1515	....	....	....	0130	....	....	....	....	....	391	a.**Gaspé** ....d.	....	....	0445	....	....	....	1350	....	....	1605	....

r– Calls by request. s–Calls to set down only. ④–Thursdays. ⑤–Fridays. ⑦–Sundays. *OEX*–Orléans Express Inc. Tel.: Montréal 514 847 4000.

Table 202 HALIFAX - SYDNEY/YARMOUTH 🚌 ALL

CA $	67		47L	57	41L	37	69			75	55 ⑤		21 ②③	21 ex②③		km	396 ↓ ↑		56	38 †	22 ③④	22 ①②⑤⑥	72		64	48L	38 ⚒	22A †		42L	76	
0.00	0800	....	0730	1300	1300	1415	1430	....	....	1645	1730	....	1815	1815	....	0	d.**Halifax** ....a.	....	1105	1230	1235	1235	1500	....	1745	1800	1945	2150	....	0010	2250	....
6.75	0935	....	0845	1455	1415	|	|	....	....	1830	1930	....	|	|	....	93	d.**Truro** ....d.	....	0925	|	|	|	1340	....	1630	1650	|	|	....	2305	2145	....
11.00	1030	....	|	1615	|	|	|	....	....	1925	2046	....	|	|	....	156	d.New Glasgow ....d.	....	0820	|	|	|	1230	....	1535	|	|	|	....	|	2050	....
14.75	1140	....	|	1700	|	|	1730	....	....	2015	2130	....	|	|	....	214	d.Antigonish ....d.	....	0730	|	|	|	1140	....	1445	|	|	|	....	|	2005	....
18.75	1250	....	|	....	|	|	1825	....	....	2110	....	....	|	|	....	277	d.Port Hawkesbury ..d.	....	....	|	|	|	1015	....	1305	|	|	|	....	|	1905	....
26.50	|	....	|	....	|	|	2035	....	....	2300	....	....	|	|	....	428	d.North Sydney ....d.	....	....	|	|	|	0755	....	|	|	|	|	....	|	1700	....
26.75	1450	....	|	....	|	|	2100	....	....	2330	....	....	|	|	....	450	a.**Sydney** ....d.	....	....	|	|	|	0730	....	1100	|	|	|	....	|	1630	....
15.50	....	....	1030	....	1605	|	....	....	....	....	....	....	|	|	....	225	a. Amherst ....d.	....	....	|	|	|	....	....	....	1505	|	|	....	2115	....	....
5.00	....	....	....	....	....	1535	....	....	....	....	....	....	1915	1915	....	69	d. Windsor ....d.	....	....	1115	1140	1140	....	....	....	....	1830	2055	....	....	....	....
8.00	....	....	....	....	....	1631	....	....	....	....	....	....	2005	2005	....	111	d. Kentville ....d.	....	....	1022	1050	1050	....	....	....	....	1737	2005	....	....	....	....
14.50	....	....	....	....	....	1835	....	....	....	....	....	....	....	2135	....	211	d. Annapolis Royal..d.	....	....	0813	....	0910	....	....	....	....	1528	1825	....	....	....	....
16.75	....	....	....	....	....	1918	....	....	....	....	....	....	....	2210	....	245	d. Digby ....d.	....	....	0730	....	0840	....	....	....	....	1445	1750	....	....	....	....
23.25	....	....	....	....	....	....	....	....	....	....	....	....	....	0005	....	352	a. **Yarmouth** ....d.	....	....	....	....	0645	....	....	....	....	....	1600	....	....	....	....

⚒– Daily except Sundays and holidays. †–Sundays and holidays. ①–Mondays. ②–Tuesdays. ③-Wednesdays. ④–Thursdays. ⑤–Fridays. ⑥–Saturdays.
ALL– Acadian Lines. Tel.: Halifax 902 453 0353.

Table 203 TORONTO - PEMBROKE 🚌 GLC

CA $			6126		km	396 ↓ ↑	6127 ex⑦			6129 ⑦
0.00	....	....	1245	....	0	d.**Toronto** ....a.	1545	....	....	2020
17.50	....	....	1515	....	88	d.Peterborough........d.	1350	....	....	1800
	....	....	1727	....		d.Bancroft........d.	1148	....	....	1608
49.50	....	....	2005	....	410	a.**Pembroke**........d.	0840	....	....	1300

⑦–Sundays. *GLC*–Greyhound Lines of Canada. Tel.: Toronto 416 393 7911.

Table 204 396 THETFORD MINES 🚌 DRU

🚌 service Montréal-St. Hyacinthe-Drummondville-Victoriaville-Thetford Mines and v.v. ❖ km. Journey: 3½ hours. Fare CA $: ❖.
From Montréal: 1010, 1715, 1815⑤, 2010⑦.
From Thetford Mines: 0715, 1630, 1830⑦.

❖–Information not available at press date. ⑤–Fridays. ⑦–Sundays. *DRU*–Autobus Drummondville Ltée. Tel.: Drummondville 477 2111.

Table 205 HALIFAX - YARMOUTH 🚌 MKB

CA $	12	4A	4 ⑤	20 ⚒	km	396 ↓ ↑	1 a	13A †	13 ⚒	19 †
0.00	0900	1745	1745	2030	0	d.**Halifax** ....a.	0815	1700	1505	2000
6.50	0935	1825	|	2103	52	d.Hubbards........d.	0737	1620	1425	1922
8.00	0955	1845	|	2112	71	d.Chester ....d.	|	1605	1410	1913
10.50	1015	1905	|	2125	97	d.Mahone Bay........d.	0715	1540	1345	1900
11.00	1030	1920	|	|	109	d.Lunenburg........d.	|	1525	1330	|
12.00	1110	1945	1915	2140	129	d.Bridgewater........d.	0700	1500	1305	1845
16.50	1150	....	2000	....	177	d.Liverpool........d.	....	....	1215	1750
22.50	1300	....	2045	....	241	d.Shelburne........d.	....	....	1115	1650
23.50	1340	....	....	....	281	d.Barrington Passage d.	....	....	1025	1600
28.50	1445	....	....	....	355	a.**Yarmouth** ....d.	....	....	0925	1500

a–Additional service on ⑤ leaving at 1530. ⚒–Daily except Sundays and holidays. †–Sundays and holidays. ⑤–Fridays.
MKB–Mackenzie Bus Line. Tel.: Bridgewater 902 543 2491.

Table 206 CHARLOTTETOWN 🚌 SMT

CA $	50		52		km	396 ↓ ↑		51		53
0.00	0745	....	1230	....	0	d.**Charlottetown** ....a.	....	1745	....	2345
5.00	0850	....	1335	....	60	d.Summerside ....d.	....	1650	....	2250
7.25	0910	....	1355	....	84	d.Borden ....d.	....	1620	....	2220
10.00	1020	....	1520	....	100	d.Cape Tormentine....d.	....	1510	....	2150
12.00	1110	....	|	....	152	a. Amherst ....d.	....	|	....	|
17.00	1155	....	1630	....	218	a.**Moncton** ....d.	....	1405	....	2005

SMT– SMT (Eastern) Ltd. ☎ Moncton 506 859 5105.

Table 211 ST. JOHN'S - BONAVISTA 🚌 CL NH

CA $			NH	CL	km	396 ↓ ↑	CL ex⑦	NH	CL ⑦	
❖	....	❖	....	1700	0	d.**St. John's**........a.	1145	....	1545	....
❖	....	|	....	1805	84	d.Whitbourne Junction d.	1020	....	1420	....
0.00	....	|	2000	2015	185	d.Clarenville ....d.	0830	0930	1230	....
4.00	....	|	2125	|	242	d.Trinity ....d.	|	0825	|	....
7.00	....	|	2215	2215	328	d.**Bonavista**........d.	0600	0730	1000	....
❖	....	❖	....	....	129	a. Carbonear........d.	....	....	....	....

⑦–Sundays. ❖–Information not available at press date. *CL*–Clarenville Transportation. Tel.: Clarenville 463 2492. *NH*–Newhook's Bus Service. Tel.: Argentia ❖.

Table 208 FORTUNE 🚌 SPM

CA $	W 🅁				km	396 ↓ ↑		W 🅁		
0.00	0800	....	....	....	0	d.**St. John's**........a.	....	1730	....	....
	|	....	....	....		d.Grand Bank........d.	....	|	....	....
❖	1230	....	....	....	247	a.**Fortune**........d.	....	1300	....	....

W–June 28-Sept. 2. 🅁–Reservation obligatory. ❖–Information not available at press date. *SPM*–SPM Tours. Tel.: St. John's 709 722 3892.

Table 212 396 DARTMOUTH 🚌 HMT

🚌 service Halifax-Dartmouth and v.v. *3* km. Journey: 15 mins. Fare: CA $: 1.30.
From Halifax: 0015②-⑥, 0028⑦, 0040②-⑥, 0625Ⓐ/0628⑥/0730† and frequent to 2340Ⓐ/2358⑥/2359†.
From Dartmouth: 0026ex①, 0608⚒/0655† and frequent to 2346†/2355⚒.

Ⓐ–Mondays to Fridays except holidays. ⚒–Daily except Sundays and holidays. †–Sundays and holidays. ①–Mondays. ②–Tuesdays. ⑥–Saturdays. *HMT*–Halifax Metro Transit. Tel.: Dartmouth 902 421 6600.

Table 210 QUÉBEC - WHITE RIVER 🚌 AQC VT

US $	VT 9096	AQC 53/22 ⚒	AQC 53/204 ⑤⑦	AQC 53/2 ex⑤⑦	km	396 ↓ ↑	AQC 53/1 ⚒	AQC 53/201 ⑤⑦	AQC 53/23 ⚒	VT 9093
	....	0630	1335	1630	0	d.**Québec** ◇ ....a.	1245	1630	2030	....
	....	0955	1640	2015	228	d.**Sherbrooke** ◇........d.	0850	1320	1700	....
	0735	....	....	....	311	d.Newport ....d.	....	....	....	1940
	0845	....	....	....	387	d.St. Johnsbury ....d.	....	....	....	1830
0.00	1025	....	....	....	495	d.**White River Junction** .d.	....	....	....	1700

◇– Additional trips from Québec: 0750①, 0950⑥, 1745⑤†, 1815†, returning from Sherbrooke at 1300†, 1430⑥, 1745④⑤⑦, 1820⑦.
⚒– Daily except Sundays and holidays. †–Sundays and holidays.
①– Mondays. ④–Thursdays. ⑤–Fridays. ⑥–Saturdays. ⑦–Sundays.
AQC– Autobus Auger Inc. ☎ Chateauguay 514 691 1654.
VT– Vermont Transit. Tel.: Burlington 802 864 6811.

Table 214 TERRENCEVILLE 🚌

CA $					km	396 ↓ ↑				
0.00	....	❖	....	....	0	d.**Terrenceville** ....a.	....	....	❖	....
❖	....	❖	....	....	❖	a.**St. John's**........d.	....	....	❖	....

❖– Information not available at press date.

Table 215 ARGENTIA 🚌 NH

CA $	⚒	†		⑦	km	396 ↓ ↑		†		
0.00	0800	1400	....	1830	0	d.**Argentia** ....a.	....	1115	....	1915
❖	0845	1445	....	1915	❖	a.**Whitbourne**........d.	....	1020	....	1820

⚒– Daily except Sundays and holidays. †–Sundays and holidays. ⑦–Sundays.
❖– Information not available at press date.
NH– Newhook's Bus Service. Tel.: Argentia ❖.

Table 220 NEWFOUNDLAND ♿ — CN

CA $	519 ⑤			503	km	396 ↓ ↑		504		522 ⑦P
0.00	1730	....	....	0800	0	d.**St. John's**.........a.	....	2215	....	....
12.50	1840	....	....	0900	84	d.Whitbourne Junction.d.	....	2018	....	....
24.25	2000	....	....	1022	187	d.Clarenville ....d.	....	1904	....	....
37.25	2156	....	....	1246	331	d.**Gander Airport**.d.	....	1702	....	....
44.25	|	....	....	|	392	d.Lewisporte.........d.	....	|	....	....
44.25	2302	....	....	1351	414	d.Bishop's Falls....d.	....	1529	....	....
46.00	2315	....	....	1415	428	d.Grand Falls ⊙...d.	....	1515	....	....
47.25	....	....	....	1436	457	d.Badger ....d.	....	1445	....	....
60.75	....	....	....	1712	639	d.Deer Lake ....d.	....	1233	....	....
64.25	....	....	....	1755	687	d.Corner Brook.....d.	....	1125	....	1730
≶22.50	....	....	....	1859	761	d.Stephenville.......d.	....	1017	....	1625
79.75	....	....	....	2105	904	a.**Port aux Basques**.d.	....	0800	....	1400

–Runs on † (except on ⑦ of holiday weekends).Will not operate May12 to September 8. –Sundays and holidays. ⑤–Fridays. ⑦–Sundays. ⊙–Windsor. ≶–Fare ex Port aux Basques. *CN*–CN Roadcruiser. Tel.: St. John's 709 737 5912.

Table 222 MONTRÉAL - BOSTON — GL VT

US $	*VT* 9122 ♣	*VT* 9424	*VT* 220 ♣	*VT* 9124	km	396 ↓ ↑	*VT* 9127 ex⑦	*VT* 231 ♣	*VT* 9321	*VT* 9523
0.00	0100**b**	....	*0745***b**	....	0	d.**Montréal** ....a.	....	1810**b**	*2315***b**	....
13.00	|	....	|	....	118	d.St. Albans ■.....d.	....	1600**b**	|	....
19.00	|	0820	1130	1430	170	d.Burlington ....d.	0700	1520	1915	2330
24.00	|	0915	1225	1525	231	d.Montpelier ....d.	0605	1405	1820	2235
25.00	|	|	|	|	242	d.Barre ....d.	0545	|	|	|
33.00	0530	1040	1350	1700	323	d.White River Junction.d.	0445	1300	1710	2130
41.00	|	|	|	1815	418	d.Concord ....d.	|	|	|	|
43.00	|	1215	1515	1840	446	d.Manchester ....d.	0220	1105	|	1925
50.00	|	|	|	1910	474	d.Nashua.............d.	|	|	|	1900
50.00	|	|	|	|	508	d.Lowell................d.	|	|	|	|
53.00	0800	1320	1630	2005	560	a.**Boston**..............d.	0115	1000	1400	1800
53.00	0820	1340	....	....	567	a.Boston Airport ≪ d.	....	....	....	....

–*GL*. ⑦–Sundays. ♣–International bus service. ≪–Logan Airport. *GL*–Greyhound Lines. Tel.: Dallas 214 789 7000. *VT*–Vermont Transit. Tel.: Burlington 802 862 9671.

Table 223 ST. ANTHONY - CORNER BROOK — VE

CA $		②④⑦			km	396 ↓ ↑			①③⑤	
0.00	....	1000	....	....	0	d.**St. Anthony**......a.	....	....	0000	....
❖	....	1140	....	....	❖	d.St. Barbe...........d.	....	....	2135	....
❖	....	1610	....	....	285	d.Deer Lake ....d.	....	....	1650	....
❖	....	....	....	....	333	a.**Corner Brook**...d.	....	....	....	....

①–Monday. ②–Tuesday. ③–Wednesdays. ④–Thursdays. ⑤–Fridays. ⑦–Sundays. ❖–Information not available at press date. *VE*–Viking Express. Tel.: St Barbe 877 2314.

Table 225 BURGEO — DBS

CA $		⚒			km	396 ↓ ↑			⚒	
0.00	....	0800	....	....	0	d.**Burgeo** ....a.	....	....	1800	....
25.00	....	1100	....	....	211	a.**Corner Brook**...d.	.....	....	1500	....

⚒–Daily except Sundays and holidays. *DBS*–Devins/Vineys Bus Services. Tel.: Burgeo ❖.

Table 226 HARBOUR BRETON — HBS

CA $		①③⑤			km	396 ↓ ↑			①③⑤	
0.00	....	0800	....	....	0	d.**Harbour Breton**a.	....	....	1900	....
25.00	....	1100	....	....	250	a.**Grand Falls**......d.	....	....	1600	....

①–Mondays. ③–Wednesdays. ⑤–Fridays. ❖–Information not available at press date. *HBS*– Hickeys Bus Service. Tel.: Harbour Breton ❖.

Table 228 SAINT JOHN - AMHERST — SMT

CA $	10		12		km	396 ↓ ↑			11	13
	....	....	1610	....		d.St Stephen ....a.	....	....	1600	....
0.00	1115	....	1740	....	0	d.**Saint John**........a.	....	....	1440	2005
	1220	....	1845	....	69	d.Sussex ....d.	....	....	1330	1905
	1400	....	2015	....	146	d.Moncton ....d.	....	....	1220	1755
	1505	....	2115	....	215	a.**Amherst** ....d.	....	....	1035	1605

SMT– SMT (Eastern) Ltd. ☎Moncton 506 859 5105.

Table 229 SUDBURY - OTTAWA - MONTRÉAL — GLC VCL

CA $	*GLC* 6104 ex⑦			*GLC* 6106 ⑦	*GLC* 6112		*GLC* 6122	*GLC* 6122	*GLC* 2764	*GLC* 6128	*GLC* 6128	km	496 ↓ ↑	*VCL* 127		*GLC* 2777	*GLC* 6103			*GLC* 6207				*GLC* 6119
0.00	....	....	....	....	0930	....	1300	....	1830	0001	....	0	d.**Sudbury** ....a.	0645**a**	....	1255	1755	....	....	1800	....	....	....	....
	....	....	....	....	1140	....	1500	1600	2020	0135	0145	124	d.North Bay.................d.	0500**a**	....	1105	1600	....	....	1620	....	....	....	....
	0840	....	....	1240	1455	....	....	1940	....	....	0450	341	d.Pembroke.................d.	0145**a**	....	....	1230	....	....	1320	....	....	....	2010
63.96	1116	....	....	1515	1715	....	....	2150	....	....	0650	502	a.**Ottawa** ≠ ....d.	2359**a**	....	....	1000	....	....	1130	....	....	....	1725
83.30	1420**b**	....	....	....	2020**b**	....	....	....	....	....	....	700	a.**Montréal** ≠ ....d.	2100	....	....	....	....	....	....	....	....	....	....

–*GLC*. b–*VCL*. Ⓐ–Mondays to Fridays except holidays. ⚒–Daily except Sundays and holidays. ⑦–Sundays. ≠–Local *VCL* services operate between Montréal and Ottawa throughout the day, from Montréal at 0001, 0600Ⓐ, 0700 and hourly to 2200, returning at 0600⚒, 0700 and hourly to 2200, 2330. *GLC*–Greyhound Lines of Canada. Tel.: Winnipeg 204 783 8840. *VCL*–Voyageur Colonial. Tel.: Ottawa 613 238 5900.

Table 231 EDMUNDSTON — SMT

CA $	20		24	26	km	396 ↓ ↑		21	23	25
0.00	0350	....	1135	2020	0	d.**Rivière du Loup** a.	....	1040	2015	0035
	0625	....	1420	2310	125	a.**Edmundston** ....d.	....	0950	1725	0001

SMT– SMT (Eastern) Ltd. Tel.: Moncton 506 859 5105.

Table 232 MONTRÉAL - NEWPORT — AVI

CA $	1 ♣Ⓒ	13 Ⓐ	5/7	9 ⑤⑦	km	396 ↓ ↑	2	6 ♣Ⓒ	14 Ⓐ	8 ⑦
0.00	1020	1100	1810	2115	0	d.**Montréal**...........a.	0920	1705	1705	2015
	1230	1310	2020	2325	131	d.Knowlton ....d.	0710	1455	1455	1805
	1255	1335	2045**a**	....	159	d.Mansonville ....d.	....	1430	1430	1740
	1302	....	....	....	165	d.Highwater ■ .....d.	....	1423	....	....
	1335	....	....	....	187	a.**Newport**...........d.	....	1350	....	....

a–⑤ only. Ⓐ–Mondays to Fridays except holidays. Ⓒ–Saturdays, Sundays and holidays. ⑤–Fridays. ⑦–Sundays. ♣–International bus service. *AVI*–Autobus Viens Inc. Tel.: Farnham 514 293 3129.

UNITED STATES OF AMERICA

See MAPS 3, 4 and 5 (p. 77, 102, 103) *9363130 sq. km.* Capital: Washington

Rail services in the USA are provided mainly by AMTRAK. Suburban services, in general, are *not* operated by AMTRAK, and on common sections of route, fares are usuall[y] different and tickets are not interavailable. AMTRAK trains offer one basic class of accommodation - coach class, shown as 'C' in the following tables. Supplements are payabl[e] for superior accommodation, such as overnight sleeping accommodation or club car (parlor car) seats, which are shown as 'S' or 'P' in the tables. Some trains conve[y] 'Slumbercoaches' (high-density sleeping cars) and these are shown as [sleeper] in the tables. Metroliners, high-speed trains operating generally between New York and Washingtor[n] charge higher basic fares, and a further supplement is payable for travel by 'Metroclub'. A few trains, on selected routes, include 'Custom Class' - a high quality coach class fo[r] which a small premium is paid. Where available this will be shown as '1' class. Children of under 2 years travel free; those of 2 but under 16 years pay 50% of basic coach fare (bu[t] full accommodation charges); those of 16 and over pay full fare. Children below 12 years are not generally permitted to travel unaccompanied, whilst those who are must pay fu[ll] fare. A network of excellent bus services, usually air-conditioned, operates throughout the country.

Table 300 NEW YORK - POUGHKEEPSIE - ALBANY

NRPC

US $ C cl.	396 1.435m.	km			63	261	69	251	281	71	283	267	257	259	289			265	49	271			277		
					C‡	1‡C‡	1‡C‡	C‡	C‡	1‡C‡	C‡	C‡	C‡	1‡C‡	1‡C‡			C‡	S‡C‡	C‡			C‡		
					◆	P	◆	🍷	◆	◆	◆	R	⚒🍷	◆	◆			🍷	◆	🍷			🍷		
	↓						⚒	①②③	④⑤⑥†	†			𝔛	①-④	⑤				Ⓡ	Ⓓ			Ⓒ		
0.00	**New York Penn. Stn.** d.	*0*	....	....	0720	0755	0830	1145	1145	1250	1435	1550	1550	1635	1635	....	....	1737	1840	2037	....	....	2335	....	....
5.25	Yonkers.............d.	*24*	....	....	0744u	|	0854u	1209u	1209u	1314u	1459u	1614u	1614u	|	|	....	....	1801u	|	2101u	....	....	|	....	....
6.75	Croton Harmon...d.	*54*	....	....	0804u	|	0914u	1229u	1229u	1334u	1519u	1634u	1634u	|	|	....	....	1821u	1927u	2121u	....	....	0017u	....	....
11.75	Poughkeepsie ....d.	*118*	....	....	0843u	|	0953u	1308u	1308u	1413u	1558u	1713u	1713u	|	|	....	....	1900u	|	2200u	....	....	0056u	....	....
	Rhinecliff ↷........d.		....	....	0858	0923	1008	1323	1323	1428	1613	1728	1728	|	|	....	....	1915	2025	2215	....	....	0111	....	....
30.00	Hudson..............d.	*184*	....	....	0920	0945	1030	1345	1345	1450	1635	1750	1750	|	|	....	....	1937	2050	2237	....	....	0133	....	....
40.00	**Albany Rensselaer** a.	*229*	....	....	0945	1015	1055	1410	1410	1515	1700	1815	1815	1847	1847	....	....	2002	2123	2302	....	....	0158	....	....

396			242		246	244	248		254	284	2048	48			286		264	68		64	270	260	288		
			C‡		1‡C‡	C‡	C‡		C‡	C‡	C‡	S‡C‡			C‡		C‡	1‡C‡		C‡	C‡	C‡	1‡C‡		
			🍷		◆	🍷	🍷		🍷	◆Ⓡ	🍷	◆			◆		🍷	◆		◆	𝔚	Q	◆		
↓			Ⓐ		Ⓐ	Ⓒ	⚒		ex①⑤⑥	①⑤⑥	𝔅	Ⓡ					⑥				†🍷		†		
Albany Rensselaer .d.	....	....	0625	....	0705	0655	0805	....	1035	1035	1235	1250	....	....	1405	....	1605	1740	....	1905	1955	1955	2050	....	....
Hudson....................d.	....	....	0649	....	|	0719	0829	....	1059	1059	1259	1315s	....	....	1429	....	1629	1804	....	1929	2019	2019	2114	....	....
Rhinecliff ↷...............d.	....	....	0711	....	|	0741	0851	....	1121	1121	1321	1342s	....	....	1451	....	1651	1826	....	1951	2041	2041	2136	....	....
Poughkeepsie ....d.	....	....	|	....	|	0756s	0906s	....	1136s	1136s	|	|	....	....	1506s	....	1706s	1841s	....	2006s	|	|	2151s	....	....
Croton Harmon.........d.	....	....	0803s	....	|	0835s	0945s	....	1215s	1215s	|	1443s	....	....	1545s	....	1745s	1920s	....	2045s	|	|	2230s	....	....
Yonkers....................d.	....	....	|	....	|	0854s	1004s	....	|	|	|	|	....	....	1604s	....	1804s	1939s	....	2104s	|	|	2249s	....	....
New York Penn. Stn....a.	....	....	0845	....	0915	0920	1030	....	1302	1302	1455	1549	....	....	1635	....	1830	2010	....	2135	2215	2215	2320	....	....

48/49– LAKE SHORE LIMITED–[sleeper]‡, [C] and ✗ Chicago(**48/49**)-New York and v.v.
63/64– THE MAPLE LEAF–[C] and ⊗ New York(**63**)-Niagara Falls(**98**)-Toronto; [C] and ⊗ Toronto(**97**)-Niagara Falls(**64**)-New York.
68– ADIRONDACK–[1C] and ⊗ Montréal(**68**)-New York.
69– ADIRONDACK–[1C] and ⊗ New York(**69**)-Montréal.
71– ADIRONDACK–[1C] and ⊗ New York(**71**)-Montréal.
246– [1C] and 🍷 Schenectady(**246**)-New York.
259– [1C] and 🍷 New York(**259**)-Schenectady.
281– [C] and 🍷 New York(**281**)-Niagara Falls.
283– [C] (also [1] on ⑤) and 🍷 New York(**283**)-Niagara Falls.
284– [C] and 🍷 Niagara Falls(**284**)-New York.
286– [C] and 🍷 Niagara Falls(**286**)-New York.
288– [1C] and 🍷 Niagara Falls(**288**)-New York.
289– [1C] and 🍷 New York(**289**)-Syracuse.
P– ⑤ July 27-Aug. 31: [1C] and 🍷 New York(**261**)-Saratoga Springs.
Q– ⑦ June 30-Aug. 25 and ⑤ July 27-Aug. 31 (also Sept. 2): [C] (also [1] on ⑤) and 🍷 Saratoga Springs(**260**)-New York.
R– ⑤ June 28-Aug. 30: [C] and 🍷 New York(**267**)-Saratoga Springs.
s– Calls to set down only.
u– Calls to take up only.
⚒– Daily except Sundays and holidays.
‡– Air-conditioned.
🍷– Light refreshments.
①– Mondays.
②– Tuesdays.
③– Wednesdays.
④– Thursdays.
⑤– Fridays.
⑥– Saturdays.
†– Sundays and holidays.
Ⓐ– Mondays to Fridays except holidays.
Ⓓ– Daily except Saturdays.
Ⓒ– Saturdays, Sundays and holidays.
Ⓡ– Reservation obligatory.
[sleeper]– Sleeping car.
[C]– Seating car.
✗– Restaurant car.
⊗– Buffet car.
𝔅– Runs May 27 and Sept. 2 only.
𝔚– Will not run on May 26, or June 30-Sept. 1.
𝔛– Will not run on ⑤ June 28-Aug. 30.
↷– Kingston.
NRPC–AMTRAK. Tel.: New York 212 582 6875.

[tram]–Tram [mountain railway]–Mountain Railway [cablecar]–Cablecar

Table 305 PORTLAND - BETHEL #### SL&A

R.T. US $ C cl.	C⊗ ⑤Ⓒ				km	496 1.435m. Dec. 26-Apr. 30 ↓ ↑			C⊗ ⑤Ⓒ	
0.00	0630	....	....	....	0	d.**Portland** ....a.	....	....	1850	....
	0715	....	....	....		d.Auburn 𝔗..........d.	....	....	1805	....
25.00	0830	....	....	....	113	a.**Bethel** ....d.	....	....	1705	....

⊗– Buffet car. ⑤–Fridays. Ⓒ–Saturdays, Sundays and holidays.
𝔗– Lewiston. *SL&A*–Sunday River Co. Inc./St. Lawrence & Atlantic Railroad.

Table 307 CAPE COD #### NRPC

US $ C cl.			234 C‡ ⑤◆		km	496 1.435m. June 28-Sept. 29 ↓ ↑		235 C‡ ⑦◆		
0.00	....	....	1833	....	304	d.**New Haven**.......a.	....	2125	....	....
	....	....	2040	....	123	d.Providence ....d.	....	1855	....	....
	....	....	2230	....	38	a.Buzzards Bay....d.	....	1657	....	....
	....	....	2243	....	25	a.Sandwich...........d.	....	1641	....	....
	....	....	2320	....	0	a.**Hyannis** ....d.	....	1615	....	....

234/5– C‡ Boston(**234/5**)-Hyannis and v.v. ⑤–Fridays. ⑦–Sundays.
▭– Seating car. ‡–Air-conditioned.
NRPC–AMTRAK. Tel.: New York 212 582 6875.

Table 310 NEW HAVEN - MONTRÉAL #### NRPC

US $ C cl.	56 C‡ ◆		142 C‡ 🍷		km	496 1.435m ↓ ↑	471 C‡		55 C‡ ◆⚒	57 C‡ ◆†
0.00	0949	....	1605	....	0	d.*New York* ....a.	1230	....	1557	1925
21.00	1143	....	1800	....		d.**New Haven**...........a.	1025	....	1405	1730
26.50	|	....	|	....		d. New London.........d.	|	....	|	|
	1320	....	1930	....		a.Springfield ....d.	0900	....	1240	1605
37.00	1425	....	|	....		d.Amherst..................d.	|	....	1104	1432
40.00	1515	....	*2120a*	....		d.Brattleboro.............d.	*0645a*	....	1016	1336
46.00	1550	....	*2150a*	....		d.Bellows Falls ....d.	*0610a*	....	0941	1301
	1613	....	*2220a*	....		d.Claremont...............d.	*0540a*	....	0919	1239
54.00	1650	....	*2250a*	....		d.White River Junction d.	*0500a*	....	0850	1210
64.00	1807	....	....	....		d.Montpelier ....d.	....	....	0727	1047
66.00	1850	....	....	....		d.Essex Junction ◇ ..d.	....	....	0645	1005
70.00	1935	....	....	....		d.St. Albans ▣.........d.	....	....	0615	0935
72.00	*2145a*	....	....	....		a.**Montréal** Central....d.	....	....	*0345a*	*0705a*

55/57– VERMONTER–C‡ and 🍷 St. Albans(**55/57**)-Washington.
56– VERMONTER–C‡ and 🍷 Washington(**56**)-St. Albans.
a–Connection by bus. ◇–Burlington. ‡–Air-conditioned. 🍷–Light refreshments.
⚒–Daily except Sundays and holidays. †–Sundays and holidays.
NRPC–AMTRAK. Tel.: New York 212 582 6875.

Table 315 396 BOSTON LOCAL SERVICES #### bus CJR MBTA PRT

ocal #### (C‡ only, 1.435m.) and bus services operate in the Boston area as follows:

rlington ζ *(MBTA)* (❖ km, US $: ❖). From Harvard: 0512Ⓐ/0518⑥/0630† and frequent to 0100, returning at 0455⚒/0607† and frequent to 0037①⑦/0042ex①⑦. Journey: 15 mins.

ttleboro θ *(MBTA)* (❖ km, US $: 3.75). From Boston South: 0525Ⓐ, 0643Ⓐ, 0645⑥, 0800Ⓐ, 0825Ⓐ, 1000⚒, 1100Ⓒ, 1220Ⓐ, 1245Ⓒ, 1415Ⓐ, 1445Ⓒ, 1550Ⓐ, 1635Ⓐ, 1645Ⓒ, 1705Ⓐ, 1740Ⓐ, 1820Ⓐ, 1845, 2020Ⓐ, 2045Ⓒ, 2155Ⓐ, 2300Ⓒ, 2359Ⓐ, returning at 0547Ⓐ, 0633Ⓐ, 0655⑥, 0709Ⓐ, 0730Ⓐ, 0800Ⓐ, 0827Ⓐ, 0855⚒, 1002Ⓐ, 1145Ⓒ, 1149Ⓐ, 1315Ⓒ, 1403Ⓐ, 1455Ⓒ, 1535Ⓐ, 1655Ⓒ, 1728Ⓐ, 1809Ⓐ, 1915Ⓒ, 2000Ⓐ, 2055Ⓒ, 2158Ⓐ, 2235Ⓒ, 2323Ⓐ. Journey: 45 mins.

elmont θ *(MBTA)* (❖ km, US $: 2.00). From Boston North: 0010②-⑥, 0725Ⓐ, 0820Ⓐ, 0830⑥, 0930†, 0935Ⓐ, 1120⑥, 1200†, 1320⚒, 1500⑥, 1530⑥, 1600Ⓐ, 1630⑥, 1650Ⓐ, 1730, 1815Ⓐ, 1930Ⓒ, 1935Ⓐ, 2045Ⓐ, 2135†, 2230Ⓐ, 2300Ⓒ, returning at 0700Ⓐ, 0744Ⓐ, 0755⑥, 0834Ⓐ, 0904Ⓐ, 0905†, 0959Ⓐ, 1035⑥, 1109†, 1140Ⓐ, 1230⑥, 1237Ⓐ, 1245†, 1420Ⓐ, 1459⑥, 1532†, 1600⑥, 1618Ⓐ, 1645Ⓐ, 1654†, 1741Ⓐ, 1809⑥, 1840†, 1850⑥, 1912Ⓐ, 2109†, 2114Ⓐ, 2129⑥. Journey: 15 mins.

helsea ζ *(MBTA)* (❖ km, US $: 1.25). From Boston: 0020⑦, 0025②-⑥, 0055, 0527Ⓐ/0557⑥/0655† and frequent to 2355, returning at 0004⑦, 0009②-⑥, 0029①, 0039ex①, 0514Ⓐ/0544⑥/0639† and frequent to 2339. Journey: 12 mins.

over ζ *(CJR)* (*112* km, US $: 12.95). From Boston: 0730Ⓐ, 0900Ⓒ, 0930Ⓐ, 1200, 1300, 1400, 1500, 1600, 1630Ⓐ, 1700Ⓒ, 1715Ⓐ, 1745Ⓐ, 1900, 2000, 2230, returning at 0410Ⓐ, 0510Ⓐ, 0540, 0610Ⓐ, 0640Ⓐ, 0740, 0940, 1040, 1140, 1240, 1440, 1555, 1655, 1840. Journey: 1¾ hours.

verett ζ *(MBTA)* (❖ km, US $: 1.25). From Sullivan: 0015, 0441⑥, 0520⑥, 0530Ⓐ, 0550Ⓐ, 0610⚒, 0615† and frequent (about hourly on †) to 2315, returning at 0045ex①, 0047①, 0510⑥, 0521Ⓐ, 0540Ⓐ, 0555⑥, 0600Ⓐ, 0615Ⓐ, 0630Ⓐ, 0640⑥, 0645⑥ and frequent (about hourly on †) to 2345⚒, 2347†. Journey: 10 mins.

itchburg θ *(MBTA)* (*81* km, US $: 4.75). From Boston North: 0010②-⑥, 0830⑥, 0850Ⓐ, 0935Ⓐ, 1120⚒, 1200†, 1320Ⓐ, 1530⑥, 1650Ⓐ, 1720Ⓐ, 1730Ⓒ, 1815Ⓐ, 2045Ⓐ, 2135†, 2230Ⓐ, 2300Ⓒ, returning at 0545Ⓐ, 0625Ⓐ, 0640⑥, 0655Ⓐ, 0715Ⓐ, 0750†, 0920⑥, 1025Ⓐ, 1115⑥, 1124Ⓐ, 1130†, 1305Ⓐ, 1415†, 1445⑥, 1505Ⓐ, 1725†, 1735⑥, 1905Ⓐ, 2230Ⓐ. Journey: 1½ hours.

ramingham θ *(MBTA)* (*34* km, US $: 3.25). From Boston South: 0550Ⓐ, 0600⑥, 0650Ⓐ, 0740Ⓐ, 0800⑥, 0905Ⓐ, 1030Ⓒ, 1105Ⓐ, 1235Ⓒ, 1255Ⓐ, 1430Ⓒ, 1440Ⓐ, 1630, 1655Ⓐ, 1705Ⓐ, 1730Ⓐ, 1800Ⓐ, 1815Ⓐ, 1830Ⓒ, 1855Ⓐ, 2020Ⓐ, 2030Ⓒ, 2205Ⓐ, 2300Ⓒ, 2305Ⓐ, returning at 0000Ⓒ, 0005Ⓐ, 0615Ⓐ, 0650Ⓐ, 0700⑥, 0702Ⓐ, 0720Ⓐ, 0745Ⓐ, 0800Ⓐ, 0835Ⓐ, 0900⑥, 1000Ⓐ, 1130Ⓒ, 1205Ⓐ, 1330Ⓒ, 1400Ⓐ, 1545, 1730Ⓒ, 1740Ⓐ, 1840Ⓐ, 1930Ⓒ, 2020Ⓐ, 2120Ⓐ, 2130Ⓒ, 2305Ⓐ. Journey: 50 mins.

ranklin θ *(MBTA)* (❖ km, US $: 3.50). From Boston South: 0350Ⓐ, 0400Ⓐ, 0720⑥, 0750Ⓐ, 0910Ⓐ, 0920⑥, 1050Ⓐ, 1120Ⓒ, 1245Ⓐ, 1320Ⓒ, 1445Ⓐ, 1520Ⓒ, 1605Ⓐ, 1630Ⓐ, 1710Ⓐ, 1720Ⓒ, 1740Ⓐ, 1815Ⓐ, 1920Ⓒ, 1935Ⓐ, 2050Ⓐ, 2120Ⓒ, 2220Ⓐ, 2320Ⓒ, 2350Ⓐ, returning at 0522Ⓐ, 0552Ⓐ, 0622Ⓐ, 0642⚒, 0713Ⓐ, 0752Ⓐ, 0842⑥, 0913Ⓐ, 1022Ⓐ, 1042Ⓒ, 1211Ⓐ, 1242Ⓒ, 1407Ⓐ, 1442Ⓒ, 1608Ⓐ, 1642Ⓒ, 1732Ⓐ, 1842Ⓒ, 1947Ⓐ, 2042Ⓒ, 2057Ⓐ, 2228Ⓐ, 2242Ⓒ, 2342Ⓐ. Journey: 50 mins.

averhill θ *(MBTA)* (*53* km, US $: 3.75). From Boston North: 0655Ⓐ, *0750*Ⓐ, 0845Ⓒ, 0850Ⓐ, 1145Ⓒ, 1320Ⓐ, 1445Ⓒ, *1520*Ⓐ, 1630Ⓐ, 1715Ⓐ, 1745Ⓒ, 1815Ⓐ, 2020Ⓐ, 2045Ⓒ, 2330Ⓒ, 2359Ⓐ, returning at 0535Ⓐ, 0608Ⓐ, 0632Ⓐ, 0700Ⓐ, 0715Ⓒ, *0715*Ⓐ, 0820Ⓐ, 1015Ⓒ, 1023Ⓐ, 1315Ⓒ, 1453Ⓐ, 1615Ⓒ, 1810Ⓐ, 1915Ⓒ, 2215Ⓒ. Journey: 65 mins.

swich θ *(MBTA)* (❖ km, US $: 3.50). From Boston North: 0700Ⓐ, 0805Ⓐ, 0940Ⓐ, 1115Ⓐ, 1130⑥, 1315Ⓐ, 1330⑥, 1515Ⓐ, 1630⚒, 1710Ⓐ, 1735Ⓐ, 1830⑥, 1845Ⓐ, 1930Ⓐ, 2120Ⓐ, 2200⑥, *2240*Ⓐ, returning at 0552Ⓐ, 0612Ⓐ, 0650Ⓐ, 0715Ⓐ, 0807Ⓐ, 0900⑥, 0948Ⓐ, 1100⑥, 1118Ⓐ, 1300⑥, 1318Ⓐ, 1500⚒, 1625Ⓐ, 1735Ⓐ, 2038⚒, *2230*Ⓐ. Journey: 1 hour.

awrence θ *(MBTA)* (*42* km, US $: 3.50). From Boston North: 0655Ⓐ, *0750*Ⓐ, 0845Ⓒ, 0850Ⓐ, 1145Ⓒ, 1320Ⓐ, 1445Ⓒ, *1520*Ⓐ, 1630Ⓐ, 1715Ⓐ, 1745Ⓒ, 1815Ⓐ, 2020Ⓐ, 2045Ⓒ, 2330Ⓒ, 2359Ⓐ, returning at 0546Ⓐ, 0619Ⓐ, 0643Ⓐ, 0711Ⓐ, *0720*Ⓐ, 0726Ⓒ, 0831Ⓐ, 1026Ⓒ, 1034Ⓐ, 1326Ⓒ, 1504Ⓐ, 1626Ⓒ, 1821Ⓐ, 1926Ⓒ, 2226Ⓒ. Journey: 55 mins.

exington ζ *(MBTA)* (❖ km, US $: 1.25). From Alewife: 0557Ⓐ, 0605Ⓐ, 0615Ⓐ, 0630⚒, 0645Ⓐ, 0700⚒, 0715Ⓐ, 0730⚒, 0745Ⓐ, 0800⚒, 0815Ⓐ and about every 30 mins. to 1900⚒, 1930Ⓐ, 2000Ⓐ, 2030Ⓐ, 2130Ⓐ, returning at 0634Ⓐ, 0648Ⓐ, 0704Ⓐ, 0717Ⓐ, 0723⑥, 0734Ⓐ, 0747Ⓐ, 0758⑥, 0804Ⓐ, 0817Ⓐ, 0832⑥, 0834Ⓐ, 0847Ⓐ, 0901⑥ and about every 30 mins. to 1902⑥, 1903Ⓐ, 1905⑥, 1917Ⓐ, 1933Ⓐ, 1954Ⓐ, 1959⑥, 2005Ⓐ, 2053Ⓐ, 2105Ⓐ, 2205Ⓐ. Journey: 25 mins.

owell θ *(MBTA)* (*52* km, US $: 3.50). From Boston North: 0550Ⓐ, 0635Ⓐ, 0725Ⓐ, 0800Ⓒ, 0805Ⓐ, 0910Ⓐ, 1000Ⓒ, 1010Ⓐ, 1110Ⓐ, 1200Ⓒ, 1210Ⓐ, 1310Ⓐ, 1400Ⓒ, 1410Ⓐ, 1510Ⓐ, 1600Ⓒ, 1610Ⓐ, 1640Ⓐ, 1710Ⓐ, 1745Ⓐ, 1800Ⓒ, 1815Ⓐ, 1930Ⓐ, 2000Ⓒ, 2030Ⓐ, 2140Ⓐ, 2240Ⓐ, 2300Ⓒ, 2359Ⓐ, returning at 0535Ⓐ, 0615Ⓐ, 0650Ⓐ, 0700Ⓒ, 0722Ⓐ, 0750Ⓐ, 0825Ⓐ, 0900Ⓒ, 0907Ⓐ, 1007Ⓐ, 1100Ⓒ, 1107Ⓐ, 1207Ⓐ, 1300Ⓒ, 1307Ⓐ, 1407Ⓐ, 1500Ⓒ, 1507Ⓐ, 1610Ⓐ, 1700Ⓒ, 1710Ⓐ, 1745Ⓐ, 1815Ⓐ, 1900Ⓒ, 1915Ⓐ, 2030Ⓐ, 2100Ⓒ, 2130Ⓐ, 2235Ⓐ. Journey: 45 mins.

ynn θ *(MBTA)* (❖ km, US $: 2.25). From Boston North: 0700Ⓐ, 0735Ⓐ, 0805Ⓐ, 0830, 0940Ⓐ, 1015, 1115Ⓐ, 1130⑥, 1215, 1315Ⓐ, 1330⑥, 1415, 1515Ⓐ, 1530Ⓐ, 1600Ⓐ, 1630⚒, 1645Ⓐ, 1710Ⓐ, 1730Ⓒ, 1735Ⓐ, 1750Ⓐ, 1805Ⓐ, 1830⑥, 1845Ⓐ, 1930Ⓐ, 2000Ⓐ, 2030Ⓒ, 2120Ⓐ, 2200⑥, 2240Ⓐ, 2330Ⓒ, 2359Ⓐ, returning at 0559Ⓐ, 0622Ⓐ, 0642Ⓐ, 0701Ⓐ, 0721Ⓐ, 0747, 0803Ⓐ, 0824Ⓐ, 0837Ⓐ, 0924Ⓐ, 0929⑥, 0955Ⓐ, 1018Ⓐ, 1047Ⓒ, 1048 Ⓐ, 1129⑥, 1148Ⓐ, 1247Ⓒ, 1248Ⓐ, 1329⑥, 1348Ⓐ, 1447Ⓒ, 1448 Ⓐ, 1529Ⓒ, 1530Ⓐ, 1656Ⓐ, 1802Ⓒ, 1823Ⓐ, 1854Ⓐ, 2017Ⓒ, 2029Ⓐ, 2107⚒, 2247Ⓒ, 2313Ⓐ. Journey: 25 mins.

alden θ *(MBTA)* (❖ km, US $: 0.85). From Boston State: 0516⚒/0600† and frequent to 0022, returning at 0516⚒/0600† and frequent to 0026. Journey: 15 mins.

Medford ζ *(MBTA)* (❖ km, US $: 1.25). From Wellington: 0000②-⑥, 0005①⑦, 0040②-⑥, 0102①⑦, 0520Ⓐ/0605†/0615⑥ and frequent (about hourly on †) to 2305Ⓒ/2320Ⓐ, returning at 0015①⑦, 0020②-⑥, 0615 and frequent (about hourly on †) to 2315Ⓒ/2340Ⓐ. Journey: 15 mins.

Melrose θ *(MBTA)* (❖ km, US $: 2.00). From Boston North: 0730Ⓐ, 0750Ⓐ, 0845Ⓒ, 0850Ⓐ, 0920Ⓐ, 1120Ⓐ, 1145Ⓒ, 1220Ⓐ, 1320Ⓐ, 1420Ⓐ, 1445Ⓒ, 1520Ⓐ, 1557Ⓐ, 1630Ⓐ, 1655Ⓐ, 1730Ⓐ, 1745Ⓒ, 1815Ⓐ, 1855Ⓐ, 1930Ⓐ, 2020Ⓐ, 2045Ⓒ, 2115Ⓐ, 2235Ⓐ, 2330Ⓒ, 2359Ⓐ, returning from Melrose Highlands at 0621Ⓐ, 0655Ⓐ, 0720Ⓐ, 0750Ⓐ, 0802Ⓒ, 0819Ⓐ, 0841Ⓐ, 0906Ⓐ, 1009Ⓐ, 1102Ⓒ, 1109Ⓐ, 1209Ⓐ, 1350Ⓐ, 1402Ⓒ, 1509Ⓐ, 1539Ⓐ, 1613Ⓐ, 1646Ⓐ, 1702Ⓒ, 1746Ⓐ, 1824Ⓐ, 1947Ⓐ, 2002Ⓒ, 2028Ⓐ, 2208Ⓐ, 2302Ⓒ, 2326Ⓐ. Journey: 20 mins.

Orient Heights θ *(MBTA)* (❖ km, US $: 0.85). From Boston State: 0528⚒/0619† and frequent to 0049, returning at 0513⚒/0603† and frequent to 0025①⑦, 0027ex①⑦. Journey: 12 mins.

Portsmouth ζ *(CJR)* (*100* km, US $: 11.75). From Boston:: 0730Ⓐ, 0900Ⓒ, 0930Ⓐ, 1030, 1200, 1300, 1400, 1500, 1600, 1630Ⓐ, 1700Ⓒ, 1715Ⓐ, 1745Ⓐ, 1800, 1900, 2000, 2230, returning at 0430Ⓐ, 0530Ⓐ, 0600, 0630Ⓐ, 0700Ⓐ, 0800, 0900, 1000, 1100, 1200, 1300, 1400, 1500, 1615, 1715, 1900. Journey: 1¼ hours.

Providence θ *(MBTA)* (*69* km, US $5.50). From Boston South: 0643Ⓐ, 1635Ⓐ, 1705Ⓐ, 1740Ⓐ, 1820Ⓐ, returning at 0612Ⓐ, 0651Ⓐ, 0710Ⓐ, 0811Ⓐ, 1753Ⓐ. Journey: 1¼ hours.

Revere ζ *(MBTA)* (❖ km, US $: ❖). From Boston: 0527Ⓐ/0557⑥/0655† and frequent to 0055, returning at 0505Ⓐ/0535⑥/0630† and frequent to 0020①⑦/0030ex①⑦. Journey: 20 mins.

Rockport θ *(MBTA)* (❖ km, US $: 4.00). From Boston North: 0735Ⓐ, 0830, 1015, 1215, 1415, 1600Ⓐ, 1700Ⓐ, 1725Ⓐ, 1730Ⓒ, 1805Ⓐ, *1845*Ⓐ, 2000Ⓐ, 2030Ⓒ, 2240Ⓐ, 2330Ⓒ, 2359Ⓐ, returning at 0511Ⓐ, 0611Ⓐ, 0648Ⓐ, 0700Ⓒ, 0724Ⓐ, 0907Ⓐ, 1000, 1200, 1400, 1540Ⓐ, 1715Ⓒ, 1734Ⓐ, 1930Ⓒ, 1940Ⓐ, 2200Ⓒ, 2224Ⓐ. Journey: 1¼ hours.

Salem θ *(MBTA)* (❖ km, US $: 2.50). From Boston North: 0650Ⓐ, 0700Ⓐ, 0735Ⓐ, 0805Ⓐ, 0820Ⓐ, 0830, 0940Ⓐ, 1015, 1115Ⓐ, 1130⑥, 1215, 1315Ⓐ, 1330⑥, 1415, 1515Ⓐ, 1530Ⓐ, 1600Ⓐ, 1630⚒, 1645Ⓐ, 1700Ⓐ, 1710Ⓐ, 1725Ⓐ, 1730Ⓒ, 1735Ⓐ, 1750Ⓐ, 1805Ⓐ, 1830⑥, 1845Ⓐ, 1930Ⓐ, 2000Ⓐ, 2030Ⓒ, 2120Ⓐ, 2200⑥, 2240Ⓐ, 2330Ⓒ, 2359Ⓐ, returning at 0549Ⓐ, 0612Ⓐ, 0632Ⓐ, 0651Ⓐ, 0711Ⓐ, 0729Ⓐ, 0737Ⓐ, 0738Ⓒ, 0753Ⓐ, 0805Ⓐ, 0814Ⓐ, 0827Ⓐ, 0914Ⓐ, 0920⑥, 0945Ⓐ, 1008Ⓐ, 1038, 1120⑥, 1138Ⓐ, 1238, 1320⑥, 1338Ⓐ, 1438, 1520⚒, 1619Ⓐ, 1629Ⓐ, 1646Ⓐ, 1753Ⓒ, 1755Ⓐ, 1813Ⓐ, 1844Ⓐ, 2008Ⓒ, 2019Ⓐ, 2058⚒, 2238Ⓒ, 2303Ⓐ. Journey: 35 mins.

Saugus ζ *(MBTA)* (❖ km, US $: ❖). From Boston: about hourly, returning about hourly. Journey: 40 mins.

Somerville ζ *(MBTA)* (❖ km, US $: ❖). From Lechmere: 0020, 0100, 0540Ⓐ/0553⑥/0620† and frequent to 2350, returning at 0014, 0044, 0524Ⓐ/0534⑥/0644† and frequent to 2344. Journey: 15 mins.

Sullivan θ *(MBTA)* (❖ km, US $: 0.85). From Boston State: 0516⚒/0600† and frequent to 0022, returning at 0520⚒/0604† and frequent to 0030. Journey: 12 mins.

Winchester θ *(MBTA)* (❖ km, US $: 2.00). From Boston North: 0550Ⓐ, 0635Ⓐ, 0725Ⓐ, 0800Ⓒ, 0805Ⓐ, 0910Ⓐ, 1000Ⓒ, 1010Ⓐ, 1110Ⓐ, 1200Ⓒ, 1210Ⓐ, 1310Ⓐ, 1400Ⓒ, 1410Ⓐ, 1510Ⓐ, 1600Ⓒ, 1610Ⓐ, 1640Ⓐ, 1710Ⓐ, 1745Ⓐ, 1800Ⓒ, 1815Ⓐ, 1930Ⓐ, 2000Ⓒ, 2030Ⓐ, 2140Ⓐ, 2240Ⓐ, 2300Ⓒ, 2359Ⓐ, returning at 0602Ⓐ, 0643Ⓐ, 0720Ⓐ, 0726Ⓒ, 0752Ⓐ, 0820Ⓐ, 0853Ⓐ, 0926Ⓒ, 0934Ⓐ, 1034Ⓐ, 1126Ⓒ, 1134Ⓐ, 1234Ⓐ, 1326Ⓒ, 1334Ⓐ, 1434Ⓐ, 1526Ⓒ, 1534Ⓐ, 1637Ⓐ, 1726Ⓒ, 1737Ⓐ, 1812Ⓐ, 1842Ⓐ, 1926Ⓒ, 1942Ⓐ, 2057Ⓐ, 2126Ⓒ, 2157Ⓐ, 2302Ⓐ. Journey: 20 mins.

Winthrop ζ *(PRT)* (❖ km, US $: ❖). From Orient Heights: 0005⑦, 0015②-⑥, 0040⑦, 0045②-⑥, 0108②-⑥, 0110⑦, 0520⚒/0740† and frequent to 2310†/2335⑥/2355Ⓐ, returning at 0020ex①, 0030②-⑥, 0055⑦, 0500⚒/0725† and frequent to 2325†/2350⑥/2359Ⓐ. Journey: 10 mins.

Worcester θ *(MBTA)* (*71* km, US $: 4.75). From Boston South: 1655Ⓐ, 1730Ⓐ, 1800Ⓐ, returning at 0545Ⓐ, 0620Ⓐ, 0715Ⓐ. Journey: 1 hour.

θ–By ####. ζ–By bus. ‡–Air-conditioned. ❖–Information not available at press date. ⑦–Sundays. Ⓐ–Mondays to Fridays except holidays. ⑥–Saturdays. †–Sundays and holidays. ⚒–Daily except Sundays and holidays. ①–Mondays. ②–Tuesdays. Ⓒ–Saturdays, Sundays and holidays. Ⓑ–Daily except Saturdays. *CJR*– C&J Trailways. Tel.: Dover 603 742 5111. *MBTA*–Massachusetts Bay Transportation Authority. Tel.: Boston 722 3200. *PRT*– Paul Revere Transportation. Tel.: 617 539 1993.

Table 320 ALBANY - MONTRÉAL #### NRPC

US $ C cl.	261 1‡C‡ ◆	69 1‡C‡ ◆ ⚒	71 1‡C‡ ◆ †	267 C‡ ◆	km	396 1.435m. ↓ ↑	68 1‡C‡ ◆		260 C‡ ◆	
0.00	0755	0830	1040	1550	0	d.*New York* ....a.	2010	....	2215	....
40.00	1030	1115	1330	1840	229	d.**Albany Rensselaer** .a.	1720	....	1940	....
45.00	|	1140	1355	|	258	d.Schenectady .....d.	1655	....	|	....
45.00	1120	1206	1418	1930	288	d.Saratoga Springs d.	1618	....	1845	....
49.00	....	1226	1438	....	320	d.Fort Edward ★..d.	1558	....	....	....
54.00	....	1251	1459	....	355	d.Whitehall ....d.	1533	....	....	....
58.00	....	1405	1606	....	436	d.Westport............d.	1422	....	....	....
65.00	....	1445a	1641a	....	479	d.Port Kent...........d.	1336a	....	....	....
65.00	....	1505	1704	....	500	d.Plattsburgh ....d.	1318	....	....	....
67.00	....	1541	1743	....	538	d.Rouses Point ▣ d.	1250	....	....	....
67.00	....	1755	1955	....	617	a.**Montréal** Central d.	1040	....	....	....

68– ADIRONDACK–1‡C‡ and ⊗ Montréal(**68**)-New York.
69– ADIRONDACK–1‡C‡ and ⊗ New York(**69**)-Montréal.
71– ADIRONDACK–1‡C‡ and ⊗ New York(**71**)-Montréal.
260– ⑦ June 30-Aug. 25 and ⑥ July 27-Aug. 31 (also Sept. 2): C‡ (also 1‡ on ⑥) and 🍷 Saratoga Springs(**260**)-New York.
261– ⑥ July 27-Aug. 31: 1‡C‡ and 🍷 New York(**261**)-Saratoga Springs.
267– ⑤ June 28-Aug. 30: C‡ and 🍷 New York(**267**)-Saratoga Springs.
– May 16-Oct. 20 only. Note r applies.
– Calls by request.
– Air-conditioned. ⚒–Daily except Sundays and holidays. ⑥–Saturdays.
– Sundays and holidays. ▭–Seating car. ⊗–Buffet car.
– Sundays. 🍷–Light refreshments. ⑤–Fridays.
★– Glens Falls.
NRPC–AMTRAK. Tel.: New York 212 582 6875.

Table 324 BOSTON - ALBANY #### NRPC

US $ C cl.				449 S‡C‡ ◆ Ⓡ	km	396 1.435m. ↓ ↑		448 S‡C‡ ◆ Ⓡ		
0.00	....	....	....	1530	0	d.**Boston** South ....a.	....	1801	....	....
	....	....	....	1539u	2	d.**Boston** Back Bay ..a.	....	1753s	....	....
7.25	....	....	....	1607u	34	d.Framingham ....d.	....	1716s	....	....
10.50	....	....	....	1637	71	d.Worcester...............d.	....	1646	....	....
19.00	....	....	....	1804	158	d.Springfield ....d.	....	1539	....	....
23.50	....	....	....	1917	239	d.Pittsfield ....d.	....	1415	....	....
37.00	....	....	....	2034	321	a.**Albany Rensselaer** .d.	....	1310	....	....
113.00	....	....	....	1230	1544	a.*Chicago*.................d.	....	2000	....	....

448/9–LAKE SHORE LIMITED–sleeping car‡ and C‡ Chicago(**48/49**)-Albany(**448/9**)-Boston and v.v.; ⊗ Albany(**448/9**)-Boston and v.v.
NRPC–AMTRAK. Tel.: Boston 617 482 3660.

Table 325 396 MOUNT WASHINGTON MWCR

Cog railway service (steam operated, 1.435m.) from Base Station to summit of Mount Washington. *5* km. Journey: R.T.: 2 hours. Fare: US $: R. T.: 45.00.

***Departures from Base Station** for summit and return: **early May-June 25**: 0900 and hourly to 3 hours before sunset; operates in accordance with demand, and as track maintenance permits. **June 26-Sept. 6**: 0800 and hourly to 3 hours before sunset. **Sept. 7-early November**: 1000 and as required to 3 hours before sunset.

*– Services may operate weekends only in May and after mid October.
MWCR–Mount Washington Cog Railway. ☎Bretton Woods 603 846 5404.

Table 330 BOSTON - NEW YORK

CDT NRPC

US $ C cl.	396 1.435m. NRPC ↓	km	CDT 3629 C‡ Ⓐ	141 C‡ ◆ Ⓐ	CDT 3639 C‡ Ⓐ	143 C‡ ◆	95 P‡C‡ ◆ ✕	171 P‡1‡C‡ ◆	93 P‡C‡ ◆ ex⑤†	99 P‡C‡ Ⓡ◆ ⑤†	145 C‡ ◆ Ⓒ	55 C‡ ◆ ✕	173 P‡1‡C‡ ◆		175 P‡1‡C‡ ◆	165 P‡C‡ ◆ Ⓐ	155 C‡ 🍷 †	57 C‡ ◆ †	157 C‡ 🍷 ⓨ	2157 C‡ ◆	177 C‡ ◆	179 C‡ ◆	234 C‡ ◆	67 S‡C‡ ◆ Ⓡ	
0.00	**Boston** South d.	*0*	....	....	....	....	0620	0730	0900	0900	....	....	1120	....	1330	1440	1440	....	1608	1608	1625	1815	1935	2130	....
	Boston Back Bay d.	*2*	....	....	....	....	0627u	0738u	0907u	0907u	....	....	1128u	....	1338u	1447u	1447u	....	1615u	1615u	1632u	1822u	1942u	2138u	....
	Route 128 d.		....	....	....	....	0639u	0751u	0920u	0920u	....	....	1141u	....	1350u	1459u	1459u	....	1628u	1628u	1645u	1836u	1953u	2150u	....
13.00	Providence d.	*69*	....	....	....	....	0707	0823	0951	0951	....	....	1213	....	1420	1530	1530	....	1658	1658	1717	1908	2022	2225	....
	Kingston d.		....	....	....	....	│	0848	│	│	....	....	1238	....	1445	│	│	....	│	│	1746	1936	....	2253	....
	Westerly d.	*140*	....	....	....	....	│	0904	│	│	....	....	1255	....	│	│	│	....	│	│	1808	1957	....	2313	....
	Mystic d.		....	....	....	....	│	0915	│	│	....	....	1306	....	│	│	│	....	│	│	1819	2008	....	│	....
25.50	New London d.	*169*	0528	....	0628	....	0804	0930	│	│	....	....	1322	....	1520	1628	1628	....	│	│	1832	2023	....	2335	....
	Old Saybrook ⚛ d.		0548	....	0648	....	│	0951	│	│	....	....	1350	....	1541	│	│	....	│	│	1852	2044	....	2355	....
35.00	New Haven ⚛ d.	*251*	0638	0642	0738	0830	0905	1045	1151	1151	1245	1420	1450	....	1630	1735	1735	1745	1901	1901	1945	2135	....	0055	....
35.00	Bridgeport d.	*218*	....	0706	....	0854	│	1110	│	│	1310	1444	1515	....	│	│	│	1810	│	│	2010	2200	....	│	....
35.00	Stamford d.	*301*	....	0733	....	0920	│	1136	1236	1236	1336	1510	1544	....	1719	1820	1820	1835	1943	1943	2036	2226	....	0147	....
45.00	New Rochelle d.	*314*	....	0758	....	0940	│	1155	│	│	1356	│	1604	....	│	│	│	│	│	│	2056	2246	....	│	....
45.00	**New York** Penn. Stn. a.	*373*	....	0835	....	1010	1036	1230	1325	1325	1432	1557	1636	....	1815	1910	1910	1925	2030	2030	2125	2315	....	0245	....
61.00	*Philadelphia 30th Street* a.	*519*	....	1034	....	1154	1229	1425	1506	1506	1629	1738	1828	....	1957	2054	....	2103	....	2214	2310	0101	....	0526	....
92.00	*Washington Union* a.	*735*	....	1229	....	1353	1425	1632	1715	1715	1836	1935	2028	....	2155	2245	....	2256	....	0012	0115	0310	....	0755	....

396 NRPC ↓		66 S‡C‡ ◆ Ⓡ		12 C‡ ◆	136 C‡ 🍷 Ⓒ	170 P‡C‡ ◆ Ⓐ	56 C‡ ◆			172 P‡1‡C‡ ◆		84 P‡C‡ ◆	2174 C‡ ◆	174 P‡1‡C‡ ◆	86 P‡C‡ ◆	CDT 3638 C‡ Ⓐ	142 C‡ ◆	CDT 3644 C‡ Ⓐ	235 C‡ ◆	94 P‡C‡ ◆ Ⓑ	176 P‡1‡C‡ ◆	168 P‡C‡ ◆		148 C‡ ◆	
Washington Union d.	....	2200	....	0300	....	0530	0615	....	....	0715	....	0905	1005	1015	1105	....	1215	....	....	1315	1415	1610	....	1708	....
Philadelphia 30th Street d.	....	0025	....	0505	....	0735	0808	....	....	0921	....	1103	1158	1215	1258	....	1415	....	....	1506	1617	1810	....	1924	....
New York Penn. Stn. d.	....	0230	....	0658	0920	0920	0949	....	....	1107	....	1250	1340	1406	1505	....	1605	....	....	1650	1805	2010	....	2125	....
New Rochelle d.	....	│	....	│	0954	0954	│	....	....	1138	....	│	│	1436	│	....	1636	....	....	│	1838	│	....	2155	....
Stamford d.	....	0319	....	0748	1017	1017	1037	....	....	1201	....	1337	1427	1458	1558	....	1659	....	....	│	1902	2058	....	2220	....
Bridgeport d.	....	│	....	│	1044	1044	1103	....	....	1228	....	│	│	1525	│	....	1726	....	....	│	1927	│	....	2247	....
New Haven ⚛ d.	....	0423	....	0907	1125	1125	1128	....	....	1313	....	1432	1523	1614	1653	1705	1750	1810	....	1833	2012	2155	....	2312	....
Old Saybrook ⚛ d.	....	0500	....	0945	1201	1201	....	....	....	1348	....	│	│	1648	│	1755	....	1900		│	2046	│	....	....	....
New London d.	....	0522	....	1008	1222	1222	....	....	....	1408	....	│	│	1708	│	1815	....	1920	....	1934	2106	2247	....	....	....
Mystic d.	....	0536	....	│	1237	1237	....	....	....	1421	....	│	│	1721	│	....	....	....	....	│	2119	│	....	....	....
Westerly d.	....	0547	....	│	1248	1248	....	....	....	1431	....	│	│	1731	│	....	....	....	....	│	2129	│	....	....	....
Kingston d.	....	0604	....	1045	1307	1307	....	....	....	1447	....	│	│	1748	│	....	....	....	....	│	2145	│	....	....	....
Providence d.	....	0640	....	1117	1332	1332	....	....	....	1510	....	1620	1729s	1812	1843	....	....	....	1910	2030	2208	2349	....	....	....
Route 128 a.	....	0723s	....	1150s	1402s	1402s	....	....	....	1533s	....	1650s	1800s	1840s	1912s	....	....	....	1938s	2059s	2236s	0012s	....	....	....
Boston Back Bay a.	....	0740s	....	1201s	1415s	1415s	....	....	....	1549s	....	1702s	1813s	1852s	1925s	....	....	....	1953s	2111s	2249s	0024s	....	....	....
Boston South a.	....	0749	....	1210	1424	1424	....	....	....	1600	....	1710	1820	1900	1933	....	....	....	2003	2120	2257	0035	....	....	....

Table 331 SPRINGFIELD - NEW HAVEN

NRPC

US $ C cl.	396 1.435m. ↓	km			141 C‡ ◆Ⓐ	143 C‡ ◆			471 C‡ ◆				145 C‡ ◆Ⓒ				55 C‡ ◆✕	473 C‡ ◆	475 C‡ ◆		57 C‡ ◆†		477 C‡ ◆		
0.00	**Springfield** d.	*0*	....	....	0500	0650	....	....	0900	....	....	....	1105	....	....	....	1240	1305	1440	....	1605	....	1800	....	....
6.00	Windsor Locks d.	*22*	....	....	0521	0711	....	....	0919	....	....	....	1127	....	....	....	│	1324	1459	....	│	....	1819	....	....
9.00	Hartford d.	*41*	....	....	0540	0730	....	....	0936	....	....	....	1145	....	....	....	1318	1340	1515	....	1641	....	1836	....	....
11.00	Berlin d.	*58*	....	....	0553	0743	....	....	0950	....	....	....	1158	....	....	....	1331	1355	1526	....	1654	....	1851	....	....
13.00	Meriden d.	*70*	....	....	0603	0753	....	....	0959	....	....	....	1209	....	....	....	1342	1404	1535	....	1705	....	1900	....	....
16.00	**New Haven** a.	*100*	....	....	0632	0820	....	....	1025	....	....	....	1235	....	....	....	1405	1430	1605	....	1730	....	1925	....	....

396 ↓				412 C‡ ◆	56 C‡ ◆							472 C‡ ◆	474 C‡ ◆			142 C‡ ◆					476 C‡ ◆			148 C‡ ◆	
New Haven d.	....	....	....	0858	1143	....	....	....	....	....	....	1303	1604	....	....	1800	....	....	....	....	2002	....	....	2322	....
Meriden d.	....	....	....	0927	1209	....	....	....	....	....	....	1330	1631	....	....	1828	....	....	....	....	2032	....	....	2349	....
Berlin d.	....	....	....	0937	1219	....	....	....	....	....	....	1344	1641	....	....	1838	....	....	....	....	2045	....	....	2359	....
Hartford d.	....	....	....	0950	1233	....	....	....	....	....	....	1357	1656	....	....	1852	....	....	....	....	2058	....	....	0013	....
Windsor Locks d.	....	....	....	1005	│	....	....	....	....	....	....	1412	1711	....	....	1907	....	....	....	....	2113	....	....	0028	....
Springfield a.	....	....	....	1027	1320	....	....	....	....	....	....	1434	1733	....	....	1930	....	....	....	....	2135	....	.....	0051	....

NOTES for Tables 202 and 203

12– FAST MAIL–C‡ and 🍷 Washington(**12**)-Boston; C‡ Washington(**12**)-New Haven(**412**)-Springfield.
55/56– VERMONTER–C‡ and 🍷 St. Albans(**55/56**)-Washington and v.v.
57– VERMONTER–C‡ and 🍷 St. Albans(**57**)-Washington.
66/67– S‡, C‡ and 🍷 Washington(**66/67**)-Boston and v.v.
84– Runs daily ex ⑦ (except May 27, Sept. 2): P‡C‡ and 🍷 Richmond(**84**)-Boston.
86– Runs on ⑦ (also May 27, Sept. 2, but not May 26, Sept. 1): P‡C‡ and 🍷 Richmond(**86**)-Boston.
93– P‡C‡ and 🍷 Boston(**93**)-Richmond.
94– P‡C‡ and 🍷 Newport News(**94**)-Boston.
95– P‡C‡ and 🍷 Boston(**95**)-Newport News.
99– P‡C‡ and 🍷 Boston(**99**)-Newport News.
141– C‡ and 🍷 Springfield(**141**)-Washington.
142– C‡ and 🍷 Washington(**142**)-Springfield.
143– C‡ and 🍷 Springfield(**143**)-Washington.
145– C‡ and 🍷 Springfield(**145**)-Washington.
148– C‡ and 🍷 Washington(**148**)-Springfield.
165– P‡C‡ and 🍷 Boston(**165**)-Washington.
168– P‡C‡ and 🍷 Washington(**168**)-Boston.
170– P‡C‡ and 🍷 Washington(**170**)-Boston.
171– P‡ 1‡C‡ and 🍷 Boston(**171**)-Washington; C‡ Springfield(**471**)-New Haven(**171**)-Washington.
172– P‡ 1‡C‡ and 🍷 Washington(**172**)-Boston; C‡ Washington(**172**)-New Haven(**472**)-Springfield.
173– P‡ 1‡C‡ and 🍷 Boston(**173**)-Washington; C‡ Springfield(**473**)-New Haven(**173**)-Washington.
174– P‡ 1‡C‡ and 🍷 Washington(**174**)-Boston; C‡ Washington(**174**)-New Haven(**474**)-Springfield.
175– P‡ 1‡C‡ and 🍷 Boston(**175**)-Washington; C‡ Springfield(**475**)-New Haven(**175**)-Washington.
176– P‡ 1‡C‡ and 🍷 Washington(**176**)-Boston; C‡ Washington(**176**)-New Haven(**476**)-Springfield.
177– C‡ and 🍷 Boston(**177**)-Washington; C‡ Springfield(**477**)-New Haven(**177**)-Washington.
179– C‡ (also 1‡ on Ⓐ) and 🍷 Boston(**179**)-Washington.
234– CAPE CODDER–⑤ June 28-Sept. 27: C‡ Boston(**234**)-Hyannis.
235– CAPE CODDER–⑦ June 30-Sept. 29: C‡ Hyannis(**235**)-Boston.
412– C‡ Washington(**12**)-New Haven(**412**)-Springfield.
471– C‡ Springfield(**471**)-New Haven(**171**)-Washington.
472– C‡ Washington(**172**)-New Haven(**472**)-Springfield.
473– C‡ Springfield(**473**)-New Haven(**173**)-Washington.
474– C‡ Washington(**174**)-New Haven(**474**)-Springfield.
475– C‡ Springfield(**475**)-New Haven(**175**)-Washington.
476– C‡ Washington(**176**)-New Haven(**476**)-Springfield.
477– C‡ Springfield(**477**)-New Haven(**177**)-Washington.
2157– Runs May 24, 27, July 3, Aug. 30, Sept. 2: C‡ and 🍷 Boston(**2157**)-Washington.
2174– Runs May 24, 27, July 3, Aug. 30, Sept. 2: C‡ and 🍷 Washington(**2174**)-Boston.
⚛– Local *CDT* #### service (C cl. only). Fare: US $: 5.00. New Haven-Old Saybrook and v.v. **From New Haven** at: 0625Ⓐ, 0800Ⓐ, 1358⑤, 1520Ⓐ, 1615Ⓐ, 1705Ⓐ, 1730Ⓐ, 1810Ⓐ, 1920Ⓐ, 2017Ⓐ, 2136Ⓐ, returning at 0528Ⓐ, 0548Ⓐ, 0648Ⓐ, 0720Ⓐ, 0748Ⓐ, 0858Ⓐ,1508⑤ 1625Ⓐ, 1715Ⓐ.
ⓨ– Runs ⑦, except May 26, Sept. 1.
CDT– Connecticut Department of Transportation. Tel.: New Haven 203 777 7433.
NRPC–AMTRAK. Tel.: New York 212 582 6875.

Table 335 396 NEW YORK LOCAL SERVICES #### 🚌 *BTL CDT HTL IBS LIRR MNR MTA NJT NYCTA PATH RTL*

ocal #### (C‡ only, 1.435m.) and 🚌 services operate in the New York area as follows:

nsonia 🚆 *(CDT)* (*174* km, US $: 12.75). From New York Grand Central: *0602Ⓐ, 0807Ⓒ, 0907Ⓐ, 1207, 1607Ⓒ, 1622Ⓐ, 1826Ⓐ, 2107*, returning at *0700Ⓐ, 0743Ⓒ, 0942Ⓐ, 1143Ⓒ, 1242Ⓐ, 1542Ⓐ, 1543Ⓒ, 1921Ⓐ, 1943Ⓒ, 2144Ⓐ*. Journey: 2 hours.

sbury Park 🚆 *(NJT)* (❖ km, US $: ❖). From New York Penn Stn.: *0037†, 0137Ⓒ, 0637Ⓒ, 0707Ⓐ, 0829Ⓐ, 0837Ⓒ, 0930Ⓐ, 0937Ⓒ, 0941Ⓐ, 1037Ⓒ, 1137Ⓒ, 1143Ⓐ, 1237Ⓒ, 1243♤, 1337Ⓒ, 1407Ⓐ, 1437Ⓒ, 1535▽, 1552Ⓐ, 1620Ⓐ, 1637Ⓒ, 1642Ⓐ, 1710Ⓐ, 1721Ⓐ, 1732Ⓐ, 1742Ⓒ, 1810Ⓐ, 1837Ⓒ, 1852♤, 1907Ⓐ, 2007Ⓐ, 2037Ⓒ, 2112Ⓐ, 2137Ⓒ, 2230Ⓐ, 2332Ⓐ, 2337Ⓒ*, returning at *0516Ⓐ, 0529Ⓒ, 0541Ⓐ, 0610Ⓐ, 0629Ⓒ, 0641Ⓐ, 0713Ⓐ, 0729Ⓒ, 0742Ⓐ, 0806Ⓐ, 0914Ⓐ, 0929Ⓒ, 1029Ⓐ, 1129Ⓒ, 1229Ⓐ, 1229Ⓒ, 1329Ⓒ, 1429Ⓒ, 1519Ⓐ, 1529Ⓒ, 1623Ⓐ, 1626⑦, 1723Ⓐ, 1726Ⓒ, 1756Ⓒ, 1826Ⓒ, 1917†, 1926⑥, 2031Ⓐ, 2045∝, 2130Ⓒ, 2208Ⓐ, 2320Ⓐ, 2343Ⓒ*. Journey: 2 hours. Also from Hoboken: 0833Ⓐ, 1110⑥, 1412Ⓐ, 1644Ⓐ, 1709Ⓐ, 1740Ⓐ, 1810Ⓐ, 1855♤, *1855♂*, returning at 0541Ⓐ, 0610Ⓐ, 0641Ⓐ, 0713Ⓐ, 0914Ⓐ, 1519Ⓐ, 2045∝. Journey: 1½ hours.

tlantic City 🚌 *(GL)* (*206* km, US $: 23.00). From New York: 0745⑥⑦, 0815, 0845⑦, 0900, 0930⑥⑦, 1000, 1030, 1100, 1130⑤⑥⑦, 1201, 1230, 1300, 1330, 1400, 1500, 1530, 1600, 1630, 1700, 1730, 1800, 1830⑤⑥, 1900, 1930⑤⑥, 2000, 2030, 2100, 2130, 2200⑤⑥, 2230⑤⑥, 2330, returning at 0030, 0100, 0200, 0230, 0330, 0400⑥⑦, 0430, 0445, 0500, 0545, 0600⑥⑦, 0630⑥⑦, 0700⑥⑦, 0800, 1000, 1130, 1230, 1330, 1430, 1530, 1630, 1700⑥⑦, 1730, 1800⑦, 1830, 1900, 1930, 2030, 2100⑤⑥⑦, 2130, 2230, 2300. Journey: 3 hours. Also *NJT* from New York: 0000, 0800, 0900, 1000, 1100, 1200, 1300, 1400, 1500, 1600, 1700, 1800, 1900, 2000, 2100, 2130, 2200, 2300⑤, returning at 0030, 0415, 0600, 0630⚒, 0700, 0800, 0900, 1000, 1100, 1200, 1300, 1400, 1500, 1600⑥⑦, 1700, 1800, 2000⑦, 2200, 2300⑤.

abylon 🚆 *(LIRR)* (*61* km, US $: 8.50). From New York Penn Stn.: 0009, 0036Ⓐ, 0038Ⓒ, 0140Ⓒ, 0146Ⓐ, 0242Ⓒ, 0313Ⓐ, 0454Ⓐ, 0510Ⓒ, 0610Ⓒ, 0636Ⓐ and frequent (about every 30 mins. on Ⓒ) to 2207Ⓐ, 2208Ⓒ, 2229Ⓐ, 2238Ⓐ, 2306Ⓐ, 2310Ⓒ, 2331Ⓐ, 2338Ⓒ, 2339Ⓐ, returning at 0055, *0103*, 0139Ⓐ, 0153Ⓒ, 0313Ⓐ, 0339Ⓐ, 0350Ⓒ, 0439Ⓐ, 0450Ⓒ, 0502Ⓐ, *0519Ⓐ*, 0520Ⓒ, 0541Ⓐ, 0550Ⓒ, 0556Ⓐ, 0609Ⓐ, 0612Ⓐ, *0615Ⓐ*, *0618Ⓒ*, 0620Ⓒ, 0632Ⓐ, 0642Ⓐ, 0650Ⓒ, *0652Ⓐ* and frequent (about every 30 mins. on Ⓒ) to *2203Ⓐ*, 2209Ⓐ, *2235Ⓒ*, 2239Ⓐ, 2241Ⓒ, 2309Ⓐ, 2339. Journey: 1¼ hours.

ay Head 🚆 *(NJT)* (*108* km, US $: 9.60). From New York Penn. Stn.: *0037†, 0137Ⓒ, 0637Ⓒ, 0707Ⓐ, 0829Ⓐ, 0837Ⓒ, 0930Ⓐ, 0937Ⓒ, 0941Ⓐ, 1037Ⓒ, 1137Ⓒ, 1143Ⓐ, 1237Ⓒ, 1243♤, 1337Ⓒ, 1407Ⓐ, 1437Ⓒ, 1535▽, 1552Ⓐ, 1620Ⓐ, 1637Ⓒ, 1642Ⓐ, 1710Ⓐ, 1721Ⓐ, 1732Ⓐ, 1742Ⓒ, 1810Ⓐ, 1837Ⓒ, 1852♤, 1907Ⓐ, 2007Ⓐ, 2037Ⓒ, 2112Ⓐ, 2137Ⓒ, 2230Ⓐ, 2332Ⓐ, 2337Ⓒ*, returning at *0454Ⓐ, 0506Ⓒ, 0516Ⓐ, 0545Ⓐ, 0617Ⓐ, 0633Ⓒ, 0649Ⓐ, 0706Ⓒ, 0717Ⓐ, 0746Ⓐ, 0849Ⓐ, 0906Ⓒ, 0952Ⓐ, 1006Ⓐ, 1106Ⓒ, 1206Ⓐ, 1208Ⓒ, 1306Ⓒ, 1406Ⓒ, 1453Ⓐ, 1506Ⓒ, 1600Ⓐ, 1602⑦, 1700Ⓐ, 1702Ⓒ, 1735Ⓒ, 1802Ⓒ, 1847†, 1902⑥, 2008Ⓐ*, 2020∝, *2106Ⓒ, 2145Ⓐ*, 2259Ⓐ, *2319Ⓒ*. Journey: 2 hours. Also from Hoboken: 0833Ⓐ, 1010Ⓒ, 1110⑥, 1412Ⓐ, 1644Ⓐ, 1709Ⓐ, 1740Ⓐ, 1810Ⓐ, 1855♤, *1855♂*, returning at 0516Ⓐ, 0545Ⓐ, 0617Ⓐ, 0633Ⓒ, 0649Ⓐ, 0849Ⓐ, 1453Ⓐ, 1735Ⓒ, 2020∝. Journey: 2 hours.

ayonne 🚌 *(BTL)* (❖ km, US $: 2.60). From New York: 0000, 0015①, 0030ex①, 0100, 0200, 0400, 0500, 0605, 0700⚒, 0728Ⓐ, 0730⑥/0800†/0900† and frequent (every 30 mins on †) to 2130Ⓒ, 2140Ⓐ, 2200, 2230, 2300, 2330, returning at 0000, 0100, 0300, 0500, 0600⚒, 0615Ⓐ, 0628Ⓐ, 0630⑥/0700†/0800† and frequent (every 30 mins. on †) to 2030Ⓒ, 2040Ⓐ, 2100, 2130, 2200, 2230, 2300, 2330⚒. Journey: 25 mins.

rewster 🚆 *(MNR)* (*83* km, US $: 10.25). From New York Grand Central: 0030, 0130, 0555Ⓒ, 0600Ⓐ, 0716Ⓐ, 0747Ⓐ, 0749Ⓐ, 0847Ⓐ, 0849Ⓒ, 0949 and hourly to 1449, 1519Ⓐ, 1548Ⓐ, 1549Ⓒ, 1554Ⓐ,, 1617Ⓐ, 1639Ⓐ, 1649Ⓒ, 1657Ⓐ, 1716Ⓐ, 1725Ⓐ, 1739Ⓐ, 1749Ⓒ, 1803Ⓐ, 1806Ⓐ, 1829Ⓐ, 1832Ⓐ, 1849Ⓒ, 1858Ⓐ, 1922Ⓐ, 1949Ⓒ, 1950Ⓐ, 2017Ⓐ, 2049, 2149, 2257, 2349, returning at 0508⚒, 0546⚒, 0609Ⓐ, 0637Ⓐ, 0708, 0715Ⓐ, 0723Ⓐ, 0744Ⓐ 0806Ⓐ, 0808Ⓒ, 0840Ⓐ,0908 and hourly to 1508, 1608Ⓒ 1610Ⓐ, 1640Ⓐ, 1706Ⓐ, 1708Ⓒ,1753Ⓐ 1808Ⓒ, 1857Ⓐ, 1908Ⓒ, 2008, 2108, 2208, 2305Ⓐ. 2323Ⓒ Journey: 1½ hours.

ridgeport 🚆 *(CDT)* (*155* km, US $: 11.75). From New York Grand Central: 0035, 0130, 0540Ⓒ, 0602Ⓐ, 0705Ⓐ, 0807 and hourly to 1407, 1502⑥, 1507, 1539Ⓐ, 1600Ⓐ, 1607, 1622Ⓐ, 1635Ⓐ, 1641Ⓐ, 1645Ⓐ, 1703Ⓐ, 1707Ⓒ, 1713Ⓐ, 1718Ⓐ, 1736Ⓐ, 1742Ⓐ, 1804Ⓐ, 1807Ⓒ, 1826Ⓐ, 1906Ⓐ, 1907Ⓒ, 1937Ⓐ, 2007, 2037Ⓐ, 2107, 2207, 2320, returning at 0515⑥, 0516Ⓐ, 0548Ⓐ, 0606Ⓐ, 0619Ⓒ, 0621Ⓐ, 0649Ⓐ, 0709Ⓐ, 0719⑥, 0723Ⓐ, 0735Ⓐ, 0750Ⓐ, 0756Ⓐ, 0808Ⓐ, 0816Ⓐ, 0819Ⓒ, 0827Ⓐ, 0915Ⓐ, 0919Ⓒ, 1019, 1119, 1219, 1319, 1419, 1519, 1616Ⓐ, 1619Ⓒ, 1719 and hourly to 2219, 2344. Journey: 1¼ hours.

rooklyn 🚆 *(NYCTA)* (❖ km, US $: ❖). Frequent service 24 hours a day from New York 42nd Street/Grand Central, 42nd Street/Times Square, 42nd Street/Avenue of the Americas and other central stations, returning from Brooklyn Atlantic Avenue/Pacific Street, Nevins and various other Brooklyn stations. Journey: 25-40 mins.

oney Island 🚆 *(NYCTA)* (❖ km, US $: ❖). From New York 42nd Street/Avenue of the Americas: frequent (about every 30 mins. at night), returning from Coney Island Stillwell Avenue frequently (about every 30 mins. at night). Journey: 40 mins.

roton Harmon 🚆 *(MNR)* (*54* km, US $: 7.50). From New York Grand Central: 0020, 0120, 0620, 0649Ⓐ, 0720, 0749Ⓐ, 0758Ⓒ, 0820, 0858, 0920, 0958, 1020, 1055 and frequent to 2020, 2100, 2120, 2155, 2220, 2300, 2320, 2355, returning at 0501Ⓐ, 0526Ⓐ, 0536Ⓒ, 0538Ⓐ, 0556Ⓐ, 0607⑥, 0620Ⓐ, 0629Ⓐ, 0633Ⓐ, 0636Ⓒ, 0651Ⓐ, 0658Ⓐ, 0707Ⓐ, 0713Ⓒ, 0721Ⓐ, 0730Ⓐ, 0736Ⓒ, and about ½hourly to 2036, 2107Ⓒ, 2131Ⓐ, 2136Ⓒ, 2213Ⓒ, 2231Ⓐ, 2236Ⓒ, 2346. Journey: 1 hour.

anbury 🚆 *(CDT)* (*104* km, US $: 11.25). From New York Grand Central: *0807, 1107Ⓒ, 1207Ⓐ, 1407Ⓒ, 1507Ⓐ*, 1700Ⓐ, *1707Ⓒ*, 1738Ⓐ, 1807Ⓐ, *1906Ⓐ, 2007, 2207Ⓐ, 2320Ⓒ*, returning at 0539Ⓐ, 0620Ⓐ, 0654Ⓐ, *0733Ⓐ, 0744Ⓒ, 1044, 1344Ⓒ, 1444Ⓐ, 1644Ⓒ, 1710Ⓐ, 1944Ⓒ, 2012Ⓐ, 2209Ⓐ, 2309Ⓒ*. Journey: 1 hour 50 mins.

erby Shelton 🚆 *(CDT)* (*171* km, US $: 12.75). From New York Grand Central: 0602Ⓐ, *0807Ⓒ, 0907Ⓐ, 1207, 1607Ⓒ, 1622Ⓐ, 1826Ⓐ, 2107*, returning at *0704Ⓐ, 0747Ⓒ, 0946Ⓐ, 1147Ⓒ, 1246Ⓐ, 1546Ⓐ, 1547Ⓒ, 1925Ⓐ, 1947Ⓒ, 2148Ⓐ*. Journey: 2 hours.

over Plains 🚆 *(MNR)* (*124* km, US $: 13.00). From New York Grand Central: *0555Ⓒ, 0716Ⓐ, 0847Ⓐ, 0849Ⓒ, 1049, 1249, 1449Ⓐ, 1549Ⓒ*, 1716Ⓐ, *1749Ⓒ, 1803Ⓐ, 1949Ⓒ, 1950Ⓐ, 2149Ⓐ*, returning at *0531Ⓐ, 0632Ⓒ*, 0633Ⓐ, *0803Ⓐ, 0832Ⓒ, 0932Ⓐ, 1132, 1332, 1532Ⓒ, 1534Ⓐ, 1700Ⓐ, 1822Ⓒ, 2032, 2229Ⓐ. 2247Ⓒ*. Journey: 2 hours.

ast Hampton 🚆 *(LIRR)* (*164* km, US $: 15.25). From New York Penn. Stn.: *0036Ⓐ, 0038Ⓒ, 0749Ⓐ, 0758Ⓒ, 1006Ⓒ, 1153Ⓒ, 1201Ⓐ, 1601⑤, 1619Ⓐ, 1751Ⓐ, 2031Ⓐ, 2043Ⓒ*, returning at *0117Ⓐ, 0603Ⓐ, 0721Ⓒ, 1112Ⓐ, 1521Ⓐ, 1557Ⓒ, 1729Ⓒ, 1957Ⓒ, 2302Ⓐ*. Journey: 2¾ hours.

ast Orange 🚆 *(NJT)* (❖ km, US $: 2.80). From Hoboken: 0037, 0145⚒, 0600Ⓐ, 0630Ⓐ, 0635⑥, 0650Ⓐ, 0702Ⓐ, 0730Ⓐ, 0737Ⓒ, 0745Ⓐ, 0813Ⓐ, 0835Ⓐ, 0837Ⓒ, 0907Ⓐ, 0937, 1002Ⓐ, 1037 and about every 30 mins. (hourly on Ⓒ) to 2007Ⓐ, 2037, 2107Ⓐ, 2137, 2207Ⓐ, 2237, 2337, returning at 0022ex①⑦, 0032①⑦, 0122⑦, 0132ex⑦, 0558Ⓐ, 0628Ⓐ, 0630⑥, 0646Ⓐ, 0714Ⓐ, 0732⑥, 0737Ⓐ, 0810Ⓐ, 0822Ⓒ, 0827Ⓐ, 0848Ⓐ, 0922Ⓒ, 0930Ⓐ, 0957Ⓐ, 1022Ⓒ, 1032Ⓐ, 1052Ⓐ and about every 30 mins. (about hourly on Ⓒ) to 2030Ⓐ, 2032Ⓒ, 2102Ⓐ, 2122Ⓒ, 2139Ⓐ, 2226Ⓐ, 2232Ⓒ, 2322Ⓐ, 2332Ⓒ. Journey: 20 mins.

lizabeth 🚆 *(NJT)* (24 km, US $: 4.15). From New York Penn Stn.: 0037, 0040, 0137, 0140 0439Ⓐ, 0503Ⓒ, 0553Ⓐ, 0608Ⓐ, 0623Ⓐ, 0632Ⓒ, 0637, 0707Ⓐ, 0713Ⓐ, 0737Ⓒ, 0745Ⓒ, 0749Ⓐ, 0810Ⓐ, 0829Ⓐ, 0837Ⓒ, 0849Ⓐ and frequent to 2112Ⓐ, 2130Ⓒ, 2137Ⓒ, 2142Ⓐ, 2230Ⓐ, 2232Ⓒ, 2237Ⓒ, 2333Ⓒ, 2337Ⓒ, 2340Ⓐ, returning at 0007①⑦, 0041②-⑥, 0051②-⑥, 0103①⑦, 0419Ⓐ, 0552Ⓐ, 0620Ⓒ, 0625Ⓐ, 0645Ⓐ, 0653Ⓒ, 0705Ⓐ, 0707Ⓒ, 0732Ⓐ, 0750Ⓐ, 0753Ⓒ and frequent to 2107Ⓒ, 2125Ⓐ, 2149Ⓐ, 2153Ⓒ, 2155Ⓐ, 2218Ⓒ, 2225Ⓐ, 2230Ⓐ, 2253Ⓒ, 2256Ⓐ, 2307Ⓒ, 2334Ⓐ, 2353Ⓒ, 2356Ⓐ. Journey: 25 mins.

nglewood 🚌 *(NJT RTL)* (❖ km, US $: 2.55). From New York: *NJT* 0000ex①⑦, 0015ex①, 0020①, 0045⑦, 0050ex①⑦, 0055ex①⑦, 0120⑦, 0130, 0550Ⓐ, 0600Ⓐ, 0615Ⓐ, 0625⑥, 0630Ⓐ, 0640Ⓐ, 0650⑥, 0655Ⓐ, 0700⚒, 0705Ⓐ, 0710Ⓐ, 0725 and frequent to 2315⑥, 2320⑥, 2325Ⓐ, 2345⑥, returning at 0003①, 0017⑦, 0031ex①⑦, 0035ex①⑦, 0451Ⓐ, 0512⑥, 0518Ⓐ, 0521Ⓐ, 0542⚒, 0551Ⓐ, 0558Ⓐ, 0602Ⓐ, 0603Ⓐ, 0612, 0618† and frequent to 2203†, 2217⑥, 2225Ⓐ, 2259Ⓐ, 2303†, 2305Ⓐ, 2317⑥, 2348Ⓐ, 2355Ⓐ; *RTL* ❖. Journey: 20-50 mins.

lushing 🚆 *(LIRR)* (❖ km, US $: 5.50). From New York Penn Stn.: 0019Ⓐ, 0020Ⓒ, 0119Ⓐ, 0120Ⓒ, 0319Ⓐ, 0350Ⓒ, 0520Ⓒ, 0529Ⓐ, 0620Ⓒ, 0631Ⓐ, 0701Ⓐ, 0720Ⓒ, 0753Ⓐ, 0820Ⓒ, 0823Ⓐ, 0850Ⓐ, 0919Ⓐ, 0920Ⓒ and about every 30 mins. (hourly on Ⓒ) to 2119Ⓐ, 2120Ⓒ, 2149Ⓐ, 2219Ⓐ, 2220Ⓒ, 2249Ⓐ, 2319Ⓐ, 2320Ⓒ, 2349Ⓐ, returning from Flushing Main Street at 0005, 0105, 0202Ⓒ, 0205Ⓐ, 0342Ⓒ, 0405Ⓐ, 0536Ⓐ, 0602Ⓐ, 0605Ⓒ, 0644Ⓐ, 0655Ⓐ, 0705Ⓒ, 0727Ⓐ, 0805Ⓒ, 0812Ⓐ, 0842Ⓐ, 0855Ⓐ, 0905Ⓒ, 0915Ⓐ, 0943Ⓐ, 1003Ⓐ, 1005Ⓒ and about every 30 mins. (hourly on Ⓒ) to 2205, 2235Ⓐ, 2305. Journey: 20 mins. Also, by *MTA/NYCTA* from New York Times Square: 0005 and frequent (every 30 mins. at night) to 2350, returning from Flushing Main Street at 0012 and frequent (every 30 mins. at night) to 2352. Journey: 40 mins.

reeport ◇🚆 *(LIRR)* (❖ km, US $: 7.00). From New York Penn Stn.: 0009, 0036Ⓐ, 0038Ⓒ, 0140Ⓒ, 0146Ⓐ, 0242Ⓒ, 0313Ⓐ, 0454Ⓐ, 0510Ⓒ, 0610Ⓒ, 0636Ⓐ and frequent to 2207Ⓐ, 2208Ⓒ, 2229Ⓐ, 2238Ⓐ, 2306Ⓐ, 2310Ⓒ, 2331Ⓐ, 2338Ⓒ, 2339Ⓐ, returning at 0008, 0123, 0208Ⓐ, 0220Ⓒ, 0330Ⓐ, 0408Ⓐ, 0419Ⓒ, 0508Ⓐ, 0519Ⓒ, 0529Ⓐ, *0547Ⓐ*, 0549Ⓒ, 0610Ⓐ, 0619Ⓒ, 0626Ⓐ, 0640Ⓐ, *0645Ⓐ*, 0649Ⓒ, 0657Ⓐ and frequent to 2208Ⓐ, 2219Ⓒ, 2238Ⓐ, 2308Ⓐ, 2310Ⓒ, 2338Ⓐ. Journey: 45 mins.

len Cove 🚆 *(LIRR)* (❖ km, US $: 7.00). From New York Penn Stn.: *0036Ⓐ, 0038Ⓒ, 0735Ⓒ, 0739Ⓐ, 0835Ⓐ, 0930Ⓒ, 1022Ⓐ, 1134Ⓒ, 1143Ⓐ, 1256Ⓐ, 1334Ⓒ, 1422Ⓐ, 1531Ⓐ, 1533Ⓒ, 1619Ⓐ, 1654Ⓐ, 1733, 1808Ⓐ, 1828Ⓒ, 1835Ⓐ, 1934Ⓒ, 1939Ⓐ, 2043Ⓐ, 2126Ⓒ, 2134Ⓐ, 2245Ⓒ, 2316Ⓐ*, returning at *0526Ⓐ, 0558Ⓐ, 0627Ⓒ, 0642Ⓐ, 0722Ⓐ, 0727Ⓒ, 0750Ⓐ, 0830Ⓐ, 0927Ⓒ, 0938Ⓐ, 1055Ⓐ, 1127Ⓒ, 1217Ⓐ, 1327Ⓒ, 1332Ⓐ, 1458Ⓐ, 1527Ⓒ, 1615Ⓐ, 1627Ⓒ, 1727Ⓒ, 1805Ⓐ, 1845Ⓐ, 1927Ⓒ, 2015Ⓐ, 2027Ⓒ, 2144Ⓐ, 2227Ⓒ, 2315Ⓐ*. Journey: 1¼ hours.

reenport 🚆 *(LIRR)* (❖ km, US $: 15.25). From New York Penn Stn.: *0739Ⓐ, 0914Ⓒ, 1414Ⓒ, 1741Ⓐ,1753Ⓐ* returning at *0529Ⓐ, 1137Ⓐ, 1240Ⓒ, 1740Ⓒ, 2137Ⓐ*. Journey: 3 hours. Also 🚌 *SE* from New York at 0830⑥, 0930⑥, 1100, 1430⚒, 1830, 2030①③⑤, 2145⑦, returning at 0545⑥, 0730⚒, 0800†, 1100⚒, 1430, 1730①③⑤, 1900⑦.

empstead 🚆 *(LIRR)* (❖ km, US $: 6.25). From New York Penn Stn.: *0036Ⓐ, 0038Ⓒ, 0140Ⓒ, 0146Ⓐ, 0300Ⓐ, 0334Ⓒ, 0530Ⓒ*, 0539Ⓐ, *0630Ⓒ*, 0655Ⓐ, *0735Ⓒ, 0739Ⓐ, 0835Ⓐ*, 0841Ⓒ, *0930Ⓒ, 0937Ⓐ, 1036Ⓐ, 1040Ⓒ, 1134Ⓒ, 1136Ⓐ, 1236Ⓐ, 1238Ⓒ, 1334Ⓒ, 1338Ⓐ, 1429Ⓐ, 1442Ⓒ, 1529Ⓒ, 1534Ⓐ*, 1632Ⓐ, *1633Ⓒ, 1642Ⓐ*, 1707Ⓐ, *1713Ⓐ, 1733Ⓒ*, 1738Ⓐ, 1751Ⓐ, *1808Ⓐ, 1828Ⓒ*, 1839Ⓐ, 1905Ⓐ, *1934Ⓒ, 1939Ⓐ, 2034Ⓐ, 2043Ⓒ, 2134Ⓐ, 2139Ⓒ, 2238Ⓐ, 2245Ⓒ, 2331Ⓐ, 2338Ⓒ*, returning at *0001, 0115, 0201Ⓐ, 0209Ⓒ, 0407Ⓐ, 0411Ⓒ, 0501Ⓐ, 0541Ⓒ, 0602Ⓐ, 0633Ⓒ*, 0638Ⓐ, 0658Ⓐ, 0714Ⓐ, *0723Ⓐ, 0724Ⓒ, 0736Ⓐ, 0800Ⓒ*, 0803Ⓐ, *0820Ⓐ, 0841Ⓒ, 0842Ⓐ, 0903Ⓐ, 0941Ⓒ, 1002Ⓐ, 1041Ⓒ, 1101Ⓐ, 1151Ⓒ, 1201Ⓐ, 1241Ⓒ, 1301Ⓐ, 1342Ⓐ, 1401Ⓐ, 1441Ⓒ, 1500Ⓐ, 1546Ⓐ, 1600Ⓐ, 1641Ⓒ, 1653Ⓐ*, 1741Ⓐ, *1745Ⓒ, 1820Ⓐ, 1843Ⓒ, 1909Ⓐ, 1947Ⓒ, 2000Ⓐ, 2041Ⓒ, 2101Ⓐ, 2148Ⓒ, 2201Ⓐ, 2208Ⓒ, 2301Ⓐ, 2302Ⓒ*. Journey: 50 mins.

oboken 🚆 *(PATH)* (*4* km, US $: ❖). From New York 33rd Street: 0012, 0042, 0112 and every 30 mins. to 0612, 0630Ⓐ, 0640Ⓐ, 0642Ⓒ, 0650Ⓐ, 0700Ⓐ, 0710Ⓐ, 0715Ⓒ and frequent to 2310Ⓐ, 2316Ⓒ, 2327Ⓐ, 2342, returning at 0026 and every 30 mins. to 0556, 0610Ⓐ, 0623Ⓐ, 0626Ⓒ, 0633Ⓐ, 0643Ⓐ, 0653Ⓐ, 0658Ⓒ, 0703Ⓐ, 0713Ⓐ, 0723Ⓐ, 0728Ⓒ, 0729Ⓐ and frequent to 2254Ⓐ, 2259Ⓒ, 2311Ⓐ, 2325Ⓒ, 2326Ⓐ, 2356. Journey: 14 mins.

untington 🚆 *(LIRR)* (❖ km, US $: 8.50). From New York Penn Stn.: 0000Ⓐ, 0001Ⓒ, 0105Ⓒ, 0107Ⓐ, *0140Ⓒ*, 0306Ⓐ, 0334Ⓒ, *0454Ⓐ*, 0530Ⓒ, 0548Ⓐ, 0630Ⓒ, 0703Ⓒ, *0739Ⓐ*, 0758Ⓒ, 0800Ⓐ, 0826Ⓐ, 0841Ⓒ, 0857Ⓐ, 0930Ⓒ, 0941Ⓐ, 1000Ⓒ, 1022Ⓐ, 1051Ⓐ, 1056Ⓒ, 1143Ⓐ, 1153Ⓒ, 1216Ⓐ, 1230Ⓒ, 1256Ⓐ, 1301Ⓒ, 1342Ⓐ, 1358Ⓒ, 1422Ⓐ, 1442Ⓒ, 1452Ⓐ, 1531Ⓐ, 1533Ⓒ, 1543Ⓐ, 1601Ⓐ, 1600Ⓒ, *1616Ⓐ*, 1631Ⓐ, *1632Ⓐ*, 1649Ⓐ, 1658Ⓒ, 1706Ⓐ, *1707Ⓐ*, 1717Ⓐ, 1735Ⓐ, 1746Ⓐ, 1743Ⓒ, *1801Ⓐ*, 1808Ⓐ, 1824Ⓐ, 1828Ⓒ, 1856Ⓐ, 1859Ⓒ, 1922Ⓐ, 1954Ⓐ, 2002Ⓒ, 2043, 2117Ⓐ, 2126Ⓒ, 2159Ⓐ, 2234Ⓐ, 2245Ⓒ, 2316Ⓐ, 2317Ⓒ, returning at 0005, 0034, 0133, 0346Ⓐ, 0348Ⓒ, 0509Ⓐ, 0527Ⓐ, 0548Ⓐ, 0552Ⓒ, 0615Ⓐ, 0631Ⓒ, *0638Ⓐ, 0649Ⓐ*, 0703Ⓒ, 0712Ⓐ, *0720Ⓐ*, 0737Ⓐ, *0745Ⓐ*, 0746Ⓒ, 0800Ⓐ, *0824Ⓐ*, 0833Ⓒ, 0859Ⓐ, 0903Ⓒ, *0913Ⓐ*, 0918Ⓐ, 0944Ⓐ, 1003Ⓒ, 1031Ⓐ, 1050Ⓒ, 1102Ⓐ, 1133Ⓒ, 1137Ⓐ, 1202Ⓒ, 1217Ⓐ, 1229Ⓐ, 1301Ⓐ, 1303Ⓒ, 1344Ⓐ, 1349Ⓒ, 1431Ⓐ, 1433Ⓒ, 1503Ⓐ, 1531Ⓒ, *1551Ⓐ*, 1603Ⓒ, 1611Ⓐ, 1651Ⓒ, 1709Ⓐ, 1735Ⓒ, 1829Ⓐ, 1830Ⓒ, 1903Ⓒ, 1938Ⓐ, 1950Ⓒ, 2003Ⓐ, 2033Ⓒ, 2040Ⓐ, 2127Ⓐ, 2132Ⓒ, 2201Ⓐ, 2203Ⓒ, 2244Ⓐ, 2332Ⓐ, 2333Ⓒ. Journey: 1¼ hours.

slip 🚆 *(LIRR)* (❖ km, US $: 9.50). From New York Penn Stn.: *0036Ⓐ, 0038Ⓒ, 0636Ⓐ, 0735Ⓒ, 0826Ⓐ, 0932Ⓐ, 0939Ⓒ, 1031Ⓐ, 1131Ⓐ, 1134Ⓒ, 1331Ⓐ, 1334Ⓒ, 1432Ⓐ, 1522Ⓐ, 1529Ⓒ, 1604Ⓐ, 1633Ⓒ, 1640Ⓐ, 1710Ⓐ, 1736Ⓐ, 1743Ⓒ, 1830Ⓐ, 1859Ⓒ, 1930Ⓐ, 2031Ⓐ, 2043Ⓒ, 2208Ⓒ, 2229Ⓐ, 2310Ⓒ*, returning at *0049, 0258Ⓐ, 0524Ⓐ, 0606Ⓒ, 0619Ⓐ, 0704Ⓐ, 0716Ⓐ, 0730Ⓒ, 0758Ⓐ, 0821Ⓐ, 0902Ⓒ, 0950Ⓐ, 1050Ⓐ, 1100Ⓒ, 1150Ⓐ, 1300Ⓒ, 1350Ⓐ, 1455Ⓐ, 1500Ⓒ, 1550Ⓐ, 1600Ⓒ, 1700Ⓐ, 1800Ⓒ, 1849Ⓐ, 1929Ⓒ, 2119Ⓒ, 2151Ⓐ, 2224Ⓒ, 2251Ⓐ*. Journey: 1¼ hours.

amaica 🚆 *(LIRR)* (*18* km, US $: 5.50). From New York Penn Stn.: 0000Ⓐ, 0001Ⓒ, 0009, 0015, 0036Ⓐ, 0038Ⓒ, 0059Ⓐ, 0105Ⓒ, 0107Ⓐ, 0114Ⓒ, 0115Ⓐ, 0140Ⓒ, 0146Ⓐ, 0242Ⓒ, 0246Ⓒ, 0300Ⓐ, 0306Ⓐ, 0313Ⓐ, 0316Ⓐ, 0334Ⓒ, 0454Ⓐ, 0510Ⓒ, 0511Ⓐ, 0514Ⓒ, 0530Ⓒ, 0539Ⓐ, 0548Ⓐ and frequent to 2306Ⓐ, 2310Ⓒ, 2314, 2316Ⓐ, 2317Ⓒ, 2331Ⓐ, 2338Ⓒ, 2339Ⓐ, returning at 0000②-⑥, 0007, 0017, 0033, 0047, 0107, 0117, 0148, 0206Ⓒ, 0207Ⓐ, 0215Ⓐ, 0219Ⓒ, 0233Ⓐ, 0244Ⓒ, 0350Ⓐ, 0430Ⓒ, 0433Ⓐ, 0435Ⓐ, 0436Ⓒ, 0443Ⓒ, 0511Ⓐ, 0533Ⓐ, 0543Ⓒ, 0551Ⓐ and frequent to 2301Ⓐ, 2307, 2316Ⓒ, 2327Ⓐ, 2333Ⓐ, 2334Ⓒ. Also, by *MTA/NYCTA* from New York Times Square: 0005 and frequent (every 30 mins. at night) to 2350, returning from Jamaica 179 Street at 0010 and frequent (every 30 mins. at night) to 2355; or from New York 42nd Street at 0007 and frequent (every 30 mins. at night) to 2352, returning from Jamaica Center at 0000 and frequent (every 30 mins. at night) to 2345. Journey: 40 mins.

Jersey City 🚆 *(PATH)* (*5* km, US $: ❖). From New York World Trade Center: 0027Ⓐ, 0030Ⓒ, 0100 and every 30 mins. to 0600Ⓐ/0700Ⓒ and frequent to 2342Ⓒ, 2357Ⓐ, returning at 0010 and every 30 mins. to 0540 and frequent to 2340Ⓐ, 2345Ⓒ. Journey: 11 mins.

Kennedy Airport 🚆. Use Jamaica Station, and connecting 🚌 service (*CCL*).

Long Branch 🚆 *(NJT)* (❖ km, US $: 9.15). From New York Penn. Stn.: 0037, 0137, 0608Ⓐ, 0637Ⓒ, 0707Ⓐ, 0737Ⓒ, 0749Ⓐ, *0829Ⓐ*, 0837Ⓒ, 0849Ⓐ, 0937Ⓒ, 0941Ⓐ, 1037Ⓒ, 1043Ⓐ, 1137Ⓒ, 1143Ⓐ, 1237Ⓒ, 1243Ⓐ, 1337Ⓒ, 1348Ⓐ, *1410Ⓐ*, 1437Ⓒ, 1454Ⓐ, 1532Ⓒ, 1552Ⓐ, *1620Ⓐ*, 1623Ⓐ, 1637Ⓒ, *1642Ⓐ*, 1655Ⓐ, *1710Ⓐ*, 1727Ⓐ, *1732Ⓐ*, 1742Ⓒ, 1749Ⓐ, 1752Ⓐ, *1810Ⓐ*, 1826Ⓐ, 1837Ⓒ, 1907Ⓐ, 1937Ⓒ, 2007Ⓐ, 2037Ⓒ, 2112Ⓐ, 2137Ⓒ, 2142Ⓐ, 2230Ⓐ, 2237Ⓒ, 2332Ⓐ, 2337Ⓒ, returning at 0447Ⓐ, 0535Ⓐ, 0540Ⓐ, 0550Ⓒ, *0555Ⓐ*, 0605Ⓐ, *0623Ⓐ*, 0632Ⓐ, 0642Ⓐ, 0650Ⓒ, *0654Ⓐ*, 0704Ⓐ, 0711Ⓐ, *0726Ⓐ*, 0735Ⓐ, 0750Ⓒ, *0755Ⓐ*, 0825Ⓐ, 0850Ⓒ, 0903Ⓐ, *0927Ⓐ*, 0950Ⓒ, 1003Ⓐ, 1048Ⓐ, 1050Ⓒ, 1148Ⓐ, 1150Ⓒ, 1248Ⓐ, 1250Ⓒ, 1348Ⓐ, 1350Ⓒ, 1448Ⓐ, 1450Ⓒ, *1532Ⓐ*, 1540Ⓐ, 1550Ⓒ, 1642Ⓐ, 1650Ⓒ, 1742Ⓐ, 1750Ⓒ, 1850Ⓒ, 1859Ⓐ, 1949Ⓐ, 1950Ⓒ, 2048Ⓐ, 2050Ⓒ, 2150Ⓒ, 2227Ⓐ, 2250Ⓒ, 2339Ⓐ, 2359Ⓒ. Journey: 1½ hours.

Matawan 🚆 *(NJT)* (❖ km, US $: 8.25). From New York Penn. Stn.: 0037, 0137, 0608Ⓐ, 0637Ⓒ, 0707Ⓐ, 0737Ⓒ, 0749Ⓐ, *0829Ⓐ*, 0837Ⓒ, 0849Ⓐ, 0937Ⓒ, 0941Ⓐ, 1037Ⓒ, 1043Ⓐ, 1137Ⓒ, 1143Ⓐ, 1237Ⓒ, 1243Ⓐ, 1337Ⓒ, 1348Ⓐ, *1410Ⓐ*, 1437Ⓒ, 1454Ⓐ, 1532Ⓒ, 1552Ⓐ, *1620Ⓐ*, 1623Ⓐ, 1637Ⓒ, *1642Ⓐ*, 1652Ⓐ, 1655Ⓐ, *1710Ⓐ*, 1727Ⓐ, *1732Ⓐ*, 1742Ⓒ, 1749Ⓐ, 1752Ⓐ, *1810Ⓐ*, 1826Ⓐ, 1837Ⓒ, 1852Ⓐ, 1907Ⓐ, 1920Ⓐ, 1937Ⓒ, 2007Ⓐ, 2034Ⓐ, 2037Ⓒ, 2112Ⓐ, 2137Ⓒ, 2142Ⓐ, 2230Ⓐ, 2237Ⓒ, 2332Ⓐ, 2337Ⓒ, returning at 0006ex①⑦, 0027①⑦, 0512Ⓐ, 0602Ⓐ, 0607Ⓐ, 0617Ⓒ, *0618Ⓐ*, 0633Ⓐ, *0648Ⓐ*, 0659Ⓐ, 0709Ⓐ, 0717Ⓒ, *0721Ⓐ*, 0726Ⓐ, 0738Ⓐ, *0750Ⓐ*, 0802Ⓐ, 0817Ⓒ, *0821Ⓐ*, 0840Ⓐ, 0851Ⓐ, 0917Ⓒ, 0929Ⓐ, *0949Ⓐ*, 1017Ⓒ, 1029Ⓐ, 1115Ⓐ, 1117Ⓒ, 1215Ⓐ, 1217Ⓒ, 1315Ⓐ, 1317Ⓒ, 1417Ⓒ, 1419Ⓐ, 1515Ⓐ, 1517Ⓒ, *1557Ⓐ*, 1607Ⓐ, 1617Ⓒ, 1709Ⓐ, 1717Ⓒ, 1810Ⓐ, 1817Ⓒ, 1917Ⓒ, 1926Ⓐ, 2015Ⓐ, 2017Ⓒ, 2114Ⓐ, 2117Ⓒ, 2155Ⓐ, 2217Ⓒ, 2253Ⓐ, 2317Ⓒ. Journey: 1 hour.

Middletown 🚆 *(MNR)* (*106* km, US $: 8.75). From Hoboken: 0907Ⓒ, 0935Ⓐ, 1250⑥, 1555Ⓐ, 1645Ⓐ, 1742Ⓐ, 1823Ⓐ, 1840Ⓒ, 1905Ⓐ, *2115Ⓐ*, 2145†, returning at 0516Ⓐ, 0555Ⓐ, 0633Ⓐ, 0712Ⓐ, 0801Ⓒ, 0908Ⓐ, 1227⑥, 1408Ⓐ, 1754Ⓒ, 2117Ⓐ, 2209⑥. Journey: 2 hours.

Milford 🚆 *(CDT)* (❖ km, US $: 11.75). From New York Grand Central: 0035, 0130, 0540Ⓒ, 0602Ⓐ, 0705Ⓐ, 0807 and hourly to 1407, 1502⑥, 1507, 1539, 1600Ⓐ, 1607, 1622Ⓐ, 1635Ⓐ, 1645Ⓐ, 1703Ⓐ, 1707Ⓒ, 1713Ⓐ, 1718Ⓐ, 1736Ⓐ, 1742Ⓐ, 1804Ⓐ, 1807Ⓒ, 1826Ⓐ, 1906Ⓐ, 1907Ⓒ, 1937Ⓐ, 2007, 2037Ⓐ, 2107, 2207, 2320, returning at 0503Ⓐ, 0535Ⓐ, 0553Ⓐ, 0608, 0636Ⓐ, 0656Ⓐ, 0708⑥, 0710Ⓐ, 0722Ⓐ, 0737Ⓐ, 0755Ⓐ, 0803Ⓐ, 0808Ⓒ, 0814Ⓐ, 0902Ⓐ, 0908Ⓒ, 1008, and hourly to 1508, 1605Ⓐ, 1608Ⓒ, 1708 and hourly to 2208, 2333. Journey: 1½ hours.

Montauk 🚆 *(LIRR)* (*188* km, US $: 15.25). From New York Penn. Stn.: *0036Ⓐ, 0038Ⓒ, 0749Ⓐ, 0758Ⓒ, 1006Ⓒ, 1153Ⓒ, 1601⑤, 1619Ⓐ, 1751Ⓐ, 2031Ⓐ, 2043Ⓒ*, returning at *0051Ⓐ, 0538Ⓐ, 0655Ⓒ, 1125Ⓐ, 1530Ⓒ, 1702Ⓒ, 1930Ⓒ, 2236Ⓐ*. Journey: 2¾ hours.

Mount Vernon 🚆 *(CDT/MNR)* (21km, US $: 5.75). From New York Grand Central to Mount Vernon: 0040, 0130, 0535Ⓐ, 0540Ⓒ, 0640, 0710Ⓐ and about every 30 mins. (hourly on Ⓒ) to 2240, 2310Ⓐ, 2340, returning at 0101, 0535Ⓐ, 0605Ⓐ, 0633Ⓐ, 0636Ⓒ, 0654Ⓐ, 0716Ⓐ, 0730Ⓐ, 0736Ⓒ and about every 30 mins. (hourly on Ⓒ) to 2036, 2106Ⓐ, 2136, 2236, 2346. Also from New York Grand Central to Mount Vernon West: 0030, 0130, 0555Ⓒ, 0600Ⓐ, 0628Ⓐ, 0651Ⓐ, 0716Ⓐ, 0727Ⓒ, 0730Ⓐ and about every 30 mins. (hourly on Ⓒ) to 2203Ⓐ. 2227. 2303Ⓐ. 2327. returning at 0023Ⓐ. 0032Ⓒ. 0521Ⓐ. 0551Ⓐ. 0554Ⓒ. 0622Ⓐ. 0639Ⓐ. 0648Ⓐ. 0655Ⓐ, 0700Ⓒ, 0704Ⓐ, 0721Ⓐ, 0723Ⓒ and about every 30 mins. (hourly on Ⓒ) to 1854Ⓐ, 1922Ⓒ, 1924Ⓐ, 2023, 2123, 2223, 2323. Journey: 25-30 mins.

Newark 🚆 *(NJT)* (*16* km, US $: 2.50). From New York Penn. Stn.: 0037, 0040, 0137, 0140, 0439Ⓐ, 0503Ⓒ, 0553Ⓐ, 0608Ⓐ, 0623Ⓐ, 0632Ⓒ, 0637Ⓒ, 0653Ⓐ, 0707Ⓐ, 0716Ⓐ, 0737Ⓒ, 0738Ⓐ, 0745Ⓒ, 0749Ⓐ and frequent to 2104Ⓐ, 2112Ⓐ, 2130Ⓒ, 2135Ⓐ, 2137Ⓒ, 2142Ⓐ, 2225Ⓐ, 2230Ⓐ, 2232Ⓒ, 2237Ⓒ, 2325Ⓐ, 2332, 2337Ⓒ, 2340Ⓐ, returning from Newark Penn. Stn. at 0000①⑦, 0003ex①⑦, 0014①⑦, 0048ex①⑦, 0058ex①⑦, 0110①⑦, 0425Ⓐ, 0550Ⓐ, 0602Ⓐ, 0615Ⓐ, 0627Ⓒ, 0636Ⓐ, 0638Ⓐ, 0642Ⓐ, 0650Ⓐ, 0655Ⓐ, 0700Ⓒ and frequent to 2100Ⓒ, 2102Ⓐ, 2114Ⓒ, 2132Ⓐ, 2156Ⓐ, 2158Ⓒ, 2202Ⓐ, 2225Ⓒ, 2237Ⓐ, 2242Ⓐ, 2300Ⓒ, 2303Ⓐ, 2314Ⓒ, 2342Ⓐ. Journey: 15 mins. Also, by *PATH* from New York World Trade Center: 0027Ⓐ, 0030Ⓒ, 0100 and every 30 mins. to 0600Ⓐ/0700Ⓒ and frequent to 2342Ⓒ, 2357Ⓐ, returning at 0000 and every 30 mins. to 0530 and frequent to 2330Ⓐ, 2335Ⓒ. Journey: 22 mins. Also by *NJT* from Hoboken at 0037, 0107②-⑥, 0145②-⑥, 0600Ⓐ/0635⑥/0737† and frequent to 2337Ⓒ/2350Ⓐ, returning from Newark Broad Street at 0026ex①⑦, 0036①⑦, 0106ex①⑦, 0136, 0602Ⓐ/0634⑥/0826† and frequent to 2326Ⓐ/ 2336Ⓒ.

New Brunswick 🚆 *(NJT)* (*53* km, US $: ❖). From New York Penn. Stn.: 0040, 0140, 0439Ⓐ, 0503Ⓒ, 0553Ⓐ, 0632Ⓒ, 0653Ⓐ, 0716Ⓐ, 0738Ⓐ, 0745Ⓒ, 0810Ⓐ, 0829Ⓐ, 0832Ⓒ, 0902Ⓐ, 0925Ⓒ, 0932Ⓐ, 1002Ⓐ, 1027Ⓒ, 1034Ⓐ, 1104Ⓐ, 1127Ⓒ, 1134Ⓐ, 1204Ⓐ, 1232Ⓒ, 1237Ⓐ, 1302Ⓐ, 1329Ⓒ, 1337Ⓐ, 1410Ⓐ, 1432Ⓒ, 1442Ⓐ, 1510Ⓐ, 1525Ⓒ, 1544Ⓐ, 1620Ⓐ, 1625Ⓒ, 1703Ⓐ, 1724Ⓐ, 1725Ⓒ, *1740Ⓐ*, 1810Ⓐ, *1823Ⓐ*, 1825Ⓒ, 1837Ⓐ, *1852Ⓐ*, 1910Ⓐ, 1925Ⓒ, 1933Ⓐ, 2014Ⓐ, 2032Ⓒ, 2044Ⓐ, 2104Ⓐ, 2130Ⓒ, 2135Ⓐ, 2225Ⓐ, 2232Ⓒ, 2325Ⓐ, 2332Ⓒ, 2340Ⓐ, returning at ❖. Journey: 50 mins.

New Haven 🚆 *(CDT)* (*116* km, US $: 13.50). From New York Grand Central: 0035, 0130, 0540Ⓒ, 0602Ⓐ, 0705Ⓐ, 0807 and hourly to 1407, 1502⑥, 1507, 1539Ⓐ, 1600Ⓐ, 1607, 1622Ⓐ, 1635Ⓐ, 1645Ⓐ, 1703Ⓐ, 1707Ⓒ, 1713Ⓐ, 1718Ⓐ, 1736Ⓐ, 1736, 1742Ⓐ, 1804Ⓐ, 1807Ⓒ, 1826Ⓐ, 1906Ⓐ, 1907Ⓒ, 1937Ⓐ, 2007, 2037Ⓐ, 2107, 2207, 2320, returning at 0452Ⓐ, 0524Ⓐ, 0542Ⓐ, 0557, 0625Ⓐ, 0645Ⓐ, 0657⑥, 0659Ⓐ, 0711Ⓐ, 0726Ⓐ, 0744Ⓐ, 0752Ⓐ, 0757Ⓒ, 0803Ⓐ, 0851Ⓐ, 0857Ⓒ, 0957, 1057, 1157, 1257, 1357, 1457, 1554Ⓐ, 1557Ⓒ, 1657 and hourly to 2157, 2322. Journey: 1¾ hours.

New Rochelle 🚆 *(CDT)* (*53* km, US $: 5.25). From New York Grand Central: 0040, 0130, 0535Ⓐ, 0540Ⓒ, 0640, 0710Ⓐ, 0740Ⓒ, 0742Ⓐ, 0810Ⓐ, 0840 then ½ hourly (hourly on Ⓒ) until 1540, 1609Ⓐ, 1629Ⓐ, 1640Ⓒ, 1654Ⓐ, 1710⑥, 1716Ⓐ, 1720Ⓐ, 1734Ⓐ, 1740Ⓒ, 1742Ⓐ, 1801Ⓐ, 1810⑥, 1819Ⓐ, 1840, 1915Ⓐ, 1940 then ½ hourly (hourly on Ⓒ) until 2340, returning at 0054, 0529Ⓐ, 0559Ⓐ, 0627Ⓐ, 0629Ⓒ, 0648Ⓐ, 0710Ⓐ, 0722Ⓐ, 0729Ⓒ, 0742Ⓐ, 0756Ⓐ, 0759⑥, 0816Ⓐ, 0829Ⓒ, 0843Ⓐ, 0854Ⓐ, 0859⑥, 0906Ⓐ, 0926Ⓐ, 0929Ⓒ, 0959Ⓐ, 1029Ⓒ, 1036Ⓐ, 1059Ⓐ, 1129, 1159Ⓐ, 1229, 1259Ⓐ, 1329, 1359Ⓐ, 1429, 1459Ⓐ, 1529, 1559Ⓐ, 1629, 1651Ⓐ, 1659Ⓐ, 1727Ⓐ, 1729Ⓒ, 1734Ⓐ, 1804Ⓐ, 1829⑥, 1834Ⓐ, 1904Ⓐ, 1929Ⓒ, 1934Ⓐ, 1959Ⓐ, 2029, 2059Ⓐ, 2129, 2229, 2339. Journey: 30 mins.

North Bergen 🚌 *(NJT)* (❖ km, US $: 1.90). From New York: 0500Ⓐ/0630⑥/0705† and frequent to 0330, returning at 0525Ⓐ/0531⑥/0625† and frequent to 0245ex①/0250①. Journey: 20 mins.

North White Plains 🚆 *(MNR)* (38 km, US $: 6.50). From New York Grand Central: 0030, 0130, 0555Ⓒ, 0600Ⓐ, 0628Ⓐ, 0651Ⓐ, 0716Ⓐ, 0730Ⓐ, 0733Ⓒ, 0752⑥, 0755Ⓐ, 0801Ⓐ, 0830Ⓐ, 0833Ⓒ, 0847Ⓒ, 0856Ⓐ, 0901Ⓐ, 0930Ⓐ, 0933Ⓒ, 0947 and frequent (twice hourly on Ⓒ) to 2347, returning at 0000Ⓐ, 0009Ⓒ, 0500Ⓐ, 0530Ⓐ, 0531Ⓒ, 0554⚒, 0617Ⓐ, 0627Ⓐ, 0632⑥, 0633Ⓐ, 0637⑥, 0641Ⓐ, 0650Ⓐ, 0657Ⓐ, 0700Ⓒ, 0702Ⓐ, 0705Ⓐ, 0716Ⓐ, 0729⑥, 0733Ⓐ, 0730⑥, 0754Ⓒ, 0800Ⓒ, 0801Ⓐ, 0804Ⓐ, 0823Ⓐ, 0830⑥, 0832Ⓐ, 0854Ⓒ, 0858Ⓐ, 0900Ⓒ, 0926Ⓐ, 0930Ⓐ, 0954Ⓒ, 1000, 1030Ⓐ, 1054, 1100, 1130Ⓐ, 1154, 1200, 1230Ⓐ, 1254, 1300, 1330Ⓐ, 1354, 1400, 1430Ⓐ, 1454, 1500, 1529Ⓐ, 1554, 1600, 1629Ⓐ, 1654Ⓒ, 1656Ⓐ, 1700Ⓒ, 1701Ⓐ, 1726Ⓐ, 1731Ⓐ, 1752Ⓐ, 1754Ⓒ, 1800Ⓒ, 1801Ⓐ, 1831Ⓐ, 1854Ⓒ, 1856Ⓐ, 1900Ⓒ, 1901Ⓐ, 1954, 2000, 2054, 2100, 2154, 2200, 2254. Journey: 50 mins.

Oyster Bay 🚆 *(LIRR)* (❖ km, US $: 7.00). From New York Penn. Stn.: *0036Ⓐ, 0038Ⓒ, 0735Ⓒ, 0739Ⓐ, 0835Ⓐ, 0930Ⓒ, 1022Ⓐ, 1134Ⓒ, 1143Ⓐ, 1258Ⓐ, 1334Ⓒ, 1422Ⓐ, 1531Ⓐ, 1533Ⓒ, 1619Ⓐ, 1654Ⓐ, 1733, 1808Ⓐ, 1828Ⓒ, 1835Ⓐ, 1934Ⓒ, 1939Ⓐ, 2043Ⓐ, 2126Ⓒ, 2134Ⓐ, 2245Ⓒ, 2316Ⓐ*, returning at *0513Ⓐ, 0545Ⓐ, 0614Ⓒ, 0629Ⓐ, 0706Ⓐ, 0714Ⓒ, 0733Ⓐ, 0815Ⓐ, 0914Ⓒ, 0924Ⓐ, 1041Ⓐ, 1114Ⓒ, 1203Ⓐ, 1314Ⓒ, 1318Ⓐ, 1444Ⓐ, 1514Ⓒ, 1602Ⓐ, 1614Ⓒ, 1714Ⓒ, 1752Ⓐ, 1832Ⓐ, 1914Ⓒ, 2002Ⓐ, 2014Ⓒ, 2131Ⓐ, 2214Ⓒ, 2302Ⓐ*. Journey: 1½ hours.

Paramus 🚌 *(HTL)* (❖ km, US $: 5.50). From New York: 0030, 0130, 0650Ⓐ, 0715, 0730Ⓐ, 0750Ⓐ and frequent (about hourly on Ⓒ) to 2015Ⓐ, 2030Ⓒ, 2045Ⓐ, 2115Ⓐ, 2130Ⓒ, 2145Ⓐ, 2215, 2245, 2330, returning at 0553Ⓒ, 0557Ⓐ, 0617Ⓐ, 0623Ⓒ, 0629Ⓐ, 0641Ⓐ, 0643Ⓐ, 0653Ⓒ, 0655Ⓐ and frequent (about hourly on Ⓒ) to 2026⑥, 2027Ⓐ, 2028†, 2123Ⓐ, 2124Ⓒ, 2229, 2320Ⓐ, 2321Ⓒ. Journey: 30 mins. Also by *IBS* from New York at 0845, 1115, 1415Ⓒ, 1455Ⓐ, 1815Ⓒ, returning at 1000, 1230, 1630, 1830Ⓒ and by *NJT* at 0020ex①⑦, 0030①, 0035①⑦, 0040⑦, 0110①⑦, 0115ex⑦, 0120, 0610Ⓐ, 0630Ⓐ, 0640Ⓐ, 0700Ⓐ, 0710⚒, 0715Ⓐ, 0730 and frequent to 2220, 2230†, 2245, 2250⑥, 2320, 2330†, 2340⑥, 2345⚒, returning at 0009ex①⑦, 0010⑦, 0011①⑦, 0015ex①⑦, 0517Ⓐ, 0532Ⓐ, 0535Ⓐ, 0542Ⓐ, 0550Ⓐ, 0552Ⓐ, 0601†, 0602⚒ and frequent to 2206⑥, 2210⑥, 2211†, 2214Ⓐ, 2215Ⓐ, 2235⚒, 2244†, 2304Ⓐ, 2306⑥, 2310⑥, 2311†, 2315Ⓐ, 2335⚒, 2344†.

Passaic 🚆 *(NJT)* (❖ km, US $: 2.80). From Hoboken: 0035, 0605Ⓐ, 0640Ⓐ, 0713Ⓐ, 0741Ⓐ, 0830Ⓐ, 0840Ⓒ, 1135Ⓐ, 1250⑥, 1335Ⓐ, 1445Ⓐ, 1535Ⓐ, 1540⑥, 1615Ⓐ, 1640†, 1715Ⓐ, 1740⑥, 1741Ⓐ, 1811Ⓐ, 1841Ⓐ, 1935Ⓐ, 1945⑥, 2035Ⓐ, 2045†, 2145⑥, 2215Ⓐ, 2320Ⓐ, returning from Passaic, Passaic Avenue at 0554Ⓐ, 0701Ⓐ, 0733Ⓐ, 0800Ⓒ, 0804Ⓐ, 0824Ⓐ, 0852Ⓐ, 0914Ⓐ, 1017Ⓐ, 1100Ⓒ, 1239Ⓐ, 1400⑥, 1439Ⓐ, 1539Ⓐ, 1639Ⓐ, 1739Ⓐ, 1800⑥, 1854Ⓐ, 1930†, 1950⑥, 2245⑥, 2305Ⓐ, 2355⑥. Journey: 25 mins.

Patchogue 🚆 *(LIRR)* (*90* km, US $: 10.75). From New York Penn Stn.: *0036Ⓐ, 0038Ⓒ, 0636Ⓐ, 0735Ⓒ, 0749Ⓐ, 0758Ⓒ, 0826Ⓐ, 0930Ⓒ, 0932Ⓐ, 1006Ⓒ, 1031Ⓐ, 1131Ⓐ, 1134Ⓒ, 1153Ⓒ, 1201Ⓐ, 1328Ⓐ, 1334Ⓒ, 1429Ⓐ, 1521Ⓐ, 1529Ⓒ, 1604Ⓐ, 1619Ⓐ, 1633Ⓒ, 1640Ⓐ, 1710Ⓐ, 1736Ⓐ, 1743Ⓒ, 1751Ⓐ, 1830Ⓐ, 1859Ⓒ, 1930Ⓐ, 1954Ⓒ, 2031Ⓐ, 2043Ⓒ, 2208Ⓒ, 2229Ⓐ, 2310Ⓒ*, returning at *0027, 0238Ⓐ, 0458Ⓐ, 0535Ⓐ, 0548Ⓒ, 0555Ⓐ, 0639Ⓐ, 0653Ⓐ, 0706Ⓒ, 0716Ⓐ, 0735Ⓐ, 0756Ⓐ, 0839Ⓒ, 0930Ⓐ, 1030Ⓐ, 1037Ⓒ, 1130Ⓐ, 1237Ⓒ, 1306Ⓐ, 1330Ⓐ, 1434Ⓐ, 1436Ⓒ, 1530Ⓐ, 1538Ⓒ, 1635Ⓐ, 1718Ⓒ, 1738Ⓒ, 1807Ⓒ, 1829Ⓐ, 1849Ⓒ, 1906Ⓒ, 1936Ⓐ, 2003Ⓒ, 2055Ⓒ, 2118Ⓒ, 2131Ⓐ, 2205Ⓒ, 2229Ⓐ*. Journey: 1½ hours.

Paterson 🚆 *(NJT)* (*26* km, US $: 3.60). From Hoboken: 0035, 0605Ⓐ, 0640Ⓐ, 0713Ⓐ, 0741Ⓐ, 0830Ⓐ, 0840⑥, 1135Ⓐ, 1250⑥, 1335Ⓐ, 1445Ⓐ, 1535Ⓐ, 1540⑥, 1615Ⓐ, 1640†, 1715Ⓐ, 1740⑥, 1741Ⓐ, 1811Ⓐ, 1841Ⓐ, 1935Ⓐ, 1945⑥, 2035Ⓐ, 2045†, 2145⑥, 2215Ⓐ, 2320Ⓐ, returning from Paterson Market Street at 0544Ⓐ, 0650Ⓐ, 0722Ⓐ, 0750Ⓒ, 0753Ⓐ, 0843Ⓐ, 0905Ⓐ, 1007Ⓐ, 1050Ⓒ, 1229Ⓐ, 1350⑥, 1429Ⓐ, 1529Ⓐ, 1629Ⓐ, 1729Ⓐ, 1750⑥, 1845Ⓐ, 1940⑥, 1950†, 2235⑥, 2256Ⓐ, 2345⑥. Journey: 35 mins.

Point Pleasant Beach 🚆 *(NJT)* (❖ km, US $: 9.45). From New York Penn Stn.: *0037†, 0137Ⓒ, 0637Ⓒ, 0707Ⓐ, 0829Ⓐ, 0837Ⓒ, 0930⑥, 0937Ⓒ, 0941Ⓐ, 1037Ⓒ, 1137Ⓒ, 1143Ⓐ, 1237Ⓒ, 1243♤, 1337Ⓒ, 1407Ⓐ, 1437Ⓒ, 1535▽, 1552Ⓐ, 1620Ⓐ, 1637Ⓒ, 1642Ⓐ, 1710Ⓐ, 1721Ⓐ, 1732Ⓐ, 1742Ⓒ, 1810Ⓐ, 1837Ⓒ, 1852♤, 1907Ⓐ, 2007Ⓐ, 2037Ⓒ, 2112Ⓐ, 2137Ⓒ, 2230Ⓐ, 2332Ⓐ, 2337Ⓒ*, returning at *0458Ⓐ, 0510Ⓒ, 0520Ⓐ, 0549Ⓐ, 0610⑥, 0621Ⓐ, 0653Ⓐ, 0710Ⓒ, 0721Ⓐ, 0748Ⓐ, 0853Ⓐ, 0910Ⓒ, 1010Ⓐ, 1110Ⓒ, 1210Ⓐ, 1310Ⓒ, 1457Ⓐ, 1510Ⓒ, 1604Ⓐ, 1706Ⓒ, 1707Ⓐ, 1806Ⓒ, 1906Ⓒ, 2012Ⓐ, 2024∝, 2110Ⓒ, 2149Ⓐ, 2302Ⓐ, 2323Ⓒ*. Journey: 2¼ hours.

Port Jervis 🚆 *(MNR)* (*140* km, US $: 11.50). From Hoboken: 0907Ⓒ, 0935Ⓐ, 1250⑥, 1555Ⓐ, 1645Ⓐ, 1742Ⓐ, 1823Ⓐ, 1840Ⓒ, 1905Ⓐ, *2115Ⓐ*, 2145†, returning at 0443Ⓐ, 0523Ⓐ, 0601Ⓐ, 0642Ⓐ, 0729Ⓒ, 0835Ⓐ, 1155⑥, 1335Ⓐ, 1722Ⓒ, *2044Ⓐ*, 2137⑥. Journey: 2¼ hours.

Port Washington 🚆 *(LIRR)* (❖ km, US $: 6.25). From New York Penn Stn.: 0019Ⓐ, 0020Ⓒ, 0119Ⓐ, 0120Ⓒ, 0319Ⓐ, 0350Ⓒ, 0520Ⓒ, 0529Ⓐ, 0620Ⓒ, 0631Ⓐ, 0720Ⓒ, 0753Ⓐ, 0820Ⓒ, 0823Ⓐ, 0850Ⓐ, 0919Ⓐ, 0920Ⓒ and about every 30 mins. (hourly on Ⓒ) to 2219Ⓐ, 2220Ⓒ, 2249Ⓐ, 2319Ⓐ, 2320Ⓒ, 2349Ⓐ, returning at 0039, 0136Ⓒ, 0139Ⓐ, 0316Ⓒ, 0339Ⓐ, 0509Ⓐ, 0536Ⓐ, 0539Ⓒ, 0617Ⓐ, 0627Ⓐ, 0639Ⓒ, 0645Ⓐ, 0720Ⓐ, 0736Ⓐ, 0739Ⓒ, 0747Ⓐ, 0806Ⓐ, 0817Ⓐ, 0839Ⓒ, 0845Ⓐ, 0911Ⓐ, 0938Ⓐ, 0939Ⓒ and about every 30 mins. (hourly on Ⓒ) to 2209Ⓐ, 2239, 2339. Journey: 45 mins.

Poughkeepsie 🚆 *(MNR)* (*118* km, US $: 13.00). From New York Grand Central: *0120*, 0649Ⓐ, 0749Ⓐ, 0758Ⓒ, 0858, 0958, 1055Ⓐ, *1058Ⓒ*, 1158, 1258, *1355Ⓒ*, 1358Ⓐ, 1458, *1555Ⓒ*, 1600Ⓐ, 1649Ⓐ, 1658Ⓒ, 1710Ⓐ, 1746Ⓐ, 1758Ⓒ, 1814Ⓐ, 1847Ⓐ, 1858Ⓒ, *1917Ⓐ*, 1953Ⓐ, *1955Ⓒ*, 2100, 2155, 2300, *2355*, returning at 0440Ⓐ, 0512⑥, 0531Ⓐ, 0600Ⓐ, *0612Ⓒ*, 0624Ⓐ, 0644Ⓐ, 0656Ⓐ, 0712Ⓒ, 0729Ⓐ, *0815Ⓐ*, 0812Ⓒ, 0912, 1012, 1112, *1212*, 1312, 1412, 1512, 1612, 1712, 1812, 1912, 2012Ⓒ, *2020Ⓐ, 2112Ⓒ, 2130Ⓐ, 2245*. Journey: 1 hour 50 mins.

Princeton 🚆 *(NJT)* (*4* km, US $: ❖). From Princeton Junction: 0027②-⑥, 0039①⑦, 0051②-⑥, 0552Ⓐ, 0632Ⓒ, 0711Ⓐ, 0734Ⓐ, 0739Ⓒ, 0806Ⓐ, 0845Ⓐ, 0852Ⓒ, 0920Ⓐ, 0939Ⓒ, 0945Ⓐ, 1015Ⓐ, 1032Ⓒ, 1045Ⓐ, 1106Ⓐ, 1140Ⓒ, 1211Ⓐ, 1234Ⓒ, 1242Ⓐ, 1311Ⓐ, 1339Ⓒ, 1346Ⓐ, 1409Ⓐ, 1436Ⓒ, 1445Ⓐ, 1518Ⓐ, 1540Ⓒ, 1555Ⓐ, 1621Ⓐ, 1640Ⓒ, 1655Ⓐ, 1722Ⓐ, 1734Ⓒ, 1745Ⓐ, 1818Ⓐ, 1832Ⓒ, 1846Ⓐ, 1904Ⓐ, 1922Ⓐ, 1935Ⓒ, 1946Ⓐ, 2020Ⓐ, 2032Ⓒ, 2141Ⓒ, 2148Ⓐ, 2208Ⓐ, 2237Ⓒ, 2239Ⓐ, 2329Ⓐ, 2340Ⓒ, returning at 0543Ⓐ, 0601Ⓐ, 0617Ⓒ, 0619Ⓐ, 0644Ⓐ, 0702Ⓐ, 0717Ⓒ, 0725Ⓐ, 0742Ⓐ, 0817Ⓒ, 0821Ⓐ, 0903Ⓐ, 0917Ⓒ,

Table 335–contd NEW YORK LOCAL SERVICES

BTL CDT HTL IBS LIRR MNR MTA NJT NYCTA PATH RTL

0929Ⓐ, 0954Ⓐ, 1017Ⓒ, 1025Ⓐ, 1054Ⓐ, 1117Ⓒ, 1157Ⓐ, 1217Ⓒ, 1228Ⓐ, 1257Ⓐ, 1317Ⓒ, 1332Ⓐ, 1355Ⓐ, 1417Ⓒ, 1431Ⓐ, 1506Ⓐ, 1517Ⓒ, 1539Ⓐ, 1605Ⓐ, 1617Ⓒ, 1639Ⓐ, 1710Ⓐ, 1717Ⓒ, 1731Ⓐ, 1801Ⓐ, 1817Ⓒ, 1827Ⓐ, 1855Ⓐ, 1917Ⓒ, 1931Ⓐ, 2005Ⓐ, 2017Ⓒ, 2123Ⓒ, 2134Ⓐ, 2157Ⓐ, 2217Ⓒ, 2305Ⓐ, 2317Ⓒ, 2359Ⓐ. Journey: 6 mins.

Princeton Junction 🚆 *(NJT)* (*78* km, US $: ❖). From New York Penn. Stn.: 0040, 0140, 0439Ⓐ, 0503Ⓒ, 0553Ⓐ, 0632Ⓒ, 0653Ⓐ, 0716Ⓐ, 0738Ⓐ, 0745Ⓒ, 0810Ⓐ, 0829Ⓐ, 0832Ⓒ, 0902Ⓐ, 0925Ⓒ, 0932Ⓐ, 1002Ⓐ, 1027Ⓒ, 1034Ⓐ, 1104Ⓐ, 1127Ⓒ, 1134Ⓐ, 1204Ⓐ, 1232Ⓒ, 1237Ⓐ, 1302Ⓐ, 1329Ⓒ, 1337Ⓐ, 1410Ⓐ, 1432Ⓒ, 1442Ⓐ, 1510Ⓐ, 1525Ⓒ, 1544Ⓐ, 1620Ⓐ, 1625Ⓒ, 1703Ⓐ, 1724Ⓐ, 1725Ⓒ, *1740*Ⓐ, 1810Ⓐ, *1823*Ⓐ, 1825Ⓒ, 1837Ⓐ, *1852*Ⓐ, 1910Ⓐ, 1925Ⓒ, 1933Ⓐ, 2014Ⓐ, 2032Ⓒ, 2044Ⓐ, 2104Ⓐ, 2130Ⓒ, 2135Ⓐ, 2225Ⓐ, 2232Ⓒ, 2325Ⓐ, 2332Ⓒ, 2340Ⓐ, returning at 0010②-⑥, 0340Ⓐ, 0535Ⓐ, 0540Ⓒ, 0600Ⓐ, *0618*Ⓐ, 0627Ⓒ, 0641Ⓐ, 0651Ⓐ, 0703Ⓐ, *0722*Ⓐ, 0727Ⓒ, 0730Ⓐ, 0741Ⓐ, 0753Ⓐ, 0827Ⓒ, 0840Ⓐ, 0915Ⓐ, 0927Ⓒ, 0940Ⓐ, 1010Ⓐ, 1027Ⓒ, 1040Ⓐ, 1120Ⓐ, 1127Ⓒ, 1150Ⓐ, 1220Ⓐ, 1227Ⓒ, 1250Ⓐ, 1320Ⓐ, 1327Ⓒ, 1350Ⓐ, 1420Ⓐ, 1427Ⓒ, 1450Ⓐ, 1520Ⓐ, 1527Ⓒ, 1550Ⓐ, 1625Ⓐ, 1627Ⓒ, 16540Ⓐ, 1720Ⓐ, 1727Ⓒ, 1750Ⓐ, 1820Ⓐ, 1827Ⓒ, 1850Ⓐ, 1910Ⓐ, 1930Ⓒ, 1940Ⓐ, 2015Ⓐ, 2027Ⓒ, 2045Ⓐ, 2115Ⓐ, 2136Ⓒ, 2145Ⓐ, 2215Ⓐ, 2227Ⓒ, 2315Ⓐ, 2327Ⓒ. Journey: 1¼ hours.

Ridgewood 🚆 *(NJT)* (*34* km, US $: 5.00). From Hoboken: 0035, 0605Ⓐ, 0640Ⓐ, 0705Ⓐ, 0713Ⓐ, 0741Ⓐ, 0830Ⓐ, 0840Ⓒ, 0907Ⓒ, 0935Ⓐ, 0955Ⓒ, 1135Ⓐ, 1235Ⓐ, 1250⑥, 1335Ⓐ, 1425Ⓐ, 1440Ⓒ, 1445Ⓐ, 1531Ⓐ, 1535Ⓐ,, 1540⑥, 1555Ⓐ, 1615Ⓐ, 1631Ⓐ, 1640Ⓒ, 1645Ⓐ, 1658Ⓐ, 1705Ⓐ, 1715Ⓐ, 1722Ⓐ, 1726Ⓐ, 1740⑥, 1741Ⓐ, 1747Ⓐ, 1754Ⓐ, 1811Ⓐ, 1829Ⓐ, 1840Ⓒ, 1841Ⓐ, 1905Ⓐ, 1935Ⓐ, 1945⑥, 2005Ⓐ, 2035Ⓐ, 2045Ⓒ, 2115Ⓐ, 2145Ⓒ, 2215Ⓐ, 2232Ⓐ, 2320Ⓐ, 2340Ⓒ, 2347Ⓐ, returning at 0534Ⓐ, 0610Ⓐ, 0632Ⓐ, 0639Ⓐ, 0640⑥, 0702Ⓐ, 0712Ⓐ, 0717Ⓐ, 0723Ⓐ, 0740Ⓒ, 0742Ⓐ, 0750Ⓐ, 0804Ⓐ, 0823Ⓐ, 0833Ⓐ, 0855Ⓐ, 0904Ⓐ, 0913Ⓒ, 0957Ⓐ, 1019Ⓐ, 1040Ⓒ, 1140Ⓒ, 1219Ⓐ, 1319Ⓐ, 1340⑥, 1419Ⓐ, 1519Ⓐ, 1533Ⓐ, 1619Ⓐ, 1637Ⓐ, 1640Ⓒ, 1719Ⓐ, 1728Ⓐ. 1740⑥, 1835Ⓐ, 1840⑥, 1900Ⓒ, 1910†, 1930⑥, 2004Ⓐ, 2125Ⓐ, 2129⑥, 2225⑥, 2228†, 2246Ⓐ, 2315⑥, 2335⑥. Journey: 40 mins.

Rockville Centre 🚆 *(LIRR)* (❖ km, US $: 7.00). From New York Penn Stn: 0009, 0036Ⓐ, 0038Ⓒ, 0140Ⓒ, 0146Ⓐ, 0242Ⓒ, 0313Ⓐ, 0454Ⓐ, 0510Ⓒ, 0610Ⓒ, 0636Ⓐ and frequent (about every 30 min.s on Ⓒ) to 2207Ⓐ, 2208Ⓒ, 2238Ⓐ, 2306Ⓐ, 2310Ⓒ, 2338Ⓒ, 2339Ⓐ, returning at 0014, 0130, 0214Ⓐ, 0226Ⓒ, 0414Ⓐ, 0425Ⓒ, 0514Ⓐ, 0525Ⓒ, 0535Ⓐ, *0553*Ⓐ, 0555Ⓒ, 0617Ⓐ, 0625Ⓒ, 0633Ⓐ, 0647Ⓐ, *0652*Ⓐ, 0655Ⓒ and frequent (about every 30 mins. on Ⓒ) to 2214Ⓐ, 2225Ⓒ, 2244Ⓐ, 2314Ⓐ, 2316Ⓒ, 2344Ⓐ. Journey: 40 mins.

Rye 🚆 *(CDT)* (39 km, US $: 6.25). From New York Grand Central: 0040, 0130, 0535Ⓐ, 0540Ⓒ, 0640, 0710Ⓐ, 0740Ⓒ, 0742Ⓐ, 0810Ⓐ, 0840 then ½ hourly (hourly on Ⓒ) until 1440, 1510Ⓐ, 1540Ⓒ, 1541Ⓐ, 1607Ⓐ, 1622Ⓐ, 1640Ⓒ, 1645Ⓐ, 1710⑥, 1713Ⓐ, 1732Ⓐ, 1740Ⓒ, 1742Ⓐ, 1755Ⓐ, 1810⑥, 1815Ⓐ, 1837Ⓐ, 1840, 1909Ⓐ, 1915Ⓐ, 1940, 2010Ⓐ, 2040, 2110Ⓐ, 2140, 2210Ⓐ, 2240, 2310Ⓐ, 2340, returning at 0041, 0516Ⓐ, 0546Ⓐ, 0614Ⓐ, 0616Ⓒ, 0635Ⓐ, 0655Ⓐ, 0713Ⓐ, 0716Ⓒ, 0726Ⓐ, 0742Ⓐ, 0746Ⓐ, 0759Ⓐ, 0816Ⓒ, 0825Ⓐ, 0846⚒, 0859Ⓐ, 0916Ⓒ, 0928Ⓐ, 0946Ⓐ, 1016, 1046Ⓐ, 1116, 1146Ⓐ, 1216, 1246Ⓐ, 1316, 1346Ⓐ, 1416, 1446Ⓐ, 1516, 1546Ⓐ, 1616, 1638Ⓐ, 1646Ⓐ, 1716Ⓒ, 1721Ⓐ, 1751Ⓐ, 1816Ⓒ, 1821Ⓐ, 1851Ⓐ, 1916Ⓒ, 1921Ⓐ, 1946Ⓐ, 2016, 2046Ⓐ, 2116, 2216, 2326Ⓐ. Journey: 45 mins.

Southampton 🚆 *(LIRR)* (*146* km, US $: 15.25). From New York Penn. Stn.: *0036*Ⓐ, *0038*Ⓒ, *0749*Ⓐ, *0758*Ⓒ, *1006*Ⓒ, *1153*Ⓒ, *1201*Ⓐ, *1601*⑤, *1619*Ⓐ, *1751*Ⓐ, *2031*Ⓐ, *2043*Ⓒ, returning at *0133*Ⓐ, *0619*Ⓐ, *0736*Ⓒ, *1207*Ⓐ, *1537*Ⓐ, *1615*Ⓒ, *1748*Ⓒ, *2016*Ⓒ, *2325*Ⓐ. Journey: 2½ hours.

South Norwalk 🚆 *(CDT)*(66 km, US $: 9.50). From New York Grand Central: 0035, 0130, 0540Ⓒ, 0602Ⓐ, 0705Ⓐ, 0807 and hourly to 1507, 1605Ⓐ, 1607, 1635Ⓐ, 1641Ⓐ, 1700Ⓐ, 1707Ⓒ, 1713Ⓐ, 1723Ⓐ, 1738Ⓐ, 1742Ⓐ, 1745Ⓐ, 1753Ⓐ, 1807, 1834Ⓐ, 1906Ⓐ, 1907Ⓒ, 1909Ⓐ, 1937Ⓐ, 2007, 2037Ⓐ, 2107, 2207, 2320, returning at 0005,0538⑥, 0539Ⓐ, 0611Ⓐ, 0632Ⓐ, 0641Ⓒ, 0645Ⓐ, 0653Ⓐ, 0708Ⓐ, 0713Ⓐ, 0722Ⓐ, 0734Ⓐ, 0741⑥, 0744Ⓐ, 0759Ⓐ, 0817Ⓐ, 0828Ⓐ, 0840Ⓒ, 0851Ⓐ, 0940Ⓒ, 0943Ⓐ, 0948Ⓐ, 1040, 1140, 1240, 1340, 1440, 1540, 1639Ⓐ, 1640Ⓒ, 1740Ⓒ, 1742Ⓐ, 1840Ⓒ, 1842Ⓐ, 1940, 2040, 2140, 2240, 2301Ⓐ. Journey: 1 hour.

Speonk 🚆 *(LIRR)* (*117* km, US $: 12.00). From New York Penn. Stn.: *0036*Ⓐ, *0038*Ⓒ, *0749*Ⓐ, *0758*Ⓒ, *1006*, *1153*Ⓒ, *1201*Ⓐ, *1619*Ⓐ, *1710*Ⓐ, *1751*Ⓐ, *1830*Ⓐ, *1859*Ⓒ, *1930*Ⓐ, *2031*Ⓐ, *2043*Ⓒ, *2208*Ⓒ, *2229*Ⓐ, *2310*Ⓒ, returning at *0209*Ⓐ, *0430*Ⓐ, *0505*Ⓐ, *0519*Ⓒ, *0530*Ⓐ, *0610*Ⓐ, *0637*Ⓒ, *0651*Ⓐ, *0727*Ⓐ, *0810*Ⓒ, *1013*Ⓒ, *1213*Ⓒ, *1242*Ⓐ, *1405*Ⓐ, *1407*Ⓒ, *1611*Ⓐ, *1653*Ⓒ, *1745*Ⓒ, *1826*Ⓒ, *2055*Ⓒ, *2103*Ⓐ, *2202*Ⓐ, *2356*Ⓐ. Journey: 2 hours.

Stamford 🚆 *(CDT)* (*66* km, US $: 8.75). From New York Grand Central: 0035, 0040, 0130, 0535Ⓐ, 0540Ⓒ, 0602Ⓐ, 0640 and frequent to 2107, 2110Ⓐ, 2140, 2207, 2210Ⓐ, 2240, 2310Ⓐ, 2320, 2340, returning at 0018, 0025, 0500Ⓐ, 0530Ⓐ, 0553Ⓐ, 0558Ⓐ, 0600Ⓒ, 0619Ⓐ, 0629Ⓐ, 0638Ⓐ, 0643Ⓐ, 0651Ⓐ, 0655 and frequent to 2100, 2153, 2200, 2253, 2310. Journey: 50-65 mins.

Suffern 🚆 *(MNR/NJT)* (*55* km, US $: 5.50). From Hoboken: 0035, 0713Ⓐ, 0741Ⓐ, 0830Ⓐ, 0840Ⓒ, 0907Ⓒ, 0935Ⓐ, 0955Ⓒ, 1135Ⓐ, 1235Ⓐ, 1250⑥, 1335Ⓐ, 1440Ⓒ, 1445Ⓐ, 1540⑥, 1555Ⓐ, 1640Ⓒ, 1645Ⓐ, 1658Ⓐ, 1722Ⓐ, 1740⑥, 1742Ⓐ, 1747Ⓐ, 1811Ⓐ, 1823Ⓐ, 1829Ⓐ, 1840Ⓒ, 1905Ⓐ, 1935Ⓐ, 1945⑥, 2005Ⓐ, 2045Ⓒ, 2115Ⓐ, 2145Ⓒ, 2232Ⓐ, 2340Ⓒ, 2347Ⓐ, returning at 0515Ⓐ, 0551Ⓐ, 0610Ⓐ, 0614Ⓐ, 0622Ⓒ, 0640Ⓐ, 0650Ⓐ, 0655Ⓐ, 0715Ⓐ, 0722Ⓒ, 0729Ⓐ, 0735Ⓐ, 0803Ⓐ, 0846Ⓐ, 0855Ⓒ, 0939Ⓐ, 1002Ⓐ, 1022Ⓒ, 1122Ⓒ, 1202Ⓐ, 1302Ⓐ, 1321⑥, 1402Ⓐ, 1502Ⓐ, 1602Ⓐ, 1622Ⓒ, 1702Ⓐ, 1722⑥, 1817Ⓐ, 1822⑥, 1848Ⓒ, 1853†, 1912⑥, 2111⑥, 2112Ⓐ, 2207⑥, 2230Ⓐ, 2303⑥, 2317⑥. Journey: 55 mins.

Tarrytown 🚆 *(MNR)* (40 km, US $: 7.50). From New York Grand Central: 0020, 0120, 0620, 0649Ⓐ, 0720, 0749Ⓐ, 0758Ⓒ, 0820,, 0858, then about ½hourly till 2020, 2100, 2120, 2155, 2220, 2300, 2320, 2355, returning at 0514Ⓐ, 0539Ⓐ, 0553Ⓐ, 0549Ⓒ, 0609Ⓐ, 0619Ⓒ, 0634Ⓐ, 0643Ⓐ, 0649Ⓒ, 0705Ⓐ, 0718Ⓐ, 0724, 0744Ⓐ, 0749Ⓒ, 0751Ⓐ, 0820Ⓐ, 0819Ⓒ, 0834Ⓐ, 0849Ⓒ, 0858Ⓐ, then about ½hourly till 2049, 2119Ⓒ, 2144Ⓐ, 2149Ⓒ, 2224Ⓒ, 2244Ⓐ, 2249Ⓒ, 2359. Journey: 50 mins.

Tom's River 🚌 *(NJT)* (*118* km, US $: ❖). From New York: 1300, 1800, 2300, returning at 1000, 1500, 1900. Journey: 1½ hours.

Trenton 🚆 *(NJT)* (*94* km, US $: ❖). From New York Penn. Stn.: 0040, 0140, 0439Ⓐ, 0503Ⓒ, 0553Ⓐ, 0632Ⓒ, 0653Ⓐ, 0716Ⓐ, 0738Ⓐ, 0745Ⓒ, 0810Ⓐ, 0829Ⓐ, 0832Ⓒ, 0902Ⓐ, 0925Ⓒ, 0932Ⓐ, 1002Ⓐ, 1027Ⓒ, 1034Ⓐ, 1104Ⓐ, 1127Ⓒ, 1134Ⓐ, 1204Ⓐ, 1232Ⓒ, 1237Ⓐ, 1302Ⓐ, 1329Ⓒ, 1337Ⓐ, 1410Ⓐ, 1432Ⓒ, 1442Ⓐ, 1510Ⓐ, 1525Ⓒ, 1544Ⓐ, 1620Ⓐ, 1625Ⓒ, 1703Ⓐ, 1724Ⓐ, 1725Ⓒ, *1740*Ⓐ, 1810Ⓐ, *1823*Ⓐ, 1825Ⓒ, 1837Ⓐ, *1852*Ⓐ, 1910Ⓐ, 1925Ⓒ, 1933Ⓐ, 2014Ⓐ, 2032Ⓒ, 2044Ⓐ, 2104Ⓐ, 2130Ⓒ, 2135Ⓐ, 2225Ⓐ, 2232Ⓒ, 2325Ⓐ, 2332Ⓒ, 2340Ⓐ, returning at 0330Ⓐ, 0525Ⓐ, 0530Ⓒ, 0550Ⓐ, *0605*Ⓐ, 0617Ⓒ, 0628Ⓐ, 0638Ⓐ, 0650Ⓐ, 0717Ⓒ, 0718Ⓐ, 0728Ⓐ, 0741Ⓐ, 0817Ⓒ, 0830Ⓐ, 0905Ⓐ, 0917Ⓒ, 0930Ⓐ, 1000Ⓐ, 1017Ⓒ, 1030Ⓐ, 1110Ⓐ, 1117Ⓒ, 1140Ⓐ, 1210Ⓐ, 1217Ⓒ, 1240Ⓐ, 1310Ⓐ, 1317Ⓒ, 1340Ⓐ, 1410Ⓐ, 1417Ⓒ, 1440Ⓐ, 1510Ⓐ, 1517Ⓒ, 1540Ⓐ, 1605Ⓐ, 1617Ⓒ, 1640Ⓐ, 1710Ⓐ, 1717Ⓒ, 1740Ⓐ, 1810Ⓐ, 1817Ⓒ, 1840Ⓐ, 1900Ⓐ, 1920Ⓒ, 1930Ⓐ, 2005Ⓐ, 2017Ⓒ, 2035Ⓐ, 2105Ⓐ, 2126Ⓒ, 2145Ⓐ, 2205Ⓐ, 2217Ⓒ, 2305Ⓐ, 2317Ⓒ, 2359Ⓐ. Journey: 1½ hours.

Union City 🚌 *(NJT)* (❖ km, US $: 1.90). From New York: 0500Ⓐ/0630⑥/0705† and frequent to 0330, returning at 0433Ⓐ/0551⑥/0637† and frequent to 0258⑦/0302⑥. Journey: 15 mins. Also by *DC* at ❖, returning at ❖.

Valley Stream 🚆 *(LIRR)* (❖ km, US $: 5.75). From New York Penn Station: *0000*Ⓐ, *0001*Ⓒ, *0009*, 0059Ⓐ, *0105*Ⓒ, *0107*Ⓐ, 0140Ⓒ, *0242*Ⓒ, 0300Ⓐ, *0313*Ⓐ, *0510*Ⓒ, *0511*Ⓐ, *0539*Ⓐ, *0548*Ⓐ, *0610*Ⓒ, *0636*Ⓐ and frequent to *2207*Ⓐ, *2208*Ⓒ, *2229*Ⓐ, *2306*Ⓐ, *2314*Ⓒ, *2316*Ⓐ, returning at *0005*, *0035*, *0101*, *0155*Ⓐ, *0159*Ⓐ, *0202*Ⓒ, *0334*Ⓐ, *0414*Ⓒ, 0520Ⓐ, *0527*Ⓒ, *0539*Ⓐ, 0555Ⓐ, *0627*Ⓒ, *0633*Ⓐ, *0649*Ⓐ, 0657Ⓐ and frequent to *2227*Ⓒ, *2235*Ⓐ, *2251*Ⓐ, *2254*Ⓒ, *2304*Ⓒ, *2340*Ⓐ, *2351*. Journey: 35 mins.

Waterbury 🚆 *(CDT)* (*200* km, US $: 12.75). From New York Grand Central: 0602Ⓐ, 0807Ⓒ, 0907Ⓐ, 1207, 1607Ⓒ, 1622Ⓐ, 1826Ⓐ, 2107, returning at 0635Ⓐ, 0718Ⓒ, 0917Ⓐ, 1118Ⓒ, 1217Ⓐ, 1517Ⓐ, 1518Ⓒ, 1856Ⓐ, 1918Ⓒ, 2119Ⓐ. Journey: 2¼ hours.

West New York 🚌 *(NJT)* (❖ km, US $: 1.90). From New York: 0500Ⓐ/0630⑥/0705† and frequent to 0330, returning at 0429Ⓐ/0546⑥/0634† and frequent to 0254⑦/0259⑥. Journey: 20 mins.

White Plains 🚆 *(MNR)* (35 km, US $: 6.50). From New York Grand Central: 0030, 0130, 0555Ⓐ, 0600Ⓐ, 0628Ⓐ, 0651Ⓐ, 0716Ⓐ, 0727Ⓒ, 0730Ⓐ, 0747Ⓐ, 0749⑥, 0758Ⓐ, 0827Ⓒ, 0830Ⓐ, 0847Ⓐ, 0849Ⓒ, 0901Ⓐ, 0927, 0949 and frequent (twice hourly on Ⓒ) to 2349, returning at 0004Ⓐ, 0013Ⓒ, 0503Ⓐ, 0533Ⓐ, 0535Ⓒ, 0557Ⓒ, 0558Ⓐ, 0604Ⓐ, 0620Ⓐ, 0630Ⓐ, 0635Ⓒ, 0636Ⓐ, 0641⑥, 0644Ⓐ, 0653Ⓐ, 0700, 0708Ⓐ, 0719Ⓐ, 0722Ⓐ, 0730⑥, 0737Ⓐ, 0739Ⓐ, 0744Ⓐ, 0749Ⓐ, 0754Ⓒ, 0805, 0808Ⓐ, 0827Ⓐ, 0830⚒, 0856Ⓐ, 0857Ⓒ, 0902, 0928⑥, 0934Ⓐ, 0957, then about ½hourly to2304. Journey: 50 mins.

Yonkers 🚆 *(MNR)* (*24* km, US $: 5.75). From New York Grand Central: 0020, 0120, 0620, 0649Ⓐ, 0720, 0749Ⓐ, 0758Ⓒ, 0820, 0858, 0920, 0958, 1020, 1055 and frequent to 2020, 2100, 2120, 2155, 2220, 2300, 2320, 2355 returning at 0017, 0532Ⓐ, 0602Ⓐ, 0607Ⓒ, 0627Ⓐ, 0630⑥, 0701Ⓐ, 0707Ⓒ, 0712Ⓐ, 0722Ⓐ, 0738Ⓐ, 0734Ⓒ, 0752Ⓐ, 0749Ⓒ, 0804Ⓐ, 0807Ⓒ and frequent to 1802, 1830, 1907Ⓐ, 1930Ⓐ, 1935Ⓒ, 2007, 2030Ⓐ, 2034Ⓒ, 2107, 2230Ⓒ, 2202Ⓐ, 2207Ⓒ, 2234Ⓒ, 2302Ⓐ, 2207Ⓒ. Journey: 50 mins.

⍚– ⑤ May 27-Sept. 2. ▽–⑤ May 27-July 1.
∝– † (ex ⑦ May 29-July 3). ✿–⑦ May 29-Sept. 4.
ⓓ– Ⓐ (ex ⑤ May 27-Sept. 2). ◇–For Jones Beach.
🚆– By ####. 🚌–By railcar.
▲– ⑥ June 1-mid October. ⊻–† (also ⑥ June 1-mid October).
●– ① June 1-Sept. 1.
⚒– ① June 1-Sept. 1 and ⑥ June 1-mid October.
BTL– Boulevard Transit Lines (Drogin Bus Co.). Tel.: New York ❖.
CCL– Carey Coach Lines. Tel.: New York 212 564 8484.
CDT– Connecticut Department of Transportation/Metro North Railroad. Tel.: New Haven 203 777 7433.
DC– DeCamp Bus Lines. Tel.: New York 212 502 2200.
GL– Greyhound Lines. Tel.: Dallas 214 744 6500.
HTL– The Short Line. Tel.: Mahwah 201 529 3666.
IBS– International Bus Services Inc. Tel.: Hoboken 201 714 9400.
LIRR– Long Island Railroad. Tel.: Jamaica 718 990 7400.
MNR– Metro-North Railroad. Tel.: New York 800 638 7646.
MTA– Metropolitan Transportation Authority. Tel.: New York 212 878 7000.
NJT– New Jersey Transit. Tel.: Newark 201 762 5100.
NYCTA–New York City Transit Authority. Tel.: New York 718 330 1234.
PATH– Port Authority Trans Hudson Corporation. Tel.: Jersey City 201 659 8823.
RTL– Rockland Coaches (Black & Tan Lines). Tel.: New York 201 38[illegible] 2400.
SE– Sunrise Express. Tel.: Greenport 516 477 1200.

'able 340 NEW YORK - PHILADELPHIA - WASHINGTON

╫╫╫╫ *NRPC SEP*

JS $ C cl.	496 1.435m. *NRPC*	km	201	101	79		103	43	105	205	181	107	207	195	141	109	209	143			111	211	95	113	193
			P‡C‡	P‡C‡	1‡C‡		P‡C‡	C‡	P‡C‡	P‡C‡	C‡	P‡C‡	P‡C‡	C‡	C‡	P‡C‡	P‡C‡	S‡C‡			P‡C‡	P‡C‡	P‡C‡	P‡C‡	C‡
			ⓇP	ⓇP	◆		ⓇP	◆	ⓇP	ⓇP		ⓇP	ⓇP		◆	ⓇP	ⓇP	◆			ⓇP	ⓇP	◆Ⓡ	ⓇP	◆
	↓	km	🍷□Ⓐ	🍷□Ⓐ			🍷□Ⓐ		🍷□Ⓐ	🍷□⑥		🍷□Ⓐ	□🍷†	⑥	Ⓐ	🍷□Ⓐ	🍷□⑥				🍷□Ⓐ	🍷□†	⚒	🍷□Ⓐ	†
	Boston................d.	*0*	....	....	....	....	....	....	....	....	....	....	....	....	....	....	....	....	....	....	....	....	0620	....	....
0.00	**New York** Penn. Stnd.	*373*	0530	0600	0615	....	0700	0715	0800	0800	0805	0900	0900	0905	0905	1000	1000	1030	....	....	1100	1100	1105	1200	1205
8.00	Newark..............d.	*389*	0544u	0614u	0632u	....	0714u	0730u	0814u	0814u	0820	0914u	0914u	0920u	0920	1014u	1014u	1045	....	....	1114u	1114u	1120	1214u	1220u
7.00	New Brunswick...d.	*426*	|	|	0655	....	|	0753	|	|	|	|	|	|	|	|	|	|	....	....	|	|	|	|	|
2.00	Princeton Junction.d.	*451*	0614	0644	0708	....	|	0806	|	|	|	|	|	0955	0955	|	|	|	....	....	|	|	|	|	|
5.00	Trenton ◇..........d.	*467*	0623	0653	0718	....	|	0816	|	|	0900	|	|	1005	1005	|	|	1125	....	....	|	|	1200	|	1300
0.00	North Philadelphiad.	*512*	|	|	0741	....	|	0838	|	|	|	|	|	|	|	|	|	|	....	....	|	|	|	|	|
0.00	**Philadelphia** 30th Str.◇.d.	*519*	0652	0722	0800	....	0815	0850	0915	0915	0935	1015	1015	1037	1037	1112	1115	1157	....	....	1212	1215	1232	1312	1332
7.00	Wilmington ....d.	*569*	0713	0743	0823	....	0836	....	0936	0936	0957	1036	1036	1059	1059	1133	1136	1219	....	....	1233	1236	1254	1333	1355
9.00	**Baltimore** Penn. Stn. d.	*670*	0758	0828	0915	....	0923	....	1023	1023	1046	1123	1123	1148	1148	1220	1223	1308	....	....	1320	1323	1343	1420	1445
9.00	BWI Airport ....d.	*687*	0812	|	0928	....	0936	....	|	1036	1059	|	1136	|	|	1233	1236	1322	....	....	|	1336	|	1433	|
4.00	New Carrollton ...a.	*716*	|	0851s	0943	....	0949s	....	|	1049s	1115s	|	1149s	1214s	1214s	|	1249s	1338s	....	....	|	1349s	1410	1446s	1511
4.00	**Washington** Uniona.	*735*	0834	0905	1000	....	1004	....	1059	1104	1130	1159	1204	1229	1229	1259	1304	1353	....	....	1359	1404	1425	1502	1525

96	47	171	115	215	93	99	117	217	641	119	219	185	145	643	121	221	55	189	645	123		223	173	647	627
	C‡	P‡1‡C‡	P‡C‡	P‡C‡	P‡C‡	P‡C‡	P‡C‡	P‡C‡	C‡	P‡C‡	P‡C‡	C‡	C‡	C‡	P‡C‡	P‡C‡	C‡	C‡	C‡	P‡C‡		P‡C‡	P‡1‡C‡	C‡	C‡
	◆	◆	ⓇP	ⓇP	◆	◆	ⓇP	ⓇP	◆	ⓇP	ⓇP		◆	◆	ⓇP	ⓇP	◆		◆	ⓇP		ⓇP	◆	◆	Ⓐ
↓			🍷□Ⓐ	🍷□†	ex⑤†	⑤†	🍷□Ⓐ	🍷□†	Ⓐ	🍷□Ⓐ	🍷□Ⓒ	Ⓐ	Ⓒ		🍷□Ⓐ	🍷□†	Ⓡ	†	Ⓐ	🍷□Ⓐ		🍷□⑥		Ⓒ	
oston....................d.	....	0730	....	....	0900	090	....	....	....	....	....	....	....	....	....	....	....	....	....	....	....	....	1120	....	....
ew York Penn. Stn..d.	1220	1255	1300	1300	1345	1345	1400	1400	1440	1500	1500	1505	1505	1550	1600	1600	1617	1617	1645	1700	....	1700	1706	1715	1715
ewark....................d.	1235u	1317	1314u	1314u	1400	1400	1414u	1414u	1455	1514u	1514u	1520u	1520	1605u	1614u	1614u	1632	1632u	1701	1714u	....	1714u	1721	1730u	1732
ew Brunswick.........d.	|	|	|	|	|	|	|	|	|	|	|	|	|	|	|	|	|	|	|	|	....	|	|	|	|
rinceton Junction....d.	|	|	|	|	|	|	|	|	|	|	|	|	|	|	|	|	|	|	1735	|	....	|	|	|	1806s
renton ◇...............d.	1315	1357	|	|	1437	1437	|	|	1534	|	|	1600	1600	|	|	|	1709	1709	1746	|	....	|	|	1810	1821s
orth Philadelphia....d.	|	|	|	|	|	|	|	|	1556	|	|	|	|	|	|	|	|	|	1810	|	....	|	1818	|	1849s
hiladelphia 30th Str. ◇d.	1350	1435	1412	1415	1518	1518	1512	1515	1605	1612	1615	1632	1632	1705	1712	1715	1741	1741	1820	1815	....	1815	1832	1840	1904
/ilmington ....d.	....	1458	1433	1436	1542	1542	1533	1536	....	1633	1636	1655	1655	....	1733	1736	1804	1804	....	1836	....	1836	1855	....	....
altimore Penn. Stn..d.	....	1550	1520	1523	1633	1633	1620	1623	....	1720	1723	1754	1754	....	1820	1823	1852	1852	....	1923	....	1923	1946	....	....
WI Airport ....d.	....	1603	|	1536	|	|	1633	1636	....	|	1736	1807	1807	....	1833	1836	|	|	....	|	....	1936	1959	....	....
ew Carrollton ....a.	....	1619s	1542s	1549s	1700	1700	1646s	1649s	....	1742s	1749s	1822s	1822s	....	1846s	1849s	1917s	1917s	....	1945s	....	1949s	2015s	....	....
/ashington Union ..a.	....	1632	1559	1604	1715	1715	1702	1704	....	1759	1804	1836	1836	....	1902	1904	1935	1935	....	2002	....	2004	2028	....	....

96	85		629	125	225	633	175				127	2165	165	57	227	191	2157	639	177			179			67
	C‡		C‡	P‡C‡	P‡C‡	C‡	P‡1‡C‡				P‡C‡	C‡	P‡C‡	C‡	P‡C‡	C‡	C‡	C‡	C‡			C‡			S‡C‡
	◆		Ⓐ	ⓇP	ⓇP	Ⓐ	◆				ⓇP	🍷	◆	◆	ⓇP		◆		◆			◆			◆
↓	Ⓡ			🍷□Ⓐ	🍷□†						🍷□Ⓐ	3	Ⓐ	†	🍷□†	♿		†							Ⓡ
oston....................d.	....	....	....	....	....	....	1330	....	....	....	....	....	1440	....	....	....	1608	....	1625	....	....	1815	....	....	2130
ew York Penn. Stn..d.	1737	....	1740	1800	1800	1807	1835	....	....	....	1900	1920	1930	1945	2000	2050	2050	2140	2145	....	....	2335	....	....	0345
ewark....................d.	1752u	....	1757	1814u	1814u	1824	1850	....	....	....	1914u	1935u	1945	2000	2014u	2105u	2105	2155u	2200	....	....	2350	....	....	0409
ew Brunswick.........d.	|	....	|	|	|	|	|	....	....	....	|	|	|	|	|	|	|	|	|	....	....	|	....	....	|
rinceton Junction....d.	|	....	1831s	|	|	1858s	|	....	....	....	|	|	|	|	|	|	|	|	|	....	....	|	....	....	|
renton ◇...............d.	|	....	1846s	|	|	1913s	1930	....	....	....	|	|	2025	2034	|	2145	2145	2233	2240	....	....	0030	....	....	0456
orth Philadelphia....d.	|	....	1914s	|	|	1941s	|	....	....	....	|	|	|	|	|	|	|	|	|	....	....	|	....	....	|
hiladelphia 30th Str.◇ d.	1856	....	1929	1912	1915	1956	2000	....	....	....	2015	|	2057	2106	2115	2217	2217	2303	2313	....	....	0103	....	....	0543
/ilmington ....d.	1918	....	....	1933	1936	....	2023	....	....	....	2036	|	2119	2128	2136	2239	2239	....	2336	....	....	0125	....	....	0607
altimore Penn. Stn..d.	2011	....	....	2020	2023	....	2112	....	....	....	2123	2143s	2208	2217	2223	2328	2328	....	0030	....	....	0221	....	....	0711
WI Airport ....d.	2024	....	....	2033	2036	....	2125	....	....	....	|	|	|	|	2236	2341	2341	....	0043	....	....	|	....	....	0725
ew Carrollton ....a.	2040	....	....	2046s	2049s	....	2141s	....	....	....	2145s	2211s	2232s	2243s	2249s	2357s	2357s	....	0059s	....	....	0250s	....	....	0740s
/ashington Union ..a.	2055	....	....	2102	2104	....	2155	....	....	....	2202	2226	2245	2256	2304	0012	0012	....	0115	....	....	0310	....	....	0755

3– PENNSYLVANIAN–C‡ and 🍷 New York(**43**)-Pittsburgh.
7– THREE RIVERS–C‡ and 🍷 New York(**47**)-Pittsburgh; C‡ New York(**47**)-Pittsburgh(**29**)-Chicago. This train may be replaced by a through Philadelphia-Chicago service from a date to be announced.
5– VERMONTER–C‡ and 🍷 St. Albans(**55**)-Washington.
7– VERMONTER–C‡ and 🍷 St. Albans(**57**)-Washington.
7– S‡, C‡ and 🍷 Boston(**67**)-Washington.
9– CAROLINIAN–1‡C‡ and 🍷 New York(**79**)-Charlotte.
5– C‡ and 🍷 New York(**85**)-Richmond.
3– P‡C‡ and 🍷 Boston(**93**)-Richmond.
5– P‡C‡ and 🍷 Boston(**95**)-Newport News.
9– P‡C‡ and 🍷 Boston(**99**)-Newport News.
41– C‡ and 🍷 Springfield(**141**)-Washington.
43– C‡ and 🍷 Springfield(**143**)-Washington.
45– C‡ and 🍷 Springfield(**145**)-Washington.
65– P‡C‡ and 🍷 Boston(**165**)-Washington.
71– P‡ 1‡C‡ and 🍷 Boston(**171**)-Washington; C‡ Springfield(**471**)-New Haven(**171**)-Washington.
73– P‡ 1‡C‡ and 🍷 Boston(**173**)-Washington; C‡ Springfield(**473**)-New Haven(**173**)-Washington.
75– P‡ 1‡C‡ and 🍷 Boston(**175**)-Washington; C‡ Springfield(**475**)-New Haven(**175**)-Washington.
77– C‡ and 🍷 Boston(**177**)-Washington; C‡ and 🍷 Springfield(**477**)-New Haven(**177**)-Washington.
79– C‡ (also 1‡ on Ⓐ) and 🍷 Boston(**179**)-Washington.
93– P‡C‡ and 🍷 New York(**193**)-Richmond.
41– C‡ New York(**641**)-Harrisburg.
43– C‡ New York(**643**)-Harrisburg.
45– C‡ New York(**645**)-Harrisburg.
47– C‡ New York(**647**)-Harrisburg.
157–Runs May 24, 27, July 3, Aug. 30, Sept. 2: C‡ and 🍷 Boston(**2157**)-Washington.
– METROLINER.
– Local ╫╫╫╫ service (*SEP*), C cl. only, Trenton-Philadelphia 30th Street (Journey 50 minutes), **from Trenton** at: 0013Ⓒ, 0544Ⓐ, 0618Ⓐ, 0636Ⓐ, 0659Ⓐ, 0701Ⓒ, 0712Ⓐ, 0733Ⓐ, 0800Ⓒ, 0808Ⓐ, 0846Ⓐ, 0904Ⓒ, 0937Ⓐ, 1000Ⓒ, 1032Ⓐ, 1110Ⓒ, 1137Ⓐ, 1200Ⓒ, 1239Ⓐ, 1300Ⓒ, 1337Ⓐ, 1400Ⓒ, 1439Ⓐ, 1500Ⓒ, 1547Ⓐ, 1600Ⓒ, 1637Ⓐ, 1700Ⓒ, 1707Ⓐ, 1752Ⓐ, 1800Ⓒ, 1832Ⓐ, 1900Ⓒ, 1901Ⓐ, 1939Ⓐ, 2000Ⓒ, 2038Ⓐ, 2100Ⓒ, 2137Ⓐ, 2201Ⓒ, 2237Ⓐ, 2300Ⓒ, 2356Ⓐ.
– Runs May 24, 27, July 3, Aug. 30, Sept. 2.
– Runs daily except May 24, 27, July 3, Aug. 30, Sept. 2.
ARC–Maryland Department of Transportation. Tel.: Washington 202 906 3104.
RPC–AMTRAK. Tel: New York 212 582 6875.
EP– Southeastern Pennsylvania Transportation Authority. Tel.: Philadelphia 580 7800.

Table 340–contd WASHINGTON - PHILADELPHIA - NEW YORK

NRPC SEP

US $ C cl.	496 NRPC	km	12	622	624	180		628	100	170		200	640	56			102		642	172	104	204	192	644	106
			C‡	C‡	C‡	C‡		C‡	P‡C‡	P‡C‡		P‡C‡	C‡	C‡			P‡C‡		C‡	P‡1‡C‡	P‡C‡	P‡C‡	C‡	C‡	P‡C‡
			◆	Ⓐ	Ⓐ			Ⓐ	ⓇP	◆		ⓇP	◆	◆			ⓇP		◆	◆	ⓇP	ⓇP		◆	ⓇP
	↓					⚒			🍷⊡Ⓐ	Ⓐ		🍷⊡Ⓐ	Ⓐ				🍷⊡Ⓐ				🍷⊡Ⓐ	🍷⊡⑥	Ⓒ		🍷⊡Ⓐ
0.00	**Washington** Union ...d.	0	0300	....	....	0440	....	....	0525	0530	....	0600	....	0615	....	....	0700	....	....	0715	0800	0800	0815	....	0900
★6.00	New Carrollton ....d.	16	|	....	....	0453u	....	....	0535u	0543u	....	0610u	....	0628u	....	....	0710u	....	....	0728u	0810u	0810u	0828u	....	0910u
★10.00	BWI Airport ....d.	48	|	....	....	0510	....	....	0550	0600	....	0625	....	|	....	....	0725	....	....	0746	|	0825	|	....	0925
★12.00	**Baltimore** Penn. Stn. d.	65	0338	....	....	0525	....	....	0603	0615	....	0638	....	0655	....	....	0738	....	....	0801	0834	0838	0855	....	0938
31.00	Wilmington ....d.	175	0427	....	....	0620	....	....	0649	0706	....	0724	....	0742	....	....	0824	....	....	0850	0920	0924	0944	....	1024
40.00	**Philadelphia** 30th Street Ω d.	216	0505	0540	0615	0650	....	0705	0715	0735	....	0747	0749	0808	....	....	0847	....	0858	0921	0943	0946	1009	1025	1047
40.00	North Philadelphia .....d.	223	|	0550u	0626u	0659	....	0715u	|	0744	....	|	0759	|	....	....	|	....	|	|	|	|	|	|	|
47.00	Trenton Ω..................d.	268	|	0620	0655	|	....	0745	|	|	....	|	0821	0838	....	....	|	....	|	0951	|	|	|	1055	|
50.00	Princeton Junction.....d.	283	|	0634	0707	|	....	0757	|	|	....	|	0831	|	....	....	|	....	|	|	|	|	|	|	|
62.00	New Brunswick..........d.	309	|	|	0723	|	....	0813	|	|	....	|	|	|	....	....	|	....	|	|	|	|	|	|	|
64.00	Newark.....................d.	345	0622	0706s	0751s	0749s	....	0838s	0814s	0835	....	0846s	0900s	0914	....	....	0945s	....	1007s	1032	1045s	1047s	1116s	1134s	1145s
64.00	**New York** Penn. Stn...a.	361	0638	0726	0812	0806	....	0859	0830	0850	....	0902	0919	0929	....	....	1002	....	1025	1047	1102	1104	1136	1150	1202
98.00	*Boston*.....................a.	735	1210	....	....	....	....	....	....	1424	....	....	....	....	....	....	....	....	....	1600	....	....	....	....	....

396	206	84	108	208	2174	174	110	210	186	86	112	142	114	214	94	184	46	116	216	176	118	218	194	120	220
	P‡C‡	P‡C‡	P‡C‡	P‡C‡	C‡	P‡1‡C‡	P‡C‡	P‡C‡	C‡	P‡C‡	P‡C‡	C‡	P‡C‡	P‡C‡	P‡C‡	P‡C‡	C‡	P‡C‡	P‡C‡	P‡1‡C‡	P‡C‡	P‡C‡	C‡	P‡C‡	P‡C‡
	ⓇP	◆	ⓇP	ⓇP	◆	◆	ⓇP	ⓇP	◆	◆	ⓇP	◆	ⓇP	ⓇP	◆	◆	◆	ⓇP	ⓇP	◆	ⓇP	ⓇP		ⓇP	ⓇP
↓	🍷⊡†	⚒	🍷⊡Ⓐ	🍷⊡⑥			🍷⊡Ⓐ	🍷⊡†	⚒	†	🍷⊡Ⓐ		🍷⊡Ⓐ	🍷⊡†	Ⓑ	⑥		🍷⊡Ⓐ	🍷⊡†		🍷⊡Ⓐ	🍷⊡Ⓒ	Ⓑ	🍷⊡Ⓐ	🍷⊡†
Washington Union .....d.	0900	0905	1000	1000	1005	1015	1100	1100	1105	1105	1200	1215	1300	1300	1315	1315	....	1400	1400	1415	1500	1500	1505	1600	1600
New Carrollton ....d.	0910u	0918	1010u	1010u	1018	1028	|	1110u	1118	1118	1210u	1228u	|	1310u	1328	1328	....	|	1410u	1428u	|	1510u	1518u	1610u	1610u
BWI Airport ....d.	0925	0935	|	1025	|	1045	1123	1125	|	|	|	1245	1323	1325	|	|	....	|	1425	1446	1523	1525	1536	|	1625
Baltimore Penn. Stn...d.	0938	0950	1034	1038	1045	1100	1136	1138	1145	1145	1234	1300	1336	1338	1353	1353	....	1432	1438	1501	1536	1538	1552	1634	1638
Wilmington ....d.	1024	1039	1120	1124	1133	1150	1222	1224	1234	1234	1320	1349	1422	1424	1442	1442	....	1518	1524	1550	1622	1624	1647	1720	1724
Philadelphia 30th Street Ωd.	1046	1103	1143	1146	1158	1215	1245	1246	1258	1258	1343	1415	1445	1446	1506	1506	1515	1541	1546	1617	1645	1646	1717	1743	1746
North Philadelphia ....d.	|	|	|	|	|	|	|	|	|	|	|	|	|	|	|	|	1525	|	|	|	|	|	1726	|	|
Trenton Ω.....................d.	|	1133	|	|	|	1245	|	|	1329	1329	|	1446	|	|	1537	1537	1546	|	|	1648	|	|	1749	|	|
Princeton Junction.......d.	|	|	|	|	|	1255	|	|	|	|	|	|	|	|	|	|	1556	|	|	|	|	|	1759	|	|
New Brunswick............d.	|	|	|	|	|	|	|	|	|	|	|	|	|	|	|	|	1609	|	|	|	|	|	1813	|	|
Newark.........................d.	1147s	1156	1242s	1247s	1302	1332	1345s	1347s	1410s	1410	1442s	1527	1545s	1547s	1615	1614s	1632s	1640s	1647s	1729	1745s	1747s	1840s	1845s	1847s
New York Penn. Stn.....a.	1204	1213	1259	1304	1320	1346	1402	1404	1430	1430	1459	1546	1602	1604	1630	1630	-1650	1659	1704	1745	1802	1804	1859	1902	1904
Boston.........................a.	....	1710	....	....	1820	1900	....	....	....	1933	....	....	....	....	2120	....	....	....	....	2257	....	....	....	....	....

396		168				122	222	42	148	124	224	80		44	126	638	226			196	96		66		
		P‡C‡				P‡C‡	P‡C‡	C‡	C‡	P‡C‡	P‡C‡	1‡C‡		C‡	P‡C‡	C‡	P‡C‡			C‡	C‡		S‡C‡		
		◆				ⓇP	ⓇP	◆	◆	ⓇP	ⓇP	◆		◆	ⓇP		ⓇP				◆		◆		
↓						🍷⊡Ⓐ	🍷⊡⑥	⚒		🍷⊡Ⓐ	🍷⊡†			†	🍷⊡Ⓐ	⑤	🍷⊡†			ex⑤†	⑤†		Ⓡ		
Washington Union .....d.	....	1610	....	....	....	1700	1700	....	1708	1800	1800	1815	....	....	1900	....	2000	....	....	2035	2050	....	2200	....	....
New Carrollton ....d.	....	1623u	....	....	....	|	1710u	....	1721u	1810u	1810u	1828	....	....	1910u	....	2010u	....	....	2048u	2103	....	2213u	....	....
BWI Airport ....d.	....	|	....	....	....	1723	1725	....	1739	|	1825	|	....	....	1925	....	2025	....	....	2105	2120	....	2231	....	....
Baltimore Penn. Stn...d.	....	1650	....	....	....	1736	1738	....	1755	1834	1838	1901	....	....	1938	....	2038	....	....	2120	2134	....	2253	....	....
Wilmington ....d.	....	1739	....	....	....	1822	1824	....	1848	1920	1924	1953	....	....	2024	....	2124	....	....	2212	2226	....	2348	....	....
Philadelphia 30th Street Ωd.	....	1810	....	....	....	1845	1846	1848	1924	1943	1946	2021	....	2030	2046	2130	2146	....	....	2236	2249	....	0025	....	....
North Philadelphia ....d.	....	|	....	....	....	|	|	1858	|	|	|	|	....	|	|	|	|	....	....	|	|	....	|	....	....
Trenton Ω.....................d.	....	1839	....	....	....	1912	|	1923	1954	|	|	2054	....	2101	|	2200	|	....	....	2307	2320	....	0057	....	....
Princeton Junction.......d.	....	|	....	....	....	1921	|	1932	|	|	|	2103	....	|	|	|	|	....	....	|	|	....	|	....	....
New Brunswick............d.	....	|	....	....	....	|	|	1945	|	|	|	|	....	|	|	|	|	....	....	|	|	....	|	....	....
Newark.........................d.	....	1922	....	....	....	1948s	1947s	2009s	2039	2045s	2047s	2135s	....	2139s	2147s	2236s	2247s	....	....	2348s	2358s	....	0144	....	....
New York Penn. Stn.....a.	....	1937	....	....	....	2005	2004	2025	2057	2102	2104	2156	....	2159	2204	2256	2304	....	....	0007	0015	....	0200	....	....
Boston.........................a.	....	0035	....	....	....	....	....	....	....	....	....	....	....	....	....	....	....	....	....	....	....	....	0749	....	....

12– [C‡] and 🍷 Washington(**12**)-Boston; [C‡] and 🍷 Washington(**12**)-New Haven(**412**)-Springfield.
42– PENNSYLVANIAN–[C‡] and 🍷 Pittsburgh(**42**)-New York.
44– PENNSYLVANIAN–[C‡] and 🍷 Pittsburgh(**44**)-New York.
46– THREE RIVERS–[C‡] and 🍷 Pittsburgh(**46**)-New York; [C‡] Chicago(**30**)-Pittsburgh(**46**)-New York. This train may be replaced by a through Chicago-Philadelphia service from a date to be announced.
56– VERMONTER–[C‡] and 🍷 Washington(**56**)-St. Albans.
66– [S‡], [C‡] and 🍷 Washington(**66**)-Boston.
80– CAROLINIAN–[1‡C‡] and 🍷 Charlotte(**80**)-New York.
84– [P‡C‡] and 🍷 Richmond(**84**)-Boston.
86– [P‡C‡] and 🍷 Richmond(**86**)-Boston.
94– [P‡C‡] and 🍷 Newport News(**94**)-Boston.
96– [C‡] and 🍷 Newport News(**96**)-New York.
142– [C‡] and 🍷 Washington(**144**)-Springfield.
148– [C‡] and 🍷 Washington(**148**)-Springfield.
168– [P‡C‡] and 🍷 Washington(**168**)-Boston.
170– [P‡C‡] and 🍷 Washington(**170**)-Boston.
172– [P‡] [1‡C‡] and 🍷 Washington(**172**)-Boston; [C‡] Washington(**172**)-New Haven(**472**)-Springfield.
174– [P‡] [1‡C‡] and 🍷 Washington(**174**)-Boston; [C‡] Washington(**174**)-New Haven(**474**)-Springfield.
176– [P‡] [1‡C‡] and 🍷 Washington(**176**)-Boston; [C‡] Washington(**176**)-New Haven(**476**)-Springfield.
184– [P‡C‡] Newport News(**184**)-New York.
186– [C‡] and 🍷 Richmond(**186**)-New York.
640– [C‡] Harrisburg(**640**)-New York.
642– [C‡] Harrisburg(**642**)-New York.
644– [C‡] Harrisburg(**644**)-New York.
2174–Runs May 24, 27, July, 3, Aug. 30, Sept. 2: [C‡] and 🍷 Washington(**2174**)-Boston.
P– METROLINER.
★– *MDT* fares are cheaper.
Ω– Local #### service (*SEP*), C cl. only, Philadelphia 30th Street-Trenton (Journey 50 minutes) at: 0504Ⓐ, 0519Ⓐ, 0553Ⓐ, 0621Ⓒ, 0637Ⓐ, 0713Ⓐ, 0721Ⓒ, 0807Ⓐ, 0821Ⓒ, 0906Ⓐ, 0921Ⓒ, 1010Ⓐ, 1021Ⓒ, 1104Ⓐ, 1121Ⓒ, 1204Ⓐ, 1221Ⓒ, 1304Ⓐ, 1321Ⓒ, 1404Ⓐ, 1421Ⓒ, 1504Ⓐ, 1516Ⓒ, 1604Ⓐ, 1621Ⓒ, 1628Ⓐ, 1654Ⓐ, 1716Ⓐ, 1721Ⓒ, 1740Ⓐ, 1754Ⓐ, 1821Ⓒ, 1823Ⓐ, 1904Ⓐ, 1921Ⓒ, 2004Ⓐ, 2021Ⓒ, 2104Ⓐ, 2121Ⓒ, 2154Ⓐ, 2216Ⓒ, 2254Ⓐ, 2354Ⓐ, 2321Ⓒ.
NRPC–AMTRAK. Tel.: New York 212 582 6875.
SEP– Southeastern Pennsylvania Transportation Authority. Tel.: Philadelphia 580 7800.

able 345 ALBANY - BUFFALO - CLEVELAND - CHICAGO

NRPC

$ cl.	29	63	69	281	71	283	259	289	49	km	396 1.435m.	30	246	284	48	286	68	64	288
	S‡C‡	C‡	1‡C‡	C‡◆	1‡C‡	C‡	1‡C‡	1‡C‡	S‡C‡		↓ ↑	S‡C‡	C‡	C‡	S‡C‡	C‡	1‡C‡	C‡	1‡C‡
	◆	◆	◆⚒	ex①②③	◆†	◆	◆①-④	◆⑤	◆			◆	◆Ⓐ	◆①⑤⑥	◆	◆	◆	◆	◆†
.00	....	0720	0830	1145	1250	1435	1635	1635	1840	0	d.*New York* .... a.	....	0915	1302	1549	1635	2010	2135	2320
6.00	....	|	|	|	|	|	|	|	1530		d. *Boston* .... a.	....	|	|	1801	|	|	|	|
.00	....	1010	1115	1435	1535	1725	1847s	1902	2153	229	d.**Albany Rensselaer** a.	....	0658	1010	1220	1340	1720	1840	2030
.00	....	1032	1140	1457	1600	1747	1917	1924	2219	258	d.Schenectady .... d.	....	0635	0944	1148	1314	1655	1814	2004
.00	....	1049	....	1514	....	1804	....	1941	|	286	d.Amsterdam .... d.	....	....	0924	|	1244	....	1754	1944
.00	....	1147	....	1612	....	1902	....	2040	2337	382	d.Utica .... d.	....	....	0828	1030	1158	....	1658	1848
.00	....	1201	....	1626	....	1916	....	2054	|	404	d.Rome .... d.	....	....	0811	|	1141	....	1641	1831
.00	....	1237	....	1702	....	1952	....	2128	0029	459	d.Syracuse .... d.	....	....	0741	0943	1111	....	1611	1801
.00	....	1400	....	1825	....	2115	....	....	0152	597	d.Rochester .... d.	....	....	0617	0818	0947	....	1447	1637
2.00	....	1456	....	1921	....	2211	....	....	0317	693	d.**Buffalo** Depew .... d.	....	....	0520	0700	0850	....	1350	1540
2.00	....	1508	....	1933	....	2223	....	....	|	706	d. **Buffalo** Exchange Street d.	....	....	0505	|	0835	....	1335	1525
2.00	....	1600	....	2024	....	2314	....	....	|	745	a. **Niagara Falls** *USA* d.	....	....	0430	|	0800	....	1300	1450
.00	....	1914	....	....	....	....	....	....	|	879	a. *Toronto* .... d.	....	....	....	|	....	....	0930	....
.00	....	....	....	....	....	....	....	....	0451	843	d.Erie .... d.	....	....	....	0515	....	....	....	....
.00	0305	....	....	....	....	....	....	....	0638	995	d.**Cleveland** Lakefront . d.	0216	....	....	0344	....	....	....	....
.00	0335	....	....	....	....	....	....	....	0710	1036	d.Elyria (Lorain) .... d.	0133	....	....	0300	....	....	....	....
	0501	....	....	....	....	....	....	....	0835	1167	a. **Toledo Central Union** d.	0014	....	....	0135	....	....	....	....
1.00	0526	....	....	....	....	....	....	....	0857		d. **Toledo Central Union** a.	0001	....	....	0113	....	....	....	....
3.00	0631	....	....	....	....	....	....	....	1003	1382	d.Elkhart .... d.	2050	....	....	2200	....	....	....	....
4.00	0658	....	....	....	....	....	....	....	1028	1409	d.South Bend .... d.	2023	....	....	2135	....	....	....	....
4.00	0803s	....	....	....	....	....	....	....	1131s	1509	d.Hammond NRPC .. d.	1920u	....	....	2032u	....	....	....	....
4.00	0905	....	....	....	....	....	....	....	1230	1544	a.**Chicago** Union ..... d.	1850	....	....	2000	....	....	....	....

/30– CAPITOL LIMITED–sleeper‡, ‡, C‡ and ✕ Washington(**29/30**)-Chicago and v.v.; C‡ New York(**47/46**)-Pittsburgh(**29/30**)-Chicago and v.v. (these cars may be replaced by a through Philadelphia-Chicago train from a date to be announced).

/49– LAKESHORE LIMITED–sleeper‡, C‡ and ✕ Chicago(**48/49**)-New York and v.v.; sleeper‡ and C‡ Chicago(**48/49**)-Albany(**448/9**)-Boston and v.v.

/64– MAPLE LEAF–C‡ and ⊗ New York(**63/64**)-Niagara Falls(**98/97**)-Toronto and v.v.

– ADIRONDACK–1‡C‡ and ⊗ Montréal(**68**)-New York.

– ADIRONDACK–1‡C‡ and ⊗ New York(**69**)-Montréal.

– ADIRONDACK–1‡C‡ and ⊗ New York(**71**)-Montréal.

46– 1‡C‡ and 🍷 Schenectady(**246**)-New York.

59– 1‡C‡ and 🍷 New York(**259**)-Schenectady.

81– C‡ and 🍷 New York(**281**)-Niagara Falls.

83– C‡ (also 1‡ on ⑥) and 🍷 New York(**283**)-Niagara Falls.

84– C‡ and 🍷 Niagara Falls(**284**)-New York.

286– C‡ and 🍷 Niagara Falls(**286**)-New York.

288– 1‡C‡ and 🍷 Niagara Falls(**288**)-New York.

289– 1‡C‡ and 🍷 New York(**289**)-Syracuse.

◇– Fare ex Albany.

NRPC–National Railroad Passenger Corporation (AMTRAK). Tel: New York 212 582 6875.

able 348 PHILADELPHIA - HARRISBURG

NRPC

JS $ C cl.	396 1.435m.	km	601	43	47	641	643	645	647	619
	↓		C‡ Ⓐ	C‡ ◆	C‡ ◆	C‡ ◆Ⓐ	C‡ ◆	C‡ ◆Ⓐ	C‡ ◆©	C‡ Ⓐ
	New York .... d.		....	0715	1220	1440	1550	1645	1715	....
0.00	**Philadelphia 30th Street** d.	0	0545	0915	1415	1635	1735	1845	1900	2015
6.00	Paoli .... d.	32	0612	0944	1444	1703	1802	1913	1928	2043
8.00	Downingtown .... d.	48	0625	0958	1457	1716	1821	1926	1941	2056
1.00	Lancaster .... d.	109	0701	1032	1531	1751	1858	2000	2016	2131
5.00	Middletown .... d.	151	0730	|	|	1820	1926	2028	2045	|
8.00	**Harrisburg** .... a.	166	0743	1111	1612	1835	1940	2043	2100	2212

96	640	642	644	46	42	616	44	618
↓	C‡ ◆Ⓐ	C‡ ◆	C‡ ◆	C‡ ◆	C‡ ◆⚒	C‡ Ⓐ	C‡ ◆†	C‡ Ⓐ
arrisburg .... d.	0530	0635	0810	1253	1624	1720	1810	1945
iddletown .... d.	0542	0647	0822	|	|	1732	|	1956
ancaster .... d.	0610	0718	0852	1336	1707	1802	1853	2025
owningtown .... d.	0642	0753	0924	1408	1740	1837	1926	2057
aoli .... d.	0659	0811	0939	1424	1756	1851	1942	2111
hiladelphia 30th Street a.	0728	0838	1005	1451	1824	1919	2009	2138
ew York .... a.	0919	1025	1150	1650	2025	....	2159	....

2-44– PENNSYLVANIAN–C‡ and 🍷 Pittsburgh(**42/44/43**)-New York and v.v.

6/47– THREE RIVERS–C‡ and 🍷 Pittsburgh(**46/47**)-New York and v.v.; C‡ Chicago(**30/29**)-Pittsburgh(**46/47**)-New York and v.v. This train may be replaced by a through Chicago-Philadelphia train from a date to be announced.

/1– C‡ Harrisburg(**640/1**)-New York and v.v.

42/3– C‡ Harrisburg(**642/3**)-New York and v.v.

44/5– C‡ Harrisburg(**644/5**)-New York and v.v.

47– C‡ New York(**647**)-Harrisburg.

RPC–National Railroad Passenger Corporation (AMTRAK). Tel.: Philadelphia 215 824 1600.

'able 349 PHILADELPHIA - ATLANTIC CITY

NJT

US $ C cl.	396 1.435m.	km	4403	4505	4607	4609	4611	4613	4515	4615	4617	4619	4621	4523	4625	4627	4629
	↓		C‡	C‡	C‡	C‡	C‡	C‡ ©	C‡ ©	C‡	C‡	C‡	C‡	C‡	C‡	C‡	C‡ ⑥
0.00	**Philadelphia 30th Street** d.	0	....	....	0635	0800	0940	1150	....	1330	1510	1642	1742	....	2030	2150	2325
3.00	Lindenwold .... d.	35	0501	0620	0716	0833	1013	1227	1411	1411	1559	1717	1816	1926	2103	2229	2358
4.60	Hammonton .... d.	65	0529	0645	0742	0851	1033	1253	1432	1432	1623	1740	1837	1947	2128	2246	0015
5.45	Egg Harbor .... d.	82	0540	0656	0754	0903	1043	1304	1443	1443	1635	1751	1848	1958	2139	2256	0024
5.50	Absecon .... d.	99	0551	0707	0805	0914	1054	1315	1454	1454	1653	1806	1859	2009	2150	2307	0034
6.00	**Atlantic City** .... a.	109	0609	0722	0820	0925	1110	1330	1510	1510	1708	1822	1914	2024	2205	2320	0050

96	4500	4600	4504	4606	4608	4610	4612	4614	4514	4616	4618	4520	4622	4624	4526	4626	4624
↓	C‡ Ⓐ	C‡ ©	C‡	C‡	C‡	C‡	C‡ ©	C‡ Ⓐ	C‡ ©	C‡	C‡	C‡	C‡	C‡	C‡ Ⓐ	C‡ ©	C‡
tlantic City .... d.	0045	0045	0445	0600	0645	0850	1140	1210	1233	1430	1532	1632	1745	1900	2045	2045	2245
bsecon .... d.	0053	0053	0456	0612	0654	0901	1151	1220	1242	1441	1541	1641	1754	1913	2055	2055	2254
gg Harbor .... d.	0103	0103	0506	0622	0709	0918	1201	1230	1252	1458	1551	1650	1804	1923	2105	2105	2309
ammonton .... d.	0114	0114	0517	0633	0720	0929	1212	1241	1307	1509	1602	1701	1815	1934	2116	2116	2320
indenwold .... a.	0136	0136	0539	0654	0740	0952	1235	1302	1327	1530	1622	1724	1840	2001	2137	2137	2341
hiladelphia 30th Street a.	....	0220	....	0735	0820	1035	1325	1340	....	1615	1700	....	1920	2040	....	2215	0020

JT– New Jersey Transit. Tel.: Newark 201 762 5100.

Table 350 WASHINGTON - PITTSBURGH - CLEVELAND

MARC NRPC

US $ C cl	*MARC* 271 C‡ Ⓐ	*MARC* 273 C‡ Ⓐ	*NRPC* 29 S‡C‡ ◆[R]	*MARC* 275 C‡ Ⓐ	*MARC* 277 C‡ Ⓐ	*MARC* 279 C‡ Ⓐ	*MARC* 281 C‡ 🍷Ⓐ		*MARC* 283 C‡ Ⓐ	*MARC* 285 C‡ Ⓐ	*MARC* 287 C‡ Ⓐ	km	396 1.435m ↓ ↑	*MARC* 270 C‡ Ⓐ	*MARC* 272 C‡ Ⓐ	*MARC* 274 C‡ Ⓐ		*MARC* 276 C‡ 🍷Ⓐ	*MARC* 278 C‡ Ⓐ	*MARC* 280 C‡ Ⓐ	*MARC* 282 C‡ Ⓐ	*NRPC* 30 S‡C‡ ◆[R]	*MARC* 284 C‡ Ⓐ	*MARC* 286 C‡ Ⓐ
0.00	0845	1300	1605	1625	1655	1710	1730	....	1813	1855	1955	*0*	d.**Washington** Union ....a.	0638	0705	0725	....	0740	0810	0830	0920	1312	1610	1750
3.00	0904	1318r	|	1644	|	1731	1750	....	1834	1916	2015r	*18*	d.Kensington ....d.	0615	0636	|	....	0717	0744	|	0857	|	1546	1727
⋐5.00	0911	1327	1627	1653	1721	1740	1800	....	1843	1925	2024	*28*	d.Rockville ....d.	0606	0627	0655	....	0708	0734	0759	0848	1230	1538	1718
3.75	0918	1335	|	1702	|	1748	1807	....	1851	1934	2032	*34*	d.Gaithersburg ....d.	0557	0619	0647	....	0659	0725	0750	0841	|	1531	1711
6.00	0956	1420	|	1747	1801	1834	1850	....	1937	2017	2112	*79*	d.Brunswick ....d.	0515	0540	0607	....	0620	0640	0713	0800	|	1500	1630
★13.00	....	....	1709	....	1811	....	1900	....	....	2026	....	*89*	d.Harper's Ferry ....d.	....	....	0555	....	....	....	0702	....	1148	....	....
Ω19.00	....	....	1731	....	1840	....	1929	....	....	2055	....	*119*	d.**Martinsburg** ....d.	....	....	0530	....	....	....	0635	....	1126	....	....
31.00	....	....	1906	....	....	....	....	....	....	....	....	*236*	d.Cumberland ....d.	....	....	....	....	....	....	....	....	1001	....	....
51.00	....	....	2121	....	....	....	....	....	....	....	....	*386*	d.Connellsville ....d.	....	....	....	....	....	....	....	....	0726	....	....
64.00	....	....	2302	....	....	....	....	....	....	....	....	*480*	a. **Pittsburgh** ....d.	....	....	....	....	....	....	....	....	0600	....	....
	....	....	2357	....	....	....	....	....	....	....	....		d. **Pittsburgh** ....a.	....	....	....	....	....	....	....	....	0520	....	....
81.00	....	....	0136	....	....	....	....	....	....	....	....	*616*	d.Alliance ⊠ ....d.	....	....	....	....	....	....	....	....	0332	....	....
82.00	....	....	0305	....	....	....	....	....	....	....	....	*704*	a.**Cleveland** ....d.	....	....	....	....	....	....	....	....	0216	....	....
89.00	....	....	0501	....	....	....	....	....	....	....	....	*872*	a.*Toledo* ....d.	....	....	....	....	....	....	....	....	0014	....	....
118.00	....	....	0905	....	....	....	....	....	....	....	....	*1280*	a.*Chicago* ....d.	....	....	....	....	....	....	....	....	1850	....	....

29/30–CAPITOL LIMITED–[sleeper]‡, [D]‡, [C‡] and ✕ Washington(**29/30**)-Chicago and v.v.; [C‡] New York(**47/46**)-Pittsburgh(**29/30**)-Chicago and v.v. (these cars may be replaced by a new Philadelphia-Chicago train from a date to be announced).

⋐– *MARC* fare: $3.75.

★– *MARC* fare: $6.75.

Ω– *MARC* fare: $7.50.

⊠– for Canton.

MARC–Maryland Department of Transportation. Tel.: Washington 202 906 3104.

NRPC–National Railroad Passenger Corporation (AMTRAK). Tel.: Washington 202 484 754[illegible]

Table 352 WASHINGTON - JACKSONVILLE - TAMPA/MIAMI

NRPC VRE

US $ C cl.	73 C‡ ◆	75 C‡ 🍷⑤†		79 1‡C‡ ◆ [R]		81 S‡C‡ ◆ [R]	91 S‡C‡ ◆ [R]	53 S‡C‡ ◆[R]	95 P‡C‡ ◆ ⚒	193 P‡C‡ ◆ †	93 P‡C‡ ◆ ex⑤†	99 P‡C‡ ◆ ⑤†	97 S‡C‡ ◆ [R]	85 C‡ ◆ ⑥	2 S‡C‡ ◆[R] ①③⑥	km	396 1.435m. *NRPC* ↓ ↑	98 S‡C‡ ◆ [R]	84 P‡C‡ ◆ ⚒	186 C‡ ◆ †	86 P‡C‡ ◆ †	52 S‡C‡ ◆ [R]	92 S‡C‡ ◆ [R]	82 S‡C‡ ◆ [R]	1 S‡C‡ ◆[R] ②⑤⑦	94 P‡C‡ ◆ ⑤	184 P‡C‡ ◆ ⑥	80 1‡C‡ ◆ [R]	96 C‡ ◆[R] ⑤†	74 C‡ ◆		78 C‡ ⑤🍷
64.00	....	....	....	0615	....	1010	....	....	1105	1205	1345	1345	1610	1737	....	*0*	d.*New York* ......a.	0945	1230	1430	1430	....	....	1830	....	1630	1630	2156	0015	....	....	....
	....	....	....	0632u	....	1034u	....	....	1120	1220u	1400	1400	1634u	1752u	....	*16*	d.*Newark* ......a.	0920s	1213	1410s	1412	....	....	1801s	....	1615	1614s	2135s	2358s	....	....	....
	....	....	....	0718	....	1122u	....	....	1200	1300	1437	1437	1719u	|	....	*94*	d.*Trenton* ......a.	0841s	1133	1329	1329	....	....	1707s	....	1537	1537	2054	2320	....	....	....
34.00	....	....	....	0800	....	1213u	....	....	1232	1332	1518	1518	1759u	1856	....	*246*	d.*Philadelphia* ......a.	0758s	1103	1258	1258	....	....	1627s	....	1506	1506	2021	2249	....	....	....
	....	....	....	0915	....	1347u	....	....	1343	1445	1633	1633	1932u	2011	....	*297*	d.*Baltimore* ......a.	0639s	0950	1145	1145	....	....	1445s	....	1353	1353	1901	2134	....	....	....
0.00	....	1000	....	1040	....	1500u	....	....	1455	1555	1745	1745	2045u	2125	....	*361*	d.**Washington** Union ⊠ a.	0530s	0835	1030	1030	....	....	1330s	....	1245	1245	1745	2020	....	....	....
5.00	....	1019	....	1057	....	1517	....	....	1513	1614	1804	1804	2104	2143	....	*361*	d.Alexandria ⊠ ......d.	0505	0810	1006	1006	....	....	1304	....	1219	1219	1720	1955	....	....	....
	....	|	....	|	....	|	....	1530	|	|	|	|	|	|	....	*396*	d. Lorton ......a.	|	|	|	|	0900	....	|	....	|	|	|	|	....	....	....
9.00	....	1045	....	1126	....	|	....	|	1543	1641	1831	1831	|	2212	....	*417*	d.Quantico ⊠ ......d.	|	0737	0936	0936	|	....	|	....	1151	1151	1654	1931	....	....	....
11.00	....	1103	....	1145	....	1607u	....	|	1601	1659	1849	1849	|	2230	....	*448*	d.Fredericksburg ⊠ . d.	|	0718	0917	0917	|	....	1216	....	1131	1131	1634	1912	....	....	....
21.00	....	1210	....	1310	....	1720	....	|	1707	1757	1947	1957	2300	2327	....	*537*	d.**Richmond** ......d.	0330	0625	0825	0825	|	....	1125	....	1041	1041	1545	1820	....	....	0001
28.00	....	1322	....	|	....	|	....	|	1812	....	....	2102	|	....	....	*625*	a. Williamsburg Boundary Street d.	|	....	....	....	|	....	|	....	0909	0909	|	1701	....	....	2254
35.00	....	1352	....	|	....	|	....	|	1844	....	....	2134	|	....	....	*668*	a. **Newport News** .. d.	|	....	....	....	|	....	|	....	0845	0645	|	1635	....	....	2230
	....	*1430c*	....	|	....	|	....	|	*1952c*	....	....	*2212c*	|	....	....		a. Norfolk ......d.	|	....	....	....	|	....	|	....	*0720c*	*0720c*	|	*1510c*	....	....	....
21.00	....	....	....	1342	....	1752	....	|	....	....	....	....	2333	....	....	*583*	d.Petersburg ......d.	0228	....	....	....	|	....	1022	....	....	....	1437	....	....	....	....
40.00	....	....	....	1507	....	1915	....	|	....	....	....	....	0056	....	....	*739*	d.Rocky Mount ......d.	0058	....	....	....	|	....	0857	....	....	....	1317	....	....	....	....
41.00	....	....	....	1525	....	|	....	|	....	....	....	....	|	....	....	*765*	d.Wilson ......d.	|	....	....	....	|	....	|	....	....	....	1300	....	....	....	....
45.00	0710	....	....	1647	....	2057	....	|	....	....	....	....	|	....	....	*805*	d. Raleigh ......d.	|	....	....	....	|	....	0736	....	....	....	1155	....	2115	....	....
49.00	0746	....	....	1725	....	|	....	|	....	....	....	....	|	....	....		d. Durham..... d.	|	....	....	....	|	....	|	....	....	....	1105	....	2025	....	....
58.00	0906	....	....	1857	....	|	....	|	....	....	....	....	|	....	....		a. Greensboro d.	|	....	....	....	|	....	|	....	....	....	0941	....	1907	....	....
75.00	....	....	....	....	....	2246	....	|	....	....	....	....	|	....	....	*962*	d. Hamlet ......d.	|	....	....	....	|	....	0529	....	....	....	....	....	....	....	....
87.00	....	....	....	....	....	0053	....	|	....	....	....	....	|	....	....	*1133*	d. Columbia ......d.	|	....	....	....	|	....	0326	....	....	....	....	....	....	....	....
71.00	....	....	....	....	....	|	....	|	....	....	....	....	0221	....	....	*884*	d.Fayetteville ......d.	2333	....	....	....	|	....	|	....	....	....	....	....	....	....	....
80.00	....	....	....	....	....	|	....	|	....	....	....	....	0307	....	....	*969*	d.Dillon ......d.	2242	....	....	....	|	....	|	....	....	....	....	....	....	....	....
82.00	....	....	....	....	....	|	....	|	....	....	....	....	0357	....	....	*1018*	d.Florence ......d.	2212	....	....	....	|	....	|	....	....	....	....	....	....	....	....
104.00	....	....	....	....	....	|	....	|	....	....	....	....	0536	....	....	*1170*	d.**Charleston** ......d.	2013	....	....	....	|	....	|	....	....	....	....	....	....	....	....
104.00	....	....	....	....	....	|	....	|	....	....	....	....	0625	....	....	*1256*	d.Yemassee ......d.	1921	....	....	....	|	....	|	....	....	....	....	....	....	....	....
115.00	....	....	....	....	....	0325	....	|	....	....	....	....	0733	....	....	*1333*	d.Savannah ......d.	1835	....	....	....	|	....	0055	....	....	....	....	....	....	....	....
130.00	....	....	....	....	....	0543	....	|	....	....	....	....	0955	....	....	*1572*	a. **Jacksonville** ......d.	1606	....	....	....	|	....	2230	....	....	....	....	....	....	....	....
	....	....	....	....	....	0615	0635	|	....	....	....	....	1025	....	1430		d. **Jacksonville** ......a.	1544	....	....	....	|	2123	2145	2005	....	....	....	....	....	....	....
148.00	....	....	....	....	....	0828	|	0900	....	....	....	....	1241	....	1640	*1797*	d. Sanford ......d.	1320	....	....	....	1530	|	1908	1715	....	....	....	....	....	....	....
150.00	....	....	....	....	....	0852	|	....	....	....	....	....	1303	....	1705	*1823*	d. Winter Park ... d.	1257	....	....	....	....	|	1841	1652	....	....	....	....	....	....	....
150.00	....	....	....	....	....	0920	|	....	....	....	....	....	1331	....	1735	*1831*	d. Orlando ◇..... d.	1242	....	....	....	....	|	1825	1638	....	....	....	....	....	....	....
152.00	....	....	....	....	....	0940	|	....	....	....	....	....	1353	....	1752	*1872*	d. Kissimmee..... d.	1209	....	....	....	....	|	1754	1610	....	....	....	....	....	....	....
153.00	....	....	....	....	....	1021	|	....	....	....	....	....	|	....	|	*1930*	d. Lakeland ......d.	|	....	....	....	....	|	1711	|	....	....	....	....	....	....	....
153.00	....	....	....	....	....	1117	|	....	....	....	....	....	|	....	|	*1978*	a. **Tampa** ......d.	|	....	....	....	....	|	1638	|	....	....	....	....	....	....	....
153.00	....	....	....	....	....	*1210*	|	....	....	....	....	....	|	....	|	2032	a. *Clearwater* c .. d.	|	....	....	....	....	|	*1535*	|	....	....	....	....	....	....	....
153.00	....	....	....	....	....	*1210*	|	....	....	....	....	....	|	....	|	2053	a. *St. Petersburg* c d.	|	....	....	....	....	|	*1535*	|	....	....	....	....	....	....	....
	....	....	....	....	....	*1520*	|	....	....	....	....	....	|	....	|		a. *Fort Myers* c .. d.	|	....	....	....	....	|	*1225*	|	....	....	....	....	....	....	....
140.00	....	....	....	....	....	....	0734	....	....	....	....	....	|	....	|	*1688*	d.Waldo ......d.	|	....	....	....	....	1950	....	|	....	....	....	....	....	....	....
145.00	....	....	....	....	....	....	0819	....	....	....	....	....	|	....	|	*1761*	d.Ocala ......d.	|	....	....	....	....	1907	....	|	....	....	....	....	....	....	....
148.00	....	....	....	....	....	....	0848	....	....	....	....	....	|	....	|	*1802*	d.Wildwood ......d.	|	....	....	....	....	1833	....	|	....	....	....	....	....	....	....
153.00	....	....	....	....	....	....	1016	....	....	....	....	....	1448	....	1847	*1907*	d.Winter Haven ......d.	1121	....	....	....	....	1707	....	1522	....	....	....	....	....	....	....
153.00	....	....	....	....	....	....	1057	....	....	....	....	....	1526	....	1925	*1973*	d.Sebring ......d.	1036	....	....	....	....	1628	....	1443	....	....	....	....	....	....	....
153.00	....	....	....	....	....	....	1132	....	....	....	....	....	1601	....	2000		d.Okeechobee ......d.	0959	....	....	....	....	1551	....	1408	....	....	....	....	....	....	....
157.00	....	....	....	....	....	....	1235s	....	....	....	....	....	1655s	....	2100s	*2138*	d.West Palm Beach . d.	0906u	....	....	....	....	1458u	....	1315u	....	....	....	....	....	....	....
161.00	....	....	....	....	....	....	1333s	....	....	....	....	....	1752s	....	2153s	*2207*	a.Fort Lauderdale .... d.	0809u	....	....	....	....	1402u	....	1219u	....	....	....	....	....	....	....
	....	....	....	....	....	....	|	....	....	....	....	....	|	....	|		d.**Miami Metrorail** .... d.	|	....	....	....	....	|	....	|	....	....	....	....	....	....	....
161.00	....	....	....	....	....	....	1415	....	....	....	....	....	1847	....	2255	*2241*	a.**Miami** AMTRAK .. d.	0725	....	....	....	....	1323	....	1140	....	....	....	....	....	....	....
	....	....	....	....	....	....	....	....	....	....	....	....	....	....	....		a.Miami International Airport d.	....	....	....	....	....	....	....	....	....	....	....	....	....	....	....

1/2– SUNSET LIMITED–[sleeper]‡, entertainment car (‡), [C‡] and ✕ Miami(**1/2**)-Los Angeles and v.v.

52/53– AUTO TRAIN–[sleeper]‡, [D]‡, cinema car, ⊗, [C‡] and [car].

73/74– PIEDMONT–[C‡] and ⊗ Raleigh(**73/74**)-Charlotte and v.v.

79/80– CAROLINIAN–[1‡C‡] and 🍷 New York(**79/80**)-Charlotte and v.v.

81/82– SILVER STAR–[sleeper]‡, [C‡] and ✕ New York(**81**)-Jacksonville(**91**)-Miami; [sleeper]‡, [C‡] and ✕ Miami(**92**)-Jacksonville(**82**)-New York; [sleeper]‡, [C] and 🍷 New York(**81/82**)-Tampa and v.v.

84– [P‡C‡] and 🍷 Richmond(**84**)-Boston.

85– [C‡] and 🍷 New York(**85**)-Richmond.

86– [P‡C‡] and 🍷 Richmond(**86**)-Boston.

91/92– SILVER STAR–[sleeper]‡, [C‡] and ✕ New York(**81**)-Jacksonville(**91**)-Miami; [sleeper]‡, [C‡] and ✕ Miami(**92**)-Jacksonville(**82**)-New York.

93– [P‡C‡] and 🍷 Boston(**93**)-Richmond.

94– [P‡C‡] and 🍷 Newport News(**94**)-Boston.

95– [P‡C‡] and 🍷 Boston(**95**)-Newport News.

96– [C‡] and 🍷 Newport News(**96**)-New York.

97/98– SILVER METEOR–[sleeper]‡, [C‡] and ✕ New York(**97/98**)-Miami and v.v.

99– [P‡C‡] and 🍷 Boston(**99**)-Newport News.

184– [P‡C‡] and 🍷 Newport News(**184**)-New York.

186– [C‡] and 🍷 Richmond(**186**)-New York.

193– [P‡C‡] and 🍷 New York(**193**)-Richmond.

c– Connection by [bus].

◇– For Disney World.

⊠– Local service *(VRE)* operates Washington-Alexandria-Lorton-Quantico-Fredericksburg and v.v. **From Washington** Union:(US$ 6.70 Fredericksburg; US$ 4.00 Alexandria) 0638Ⓐ, 0655Ⓐ♧, 0800Ⓐ♧, 1542Ⓐ, 1552Ⓐ♧, 1631Ⓐ♧, 1640Ⓐ, 1705Ⓐ♧, 1715Ⓐ, 1735Ⓐ♧, 1755Ⓐ, 1825Ⓐ♧, 1840Ⓐ; **from Fredericksburg**: 0520Ⓐ, 0555Ⓐ, 0625Ⓐ, 0700Ⓐ, 0800Ⓐ, 1720Ⓐ; **from Alexandria only**: 0605Ⓐ, 0637Ⓐ, 0707Ⓐ, 0744Ⓐ, 0809Ⓐ, 0907Ⓐ 1755Ⓐ.

♧– Washington-Alexandria only.

NRPC–National Railroad Passenger Corporation (AMTRAK). Tel.: Washington 202 484 754[illegible]

VRE– Virginia Railway Express. Tel.: Washington 703 497 7777.

Table 355 NEW ORLEANS/CHICAGO #### NRPC

JS $ C cl.	79	51	19	73	km	396 1.435m.	74	20	80	50
	1‡C‡	S‡C‡	S‡C‡	C‡			C‡	S‡C‡	1‡C‡	S‡C‡
	◆	◆Ⓡ	◆	◆			◆	◆	◆	◆Ⓡ
	Ⓡ	③⑤⑦	Ⓡ			↓ ↑		Ⓡ		②④⑥
4.00	0615	....	1410	....	0	d.*New York* ....a.	....	1355	2156	....
0.00	1040	1100	1848u	....	361	d.**Washington** Union a.	....	0915s	1745	2010
5.00	1057	1119	1907	....	375	d.Alexandria ....d.	....	0842s	1720	1942s
3.00	|	1229	2012r	....	470	d.Culpeper...........d.	....	0738r	|	1815
	|	*1150*b	|	....		d. Richmond ...a.	....	|	|	*1845*b
2.00	|	1335	2105	....	542	d.Charlottesville....d.	....	0648	|	1711
5.00	a	|	2225	....	639	d.Lynchburg ....d.	....	0533	a	|
0.00	|	|	2333	....	741	d.Danville ....d.	....	0415	|	|
3.00	1857	|	0113	0906	818	d.Greensboro ....d.	1907	0315	0941	|
2.00	1911	|	0126	0920	843	d.High Point ....d.	1852	0237	0923	|
3.00	1950	|	0208	0957	899	d.Salisbury ....d.	1816	0155	0845	|
5.00	2045	|	0258	1055	966	d.Charlotte ....d.	1730	0104	0800	|
9.00	....	|	0328r	....	1004	d.Gastonia............d.	....	0032r	....	|
3.00	....	|	0430	....	1090	d.Spartanburg ......d.	....	2332	....	|
1.00	....	|	0535	....	1140	d.Greenville ....d.	....	2255	....	|
2.00	....	|	0730	....	1302	d.Gainesville.........d.	....	2038	....	|
9.00	....	|	0830	....	1381	a. **Atlanta** .... d.	....	1945	....	|
	....	|	0845c	....		d. **Atlanta** .... a.	....	1920d	....	|
2.00	....	|	1005c	....	1544	d.Anniston ....d.	....	1550d	....	|
0.00	....	|	1203c	....	1647	d.Birmingham ....d.	....	1420d	....	|
7.00	....	|	1313c	....	1736	d.Tuscaloosa........d.	....	1240d	....	|
8.00	....	|	1515c	....	1892	d.Meridian ....d.	....	1105d	....	|
0.00	....	|	1614c	....	1986	d.Laurel ....d.	....	0952d	....	|
7.00	....	|	1645c	....	2029	d.Hattiesburg........d.	....	0921d	....	|
0.00	....	|	1928c	....	2218	a.**New Orleans** ....d.	....	0705d	....	|
8.00	....	1433	....	....	248	d. Staunton ....d.	....	....	....	1552
3.00	....	1543	....	....	339	d. Clifton Forge ...d.	....	....	....	1441
7.00	....	1632	....	....	394	d. White Sulphur Springs d.	....	....	....	1346
5.00	....	2005	....	....	622	d. Charleston ......d.	....	....	....	1035
2.00	....	2103	....	....	704	d. Huntington ......d.	....	....	....	0932
3.00	....	2123	....	....	721	d. Catlettsburg ....d.	....	....	....	0911
6.00	....	2225	....	....	778	d. South Portsmouth d.	....	....	....	0803
2.00	....	0110	....	....	965	d. **Cincinnati** ......d.	....	....	....	0555
8.00	....	0200	....	....	1008	d. Hamilton..........d.	....	....	....	0430
2.00	....	0405	....	....	1167	d. **Indianapolis**...d.	....	....	....	0105
6.00	....	0511	....	....	1242	d. Crawfordsville .d.	....	....	....	2318
8.00	....	0544	....	....	1285	d. Lafayette.........d.	....	....	....	2248
8.00	....	0915	....	....	1479	a. **Chicago** Union.d.	....	....	....	2010

/20– CRESCENT–sleeper‡, coach and ✕ New York(**19/20**)-Atlanta and v.v.; conveys on ②④⑤⑥: sleeper‡, coach and ✕ New York(**19**)-New Orleans; on ①④⑥⑦: sleeper‡, coach and ✕ New Orleans(**20**)-New York. Additional trains may operate on this route during the 1996 Olympic Games.
/51– CARDINAL–sleeper‡, lounge, coach and ⊗ Chicago(**50/51**)-Washington and v.v.
/74– PIEDMONT–coach and ⊗ Raleigh(**73/74**)-Charlotte and v.v.
/80– CAROLINIAN–coach and 🍷 New York(**79/80**)-Charlotte and v.v. via Raleigh. **b**–Connection by bus. **c**–③⑤⑥⑦. **d**–①④⑥⑦.
RPC–National Railroad Passenger Corporation (AMTRAK). Tel.: Chicago 312 558 1075.

Table 357 396 PHILADELPHIA AIRPORT #### SEP

Local #### service (C cl. only) Philadelphia-Philadelphia Airport and v.v. *13* km. Journey: 20 mins. Fare: US $: 6.00.
From Philadelphia 30th Street: 0534 and every 30 mins. to 2334.
From Philadelphia Airport: 0010, 0610 and every 30 mins to 2340.
SEP– Southeastern Pennsylvania Transportation Authority. Tel.: Philadelphia 580 7800.

Table 358 HARRISBURG - CHICAGO #### NRPC

US $ C cl.	43		47	29	km	396 1.435m.	30	46	42	44
	C‡		C‡	S‡C‡			S‡C‡	C‡	C‡	C‡
	◆		◆	◆Ⓡ		↓ ↑	◆Ⓡ	◆	◆ ⚒	◆ †
0.00	0715	....	1220	....	0	d.*New York* ....a.	....	1650	2025	2159
30.00	0915	....	1415	....	145	d.*Philadelphia*.......a.	....	1451	1824	2009
44.00	1121	....	1620	....	310	d.**Harrisburg**........a.	....	1242	1611	1756
82.00	1357	....	1900	....	521	d.Altoona..............d.	....	0958	1330	1515
88.00	1455	....	2000	....	584	d.Johnstown ....d.	....	0856	1230	1415
88.00	1654	....	2200	....	710	a. **Pittsburgh** .... d.	....	0720	1055	1240
	....	....	....	2357		d. **Pittsburgh** .... a.	0520	....	....	....
90.00	....	....	....	|	832	d.Youngstown ......d.	|	....	....	....
90.00	....	....	....	a	920	d.Akron ....d.	a	....	....	....
97.00	....	....	....	|	1080	d.Fostoria ....d.	|	....	....	....
102.00	....	....	....	|	1232	d.Garrett................d.	|	....	....	....
105.00	....	....	....	|	1312	d.Nappanee...........d.	|	....	....	....
124.00	....	....	....	0803s	1440	d.Hammond NRPC d.	1920u	....	....	....
124.00	....	....	....	0905	1465	a.**Chicago** Union..d.	1850	....	....	....
	....	....	....	*1130*		a. *Rockford* ▽ ......d.	*1515*	....	....	....
	....	....	....	*1315*		a. *Madison* ▽ ....d.	*1330*	....	....	....

29/30– CAPITOL LIMITED sleeper‡, Ⓓ‡, coach and ✕ Washington(**29/30**)-Chicago and v.v.
42-44– PENNSYLVANIAN–coach and 🍷 Pittsburgh(**42/44/43**)-New York and v.v.
46/47– THREE RIVERS–coach and 🍷 Pittsburgh(**46/47**)-New York and v.v.; coach Chiacgo(**30/29**)-Pittsburgh(**46/47**)-New York and v.v. (these cars may be replaced by a through Philadelphia-Chicago train from a date to be announced).
a– Via Cleveland.
▽– Connection by bus.
NRPC–National Railroad Passenger Corporation (AMTRAK). Tel.: Chicago 312 558 1075.

Table 359 CHICAGO - DETROIT/PORT HURON #### NRPC

JS $ C cl.	350	364					352		354			km	396 1.435m.		351		353			365	355		367	
	1‡C‡	C‡					1‡C‡		1‡C‡						1‡C‡		1‡C‡			C‡	1‡C‡		C‡	
	◆Ⓡ	◆					◆Ⓡ		◆Ⓡ						◆Ⓡ		◆Ⓡ			◆Ⓡ	◆Ⓡ		◆Ⓡ	
	🍷	Ⓡ					🍷		🍷				↓ ↑		🍷		🍷			⚒	🍷		†	
0.00	0700	0950	....	....	....	....	1405	....	1815	....	....	0	d.**Chicago** Union..........a.	....	1140	....	1455	....	....	1838	2157	....	2230	....
4.00	0727	1017	....	....	....	....	1432	....	1842	....	....	25	d.Hammond NRPC.......a.	....	1101	....	1412	....	....	1800	2118	....	2145	....
3.00	|	|	....	....	....	....	|	....	1922	....	....	34	d.Michigan City............d.	....	1018	....	|	....	....	|	|	....	|	....
3.00	0941	1231	....	....	....	....	1646	....	2057	....	....	141	d.Niles.........................d.	....	1045	....	1401	....	....	1749	2107	....	2134	....
6.50	1033	1323	....	....	....	....	1738	....	2152	....	....	221	d.Kalamazoo ....d.	....	0955	....	1314	....	....	1702	2020	....	2047	....
9.00	1103	1358	....	....	....	....	1808	....	2222	....	....	258	d.Battle Creek ....d.	....	0923	....	1242		....	1630	1948	....	2015	....
0.00	*1315*b	1457	....	....	....	....	*2015*b	....	*2350*b	....	....	335	d. East Lansing ....d.	....	*0730*b	....	*1030*b	....	....	1515	|	....	1900	....
0.00	|	1527	....	....	....	....	|	....	|	....	....	382	d. Durand ....d.	....	|	....	|	....	....	1445	|	....	1830	....
0.00	*1455*b	1554	....	....	....	....	*2130*b	....	*0115*b	....	....	409	d. Flint..........................d.	....	*0600*b	....	*0915*b	....	....	1423	|	....	1808	....
7.00	|	1735	....	....	....	....	|	....	|	....	....	513	d. **Port Huron** 🛃 ....d.	....	|	....	|	....	....	1315	|	....	1700	....
9.00	|	1755	....	....	....	....	|	....	|	....	....	518	a. Sarnia 🛃................d.	....	|	....	|	....	....	1210	|	....	1555	....
5.00	|	2251	....	....	....	....	|	....	|	....	....	796	a. *Toronto* ....d.	....	|	....	|	....	....	0750	|	....	1150	....
9.00	1152	....	....	....	....	....	1901	....	2311	....	....	331	d.Jackson......................d.	....	0833	....	1148	....	....	....	1858	....	....	....
9.00	1233	....	....	....	....	....	1942	....	2352	....	....	390	d.Ann Arbor...................d.	....	0755	....	1110	....	....	....	1820	....	....	....
9.00	1308s	....	....	....	....	....	2017s	....	0027s	....	....	439	d.Dearborn ....d.	....	0721u	....	1036u	....	....	....	1746u	....	....	....
9.00	1331	....	....	....	....	....	2042	....	0050	....	....	450	a. Detroit Woodward Avenue d.	....	0653	....	1008	....	....	....	1718	....	....	....
	1335	....	....	....	....	....	2047	....	0054	....	....		d. Detroit Woodward Avenue a.	....	0649	....	1004	....	....	....	1714	....	....	....
5.00	1430	....	....	....	....	....	2140	....	0145	....	....	494	a.Pontiac.......................d.	....	0605	....	0920	....	....	....	1630	....	....	....

0/1– WOLVERINE. **352/3**–LAKE CITIES. **354/5**–TWILIGHT LIMITED.
4– INTERNATIONAL–coach and ⊗ Chicago(**364**)-Sarnia(**88**)-Toronto.
5– INTERNATIONAL–coach and ⊗ Toronto(**85**)-Sarnia(**365**)-Chicago.
7– INTERNATIONAL–coach and ⊗ Toronto(**685**)-Sarnia(**367**)-Chicago.
b– Connection by bus.
NRPC–National Railroad Passenger Corporation (AMTRAK). Tel.: Chicago 312 558 1075.

Table 360 MINNEAPOLIS - CHICAGO #### NRPC

JS $ C cl.	330		332		334	336	8	338		340		km	396 1.435m.	331	333	335	337	7		339		341		
	C‡		C‡		C‡	C‡	S‡C‡	C‡		C‡				C‡	C‡	C‡	C‡	S‡C‡		C‡		C‡		
	◆ ⚒		◆		◆	◆	◆Ⓡ	◆		◆			↓ ↑	◆ ⚒	◆	◆	◆	◆Ⓡ		◆		◆		
2.00	....	....	....	....	....	....	0820	....	....	....	....	0	d.St. Paul/Minneapolis Midway ..a.	....	....	....	....	2310	....	....	....	....	....	....
2.00	....	....	....	....	....	....	0924	....	....	....	....	76	d.Red Wing ....d.	....	....	....	....	2145	....	....	....	....	....	....
0.00	....	....	....	....	....	....	1029	....	....	....	....	177	d.Winona.......................d.	....	....	....	....	2043	....	....	....	....	....	....
6.00	....	....	....	....	....	....	1105	....	....	....	....	221	d.La Crosse...................d.	....	....	....	....	2010	....	....	....	....	....	....
3.00	....	....	....	....	....	....	1146	....	....	....	....	287	d.Tomah........................d.	....	....	....	....	1926	....	....	....	....	....	....
1.00	....	....	....	....	....	....	1227	....	....	....	....	359	d.Wisconsin Dells.........d.	....	....	....	....	1848	....	....	....	....	....	....
7.00	....	....	....	....	....	....	1245	....	....	....	....	386	d.Portage ....d.	....	....	....	....	1830	....	....	....	....	....	....
6.50	....	....	....	....	....	....	1318	....	....	....	....	432	d.Columbus ....d.	....	....	....	....	1801	....	....	....	....	....	....
6.00	0620	....	0800	....	1035	1235	1440s	1505	....	1740	....	536	d.**Milwaukee** ....d.	0957	1202	1405	1637	1651u	....	1845	....	2137	....	....
5.00	0644	....	0824	....	1059	1259	|	1529	....	1804	....	574	d.Sturtevant (Racine) ...d.	0926	1131	1334	1606	|	....	1813	....	2106	....	....
5.00	0725	....	0902	....	1137	1337	1540s	1607	....	1842	....	645	d.Glenview ◇............ d.	0848	1053	1256	1528	1539u	....	1732	....	2028	....	....
0.00	0757	....	0932	....	1207	1407	1620	1637	....	1912	....	673	a.**Chicago** Union.........d.	0825	1030	1233	1505	1515	....	1708	....	2005	....	....

3–EMPIRE BUILDER–coach and 🍷 Chicago(**7/8**)-Minneapolis and v.v.; conveys on ①③⑤⑥: sleeper‡, coach and ✕ Chicago(**7/8**)-Seattle and v.v.; sleeper‡, entertainment car‡, ⊗ and coach icago(**7/8**)-Spokane(**27/28**)-Portland and v.v. **330-341**–HIAWATHA. ◇–Local passengers not carried Glenview-Chicago or v.v. unless connecting at Chicago with other *NRPC* trains.
RPC–National Railroad Passenger Corporation (AMTRAK). Tel.: Chicago 312 558 1075.

Table 365 396 CHICAGO LOCAL SERVICES

Local ╫╫╫ (C‡ only, 1.435m.) and 🚌 services operate in the Chicago area as follows:

Arlington Park ⋖ *(MR)* (*30* km, US $: 3.30). From Chicago Madison Street: 0030, 0555Ⓐ, 0630Ⓐ, 0713Ⓐ, 0730Ⓐ, 0830Ⓑ, 0900Ⓐ, 1030, 1130✕, 1230, 1310Ⓑ, 1330Ⓐ, 1430, 1530✕, 1610Ⓐ, 1630Ⓒ, 1639Ⓐ, 1658Ⓐ, 1705Ⓑ, 1706Ⓐ, 1716Ⓐ, 1720✕, 1723Ⓐ, 1733Ⓐ, 1747Ⓐ, 1820Ⓐ, 1830, 1930Ⓐ, 2030, 2130Ⓐ, 2230Ⓐ, 2330Ⓑ, returning at 0024②-⑥, 0519Ⓐ, 0549Ⓐ, 0609Ⓐ, 0632Ⓐ, 0641Ⓐ, 0643Ⓐ, 0648Ⓑ, 0652Ⓐ, 0711Ⓐ, 0722Ⓑ, 0728Ⓑ, 0729Ⓐ, 0740Ⓐ, 0755Ⓑ, 0756Ⓐ, 0801Ⓐ, 0808Ⓑ, 0828✕, 0928, 1028✕, 1128, 1228✕, 1328†, 1428✕, 1528Ⓑ, 1628Ⓐ, 1728, 1816Ⓐ, 1828Ⓐ, 1928†, 2028✕, 2128. Journey: 50 mins.

Aurora ⋖ *(MR)* (*62* km, US $: 4.45). From Chicago Union: 0035, 0615Ⓐ, 0630Ⓑ, 0740Ⓐ, 0830Ⓒ, 0850Ⓐ, 1030, 1230, 1330✕, 1430, 1520Ⓐ, 1530Ⓑ, 1558Ⓐ, 1628Ⓐ, 1630Ⓒ, 1646Ⓐ, 1702Ⓐ, 1710Ⓐ, 1728Ⓐ, 1730✕, 1734Ⓐ, 1742Ⓐ, 1810Ⓐ, 1820Ⓐ, 1830Ⓒ, 1850Ⓐ, 1930Ⓐ, 2030, 2130Ⓐ, 2230, 2335Ⓐ, returning at 0450Ⓐ, 0520Ⓑ, 0530Ⓐ, 0540Ⓐ, 0602Ⓐ, 0620Ⓒ, 0621Ⓐ, 0627Ⓐ, 0641Ⓐ, 0642Ⓑ, 0701Ⓐ, 0707Ⓐ, 0720Ⓑ, 0721Ⓐ, 0722Ⓑ, 0741Ⓐ, 0800Ⓐ, 0820Ⓒ, 0920, 1020, 1120Ⓑ, 1220, 1420, 1520Ⓐ, 1600Ⓐ, 1620Ⓒ, 1648Ⓐ, 1720Ⓐ, 1820, 2020, 2220Ⓐ, 2320. Journey: 1 hour.

Barrington ⋖ *(MR)* (*52* km, US $: 4.10). From Chicago Madison Street: 0030, 0555Ⓐ, 0630Ⓐ, 0713Ⓐ, 0730Ⓐ, 0830Ⓑ, 0900Ⓐ, 1030, 1130✕, 1230, 1310Ⓑ, 1330Ⓐ, 1430, 1530✕, 1610Ⓐ, 1630Ⓒ, 1639Ⓐ, 1645Ⓐ, 1648Ⓐ, 1658Ⓐ, 1705Ⓑ, 1706Ⓐ, 1712Ⓐ, 1720✕, 1723Ⓐ, 1733Ⓐ, 1747Ⓐ, 1801Ⓐ, 1820Ⓐ, 1830, 1930Ⓐ, 2030, 2130Ⓐ, 2230Ⓐ, 2330Ⓑ, returning at 0012②-⑥, 0507Ⓐ, 0537Ⓐ, 0557Ⓐ, 0618Ⓐ, 0627Ⓐ, 0634Ⓐ, 0636Ⓑ, 0638Ⓐ, 0707Ⓑ, 0711Ⓐ, 0715Ⓐ, 0716Ⓑ, 0724Ⓐ, 0727Ⓐ, 0742Ⓐ, 0743Ⓑ, 0747Ⓐ, 0754Ⓐ, 0756Ⓑ, 0804Ⓐ, 0816✕, 0916, 1016✕, 1116, 1216✕, 1316†, 1416✕, 1516Ⓑ, 1616Ⓐ, 1716, 1805Ⓐ, 1816Ⓐ, 1916†, 2016✕, 2116. Journey: 1 hour.

Downers Grove ⋖ *(MR)* (❖ km, US $: 3.30). From Chicago Union: 0035, 0615Ⓐ, 0630Ⓑ, 0645Ⓐ, 0710Ⓐ, 0727Ⓐ, 0740Ⓐ, 0830Ⓒ, 0850Ⓐ, 1030, 1230, 1330✕, 1430, 1520Ⓐ, 1530Ⓑ, 1558Ⓐ, 1602Ⓐ, 1628Ⓐ, 1630Ⓒ, 1646Ⓐ, 1652Ⓐ, 1706Ⓐ, 1726Ⓐ, 1730Ⓑ, 1734Ⓐ, 1746Ⓐ, 1810Ⓐ, 1820Ⓐ, 1830Ⓒ, 1850Ⓐ, 1930Ⓐ, 2030, 2130Ⓐ, 2230, 2335Ⓐ, returning at 0514Ⓐ, 0544Ⓑ, 0600Ⓐ, 0604Ⓐ, 0626Ⓐ, 0640Ⓐ, 0644Ⓒ, 0652Ⓐ, 0700Ⓐ, 0720Ⓐ, 0732Ⓐ, 0740Ⓐ, 0744Ⓑ, 0800Ⓐ, 0810Ⓐ, 0824Ⓐ, 0844Ⓒ, 0944✕, 1044, 1144Ⓑ, 1244, 1444, 1544Ⓐ, 1624Ⓐ, 1644Ⓒ, 1656Ⓐ, 1744Ⓐ, 1844, 2044, 2244Ⓐ, 2344. Journey: 50 mins.

Elgin ⋖ *(MR)* (❖ km, US $: 4.45). From Chicago Union: 0030, 0545Ⓐ, 0625Ⓐ, 0713Ⓐ, 0730Ⓑ, 0755Ⓐ, 0830, 0930Ⓐ, 1030, 1130Ⓐ, 1230, 1340Ⓐ, 1430, 1540Ⓐ, 1625Ⓐ, 1630Ⓒ, 1650Ⓐ, 1705Ⓐ, 1717Ⓐ, 1730Ⓑ, 1740Ⓐ, 1805Ⓐ, 1830Ⓒ, 1840Ⓐ, 1930Ⓐ, 2030, 2130Ⓐ, 2230, returning at 0425Ⓐ, 0500Ⓐ, 0536Ⓐ, 0555Ⓒ, 0556Ⓐ, 0625Ⓐ, 0655Ⓑ, 0658Ⓐ, 0727Ⓐ, 0742Ⓐ, 0755Ⓒ, 0843Ⓐ, 0855Ⓑ, 0929Ⓐ, 0955Ⓒ, 1029Ⓐ, 1129Ⓐ, 1155Ⓒ, 1229Ⓐ, 1329Ⓐ, 1355Ⓒ, 1429Ⓐ, 1529Ⓐ, 1555Ⓒ, 1600Ⓐ, 1715Ⓐ, 1755Ⓒ, 1809Ⓐ, 1909Ⓐ, 1955Ⓒ, 2009Ⓐ, 2108Ⓐ, 2155Ⓒ, 2208Ⓐ Journey: 1¼ hours.

Elmwood Park ⋖ *(MR)* (❖ km, US $: 2.55). From Chicago Union: 0030, 0545Ⓐ, 0625Ⓐ, 0713Ⓐ, 0730Ⓑ, 0755Ⓐ, 0830, 0930Ⓐ, 1030, 1130Ⓐ, 1230, 1340Ⓐ, 1430, 1540Ⓐ, 1610Ⓐ, 1630Ⓒ, 1634Ⓐ, 1705Ⓐ, 1727Ⓐ, 1730Ⓑ, 1805Ⓐ, 1830Ⓒ, 1840Ⓐ, 1930Ⓐ, 2030, 2130Ⓐ, 2230, returning at 0509Ⓐ, 0547Ⓐ, 0639Ⓒ, 0649Ⓐ, 0720Ⓐ, 0739Ⓑ, 0744Ⓐ, 0811Ⓐ, 0839Ⓒ, 0927Ⓐ, 0939Ⓑ, 1013Ⓐ, 1039Ⓒ, 1113Ⓐ, 1213Ⓐ, 1239Ⓒ, 1313Ⓐ, 1413Ⓐ, 1439Ⓒ, 1513Ⓐ, 1613Ⓐ, 1639Ⓒ, 1644Ⓐ, 1759Ⓐ, 1839Ⓒ, 1853Ⓐ, 1953Ⓐ, 2039Ⓒ, 2053Ⓐ, 2153Ⓐ, 2239Ⓒ, 2253Ⓐ. Journey: 25 mins.

Evanston ⋖ *(MR)* (*19* km, US $: 2.55). From Chicago Madison Street: 0035, 0624Ⓐ, 0635✕, 0650Ⓐ, 0709Ⓐ, 0725Ⓐ, 0800Ⓐ, 0835✕, 1035, 1135Ⓐ, 1235, 1335Ⓐ, 1435, 1535Ⓐ, 1615Ⓐ, 1630Ⓐ, 1635, 1710Ⓐ, 1715Ⓐ, 1721Ⓐ, 1735✕, 1800Ⓐ, 1831Ⓐ, 1835Ⓑ, 1935✕, 2035Ⓑ, 2135✕, 2235, 2335Ⓐ, returning from Evanston Davis Street at 0045②-⑥, 0549✕, 0619Ⓐ, 0651Ⓐ, 0700Ⓑ, 0713Ⓐ, 0719Ⓐ, 0739Ⓐ, 0745Ⓐ, 0753Ⓐ, 0759Ⓐ, 0800Ⓒ, 0810Ⓐ, 0835Ⓐ, 0857Ⓐ, 0900Ⓑ, 0929Ⓐ, 1000, 1100✕, 1145†, 1300, 1400Ⓐ, 1500, 1600Ⓐ, 1700, 1735Ⓐ, 1800Ⓐ, 1806Ⓐ, 1900Ⓐ, 2000, 2100Ⓐ, 2200Ⓐ, 2300†, 2330✕; also by *CTA* from Chicago Van Buren (change at Howard except during Ⓐ peak hours): frequent (about every 40 mins. at night), returning from Evanston Davis Street frequent (about every 40 mins. at night). Journey: 40 mins.

Fox Lake ⋖ *(MR)* (*81* km, US $: 5.25). From Chicago Union: 0025, 0705Ⓐ, 0835, 1035, 1235, 1435✕, 1535Ⓐ, 1620Ⓐ, 1645✕, 1710Ⓐ, 1725Ⓐ, 1730Ⓐ, 1735Ⓒ, 1748Ⓐ, 1850Ⓐ, 1935, 2035Ⓐ, 2135Ⓒ, 2205Ⓐ, returning at 0450Ⓐ, 0518✕, 0548Ⓐ, 0612Ⓐ, 0620Ⓐ, 0632Ⓐ, 0642, 0655Ⓐ, 0700Ⓐ, 0720Ⓐ, 0842, 1042, 1242✕, 1442, 1605Ⓐ, 1642Ⓒ, 1915, 2205. Journey: 1½ hours.

Franklin Park ⋖ *(MR)* (❖ km, US $: 2.55). From Chicago Union: 0030, 0545Ⓐ, 0625Ⓐ, 0713Ⓐ, 0730Ⓑ, 0755Ⓐ, 0830, 0930Ⓐ, 1030, 1130Ⓐ, 1230, 1340Ⓐ, 1430, 1540Ⓐ, 1610Ⓐ, 1625Ⓐ, 1630Ⓒ, 1634Ⓐ, 1650Ⓐ, 1655Ⓐ, 1705Ⓐ, 1727Ⓐ, 1730Ⓑ, 1740Ⓐ, 1805Ⓐ, 1830Ⓒ, 1840Ⓐ, 1930Ⓐ, 2030, 2130Ⓐ, 2230, returning at 0504Ⓐ, 0542Ⓐ, 0634Ⓒ, 0639Ⓐ, 0643Ⓐ, 0707Ⓐ, 0714Ⓐ, 0727Ⓐ, 0732Ⓐ, 0734Ⓑ, 0738Ⓐ, 0755Ⓐ, 0800Ⓐ, 0805Ⓐ, 0826Ⓐ, 0834Ⓒ, 0922Ⓐ, 0934Ⓑ, 1008Ⓐ, 1034Ⓒ, 1108Ⓐ, 1208Ⓐ, 1234Ⓒ, 1308Ⓐ, 1408Ⓐ, 1434Ⓒ, 1508Ⓐ, 1608Ⓐ, 1634Ⓒ, 1639Ⓐ, 1753Ⓐ, 1834Ⓒ, 1848Ⓐ, 1948Ⓐ, 2034Ⓒ, 2048Ⓐ, 2147Ⓐ, 2234Ⓒ, 2247Ⓐ. Journey: 30 mins.

Gary ⋖ *(NICD)* (*50* km, US $: 4.45). From Chicago Randolph Street: 0045, 0730Ⓐ, 0800Ⓒ, 0845Ⓐ, 1000Ⓒ, 1015Ⓐ, 1159Ⓒ, 1225Ⓐ, 1400Ⓒ, 1425Ⓐ, 1520Ⓐ, 1558Ⓐ, 1600Ⓒ, 1625Ⓐ, 1656Ⓐ, 1710Ⓐ, 1728Ⓐ, 1732Ⓐ, 1758Ⓐ, 1800Ⓒ, 1858Ⓐ, 2000Ⓒ, 2015Ⓐ, 2200Ⓒ, 2215Ⓐ, returning from Gary CSSB at 0445Ⓐ, 0542Ⓐ, 0604Ⓒ, 0638Ⓐ, 0650Ⓐ, 0709Ⓐ, 0742Ⓐ, 0757Ⓐ, 0804Ⓒ, 0929Ⓐ, 1004Ⓒ, 1012Ⓐ, 1114Ⓐ, 1204Ⓒ, 1223Ⓐ, 1325Ⓐ, 1404Ⓒ, 1520Ⓐ, 1604Ⓒ, 1635Ⓐ, 1725Ⓐ, 1804Ⓒ, 2004Ⓒ, 2104Ⓐ, 2204Ⓒ. Journey: 1 hour.

Geneva ⋖ *(MR)* (*75* km, US $: 4.45). From Chicago Madison Street: 0040②-⑦, 0620Ⓐ, 0650Ⓐ, 0740Ⓑ, 0840✕, 1040✕, 1240, 1440✕, 1540Ⓑ, 1614Ⓐ, 1640Ⓑ, 1704Ⓐ, 1717Ⓐ, 1732Ⓐ, 1740Ⓒ, 1810Ⓐ, 1840✕, 1940Ⓐ, 2040, 2140Ⓐ, 2240✕, 2340Ⓑ, returning at 0500Ⓐ, 0541Ⓐ, 0605Ⓑ, 0606Ⓐ, 0637Ⓐ, 0654Ⓐ, 0705Ⓑ, 0725Ⓐ, 0740Ⓐ, 0805✕, 0905Ⓑ, 1005✕, 1205✕, 1405, 1605✕, 1705Ⓑ, 1805✕, 1905†, 2005Ⓑ, 2105Ⓐ, 2205. Journey: 1¼ hours.

Hammond ⋖ *(NICD)* (*34* km, US $: 3.65). From Chicago Randolph Street: 0045, 0730Ⓐ, 0800Ⓒ, 0845Ⓐ, 1000Ⓒ, 1015Ⓐ, 1159Ⓒ, 1225Ⓐ, 1400Ⓒ, 1425Ⓐ, 1520Ⓐ, 1558Ⓐ, 1600Ⓒ, 1625Ⓐ, 1656Ⓐ, 1710Ⓐ, 1728Ⓐ, 1732Ⓐ, 1758Ⓐ, 1800Ⓒ, 1858Ⓐ, 2000Ⓒ, 2015Ⓐ, 2200Ⓒ, 2215Ⓐ, returning from Hammond CSSB at 0502Ⓐ, 0559Ⓐ, 0620Ⓒ, 0655Ⓐ, 0710Ⓐ, 0723Ⓐ, 0756Ⓐ, 0815Ⓐ, 0820Ⓒ, 0945Ⓐ, 1020Ⓒ, 1030Ⓐ, 1130Ⓐ, 1220Ⓒ, 1240Ⓐ, 1342Ⓐ, 1420Ⓒ, 1537Ⓐ, 1620Ⓒ, 1652Ⓐ, 1742Ⓐ, 1820Ⓒ, 2020Ⓒ, 2121Ⓐ, 2220Ⓒ. Journey: 40 mins.

Harlem ⋖ *(CTA)* (❖ km, US $: ❖). From Chicago Jackson: frequent service day and night, returning frequent day and night. Journey: 30 mins.

Harvard ⋖ *(MR)* (*101* km, US $: 6.40). From Chicago Madison Street: 0030, 0730Ⓐ, 0830Ⓑ, 1030†, 1130✕, 1310Ⓑ, 1330Ⓐ, 1430Ⓒ, 1530Ⓐ, 1610Ⓐ, 1630†, 1716Ⓐ, 1733Ⓐ, 1830, 2030, 2130Ⓐ, returning at 0548Ⓐ, 0621Ⓑ, 0622Ⓐ, 0659Ⓑ, 0708Ⓐ, 0735✕, 0835†, 0935Ⓐ, 1035Ⓒ, 1235†, 1335✕, 1635, 1735Ⓐ, 1835†, 2035. Journey: 1¾ hours.

Joliet ⋖ *(MR)* (*60* km, US $: 4.45). From Chicago La Salle Street: 0030ex①, 0657Ⓐ, 0745Ⓐ, 0830, 0930Ⓐ, 1030, 1130Ⓐ, 1230, 1330Ⓐ, 1430, 1545Ⓐ, 1610Ⓐ, 1630Ⓒ, 1635Ⓐ, 1710Ⓐ, 1720Ⓐ, 1730Ⓑ, 1740Ⓐ, 1815Ⓐ, 1840, 1940Ⓐ, 2045, 2145Ⓐ, 2255, returning from Joliet Union at 0504Ⓐ, 0533Ⓐ, 0550Ⓐ, 0604Ⓒ, 0612Ⓐ, 0632Ⓐ, 0648Ⓐ, 0704Ⓐ, 0719Ⓐ, 0724Ⓑ, 0737Ⓐ, 0824, 0924Ⓐ, 1024, 1124Ⓐ, 1224, 1324Ⓐ, 1424, 1524Ⓐ, 1624, 1713Ⓐ, 1818Ⓐ, 1824Ⓒ, 1918Ⓐ, 2024Ⓒ, 2124Ⓐ, 2224✕. Journey: 1¼ hours. Also from Chicago Union at 1650Ⓐ, 1725Ⓐ, returning at 0625Ⓐ, 0705Ⓐ.

Kenosha ⋖ *(MR)* (*84* km, US $: 5.60). From Chicago Madison Street: 0035, 0635✕, 1035Ⓑ, 1235✕, 1435†, 1615Ⓐ, 1635Ⓒ, 1707Ⓐ, 1710Ⓐ, 1735✕, 1831Ⓐ, 2135✕, returning at 0549Ⓑ, 0555Ⓐ, 0620Ⓐ, 0649Ⓒ, 0653Ⓐ, 0715Ⓐ, 0753Ⓐ, 0847Ⓑ, 0849Ⓑ, 1449Ⓐ, 1749Ⓐ, 1849Ⓒ, 2220Ⓑ, 2335Ⓐ. Journey: 1¾ hours.

Maywood ⋖ *(MR)* (❖ km, US $: 2.55). From Chicago Madison Street: 0040②-⑥, 0620Ⓐ, 0715Ⓐ, 0740Ⓐ, 0840✕, 1140Ⓐ, 1240Ⓑ, 1340Ⓐ, 1540Ⓐ, 1620Ⓐ, 1640Ⓑ, 1717Ⓐ, 1744Ⓐ, 1840✕, 2040Ⓐ, 2240✕, returning at 0545Ⓐ, 0639Ⓐ, 0706Ⓐ, 0745Ⓐ, 0749Ⓑ, 0814Ⓐ, 0852Ⓐ, 1049✕, 1349Ⓐ, 1449Ⓑ, 1549Ⓐ, 1650Ⓐ, 1751Ⓐ, 1849Ⓑ, 1949Ⓐ, 2148Ⓐ, 2249Ⓑ. Journey: 20 mins.

McHenry ⋖ *(MR)* (*83* km, US $: 5.60). From Chicago Madison Street: 0555Ⓐ, 1645Ⓐ, 1720✕, returning at 0553Ⓐ, 0654Ⓐ, 0730Ⓑ, 0736Ⓐ. Journey: 1½ hours.

Morton Grove ⋖ *(MR)* (❖ km, US $: 2.55). From Chicago Union: 0025, 0635Ⓐ, 0705Ⓐ, 0724Ⓐ, 0740Ⓐ, 0835, 0935Ⓐ, 1035, 1135Ⓐ, 1235, 1335Ⓐ, 1435✕, 1535Ⓐ, 1620Ⓐ, 1645✕, 1652Ⓐ, 1715Ⓐ, 1730Ⓐ, 1735Ⓒ, 1755Ⓐ, 1850Ⓐ, 1935, 2035Ⓐ, 2135Ⓒ, 2205Ⓐ, returning at 0545Ⓐ, 0615✕, 0648Ⓐ, 0705Ⓐ, 0713Ⓐ, 0726Ⓐ, 0734Ⓐ, 0736†, 0737Ⓒ, 0746Ⓐ, 0806Ⓐ, 0814Ⓐ, 0831Ⓐ, 0936Ⓑ, 0937Ⓑ, 1036Ⓐ, 1136Ⓑ, 1137Ⓑ, 1236Ⓐ, 1336Ⓐ, 1337Ⓒ, 1436Ⓐ, 1536Ⓑ, 1537Ⓑ, 1636Ⓐ, 1659Ⓐ, 1734Ⓑ, 1736†, 1806Ⓐ, 1836Ⓐ, 1906Ⓐ, 2009Ⓑ, 2010Ⓑ, 2259Ⓑ, 2300Ⓑ. Journey: 30 mins.

Naperville ⋖ *(MR)* (❖ km, US $: 4.45). From Chicago Union: 0035, 0615Ⓐ, 0630Ⓑ, 0740Ⓐ, 0830Ⓒ, 0850Ⓐ, 1030, 1230, 1330✕, 1430, 1520Ⓐ, 1530Ⓑ, 1558Ⓐ, 1628Ⓐ, 1630Ⓒ, 1646Ⓐ, 1652Ⓐ, 1702Ⓐ, 1706Ⓐ, 1722Ⓐ, 1730Ⓑ, 1734Ⓐ, 1742Ⓐ, 1746Ⓐ, 1810Ⓐ, 1820Ⓐ, 1830Ⓒ, 1850Ⓐ, 1930Ⓐ, 2030, 2130Ⓐ, 2230, 2335Ⓐ, returning at 0503Ⓐ, 0533Ⓑ, 0545Ⓐ, 0553Ⓐ, 0615Ⓐ, 0633Ⓒ, 0639Ⓐ, 0641Ⓐ, 0659Ⓐ, 0719Ⓐ, 0721Ⓐ, 0733Ⓑ, 0739Ⓐ, 0759Ⓐ, 0813Ⓐ, 0833Ⓒ, 0933✕, 1033, 1133Ⓑ, 1233, 1433, 1533Ⓐ, 1613Ⓐ, 1633Ⓒ, 1733Ⓐ, 1833, 2033, 2233Ⓐ, 2333. Journey: 1 hour.

Norridge ≠ *(CTA/PACE)* (❖ km, US $: ❖). From Harlem: 0450Ⓐ/0455Ⓑ/0640† and frequent to 2155Ⓒ/2355Ⓐ, returning at 0520✕/0725† and frequent to 2230†/2235Ⓐ/0025②-⑥. Journey: 10 mins.

Northlake ≠ *(CTA/PACE)* (❖ km, US $: ❖). From Harlem: ❖, returning at ❖. Journey: ❖.

Oak Park ⋖ *(MR)* (❖ km, US $: 1.75). From Chicago Madison Street: 0030ex①, 0620Ⓐ, 0650Ⓐ, 0715Ⓐ, 0740Ⓑ, 0840✕, 0940†, 1040✕, 1140Ⓐ, 1240, 1340Ⓐ, 1440✕, 1540Ⓑ, 1620Ⓐ, 1638Ⓐ, 1640Ⓑ, 1713Ⓐ, 1717Ⓐ, 1732Ⓐ, 1740Ⓒ, 1744Ⓐ, 1810Ⓐ, 1840✕, 1940Ⓐ, 2040, 2140Ⓐ, 2240✕, 2340Ⓑ, returning from Oak Park Marion Street at 0550Ⓐ, 0615Ⓐ, 0629Ⓐ, 0646Ⓐ, 0654Ⓑ, 0655Ⓐ, 0712Ⓐ, 0731Ⓐ, 0751Ⓐ, 0753†, 0754Ⓑ, 0759Ⓐ, 0820Ⓐ, 0854Ⓑ, 0857Ⓐ, 0954Ⓑ, 1054✕, 1153†, 1254✕, 1354Ⓐ, 1453†, 1454✕, 1554Ⓐ, 1654Ⓑ, 1655Ⓐ, 1753†, 1757Ⓐ, 1836Ⓐ, 1854Ⓑ, 1855Ⓐ, 1953†, 1955Ⓐ, 2053Ⓐ, 2054Ⓑ, 2153Ⓐ, 2253Ⓑ, 2254Ⓑ. Journey: 20 mins.

Orland Park ⋖ *(MR)* (❖ km, US $: 3.30). From Chicago Union: 1345Ⓐ, 1500Ⓐ, 1630Ⓐ, 1657Ⓐ, 1730Ⓐ, 1845Ⓐ, returning from Orland Park 153rd Street at 0529Ⓐ, 0626Ⓐ, 0701Ⓐ, 0734Ⓐ, 1510Ⓐ, 1620Ⓐ. Journey: 1 hour. Also (≠) *PACE* from Chicago (Monroe/Wabash) at 1110Ⓐ, 112150Ⓐ, 1545Ⓐ, 1615Ⓐ, 1650Ⓐ, 1705Ⓐ, 1715Ⓐ, 1735Ⓐ, 1800Ⓐ, 1835Ⓐ, 1915Ⓐ, 2015Ⓐ, 2130Ⓐ, returning at 0522Ⓐ, 0553Ⓐ, 0609Ⓐ, 0649Ⓐ, 0813Ⓐ, 0926Ⓐ, 1038Ⓐ.

Park Ridge ⋖ *(MR)* (❖ km, US $: 2.55). From Chicago Madison Street: 0030, 0555Ⓐ, 0630Ⓐ, 0713Ⓐ, 0730Ⓐ, 0830Ⓑ, 0900Ⓐ, 1030, 1130✕, 1230, 1310Ⓑ, 1330Ⓐ, 1430, 1530✕, 1610Ⓐ, 1630Ⓒ, 1639Ⓐ, 1648Ⓐ, 1705Ⓑ, 1712Ⓐ, 1723Ⓐ, 1747Ⓐ, 1820Ⓐ, 1830Ⓒ, 1930Ⓐ, 2030, 2130Ⓐ, 2230Ⓐ, 2330Ⓑ, returning at 0541Ⓐ, 0611Ⓐ, 0633Ⓐ, 0702Ⓐ, 0710Ⓑ, 0716Ⓐ, 0721Ⓐ, 0750✕, 0806Ⓐ, 0815Ⓑ, 0821Ⓐ, 0830Ⓑ, 0850✕, 0950, 1050✕, 1150, 1250✕, 1350†, 1450✕, 1550Ⓑ, 1650Ⓐ, 1750, 1829Ⓐ, 1850Ⓐ, 1950†, 2050✕, 2150. Journey: 30 mins.

Ravinia Park ▮ ⋖ *(MR)* (*36* km, US $: 3.30). From Chicago Madison Street: 1235†, 1435†, 1635Ⓒ, 1735Ⓑ, 1800Ⓐ, 1835Ⓑ, 1935✕, 2035Ⓑ, 2135✕, 2235, 2335Ⓐ, returning at 0023②-⑥, 1638Ⓒ, 1738Ⓐ, 1838Ⓐ, 1938✕, 2138Ⓐ, 2238†, 2308✕. Journey: 50 mins.

River Forest ⋖ *(MR)* (❖ km, US $: 3.70). From Chicago Madison Street: 0040ex①, 0620Ⓐ, 0650Ⓐ, 0715Ⓐ, 0740Ⓑ, 0840✕, 0940†, 1040✕, 1140Ⓐ, 1240, 1340Ⓐ, 1440✕, 1540Ⓑ, 1620Ⓐ, 1638Ⓐ, 1640Ⓑ, 1717Ⓐ, 1740Ⓒ, 1744Ⓐ, 1840✕, 1940Ⓐ, 2040, 2140Ⓐ, 2240✕, 2340Ⓑ, returning at 0547Ⓐ, 0611Ⓐ, 0626Ⓐ, 0642Ⓐ, 0651Ⓑ, 0708Ⓐ, 0716Ⓐ, 0747Ⓐ, 0751Ⓒ, 0755Ⓐ, 0816Ⓐ, 0851Ⓑ, 0854Ⓐ, 0950†, 0951Ⓐ, 1051✕, 1150†, 1251✕, 1351Ⓐ, 1450†, 1451✕, 1551Ⓐ, 1651Ⓑ, 1652Ⓐ, 1750†, 1753Ⓐ, 1851✕, 1950†, 1951Ⓐ, 2050Ⓐ, 2051Ⓑ, 2150Ⓐ, 2250Ⓑ, 2251Ⓑ. Journey: 55 mins.

Skokie ⋖ *(CTA)* (❖ km, US $: ❖). From Chicago Jackson: *0003②-⑥*, *0515Ⓐ/0520Ⓑ/0630†* and frequent (every 30 mins, on †) to *2300†/2303Ⓑ/2333Ⓐ*, returning from Skokie Dempster at *0000②-⑥*, *0030②-⑥*, *0455✕/0703†* and frequent (about every 30 mins. on †) to *2330✕/2335Ⓐ*. Journey: 20 mins.

University Park ⋖ *(MR)* (*55* km, US $: 4.10). From Chicago Randolph Street: 0050, 0515✕, 0530†, 0630†, 0635✕, 0753✕, 0830Ⓑ, 0930✕, 1030, 1130✕, 1230, 1330✕, 1430, 1520✕, 1538✕, 1608✕, 1630†, 1632Ⓐ, 1638Ⓑ, 1647Ⓐ, 1702Ⓐ, 1708Ⓐ, 1717Ⓐ, 1737Ⓐ, 1738Ⓑ, 1808✕, 1830†, 1838✕, 1925✕, 2020✕, 2030†, 2120✕, 2220✕, 2230†, 2320✕, returning at 0420✕, 0445†, 0515✕, 0550✕, 0634Ⓐ, 0640Ⓐ, 0644Ⓑ, 0645†, 0655Ⓐ, 0710Ⓐ, 0714Ⓑ, 0725Ⓐ, 0744Ⓑ, 0745Ⓑ, 0751Ⓐ, 0801Ⓐ, 0826Ⓑ, 0856✕, 0945†, 0956✕, 1056✕, 1145†, 1156✕, 1256✕, 1345†, 1356✕, 1456✕, 1545†, 1556✕, 1640✕, 1740✕, 1745†, 1838✕, 1938✕, 1945†, 2038✕, 2138✕, 2145†, 2238✕, 2338✕, 2345†. Journey: 1¼ hours.

Waukegan ⋖ *(MR)* (*58* km, US $: 4.45). From Chicago Madison Street: 0035, 0635✕, 0725Ⓐ, 0835✕, 1035, 1135Ⓐ, 123[illegible], 1335Ⓐ, 1435, 1535Ⓐ, 1615Ⓐ, 1635, 1707Ⓐ, 1710Ⓐ, 1715Ⓐ, 1735✕, 1745Ⓐ, 1800Ⓐ, 1831Ⓐ, 1835Ⓑ, 1935✕, 2035Ⓑ, 2135[illegible], 2235, 2335Ⓐ, returning at 0500✕, 0530Ⓐ, 0558Ⓐ, 0610Ⓑ, 0617Ⓐ, 0641Ⓐ, 0709Ⓐ, 0710Ⓒ, 0715Ⓐ, 0720Ⓐ, 0737Ⓐ, 0747[illegible], 0810Ⓑ, 0814Ⓐ, 0908Ⓑ, 0910Ⓑ, 1010✕, 1055†, 1210, 1310Ⓐ, 1410, 1510Ⓐ, 1610, 1710Ⓐ, 1810Ⓐ, 1910, 2010Ⓐ, 2110[illegible], 2240✕, 2355Ⓐ. Journey: 1¼ hours.

West Chicago ⋖ *(MR)* (❖ km, US $: 3.70). From Chicago Madison Street: 0040ex①, 0620Ⓐ, 0650Ⓐ, 0740Ⓑ, 0840✕, 094[illegible], 1040✕, 1140Ⓐ, 1240, 1340Ⓐ, 1440✕, 1540Ⓑ, 1614Ⓐ, 1638Ⓐ, 1640Ⓑ, 1709Ⓐ, 1713Ⓐ, 1732Ⓐ, 1740, 1810Ⓐ, 1840✕, 1940[illegible], 2040, 2140Ⓐ, 2240✕, 2340Ⓑ, returning at 0508Ⓐ, 0533Ⓐ, 0550Ⓐ, 0605Ⓐ, 0613Ⓑ, 0615Ⓐ, 0626Ⓐ, 0646Ⓐ, 0653Ⓐ, 071[illegible], 0719Ⓐ, 0734Ⓐ, 0749Ⓐ, 0813✕, 0913Ⓑ, 1013✕, 1113†, 1213✕, 1313Ⓐ, 1413, 1513Ⓐ, 1613✕, 1713Ⓑ, 1813✕, 191[illegible], 2013✕, 2113Ⓐ, 2213. Journey: 55 mins.

⋖– By ╫╫╫. ≠–By 🚌.
▮– Open June 23-Sept. 3 only, and only for concerts/meetings.
CTA– Chicago Transit Authority. Tel.: Chicago 664 7200.
MR– Metropolitan Rail. Tel.: Chicago 312 322 6777.
NICD– Northern Idiana Commuter Transportation District ("The South Shore Line"). Tel.: Chesterton 219 926 5744.
PACE–PACE. Tel.: Chicago 312 364 7223.

able 366 496 PHILADELPHIA LOCAL SERVICES

╫╫╫╫ *NJT PAT SEP*

cal ╫╫╫╫ (C‡ cl. only, 1.435m. [Φ–1.580m.]), 🚋 and 🚌 services operate in the Philadelphia area as follows:

co O *(NJT)* (45 km, US $: 3.85). From Philadelphia 30th Street: 0501ω, 0620ω, 0635, 0800, 0940, 1150Ⓒ, 1330Ⓐ, 1411ωⒸ, 1510, 1642, 1742, 1926ω, 2030, 2150, 2325Ⓐ, returning at 0127πⒶ, 0127Ⓒ, 0531π, 0646, 0733, 0945, 1225Ⓒ, 1254Ⓐ, 1320πⒸ, 1522, 1615, 1715π, 1832, 1953, 2129Ⓒ, 2129πⒶ, 2333. Journey: 40 mins.

thayres O *(SEP)* (27 km, US $: 4.00). From Philadelphia 30th Street: 0528Ⓐ, 0620Ⓐ, 0630Ⓑ, 0715Ⓐ, 0730Ⓒ, 0812Ⓐ, 0830Ⓒ, 0914Ⓐ, 0930Ⓒ, 1010Ⓐ, 1030Ⓒ, 1110Ⓐ, 1130Ⓒ, 1210Ⓐ, 1230Ⓒ, 1310Ⓐ, 1330Ⓒ, 1410Ⓐ, 1430Ⓒ, 1510Ⓐ, 1530Ⓒ, 1550Ⓐ, 1620Ⓐ, 1630Ⓒ, 1640Ⓐ, 1650Ⓐ, 1709Ⓐ, 1714Ⓐ, 1730Ⓒ, 1742Ⓐ, 1823Ⓐ, 1830Ⓒ, 1912Ⓐ, 1930Ⓒ, 2014Ⓐ, 2030Ⓒ, 2114Ⓐ, 2130Ⓒ, 2233Ⓐ, 2300Ⓒ, 2333Ⓐ, returning at 0617Ⓐ, 0644Ⓐ, 0703Ⓐ, 0717Ⓐ, 0721Ⓑ, 0733Ⓐ, 0746Ⓐ, 0804Ⓐ, 0814Ⓐ, 0821Ⓒ, 0914Ⓐ, 0921Ⓒ, 1004Ⓐ, 1021Ⓒ, 1104Ⓐ, 1121Ⓒ, 1204Ⓐ, 1221Ⓒ, 1304Ⓐ, 1321Ⓒ, 1404Ⓐ, 1421Ⓒ, 1504Ⓐ, 1521Ⓒ, 1620Ⓐ, 1621Ⓒ, 1716Ⓐ, 1721Ⓒ, 1746Ⓐ, 1821, 1919Ⓐ, 1921Ⓒ, 2021, 2108Ⓐ, 2121Ⓒ, 2208Ⓐ, 2221Ⓒ, 2308Ⓐ. Journey: 35 mins.

mden O *(PAT)* (6 km, US $:0.75). From Philadelphia 15/16 & Locust: frequent service 24 hours a day, returning from Camden Broadway frequently 24 hours a day. Journey: 10 mins.

wningtown O *(SEP)* (48 km, US $: 5.00). From Philadelphia 30th Street: 0732Ⓐ, 0819Ⓑ, 0949⚒, 1119Ⓐ, 1149Ⓑ, 1319⚒, 1419Ⓑ, 1519Ⓐ, 1549Ⓑ, 1612Ⓐ, 1654Ⓐ, 1713Ⓐ, 1740Ⓐ, 1749Ⓑ, 1810Ⓐ, 1919Ⓐ, 1949Ⓑ, 2019Ⓐ, 2119Ⓐ, 2149Ⓑ, 2219Ⓐ, 2249Ⓑ, returning at 0600Ⓐ, 0634Ⓐ, 0647Ⓑ, 0659Ⓐ, 0718Ⓐ, 0737Ⓐ, 0817Ⓑ, 0909Ⓐ, 0947Ⓑ, 1117⚒, 1317Ⓑ, 1417Ⓐ, 1444⚒, 1547Ⓑ, 1644Ⓐ, 1717Ⓑ, 1747Ⓐ, 1917Ⓑ, 2047Ⓐ, 2117Ⓑ, 2147Ⓐ, 2247Ⓐ. Journey: 1 hour.

rn Rock O *(SEP)* (❖ km US $:3.00). From Philadelphia 30th Street: 0000, 0030, 0459Ⓐ, 0528Ⓐ, 0535Ⓐ, 0615Ⓐ, 0620Ⓐ, 0630Ⓒ, 0633Ⓐ and frequent to 2300Ⓒ, 2314Ⓐ, 2333Ⓐ, 2345Ⓐ, returning at 0008②-⑥, 0508, 0538, 0555Ⓐ, 0608, 0625Ⓐ, 0633Ⓐ and frequent to 2308, 2319Ⓐ, 2353. Journey: 25 mins.

ankford ▶Φ *(SEP)* (❖ km, US $: ❖). From Philadelphia 30th Street: frequent service 24 hours a day (by 🚌 0026-0459), returning frequently (by 🚌 2359-0439). Journey: 30 mins.

rmantown O *(SEP)* (13 km, US $: 3.00). From Philadelphia 30th Street: 0043, 0636Ⓐ, 0727Ⓐ, 0748Ⓒ and about hourly (every 2 hours on †) to 2126Ⓐ, 2148Ⓒ, 2226Ⓐ, 2248Ⓑ, 2326Ⓐ, 2348Ⓒ, returning at 0028, 0611Ⓐ, 0646Ⓐ, 0655Ⓒ, 0715Ⓐ, 0740Ⓐ, 0755Ⓑ, 0801Ⓐ,. 0819Ⓐ, 0839Ⓐ, 0855Ⓒ and about hourly (every 2 hours on †) to 2037Ⓐ, 2050Ⓒ, 2138Ⓐ, 2150Ⓑ, 2238Ⓐ, 2255Ⓒ, 2338Ⓐ. Journey: 25 mins.

nkintown O *(SEP)* (20 km, US $: 4.00). From Philadelphia 30th Street: 0000, 0030, 0459Ⓐ, 0528Ⓐ, 0535Ⓐ and frequent to 2300Ⓒ, 2314Ⓐ, 2333Ⓐ, 2345Ⓐ, returning from Jenkintown Wyncote Station at 0001, 0501, 0531, 0548Ⓐ, 0601, 0618Ⓐ, 0627Ⓐ, 0631 and frequent to 2301, 2317Ⓐ. Journey: 30 mins.

ndenwold O *(PAT)* (23 km, US $: 1.60). From Philadelphia 15/16 & Locust: frequent service 24 hours a day, returning frequently 24 hours a day. Journey: 25 mins.

anayunk O *(SEP)* (15 km, US $: 3.50). From Philadelphia 30th Street: 0550Ⓐ, 0628Ⓐ, 0703Ⓐ, 0724Ⓐ, 0738Ⓒ, 0808Ⓐ, 0820Ⓑ, 0850Ⓐ, 0918Ⓐ, 0920Ⓒ, 1020Ⓒ, 1034Ⓐ, then hourly to 1520Ⓒ, 1522Ⓐ, 1557Ⓐ, 1620Ⓒ, 1627Ⓐ, 1657Ⓐ, 1720Ⓒ, 1730Ⓐ, 1757Ⓐ, 1820Ⓒ, 1839Ⓐ, 1920Ⓒ, 1928Ⓐ, 2020Ⓒ, 2033Ⓐ, 2120Ⓒ, 2133Ⓐ, 2233Ⓐ, 2235Ⓒ, 2333Ⓐ, 2335Ⓒ, returning at 0617Ⓐ, 0648Ⓐ, 0702Ⓒ, 0726Ⓐ, 0757Ⓐ, 0802Ⓒ, 0827Ⓐ, 0902, 0940Ⓐ, 1002Ⓒ, 1012Ⓐ, then about hourly to 1602Ⓒ, 1610Ⓐ, 1655Ⓐ, 1702Ⓒ, 1724Ⓐ, 1759Ⓐ, 1802Ⓒ, 1829Ⓐ, 1902Ⓒ, 1925Ⓐ, 2002Ⓑ, 2010Ⓐ, 2047Ⓒ, 2110Ⓐ, 2147Ⓒ, 2210Ⓐ, 2247Ⓒ, 2314Ⓐ, 2357Ⓐ. Journey: 25 mins.

rberth O *(SEP)* (❖ km, US $: 3.50). From Philadelphia 30th Street: 0019, 0619Ⓐ, 0649Ⓐ, 0719Ⓐ, 0732Ⓐ, 0749⚒, 0819Ⓒ, 0822Ⓐ, 0849⚒, 0919, 0949⚒, 1019, 1049⚒, 1119, 1149⚒, 1219, 1249⚒, 1319, 1349⚒, 1419, 1449⚒, 1519, 1549⚒, 1619Ⓒ, 1620Ⓐ, 1644Ⓐ, 1649Ⓑ, 1701Ⓐ, 1719Ⓒ, 1725Ⓐ, 1746Ⓐ, 1749Ⓑ, 1800Ⓐ, 1818Ⓐ, 1819†, 1849⚒, 1919Ⓑ, 1949⚒, 2019Ⓑ, 2049⚒, 2119Ⓑ, 2149Ⓑ, 2219Ⓑ, 2249Ⓑ, 2319Ⓐ, returning at 0559Ⓐ, 0624Ⓐ, 0657Ⓐ, 0717Ⓐ, 0731Ⓑ, 0741Ⓐ, 0757Ⓐ, 0801Ⓒ, 0819Ⓐ, 0831Ⓑ, 0844Ⓐ, 0900Ⓐ, 0901Ⓒ, 0930Ⓐ, 0931Ⓑ, 0958Ⓐ, 1001Ⓒ, 1031⚒, 1101, 1131⚒, 1201, 1231⚒, 1301, 1331⚒, 1401, 1431⚒, 1501, 1528Ⓑ, 1531Ⓐ, 1601, 1629Ⓐ, 1631Ⓑ, 1659Ⓐ, 1701Ⓒ, 1731Ⓐ, 1801Ⓒ, 1806Ⓐ, 1831Ⓐ, 1857Ⓐ, 1901Ⓒ, 1931Ⓐ, 2001Ⓒ, 2031Ⓐ, 2101Ⓒ, 2131Ⓐ, 2201Ⓒ, 2231Ⓐ, 2301Ⓒ, 2331Ⓐ. Journey: 15 mins.

rristown O *(SEP)* (29 km, US $: 4.00). From Philadelphia 30th Street: 0550Ⓐ, 0628Ⓐ, 0703Ⓐ, 0724Ⓐ, 0738Ⓒ, 0808Ⓐ, 0820Ⓑ, 0850Ⓐ, 0920Ⓒ, 0918Ⓐ, 1020Ⓒ, 1034Ⓐ, 1120Ⓒ, 1133Ⓐ, 1220Ⓒ, 1233Ⓐ, 1320Ⓒ, 1334Ⓐ, 1420Ⓒ, 1433Ⓐ, 1520Ⓒ, 1522Ⓐ, 1557Ⓐ, 1620Ⓒ, 1627Ⓐ, 1657Ⓐ, 1709Ⓐ, 1720Ⓒ, 1730Ⓐ, 1757Ⓐ, 1820Ⓒ, 1839Ⓐ, 1920Ⓒ, 1928Ⓐ, 2020Ⓒ, 2033Ⓐ, 2120Ⓒ, 2133Ⓐ, 2233Ⓐ, 2235Ⓒ, 2333Ⓐ, 2335Ⓒ, returning from Norristown Transportation Center [Lafayette & Swede] (5 mins. earlier from Elm Street Station) at 0600Ⓐ, 0630Ⓐ, 0645Ⓒ, 0705Ⓐ, 0708Ⓐ, 0738Ⓐ, 0745Ⓒ, 0808Ⓐ, 0845, 0923Ⓐ, 0945Ⓒ, 0955Ⓐ, 1045Ⓒ, 1055Ⓐ, 1145Ⓒ, 1147Ⓐ, 1245Ⓒ, 1255Ⓐ, 1345Ⓒ, 1347Ⓐ, 1445Ⓒ, 1447Ⓐ, 1545Ⓒ, 1553Ⓐ, 1638Ⓐ, 1645Ⓒ, 1707Ⓐ, 1740Ⓐ, 1745Ⓒ, 1812Ⓐ, 1845Ⓒ, 1908Ⓐ, 1945Ⓑ, 1953Ⓐ, 2030Ⓒ, 2053Ⓐ, 2130Ⓒ, 2153Ⓐ, 2230Ⓒ, 2257Ⓐ, 2340Ⓐ. Journey: 45 mins. Also (▶) from Philadelphia 69th Street: 0007ex①⑦, 0012①⑦, 0120, 0430Ⓐ, 0445Ⓒ, 0500Ⓐ, 0525Ⓐ, 0530Ⓒ, 0545Ⓐ, 0600Ⓐ, 0605Ⓒ and frequent to 2307, 2337, returning at 0010, 0040, 0150, 0458Ⓐ, 0511Ⓒ, 0528Ⓐ, 0555Ⓐ, 0558Ⓒ, 0619Ⓐ, 0633 and frequent to 2310, 2340.

rth Philadelphia O *(SEP)* (7 km, US $: 3.00). From Philadelphia 30th Street: 0504Ⓐ, 0519Ⓐ, 0553Ⓐ, 0621Ⓒ, 0637Ⓐ and frequent to 2154Ⓐ, 2154Ⓐ, 2249Ⓐ, 2254Ⓐ, 2354Ⓐ returning at 0025②-⑥, 0049①⑦, 0625Ⓐ, 0701Ⓐ, 0737Ⓒ and frequent to 2304Ⓐ, 2337Ⓒ. Journey: 10 mins.

ak Lane P *(SEP)* (❖ km, US $: ❖). From Fern Rock: ❖, returning at ❖. Journey: ❖.

oli O *(SEP)* (32 km, US $: 4.50). From Philadelphia 30th Street: 0019, 0619Ⓐ/0749Ⓑ/0819† and frequent to 2219†/2249Ⓑ/2319Ⓐ, returning at 0529Ⓐ/0704Ⓑ/0734† and frequent to 2234Ⓒ/2304Ⓐ. Journey: 45 mins.

iladelphia International Airport O *(SEP)* (13 km, US $: 6.00). From Philadelphia 30th Street: 0534 and every 30 mins. to 2334, returning at 0610 and every 30 mins. to 0010. From Philadelphia 69th Street 0037, 0545 then ½hourly to 1745, 1835, 1935, 2035, 2137, 2237, 2337 returning at 0030, 0125, 0605, 0635, 0710, 0745, 0745 then about ½hourly to 1840, 1930 then hourly to 2330.

cklerville P *(NJT)* (❖ km, US $: ❖). From Philadelphia: ❖, returning at ❖. Journey: ❖.

cony O *(SEP)* (20 km, US $: 3.50). From Philadelphia 30th Street: 0004Ⓐ, 0040Ⓒ, 0504Ⓐ, 0519Ⓐ, 0553Ⓐ, 0621Ⓒ, 0637Ⓐ, 0713Ⓐ, 0721Ⓒ, 0807Ⓐ, 0821Ⓒ, 0906Ⓐ, 0921Ⓒ, 1004Ⓐ, 1021Ⓒ, 1104Ⓐ, 1121Ⓒ, 1204Ⓐ, 1221Ⓒ, 1304Ⓐ, 1321Ⓒ, 1404Ⓐ, 1421Ⓒ, 1504Ⓐ, 1516Ⓒ, 1604Ⓐ, 1621Ⓒ, 1628Ⓐ, 1721Ⓐ, 1721Ⓒ, 1754Ⓐ, 1821Ⓒ, 1823Ⓐ, 1904Ⓐ, 1921Ⓒ, 2004Ⓐ, 2021Ⓒ, 2104Ⓐ, 2121Ⓒ, 2204Ⓐ, 2216Ⓒ, 2304Ⓐ, 2321Ⓒ, returning at 0014Ⓐ, 0614Ⓐ, 0649Ⓐ, 0728Ⓒ, 0730Ⓐ, 0804Ⓐ, 0827Ⓒ, 0835Ⓐ, 0913Ⓐ, 0931Ⓒ, 1006Ⓐ, 1027Ⓒ, 1058Ⓐ, 1127Ⓒ, 1201Ⓐ, 1227Ⓒ, 1305Ⓐ, 1327Ⓒ, 1402Ⓐ, 1427Ⓒ, 1457Ⓐ, 1527Ⓒ, 1612Ⓐ, 1630Ⓒ, 1706Ⓐ, 1727Ⓒ, 1736Ⓐ, 1820Ⓐ, 1827Ⓒ, 1853Ⓐ, 1927Ⓒ, 1928Ⓐ, 2002Ⓐ, 2027Ⓒ, 2102Ⓐ, 2127Ⓒ, 2207Ⓐ, 2228Ⓒ, 2253Ⓐ, 2327Ⓒ. Journey: 20 mins.

est Trenton O *(SEP)* (❖ km, US $: ❖). From Philadelphia 30th Street: 0528Ⓐ, 0620Ⓐ, 0630Ⓑ, 0715Ⓐ, 0730Ⓒ, 0812Ⓐ, 0830Ⓒ, 0914Ⓐ, 0930Ⓒ, 1010Ⓐ, 1030Ⓒ, 1110Ⓐ, 1130Ⓒ, 1210Ⓐ, 1230Ⓒ, 1310Ⓐ, 1330Ⓒ, 1410Ⓐ, 1430Ⓒ, 1510Ⓐ, 1530Ⓒ, 1550Ⓐ, 1620Ⓐ, 1630Ⓒ, 1640Ⓐ, 1650Ⓐ, 1709Ⓐ, 1714Ⓐ, 1730Ⓒ, 1742Ⓐ, 1823Ⓐ, 1830Ⓒ, 1912Ⓐ, 1930Ⓒ, 2014Ⓐ, 2030Ⓒ, 2114Ⓐ, 2130Ⓒ, 2233Ⓐ, 2300Ⓒ, 2333Ⓐ, returning at 0547Ⓐ, 0614Ⓐ, 0636Ⓐ, 0647Ⓐ, 0656Ⓑ, 0706Ⓐ, 0716Ⓐ, 0737Ⓐ, 0744Ⓐ, 0756Ⓒ, 0844Ⓐ, 0856Ⓒ, 0938Ⓐ, 0956Ⓒ, 1038Ⓐ, 1056Ⓒ, 1138Ⓐ, 1156Ⓒ, 1238Ⓐ, 1256Ⓒ, 1338Ⓐ, 1356Ⓒ, 1438Ⓐ, 1456Ⓒ, 1554Ⓐ, 1556Ⓒ, 1650Ⓐ, 1656Ⓒ, 1720Ⓐ, 1755Ⓐ, 1756Ⓒ, 1853Ⓐ, 1856Ⓒ, 1955Ⓐ, 1956Ⓒ, 2042Ⓐ, 2056Ⓒ, 2142Ⓐ, 2156Ⓒ, 2242Ⓐ. Journey: 1 hour.

– By ╫╫╫╫.
– By 🚌. ▶–By 🚋.
– From Lindenwold. π–To Lindenwold only.

NJT– New Jersey Transit. Tel.: Newark 201 762 5100.
PAT– Port Authority Transit PATCO. Tel.: Philadelphia 215 922 4600.
SEP– Southeastern Pennsylvania Transportation Authority. Tel.: Philadelphia 580 7800.

able 367 396 WASHINGTON LOCAL SERVICES

╫╫╫╫ *DILL MARC MCT WMATA*

cal ╫╫╫╫ (C‡ cl. only, 1.435m.) and 🚌 services operate in the Washington area as follows:

nnapolis ℨ *(DILL)* (❖ km, US $: ❖). From Washington: 1625Ⓐ, 1629Ⓐ, 1649Ⓐ, 1650Ⓐ, 1704Ⓐ, 1719Ⓐ, 1813Ⓐ, returning at 0600Ⓐ, 0628Ⓐ, 0640Ⓐ, 0650Ⓐ, 0659Ⓐ,0726Ⓐ. Journey: 1½ hours. Also from New Carrollton at 0636Ⓐ, 0706Ⓐ, 0840Ⓐ, 1000Ⓐ, 1500Ⓐ, 1630Ⓐ, 1720Ⓐ, 1806Ⓐ, 1850Ⓐ, 1950Ⓐ, returning at 0554Ⓐ, 0624Ⓐ, 0732Ⓐ, 0802Ⓐ, 0926Ⓐ, 1430Ⓐ, 1650Ⓐ, 1740Ⓐ, 1826Ⓐ.

ltimore ℌ *(MARC)* (60 km, US $: 5.75). From Washington Union to Baltimore Camden: 0652Ⓐ, 0720Ⓐ, 0800Ⓐ, 0830Ⓐ, 1130Ⓐ, 1630Ⓐ, 1712Ⓐ, 1735Ⓐ, 1800Ⓐ, 1907Ⓐ, 2000Ⓐ. Journey: 1 hour. Also from Washington Union to Baltimore Penn. Station at 0631Ⓐ, 0730Ⓐ, 0825Ⓐ, 0940Ⓐ, 1025Ⓐ, 1130Ⓐ, 1225Ⓐ, 1340Ⓐ, 1440Ⓐ, 1545Ⓐ, 1615Ⓐ, 1640Ⓐ, 1715Ⓐ, 1748Ⓐ, 1810Ⓐ, 1849Ⓐ, 2005Ⓐ, 2148Ⓐ.

ethesda ℌ *(WMATA)* (❖ km, US $: ❖). From Washington Metro Center: 0530⚒/0800† and frequent to 2355, returning at 0545⚒/0815† and frequent to 2347. Journey: 18 mins.

WI Airport ℌ *(MARC)* (48 km, US $: 5.25). From Washington Union: 0631Ⓐ, 0730Ⓐ, 0825Ⓐ, 0940Ⓐ, 1025Ⓐ, 1130Ⓐ, 1225Ⓐ, 1340Ⓐ, 1440Ⓐ, 1545Ⓐ, 1615Ⓐ, 1640Ⓐ, 1715Ⓐ, 1748Ⓐ, 1810Ⓐ, 1849Ⓐ, 2005Ⓐ, 2148Ⓐ, returning at 0536Ⓐ, 0609Ⓐ, 0633Ⓐ, 0700Ⓐ, 0705Ⓐ, 0741Ⓐ, 1107Ⓐ, 1202Ⓐ, 1410Ⓐ, 1507Ⓐ, 1811Ⓐ. Journey: 40 mins.

hevy Chase ℨ *(MCT)*. From Bethesda: 0600 and frequent to 2200, returning at 2230 and frequent to 2130. Journey: 10 mins.

yattsville ℌ *(WMATA)* (❖ km, US $: ❖). From Washington Gallery Place: 0530⚒/0800† and frequent to 2355, returning from West Hyattsville at 0545⚒/0815† and frequent to 2347. Journey: 18 mins.

aurel ℌ *(MARC)* (31 km, US $: 4.00). From Washington Union: 0652Ⓐ, 0720Ⓐ, 0800Ⓐ, 0830Ⓐ, 1130Ⓐ, 1630Ⓐ, 1712Ⓐ, 1735Ⓐ, 1800Ⓐ, 1907Ⓐ, 2000Ⓐ, returning at 0607Ⓐ, 0628Ⓐ, 0706Ⓐ, 0739Ⓐ, 0836Ⓐ, 1131Ⓐ, 1614Ⓐ, 1643Ⓐ, 1725Ⓐ, 1820Ⓐ, 1907Ⓐ. Journey: 35 mins.

ount Rainier ℨ *(MARC/MCT/WMATA)*. From Washington: ❖, returning at ❖. Journey: ❖.

ew Carrollton ℌ *(WMATA)* (19 km, US $: 2.25). From Washington Metro Center: 0530⚒/0800† and frequent to 0006, returning at 0545⚒/0815† and frequent to 2336. Journey: 30 mins.

lver Spring ℌ *(WMATA)* (11 km, US $: 1.85). From Washington Metro Center: 0530⚒/0800† and frequent to 0006, returning at 0545⚒/0815† and frequent to 2346. Journey: 20 mins.

akoma ℌ *(WMATA)* (11 km, US $: 1.85). From Washington Metro Center: 0530⚒/0800† and frequent to 0006, returning at 0548⚒/0818† and frequent to 2349. Journey: 18 mins.

– By ╫╫╫╫. ℨ–By 🚌.
ILL– Dillon's Bus Service Inc. Tel.: Annapolis 827 3490.
ARC–Maryland Department of Transportation. Tel.: Washington 202 906 3104.
MCT– Montgomery County Transit. Tel.: Rockville 217 2185.
WMATA–Washington Metropolitan Area Transit Authority. Tel.: Washington 202 962 1234.

Table 370 CHICAGO - OMAHA ♿ #### NRPC

US $ C cl.	35	5	347		km	396 1.435m.	348	346	36	6
	S‡C‡	S‡C‡	1‡C‡				1‡C‡	1‡C‡	S‡C‡	S‡C‡
	◆🅁	◆🅁	◆				◆	◆	◆🅁	◆🅁
	①④⑥	②③⑤⑦	🍷		km	↓ ↑	🍷ex⑦	🍷⑦	②④⑥	①③⑤⑦
0.00	1505	1505	1755	....	0	d.**Chicago** Union..a.	1035	1150	1615	1615
	1541u	1541u	1832u	....	41	d.Naperville..........d.	0940s	1055s	1451s	1451s
23.00	1651	1651	1941	....		d.Princeton..........d.	0831	0946	1339	1339
30.00	|	|	2004	....	211	d.Kewanee..........d.	0808	0923	|	|
37.00	1753	1753	2036	....	261	d.Galesburg S. Seminary Str.d.	0740	0855	1247	1247
37.00	|	|	2116	....	326	a. Macomb..........d.	0700	0815	|	|
45.00	|	|	2218	....	424	a. **Quincy**..........d.	0612	0727	|	|
51.00	1844	1844	....	....	330	d.Burlington..........d.	....	....	1153	1153
64.00	2005	2005	....	....	450	d.Ottumwa..........d.	....	....	1033	1033
87.00	2158	2158	....	....	632	d.Creston..........d.	....	....	0834	0834
100.00	0012	0012	....	....	798	a.**Omaha**..........d.	....	....	0644	0644
163.00	0845	0845	....	....	1664	a.*Denver*..........d.	....	....	2030c	2030a
211.00	0001	0001	....	....	2582	a.*Salt Lake City*....d.	....	....	0430c	0430a
262.00	....	1740	....	....	3895	a.*Oakland*..........d.	....	....	....	0900b

5/6– CALIFORNIA ZEPHYR–‡, entertainment car (‡), and ✕ Chicago(**5/6**)-Oakland and v.v.; conveys on ②⑦: ‡ and Chicago(**5**)-Denver(**25**)-Seattle; conveys on ②④⑦ (from Denver): ‡ and Seattle(**26**)-Denver(**6**)-Chicago.
35/36– DESERT WIND–‡, ✕ and Chicago(**35/36**)-Los Angeles and v.v.; conveys on ④: ‡ and Chicago(**35**)-Denver(**25**)-Seattle.
346-8– ILLINOIS ZEPHYR.
a– ②④⑥⑦.
b– ①③⑤⑥.
c– ①③⑤.
NRPC–National Railroad Passenger Corporation (AMTRAK). Tel.: Chicago 312 558 1075.

Table 373 CHICAGO - KANSAS CITY ♿ #### NRPC

US $ C cl.		3			km	396 1.435m.			4	
		S‡C‡							S‡C‡	
		◆							◆	
		🅁			km	↓ ↑			🅁	
0.00	....	1710	....	....	0	d.**Chicago** Union..a.	....	....	1545	....
10.00	....	1806	....	....	60	d.Joliet Union.......d.	....	....	1424	....
31.00	....	1926	....	....	209	d.Chillicothe..........d.	....	....	1258	....
37.00	....	2012	....	....	285	d.Galesburg North Broad Street d.	....	....	1212	....
59.00	....	2107	....	....	377	d.Fort Madison.....d.	....	....	1119	....
79.00	....	0042	....	....	725	a.**Kansas City**.....d.	....	....	0758	....
207.00	....	1705	....	....	2174	a.*Albuquerque*......d.	....	....	1339	....
253.00	....	0800	....	....	3604	a.*Los Angeles*......d.	....	....	2055	....

3/4– SOUTHWEST CHIEF–‡, entertainment car (‡), and ✕ Chicago(**3/4**)-Los Angeles and v.v.
NRPC–National Railroad Passenger Corporation (AMTRAK). Tel.: Chicago 312 558 1075.

Table 374 CHICAGO - ST. LOUIS ♿ #### NRPC

US $ C cl.	396 1.435m.	km	301	311	303	305		3	21	321
			1‡C‡	C‡	1‡C‡	1‡C‡		S‡C‡	S‡C‡	C‡
			◆	◆	◆	◆		◆	◆	◆
	↓	km	🍷	Ⓐ	🍷	🍷		🅁	②⑤⑦	
0.00	**Chicago** Union....d.	0	....	0820	1030	1530	....	1710	1830	1830
11.00	Joliet Union..........d.	60	....	0910	1120	1620	....	1806	1925	1925
17.00	Pontiac..........d.	148	....	1003	1211	1711	....	|	2017	2017
23.00	Bloomington..........d.	204	....	1030	1240	1740	....	a	2050	2050
27.00	Lincoln..........d.	252	....	1059	1313	1813	....	|	2125	2125
34.00	Springfield..........d.	298	....	1150	1350	1850	....	|	2202	2202
38.00	Carlinville..........d.	360	....	....	1430	1930	....	|	2042	2242
40.50	Alton..........d.	414	....	....	1500	2000	....	|	2313	2313
★17.00	Carbondale........d.	◇103	....	....	|	|	....	|	|	|
44.50	**St. Louis**..........a.	457	....	....	1605	2105	....	|	0025	0025
0.00	**St. Louis**..........d.	457	0730	....	1630	....	....	|	....	....
5.00	Kirkwood..........d.	480	0755	....	1655	....	....	|	....	....
25.00	Jefferson City.......d.	658	0950	....	1855	....	....	|	....	....
35.00	Sedalia..........d.	760	1101	....	2005	....	....	|	....	....
40.00	**Kansas City**........a.	912	1300	....	2200	....	....	0042	....	....

396		300		322	22	4	312	304		306
		1‡C‡		C‡	S‡C‡	S‡C‡	C‡	1‡C‡		1‡C‡
		◆		◆	◆	◆	◆	◆		◆
↓		🍷			①③⑤	🅁	Ⓐ	🍷		🍷
Kansas City..........d.	....	....	....	....	....	0758	....	0820	....	1530
Sedalia..........d.	....	....	....	....	....	|	....	1010	....	1724
Jefferson City..........d.	....	....	....	....	....	|	....	1121	....	1831
Kirkwood..........d.	....	....	....	....	....	|	....	1311	....	2021
St. Louis..........a.	....	....	....	....	....	|	....	1350	....	2100
St. Louis..........d.	....	0430	....	0700	0700	|	....	1415	....	....
Carbondale..........a.	....	|	....	|	|	|	....	|	....	....
Alton..........d.	....	0520	....	0748	0748	|	....	1505	....	....
Carlinville..........d.	....	0550	....	0818	0818	|	....	1535	....	....
Springfield..........d.	....	0635	....	0908	0908	|	1500	1620	....	....
Lincoln..........d.	....	0705	....	0938	0938	|	1528	1650	....	....
Bloomington..........d.	....	0738	....	1025	1025	a	1600	1723	....	....
Pontiac..........d.	....	0806	....	1053	1053	|	1627	1751	....	....
Joliet Union..........d.	....	0858	....	1145	1145	1424	1725	1843	....	....
Chicago Union..........a.	....	1000	....	1305	1305	1545	1830	1945	....	....

3/4– SOUTHWEST CHIEF–‡, entertainment car (‡), and ✕ Chicago(**3/4**)-Los Angeles and v.v.
21/22– THE TEXAS EAGLE–runs daily from Chicago to St Louis and v.v.; ①③⑥ (②⑤⑦ from Chicago) from St Louis to Los Angeles; ②⑤⑦ from Los Angeles (②④⑦ from San Antonio) to St Louis and Chicago. Conveys on ①③④⑥: and 🍷 Chicago(**321**)-St Louis; on ②④⑦: ✕ San Antonio(**22**)-Chicago; on ②④⑥⑦: and 🍷 St Louis(**322**)-Chicago; on ②⑤⑦: ‡, entertainment car (‡) and Chicago(**21**)-San Antonio(**1**)-Los Angeles; ‡, entertainment car (‡) and Los Angeles(**2**)-San Antonio(**22**)-Chicago; ✕ Chicago(**21**)-San Antonio.
300/5– STATE HOUSE. **301**–KANSAS CITY MULE. **303/4**–ANN RUTLEDGE.
311/2– THE LOOP. This train will be discontinued after 28 June.
321/2– THE TEXAS EAGLE–see also trains **21/22**.
a– Via Galesburg (Table **236**). ◇–Km ex St. Louis. ★–Fare ex St. Louis.
NRPC–National Railroad Passenger Corporation (AMTRAK). Tel.: Chicago 312 558 1075

Table 377 CHICAGO - SOUTH BEND #### NICD

US $ C cl.	396 1.435m.	km	101/601	505	7	507	107	509	109	511	111	113	513	115	117	19	119		121	515	23	517	123	619	125
			C‡	C‡	C‡	C‡	C‡	C‡	C‡	C‡	C‡	C‡	C‡	C‡	C‡	C‡	C‡		C‡	C‡	C‡	C‡	C‡	C‡	C‡
	↓	km		Ⓒ	Ⓐ	Ⓒ	Ⓐ	Ⓒ	Ⓐ	Ⓒ	Ⓐ	Ⓐ	Ⓒ	Ⓐ	Ⓐ	Ⓐ	Ⓐ		Ⓐ	Ⓒ	Ⓐ	Ⓒ	Ⓐ	Ⓒ	Ⓐ
0.00	Chicago Randolph Street d.	0	0045	0800	0845	1000	1015	1159	1225	1400	1425	1558	1600	1625	1656	1710	1728	....	1758	1800	1858	2000	2015	2200	2215
6.30	Michigan City 11th Street d.	90	0220	0935	1015	1135	1150	1335	1400	1535	1600	1733	1735	1801	1835	1845	1900	....	1933	1935	2033	2135	2145	2335	2345
8.65	**South Bend**.......a.	141	....	1020	1100	1220	....	1420	....	1620	....	....	1820	....	....	1927	....	....	....	2020	2115	2220	....	....	....

396	102	104	600	106	108	10	110		502	12	504		114	506		16	508	116	510		118	512	514	20	516
	C‡	C‡	C‡	C‡	C‡	C‡	C‡		C‡	C‡	C‡		C‡	C‡		C‡	C‡	C‡	C‡		C‡	C‡	C‡	C‡	C‡
↓	Ⓐ	Ⓐ	Ⓒ	Ⓐ	Ⓐ	Ⓐ	Ⓐ		Ⓒ	Ⓐ	Ⓒ		Ⓐ	Ⓒ		Ⓐ	Ⓒ	Ⓐ	Ⓒ		Ⓐ	Ⓒ	Ⓒ	Ⓐ	Ⓒ
South Bend............d.	....	....	....	....	....	0545	....	....	0640	0805	0840	....	....	1040	....	1201	1240	....	1440	....	....	1640	1840	1938	2040
Michigan City 11th Street..d.	0407	0502	0525	0558	0610	0630	0702	....	0725	0850	0925	....	1034	1125	....	1246	1325	1440	1525	....	1645	1725	1925	2023	2125
Chicago Randolph Street .a.	0540	0638	0700	0735	0747	0805	0836	....	0900	1025	1100	....	1210	1300	....	1422	1500	1615	1700	....	1822	1900	2100	2158	2300

NICD–Northern Indiana Commuter Transportation District ("The South Shore Line"). Tel.: Chesterton 219 926 5744.

Table 378 CHICAGO - NEW ORLEANS #### NRPC

US $ C cl.	391		59		km	396 1.435m.		58		392
	1‡C‡		S‡C‡					S‡C‡		1‡C‡
	◆		◆🅁					◆🅁		◆
	🍷		ex②		km	↓ ↑		ex②		🍷
	....	....	*1330*	....		d.*Madison* ◇........a.	....	*1600*	....	....
	....	....	*1515*	....		d.*Rockford* ◇........a.	....	*1410*	....	....
0.00	1600	....	1950	....	0	d.**Chicago** Union..a.	....	0910	....	2130
13.00	1710	....	2106	....	92	d.Kankakee..........d.	....	0739	....	1956
24.00	1829	....	2221	....	208	d.Champaign Urbana d.	....	0630	....	1852
40.00	1933	....	2327	....	323	d.Effingham..........d.	....	0521	....	1737
52.00	2021	....	0018	....	408	d.Centralia..........d.	....	0427	....	1653
58.50	2130	....	0138	....	498	d.Carbondale........d.	....	0325	....	1600
84.00	....	....	0425	....	725	d.Newbern ▶.......d.	....	0024	....	....
95.00	....	....	0635	....	850	d.**Memphis**..........d.	....	2242	....	....
104.00	....	....	0840	....		d.Greenwood........d.	....	1957	....	....
112.00	....	....	0940	....		d.Yazoo City.........d.	....	1857	....	....
116.00	....	....	1115	....	1191	d.Jackson..........d.	....	1757	....	....
125.00	....	....	1243	....	1316	d.McComb..........d.	....	1609	....	....
133.00	....	....	1341	....	1400	d.Hammond..........d.	....	1513	....	....
136.00	....	....	1505	....	1486	a.**New Orleans**....d.	....	1410	....	....
	....	....	*1900*	....		a.*Baton Rouge* ◇ d.	....	*0930*	....	....

58/59– CITY OF NEW ORLEANS–‡, ‡, and ✕ New Orleans(**58/59**)-Chicago and v.v.
391/2– ILLINI. ▶–For Dyersburg. ◇–Connection by .
NRPC–National Railroad Passenger Corporation (AMTRAK). Tel.: Chicago 312 558 1075.

Table 379 MINNEAPOLIS - SPOKANE ♿ #### NRPC

US $ C cl.			7		km	396 1.435m.			8	
			S‡C‡						S‡C‡	
			◆🅁						◆🅁	
			①③⑤⑥		km	↓ ↑			①③⑤⑥	
0.00	....	....	1515	....	0	d.*Chicago*..........a.	....	....	1620	....
64.00	....	....	2355	....	673	d.Minneapolis/St Paul Midway a.	....	....	0740	....
83.00	....	....	0129	....	785	d.St. Cloud..........d.	....	....	0553	....
107.00	....	....	0435	....	1069	d.Fargo..........d.	....	....	0244	....
121.00	....	....	0556	....	1194	d.Grand Forks......d.	....	....	0123	....
131.00	....	....	0719	....	1337	d.Devils Lake.......d.	....	....	2355	....
136.00	....	....	1004	....	1528	d.Minot..........d.	....	....	2141	....
151.00	....	....	1207	....	1720	d.Williston..........d.	....	....	1910	....
184.00	....	....	1431	....	2077	d.Malta..........d.	....	....	1446	....
202.00	....	....	1624	....	2218	d.Havre..........d.	....	....	1332	....
215.00	....	....	1803	....	2386	d.Shelby..........d.	....	....	1117	....
227.00	....	....	1931b	....	2501	d.Glacier Park......d.	....	....	0946b	....
238.00	....	....	2155	....	2628	d.Whitefish..........d.	....	....	0740	....
245.00	....	....	0029	....	2927	d.Sandpoint..........d.	....	....	0249	....
245.00	....	....	0208	....	3034	a.**Spokane**..........d.	....	....	0130	....
245.00	....	....	1030	....	3671	a.*Seattle*..........d.	....	....	1650a	....

7/8– EMPIRE BUILDER–‡, and ✕ Chicago(**7/8**)-Seattle and v.v.; entertainment car‡, ⊗ and Chicago(**7/8**)-Spokane(**27/28**)-Portland and v.v.
a– ②④⑤⑦.
b– May 5-Oct. 5.
NRPC–National Railroad Passenger Corporation (AMTRAK). Tel.: Chicago 312 558 1075

Table 380 CHICAGO - GRAND RAPIDS — NRPC

US $ C cl.	370 C‡ ◆	km	396 1.435m.	371 C‡ ◆🍷
0.00	1735	0	d.Chicago Union..a.	1040
…4.00	1802	25	d.Hammond NRPC d.	0958
…5.00	2020	140	d.Benton Harbor ◇d.	0941
…8.00	2135	241	d.Holland..........d.	0825
…1.00	2230	282	a.**Grand Rapids** ..d.	0745

…70/1– PERE MARQUETTE. ◇–Benton Harbor (*St. Joseph*).
…RPC–National Railroad Passenger Corporation (AMTRAK). Tel.: Chicago 312 558 1075.

Table 382 ST. LOUIS - SAN ANTONIO — NRPC

US $ C cl.	21 S‡C‡ ◆R ①③⑥	km	396 1.435m.	22 S‡C‡ ◆R ②④⑦
…9.00	1830a	0	d.*Chicago*..........a.	1305
0.00	0100	457	d.**St. Louis**..........a.	0620
…8.00	0448	717	d.Poplar Bluff..........d.	0209
…3.00	0542	813	d.Walnut Ridge.....d.	0105
…4.00	0808	1007	d.Little Rock..........d.	2302
…1.00	0914	1127	d.Arkadelphia........d.	2127
…6.00	1039	1240	d.Texarkana..........d.	2012
…09.00	1154	1347	d.Marshall..........d.	1848
…09.00	1229	1384	d.Longview..........d.	1816
…34.00	1515	1588	d.**Dallas**..........d.	1533
…60.00	*1715b*	1995	a. **Houston**..........d.	*1300b*
…34.00	1668	1638	d.**Fort Worth**..........d.	1425
❖	1935	1844	d.Temple..........d.	1125
…57.00	2034	1906	d.Taylor..........d.	1020
…60.00	2128	1962	d.Austin..........d.	0930
…60.00	2207	2011	d.San Marcos........d.	0840
…71.00	2359	2090	a.**San Antonio**.....d.	0700

…1/22–THE TEXAS EAGLE–Runs on ①③⑥ (②⑤⑦ from Chicago) from St Louis to Los Angeles (②④⑦ from San Antonio) to St Louis and Chicago. Conveys on ②④⑦: ✕ San Antonio(22)-Chicago; on ②⑤⑦: (sleeper)‡, entertainment car (‡) and (coach) Chicago(21)-San Antonio(1)-Los Angeles; (sleeper)‡, entertainment car (‡) and (coach) Los Angeles(2)-San Antonio(22)-Chicago; ✕ Chicago(21)-San Antonio.
…–②⑤⑦. b–Connection by (coach-bus).
…RPC–National Railroad Passenger Corporation (AMTRAK). Tel.: Chicago 312 558 1075.

Table 385 JACKSONVILLE - EL PASO — NRPC

US $ C cl.	1R S‡C‡ ◆ ②⑤⑦	km	396 1.435m.	2R S‡C‡ ◆ ①③⑥
11.00	2030	996	d.**Jacksonville**.....a.	1405
…65.00	2344	727	d.Tallahassee........d.	1025
…45.00	0325	399	d.Pensacola..........d.	0455
…45.00	0554	234	d.Mobile..........d.	0156
0.00	1010	0	a. **New Orleans** d.	2255
	1245		d. **New Orleans** a.	1935
…28.00	1527	202	d.New Iberia..........d.	1558
…30.00	1553	237	d.Lafayette..........d.	1533
…52.00	1717	352	d.Lake Charles.....d.	1406
…57.00	1840	451	d.Beaumont..........d.	1242
…73.00	2115	583	d.**Houston** Union .d.	1055
	|		a. *Dallas*..........d.	|
…20.00	0220	922	d.San Antonio........d.	0615
…33.00	0522	1194	d.Del Rio..........d.	0142
…56.00	0955	1544	d.Alpine..........d.	2134
…56.00	1250	1895	a.**El Paso**..........d.	1700
…30.00	2105	2590	a.*Phoenix*..........d.	0708
…30.00	0615	3271	a.*Los Angeles*......d.	2230a

…/2– SUNSET LIMITED–(sleeper)‡, entertainment car (‡), (coach) and ✕ Miami(1/2)-Los Angeles and v.v. Also conveys cars of THE TEXAS EAGLE, see trains **21/22** on Table **374**. a–②⑤⑦. *NRPC*–National Railroad Passenger Corporation (AMTRAK). Tel.: Los Angeles 213 624 0171.

Table 390 OMAHA - DENVER — NRPC

US $ C cl.	35 S‡C‡ ◆R ②⑤⑦	5 S‡C‡ ◆R ①③④⑥	km	396 1.435m.	6 S‡C‡ ◆R ②④⑥⑦	36 S‡C‡ ◆R ①③⑤
0.00	1505c	1505b	0	d.*Chicago*..........a.	1615	1615
	1830a	*1830b*		d. *Kansas City*.....a.	*1200a*	*1200a*
…05.00	0037	0037	798	d.**Omaha**..........d.	0619	0619
…20.00	0151	0151	886	d.Lincoln..........d.	0454	0454
…25.00	0328	0328	1042	d.Hastings..........d.	0311	0311
…43.00	0526	0526	1254	d.McCook..........d.	0113	0113
…63.00	0648	0648	1538	d.Fort Morgan......d.	2148	2148
…63.00	0845	0845	1664	a.**Denver**..........d.	2030	2030
…17.00	0001	0001	2582	a.*Salt Lake City*....d.	0430	0430

…/6–CALIFORNIA ZEPHYR–(sleeper)‡, entertainment car (‡), (coach) and ✕ Chicago(5/6)-Oakland and v.v.; conveys on ②⑦ (from Chicago): (sleeper)‡ and (coach) Chicago(5)-Denver(25)-Seattle; conveys on ②④⑦ (from Denver): (sleeper)‡ and (coach) Seattle(26)-Denver(6)-Chicago.
…5/36–DESERT WIND–(sleeper)‡, ✕ and (coach) Chicago(35/36)-Los Angeles and v.v.; conveys on ④ (from Chicago): (sleeper)‡ and (coach) Chicago(35)-Denver(25)-Seattle.
…–Connection by (coach-bus). b–②⑤⑦. c–①④⑥.
…RPC–National Railroad Passenger Corporation (AMTRAK). Tel.: Chicago 312 558 1075.

Table 392 GRAND CANYON — GCR

R.T. US $ C cl.	1PC P 🍷	km	396 1.435m.	1PC P 🍷
0.00	0930	0	d.**Williams**..........a.	1730
…47.00	1145	103	a.**Grand Canyon**.d.	1515

…–⑤⑥⑦ Feb. 1-28; ex①② Mar. 1-20; daily Mar. 23-Oct. 30; ⑤⑥⑦ Nov. 1-31; ⑥⑦ Dec. 1-18; daily Dec. 26-Jan. 1. *GCR*–Grand Canyon Railroad. Tel.: Williams 602 635 4000.

Table 395 KANSAS CITY - LOS ANGELES — NRPC

US $ C cl.	3 S‡C‡ ◆ R	35 S‡C‡ ◆R ①③⑤	km	496 1.435m.	36 S‡C‡ ◆R ②④⑦	4 S‡C‡ ◆ R
0.00	1710	....	0	d.*Chicago*..........a.	....	1545
77.00	0107	....	725	d.**Kansas City**.....a.	....	0733
90.00	0209	....	789	d.Lawrence..........d.	....	0605
96.00	0243	....	831	d.Topeka..........d.	....	0535
108.00	0348	....	930	d.Emporia..........d.	....	0423
124.00	0500	....	1047	d.Newton..........d.	....	0317
129.00	0534	....	1100	d.Hutchinson........d.	....	0239
144.00	0718	....	1294	d.Dodge City........d.	....	0051
151.00	0803	....	1374	d.Garden City.......d.	....	2359
163.00	0825	....	1535	d.Lamar..........d.	....	2140
169.00	0947	....	1619	d.La Junta..........d.	....	2051
179.00	1104	....	1751	d.Trinidad..........d.	....	1911
179.00	1211	....	1787	d.Raton..........d.	....	1814
194.00	1356	....	1964	d.Las Vegas........d.	....	1628
207.00	1538	....	2067	d.Lamy..........d.	....	1445
	1603a	....		a. *Santa Fe*.......d.	....	*1400a*
207.00	1730	....	2174	d.**Albuquerque**....d.	....	1339
238.00	1950	....	2433	d.Gallup..........d.	....	1033
245.00	2027	....	2638	d.Winslow..........d.	....	0756
	1700a	....		d. Grand Canyon a.	....	*1010a*
245.00	2132	....	2732	d.**Flagstaff**..........d.	....	0659
	|	....		a. Phoenix........d.	....	|
253.00	0030	....	3011	d.Kingman..........d.	....	0412
253.00	0124	....	3106	d.Needles..........d.	....	0247
253.00	0359	1140	3378	d.Barstow..........d.	1420	0021
	0436	1215		d.Victorville..........d.	1325	2342
253.00	0546	1320	3509	d.San Bernardino .d.	1223	2237
253.00	0654s	1428s		d.Fullerton..........d.	1120u	2135
253.00	0800	1535	3604	a.**Los Angeles** Uniond.	1045	2055

3/4– SOUTHWEST CHIEF–(sleeper)‡, entertainment car (‡), (coach) and ✕ Chicago(3/4)-Los Angeles and v.v.
35/36– THE DESERT WIND–(sleeper)‡, ✕ and (coach) Chicago(35/36)-Los Angeles and v.v.
a– Connection by (coach-bus).
NRPC– National Railroad Passenger Corporation (AMTRAK). Tel.: Los Angeles 213 624 0171.

Table 400 DENVER - SAN FRANCISCO — DRG NRPC

US $ C cl.	NRPC 731 C‡ ◆ ©	DRG 1 C‡ P ⊗	NRPC 35 S‡C‡ ◆R ②⑤⑦	NRPC 5 S‡C‡ ◆R ①③④⑥	km	396 1.435m.	DRG 2 C‡ P ⊗	NRPC 6 S‡C‡ ◆R ①③⑤⑥	NRPC 36 S‡C‡ ◆R ①③⑤	NRPC 726 C‡ ◆
0.00	....	....	1505c	1505a	0	d.*Chicago*..........a.	....	1615	1615	....
163.00	....	0715	0935	0935	1664	d.**Denver** Union....a.	1830	1910	1910	....
191.00	....	1000	1130	1130	1763	d.Winter Park........d.	1615	1625	1625	....
191.00	....	▬	1200	1200	1784	d.Granby..........d.	....	1600	1600	....
201.00	....	....	1515	1515	1961	d.Glenwood Springs d.	....	1250	1250	....
204.00	....	....	1720	1720	2106	d.Grand Junction..d.	....	1105	1105	....
217.00	....	....	2025	2025	2401	d.Helper..........d.	....	0725	0725	....
217.00	....	....	2230	2230	2510	d.Provo..........d.	....	0520	0520	....
217.00	....	....	0001	0001	2582	a. **Salt Lake City** d.	....	0430	0430	....
	....	....	....	0100	2582	d. **Salt Lake City** a.	....	0315	....	....
262.00	....	....	....	0413	2976	d.Elko..........d.	....	2123	....	....
262.00	....	....	....	0620	3229	d.Winnemucca.....d.	....	1918	....	....
262.00	....	NRPC	....	0955	3504	d.Sparks..........d.	....	1640	....	....
262.00	....	723	....	1006	3511	d.Reno..........d.	....	1605	....	....
262.00	....	C‡	....	1059	3566	d.Truckee..........d.	....	1508	....	....
262.00	....	◆©	....	1307	3672	d.Colfax..........d.	....	1257	....	....
	0630	0715	....	1413	3731	d.Roseville..........d.	....	1207	....	2020
262.00	0657	0742	....	1505	3757	a.**Sacramento**.......d.	....	1140	....	1947
262.00	0918	1003	....	1740	3895	a.*Oakland*..........d.	....	0900	....	1720
262.00	*0915b*	*1005b*	....	*1730b*	3907	a.*San Francisco*...d.	....	*0845b*	....	*1700b*

5/6– CALIFORNIA ZEPHYR–(sleeper)‡, entertainment car (‡), (coach) and ✕ Chicago(5/6)-Oakland and v.v.
35/36– DESERT WIND–(sleeper)‡, ✕ and (coach) Chicago(35/36)-Los Angeles and v.v.
723/6/731–CAPITOL–(coach) and 🍷 Roseville(723/731/726)-Oakland/San Jose and v.v.
P– ⑥⑦ Dec. 18-Apr. 3 only. a–②③⑤⑦. b–Connection by (coach-bus). c–①④⑥.
DRG– Denver and Rio Grande Western Railroad. Tel.: Denver 303 595 2230.
NRPC–National Railroad Passenger Corporation (AMTRAK). Tel.: Chicago 312 558 1075.

Table 402 PIKE'S PEAK — MPP

R.T. US $	396 1.435m.	km	C Q	C R	C T	C T	C R	C T	C T	C Q
0.00	Manitou Ω..........d.	0	0800	0920	1040	1200	1320	1440	1600	1720
◇	Summit (Pike's Peak) a.	14	0915	1035	1155	1315	1435	1555	1715	1835
	Summit (Pike's Peak) d.		1000	1120	1240	1400	1520	1640	1800	1920
17.00	Manitou Ω..........a.	28	1110	1230	1350	1510	1630	1750	1910	2030

Q– June 1-Aug. 31. R–May 1-Oct. 31.
T– June 1-Aug. 31, also, if required, May 15-31 and Sept. 1-Oct. 31.
◇– Round trip fares only; all services operate subject to weather conditions. Passengers should be at Manitou station 30 mins. before scheduled departure; advance reservations advised. Services will not operate if there are less than 20 passengers.
Ω– Manitou is *10* km from Colorado Springs.
MPP– Manitou and Pike's Peak Railway. Tel.: Manitou Springs 719 685 5401.

Table 404 DURANGO - SILVERTON — DSRR

R.T. US $ C cl.	SJE C🍷 T	1 Ca🍷 S	2 PC🍷 UH	3 C🍷 V	km	396 0.914m.	SJE C🍷 T	1 Ca🍷 S	2 PC🍷 UH	3 C🍷 V
0.00	0730	0830	0915	1010	0	d.**Durango** ℜ.......a.	1605	1725	1825	1910
42.70	1045	1145	1240	1330	81	a.**Silverton**..........d.	1245	1400	1500	1545

OW fares sold only if space is available at time of departure.
S– Apr. 27-Oct. 11. T–June 20-Aug. 17. U–May 16-Oct. 28.
V– June 5-Aug. 17 and Sept. 2-Oct. 1. a–Conveys (coach) and H May 2-22.
ℜ– A daily excursion service is available as far as Cascade Canyon (Durango dep. 1000).
DSRR–Durango and Silverton Railroad. Tel.: Durango 970 247 2733.

Table 405 LOS ANGELES - SAN DIEGO

CSTR NRPC

US $	570	572	772		574	774	776	578	780		782	584		786			396 1.435m.		769	771	573	775	577	779		781	791	583		585	587	
C cl.	1‡C‡	1‡C‡	1‡C‡		1‡C‡	1‡C‡	1‡C‡	1‡C‡	1‡C‡		1‡C‡	1‡C‡		1‡C‡					1‡C‡	1‡C‡	1‡C‡	1‡C‡	1‡C‡	1‡C‡		1‡C‡	1‡C‡	1‡C‡		1‡C‡	1‡C‡	
	🍷R	🍷R©	■Ⓐ		🍷RⒶ	■©	◆	🍷R	■Ⓐ		■©	⑥🍷R		■		km	↓ *NRPC* ↑		■©	■Ⓐ	Ⓐ🍷R	■	🍷R	◆		■Ⓐ	■©	🍷R		🍷R	🍷⑥R	
0.00	0635	0835	0835	....	1035	1035	1230	1430	1710	....	1715	1810	....	2135	....	*0*	d.**Los Angeles** Union a.	....	0858	0858	1025	1120	1320	1507	....	1730	1735	1925	....	2155	2335	....
4.00	ǀ	ǀ	ǀ	....	1051	1051	ǀ	ǀ	ǀ	....	ǀ	1826	....	ǀ	....		d.Commerce .... d.	....	ǀ	ǀ	1002	ǀ	1254	ǀ	....	ǀ	ǀ	1905	....	ǀ	ǀ	....
7.00	0709	0914	0914	....	1109	1109	1303	1504	1742	....	1747	1846	....	2208	....	*40*	d.Fullerton .... d.	....	0817	0822	0944	1036	1236	1426	....	1648	1654	1850	....	2116	2255	....
8.00	0718	0924	0924	....	1119	1119	1313	1514	ǀ	....	1756	1855	....	2217	....	*47*	d.Anaheim *(Disneyland)* d.	....	0808	ǀ	0935	1026	1226	1415	....	1638	1644	1840	....	2106	2245	....
9.00	0732	0934	0934	....	1129	1129	1323	1524	1757	....	1806	1903	....	2226	....	*57*	d.Santa Ana .... d.	....	0758	0805	0926	1018	1216	1406	....	1627	1634	1830	....	2056	2235	....
11.00	0744	0946	0946	....	1141	1141	1335	1536	ǀ	....	1818	1914	....	2237	....		d.Irvine .. .. d.	....	0746	ǀ	0914	1006	1204	1355	....	1615	1622	1814	....	2044	2223	....
13.00	0758	1003	1003	....	1158	1158	1357	1550	ǀ	....	1829	1927	....	2248	....		d.San Juan Capistrano d.	....	0731	ǀ	0900	0952	1150	1342	....	1602	1609	1800	....	2030	2209	....
14.00	ǀ	1015	1015	....	ǀ	ǀ	ǀ	ǀ	ǀ	....	ǀ	ǀ	....	ǀ	....		d.San Clemente ...... d.	....	ǀ	ǀ	ǀ	ǀ	ǀ	ǀ	....	1543	1558	ǀ	....	ǀ	ǀ	....
18.00	0829	1035	1035	....	1225	1225	1428	1621	1846	....	1859	2001	....	2318	....	*139*	d.Oceanside ℜ .... d.	....	0658	0717	0828	0922	1120	1312	....	1524	1539	1722	....	1952	2149	....
20.00	0842	1049	1049	....	1238	1238	1441	1634	1901	....	1912	2014	....	2331	....	*167*	d.Solana Beach ♁ℜ d.	....	0642	0704	0814	0906	1104	1258	....	1510	1525	1704	....	1934	2134	....
24.00	0925	1130	1130	....	1320	1320	1520	1715	1935	....	1958	2055	....	0015	....	*205*	a.**San Diego** ℜ....... d.	....	0600	0633	0730	0830	1030	1225	....	1435	1450	1630	....	1900	2100	....

776/9– SAN DIEGAN–1‡C‡ and 🍷 San Luis Obispo(**776/9**)-San Diego and v.v.
■– SAN DIEGAN–1‡C‡ and 🍷 San Diego-Santa Barbara and v.v.
R– SAN DIEGAN.
♁– for Del Mar.
ℜ– Local rail service *(CSTR)* operates Oceanside-San Diego and v.v.; **from Oceanside**: 0530Ⓐ, 0612Ⓐ, 0638Ⓐ, 0718Ⓐ, 0748Ⓐ, 1105Ⓐ, 1505Ⓐ, 1726Ⓐ, 1830⑥, 2140⑥, returning at 0641Ⓐ, 0950Ⓐ, 1350Ⓐ, 1620Ⓐ, 1650Ⓐ, 1720Ⓐ, 1750Ⓐ, 1835Ⓐ, 1950⑥, 2255⑥. Journey: 1 hour.
CSTR–Coaster. Tel.: Oceanside 619 967 2828.
NRPC–National Railroad Passenger Corporation (AMTRAK). Tel.: Los Angeles 213 624 0171

Table 406 ANTONITO - CHAMA

CTSR

R.T. US $ C cl.		C 🍷	C 🍷		km	396 0.914m. **end May-Oct. 15** ↓ ↑		C 🍷	C 🍷	
0.00	....	1000	....	....	*0*	d.**Antonito** ....a.	....	....	1700	....
◇32.00	....	1315	....	....	*61*	a. Osier ✕ .... d.	....	....	1415	....
	....	....	1330	....		d. Osier ✕ .... a.	....	1300	....	....
◇50.00	....	....	1630	....	*103*	a.**Chama** ....d.	....	1030	....	....

◇– Special inclusive round-trip facilities are available, one way by ####, one way by 🚌 and intermediately.
CTSR–Cumbres and Toltec Scenic Railroad. Tel.: Antonito 719 376 5483.

Table 408 DENVER - PORTLAND ♿

NRPC

US $ C cl.				25 S‡C‡ 🅁◆ ①③⑤	km	396 1.435m. ↓ ↑		26 S‡C‡ 🅁◆ ①③⑥		
0.00	....	....	....	1010	*0*	d.**Denver** Union....a.	....	1805	....	....
22.00	....	....	....	1215		d.Cheyenne ◇ .....d.	....	1445	....	....
30.00	....	....	....	1319		d.Laramie ....d.	....	1350	....	....
51.00	....	....	....	1509		d.Rawlins ....d.	....	1159	....	....
70.00	....	....	....	1649		d.Rock Springs.....d.	....	1019	....	....
	....	....	....	*2010*a		d. Salt Lake City .a.	....	*0700*a	....	....
98.00	....	....	....	2151		d.**Ogden** ....d.	....	0638	....	....
137.00	....	....	....	0024		d.Pocatello ....d.	....	0316	....	....
150.00	....	....	....	0205		d.Shoshone ....d.	....	0136	....	....
161.00	....	....	....	0424		d.Boise ....d.	....	2326	....	....
161.00	....	....	....	0523		d.Nampa *(Caldwell)*d.	....	2246	....	....
161.00	....	....	....	0653		d.Baker ....d.	....	1858	....	....
161.00	....	....	....	0801		d.La Grande ....d.	....	1758	....	....
161.00	....	....	....	1033		d.Pendleton ....d.	....	1540	....	....
161.00	....	....	....	1240		d.The Dalles ....d.	....	1322	....	....
161.00	....	....	....	1430		a.**Portland** ....d.	....	1140	....	....
161.00	....	....	....	1900		a.*Seattle* ....d.	....	0730	....	....

25– PIONEER–🛏‡, 🚃 and ✕ Chicago(5[35 on ④])-Denver(**25**)-Seattle.
26– PIONEER–🛏‡, 🚃 and ✕ Seattle(**26**)-Denver(**6**)-Chicago.
a– Connection by 🚌.
◇– Borie.
NRPC–National Railroad Passenger Corporation (AMTRAK). Tel.: Los Angeles 213 624 0171.

Table 409 SALT LAKE CITY - LOS ANGELES ♿

NRPC

US $ C cl.	3 S‡C‡ ◆ 🅁		35 S‡C‡ ◆🅁 ①③⑥		km	396 1.435m. ↓ ↑		36 S‡C‡ ◆🅁 ②④⑦		4 S‡C‡ ◆ 🅁
0.00	....	....	0100	....	*0*	d.**Salt Lake City** ..a.	....	0320	....	....
47.00	....	....	0407	....	*333*	d.Milford *(Cedar City)* d.	....	2320	....	....
57.00	....	....	0510	....		d.Caliente ....d.	....	2020	....	....
89.00	....	....	0820	....	*724*	d.**Las Vegas** ....d.	....	1750	....	....
111.00	0359	....	1140	....	*1020*	d.Barstow ....d.	....	1420	....	0021
111.00	0436	....	1215	....		d.Victorville...........d.	....	1325	....	2342
111.00	0546	....	1320	....	*1152*	d.San Bernardino .d.	....	1223	....	2237
111.00	0654s	....	1428s	....	*1227*	d.Fullerton ....d.	....	1120u	....	2135
111.00	0800	....	1535	....	*1247*	a.**Los Angeles** Union d.	....	1045	....	2055

3/4– SOUTHWEST CHIEF–🛏‡, entertainment car (‡), 🚃 and ✕ Chicago(**3/4**)-Los Angeles and v.v.
35/36– THE DESERT WIND–Entertainment car (‡) Salt Lake City(**35/36**)-Los Angeles and v.v; 🛏‡, ✕ and 🚃 Chicago(**35/36**)-Los Angeles and v.v.
NRPC–National Railroad Passenger Corporation (AMTRAK). Tel.: Los Angeles 213 624 0171.

Table 411 396 LOOKOUT MOUNTAIN

🚞 *LMIR*

🚞 service (1.600m.) Chattanooga-Lookout Mountain and v.v. *3* km. Journey: 8 mins. Fare: US $: 10.00.
From Chattanooga St Elmo Avenue: 0900 and frequent to 1600 winter/1800 summer.
From Lookout Mountain: 0930 and frequent to 1630 winter/1830 summer.
LMIR– Lookout Mountain Incline Railway. Tel.: Chattanooga 615 821 4224.

Table 412 396 PALM SPRINGS

🚡 *MSJ*

🚡 service Palm Springs-Mount San Jacinto and v.v. *4* km. Journey: 15 mins. Fare: R.T. US $:16.95.
From Palm Springs: 0800©/1000Ⓐ-2000.Ω.
From Mount San Jacinto: 0830©/1030Ⓐ-2145..Ω.
Ω– No service first ① in August for two weeks.
MSJ– Palm Springs Aerial Tramway. Tel.: Palm Springs 619 325 1449.

Table 414 EL PASO - LOS ANGELES ♿

NRPC

US $ C cl.			1 S‡C‡ ◆🅁 ②④⑦		km	396 1.435m. ↓ ↑			2 S‡C‡ ◆🅁 ②⑤⑦	
164.00	....	....	1245a	....	*0*	d.*New Orleans* .....a.	....	....	1935b	....
0.00	....	....	1310	....	*1895*	d.**El Paso**.............a.	....	....	1640	....
29.50	....	....	1525	....	*2134*	d.Lordsburg..........d.	....	....	1349	....
67.00	....	....	1620	....	*2304*	d.Benson...............d.	....	....	1053	....
78.00	....	....	1720	....	*2395*	d.Tucson ....d.	....	....	0935	....
91.00	....	....	2105	....	*2590*	d.**Phoenix**............d.	....	....	0708	....
120.00	....	....	0013	....	*2869*	d.Yuma ....d.	....	....	0258	....
154.00	....	....	0204	....	*3065*	d.Indio ....d.	....	....	0109	....
154.00	....	....	0401	....	*3220*	d.Pomona.............d.	....	....	2314	....
154.00	....	....	0615	....	*3271*	a.**Los Angeles** Union d.	....	....	2230	....

1/2– SUNSET LIMITED–🛏‡, entertainment car (‡), 🚃 and ✕ Miami(**1/2**)-Los Angeles and v.v.. Also, as TEXAS EAGLE, runs on ②⑤⑦ from Chicago to Los Angeles, and on ②⑤⑦ from Los Angeles to St Louis and Chicago. See Table **374**.
a– ①③⑥. **b**–Next day.
NRPC–National Railroad Passenger Corporation (AMTRAK). Tel.: Los Angeles 213 624 0171.

Table 415 WINE TRAIN

NVR

R.T. US $ C cl.	C⊗ ©	C✕ □	C✕ ©	C✕ ②-⑤	km	396 1.435m. ↓	
0.00	0855	1130	1800	1830	*0*	d.**Napa**	Passengers board about 30 mins. earlier
	ǀ	ǀ	ǀ	ǀ		d.**St. Helena**...........	Passengers remain on train
70.00	1130	1430	2100	2130		a.**Napa**	Leave train on arrival

□– Runs 1 hour later on ©.
NVR– Napa Valley Railroad. Tel.: Napa 707 253 2111.

Table 418 SPOKANE - SEATTLE ♿

NRPC

US $ C cl.			7 S‡C‡ ◆🅁 ①③⑤⑦	27 S‡C‡ ◆🅁 ①③⑤⑦	km	396 1.435m. ↓ ↑			8 S‡C‡ ◆🅁 ②④⑤⑦	28 S‡C‡ ◆🅁 ②④⑤⑦
238.00	....	....	1515a	1515a	*0*	d.*Chicago* ....a.	....	....	1620	1620
238.00	....	....	2355a	2355a	*673*	d.*Minneapolis/St Paul* a.	....	....	0740	0740
0.00	....	....	0240	0255	*3034*	d.**Spokane** ....a.	....	....	0053	0036
39.00	....	....	0555	ǀ	*3268*	d.Wenatchee ....d.	....	....	2110	ǀ
64.00	....	....	0901	ǀ	*3412*	d.Everett................d.	....	....	1803	ǀ
73.00	....	....	1030	ǀ	*3671*	a.**Seattle** ....d.	....	....	1650	ǀ
31.00	....	....	....	0541	*3528*	d. Pasco...............d.	....	....	....	2130
73.00	....	....	....	0929	*3627*	d. Vancouver.......d.	....	....	....	1739
73.00	....	....	....	1015	*3643*	a. **Portland** ....d.	....	....	....	1710

7/8– EMPIRE BUILDER–🛏‡, 🚃 and ✕ Chicago(**7/8**)-Seattle and v.v.
27/28– EMPIRE BUILDER–🛏‡, entertainment car‡ and 🚃 Chicago(**7/8**)-Spokane(**27/28**)-Portland and v.v.; ⊗ Spokane(**27/28**)-Portland and v.v.
a– ①③⑤⑥.
NRPC–National Railroad Passenger Corporation (AMTRAK). Tel.: Chicago 312 558 1075.

Table 419 396 TIJUANA

🚋 *SDT*

🚋 service San Diego-San Ysidro 🛃 (for Tijuana) and v.v. *16* km. Journey: 45 mins. Fare: US $: 2.25.
From San Diego American Plaza: 0013, 0043⑦, 0108⑦, 0208⑦, 0308⑦, 0413⑦, 0458Ⓐ, 0508Ⓐ, 0513©, 0518Ⓐ, 0528Ⓐ, 0538Ⓐ, 0543© and frequent 2313, 2343.
From San Ysidro: 0002, 0032, 0102, 0132⑦, 0202⑦, 0302⑦, 0402⑦, 0447Ⓐ, 0502, 0517Ⓐ, 0532, 0545Ⓐ and frequent to 2302, 2332.
SDT– San Diego Trolley. Tel.: San Diego 595 4949.

Table 420 SAN JOSE - OAKLAND - BAKERSFIELD/SACRAMENTO

NRPC

$	712	722	732		6	714	716	724	726		718	728	14	734			396 1.435m	721	11	731	723	733	711	725	713	5	715	735	727	717		
.	1‡C‡	C‡	C‡		S‡C‡	C‡	C‡	C‡	C‡		C‡	C‡	S‡C‡	C‡				C‡	S‡C‡	C‡	C‡	C‡	C‡	C‡	C‡	S‡C‡	C‡	C‡	C‡	1‡C‡		
	◆	✉🍷	✉🍷		◆®	◆	◆	✉	◆		◆	✉	◆♫	✉🍷				✉🍷	◆♫	◆🍷	◆🍷	✉🍷	◆	✉◆	◆®	◆	◆🍷	✉🍷	✉🍷	◆		
	🍷	Ⓑ	Ⓑ		①③⑤⑥	🍷	🍷	🍷			🍷	🍷	®	Ⓒ		km	↓ ↑	Ⓐ	®	Ⓒ	Ⓐ	Ⓒ	🍷	🍷	🍷	②④⑤⑦	🍷	⑤⑥⑦	①-④	🍷		
	....	....	....	....	....	....	....	*1000b*	*1425b*	....	....	....	....	....	....		d. Monterey .... a.	....	....	*1250b*	....	....	....	....	....	....	....	....	....	....	....	....
	....	....	....	....	....	....	....	*1035b*	*1500b*	....	....	....	....	....	....		d. Salinas .... a.	....	....	*1215b*	....	....	....	....	....	....	....	....	....	....	....	....
	....	*0545b*	0620	....	....	....	....	1300	*1540b*	....	....	1735	1915	2145	....	*71*	d.**San Jose** .... a.	*0925b*	1030	1027	1113	*1225b*	....	1635	....	....	....	2115	*2140b*	....	....	....
	0610	*0700*	*0700*	....	*0845*	*1020*	*1340*	*1340*	*1700*	....	*1710*	*1810*	*2030*	|	....		d. San Francisco Ferry Terminal a.	*0750*	*0855*	*0915s*	*1005*	*1040*	*1110*	*1520*	*1600*	*1730*	*1815*	*2000*	*2000*	*2300*	....	....
0	0630	0715	0715	....	0900	|	|	1355	1720	....	1730	1830	2025	2245	....	*0*	d.Oakland Jack London Square. a.	0800	0920	0918	1003	1100	1125	1523	|	1740	|	2003	2015	2310	....	....
	0652	0737	0737	....	0930	1055	1410	1417	1742	....	1752	1852	2115	....	....		d.Emeryville .... a.	0728	0830	0858	0943	1028	1049	1503	1535	1655s	1750	1943	1944	2244	....	....
5	0706	0750	0751	....	0941	1109	1424	1430	1755	....	1806	1905	|	....	....	*27*	d.Richmond .... d.	0714	|	0844	0929	1014	1035	1449	1507	1640s	1728	1929	1929	2230	....	....
0	0739	0821	0821	....	1013	1141	1456	1501	1826	....	1838	1936	2153	....	....	*46*	d.Martinez .... d.	0645	0745	0815	0900	0945	1006	1420	1438	1611s	1659	1900	1900	2201	....	....
	|	0843	0843	....	1035	|	|	1523	1848	....	|	1958	|	....	....	*74*	d. Suisun Fairfield ▶d.	0620	|	0750	0835	0920	|	1355	|	1549s	|	1835	1835	|	....	....
	|	0913	0913	....	1103	|	|	1553	1918	....	|	2028	2243	....	....	*117*	d. Davis .... d.	0550	0650	0720	0805	0850	|	1325	|	1525s	|	1805	1805	|	....	....
	|	0945	0945	....	1140	|	|	1630	1944	....	|	2105	2337	....	....	*138*	a. **Sacramento** .... d.	0530	0630	0700	0745	0830	|	1305	|	1505	|	1745	1745	|	....	....
0	0841	....	....	....	....	1242	1600	....	....	....	1939	....	....	....	....	*125*	d Stockton .... d.	....	....	....	....	....	0907	....	1338	....	1556	....	....	2100	....	....
0	0909	....	....	....	....	1310	1627	....	....	....	2005	....	....	....	....	*166*	d Riverbank *(Modesto)* d.	....	....	....	....	....	0834	....	1307	....	1527	....	....	2028	....	....
0	0949	....	....	....	....	1352	1707	....	....	....	2049	....	....	....	....	*230*	d.Merced .... d.	....	....	....	....	....	0756	....	1229	....	1448	....	....	1945	....	....
	1245b	....	....	....	....	*1845b*	|	....	....	....	|	....	....	....	....		a. Yosemite Lodge. d.	....	....	....	....	....	|	....	*0900b*	....	|	....	....	*1530b*	....	....
	1020	....	....	....	....	1427	1738	....	....	....	2120	....	....	....	....		d.Madera .... d.	....	....	....	....	....	0722	....	1156	....	1411	....	....	1912	....	....
0	1045	....	....	....	....	1452	1804	....	....	....	2145	....	....	....	....	*323*	d.Fresno .... d.	....	....	....	....	....	0700	....	1135	....	1350	....	....	1850	....	....
0	1121	....	....	....	....	1525	1839	....	....	....	2219	....	....	....	....	*362*	d.Hanford .... d.	....	....	....	....	....	0620	....	1055	....	1312	....	....	1808	....	....
0	1300	....	....	....	....	1700	2015	....	....	....	2355	....	....	....	....	*501*	a.**Bakersfield** .... d.	....	....	....	....	....	0500	....	0930	....	1145	....	....	1640	....	....
	1530	....	....	....	....	*1930*	*2245*	....	....	....	*0235*	....	....	....	....	*686*	a.*Los Angeles* b...... d.	....	....	....	....	....	*0140*	....	*0700*	....	*0915*	....	....	*1410*	....	....

- CALIFORNIA ZEPHYR–🛏‡, entertainment car (‡), 🚃 and ✕ Chicago(**5/6**)-Oakland and v.v.®.
14– COAST STARLIGHT–🛏‡, entertainment car (‡), 🚃 and ✕ Seattle(**11/14**)-Los Angeles and v.v.
-8– SAN JOAQUIN.
/31–CAPITOL–🚃 and 🍷 Roseville(**723/31**)-San Jose.
– CAPITOL–🚃 and 🍷 Oakland(**726**)-Roseville.
CAPITOL.
Connection by 🚌 at Emeryville. b–Connection by 🚌.
From a date to be announced, this train may be altered to run Vancouver *(Canada)*-Los Angeles and v.v.

▶– For Travis Air Force Base.
NRPC–National Railroad Passenger Corporation (AMTRAK). Tel.: Los Angeles 213 624 0171.

Table 421 396 LOS ANGELES LOCAL SERVICES

🚎 🚌 *MTL SCRTD*

🚎 (C‡ cl. only, 1.435m.) and 🚌 services operate in the Los Angeles area as follows:

mbra ≠ *(SCRTD)* (❖ km, US $: ❖). From Los Angeles: ❖, returning at ❖. Journey: ❖.

eim ⅇ ● *(MTL)* (47 km, US $: ❖). From Los Angeles Union: 1539Ⓐ, 1635Ⓐ, 1737Ⓐ, 1829Ⓐ, returning at 0551Ⓐ, 0632Ⓐ, 729Ⓐ, 0753Ⓐ. Journey: 45 mins. Also by ≠ *(SCRTD)* from Los Angeles: ❖, returning at ❖. Journey: ❖.

rly Hills ≠ *(SCRTD)* (❖ km, US $: ❖). From Los Angeles: ❖, returning at ❖. Journey: ❖.

a Park ≠ *(SCRTD)* (❖ km, US $: ❖). From Los Angeles: ❖, returning at ❖. Journey: ❖.

ank ● *(MTL)* (❖ km, US $: 3.50). From Los Angeles Union: 0632Ⓐ, 0646Ⓐ, 0730Ⓐ, 0802Ⓐ, 0830Ⓐ, 0851Ⓐ, 1305Ⓐ, 1356Ⓐ, 545Ⓐ, 1610Ⓐ, 1626Ⓐ, 1657Ⓐ, 1705Ⓐ, 1733Ⓐ, 1741Ⓐ, 1814Ⓐ, 1824Ⓐ, 2026Ⓐ, returning at 0558Ⓐ, 0603Ⓐ, 0643Ⓐ, 0652Ⓐ, 722Ⓐ, 0733Ⓐ, 0753Ⓐ, 0812Ⓐ, 0822Ⓐ, 0922Ⓐ, 1011Ⓐ, 1537Ⓐ, 1556Ⓐ, 1653Ⓐ, 1740Ⓐ, 1954Ⓐ. Journey: 25 mins. Also ≠ *(SCRTD)* from Los Angeles: ❖, returning at ❖.

arillo ● *(MTL)* (❖ km, US $: 7.50). From Los Angeles Union: 1626Ⓐ, 1705Ⓐ, returning at 0539Ⓐ, 0629Ⓐ. Journey: 1¼ hours.

mont ● *(MTL)* (❖ km, US $: 5.50). From Los Angeles Union: 0618Ⓐ, 0854Ⓐ, 0910⑥, 1113Ⓐ, 1228⑥, 1302Ⓐ, 1520Ⓐ, 620Ⓐ, 1625⑥, 1651Ⓐ, 1723Ⓐ, 1751Ⓐ, 1842Ⓐ, 1923Ⓐ, 1945⑥, 2045Ⓐ, returning at 0457Ⓐ, 0547Ⓐ, 0624Ⓐ, 0653Ⓐ, 0734Ⓐ, 758⑥, 0802Ⓐ, 1106Ⓐ, 1125⑥, 1357Ⓐ, 1510Ⓐ, 1520⑥, 1744Ⓐ, 1840⑥, 1940Ⓐ. Journey: 50 mins.

merce ● *(MTL)* (❖ km, US $: 3.50). From Los Angeles Union: 1635Ⓐ, 1737Ⓐ, returning at 0657Ⓐ. Journey: 20 mins.

na ≠ *(SCRTD)* (❖ km, US $: ❖). From Los Angeles: ❖, returning at ❖. Journey: ❖.

a ● *(MTL)* (❖ km, US $: 4.50). From Los Angeles Union: 0854Ⓐ, 0910⑥, 1113Ⓐ, 1228⑥, 1302Ⓐ, 1520Ⓐ, 1620Ⓐ, 1625⑥, 651Ⓐ, 1723Ⓐ, 1751Ⓐ, 1842Ⓐ, 1923Ⓐ, 1945⑥, 2045Ⓐ, returning at 0511Ⓐ, 0601Ⓐ, 0640Ⓐ, 0708Ⓐ, 0747Ⓐ, 0812⑥, 0816Ⓐ, 21Ⓐ, 1139⑥, 1411Ⓐ, 1534⑥, 1854⑥. Journey: 40 mins.

onte ● *(MTL)* (25 km, US $: 4.50). From Los Angeles Union: 0618Ⓐ, 0854Ⓐ, 0910⑥, 1113Ⓐ, 1228⑥, 1302Ⓐ, 1520Ⓐ, 1620Ⓐ, 625⑥, 1651Ⓐ, 1723Ⓐ, 1751Ⓐ, 1842Ⓐ, 1923Ⓐ, 1945⑥, 2045Ⓐ, returning at 0524Ⓐ, 0614Ⓐ, 0653Ⓐ, 0721Ⓐ, 0800Ⓐ, 0825⑥, 28Ⓐ, 1134Ⓐ, 1152⑥, 1424Ⓐ, 1539Ⓐ, 1547⑥, 1648Ⓐ, 1809Ⓐ, 1907⑥, 2011Ⓐ. Journey: 25 mins. Also ≠ *(SCRTD)* from Los Angeles: ❖, returning at ❖. Journey: ❖.

rton ● *(MTL)* (40 km, US $: 4.50). From Los Angeles Union: 1539Ⓐ, 1635Ⓐ, 1737Ⓐ, 1829Ⓐ, returning at 0559Ⓐ, 0640Ⓐ, 738Ⓐ, 0801Ⓐ. Journey: 40 mins.

dale ● *(MTL)* (9 km, US $: 3.50). From Los Angeles Union: 0632Ⓐ, 0646Ⓐ, 0730Ⓐ, 0802Ⓐ, 0830Ⓐ, 0851Ⓐ, 1305Ⓐ, 1356Ⓐ, 545Ⓐ, 1610Ⓐ, 1626Ⓐ, 1657Ⓐ, 1705Ⓐ, 1733Ⓐ, 1741Ⓐ, 1814Ⓐ, 1824Ⓐ, 2026Ⓐ, returning at 0604Ⓐ, 0609Ⓐ, 0649Ⓐ, 0658Ⓐ, 728Ⓐ, 0739Ⓐ, 0759Ⓐ, 0818Ⓐ, 0828Ⓐ, 0928Ⓐ, 1017Ⓐ, 1544Ⓐ, 1602Ⓐ, 1700Ⓐ, 1724Ⓐ, 1746Ⓐ, 2000Ⓐ. Journey: 15 mins.

wood ≠ *(SCRTD)* (24 km, US $: ❖). From Los Angeles: ❖, returning at ❖. Journey: ❖.

e ● *(MTL)* (❖ km, US $: 6.50). From Los Angeles Union: 1539Ⓐ, 1635Ⓐ, 1737Ⓐ, 1829Ⓐ, returning at 0532Ⓐ, 0613Ⓐ, 0709Ⓐ, 733Ⓐ. Journey: 1¼ hours.

aster ● *(MTL)* (❖ km, US $: 6.50). From Los Angeles Union: 1545Ⓐ, 1657Ⓐ, 1733Ⓐ, 2026Ⓐ, returning at 0437Ⓐ, 0531Ⓐ, 01Ⓐ, 0632Ⓐ. Journey: 2 hours.

Beach ≡ *(SCRTD)* (35 km, US $: 1.50). From Los Angeles 7th Street: 0500 and frequent to 2240, returning from Long each Mall at 0500 and frequent to 2120. Journey: 1 hour. Also ≠ from Los Angeles and Long Beach frequent through the day d night.

clair ● *(MTL)* (❖ km, US $: 5.50). From Los Angeles Union: 0854Ⓐ, 0910⑥, 1113Ⓐ, 1228⑥, 1302Ⓐ, 1520Ⓐ, 1620Ⓐ, 1625⑥, 51Ⓐ, 1723Ⓐ, 1751Ⓐ, 1842Ⓐ, 1923Ⓐ, 1945⑥, 2045Ⓐ, returning at 0454Ⓐ, 0544Ⓐ, 0620Ⓐ, 0650Ⓐ, 0730Ⓐ, 0754⑥, 0759Ⓐ, 02Ⓐ, 1121⑥, 1507Ⓐ, 1516⑥, 1618Ⓐ, 1836Ⓐ. Journey: 50 mins.

ort Beach ≠ *(SCRTD)* (❖ km, US $: ❖). From Los Angeles: ❖, returning at ❖. Journey: ❖.

Hollywood ≠ *(SCRTD)* (❖ km, US $: ❖). From Los Angeles: ❖, returning at ❖. Journey: ❖.

dena ≠ *(SCRTD)* (❖ km, US $: ❖). From Los Angeles: ❖, returning at ❖. Journey: ❖.

ona ● *(MTL)* (❖ km, US $: 5.50). From Los Angeles Union: 0618Ⓐ, 0854Ⓐ, 0910⑥, 1113Ⓐ, 1228⑥, 1302Ⓐ, 1520Ⓐ, 1620Ⓐ, 625⑥, 1651Ⓐ, 1723Ⓐ, 1751Ⓐ, 1842Ⓐ, 1923Ⓐ, 1945⑥, 2045Ⓐ, returning at 0501Ⓐ, 0551Ⓐ, 0628Ⓐ, 0657Ⓐ, 0737Ⓐ, 0802⑥, 05Ⓐ, 1110Ⓐ, 1129⑥, 1401Ⓐ, 1514Ⓐ, 1524⑥, 1844⑥. Journey: 50 mins. Also ≠ *(SCRTD)* from Los Angeles: ❖, returning at . Journey: ❖.

● *(MTL)* (❖ km, US $: 7.50). From Los Angeles Union: 0854Ⓐ, 0910⑥, 1123Ⓐ, 1228⑥, 1302Ⓐ, 1625⑥, 1651Ⓐ, 1723Ⓐ, 751Ⓐ, 1842Ⓐ, 1923Ⓐ, 1945⑥, 2045Ⓐ, returning at 0430Ⓐ, 0519Ⓐ, 0555Ⓐ, 0625Ⓐ, 0703Ⓐ, 0730⑥, 1038Ⓐ, 1057⑥, 1329Ⓐ, 43Ⓐ, 1452⑥, 1812⑥, 1835Ⓐ. Journey: 1¼ hours.

side ● *(MTL)* (❖ km, US $: 7.50). From Los Angeles Union: 0555Ⓐ, 1320Ⓐ, 1614Ⓐ, 1655Ⓐ, 1730Ⓐ, 1835Ⓐ, returning at 00Ⓐ, 0610Ⓐ, 0640Ⓐ, 0735Ⓐ, 1447Ⓐ, 1729Ⓐ. Journey: 1¼ hours.

San Bernardino ● *(MTL)* (95 km, US $: 7.50). From Los Angeles Union: 0854Ⓐ, 0910⑥, 1113Ⓐ, 1228⑥, 1302Ⓐ, 1625⑥, 1651Ⓐ, 1723Ⓐ, 1751Ⓐ, 1842Ⓐ, 1923Ⓐ, 1945⑥, 2045Ⓐ, returning at 0422Ⓐ, 0511Ⓐ, 0547Ⓐ, 0617Ⓐ, 0655Ⓐ, 0723⑥, 1030Ⓐ, 1050⑥, 1321Ⓐ, 1435Ⓐ, 1445⑥, 1805⑥, 1828Ⓐ. Journey: 1½ hours.

San Juan Capistrano ● *(MTL)* (❖ km, US $: 7.50). From Los Angeles Union: 1539Ⓐ, 1635Ⓐ, 1737Ⓐ, 1829Ⓐ, returning at 0520Ⓐ, 0600Ⓐ, 0721Ⓐ. Journey: 1¼ hours.

San Pedro ≠ *(SCRTD)* (❖ km, US $: ❖). From Los Angeles: ❖, returning at ❖. Journey: ❖.

Santa Ana ● *(MTL)* (57 km, US $: 6.50). From Los Angeles Union: 1539Ⓐ, 1635Ⓐ, 1737Ⓐ, 1829Ⓐ, returning at 0542Ⓐ, 0623Ⓐ, 0720Ⓐ, 0744Ⓐ. Journey: 55 mins.

Santa Clarita ● *(MTL)* (❖ km, US $: 5.50). From Los Angeles Union: 0632Ⓐ, 0730Ⓐ, 1356Ⓐ, 1545Ⓐ, 1610Ⓐ, 1657Ⓐ, 1733Ⓐ, 1814Ⓐ, 2026Ⓐ, returning at 0529Ⓐ, 0623Ⓐ, 0653Ⓐ, 0724Ⓐ, 0753Ⓐ, 0853Ⓐ, 1526Ⓐ, 1709Ⓐ, 1925Ⓐ. Journey: 50 mins.

Simi Valley ● *(MTL)* (❖ km, US $: 5.50). From Los Angeles Union: 1305Ⓐ, 1626Ⓐ, 1705Ⓐ, 1741Ⓐ, 1824Ⓐ, returning at 0525Ⓐ, 0605Ⓐ, 0655Ⓐ, 0735Ⓐ, 1452Ⓐ. Journey: 70 mins.

Van Nuys ● *(MTL)* (❖ km, US $: 4.50), From Los Angeles Union: 0851Ⓐ, 1305Ⓐ, 1626Ⓐ, 1705Ⓐ, 1741Ⓐ, 1824Ⓐ, returning at 0551Ⓐ, 0631Ⓐ, 0721Ⓐ, 0800Ⓐ, 0959Ⓐ, 1525Ⓐ. Journey: 30 mins.

By ####. ⅇ–For Disneyland.
By 🚎. ≠–By 🚌.

MTL– Metrolink (Southern California Regional Rail Authority). Tel.: Los Angeles ❖.

SCRTD–Los Angeles County Metropolitan Transportation Authority. Tel.: Los Angeles ❖.

Table 423 SEATTLE - PORTLAND ♿

NRPC

$	26	11	753	751									396 1.435m.	750	25	14	752							
d.	S‡C‡	S‡C‡	C‡	C‡										C‡	S‡C‡	S‡C‡	C‡							
	◆®	◆ℜ	◆®	◆®										◆®	◆®	◆ℜ	◆®							
	①③⑥	®	🍷	🍷								km	↓ ↑	🍷	②④⑥	®	🍷							
	....	*0600a*	*0730a*	*1230a*	....	....	....	....	....	....	....		d. *Vancouver Canada* .a.	*1645a*	....	*2350a*	....	....	....	....	....	....	....	....
	....	|	|	*1030a*	....	....	....	....	....	....	....		d.*Spokane* ....a.	*1835a*	....	|	....	....	....	....	....	....	....	....
	....	|	|	*1415a*	....	....	....	....	....	....	....		d.*Ellensburg* ....a.	*1510a*	....	|	....	....	....	....	....	....	....	....
00	0730	0945	1130	1710	....	....	....	....	....	....	....	*0*	d.**Seattle** King Street....a.	1245	1900	2010	2150	....	....	....	....	....	....	....
00	0826	1042	1220	1805	....	....	....	....	....	....	....	*64*	d.Tacoma ....d.	1139	1758	1847	2049	....	....	....	....	....	....	....
50	0908	1129	1302	1847	....	....	....	....	....	....	....	*121*	d.Olympia ....d.	1053	1712	1758	2003	....	....	....	....	....	....	....
50	0930	1153	1323	1908	....	....	....	....	....	....	....	*151*	d.Centralia.....................d.	1033	1651	1735	1943	....	....	....	....	....	....	....
00	1015	1240	1407	1952	....	....	....	....	....	....	....	*217*	d.Kelso Longview ....d.	0950	1607	1647	1900	....	....	....	....	....	....	....
50	1056	1324	1445	2030	....	....	....	....	....	....	....	*280*	d.Vancouver *WA* ....d.	0911	1527	1604	1821	....	....	....	....	....	....	....
50	1125	1410	1525	2105	....	....	....	....	....	....	....	*294*	a.**Portland** ....d.	0850	1505	1540	1800	....	....	....	....	....	....	....
00	1805b	|	....	....	....	....	....	....	....	....	....	*1738*	a. *Denver* ....d.	....	1010c	|	....	....	....	....	....	....	....	....
00	....	0920	....	....	....	....	....	....	....	....	....	*1482*	a.*Oakland* ....d.	....	....	2025	....	....	....	....	....	....	....	....
00	....	2115	....	....	....	....	....	....	....	....	....	*2233*	a.*Los Angeles* ....d.	....	....	0930	....	....	....	....	....	....	....	....

4– COAST STARLIGHT–🛏‡, entertainment car (‡), 🚃 and ✕ Seattle(**11/14**)-Los Angeles and v.v.
PIONEER–🛏‡, 🚃 and ✕ Chicago(**5**[**35** on ④])-Denver(**25**)-Seattle.
PIONEER–🛏‡, 🚃 and ✕ Seattle(**26**)-Denver(**6**)-Chicago.
1– CASCADIA–🚃 and 🍷 Eugene(**750/1**)-Seattle and v.v.
3– MOUNT ADAMS.

a– Connection by 🚌. b–Next day. c–①③⑤.
ℜ– From a date to be announced, this train may be altered to run Vancouver *(Canada)*-Los Angeles and v.v.
NRPC–National Railroad Passenger Corporation (AMTRAK). Tel.: Los Angeles 213 624 0171.

Table 425 SAN FRANCISCO - LOS ANGELES ♿ #### *NRPC*

US $	772		774	776			782	780	11	786			396 1.435m.		771	769	14	775		779		781	791	
C cl.	1‡C‡		1‡C‡	1‡C‡			1‡C‡	1‡C‡	S‡C‡	1‡C‡					1‡C‡	1‡C‡	S‡C‡	1‡C‡		1‡C‡		1‡C‡	1‡C‡	
	▣Ⓐ		▣Ⓒ	◆			▣Ⓒ	▣Ⓐ	◆🛏	▣					▣Ⓐ	▣Ⓒ	◆𝔊	▣		◆		▣Ⓐ	▣Ⓒ	
									[R]			km	↓ ↑				[R]							
	....	....	....	....	....	....	....	....	0945	....	....	*0*	d.*Seattle*........a.	....	....	....	2010	....	....	....	....	....	....	....
	....	....	....	....	....	....	....	....	1430	....	....	*294*	d.*Portland*........a.	....	....	....	1515	....	....	....	....	....	....	....
	....	....	....	....	....	....	....	....	*0850*	....	....	*1471*	d.*San Francisco Ferry Terminal* ⊠ .a.	....	....	....	*2045*	....	....	....	....	....	....	....
0.00	....	....	....	....	....	....	....	....	0935	....	....	*1482*	d.*Oakland*........a.	....	....	....	2010	....	....	....	....	....	....	....
13.00	....	....	....	....	....	....	....	....	1030	....	....	*1553*	d.**San Jose**........a.	....	....	....	1915	....	....	....	....	....	....	....
24.50	....	....	....	....	....	....	....	....	1201	....	....	*1660*	d.Salinas........d.	....	....	....	1740	....	....	....	....	....	....	....
48.50	....	....	....	0715	....	....	....	....	1530	....	....	*1876*	d.San Luis Obispo........d.	....	....	....	1450	....	....	2048	....	....	....	....
65.00	0630	....	0745	0940	....	....	1415	1415	1815	1850	....	*2068*	d.Santa Barbara........d.	....	1136	1151	1200	1415	....	1803	....	2030	2040	....
	0636	....	0821	1015	....	....	│	│	│	1926	....		d.Ventura........d.	....	│	1102	│	1331	....	1711	....	1942	1949	....
65.00	0650	....	0835	1027	....	....	1502	1502	1905	1945	....	*2127*	d.Oxnard........d.	....	1036	1048	1101	1317	....	1657	....	1928	1935	....
	0756	....	0943	1147	....	....	1608	1608	│	2053	....		d.Burbank Airport........d.	....	0932	0939	│	1159	....	1545	....	1813	1821	....
66.00	│	....	0958	1155	....	....	1620	1620	2100s	2105	....	*2224*	d.Glendale........d.	....	0922	0928	0948	1148	....	1534	....	│	1809	....
66.00	0820	....	1015	1210	....	....	1655	1655	2115	2125	....	*2233*	a.**Los Angeles** Union ..d.	....	0910	0915	0930	1135	....	1520	....	1750	1755	....

11/14– COAST STARLIGHT–🛏‡, entertainment car (‡), 🚃 and ✕ Seattle(**11/14**)-Los Angeles and v.v.
776/9– SAN DIEGAN–🚃 and 🍷 San Luis Obispo(**776/9**)-San Diego and v.v.
▣– SAN DIEGAN–🚃 and 🍷 Santa Barbara-San Diego and v.v.
⊠– Connection by 🚌.
𝔊– Froma date to be announced, this train may be altered to run Vancouver *(Canada)*-Los Angeles and v.v.
NRPC–National Railroad Passenger Corporation (AMTRAK). Tel.: Los Angeles 213 624 01

Table 427 PORTLAND - OAKLAND ♿ #### *NRPC*

US $			11	751		396 1.435m.	750		14	
C cl.			S‡C‡	C‡			C‡		S‡C‡	
			◆𝔗[R]	◆[R]	km	↓ ↑	◆[R]		◆𝔗[R]	
	....	....	0945	1710	*0*	d.*Seattle*........a.	1245	....	2010	....
0.00	....	....	1430	2110	*294*	d.**Portland**........a.	0845	....	1515	....
9.75	....	....	1545	2221	*379*	d.Salem........d.	0727	....	1315	....
21.00	....	....	1707	2345	*493*	d.Eugene........d.	0610	....	1155	....
56.00	....	....	2207	....	*809*	d.Klamath Falls ....d.	....	....	0737	....
73.00	....	....	0031	....	*978*	d.Dunsmuir........d.	....	....	0434	....
80.00	....	....	0219	....	*1070*	d.Redding........d.	....	....	0247	....
85.00	....	....	0333	....	*1189*	d.Chico........d.	....	....	0124	....
91.00	....	....	0416	....	*1260*	d.Marysville........d.	....	....	0041	....
94.00	....	....	0630	....	*1343*	a.**Sacramento**......d.	....	....	2337	....
102.00	....	....	0920	....	*1482*	a.*Oakland*........d.	....	....	2025	....
102.00	....	....	*0855*	....	*1493*	a.*San Francisco Ferry Terminal* ⊠ d.	....	....	*2030*	....
146.00	....	....	2115	....	*2233*	a.*Los Angeles*......d.	....	....	0930	....

11/14–COAST STARLIGHT–🛏‡, entertainment car (‡), 🚃 and ✕ Seattle(**11/14**)-Los Angeles and v.v. **750/1**–CASCADIA–🚃 and 🍷 Eugene(**750/1**)-Seattle and v.v. ⊠–Connection by 🚌. 𝔗–Ata date to be announced, this train may be altered to run Vancouver *(Canada)*-Los Angeles and v.v. *NRPC*–National Railroad Passenger Corporation (AMTRAK). Tel.: Los Angeles 213 624 0171.

Table 428 FORT BRAGG - WILLITS #### *CWR*

R.T. US $ C cl.	11			9		396 1.435m.	8	10	10	
	🚃			🚃			🚃	🚃	🚃	
	C			C◆			C◆	C◆	C◆	
	◆☆			Q■	km	↓ ↑	Q■	P☆	Q	
0.00	0920	....	....	1340	*0*	d.**Fort Bragg**........a.	1230	1530	1545	....
26.00	1130	....	....	1725	*65*	a.**Willits**........d.	0900	1320	1325	....

8/11– SKUNK.
P– Jan. 2-June 9 and Sept. 10-Dec. 31.
Q– June 10-Sept. 9.
☆– Steam on certain ⑥ in Apr., May, Sept., and Oct.
■– Steam on ②③④⑥ (ex July 4,5,6 and Sept 5,6,7).
CWRR–California Western Railroad. Tel.: Fort Bragg 707 964 6371.

Table 429 396 SAN FRANCISCO AREA #### *BART CT*

service (C‡ cl. only) *(CT)*, 1.435m., San Francisco-San Mateo-Redwood City-Palo Alto-Sunnyvale-San Jose and v.v. *75* km. Journey: 1½ hours. Fare: US $: 4.50.

From San Francisco 4th & Townsend: 0001⑥⑦, 0500Ⓐ, 0600Ⓐ, 0630Ⓐ, 0655Ⓐ, 0700⚒, 0725Ⓐ, 0730Ⓐ, 0800, 0900Ⓐ, 1000, 1100Ⓐ, 1200, 1300Ⓐ, 1400, 1500⚒, 1545Ⓐ, 1600Ⓒ, 1625 1630Ⓐ, 1650Ⓐ, 1655Ⓐ, 1700⑥, 1720Ⓐ, 1725Ⓐ, 1730Ⓐ, 1735Ⓐ, 1800, 1820Ⓐ, 1900, 2000, 2100Ⓐ, 2200.

From San Jose Cahill: 0450Ⓐ, 0540Ⓐ, 0555Ⓐ, 0605Ⓐ, 0610Ⓐ, 0630⚒, 0635Ⓐ, 0650Ⓐ, 0700Ⓐ, 0710Ⓐ, 0730⑥, 0755Ⓐ, 0800⚒, 0900, 1000, 1100, 1200, 1300⚒, 1400, 1500Ⓐ, 1530Ⓐ, 16 1630Ⓐ, 1700Ⓐ, 1715Ⓐ, 1745Ⓐ, 1800Ⓒ, 1815Ⓐ, 1900Ⓐ, 2000, 2200.

service (C cl. only) *(BART)*, 1.676m., Daly City-San Francisco-Oakland-Fremont/Concord and v.v.Frequent service 0354Ⓐ/0600⑥/0750†-0120②-⑥/0125①⑦.

BART–Bay Area Rapid Transit. Tel.: Oakland 510 464 7133. *CT*–CalTrain. Tel.: San Carlos 415 508 6200.

Table 430 396 DALLAS and FORT WORTH LOCAL SERVICES 🚌 *DART FWTA GL TNO*

Local 🚌 services operate in the Dallas and Fort Worth areas as follows:
Arlington (*18* km, US $: ❖). From Fort Worth: *GL* at 0630, 1020, 1430, 1835, 1930 and *TNO* at 1105, 1750, returning at *GL* 0840, 1325, 1840 and *TNO* 1325, 1910. Journey: 25 mins. Also from Dallas at *GL* 0800, 1245, 1300, 1815 and *TNO* 1300, 1845, returning at *GL* 0655, 1045, 1455, 1900, 2000 and *TNO* 1135, 1820. Journey: 30 mins.
Benbrook (❖ km, US $: ❖). From Fort Worth: ❖, returning at ❖. Journey: ❖.
Grapevine (❖ km, US $: ❖). From Dallas: ❖, returning at ❖.
Haltom City *(FWTA)* (❖ km, US $: ❖). From Fort Worth: ❖, returning at ❖. Journey: ❖.
Hurst (❖ km, US $: ❖). From Fort Worth: ❖, returning at ❖. Journey: ❖.
North Richland Hills (❖ km, US $: ❖). From Fort Worth: ❖, returning at ❖. Journey: ❖.
River Oaks *(FWTA)* (❖ km, US $: ❖). From Fort Worth: ❖, returning at ❖. Journey: ❖.
White Settlement *(FWTA)* (❖ km, US $: ❖). From Fort Worth: ❖, returning at ❖. Journey: ❖.

DART–Dallas Area Transit. Tel.: Dallas 658 6284. *GL*– Greyhound Lines. Tel.: Dallas 214 744 6500.
FWTA–Fort Worth Transportation Authority. Tel.: Fort Worth 870 6200. *TNO*– TNM&O Coaches. Tel.: Dallas 214 655 7084.

Table 433 SKAGWAY - WHITEHORSE #### *WPY*

US $	1	99	99	5		396 0.914m.	2	100	6	100A
C cl.	C[R]	C[R]	C[R]	C[R]		**May 16-Sept. 23**	C[R]	C[R]	C[R]	C[R]
		◇🚫	◆		km	↓ ↑		◆		◇🚫
0.00	0845	1240	1240	1315	*0*	d.**Skagway**........a.	1135	1200	1605	1830
33.50	1000	│	│	1450	*44*	a.White Pass 🏠 ...d.	1020	│	1500	│
61.50	....	1430	1430	....	*62*	a.**Fraser**........d.	....	1020	....	1630
67.00	....	1515	│	....	*88*	a. Bennett (**b**)🚫 ..d.	....	│	....	1545
95.00	....	....	*1800***a**	....	*179*	a.**Whitehorse**......d.	....	*0815***a**	....	....

a– Connection by 🚌.
b– For hikers using Chilkoot Trail to/from Lake Bennett.
◇- June 1-Sept. 4.
🚫– Service to Bennett will not operate during 1996.
◆– May 22-Sept. 13.
WPY– White Pass & Yukon Route. Tel.: Skagway 907 983 2217.

Table 434 ANCHORAGE - FAIRBANKS #### *ARR*

US $	4	10	2	4		396 1.435m.	3	9	1	3
C cl.	🚃	🚃		🚃			🚃	🚃		🚃
	C‡R	C‡S	C‡	C‡R			C‡R	C‡S	C‡	C‡
	③⑥	⑥	R⊗	⑦	km	↓ ↑	③⑥	⑦	R⊗	⑦
0.00	0630	0830	0830	1201	*0*	d.**Anchorage**........a.	1630	2000	2030	22
14.00	0750	0950	0950	1320	*74*	d.Wasilla........d.	1440	1718r	1800	20
31.50	0930	1121	1120	1500	*180*	d.Talkeetna........d.	1300	1559	1630	18
44.00	1050	1310r	│	1620	*267*	d.Hurricane Gulch d.	1140	1405r	│	172
	....	│	│	....		d.Cantwell........d.	....	│	│	....
◇88.00	....	1512r	1615	....	*377*	d.Denali Park........d.	....	1205r	1230	....
	....	1559r	│	....	*393*	d.Healy........d.	....	1120r	│	....
	....	1714r	1800	....	*478*	d.Nenana........d.	....	1003r	1000	....
★129.00	....	1900	2030	....	*572*	a.**Fairbanks**........d.	....	0830	0830	....

R– May 18-Sept. 19. **S**–Sept. 20-May 17.
◇– Off peak fare US$65 May 18 - June 15 & Sept. 1 - 19.
★– Off peak fare US$99 May 19 - June 15 & Sept. 1 - 19.
ARR– Alaska Railroad. Tel.: Anchorage 907 265 2494.

Table 435 ANCHORAGE - WHITTIER #### *ARR*

US $		🚃											396 1.435m.											🚃
C cl.	C	C🍷	C		C	C	C	C	C	C	C			C	C	C	C	C		C	C	C	C	C
	XW	T	XW		VW	U⑥	U⑤⑦	VW	U⑤⑦	VW	VW	km	↓ ↑	XW	XW	VW	U⑥	VW		U⑤⑦	VW	U⑤⑦	VW	T
	....	0645	....	....	*1145***a**	....	....	....	....	....	....	*0*	d.**Anchorage**........a.	....	....	....	....	*1730***a**	....	....	....	....	....	22
0.00	0800	│	1045	....	1330	1415	1520	1700	1820	1900	2130	*82*	d.Portage 𝔊........d.	0700	1000	1230	1355	1600	....	1750	1830	2010	2100	│
◇8.00	0830	│	1115	....	1400	1455	1600	1735	1900	1930	2200	*101*	a.**Whittier** 𝔊........d.	0630	0930	1200	1315	1530	....	1710	1800	1930	2030	│
★50.00	....	1100	....	....	....	....	....	....	....	....	....	*210*	a. Seward........d.	....	....	....	....	....	....	....	....	....	....	18

T– May 20-Sept. 4 and ⑥⑦ Sept. 9-24.
U– Sept. 24-April 30. **V**–May 1-Sept. 23.
W– 🚃 and 🚗.
X– Ex ②③ May 10-Sept. 20.
a– Connection by 🚌.
◇– Fare ex Portage.
★– Fare ex Anchorage.
𝔊– Additional trips, from Portage (U⑥ only, 🚗 only): 0700, 0900, 1935, 2145, return at 0600, 0800, 1830, 2030.
ARR– Alaska Railroad. Tel.: Anchorage 907 265 2494.

able 450 396 NANTUCKET ISLAND *TSA*

 service Hyannis–Nantucket Island and v.v.. ❖ km. Journey: 2¼ hours. Fare: US $: 10.00.
om **Hyannis**: 0745a, 0915b, 1315a, 1445, 1845a, 2015b.
om **Nantucket Island**: 0630, 1030a, 1200b, 1600a, 1730b, 2125a.

May 18–Sept. 20. b–Mar. 16–Nov. 1.
\- Sails to Wood's Hole (not Hyannis) on Sept. 20.
A– The Steamship Authority (Wood's Hole, Martha's Vineyard and Nantucket Steamship Authority). Wood's Hole 508 540 2022.

able 451 396 MARTHA'S VINEYARD ♿ *CIE TSA*

 (TSA) service Wood's Hole–Vineyard Haven and v.v. ❖ km. Journey: 45 mins. Fare: US $: 4.75.
om **Wood's Hole**: 5-14 sailings 0715-2245 throughout the year.
m **Vineyard Haven**: 5-14 sailings 0600-2145 throughout the year.
 (TSA) service Nantucket Island-Oak Bluffs and v.v. ❖ km. Journey: 45 mins. Fare: US $: 4.00/4.50. **June 15-Sept. 10 only.**
om **Nantucket Island**: 0945, 1215, 1445, 1715.
om **Oak Bluffs**: 1100, 1330, 1600, 1830.
 (CIE) service New Bedford-Vineyard Haven and v.v. *36* km. Journey: 1½ hours. Fare: US $: 9.00.(no service Sept 13)
y 18-June 22 (except May 26, 29) and Sept. 6-Oct. 9 (except Oct 6, 9).
om **New Bedford**: 0900, 1300⑤⑥⑦, 1700⑥⑦, 1900⑤.
om **Vineyard Haven**: 1100⑤⑥⑦, 1500⑥⑦, 1600①-④, 1700⑤, 2245⑤.
y 26, 29: June 23-Sept. 5 and Oct. 6, 9.
om **New Bedford**: 0900, 1300, 1700, 2100⑤.
om **Vineyard Haven**: 1100, 1500, 1845, 2245⑤.

– Cape Island Express Lines. New Bedford 508 997 1688.
A– The Steamship Authority (Wood's Hole, Martha's Vineyard and Nantucket Steamship Authority). Wood's Hole 508 540 2022.

able 452 396 SHELTER ISLAND *NF*

 service Greenport-Shelter Island and v.v. *1* km. Journey: 10 mins. Fare: US $: 0.50.
om **Greenport**: 0600 and frequent to 0000.
om **Shelter Island**: 0540 and frequent to 2345.

– North Ferry. Tel.: Shelter Island Heights Ø.

able 453 396 CHAMPLAIN FERRIES *LCTC*

 service Burlington-Port Kent and v.v. ❖ km. Journey: 1 hour. Fare: US $: 3.00.
om **Burlington**: 8-10 journeys daily 0745-1900, May 18–Oct. 15.
om **Port Kent**: 8-10 journeys daily 0905-2015, May 18-Oct. 15.
her local services operate Charlotte-Essex (about every 30 mins. 0630-2200 Apr. 1-Jan. 7) and Grand Isle-Plattsburgh every 20 mins. 0500-0120 throughout the year.

TC–Lake Champlain Transportation Co. Tel.: Burlington 802 864 9804.

able 454 396 ERIE CANAL *ACCL*

 (ACCL) SAGUENAY cruise: Warren RI - via New York Harbor, Hudson River, Erie Canal, Lake Ontario - Clayton - Upper Canada Village - Montréal - via Saguenay Fjord - Québec - to Warren RI or v.v.. ❖ km. Duration (RT) 12 days. Fares (RT) from US $ 1622. Sold on RT basis Warren-Warren only.
om **Warren RI** (by , returning by): 1500 June. 4.July 30. Aug 27
om **Warren RI** (by , returning by): 0715 June 16 Aug 11 Sept 8
 (ACCL) FALL FOLIAGE cruise: Warren RI - via New York Harbor, Hudson River - West Point - Kingston - via Erie Canal, Lake Ontario - Clayton - Upper Canada Village - Montréal - Québec - to Warren RI or v.v.. ❖ km. Duration (RT) 12 days. Fares (RT) from US $ 1622. Sold on RT basis Warren-Warren only.
om **Warren RI** (by , returning by): 1500 Sept. 24, 25.
om **Warren RI** (by , returning by): 0715 Oct. 6, 7.

CL–American Canadian Caribbean Line. Warren (Rhode Island) 401 247 0955. Fax: 401 5 8303.

able 456 396 LONG ISLAND *BPJ CSF*

 (BPJ) service Bridgeport-Port Jefferson and v.v. ❖ km. Journey: 1½ hours. Fare: US $ 11.00.
om **Bridgeport**: 0730ex⑦, 0900⑥, 1030, 1200⑥, 1330, 1500⑥, 1630ex⑤⑦, 1645⑤⑦, 1800①-④, 1830⑤⑦, 1930ex⑤⑦, 2000⑤⑦, 2130⑤⑦.
om **Port Jefferson**: 0600ex⑦, 0730⑥, 0900, 1030⑥, 1200, 1330⑥, 1500, 1630①-④, 1645⑤⑦, 1800ex⑤⑦, 1830⑤⑦, 2000⑤⑦.
 (CSF) service New London-Orient Point ★ and v.v. ❖ km. Journey: 1½ hours. Fare: US $: 8.50.
om **New London**: 0700 and 4-14 sailings until 1900.
om **Orient Point**: 0900 and 4-14 sailings 2045.

\- For Greenport.
J– Bridgeport & Port Jefferson Steamboat Co. Port Jefferson 516 473 0286.
F– Cross Sound Ferry Services Inc. New London 446 443 5281.

able 457 396 FISHERS ISLAND *FIF*

 service New London-Fishers Island and v.v. *11* km. Journey: 45 mins. Fare: US $: 3.50. (US $ 4.50 on certain early morning, late afternoon and evening sailings).
Apr. 28-Oct. 29.
om **New London and Fishers Island**: 4-9 sailings daily.

– Fishers Island Ferry District. Fishers Island 516 788 7463.

able 458 396 BLOCK ISLAND *INC NNC*

 (INC) service Galilee (Point Judith)-Block Island and v.v. *40* km. Journey: 1 hour 10 mins. Fare: US $: 6.60.
om **Galilee**: 1100 (up to 8 additional sailings during peak periods).
om **Block Island**: 1400⚒, 1500† (up to 8 additional sailings during peak periods).
 (NNC) service New London-Block Island and v.v. *105* km. Journey: 2 hours. Fare: US $: 13.50.
Operates June 12-Sept. 12 only.
om **New London**: 0900, 1915⑤.
om **Block Island**: 1630.

C– Interstate Navigation Company. Galilee 401 789 3502.
IC–Nelseco Navigation Company. New London 203 442 7891.

Table 459 396 MAINE FERRIES *MSF*

Local service Rockland-Vinalhaven and v.v. *24* km. Journey: 1¼ hours. Fare: US.$: 6.00.
From Rockland: 0700▾, 0845, 1115⇨, 1200⌂, 1300♣, 1345♜, 1500♣, 1515⛵, 1630♣.
From Vinalhaven: 0700, 0845▾, 1030⌂, 1115♣, 1300♣, 1345⛵, 1500♣, 1515♜, 1630♣.
Local service Rockland-Matinicus Island and v.v. *55* km. Journey: 2¼ hours. Fare: US $: 6.00.
From Rockland: ω. **From Matinicus Island**: ω.
Local service Rockland-North Haven and v.v. *20* km. Journey: 1 hour. Fare: US $: 6.00.
From Rockland: 0930, 1330**M**, 1700.
From North Haven: 0800, 1215**M**, 1545.
Local service Bass Harbor-Swans Island and v.v. *11* km. Journey: 40 mins. Fare: US $: 6.00.
From Bass Harbor: 0730ex⑦, 0900⑦, 0930+, 1030=, 1100⚒, 1415§, 1500♂, 1515μ, 1545*, 1630♂, 1645μ, 1715Π.
From Swans Island: 0645ex⑦, 0815, 0945=, 1015+, 1145④, 1330§, 1415♂, 1430④, 1500÷, 1545♂, 1600μ, 1630Π.
Local service Bass Harbor-Frenchboro and v.v. *18* km. Journey: 50 mins. Fare: US $: 6.00.
From Bass Harbor: 0900③, 1230④.
From Frenchboro: 1000③, 1330④.
Local service Lincolnville-Islesboro and v.v. *5* km. Journey: 20 mins. Fare: US $: 3.00.
From Lincolnville: 0800ex⑦, 0900, 1000⊗, 1100⩾, 1300, 1400⩾, 1500⊗, 1600⛺, 1700.
From Islesboro: 0730ex⑦, 0830, 0930⊗, 1030⩾, 1230, 1330⩾, 1430⊗, 1530⛺, 1630.

M– ⚒ (daily July 1-Oct. 31). =–⑦ May 28-Oct. 8. +–①②④⑤⑥ May 26-Oct. 14.
÷– ⑦ (also ①②③⑤⑥ May 26-Oct. 14). §–ex④⑦ May 26-Oct. 14. Π–May 26-Oct. 14.
ω– 24 trips per year. *–⑦ (daily May 26-Oct. 14).
♂– ex④⑦ Jan. 1-May 24 and Oct. 16-Dec. 31. μ–④ Jan. 1-May 25 and Oct. 19-Dec. 31.
▾– ⚒ (daily Apr. 1-Oct. 31). ♣–Apr. 1-Oct. 31.
⛺– Daily Jan. 1-Sept. 30; ⑦ Oct. 1-Dec. 31. ⛵–Jan. 1-Mar. 31 and Nov. 1-Dec. 31.
♜– ⚒ Jan. 1-Mar. 31 and Nov. 1-Dec. 31. ⩾–May 14-Sept. 30.
⊗– ⚒ (daily May 15-Sept. 30). ⇨–⚒ Apr. 1-Oct. 31 (also † July 1-Oct. 31).
⌂– ⚒ Jan. 1-Mar. 31; daily Nov. 1-Dec. 31.
MSF– Maine State Ferry Service. Tel.: Rockland 207 596 2202.

Table 460 396 NEW YORK *CBB CL HSH NYC PIF SLC TNT*

Regular tours *(CL)* round Manhattan Island and surrounding areas Mar. 6–Dec. 27. *56* km. Journey: 3 hours (day cruises)/ 2 hours (Harbor Lights cruise). Fare: US$ 16.00.
From New York W. 42nd Street Pier: 2-11 sailings daily (no sailings Nov. 26 or Dec. 25).
Regular tours *(SLC)* round south end of Manhattan Island and Liberty Mar. 16–Dec. 22. ❖ km. Journey: 1 hour. Fare: US $ 10.00.
From New York South Street Pier 16: 3-5 sailings daily.
Local service *(PIF)* Hoboken-New York City and v.v. *3* km. Journey: 8 mins. Fare: US $: 2.00.
From Hoboken Ferry Terminal: 0650Ⓐ/1000© and frequent to 2200©/2250Ⓐ. φ.
From New York World Financial Centre: 0700Ⓐ/1020© and frequent to 2210©/2300Ⓐ. φ.
Local service *(PIF)* New York City-Liberty State Park. *1* km. Journey: 5 mins. Fare US $ (RT): 5.00.
From New York World Financial Centre: 1010© and every 30 mins. to 1840©.
From Jersey City Liberty State Park: 1015© and every 30 mins. to 1845©.
Local service *(NYC)* Staten Island-New York City and v.v. *4* km. Journey: 25 mins. Fare: US $: 0.50.
From Staten Island St George: 0000, 0100, 0200, 0300, 4000, 0500, 0600, 0620Ⓐ, 0640Ⓐ, 0700, 0720Ⓐ, 0740Ⓐ, 0800, 0900, 0930Ⓐ, 1000, 1030Ⓐ, 1100 and every 30 mins. to 1530, 1550Ⓐ, 1600©, 1610Ⓐ, 1630, 1650Ⓐ, 1700©, 1710Ⓐ, 1730, 1745Ⓐ, 1800, 1830, 1845Ⓐ, 1900, 1930Ⓐ, 2000, 2030Ⓐ, 2100, 2130Ⓐ, 2200, 2230Ⓐ, 2300.
From New York South Ferry Whitehall: 0030, 0130, 0230, 0330, 0430, 0530, 0630, 0650Ⓐ, 0710Ⓐ, 0730, 0750Ⓐ, 0810Ⓐ, 0830, 0845Ⓐ, 0900Ⓐ, 0915Ⓐ, 0930, 1000Ⓐ, 1030, 1100Ⓐ, 1130 and every 30 mins. to 1600, 1620Ⓐ, 1630©, 1640Ⓐ, 1700, 1715Ⓐ, 1730, 1745Ⓐ, 1800, 1815Ⓐ, 1830, 1845Ⓐ, 1900, 1920Ⓐ, 1930©, 1940Ⓐ, 2000Ⓐ, 2030, 2100Ⓐ, 2130, 2200Ⓐ, 2230, 2300Ⓐ, 2330.
Local service *(CBB)* Jersey City-New York City and v.v. 7 km. Journey: 12 mins. Fare: US $: 5.00.
From Jersey City Port Liberte': 0645Ⓐ, 0715Ⓐ, 0745Ⓐ, 0815Ⓐ, 0845Ⓐ, 0915Ⓐ, 1615Ⓐ, 1645Ⓐ, 1715Ⓐ, 1745Ⓐ, 1815Ⓐ, 1910Ⓐ.
From New York South Ferry: 0700Ⓐ, 0730Ⓐ, 0800Ⓐ, 0830Ⓐ, 0900Ⓐ, 1635Ⓐ, 1705Ⓐ, 1735Ⓐ, 1805Ⓐ, 1835Ⓐ, 1930Ⓐ.
Local service *(TNT)* Highlands-New York City and v.v. *16* km. Journey: 45 mins. Fare: US $: 15.00.
From Highlands to New York: 0615Ⓐ, 0755Ⓐ, 1030©, 1725Ⓐ.
From Atlantic Highlands to New York: 0700Ⓐ, 1740Ⓐ.
From New York Wall Street Pier 11 to Highlands: 0700Ⓐ, 1640Ⓐ, 1730⚒, 1830Ⓐ.
From New York Wall Street Pier 11 to Atlantic Highlands: 1640Ⓐ, 1730Ⓐ, 1830Ⓐ.
Local service *(HSH)* New York-La Guardia Airport and v.v. *14* km. Journey: 30 mins. (45 mins. to/from Wall Street). Fare: US $: 20.00.
From New York Wall Street Pier 11 (15 mins. later from East 34th Street): 0830Ⓐ, 0930Ⓐ, 1430Ⓐ, 1530Ⓐ, 1630Ⓐ, 1730Ⓐ.
From La Guardia Airport Marine Air Terminal to E 34 and Wall Street: 0745Ⓐ, 0845Ⓐ, 0945Ⓐ, 1045Ⓐ, 1545Ⓐ, 1645Ⓐ, 1745Ⓐ, 1845Ⓐ.
Local service *(TNT)* Brooklyn-New York City and v.v. *5* km. Journey: 15 mins. Fare: US $: 5.00.
From Brooklyn Bay Ridge 69th Street Pier: 0735Ⓐ, 0810Ⓐ, 0840Ⓐ.
From New York Wall Street Pier 11: 1650Ⓐ, 1730Ⓐ, 1830Ⓐ.
Local service *(PIF)* Weehawken-New York City and v.v. *2* km. Journey: 10 mins. (5 mins. to/from Port Imperial) Fare: US $: 4.50.
From Weehawken Lincoln Harbor: 0715Ⓐ and frequent to 2145Ⓐ.
From Weehawken Port Imperial: 0000⑥⑦, 0015⑥⑦, 0030⑥⑦, 0045⑥⑦, 0100⑥⑦, 0645Ⓐ, 0700Ⓐ, 0710Ⓐ, 0720Ⓐ, 0730Ⓐ, 0740Ⓐ, 0750Ⓐ, 0800⚒, 0810Ⓐ, 0815©, 0820Ⓐ, 0830⚒, 0840Ⓐ, 0845©, 0850Ⓐ, 0900 and frequent to 2345.
From New York Pier 78 West 38th Street to Port Imperial: 0008⑥⑦, 0023⑥⑦, 0038⑥⑦, 0053⑥⑦, 0108⑥⑦, 0655Ⓐ, 0710Ⓐ, 0720Ⓐ, 0730Ⓐ, 0740Ⓐ, 0750Ⓐ, 0800Ⓐ, 0808©, 0810Ⓐ, 0820Ⓐ, 0823©, 0830Ⓐ, 0838©, 0840Ⓐ, 0850Ⓐ, 0853©, 0900Ⓐ, 0908 and frequent to 2353.
From New York Pier 78 West 38th Street to Lincoln Harbor: 0705Ⓐ and frequent to 2137Ⓐ.

φ– On ©, service extends from Battery Park to/from Statue of Liberty until 1845.
CBB– Chris's Bay Bus Inc. Tel.: Jersey City 201 433 1444.
CL– Circle Line. New York 212 563 3200.
HSH– Harbor Shuttle. Tel.: Eatontown Ø.
NYC– New York City Department of Transportation. Tel.: New York 718 390 5253.
PIF– NY Waterway. Tel.: Weehawken 201 420 6307.
SLC– Seaport Liberty Cruises. Tel.: 212 748 8782.
TNT– TNT Hydrolines. Tel.: Atlantic Highlands 908 872 2628.

Table 462 396 PHILADELPHIA - CAMDEN *RB*

 ferry service Philadelphia-Camden and v.v. *1* km. Journey: 10 mins. Fare: US $: 2.00.
From Philadelphia Penn's Landing: 0815Ⓐ/0915© and every 30 mins. to 1745ζ/1945φ/2015ω/2115ð/2345σ.
From Camden Aquarium: 0800Ⓐ/0900© and every 30 mins. to 1730ζ/1930φ/2000ω/2100ð/2330σ.

ζ– ① in winter. φ–⑥ in winter. ω–①②④ in summer.
ð– ③⑤⑦ in summer. σ–⑥ in summer. *RB*–Riverbus Inc. Tel.: Camden 609 365 1400.

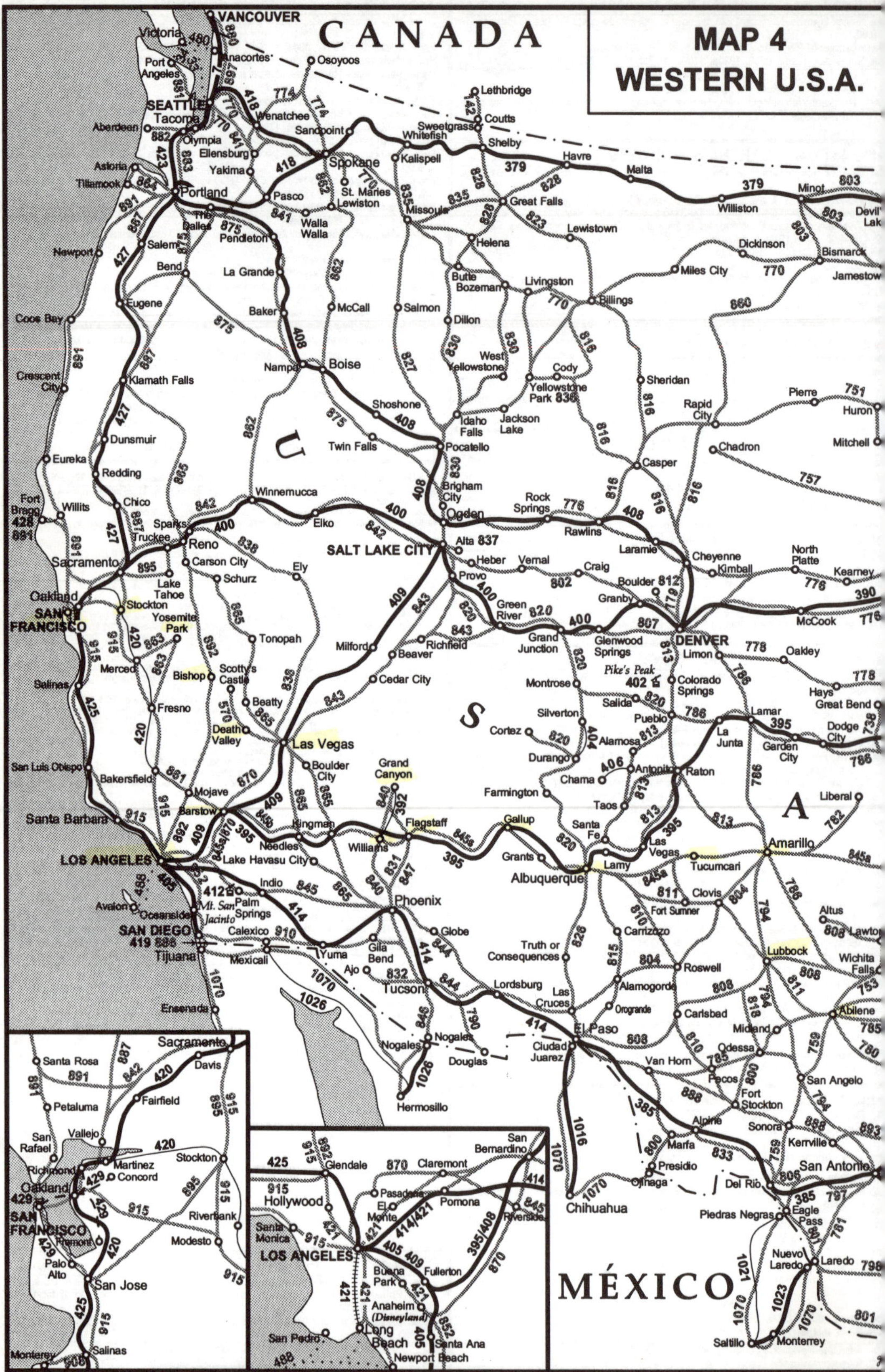

For key to map symbols see page 63

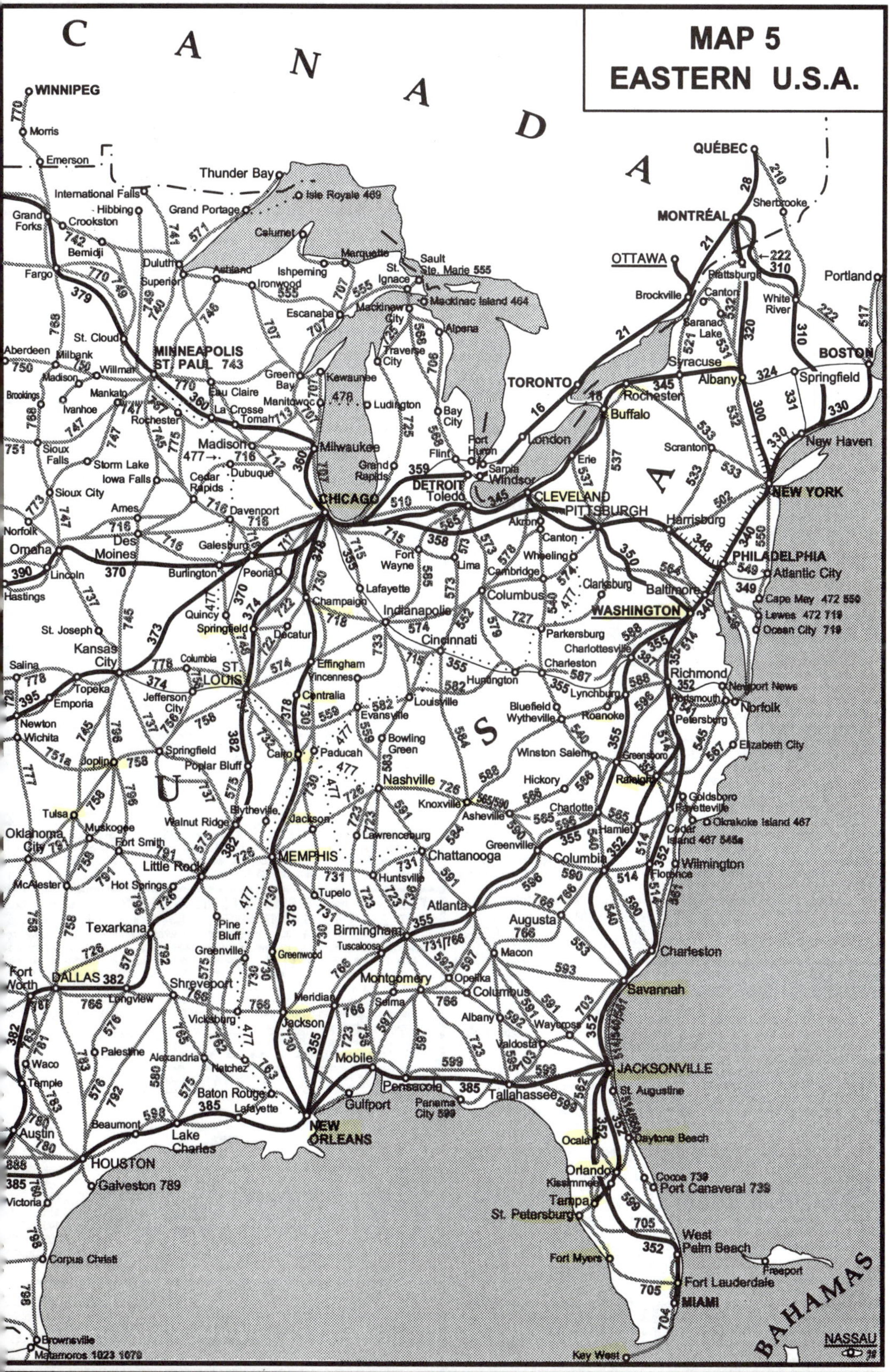

For key to map symbols see page 63

Table 464 396 MACKINAC ISLAND — AT SMIF

and catamaran service *(AT)* service Mackinaw City-Mackinac island and v.v. *11* km. Journey: 35 mins. Fare: US $: 7.00.
From Mackinaw City: 0800⧺, 0830∞, 0900⧺, 0930≺, 1000⧺, 1030∊, 1100⧺, 1130≺, 1200⧺, 1230∊, 1300⧺, 1330∍, 1345⧺, 1430∊, 1445⧺, 1530≺, 1545⧺, 1630≺, 1645⧺, 1730≺ 1745⧺, 1830∃, 1845⧺, 1930∃, 2030∃, 2230△.
From Mackinac Island to Mackinaw City: 0830⧺, 0900∞, 0930⧺, 1000∍, 1030⧺, 1045⧺, 1100∞, 1130⧺, 1145⧺, 1200∍, 1230⧺, 1245⧺, 1300∞, 1330⧺, 1345⧺, 1400∍, 1430⧺, 1500∊ 1530⧺, 1600≺, 1630⧺, 1700∊, 1730⧺, 1800≺, 1830⧺, 1900∃, 1930⧺, 2000∃, 2100∃, 2300△.
and catamaran service *(AT)* service St. Ignace-Mackinac island and v.v. *10* km. Journey: 30 mins. Fare: US $: 7.00.
From St. Ignace: 0730∊, 0830≺, 0900⍋, 0930≺, 1000⍋, 1030≺, 1100⧺, 1130≺, 1200⍋, 1230≺, 1315⧺, 1330∍, 1400⧺, 1415⧺, 1430∞, 1500⧺, 1515⧺, 1530∍, 1600⧺, 1615⧺ 1630∞, 1700⧺, 1715⧺, 1730∍, 1800⧺, 1815⧺, 1830•, 1900⧺, 1930•, 2030∃, 2230△. A limited service is provided Nov. 2-May 10.
From Mackinac Island to St. Ignace: 0800∊, 0900≺, 0930◧, 1000∊, 1015⧺, 1030◧, 1100≺, 1115⧺, 1200≺, 1215⧺, 1230◧, 1300≺, 1315⧺, 1400≺, 1430⧺, 1500∊, 1530⧺, 1600≺ 1630⧺, 1700∊, 1730⧺, 1800≺, 1830⧺, 1900∃, 2000∃, 2100∃, 2300△. A limited service is provided Nov. 2-May 10.
(SMIF) service Mackinaw City and St. Ignace-Mackinac Island and v.v. *11* km. Journey: 16 mins. Fare: (RT) US $: 9.00. ♿.
From Mackinaw City: 5-31 sailings daily May 1-Oct. 31.
From St. Ignace: 5-27 sailings daily May 1-Oct. 31.
From Mackinac Island to Mackinaw City: 5-31 sailings daily May 1-Oct. 31.
From Mackinac Island to St. Ignace: 5-27 sailings daily May 1-Oct 31.

⧺–June 4-Sept. 5. ∞–May 11-June 3, Sept. 6-Nov. 1. ≺–May 11-Oct. 16. ∊–May 11-Nov. 1. ∍–May 11-June 3, Sept. 6-Oct. 16. ∃–june 4-Sept. 5, also ⑤⑥ Sept. 6-Oct. 15. △–⑤⑥ June 24-Oct. 15. ⍋–June 4-Sept. 5, Oct. 17-Nov. 1. •–⑤⑥ Sept. 6-Oct. 15. ◧–Oct. 17-Nov. 1. *AT*–Arnold Transit. Tel.: Mackinac Island 906 847 3351. *SMIF*–Shepler's Mackinac Island Ferry. ☎Mackinaw City 616 436 5023.

Table 466 396 BEAVER ISLAND — BIB

Local service Charlevoix-Beaver Island and v.v. *15* km. Journey: 2½ hours. Fare: US $: 16.00.
From Charlevoix: 0830◙, 1130❍, 1200⊨, 1430♈, 1730⁄.
From Beaver Island: 0830↩, 1130♈, 1230●, 1430ς, 1730♈.
◙–May 13, 20, 27, 28, 30, June 3, 10, 13-30, July 1-Sept. 8. ❍–May 27, June 10, Oct. 1-3, 5-10, 12-17, 19-24, 26-31, Nov. 2-5, 7, 9-14, 16-21, 23, 25, 28, 30, Dec. 2, 5, 7, 9, 12, 14, 16, 19, 21. ⊨–Apr. 13, 15, 1,8 20, 22, 25, 27, 29, May 1, 2, 4-9, 11-26, 28-31, Jun. 1-9, 11-13, Sept. 9-30. ♈–Jun. 16-Sept. 4. ⁄–May 27, Jun. 10. ↩–Apr. 13, 15, 18, 20, 22, 25, 27, 29, May 1, 2, 4-9, 11-31, Jun. 1-13, 16-30, July 1, 2, 4, 8, 9, 15, 16, 18, 22, 23, 25, 29, 30, Aug. 1, 5, 6, 8, 12-15, 19, 20, 22, 26, 27, Sept. 2, 5, 9-30, Oct. 1-3, 5-10, 12-17, 19-24, 26-31, Nov. 2-5, 7, 9-14, 16-21, 23, 25, 26, 28, 30, Dec. 2, 5, 7, 9, 12, 14, 16, 19, 21. ●–May 13, 20, 27, 28, 30, Jun. 3, 10, 13. ς–May 27, Jun. 10, 14, 15, Sept. 6-8.
BIB–Beaver Island Boat Co. Tel.: Charlevoix 616 547 2311.

Table 467 396 OCRACOKE ISLAND — NCDT

service Cedar Island-Okracoke and v.v. *35* km. Journey: 2¼ hours. Fare: US $: 1.00.
From Cedar Island: 0700, 0815⍓, 0930♈, 1000ɋ, 1200♈, 1300ɋ, 1315⍓, 1500♈, 1600ɋ, 1800♈, 2030♈.
From Ocracoke: 0700, 0930♈, 1000ɋ, 1045⍓, 1200♈, 1300ɋ, 1500♈, 1600ɋ, 1615⍓, 1800♈, 2030♈.
service Swan Quarter-Ocracoke and v.v. *50* km. Journey: 2½ hours. Fare: US $: 1.00.
From Swan Quarter: 0930, 1600. **From Ocracoke**: 0630, 1230.
⍓– May 24-Oct. 3. ♈–Apr. 12-23, May 10-Oct. 31.
ɋ– Jan. 1-Apr. 11, Apr. 24-May 9 and Nov. 1-Dec. 31.
NCDT–North Carolina Department of Transportation. ☎Ocracoke 919 928 3841.

Table 468 396 CASCO BAY — CBL

Local service Portland-Chebeauge Island and v.v. ❖ km. Journey: 50 mins. Fare: US $: 5.00.
From Portland: 0515Ⓐ, 0645⑥, 1000, 1445, 1745, 2230⑤.
From Chebeague Island: 0630Ⓐ, 0810⑥, 1135, 1620, 1845, 2335⑤.
Local service Portland-Cliff Island and v.v. ❖ km. Journey: 50 mins. Fare: US $: 5.00.
From Portland: 0515Ⓐ, 0645⑥, 1000, 1445, 1745, 2230⑤.
From Cliff Island: 0615Ⓐ, 0755⑥, 1155, 1600, 1900, 2350⑤.
Local service Portland-Long Island, Little Diamond and Great Diamond and v.v. ❖ km. Journey: 1½ hours. Fare: US $: 5.00.
From Portland (to all three): 0515Ⓐ, 0645⑥, 0740Ⓐ, 1000, 1445, 1745, 2030, 2230⑤.
From Long Island: 0015⑥, 0650Ⓐ, 0825Ⓐ, 0830⑥, 1220, 1640, 1920, 2115.
From Little Diamond: 0050⑥, 0710Ⓐ, 0845Ⓐ, 0850⑥, 1240, 1710, 1940, 2145.
From Great Diamond: 0045⑥, 0705Ⓐ, 0840Ⓐ, 0845⑥, 1235, 1705, 1935, 2140.
Local service Portland-Peaks Island and v.v. ❖ km. Journey: 20 mins. Fare: US $: 5.00.
From Portland: 0545⚒, 0645⚒, 0745⚒, 0830†, 0930, 1045, 1215, 1415, 1515, 1620, 1735, 1835⑤, 1915ex⑤, 2015, 2115, 2230⚒, 2330⑤⑥.
From Peaks Island: 0615⚒, 0715⚒, 0815⚒, 0900†, 1000, 1115, 1245, 1445, 1545, 1700, 1800, 1900⑤, 1945ex⑤, 2045, 2145, 2255⚒, 2355⑤⑥.
Local service Portland-Diamond Cove and v.v. ❖ km. Journey: 20 mins. Fare: US $: 5.00.
From Portland: 0600⚒, 0730†♣, 0740Ⓐ❄, 0900Ⓒ♣, 1000, 1100♣, 1315♣, 1515♣, 1730♣, 1830, 2030, 2130♣, 2230◨, 2330⚒♣.
From Diamond Cove: 0030⑥❄, 0630⚒, 0800†♣, 0815Ⓐ, 1000Ⓒ♣, 1135♣, 1350♣, 1605♣, 1650❄, 1800♣, 1900, 2125, 2200♣, 2300♠, 2359⑤⑥♣.
❄– Winter sailing only. ♣–Summer sailing only. ◨–⑤Ⓒ only (daily in summer).
♠– ④Ⓒ only (daily in summer). *CBL*–Casco Bay Lines. Tel.: Portland 207 774 7871.

Table 469 396 ISLE ROYALE — GPIR IRFS IRNP

(IRNP) service Houghton-Rock Harbor and v.v. *118* km. Journey: 6 hours. Fare: US $: 30.00. **June 2-Sept. 12.**
From Houghton: 0900②⑤. **From Rock Harbor**: 0900③⑥.
(IRFS) service Copper Harbor-Rock Harbor and v.v. *90* km. Journey: 4½ hours. Fare: US $: 28.00. **May 11-June 10 and Sept. 5-30**
From Copper Harbor: 0800①⑤. **From Rock Harbor**: 1400①⑤.
June 11-Sept. 4
From Copper Harbor: 0800 (ex③④ June 11-July 31; ex⑦ June 11-30).
From Rock Harbor: 1530 (ex③④ June 11-July 31; ex⑦ June 11-30).
(GPIR) service Grand Portage-Windigo and v.v. *35* km. Journey: 3 hours. Fare: US $: 25.00. **June 11-Sept. 5**
From Grand Portage: 0930. **From Windigo**: 1400.
(GPIR) service Grand Portage-Windigo-Rock Harbor and v.v. *125* km. Journey: 6 hours. Fare: US $: 35.00. **May 7-Oct. 31.**
From Grand Portage: 0930③⑥; also ① May 30-Sept. 5.
From Rock Harbor: 0700④⑦; also ② May 31-Sept. 6.
GPIR–Grand Portage-Isle Royale Transportation Lines. ☎Duluth 218 728 1237. *IRFS*–Isle Royale Ferry Service. ☎Copper Harbor 906 289 4437 (summer), 906 482 4950 (winter). *IRNP*–Isle Royale National Park. ☎Houghton 906 482 0984.

Table 471 396 SEATTLE - BAINBRIDGE — WSF

Local service Seattle-Bainbridge Island and v.v. ❖ km. Journey: 35 mins. Fare: US $: ❖.
From Seattle: 0040, 0210, 0620, 0700Ⓐ, 0750, 0840⚒, 0925, 1015, 1120, 1230, 1315, 1410, 1500, 1550, 1640, 1725, 1815, 1900, 1945, 2030, 2110, 2150, 2245, 2315.
From Bainbridge Island: 0000, 0120, 0535, 0620Ⓐ, 0710, 0750⚒, 0840, 0925, 1010, 1120, 1220, 1315, 1410, 1500, 1550, 1635, 1725, 1810, 1900, 1945, 2025, 2110, 2200, 2230.
WSF– Washington State Ferries. Tel.: Seattle 206 464 6400.

Table 472 396 CAPE MAY - LEWES — CMLF

Local service Cape May-Lewes and v.v. 27 km. Journey: 1¼ hours. Fare: US $: 4.50
From Cape Mayℌ: 0620, 0820**P**, 0940, 1040**Q**, 1140, 1300**R**, 1400**Q**, 1500, 1620**R**, 1820 1940**P**.
From Lewesℌ: 0800, 1000**P**, 1120, 1220**Q**, 1320, 1440**R**, 1540**Q**, 1640, 1800**R**, 2000 2120**P**.
P– May 19-Oct. 9. Q–June 16-Sept. 18. R–Apr. 7-Nov. 6.
ℌ– Additional sailings may operate at peak times.
CMLF–Cape May-Lewes Ferry. ☎Cape May 609 886 2718.

Table 473 396 MARYLAND FERRIES — ATF CEV RTF

Local service *(RTF)* Crisfield-Tangier Island and v.v. ❖ km. Journey: 2 hours. Fare: US $: 16.00
From Crisfield: 1230*.
From Tangier Island: 1715*
Local service *(CEV)* Reedville-Smith Island and v.v. ❖ km. Journey: 1½ hours. Fare: US $: 18.00.
From Reedville: 1000η. **From Smith Island**: 1600η.
Local service *(ATF)* Point Lookout-Smith Island and v.v. ❖ km. Journey: 1½ hours Fare: US $: 17.00.
From Point Lookout: 1000σ.
From Smith Island: 1600σ.
Local service *(ATF)* Crisfield-Smith Island and v.v. ❖ km. Journey: 1½ hours. Fare: US $: 15.00.
From Crisfield: 1230**K**. **From Smith Island**: 1730**K**.
K– Memorial Day-Oct. 31. σ–May 31-Sept .1. η–May 1-Oct. 15. *–May 15-Oct. 31 *ATF*–Allen Tyler Ferry. Tel.: Rhodes Point 410 425 2771. *CEV*–Captain Evans (Smith Island & Chesapeake Bay Cruises. Tel.: Reedville 804 453 3430. *RTF*–Rudy Thomas Ferries Tangier Island Cruises). Tel.: Crisfield 410 968 2338.

Table 474 396 HAWAIIAN ISLANDS

Local services link Kauai (Kapaa), Oahu (Honolulu), Molokai (Kepuhi), Lana (Kaumalapau), Maui (Wailuku) and Hawaii (Hilo), with regular tours and excursion throughout the year. Few services operate as real "transport", and most trips will take yo back where you started after your visits have finished.

Table 476 396 PORTSMOUTH - GOSPORT — IOS

service Portsmouth-Gosport Harbor and v.v. ❖ km. Journey: 1 hour. Fare: US $: 9.0
From Portsmouth: 0730**N**, 0930**O**, 1100**P**, 1400**Q**, 1630**R**, 1800**S**, 1900T, 2100**U**.
From Gosport Harbor: 1030**N**, 1345V, 1430**W**, 1530**O**, 1645**X**, 2000**S**, 2030**R**, 2200T 2300**U**.
N–June 17-Sept. 4. O–June 17-Sept. 4, also ⑥⑦ Sept. 5-30. P–June 17-Oct. 31. Q– June 17-Sept. 4, also ⑥⑦ Oct. 1-31. R–①③ June 17-Sept. 4. S–Ex ③ June 17-Sept. 4 T–③④⑤⑥ June 17-Sept. 4. U–④⑤⑥ June 17-Sept. 4. V–June 17-Sept. and Oct. 1-31 W–①-⑤ Sept. 5-30. X–June 17-Sept. 4, also ⑥⑦ Sept. 5-Oct. 31. *IOS*–Isles of Shoals Steamship Co. Tel.: Portsmouth 603 431 5500.

Table 477 396 MISSISSIPPI RIVERBOATS — ACCL DQS

Cruises, often using sternwheel steamers, are operated out of many ports on the Mississipp and there are occasional trips by *ACL* and *DQS* which operate over longer distances taking anything from 3 to 10 days for the complete voyage. The major ports served ar New Orleans, Baton Rouge, St. Francisville, Natchez, Vicksburg, Greenville, Memphis Cairo, St Louis, Hannibal, Burlington, Davenport, Dubuque, La Crosse and St. Paul. Ther are also local cruises, with occasional long-distance services, on the Cumberland Rive between Cairo, Paducah and Nashville, on the Tennessee River between Cairo, Paducah Florence, Decatur and Chattanooga, and on the Ohio between Cairo, Paducah, Evansville Louisville, Cincinnati, Huntington and Pittsburgh.
ACCL– American Canadian Caribbean Line. Tel.: Warren 401 247 0955.
DQS– Delta Queen Steamboat Co.♿. Tel.: New Orleans 504 586 0631.

Table 478 LAKE MICHIGAN FERRIES ♿

US $						km	396 ↓ ↑					
0.00	....	....	....	....	....	0	d.**Ludington** ....a.	....	....	....	....	....
25.00	....	....	....	....	....	40	a.**Manitowoc**.............d.	....	....	....	....	....

Table 479 396 SEATTLE - BREMERTON — WSF

Local service Seattle-Bremerton and v.v. *40* km. Journey: 1 hour. Fare: US $: 3.30.
From Seattle: 0040, 0115Ⓒ, 0525, 0615Ⓐ, 0640⚒, 0740, 0900, 1030, 1100Ⓒ, 1145, 1245Ⓒ 1300†, 1330, 1430, 1540, 1615, 1710, 1740Ⓐ, 1830, 1930, 2050, 2100Ⓐ, 2140†, 2300.
From Bremerton: 0000Ⓒ, 0010, 0130, 0500Ⓐ, 0530⚒, 0630, 0715Ⓐ, 0750, 0915, 1030 1145, 1305, 1400, 1445, 1600, 1640, 1720, 1820, 1900Ⓐ, 1940, 2035†, 2155, 2200Ⓐ.
WSF–Washington State Ferries. Tel.: Seattle 206 464 6400.

Table 480 ANACORTES - SIDNEY — WSF

US $					km	↓ 496 ↑				
0.00	0845	....	....	....	0	d.**Anacortes**..............a.	....	1520	....	....
6.05	1140	....	....	....	93	a.**Sidney** ....d.	....	1201	....	....

WSF–Washington State Ferries. Tel.: Seattle 206 464 6400.

⛰–Mountain Railway ⍋–Cablecar ▭–Through carriage

able 485 WASHINGTON LOCAL FERRIES — WSF

cal services operate Edmonds-Kingston and v.v. *5* km. Journey: 30 mins. Fare: US $: ❖.
om Edmonds: 0100, 0550⚒, 0630⑧, 0710, 0800⚒, 0840, 0925, 1010 and about every 40 mins. to 2040, 2115, 2200©, 2235, 2320†, 2345.
om Kingston: 0020, 0510⚒, 0550⑧, 0630, 0710⚒, 0750, 0840, 0925, 1010 and about every 40 mins. to 2000, 2035, 2120©, 2155, 2240†, 2310.
SF– Washington State Ferries. Tel.: Seattle 206 464 6400.

able 488 496 SANTA CATALINA ISLAND — CC CE CP CPS SJC

service *(CE)* San Pedro-Avalon and v.v. *35* km. Journey: 1¼ hours. Fare: US $ 17.50.
om San Pedro: 0715∅, 0730⋗, 0900⩽, 0915∅, 0930⋖, 1045⩾, 1145⊗, 1245∅, 1415∅, 1430∧, 1500⩽, 1615∅, 1630⊖, 1645⊗, 1745∅, 1800∧, 1945⊙, returning at 0900⩾, 1100⪅, 1230⩾, 1330⊗, 1430∅, 1600≠, 1700⩽, 1800÷, 1845⊗, 1930≠, 2115⊙.
service *(CE)* San Pedro-Two Harbors and v.v. *38* km. Journey: 1½ hours. Fare: US $ 17.50.
om San Pedro: 0745⊗, 0815∅, 0830⧺, 1015∞, 1145⊗, 1215≺, 1445∊, 1645≺, 1845∍, returning at 0945⊗, 1015≺, 1200∊, 1415∃, 1430△, 1645∍, 1845♿, 2030∍.
service *(CE)* Avalon-Two Harbors and v.v. *15* km. Journey: 45 mins. Fare: US $ 12.50.
om Avalon: 0930∃, 1015•, 1100∊, 1130◧, 1330⊗, 1730⊗, 1800⬬, 2050⋖, returning at 0830∃, 1000∊, 1630⊗, 1700⬬.
service *(CC)* Long Beach-Avalon and v.v. *35* km. Journey: 2/2½ hours. Fare: US $ 17.75.
om Long Beach: *CC* 0700⧗, 0800**A**, 0900, 1000▣, 1100**B**, 1130**C**, 1245**A**, 1330**D**, 1445**F**, 1630⧗, 1700⧖, 1730**G**, 1830◇, 1930**H**.
om Avalon: 0915⧗, 1015**A**, 1115⛴, 1215**L**, 1315⧖, 1500★, 1600**M**, 1700, 1800▭, 1830†, 1845⧗, 1915⧖, 1945**G**, 2045◇, 2130**H**.
service *(CC and CE)* Long Beach-Two Harbors and v.v. *57* km. Journey: 2/2½ hours. Fare: US $ 17.75.
om Long Beach: *CC* 0900**E**, 1100**B**, 1130†, 1330**D**, 1930**H**; *CE* 0900•, 1015◧, 1430●, 1930⋖.
om Two Harbors: *CC* 1230**J**, 1430⧖, 1500**K**, 1515†, 1530▭, 1545**D**, 2245**H**; *CE* 1115•, 1230◧, 1800●, 2255⋖.
service *(CE)* Long Beach-Avalon and v.v. *35* km. Journey: 1 hour. Fare: US $ 17.75.
om Long Beach: 0700, 0845∅, 0900▣, 1015, 1215∅, 1230●, 1345∅, 1400▣, 1545∅, 1600▣, 1715∅, 1730∧, 1915∅, 1930⋖, 2030∍, returning at 0830. 1015⊗, 1030⛟, 1130◧, 1200⛟, 1400/, 1530, 1730, 1900↩, 2045∅, 2200△.
service *(CPS)* Newport Beach-Avalon and v.v. *35* km. Journey: 1¼ hours. Fare (RT): US $ 33.00.
om Newport Beach: 0900Ω. **From Avalon:** 1630Ω.
service *(CP)* San Diego-Avalon and v.v. *140* km. Journey: ❖. Fare (RT): US $ 49.00.
om San Diego: ❖. **From Avalon:** ❖.
service *(SJC)* San Diego-Avalon and v.v. *140* km. Journey: ❖. Fare (RT): US $ 49.00.
om San Diego: ❖. **From Avalon:** ❖.

–⑤⑥⑦ June 23-Sept. 4; ⑥ Sept. 5-Oct. 29. **B**–①-⑤ June 23-Sept. 4; ⑦ Sept. 5-Oct. 29. **C**–⑥⑦ June 23-Sept. 4. **D**–Ex⑥ June 23-Sept. 4. **E**–⑥ June 23-Sept. 4; ①②⑤⑥ Sept. 5-Oct. 29. **F**–⑥ June 23-Sept. 4; ex⑥ Sept. 5-Oct. 29; ily Oct. 30-Nov. 21. **G**–⑦ June 23-Oct. 29. **H**–⑤ June 23-Nov. 21. **J**–⑥ June 23-Sept. 4; ①③⑤ Sept. 5-Nov. 21. **K**–⑦ Sept. 5-Nov. 21. **L**–⑦ June 23-Sept. 4; ②④⑦ Sept. 5-Nov. 21. **M**–Oct. 30-June 22; ⑥⑦ June 23-Sept. 4; ⑥ pt. 5-Oct. 29. ⛟–ex⑤ (daily Apr. 2-Oct. 30). △–⑥⑦ Apr. 2-Oct. 30. α–①②③④ Apr. 2-Oct. 30. ♿–ex⑤ Apr. 2-Oct. 30. /–⑦ (daily Apr. 2-Oct. 30). ↩–⑥⑦ (daily Apr. 2-Oct. 30). ⛟–②④⑥⑦ (daily Apr. 2-Oct. 30). ∍–⑥⑦– r. 2-Oct. 30. ∊–⑤⑥⑦ Apr. 20-Oct. 30. ▣–Oct. 31-Apr. 1. •–⑥ Oct. 31-Apr. 1. ⬬–ex⑥ Apr. 2-Oct. 30. ◧–①③⑤ Oct. 31-Apr. 1. ≺–ex ⑤⑥ Apr. 2-Oct. 30. ∞–⑤ Apr. 2-Oct. 30. ⧺–⑦ Apr. 2-Oct. 30. ●–⑦ Oct. 31-Apr. 1. –①⑤ (daily Apr. 2-Oct. 30). ≠–⑤⑥ (daily Apr. 2-Oct. 30). ⪅–⑤ (⑤⑥ Oct. 31-Dec. 31 and Mar. 1-Apr. 1, daily Apr. 2-Oct. 30). ⊙–⑤ (⑤⑥⑦ Apr. 2-Oct. 30). ⊖–①⑤ Oct. 31-Apr. 1. ∧–⑥⑦ Oct. 31-Apr. 1. ⊗–⑤ Apr. 2-Oct. 30. –①⑥⑦ Oct. 31-Apr. 1 (daily Apr. 2-Oct. 30). ⋖–⑤ Oct. 31-Apr. 1. ⩽–⑤⑥ Oct. 31-Dec. 31 and Mar. 1-Apr. 1. ⋗–①⑥⑦ Oct. 31-Apr. 1. ∅–Apr. 2-Oct. 30. ▣–⑥⑦ June 23-Sept. 4; ⑥ Sept. 5-Oct. 29. ⧗–⑥ June 23-Sept. 4. –①-⑤ June 23-Sept. 4. ◇–⑥ June 23-Oct. 29. †–⑦ June 23-Sept. 4. ⛴–June 23-Sept. 4. ★–⑤ June 23-Sept. 4. ▭–⑥ Sept. 5-Oct. 29. Ω–Jan. 1, ①④⑤⑥⑦ Jan. 22-Feb. 28, daily Mar. 1-Nov. 27 and Dec. 26-31. *CC*– talina Cruises. ☎Long Beach 213 253 9800. *CE*–Catalina Express. ☎San Pedro 310 519 1212. Fax: 310 548 7389. *CP*–Catalina Pacifica. ☎Avalon 619 224 7688. Fax: 619 224 7561. *CPS*–Catalina Passenger Service. ♿. ☎ lboa 714 673 5245. *SJC*–SeaJet Cruise Lines. ☎Avalon 619 696 0088.

able 490 BELLINGHAM/PRINCE RUPERT - ALASKA — AMH

S $	496 ↓		km	Pa	Pb	Pc	Pd	Pe	Pf	Pg	Ph	Pi	Pj	Pk	Pl	Pm	Pn	Po	Pp	Pq	Pr	Ps	Pt	Pu	Pv	Pw
	Bellingham	d.	*0*	A	....	....	....	....	....	....	....	....	....	....	....	....	....	....	....	....	....	....	....	....	....	....
0.00	**Prince Rupert**	d.	*900*	|	A	A	A	A	A	A	A	A	A	A	A	A	A	....	....	....	....	....	....	....	....	....
	Stewart/Hyder	d.		|	|	|	|	|	|	|	|	|	|	|	|	|	|	A	....	....	....	....	....	....	....	....
38.00	Ketchikan	d.	*1200*	C	A	A	A	B	A	A	A	A	B	B	A	A	B	B	....	....	....	....	....	....	....	....
2.00	Hollis	d.	*1170*	|	|	|	|	|	|	|	|	|	|	|	|	|	|	....	....	....	....	....	....	....	....	....
56.00	Wrangell	d.	*1300*	C	A	A	A	|	A	B	B	A	B	B	B	|	B	....	....	....	....	....	....	....	....	....
58.00	**Petersburg**	d.	*1350*	C	B	B	B	|	B	B	B	B	B	B	B	|	B	....	A	A	A	A	....	....	....	....
30.00	Kake	d.	*1450*	|	|	|	|	|	|	|	B	B	B	|	|	|	B	....	|	A	|	B	....	....	....	....
36.00	Sitka	d.	*1650*	|	|	|	|	|	B	B	|	|	|	|	|	|	B	....	A	A	A	B	A	....	....	....
04.00	**Juneau**/Auke Bay	d.	*1600*	D	B	B	B	B	C	C	B	B	C	B	B	B	C	....	B	B	B	C	B	....	A	A
18.00	Haines	d.	*1750*	D	B	B	B	C	C	C	B	B	C	C	B	B	....	....	B	....	B	....	....	....	A	B
24.00	**Skagway**	a.	*1770*	D	B	C	B	C	C	C	C	B	C	C	B	B	....	....	B	....	B	....	....	....	A	B

96 ↓		Qa	Qb	Qc	Qd	Qe	Qf	Qg	Qh	Qi	Qj	Qk	Ql	Qm	Qn	Qo	Qp	Qq	Qr	Qs	Qt	Qu	Qv	Qw	Qx	Qy
kagway	d.	A	A	A	A	A	A	A	A	A	A	A	A	A	A	A	A	....	....	....	....	....	....	....	....	....
aines	d.	A	|	A	A	A	A	A	A	B	A	A	A	A	A	B	A	....	....	....	....	....	....	....	....	....
uneau/Auke Bay	d.	A	A	A	B	B	A	A	A	B	A	A	A	B	A	B	A	A	A	A	A	A	A	....	....	....
itka	d.	....	....	B	|	|	A	B	B	B	|	|	|	B	A	B	A	B	A	B	B	B	B	A	....	....
ake	d.	....	....	....	|	|	B	B	B	|	|	|	|	|	|	|	|	....	....	C	B	|	|	|	....	....
etersburg	d.	....	....	....	B	B	B	B	B	C	B	A	B	C	B	C	|	....	....	C	B	B	C	|	....	....
Vrangell	d.	....	....	....	B	B	B	C	B	C	B	A	B	C	B	C	|	....	....	....	....	....	....	B	....	....
ollis	d.	....	....	....	|	|	|	|	|	|	|	|	|	|	|	|	|	....	....	....	....	....	....	|	A	....
etchikan	d.	....	....	....	C	B	B	C	C	C	B	B	B	C	B	C	B	....	....	....	....	....	....	|	A	....
tewart/Hyder	d.	....	....	....	|	|	|	|	|	|	|	|	|	|	|	|	|	....	....	....	....	....	....	|	....	....
rince Rupert	d.	....	....	....	C	C	C	C	C	D	C	B	B	|	|	|	|	....	....	....	....	....	....	B	....	....
ellingham	a.	....	....	....	....	....	....	....	....	....	....	....	....	E	D	E	D	....	....	....	....	....	....	....	....	....

egular services are operated throughout the year from Bellingham and Prince Rupert to Alaskan ports and v.v.. Days of operation for summer 1995 are shown below (**A** = day 1, **B** = day 2, etc); a reduced service operates in winter. Timings vary according to tides and should be checked with operator.
a–⑤ Mar. 31-Sept. 22. **Pb**–① Apr. 3-Sept. 25.exPc; May 29 terminates Juneau. **Pc**–Aug. 21; Sept. 4, 11; **Pd**–⑥ Apr 1-Sept. 23. **Pe**–⑥Aug 26; Sept 9 **Pf**–② Apr. 25; May 2; June 6; Sept , 12 ③ Aug. 23, 30 Sept. 6. **Pg**–②Apr . 4, 11, 18. May 16-30, June 4 Aug 1-29; Sept 19, 26. **Ph**– ④ Apr. 6, 27. Aug. 31♧ **Pi**–④ Apr. 13, 20, May 4-25. **Pj**–③May 31-Aug. 16. ④ Aug. 24; ept. 7. **Pk**–⑦May 28. **Pl**–④ June 1 - Aug. 17; Sept. 14-28. **Pm**–Sept. 3. **Pn**–⑦ June 4-25; July 23; Aug. 13; July 2-30♡. Aug. 6♡. **Po**–② May 23–Sept. 5. **Pp**–② June 6,20; July 4, 8; Aug. 1, 15. **Pq**–② Apr. 11–May 30; Aug. 22, 29; Sept. 12,26. **Pr**–① June 12, 26; July 24; Aug. 7; . **Ps**–① Sept. 4, 18. **Pt**–⑥ Apr. 3-Sept 23 ; ④June 8–Sept. 14 . **Pu.** **Pv**–⑥June 3–ug 22; ① May 5–Aug. 21; Aug. 20. **Pw**–May 25. **Qa**–May25; June 13; July 17, 24, 31; Aug. 7, 14, 19, 21; Sept. 21◇,29. **Qb**–⑥ June 3–July 8. ① June 5–July 10. July 14◇, 22, 28◇; ug. 5, 11◇,19. **Qc**–⑤Apr.7–May 26 ; (May 12,26◇.) ③ June7–Aug. 16; (June 7◇; Jul. 5,19◇; Aug. 2, 16◇.) **Qd**–⑦ April 2–July 2; Aug. 6– Sept. 24. Aug 20 ♤; July 30; Sept. 26. **Qe**–⑥ une 3– Aug 12; June 22; July 6; Aug. 3, 10, 17, 24 Sept. 7, 19. **Qf**– ⑥April 8–May27 . **Qg**–⑤ June 2–23; July 21; Aug. 11; Sept. 9. **Qh**–June 30; July 7, 14, 28; Aug. 26 ; Sept 2. **Qi**–ept. 16,22. **Qj**–④ Apr. 6– May18;. May 26, 30; Jun. 1, 15, 29; Aug. 20, 31; Sept. 1, 4, 11, 14, 21, 28. **Qk**–Sept. 6. **Ql**– Sept. 8, 13. **Qm**–①Apr. 3–May29; Sept. 4–25. **Qn**–② July 18–ug. 22. **Qo**–Aug. 28. **Qp**–② June 6–July 11. **Qq**–③ Apr.12, 26; May 10, 24; Aug. 23, 30; Sept. 13,27. ⑤ June 2–Sept 22. **Qr**–Apr. 19; May 3, 17, 31; Sept 6, 20, 30. **Qs**–Apr. 9, 23; ug. 20, 27; Sept. 10,24 **Qt**–May 14, 28; Sept 3, 17. **Qu**– Jun. 5, 11, 25; Jul. 9, 23; Aug. 6. June19 ♧, Jul. ♧, **Qv**–July 2, 30; Aug 13. **Qw**–② May 23-Sept. 5. **Qx**–May 23–Sept. 5. **y**. ◇–Arrives/calls Juneau 1 day later. ♧–Calls Sitka 1 day earlier. ♡–Arrives Ketchikan 1 day earlier. ♤–Arrives Juneau 1 day earlier
Daily schedule runs between Ketchikan, Metlakatla and Hollis with several sailings a day
ares ex Bellingham add US$ 126. Stewart/Hyder to Ketchikan US$ 40
MH–Alaska Marine Highway. ☎Juneau 907 465 3941. Fax: 907 277 4829.

Table 493 WHITTIER - VALDEZ - CORDOVA — AMH

US$		G	H	I	J	K	L	M	N	O	P	km	495 ↓	↑		Q	R	S	T	U	V	W	X	Y	Z
		③	③⑤⑦	⑥		①⑤	②⑥	⑦	④							⑥	②⑥	①⑤	⑦		②④		⑥	③	
0.00	....	....	....	1100	....	1445	1445	1445	1445	....	....	*0*	d. **Whittier**	a.	....	0730	1400	1400	1400	....	....	....	....	....	....
56.00	....	0645	0845	1800	....	|	2130	2345	0015	....	....	*130*	d. Valdez	d.	....	|	0715	|	0715	....	1400	....	1845	2355	....
56.00	....	1230	1400	....	....	2145	....	0530	0600	....	....	*325*	a. **Cordova**	d.	....	0030	0030	0700	....	....	0845	....	1300	1830	....

, V & X effective April 1-30 and September 23-30 **G, K, L, M, N, R, S, T & Y** effective May 1–September 22 **Q & I** effective 13 May only
MH–Alaska Marine Highway. ☎ Juneau 907 465 3941. Fax: 907 277 4829.

Table 495 396 KODIAK - HOMER - SELDOVIA

AMH RT

(AMH) service Kodiak - Homer - Seldovia and v.v. *200* km. Journey 15-16 hours. Fare US$ 52.00. Timings vary and should be checked with operator.

From Kodiak: May 2, 6v, 7h, 9, 15, 20**v**, 21h, 23**h**, 27**v**, 28**h**, 29**h**, 31; June 1, 3, 4h, 6, 7, 12, 17**v**, 18h, 20, 24**v**, 25h, 27; July 1**v**, 2h, 4, 8**v**, 9**h**, 11, 12, 17, 22**v**, 23h, 25, 29**v** 30h; Aug. 5v, 6 8, 9, **14**, **19v**, 20h, 22, 26**v**, 27h, 29; Sept. 2**v**, 3h, 5, 9**v**, 10h, 12, 13, 18, 23**v**, 24h, 26, 27, returning from Seldovia: May 1h, 2v, 7, 8h, 9, 16, 21, 22h, 23v, 28, 29h, 30h, 31; June 2, 4, 5h, 13, 18, 19h, 20v, 25, 26**h**, 27**v**; July 2, 3**h**, 4**v**, 9, 10h, 11v, 18v, 23, 24h, 25v, 30, 31h; Aug. 1v, 6, 7**h**, 8, 15v, 20, 21h, 22v, 27, 28**h**, 29**v**; Sept. 5, 4**h**, 5**v**, 10, 11**h**, 19v, 24, 25**h**, 26.

(RT) service Homer-Seldovia and v.v. *30* km. Journey: 2 hours. Fare US $: 20.00. **Service operates June 20-Sept. 1.**

From Homer: 1100. **From Seldovia:** 1600.

h–To/from Homer, not Seldovia. v–To/from Valdez. *AMH*–Alaska Marine Highway. ☎ Juneau 907 465 3941. Fax: 907 277 4829. *RT*–Rainbow Tours. ☎ Homer 907 235 7272.

Table 497 396 ALEUTIAN ISLANDS

AMH

service Kodiak - Chignik - Sand Point - King Cove - Cold Bay - Unalaska and v.v. *930* km. Journey 58 hours. Fare US$ 202.00.

From Kodiak: 1700 April 12; May 10; June 7; July 12; Aug. 9; Sept. 13, 27. **From Unalaska:** 0800 April 15; May 13; June 10; July 15; Aug. 12; Sept. 16, 30.

AMH–Alaska Marine Highway. ☎ Juneau 907 465 3941. Fax: 907 277 4829.

Table 500 CLEVELAND - DETROIT/CHICAGO

GL

US $	1319	4445	1323	4415 ⑧	1607	4439	1601	4175	4401	1329	4449	km	396	1318	4404	1612	4440	1320	4444	4414	4176	4436	1606	1626
0.00	0045	0045	0715	0730	0945	1015	1015	1201	1201	1720	1720	0	d.**Cleveland** a.	1035	1035	1420	1435	1700	1700	1940	0005	2330	2355	0735
	|	|	0835	0855	|	|	1140	|	1325	1840	1840		d.Sandusky d.	|	0910	|	|	1530	|	1815	2250	|	|	|
	|	|	0950	1010	|	1225	1255	1410	1440	1940	|		a. **Toledo** d.	0825	0800	1215	1230	1410	1435	1700	2140	2120	|	|
	|	|	1000	1020	|	1230	1305	1415	1450	1950	|		d. **Toledo** a.	0815	0750	1201	1220	1400	1425	1650	2130	2110	|	|
	|	0355	|	1130	|	1355	|	|	1610	|	2055	256	a. **Detroit** d.	|	0630	|	1100	|	1305	1540	|	2000	|	|
	|	....	1250	....	|	....	1605	|	....	|	....		d.Elkhart d.	|	....	|	....	1105	....	....	1835	....	|	|
	|	....	1325	....	|	....	1640	|	....	|	....		d.South Bend d.	|	....	|	....	1030	....	....	1800	....	|	|
	|	....	|	....	|	....	1650	|	....	|	....		d.Gary d.	|	....	|	....	0815	....	....	1545	....	|	|
	|	....	|	....	|	....	1710	|	....	|	....		a.Hammond d.	|	....	|	....	0755	....	....	1525	....	|	|
	0600	....	1400	....	1515	....	1815	1805	....	2350	....	533	a.**Chicago** d.	0230	....	0615	....	0700	....	....	1430	....	1630	0001

GL– Greyhound Lines. Tel.: Dallas 214 789 7000.

Table 501 NEW YORK/WASHINGTON - CHICAGO

GL

US $	396	km		1323	1624	4415 ⑧	1605 ⑤	1607	4439	1601	4175	4401	1329		4449	1620	1319	4445		1622					1321
0.00	**New York** d.	0	....	2100	....	....	2100	2345	....	....	....	....	....	....	....	....	1330	....	....	....	....	....	....	....	1700
	Newark d.		....	2130	....	....	2130	|	....	....	....	....	....	....	....	....	1405	....	....	....	....	....	....	....	1745
	DuBois d.		....	|	....	....	|	|	....	....	....	....	....	....	....	....	|	....	....	....	....	....	....	....	|
❖	**Washington** d.	❖	....	|	2145	....	|	|	0035	....	....	....	0630	....	....	1100	|	1400	....	1815	....	....	....	....	|
67.00	**Pittsburgh** d.	618	....	|	0345	....	|	|	0700	....	....	....	1300	....	....	1815	|	2130	....	0015	....	....	....	....	|
82.00	**Cleveland** d.	811	....	0715	0655	0730	0730	0945	1015	1015	1201	1201	1720	....	1720	2205	0045	0045	....	0315	....	....	....	....	0400
❖	Toledo d.	❖	....	1000	....	1020	1020	|	1230	1305	1415	1450	1950	....	|	....	|	|	....	0530	....	....	....	....	0615
92.00	**Detroit** a.	1067	....	|	....	1130	1130	|	1355	|	|	1610	|	....	2055	....	|	0355	....	0640	....	....	....	....	|
98.00	**Chicago** a.	1344	....	1400	....	....	....	1515	....	1815	1805	....	2350	....	....	....	0600	....	....	....	....	....	....	....	1050

296	4404	1318			4440		1612	1320	4444	4414		1322		1326	4176	4436	1606		4436	4448	1610			1626	
Chicago d.	....	0230	....	....	....	....	0615	0700	....	....	....	1100	....	1430	1430	....	1630	....	1630	....	....	....	....	0001	....
Detroit d.	0630	|	....	....	1100	....	|	|	1305	1540	....	|	....	|		....	|	....	|	2015	....	....	....	|	....
Toledo d.	0800	0825	....	....	1230	....	1215	1410	1435	1615	....	1720	....	|	2140	2000	|	....	2340	2330	....	....	....	|	....
Cleveland d.	1100	1145	....	....	1435	....	1500	1700	1815	1940	....	2030	....	2045	0005	0045	0045	....	0125	0215	....	....	....	0815	....
Pittsburgh d.	1445	|	....	....	....	....	1845	....	2145	....	....	0045	....	|	....	|	|	....	....	0545	0845	....	....	1130	....
Washington a.	2135	|	....	....	....	....	0015	....	0235	....	....	0535	....	|	....	|	|	....	....	1155	1515	....	....	1645	....
DuBois d.	....	1540	....	....	....	....	....	....	....	....	....	....	....	|	....	|	|	....	....	....	....	....	....	....	....
Newark a.	....	2140s	....	....	....	....	....	....	....	....	....	....	....	|	....	|	|	....	....	....	....	....	....	....	....
New York a.	....	2215	....	....	....	....	....	....	....	....	....	....	....	0755	....	1010	1010	....	....	....	....	....	....	....	....

GL– Greyhound Lines. Tel.: Dallas 214 789 7000.

Table 502 NEW YORK - PITTSBURGH

CPB GL PPB

US $		GL 4375	PPB 2515	GL 1371	GL 4459	CPB 201	GL 473	CPB 203	PPB 2527	GL 1355	GL 1377	CPB 205	GL 1379		GL 1369	km	396
0.00	....	....	0700	0645	0730	0845	1000	1300	1300	1400	1700	1725	2100	....	0030	0	d.**New York** a.
	....	....	|	0725	0805	|	1035	|	|	|	1745	|	2135	....	|		d.**Newark** a.
19.00	....	0730	0935a	1000	|	|	1335	|	1450a	1635	2020	|	0001	....	0315	149	d.**Philadelphia** a.
22.00	....	0815	1010a	1040	|	1110	1415	1530	1530a	1725	|	1950	|	....	|		d.King of Prussia d.
	....	|	|	|	0925	|	|	|	|	|	|	|	|	....	|		d. Easton d.
18.00	....	|	|	|	0950	|	|	|	|	|	|	|	|	....	|		d. Bethlehem d.
19.00	....	|	|	|	1015	|	|	|	|	|	|	|	|	....	|		d. Allentown d.
32.00	....	1015	1340a	1250	1159	1340	1630	1800	1830a	1925	2235	2210	|	....	0540		d.Harrisburg d.
67.00	....	1500	....	1700	....	....	2040	....	....	2325	0225	....	0600	....	1055	618	a.**Pittsburgh** d.

396	CPB 202		GL 1346	CPB 204	GL 1374	CPB 402	GL 1376	CPB 402	GL 4690	CPB 208	GL 1328	GL 1366		GL 1368	GL 1360
d.**New York** a.	1055	....	1215	1545	1530	1700b	1940	2130	2205	2005	2120	0030	....	0335	0820
d.**Newark** a.	|	....	|	|	|	|	1900	|	2130	|	2030	2345	....	|	|
d.**Philadelphia** a.	|	....	0930	|	1210	1400	1635	1825	1855	|	|	2140	....	0110	0525
d.King of Prussia d.	0835	....	|	1325	1130	1325	1555	1750	1815	1750	|	2105	....	|	|
d. Easton d.	|	....	|	|	|	|	|	|	|	|	1900	|	....	|	|
d. Bethlehem d.	|	....	|	|	|	|	|	|	|	|	1830	|	....	|	|
d. Allentown d.	|	....	|	|	|	|	|	|	|	|	1800	|	....	|	|
d.Harrisburg d.	0600	....	0715	1045	0940	0900	1410	1410	1630	1500	1635	1930	....	2305	|
a.**Pittsburgh** d.	....	....	0300	....	0520		0915	....	0845	....	1145	1500	....	1830	2315

a– *CPB*. b–*PPB*. *CPB*–Capitol Trailways. Tel.: Harrisburg 717 233 7673. *GL*–Greyhound Lines. Tel.: 214 789 7000. *PPB*–Peter Pan Trailways. Tel.: Springfield 413 781 2900

Table 503 WASHINGTON - PITTSBURGH - CLEVELAND

GL

US $	4439	4367	4357	1329	4375	1620		4445	1622		1624	km	396		4448	4704	4366	1626	4404	4374	1612	4372	4444	1322
0.00	0035	....	....	0630	....	1100	....	1400	1815	....	2145	0	d.**Washington** a.	....	1155	....	....	1645	2135	....	0015	....	0235	0535
	|	....	....	|	....	1130	....	1430	|	....	|		d.Silver Spring d.	....	1125	....	....	1615	2050s	....	|	....	|	|
	|	....	....	0800	....	1320	....	1635	|	....	2345		d.Hagerstown d.	....	0950	1300	....	1515	1915	....	2250	....	|	|
	0545	....	....	1150	....	1725	....	2025	2325	....	0315		a. **Pittsburgh** d.	....	0545	0830	....	1130	1445	....	1845	....	2145	0045
	0700	0700	1230	1300	1545	1815	....	2130	0015	....	0345		d. **Pittsburgh** a.	....	0445	....	1040	1055	1340	1745	1740	2115	2055	2345
	|	0850	1430	|	1730	1955	....	|	|	....	0525		d.Youngstown d.	....	|	....	0900	|	|	1605	|	1920	|	|
	|	0920	|	|	1800	|	....	|	|	....	|		d.Warren d.	....	|	....	|	|	|	1530	|	|	|	|
	|	1020	1530	|	1900	2100	....	|	|	....	|		d.Akron d.	....	|	....	0740	|	|	1435	|	1815	|	2130
	0930	1120	1615	1540	1945	2205	....	2359	0245	....	0655		a.**Cleveland** d.	....	0215	....	0645	0815	1100	1330	1500	1720	1815	2030

GL– Greyhound Lines. Tel.: Dallas 214 789 7000.

Table 505 SYRACUSE - ELMIRA

NYT

US$	975 ⑤⑦	963 ⑤⑦	969	971 ⑦	km	396	960	966 ⑤⑦	974 ⑤⑦	
0.00	0930	1400	1630	2015	0	d.**Syracuse** a.	1250	1800	2210	....
	1015	1445	1715	2100		d.Cortland d.	1205	1715	2125	....
	1055	1525	1755	2140		d.Ithaca d.	1125	1630	2040	....
	1150	....	1850	....		a.**Elmira** d.	1030	....	1945	....

NYT– New York Trailways. Tel.: Kingston 914 339 4230.

Table 506 CARIBOU - BANGOR

CJT

US $		2			km	396			1	
❖	....	0700	....	....	0	d.**Caribou** a.	....	....	2230	....
❖	....	0725	....	....	25	d.Presque Isle d.	....	....	2205	....
❖	....	0830	....	....	193	d.Houlton d.	....	....	2110	....
❖	....	|	....	....	❖	d.Lincoln d.	....	....	|	....
0.00	....	1120	....	....	390	a.**Bangor** d.	....	....	1800	....

CJT– Cyr Bus Line. Tel.: Old Town 207 827 2335.

Table 512 KENNEBUNKPORT

CJR

US$			Ⓒ	Ⓐ	km	396				
0.00	....	0945	*1615*	*1700*	0	d.Logan Airport a.	....	1035	1535	....
	....	1030	1715	1800		d.**Boston** a.	....	1020	1520	....
	....	1115	1800	1845		d.Newburyport d.	....	0930	1430	....
	....	1140	1845	1910		d.Portsmouth d.	....	0900	1400	....
	....	1210	1940	1940		a.Ogunquit d.	....	0825	1325	....
	....	1220	1950	1950		a.**Wells** d.	....	0815	1315	....
	....	1235	2005	2005		a.**Kennebunkport** d.	....	0800	1300	....

CJR– C & J Trailways. Tel.: Dover 603 742 5111.

⊗–Buffet car 🍸–Light refreshments OB–Observation car

Table 514 NEW YORK - FLORIDA

CCC GL SES

US $	396	km	GL 1047	SES 204		GL 1015	CCC 509	CCC 507	SES 205	CCC 517	SES 201		GL 1003		GL 1043	SES 208	GL 1017	GL 1005	GL 1007	SES 202	GL 1011	GL 1045 ⑥		SES 209	CCC 503
0.00	**New York** d.	0	....	....	....	....	....	....	....	....	....	....	1400	....	....	....	1800	2130	....	....	....	....	....	....	....
37.00	**Washington** d.	❖	....	....	....	....	....	....	....	....	....	....	|	....	....	....	|	|	....	....	....	....	....	....	....
53.00	Richmond d.	❖	0100	....	....	1030	1330	1600	....	1800	....	....	2130	....	0105	....	0120	|	0410	....	0410	0410	....	....	0630
56.00	Petersburg d.	❖	1035	....	....	1110	1405	|	....	1835	....	....	|	....	|	....	|	|	|	....	0445	|	....	....	0705
τ25.50	Henderson d.		|	....	....	1245	1545	|	....	2015	....	....	|	....	|	....	|	|	|	....	0620	|	....	....	0845
	Rocky Mount d.	❖	1250	....	....	|	|	|	....	|	....	....	|	....	0330	....	|	|	|	....	|	0645	....	....	|
73.00	Raleigh d.	❖	|	....	....	1400	1710	|	....	2130	....	....	|	....	|	....	|	|	|	....	0740	|	....	....	1000
77.00	Fayetteville d.	❖	|	1600	....	1605	1830	2015b	2010	2330b	0145	....	0145	....	|	0515	0515	0815	0815	0800	1000	|	....	1150	1205b
85.00	Florence d.	❖	|	1810	....	1830	....	|	2200	|	0315	....	|	....	|	0655	|	|	1015	0950	1315	|	....	1335	1415b
92.00	North Charleston d.	❖	2115	|	....	2045	....	|	|	|	|	...	|	....	1145	|	|	|	|	|	1530	1530	....	|	|
92.00	Sumter d.	❖	|	|	....	....	....	|	2245	|	0405	....	|	....	|	|	|	|	1105	1035	....	....	....	1420	1505b
92.00	Columbia a.	❖	|	2000	....	....	....	|	2345	|	0500	....	|	....	|	0830	|	|	|	1135	....	....	....	1530	|
98.00	Orangeburg d.	❖	|	....	....	....	....	|	....	|	....	....	|	....	|	....	|	|	|	....	....	....	....	....	1635b
104.00	Savannah d.	❖	0020	....	....	....	....	0100b	....	|	....	....	0645	....	1500	....	|	|	1510	....	....	....	....	....	1925b
	Brunswick d.	❖	0230	....	....	....	....	|	....	|	....	....	|	....	1715	....	1100s	|	1630	....	....	....	....	....	2045b
118.00	Jacksonville a.	❖	0345	....	....	....	....	0320b	....	0615b	....	....	0915	....	1830	....	1230	|	1800	....	....	....	....	....	2215b
142.00	**Miami** a.	❖	....	....	....	....	....	1145b	....	....	....	....	1705	....	....	....	2010	|	....	....	....	....	....	....	....
131.00	Orlando a.	❖	....	....	....	....	....	*0715*	....	....	....	....	....	....	....	....	....	1730	....	....	....	....	....	....	....
131.00	Tampa a.	❖	....	....	....	....	....	*1150*	....	....	....	....	....	....	....	....	....	1955	....	....	....	....	....	....	....

296	GL 1016	GL 1046	SES 102	GL 1018	SES 108					GL 1012	GL 1044	GL 1002	SES 106	GL 1014	GL 516		SES 107	GL 1024	SES 105	GL 506	CCC 502	GL 500	SES 101	GL 1048 ⑦	
Tampa d.	....	....	....	....	....	....	....	....	....	....	....	....	....	....	....	....	....	....	....	....	....	....	....	....	....
Orlando d.	....	....	....	....	....	....	....	....	....	....	....	1330	....	....	....	....	....	....	....	....	....	....	....	....	....
Miami d.	....	....	....	....	....	....	....	....	....	....	....	|	....	....	0915	....	....	1330	....	....	....	1900	....	....	....
Jacksonville d.	....	0315	....	0730	....	....	....	....	....	1415	....	|	....	1345	1715	....	....	2130	....	0015	....	0315	....	....	....
Brunswick d.	....	|	....	0900	....	....	....	....	....	|	....	|	....	1515	|	....	....	|	....	|	....	|	....	....	....
Savannah d.	....	0615	....	1100	....	....	....	....	....	|	....	1845	....	1715	2015	....	....	0020	....	|	....	|	....	....	....
Orangeburg d.	....	|	....	1315	....	....	....	....	....	|	....	|	....	|	|	....	....	|	....	|	....	|	....	....	....
Columbia d.	....	|	1335	|	1800	....	....	....	....	|	....	|	2035	|	|	....	0105	|	0400	|	....	|	0845	....	....
Sumter d.	....	|	|	1445	1900	....	....	....	....	|	....	|	2135	|	|	....	0155	|	|	|	....	|	0945	....	....
North Charleston d.	0915	0915	|	|	|	....	....	....	....	|	1615	|	|	2015	|	....	|	|	|	|	....	|	|	0615	....
Florence d.	1201	|	1515	1605	1945	....	....	....	....	|	|	|	2215	2245	|	....	0235	|	0530	|	....	|	1030	|	....
Fayetteville d.	1530	|	1705	1845	2200	....	....	....	....	2300	|	2345	2345	0115	0115a	....	0415	0525	0715	0745a	0745	1045a	1215	|	....
Raleigh d.	1705	|	....	2035	....	....	....	....	....	|	|	|	....	|	|	....	....	|	....	|	0930	|	....	|	....
Rocky Mount d.	|	1750	....	|	....	....	....	....	....	|	0025	|	....	|	|	....	....	|	....	|	|	|	....	1500	....
Henderson d.	1830	|	....	2130	....	....	....	....	....	|	|	|	....	|	|	....	....	|	....	|	1055	|	....	|	....
Petersburg d.	2005	1950	....	2305	....	....	....	....	....	|	|	|	....	|	|	....	....	0835	....	|	1230	as	....	1700	....
Richmond a.	2045	2030	....	2345	....	....	....	....	....	0230	0245	|	....	0445	0445a	....	....	0915	....	1115a	1310	1430a	....	1740	....
Washington a.	....	....	....	....	....	....	....	....	....	|	....	|	....	....	|	....	....	....	....	....	....	....	....	....	....
New York a.	....	....	....	....	....	....	....	....	....	1020	....	0945	....	....	1220	....	....	....	....	....	....	....	....	....	....

a– *CCC*. b–*GL*. τ–Fare ex Richmond. *CCC*–Carolina Trailways. Tel.: Raleigh 919 833 3601.
GL– Greyhound Lines. Tel.: Dallas 214 789 7000. *SES*–Southeastern Stages. Tel.: Atlanta 404 874 2741.

Table 517 BANGOR - PORTLAND - BOSTON

CLI GL PPB SMT WTI

US $	GL 9641	CLI 51	GL 9639	GL 9623	CLI	CLI 55	GL 0221	GL 9685	CLI	GL 9631	WTI	GL 9627	CLI	GL 9601 ⑤⑦	SMT 11	km	396	GL 9624	CLI	GL 9620	GL 9626	CLI 52	GL 9628	CLI	CLI 56	GL 0222	GL 9644	WTI	CLI	GL 9646	SMT 12	GL 9648 ⑤⑦
19.75	....	....	....	....	....	....	....	....	....	....	....	....	....	....	1440	❖	d. **Saint John** a.	....	....	....	....	....	....	....	....	....	....	....	....	....	1730	....
	....	....	....	....	....	....	....	....	....	....	....	....	....	....	|		d. Black's Harbour d.	....	....	....	....	....	....	....	....	....	....	....	....	....	|	....
11.25	....	....	....	....	....	....	....	....	....	....	....	....	....	....	1605	❖	d. St. Stephen 🛃 a.	....	....	....	....	....	....	....	....	....	....	....	....	....	1610	....
18.00	....	....	....	....	....	....	....	....	....	....	0930	....	....	....	|	❖	d. Calais 🛃 a.	....	....	....	....	....	....	....	....	....	....	1900	....	....	|	....
	....	....	....	....	....	....	....	....	....	....	|	....	....	....	|		d. Eastport a.	....	....	....	....	....	....	....	....	....	....	|	....	....	|	....
14.00	....	....	....	....	....	....	....	....	....	....	1100	....	....	....	|	❖	d. Machias a.	....	....	....	....	....	....	....	....	....	....	1730	....	....	|	....
	....	....	....	....	....	....	....	....	....	....	|	....	....	....	|		d. Bass Harbor a.	....	....	....	....	....	....	....	....	....	....	|	....	....	|	....
	....	....	....	....	....	....	....	....	....	....	|	....	....	....	|	❖	d. Bar Harbor a.	....	....	....	....	....	....	....	....	....	....	|	....	....	|	....
7.00	....	....	....	....	....	....	....	....	....	....	1225	....	....	....	|	❖	d. Ellsworth d.	....	....	....	....	....	....	....	....	....	....	1605	....	....	|	....
0.00	....	....	....	0600	0715	0715	0800	....	1115	1215	1315	1340	1515	1600	1830f	*0*	d. **Bangor** d.	1230	1415	1435c	1740	1800	1750	1830	2215	2130	....	1510	2230	....	1145g	....
11.00	....	....	....	0705	|	|	0905	....	|	|	▬	1440	|	|	....	*99*	d. Waterville d.	1130	|	|	1640	|	|	|	|	s	....	▬	|	....	▬	....
13.00	....	....	....	0735	|	|	0935	....	|	|	....	1515	|	|	....	*132*	d. Augusta d.	1055	|	|	1605	|	|	|	|	2000	....	....	|	....	....	....
20.00	0610	....	....	0825	|	|	|	....	|	1405	....	1605	|	1750	....	*181*	d. Lewiston d.	1010	|	sc	|	|	1600	|	|	1925	1955	....	|	....	....	....
8.00	|	....	....	|	|	0810	|	....	1210	|	....	|	|	|	....	*34*	d. Belfast d.	|	|	|	|	1700	|	|	2115	|	|	....	|	....	....	....
	|	....	....	|	|	0825r	|	....	1225r	|	*CLI*	|	|	|	....		d. Lincolnville d.	|	|	|	|	1645r	|	|	2100r	|	|	....	|	....	....	....
13.00	|	....	....	|	|	0855	|	....	|	|	59	|	|	|	....	*95*	d. Rockland d.	|	|	|	|	1615	|	|	2030	|	|	....	|	....	....	....
21.00	|	0645	0730	|	|	1045	1020	....	|	|	1445	|	|	|	....	*184*	d. Brunswick d.	|	|	|	1520	1435	|	|	1845	|	s	*CLI*	|	2240	*CLI*	....
24.00	0705	0730	0805	0925	0930	1130	1105	1230	1330	1515	1530	1700	1730	1915	....	*246*	d. **Portland** d.	0920	1201	1220	1445	1400	1515	1615	1815	1835	1905	1910	2015	2205	2210	2345
26.00	|	|	|	|	|	|	|	|	|	|	|	|	|	|	....	*275*	d. Biddeford d.	|	|	|	|	|	|	|	|	|	|	|	|	|	|	|
38.00	|	|	0910	|	|	|	1205	|	|	|	|	1800	|	|	....	*322*	d. Portsmouth d.	0805	|	1110	1325	|	|	|	|	1715	|	|	|	2100	|	|
41.00	|	|	|	|	|	|	|	|	|	|	|	1825	|	|	....	*361*	d. Newburyport d.	0735	|	|	1250	|	|	|	|	|	|	|	|	2035	|	|
41.00	0905	0925	1030	1130	1125	1325	1315	1430	1525	1715	1725	1930	1925	2115	....	*424*	a. **Boston** d.	0645	1000	1000	1201	1201	1300	1415	1615	1600	1700	1715	1815	1950	2015	2145
41.00	*1420*	*1405c*	*1520*	*1630*	1605c	*1805c*	*1830*	....	*2005c*	*2230*	*2005c*	*0020e*	*0005c*	*0220*	....	*794*	a. *New York* d.	*0030*	*0355c*	....	*0700*	*0610c*	*0800*	*0830c*	1130c	*1100*	*1201*	....	*1330c*	*1500*	*1530c*	....

a– *GL*. c–*PPB*. c–⑤⑦. d–ex ⑦. e–ex ②③. f–⑤⑥. g–⑤⑦.
CLI– Concord Trailways. Tel.: Concord 603 228 3300.
GL– Greyhound Lines. Tel.: Dallas 214 789 7000.
PPB– Peter Pan Trailways. Tel.: Springfield 413 781 2900.
SMT– SMT (Eastern) Ltd. Tel.: Dieppe 506 8569 5100.
WTI– West's Transportation Inc. Tel.: Milbridge ❖.

Table 518 BOSTON - NEWPORT

BZ

US $	371 ⚒	351	355	357	359 ④		361 ④	363	365	367 †		km	396	350 ④	352 ⚒	354 ④	356		358		362	364	366	368 †
0.00	0800	1000	1400	1600	1700	....	1730	1800	2000	2200	....	*0*	d. **Boston** ◇ a.	0725	0745	0835	0940	....	1140	....	1540	1740	1940	2140
8.95	0900	1100	1500	1700	1800	....	1830	1900	2100	2300	....	*66*	a. Fall River d.	0620	0640	0730	0840	....	1040	....	1440	1640	1840	2040
13.00	0935	1135	1535	1735	....	....	1905	1935	2135	2335	....	*95*	a. **Newport** d.	...	0600	0650	0800	....	1000	....	1400	1600	1800	2000

◇– Service also operates Boston-Providence and v.v. *70* km. Journey: 1 hour. Fare: US $: 7.75. **From Boston**: 0015, 0630①⑥, 0650, 0730⚒, 0800†, 0900⚒, 1000, 1100, 1201, 1300, 1400, 1500, 1600, 1700, 1800, 1900, 2000, 2100, 2300. **From Providence**: 0520①⑥, 0600, 0715⚒, 0830, 0930 and hourly to 2130, 2315.
BZ– Bonanza Bus Lines. Tel.: Providence 401 331 7500.

Table 519 RUTLAND - BOSTON

VT

US$	123	9052	9056		km	396	9059		9055	
11.50	....	....	*1100*	....	0	d. *Burlington* a.	*1920*	....	*2315*	....
0.00	....	0645	1315	....		d. **Rutland** a.	1635	....	2115	....
6.50	....	0710	1350	....		d. Ludlow d.	1545	....	2040	....
11.50	0850	0805	1440	....		d. Bellows Falls d.	1505	....	1950	....
21.00	0930	0900	1515	....		d. Keene d.	1410	....	1855	....
29.00	....	1010	1630	....		d. Fitchburgh d.	1250	....	1735	....
34.00	....	1110	1750	....		a. **Boston** d.	1145	....	1630	....
40.00	....	....	....	....		a. Boston Airport d.	....	....	1430	....

VT–Vermont Transit. Tel.: Burlington 802 862 9671.

Table 520 WHITE RIVER - NEW YORK

GL VT

US$	VT 123	VT 127	VT 129	VT 133 ⑤⑦	km	396 ↓ ↑	VT 122	GL 124	GL 128	GL 134 ⑤⑦
0.00	0745	1040	1355	1700	0	d.**White River Junction** .a.	1245	1635b	2040b	0050b
	0850	1130	1440	|		d.Bellows Falls ....a.	1201	1520b	1955b	2350b
	1005	1205	1520	1810		d.Brattleboro..............d.	1125	1420b	1855b	2255b
	1035	1235	1550	1840		d.Greenfield...............d.	1055	1345b	1825b	2225b
	1105s	1305	s	1910s		d.Northampton ....d.	1030	1315b	1800b	2200b
	1201a	1330	1720a	1935a		d.**Springfield** ....d.	1005	1250b	1735b	2140b
	1300a	1500a	1815a	2010a		d.Hartford..................d.	0810	1155	1550	2100
	|	*1615*a	1905a	|		d.New Haven ....d.	|	1050	1440	|
	|	*1645*a	1925a	|		d.Bridgeport...............d.	|	1010	1400	|
	|	*1715*a	2005a	|		d.Stamford ....d.	|	0935	1325	|
	1555a	*1825*a	2100a	*0025*a		a.**New York**...............d.	*0515*a	0800	1201	*1730*

a–*GL*. b–*VT*. *GL*–Greyhound Lines. Tel.: Dallas 214 789 7000.
VT–Vermont Transit. Tel.: Burlington 802 862 9671.

Table 521 SYRACUSE - MALONE

ADT GL

US$	ADT 119		GL 4154	GL 4304	km	396 ↓ ↑	GL 4311		GL 4157	ADT 106B
0.00	....	....	0815	1900	0	d.**Syracuse** ....a.	1159	....	1735	....
8.00	....	....	0910	1955	55	d.Pulaski ....d.	1105	....	1640	....
11.00	....	....	0935	2020	84	d.Adams.......................d.	1045	....	1620	....
13.00	....	....	1005	2050	113	d.Watertown...............d.	1015	....	1550	....
21.00	....	....	1020	2145	173	d.Gouverneur ....d.	0910	....	1440	....
24.00	0830	....	1135	2220	210	d.Canton ....d.	0835	....	1405	2000
25.00	0845	....	1210	2245	228	d.Potsdam...................d.	0815	....	1345	1945
	|	....	|	....		d. Ogdensburg.......a.	....	....	|	|
30.00	0925	....	1240	....	259	d. Massena ....d.	....	....	1315	1910
32.00	1015	....	....	....	294	a.**Malone**...................d.	....	....	....	1820

ADT– Adirondack Trailways. Tel.: Kingston 914 339 4230.
GL– Greyhound Lines. Tel.: Dallas 214 789 7000.

Table 522 CAPE COD

BZ PLB

service *(PLB)* Boston (South Station) ★-North Plymouth-Hyannis and v.v. *113* km. Journey: $1^3/_4$-2 hours. Fare: US$: 5.70.

From Boston: 0655Ⓐ, 0705©, 0915, 1015, 1115, 1215, 1315, 1415, 1510Ⓐ, 1520©, 1530Ⓐ, 1545Ⓐ, 1600Ⓐ, 1615, 1630Ⓐ, 1650Ⓐ, 1700Ⓐ, 1715, 1725Ⓐ, 1745Ⓐ, 1800Ⓐ, 1815, 1845Ⓐ, 1915, 2015, 2115Ⓐ, 2215© 2340.

From Hyannis: 0430, 0445Ⓐ, 0500Ⓐ, 0515Ⓐ, 0525Ⓐ, 0530©, 0535Ⓐ, 0540Ⓐ, 0545Ⓐ, 0555Ⓐ, 0605Ⓐ, 0615Ⓐ, 0630, 0640Ⓐ, 0700Ⓐ, 0720Ⓐ, 0730©, 0750Ⓐ, 0830, 0930, 1030, 1130, 1230, 1330, 1430, 1530, 1630, 1830©, 1930Ⓐ, 2030©.

US$		400		402	km	292 *BZ* ↓ ↑	401		403	
0.00	....	1201	....	1815	0	d.**Springfield** ....a.	1210	....	1755	....
	....	1340	....	1955	146	a.**Providence**............d.	1030	....	1615	....

US$	800		810		km	196 *PLB* ↓ ↑	803		809	
0.00	0650	....	1450	....	0	d.**Provincetown**........a.	1245	....	1910	....
	0830	....	1630	....	82	d.Hyannis ....d.	1115	....	1745	....
	1015	....	1815	....		a.**Boston**...................d.	0915	....	1530a	....

US$	501 ex⑦	505	507	509	511 Ⓐ	513	523 Ⓐ	515	517	519	521	km	396 *BZ* ↓ ↑	500 ex⑦	502	504 Ⓐ	508	524 Ⓐ	510	512	514	516	518	520
0.00	0800	1000	1201	1400	1515	1615	1645	1715	1815	2000	2200	0	d.**Boston** ★.......................a.	0645	0730	0825	0940	1110	1205	1340	1605	1655	1835	2105
❖	0925	1125	1325	1525	1640	1740	1815	1840	1940	2130	2335	106	d.Falmouth.........................d.	0520	0600	0700	0810	0940	1040	1210	1440	1530	1710	1940
13.25	0935	1135	1335	1535	1650	1750	1825	1850	1950	2140	2345	120	a.**Wood's Hole** ....d.	....	....	0645	0800	0930	1030	1201	1430	1520	1700	1930

US$	200		202	204	206	208		212	214	216 ex⑤	216 ⑤	km	294 *BZ* ↓ ↑	201	203		205	207	209	211	213 Ⓐ		215	
0.00	0545	....	0900	1145	1345	1545	....	1745	2000	2200	2200	0	d.**Providence**.....................a.	0720	0830	....	1030	1230	1430	1730	1835	....	1930	....
3.95	s	....	0925	1210	1410	1610	....	1810	2025	2225	2225	26	d.Fall River.........................d.	0655	0800	....	1000	1201	1400	1650	1810	....	1900	....
6.90	0630	....	0945	1230	1430	1630	....	1830	2045	2245	2245	50	d.New Bedford ....d.	0630	0735	....	0935	1135	1335	1625	....	....	1835	....
17.15	....	....	1050	1335	1535	1735	....	1935	2145	....	2345	127	a.**Hyannis** ....d.	....	0630	....	0830	1030	1230	1520	....	....	1730	....

★–Certain trips operate to/from Logan Airport. a–leaves 15 minutes earlier on © *BZ*–Bonanza Bus Lines. Tel.: Providence 401 331 7500. *PLB*–Plymouth and Brockton Street Railway. Tel.: Plymouth 508 746 4795.

Table 523 NEW YORK - RUTLAND

BZ GL VT

US$		VT 9047	VT 9324	BZ 750		VT 9043	VT 9072	VT 9045	BZ 752	BZ 754	BZ 728 ⑤	km	396 ↓ ↑	BZ 751	BZ 753	VT 9042	BZ 711 ⑤	VT 9075	VT 9044		BZ 755	VT 9071	VT 9046	
0.00	....	*0600*d	....	*0845*	....	*1130*d	....	*1330*d	1415	1715	1930	0	d.**New York**........................a.	1225	1425	*1520*d	1745	....	*1920*d	....	*2050*	....	*0120*d	....
4.30	....	*0635*d	....	|	....	*1205*d	....	*1405*d	|	|	|	30	d.Ridgewood ....d.	|	|	*1435*d	|	....	*1835*d	....	|	....	|	....
11.45	....	|	....	1030	....	|	....	|	1545	1845	2055	134	d. Danbury.........................a.	1100	1300	|	1620	....	|	....	1915	....	|	....
28.20	....	|	....	1325	....	|	....	|	1815	2115	2325	250	d. Pittsfield.........................d.	0830	1030	|	1330	....	|	....	1645	....	|	....
19.95	....	0910	....	|	....	1435	....	1900	....	|	....	263	d.**Albany** ....a.	....	|	1145	....	....	1545	....	|	....	2115	....
22.05	....	r	....	|	....	r	....	r	....	|	....	271	d.Troy.....................................d.	....	|	s	....	....	s	....	|	....	s	....
28.75	....	1015	....	1420	....	1545	....	2005	....	2200	....	313	d.Bennington ....d.	....	0930	1040	....	....	1435	....	1530	....	2005	....
37 90	....	1201	1215	....	....	1720	1830	2130	....	....	....	406	d.**Rutland**.............................d.	....	....	0930	....	1155	1315	....	....	1815	1840	....
47.70	....	1355	|	....	....	1920	|	2315	....	....	....	512	a.Burlington ....d.	....	....	0735	....	|	1100	....	....	|	1630	....
❖	....	....	1330	....	....	....	1940	....	....	....	....	660	a. White River Junction d.	....	....	....	....	1040	....	....	....	1700	....	....

c–*VT*. d–*GL*. *BZ*–Bonanza Bus Lines. Tel.: Providence 401 331 7500. *GL*–Greyhound Lines. Tel.: Dallas 214 789 7000. *VT*–Vermont Transit. Tel.: Burlington 802 862 9671.

Table 524 BOSTON - ALBANY - CLEVELAND

ADT BZ GL LFL NYT PPB

US $	396 ↓	km	GL 0302	GL 4185	ADT 500A	GL 4181	ADT 502	ADT 510	GL 0306	GL 4179	PPB 321	GL 4173 ⑤⑦	BZ 401	ADT 524	ADT 512	PPB 329	GL 1387	ADT 506 ⑤⑦	PPB 335	BZ 403	ADT 514	ADT 518	GL 4177	ADT 508	GL 4175
0.00	**Boston** ⊠.........d.	0	....	....	....	....	....	....	....	0715	0800	....	....	......	....	1201	1201	....	1500	....	....	....	1700	....	2030
	Worcester ⊠......d.	71	....	....	....	....	....	....	....	0825	0905	....	....	....	....	|	1310	....	|	....	....	....	1810	....	2140
8.45	**Springfield** ⊠ ...d.	188	....	....	....	....	....	....	....	0935	1015	....	1215	....	....	1410	1420	....	1715	1815	....	....	1920	....	|
	Pittsfield ....d.		....	....	....	....	....	....	....	|	1125	....	1320	....	....	1520	|	....	1825	1925	....	....	|	....	|
	New York..........d.		2330	....	....	0600	*0700*	0900	0745	*0830*	*1000*d	*1030*	|	1115	*1300*	|	*1330*	*1300*	|	|	*1745*	1930	*1830*	2215	*2130*
	Albany ....d.		|	....	0710	0905	1015	|	|	1235	1300d	1430	1415	1430	1600	1620	1635	1640	1925	2020	2100	|	2230	|	0030
	Schenectady ......d.		|	....	0735	0935	1040	|	|	1305	1325d	1500	....	|	1625	....	1705	1705	....	....	2125	|	|	|	|
	Utica.....................d.		|	....	0905	1110	1220	|	|	1445	1505d	1640	....	1615	1755	....	1840	1850	....	....	2255	|	|	|	|
	Syracuse ....d.		0435	0715	1035c	1315	1335	1350c	1330	1625	1620c	1815	....	1740c	1920c	....	2005	2000c	....	....	0010	0030c	0050	0300c	0330
	Rochester...........d.		|	0915	1230c	1510	....	1540c	|	1820	1815c	2010	....	1930c	2105c	....	2200	2145c	....	....	....	0210c	|	0440c	0525
	Buffalo ....d.		0715	1130	1410c	1725	....	1710c	1610	2020	1950c	2140	....	*2055*c	2230c	....	0001	2315c	....	....	....	0340c	0430	0605c	0730
	Erie ....d.		....	1330	*1635*e	1935	....	....	....	2220	....	....	....	....	....	....	|	....	....	....	....	....	0630	....	0930
	Ashtabula ....d.		....	1420	|	|	....	....	....	|	....	....	....	....	....	....	|	....	....	....	....	....	|	....	1020
	Cleveland..........a.		....	1530	*1830*e	2115	....	....	....	2359	....	....	....	....	....	....	0330	....	....	....	....	....	0820	....	1130

296 ↓	GL 4182	GL 0311	GL 0303	NYT 941	NYT 939	NYT 931	BZ 400	GL 4176	NYT 901	ADT 515 ⑤	PPB 322	BZ 402	GL 4174 ⑤⑦	GL 4188	NYT 903	PPB 330	NYT 925	ADT 505	GL 4186	ETW 620 ⑤⑦	GL 0301	NYT 935	GL 4275	NYT 907 P	GL 4184
Cleveland................d.	2015	....	....	....	1710e	....	....	0045	....	....	....	....	....	....	....	....	....	....	0800	....	....	....	1115	....	1500
Ashtabula ....d.	2125	....	....	....	|	....	....	|	....	....	....	....	....	....	....	....	....	....	0910	....	....	....	|	....	|
Erie ....d.	2215	....	....	....	1905e	....	....	|	....	....	....	....	....	....	....	....	....	....	1010	....	....	....	1305	....	1650
Buffalo ....d.	0040	2245	2330	2330	2300	0230	....	0445	0540	....	....	....	1000	0820	0915	....	1130	....	1230	1310	1315	1430	1515	1630	1915
Rochester....................d.	0215	|	|	|	0030	0405	....	0615	0740	....	....	....	|	1000	1105	....	1305	....	1410	|	|	1620	1655	1820	2055
Syracuse ....d.	0415	0140	0210	0230d	0230d	0600d	....	0830	0920d	0920	....	....	1300	1230	1320d	....	1515d	1500	1610	1600d	1630	1820d	1855	....	2235
Utica............................d.	|	|	|	|	0335d	0705d	....	0935	1035d	1025	....	....	|	1335	1425d	....	|	1620	1710	|	|	1935d	2005	....	....
Schenectady ....d.	|	|	|	|	0505d	0850d	....	1110	1215d	1155	....	....	|	1515	1555d	....	|	1800	1855	|	|	2115d	2140	....	....
Albany.......................d.	0735	|	|	|	0545g	0915d	0930	1215	1245d	1245	1250	1545	|	1615	1620d	1640	|	1845	1945	|	|	2200d	2210	....	....
New York...................a.	|	0630	0715	0715d	*0905*d	*1250*d	|	*1520*	*1550*d	1535	|	|	1815	*1920*	*1950*d	|	2000d	2205	|	2100d	2145	0105d	*0120*	....	....
Pittsfield ....d.	|	....	....	....	0640g	....	1030	|	....	....	1350	1645	....	|	....	1740	....	....	|	....	....	....	....	....	....
Springfield ⊠ ....d.	0935	....	....	....	0815g	....	1140	1410	....	....	1515	1800	....	1815	....	1915	....	....	2145	....	....	....	....	....	....
Worcester ⊠...............d.	1040	....	....	....	|	....	|	1515	....	....	|	....	....	1925	....	2015	....	....	|	....	....	....	....	....	....
Boston ⊠..................a.	1150	....	....	....	1000g	....	*1400*g	1615	....	....	1700	....	....	2035	....	2120	....	....	2330	....	....	....	....	....	....

P–Runs on ⑤† (ex on ⑦ of holiday weekends). a–⑤⑦. b–①⑤. c–NYT. d–*ADT*. e–*LFL*. f–⑥ only. g–*PPB*. ⊠–Complete service *(PPB)* Boston-Springfield and v.v.; **from Boston**: 0015, 0340, 0540, 0800, 1000, 1100, 1200, 1400, 1500, 1615, 1715, 1830, 1930, 2015⑥, 2115, 2215†; **from Springfield**: 0230, 0615, 0645, 0815, 0915, 1015, 1215, 1315, 1415, 1515, 1610, 1715, 1815⑥, 1915, 2130, 2330. *ADT*–Adirondack Trailways. Tel.: Kingston 914 339 4230. *BZ*–Bonanza Bus Lines. Tel.: Providence 401 331 7500. *GL*–Greyhound Lines. Tel.: Dallas 214 789 7000. *LFL*–Lake Front Trailways. Tel.: Cleveland 216 267 8810. *NYT*–New York Trailways. Tel.: Kingston 914 339 4230. *PPB*–Peter Pan Trailways. Tel.: Springfield 413 781 2900.

Table 525 ALBANY - BINGHAMTON

GL

US$			9669		km	396		9670		
						↓ ↑				
0.00	....	....	1450	....	0	d.**Albany** ....a.	....	1355	....	....
	....	....	1515	....		d.Schenectady .....d.	....	1325	....	....
	....	....	1650	....		d.Oneonta ....d.	....	1150	....	....
	....	....	1805	....		a.**Binghamton** .....d.	....	1030	....	....

GL– Greyhound Lines. Tel.: Dallas 214 789 7000.

Table 528 UTICA - BINGHAMTON

CVB

US $		11		13	km	396			10	12
						↓ ↑				
0.00	0800	....	....	1700	0	d.**Utica** ....a.	....	....	1700	2315
	0905	1205	....	1805		d.Hamilton ....d.	....	1115	1545	2210
8.55	1050	1350	....	1950	148	a.**Binghamton** .....d.	....	0930	1400	2025

CVB– Chenango Valley Bus Lines Inc. Tel.: Binghamton 607 724 1000.

Table 530 BUFFALO - PITTSBURGH

FAB

US $	600	530	815	730	km	396	705	510	805	605
						↓ ↑				
0.00	....	1430	....	....	0	d.**Buffalo**..............a.	....	1255	....	....
	0625	|	1720	....		d. State College ..a.	....	|	0955	2040
28.00	0810	1855	1905	1925		d.DuBois ....d.	0810	0825	0825	1915
32.00	0840	....	....	1955		d.Punxsutawney ...d.	0735	....	....	1810
35.00	0935	....	....	2040		d.Indiana ....d.	0650	....	....	1725
39.00	1020	....	....	2125		d.Vandergrift.........d.	0605	....	....	1640
39.00	1125	....	....	2235		a.**Pittsburgh** ....d.	0500	....	....	1530

FAB– Fullington Trailways. Tel.: Clearfield 814 765 7871.

Table 531 NEW YORK - CANTON

ADT

US $	396	km	102A	106A	108A	114	116A	618A ⑤	122	126
	↓									
0.00	**New York** ....d.	0	*0700*	*1000*	*1300*	*1400*	*1600*	*1745*	2000	2330
	Ridgewood (u)......d.		*0730*	*1030*	*1330*	*1430*	*1630*	*1815*	2030	2359
23.05	**Albany** ....d.	226	1010	*1315*	1610	1730	1915	2040	2305	0235
29.60	Saratoga Springs .d.	275	1055	*1400*	1700	1825	2000	2125	2350	....
31.85	Glens Falls ....d.	323	1120	1430	1730	1900	2025	2150	0015	....
46.20	Lake Placid ....d.	451	....	1705	....	....	....	0010	....	....
47.70	Saranac Lake ....d.	466	....	1720	....	....	....	0025	....	....
52.90	Malone ....d.	541	....	1820	....	....	....	....	....	....
	Potsdam..............a.	605	....	1945	....	....	....	....	....	....
	Canton ....a.	621	....	2000	....	....	....	....	....	....

296	101	103 ex⑥⑦	109	111	115	119	123	505	627 ⑦	129
↓										
Canton ....d.	....	....	....	....	....	0830	....	....	....	....
Potsdam.....................d.	....	....	....	....	....	0845	....	....	....	....
Malone ....d.	....	....	....	....	....	1015	....	....	....	....
Saranac Lake ....d.	....	....	....	....	....	1115	....	....	1630	....
Lake Placid ....d.	....	....	....	....	....	1135	....	....	1650	....
Glens Falls ....d.	....	0545	0820	....	1130	*1415*	1510	....	1905	2035
Saratoga Springs ....d.	....	0615	0845	....	1201	*1450*	1540	....	1930	2100
Albany.......................d.	0600	0800	1000	1100	1300	*1535*	1700	1845	2015	2200
Ridgewood (s)............a.	s	s	s	s	s	s	s	s	s	s
New York ....a.	0905	*1055*	1250	1350	*1550*	*1850*	*1950*	2205	*2320*	*0105*

ADT– Adirondack Trailways. Tel.: Kingston 914 339 4230.

Table 532 NEW YORK - MONTRÉAL

GL

US $	4004 ♣	4181	4028 ♣⑥	4008 ♣	4082	3026 ♣	4014 ♣	3214	3248	4076 ♣	3226 ♣	km	396	4021 ♣	4073	4075	4007 ♣	3519	4003 ♣	4077	4009 ♣	4023 ⑤⑦	4013 ♣	4015 ♣
													↓ ↑											
0.00	0030	0600	0730	0830	1030	1130	1330	1530	1730	1830	2130	0	d.**New York**.................a.	0715	1120	1320	1520	1620	1720	1820	1920	2020	2105	0120
	|	0635	0805	|	1105	1205	1405	1605	1805	1905	2205		d.Ridgewood ....d.	|	1035s	1235s	1435s	|	1650s	0735s	1835s	|	2020s	|
26.00	0330	0850	1100	1201	1320	1450	1640	1820	2020	2205	0050	250	d.**Albany** ◇ ....d.	0430	0830	1030	1230	1330	1430	1530	1630	1730	1815	2230
32.00	0430	....	|	1250	....	1545	1745	....	....	2255	0140	300	d.Saratoga Springs ◇ ..d.	0320	....	....	1100	....	1320	....	1520	....	1705	2110
34.00	|	....	|	1325	....	1620	|	....	....	|	|	348	d.Glens Falls ◇ ....d.	|	....	....	|	....	1225	....	1445	....	|	|
53.00	0655	....	1355	1545	....	1840	2010	....	....	0115s	0400s	508	d.Plattsburgh ....d.	0100	....	....	0825	....	1010	....	1210	....	1440	1840
	|	....	|	|	....	|	|	....	....	|	|		a. Lake Placid ....d.	|	....	....	|	....	|	....	|	....	|	
	|	....	|	|	....	|	|	....	....	|	|		a. Saranac Lake..........d.	|	....	....	|	....	|	....	|	....	|	|
61.00	0855	....	1555	1745	....	2040	2210	....	....	0315	0600	610	a.**Montréal** ....d.	2245	....	....	0615	....	0800	....	1000	....	1230	1630

◇– Local traffic not carried between Albany and Glens Falls. GL–Greyhound Lines. Tel.: Dallas 214 789 7000.

Table 533 NEW YORK - BINGHAMTON - BUFFALO

ADT CPB CVB GL GLC HTL NYT

US $	396	km	ADT 528 ♣	GL 4260			GL 0306	NYT 972 ⑤⑦	ADT 510 ♣	CPB 1	HTL 101	GL 0300	CVB 103	HTL 103	GL 4304	GL 0316	CPB 3	CPB 193	HTL 107	ADT 108 ♣	GL 4278	HTL 111	GL 4252		HTL 113	GL 4264	GL 4280	ADT 518 ♣	GL 3500		HTL 119	CPB 7	ADT 508 ♣	HTL 125
	↓																																	
0.00	**New York** d.	0	0045	0230	....	....	0745	....	0900	....	0830	0945	....	1015	....	1145	....	....	1230	1300	1330	1430	1445	....	1630	1630	1830	1930	....	....	1830	....	2215	2300
❖	**Washington** d.		|	|	....	....	|	....	|	0415	|	|	....	|	0650	|	0815	....	|	|	|	|	|	....	|	|	|	|	1315	....	|	1745	|	|
	Ridgewood d.		|	|	....	....	|	....	|	|	0855	|	....	1040	|	|	|	....	1255	|	|	1455	|	....	1655	|	|	|	|	....	1855	|	|	|
❖	Mahwah.. d.		|	|	....	....	|	....	|	|	|	|	....	|	|	|	|	....	|	|	|	|	|	....	|	|	|	|	|	....	1910	|	|	|
❖	**Baltimore** d.		|	|	....	....	|	....	|	0515	|	|	....	|	0800	|	0925	....	|	|	|	|	|	....	|	|	|	|	1425	....	|	1900	|	|
❖	York...... d.		|	|	....	....	|	....	|	0625	|	|	....	|	0910	|	1055	....	|	|	|	|	|	....	|	|	|	|	1535	....	|	2025	|	|
❖	Harrisburg d.		|	|	....	....	|	....	|	0730	|	|	....	|	1005	|	1135	1135	|	|	|	|	|	....	|	|	|	|	1630	....	|	2110	|	|
❖	Pottsville d.		|	|	....	....	|	....	|	0905	|	|	....	|	|	|	1325	|	|	|	|	|	|	....	|	|	|	|	|	....	|	2255	|	|
❖	Sunbury d.		|	|	....	....	|	....	|	|	|	|	....	|	1110	|	|	|	|	|	|	|	|	....	|	|	|	|	1800	....	|	|	|	|
❖	Hazleton d.		|	|	....	....	|	....	|	1005	|	|	....	|	|	|	1425	|	|	|	|	|	|	....	|	|	|	|	|	....	|	2350	|	|
❖	Wilkes Barre d.		|	|	....	....	|	....	|	1050	|	|	....	|	1325	|	1510	|	|	|	|	|	|	....	|	|	|	|	2010	....	|	0030	|	|
❖	Scranton d.		|	|	....	....	|	....	|	1130	|	|	....	|	1415	|	1600	|	|	|	1600	|	|	....	|	|	2100	|	2100	....	|	0110	|	|
24.40	Monticello d.	200	|	|	....	....	|	....	|	|	1025	|	....	1210	|	|	|	|	1425	|	|	1625	|	....	1825	|	|	|	....	....	2025	|	|	0105
27.95	Liberty .... d.	220	|	|	....	....	|	....	|	|	|	|	....	|	|	|	|	|	|	|	|	|	|	....	|	|	|	|	....	....	2055	|	|	0120
32.00	Binghamton d.	309	|	0610	....	....	1130	....	|	1250	1235e	1345	1405	1350	1540	1540	|	|	1620e	|	1730	1815	1830	....	2015e	2015	2225	|	....	....	2215	0220	|	0300e
33.00	Cortland d.		|	|	....	....	1220	....	|	1340	|	*1420*	|	|	1630	|	|	|	|	|	1815	|	|	....	|	2105	2315	|	....	....	|	s	|	|
42.00	**Syracuse** a.	435	0635	|	....	....	1305	....	1350	1425	|	*1505*	|	|	1715	|	|	|	|	1900	1900	|	|	....	|	2150	2359	0010	....	....	|	0400	0255	|
39.00	Ithaca..... d.	396	|	0730	....	....	|	....	|	....	1340e	1500	1515	|	....	1655	|	|	1730e	|	....	|	1945	....	2140e	....	....	|	....	....	|	|	|	0410e
48.90	Geneva... d.	468	|	0825	....	....	|	....	|	....	....	1555	....	|	....	1750	|	|	....	|	....	|	2040	....	....	....	....	|	....	....	|	|	|	....
	Canandaigua d.		|	0855	....	....	|	....	|	....	....	1625	....	|	....	1820	|	|	....	|	....	|	2110	....	....	....	....	|	....	....	|	|	|	....
	Owego d.		|	|	....	....	|	....	|	....	....	|	....	1437u	....	|	|	|	....	|	....	1850	|	....	....	....	....	|	....	....	2250	|	|	....
37.00	Elmira. d.	427	|	|	....	....	|	1215	|	....	....	|	....	1540	....	|	1835	1550a	....	|	....	1945	|	....	....	....	....	|	....	....	2340	|	|	....
37.00	Corning d.	453	|	|	....	....	|	1240	|	....	....	|	....	1610	....	|	....	1615a	....	|	....	2005	|	....	....	....	....	|	....	....	0000	|	|	....
	Olean a.		|	|	....	....	|	|	|	....	....	|	....	1851	....	|	....	|	....	|	....	....	|	....	....	....	....	|	....	....	....	|	|	....
53.00	Rochester a.	544	0830a	0935	....	....	|	1530	1530a	....	....	1715	....	....	....	1900	....	1900a	....	2100a	....	....	2150	....	....	....	....	0210a	....	....	....	|	0440a	....
59.00	**Buffalo**... a.	662	1025a	1115	....	....	1610	....	1710a	....	....	1845	....	....	....	2040	....	....	....	2230a	....	....	*2330*	....	....	....	....	0340a	....	....	....	0745f	0605a	....
❖	*Toronto*... a.	815	1400f	....	....	....	2000	....	2055f	....	....	2200	....	....	....	2345	....	....	....	0100f	....	....	....	....	....	....	....	0650f	....	....	....	1100f	0905f	....

396	ADT 523 ♣	HTL 100			CPB 6		CVB 102	GL 4307	GL 4251	GL 4259		HTL 104	CPB 8	NYT 198		CVB 108	HTL 108		GL 4311	GL 4253	GL 4273	ADT 509 ♣	GL 309 ♣		ADT 525 ♣	HTL 116	HTL 118	GL 0301	GL 4261	CVB 122		NYT 504 ⑤⑦		NYT 937 ♣
↓																																		
Toronto...... d.	2330f	....	....	....	....	....	....	....	....	....	....	....	....	....	....	....	....	....	....	....	....	0700f	0715	....	0800	....	....	1015	....	....	....	....	....	1630f
Buffalo...... d.	0230	....	....	....	....	....	....	....	0445	....	....	....	....	0540	....	....	....	....	....	0805	....	0930	1015	....	1140	....	....	1315	....	....	....	1430	....	2030
Rochester... d.	|	....	....	....	....	....	....	....	0625	....	....	....	....	0845	....	....	....	....	....	0945	....	1120	1155	....	1315	....	....	|	....	....	....	1815	....	2220
Olean ... d.	|	....	....	....	....	....	....	....	|	....	....	....	....	|	....	....	0845	....	....	|	....	|	|	....	|	....	....	|	....	....	....	|	....	|
Corning . d.	|	....	....	....	....	....	....	....	|	....	....	0843	....	1125	....	....	1123	....	....	|	....	|	|	....	|	....	1530	|	....	....	....	1900	....	|
Elmira.... d.	|	....	....	....	0545	....	....	....	|	....	....	0915	....	1215c	....	....	1217	....	....	|	....	|	|	....	|	....	1600	|	....	....	....	1930	....	|
Owego... d.	|	....	....	....	|	....	....	....	|	....	....	1010	....	|	....	....	1308	....	....	|	....	|	|	....	|	....	1650	|	....	....	....	....	....	|
Canandaigua d.	|	....	....	....	|	....	....	....	0705	....	....	|	....	|	....	....	|	....	....	1025	....	|	1235	....	|	....	|	|	....	....	....	....	....	|
Geneva...... d.	|	....	....	....	|	....	....	....	0735	....	....	|	....	|	....	....	|	....	....	1105	....	|	1315	....	|	....	|	|	....	....	....	....	....	|
Ithaca........ d.	|	....	....	....	|	....	0720	....	0835	....		|	....	|	....	1240	|	....	....	1215	....	|	1420	....	|	....	|	|	....	1845	....	....	....	|
Syracuse d.	0600	....	....	....	|	....	|	0730	|	1000		|	0925	|	....	|	|	....	1230	|	1300	1320	|	....	1515	....	|	1630	1815	|	....	....	....	0030c
Cortland .. d.	|	....	....	....	|	....	|	0815	|	1045		|	1010	|	....	|	|	....	1315	|	1345	|	|	....	|	....	|	1715	1900	|	....	....	....	0115c
Binghamton d.	|	0610	....	....	|	....	0840g	0920	0955	1145		1110	1110	|	....	1350	1410	....	1415	1345	1445	|	1545	....	|	1610	1750	1815	2000	2005g	....	....	....	0210c
Liberty .... d.	|	|	....	....	|	....	|	|	|	|	....	|	|	|	....	....	|	....	|	|	|	|	|	....	|	|	1935	|	|	2140g	....	....	....	|
Monticello... d.	|	0800	....	....	|	....	1030g	|	|	|	....	1300	|	|	....	....	1600	....	|	|	|	|	|	....	|	1800	2000	|	|	2200g	....	....	....	|
Scranton ... d.	|	|	....	....	0845	....	|	1045	1120	1310	....	|	1235	|	....	....	|	....	1545	|	|	|	|	....	|	|	|	|	2125	|	....	....	....	0335c
Wilkes Barre d.	|	|	....	....	0915	....	|	1120	|	|	....	|	1310	|	....	....	|	....	1620	|	|	|	|	....	|	|	|	|	|	|	....	....	....	0410c
Hazleton ... d.	|	|	....	....	1000	....	|	|	|	|	....	|	1355	|	....	....	|	....	1705	|	|	|	|	....	|	|	|	|	|	|	....	....	....	0455c
Sunbury ... d.	|	|	....	....	|	....	|	1330	|	|	....	|	|	|	....	....	|	....	|	|	|	|	|	....	|	|	|	|	|	|	....	....	....	|
Pottsville ... d.	|	|	....	....	1100	....	|	|	|	|	....	|	1455	|	....	....	|	....	|	|	|	|	|	....	|	|	|	|	|	|	....	....	....	0555c
Harrisburg . d.	|	|	....	....	1300	....	|	1450	|	|	....	|	1700	1615c	....	....	|	....	1900	|	|	|	|	....	|	|	|	|	|	|	....	....	....	0740c
York......... d.	|	|	....	....	1340	....	|	1530	|	|	....	|	1750	....	....	....	|	....	1940	|	|	|	|	....	|	|	|	|	|	|	....	....	....	0830c
Baltimore . d.	|	|	....	....	1505	....	|	1645	|	|	....	|	1900	....	....	....	|	....	2055	|	|	|	|	....	|	|	|	|	|	|	....	....	....	0950c
Mahwah..... a.	|	|	....	....	|	....	|	|	|	|	....	|	|	....	....	....	|	....	|	|	|	|	|	....	|	|	2105	|	|	2317g	....	....	....	|
Ridgewood . d.	|	0920s	....	....	|	....	1148s	|	|	|	....	1410s	|	....	....	....	1720s	....	|	|	|	|	|	....	|	1915s	2115s	|	|	2323s	....	....	....	|
Washington a.	|	|	....	....	1615	....	|	1755	|	|	....	|	2015	....	....	....	|	....	2155	|	|	|	|	....	|	|	|	|	|	|	....	....	....	1055c
New York .. a.	1230	0950	....	....	....	....	1220g	....	1340	1530	....	1450	....	....	....	....	1755	....	....	1725	1815	1850	1915	....	2000	1950	2150	2145	2345	2359g	....	....	....	....

a– *NYT.*
c– *CPB.* e–*CVB.*
f– *GLC.* g–*HTL.*
h– *ADT.*
ADT– Adirondack Trailways. Tel.: Kingston 914 339 4230.
CPB– Capitol Trailways. Tel.: Harrisburg 717 233 7673.
CVB– Chenango Valley Bus Lines Inc. Tel.: Binghamton 607 724 1000.
GL– Greyhound Lines. Tel.: Dallas 214 789 7000.
GLC– Greyhound Lines of Canada. Tel.: Toronto 416 393 7911.
HTL– The Short Line. Tel.: Mahwah 201 529 3666.
NYT– New York Trailways. Tel.: Kingston 914 339 4230.

Table 537 BUFFALO - PITTSBURGH

CARTS FAB GL LCL NSB

US $	GL 7929	CARTS 8-2 Ⓐ	NSB 1001	NSB 1003	GL 4637	FAB 570	NSB 1005	FAB 530	GL 4641 ⑤⑦	NSB 1007	NSB 1009	km	396 ↓ ↑		NSB 1000	NSB 1002	FAB 510	NSB 1004	NSB 1006	FAB 550	GL 4646	CARTS 12-3 Ⓐ	NSB 1008	GL 4640 ⑤⑦	GL 7928
0.00	*0730*	....	0815	1110	*1255*	....	1400	1430	*1725*	1715	2130	*0*	d.**Buffalo**	a.	0800	1045	*1255*	1300	1600	....	*1700*	....	1950	*2220*	....
9.00	|	0910	0915	1210	|	....	1458	|	|	1815	2240	*73*	d. Dunkirk	d.	0659	0935	|	1130	1455	....	|	1655	1840	|	....
	|	0930	0940	1240	|	....	1524	|	|	1845	2310		d. Cassadaga	d.	0630	0910	|	1105	1425	....	|	1615	1810	|	....
18.00	0930	|	|	|	1500	1515	|	|	2035	|	|	*159*	d.Erie	d.	|	|	|	|	|	1205	1440	|	|	1850	2230
23.00	1030	|	|	|	1555	1615	|	|	2130	|	|	*225*	d.Meadville	d.	|	|	|	|	|	1105	1340	|	|	1755	2130
28.00	1115	|	|	|	1640	|	|	|	2215	|	|	*279*	d.Mercer	d.	|	|	|	|	|	|	1255	|	|	1710	2045
12.70	|	1020	1010	1310	|	|	1600	|	|	1915	2335	*115*	d. Jamestown	d.	0605	0845	|	1040	1400	|	|	1540	1745	|	|
26.00	|	....	....	....	|	1700	....	|	|	....	....	*237*	d. Franklin	d.	....	....	|	....	....	1020	|	....	....	|	|
28.00	|	....	....	....	|	1715	....	|	|	....	....	*254*	d. Oil City	d.	....	....	|	....	....	1005	|	....	....	|	|
	|	....	....	....	|	1855	....	1855	|	....	....		a. DuBois	d.	....	....	0825	....	....	0825	|	....	....	|	|
34.00	|	....	....	....	|	|	....	|	|	....	....	*324*	d. Butler ◇	d.	....	....	|	....	....	|	|	....	....	|	|
39.00	1330	....	....	....	1815	*2235*	....	*2235*	2340	....	....	*376*	a.**Pittsburgh** ◇	d.	....	....	*0500*	....	....	*0500*	1130	....	....	1545	1830

◇– Local service *(LCL)* operates Pittsburgh-Butler and v.v., **from Pittsburgh**: 0730Ⓐ, 1040⑥, 1220Ⓐ, 1455Ⓐ, 1500⑥, 1605Ⓐ, 1630⑦, 1710Ⓐ, 1730⑥, 1740Ⓐ, 2015Ⓐ; **from Butler**: 0600Ⓐ, 0650Ⓐ, 0900Ⓐ, 0915⑥, 1330⑥, 1335Ⓐ, 1615⑥, 1620Ⓐ, 1845⑥, 1900Ⓐ.

CARTS–Chautauqua Area Rural Transit System. Tel.: Falconer ❖.

FAB– Fullington Trailways. Tel.: Clearfield 814 765 9572.
GL– Greyhound Lines. Tel.: Dallas 214 789 7000.
LCL– Lincoln Coach Lines. Tel.: Irwin ❖.
NSB– Niagara Scenic Bus Lines. Tel.: Hamburg 716 648 1500.

Table 538 BOSTON - LITTLETON

CLI

US $												km	396 ↓ ↑												†
	....	....	0915	....	1215	....	1515	1600	1630	....	1915	*7*	d.Boston Logan Airport 🚗	a.	....	1045	1135	1250	1545	....	....	1850	....	....	2150
0.00	....	....	1000	....	1300	....	1615	1715	1745	....	2015	*0*	d.**Boston** 🚗	a.	....	1030	1115	1230	1525	....	....	1830	....	....	2130
8.35	....	....	1100	....	1405	....	|	1855	|	....	2120	*113*	d.Manchester 🚗	d.	....	0930	|	1130	|	....	....	1730	....	....	2030
9.90	....	....	1130	....	1435	....	1740	1900	1900	....	2140	*140*	d.Concord 🚗	d.	....	0900	1000	1100	1400	....	1700	1700	....	....	2000
12.70	....	....	1201s	....	1505	....	1805	1920s	|	....	2205a	*171*	d.Franklin (Tilton Junction)	d.	....	0825	|	1030	1325	....	1625	|	....	....	1925
13.50	....	....	1215s	....	1520	....	|	1935	|	....	2225a	*190*	d. Laconia	d.	....	0810	|	|	1310	....	1610	|	....	....	1910
	....	....	1325	....	....	....	|	....	2055	....	....		d. Conway	d.	....	....	0750	|	....	....	....	1450	....	....	....
18.10	....	....	....	....	....	....	|	....	2105	....	....	*256*	d. North Conway	d.	....	....	|	|	....	....	....	....	....	....	....
22.15	....	....	....	....	....	....	|	....	2155	....	....	*312*	a. **Berlin**	d.	....	....	0650	|	....	....	....	....	....	....	....
14.40	....	....	....	....	....	....	1830	....	....	....	....	*203*	d.Plymouth	d.	....	....	....	1000	....	....	....	....	....	....	....
17.55	....	....	....	....	....	....	1920s	....	....	....	....	*258*	d.Franconia	d.	....	....	....	0900	....	....	....	....	....	....	....
18.60	....	....	....	....	....	....	1930	....	....	....	....	*271*	a.**Littleton** ◇	d.	....	....	....	0850	....	....	....	....	....	....	....

a– ⑤†only ◇–For Mt. Washington Cog Railway. 🚗–Regular local service about hourly. *CLI*–Concord Trailways. Tel.: 603 228 3300.

Table 540 CLEVELAND - CHARLESTON - JACKSONVILLE

BRI GL LFL

US $		GL 1093		BRI 101		GL 1099	LFL 13 ①⑤⑥⑦	GL 1097		LFL 11		km	396 ↓ ↑		BRI 102	LFL 12 ④-⑦		GL 1096	LFL 10				GL 1090		GL 1092
0.00	....	....	....	....	....	1100	1630	1630	....	1920	....	*0*	d.**Cleveland**	a.	....	1210	....	....	1550	....	....	....	1750	....	0025
8.00	....	....	....	....	....	1225	1720	1745	....	2010	....	*55*	d.Akron	d.	....	1125	....	....	1445	....	....	....	1635	....	2345
12.00	....	....	....	....	....	1300	....	1820	....	....	....	*94*	d.Canton	d.	....	....	....	....	....	....	....	....	1600	....	2315
24.00	....	....	....	....	....	1450	....	1955	....	....	....	*293*	d.Cambridge	d.	....	....	....	....	....	....	....	....	1440	....	2210
34.00	....	....	....	....	....	1620	....	2125	....	....	....	*397*	d.Parkersburg	d.	....	....	....	....	....	....	....	....	1235	....	2040
43.00	....	0630	....	....	....	1815	....	2315	....	....	....	*518*	d.**Charleston**	d.	....	....	....	0315	....	....	....	....	1100	....	1915
	....	0820	....	....	....	2000	....	0040	....	....	....		d.Beckley	d.	....	....	....	0205	....	....	....	....	0900	....	1730
61.00	....	0925	....	....	....	2105	....	0145	....	....	....	*658*	d.Bluefield	d.	....	....	....	0045	....	....	....	....	0700	....	1540
67.00	....	1055	....	....	....	2230	....	0315	....	....	....	*758*	d.Wytheville	d.	....	....	....	2345	....	....	....	....	0600	....	1440
77.00	....	1310	....	....	....	0045	....	|	....	....	....	*887*	d.Winston Salem	d.	....	....	....	2125	....	....	....	....	|	....	1230
82.00	....	1545	....	2040	....	0315	....	0645	....	....	....	*1002*	d.Charlotte	d.	1130	....	....	1915	....	....	....	....	0315	....	1015
92.00	....	1815	....	2225	....	0545	....	0900	....	....	....	*1146*	d.Columbia	d.	0955	....	....	1630	....	....	....	....	0035	....	0715
	....	1910	....	2320	....	|	....	0955	....	....	....		d.Orangeburg	d.	0845	....	....	1450	....	....	....	....	2325	....	|
104.00	....	2330	....	....	....	0925	....	1340	....	....	....	*1381*	d.Savannah	d.	....	....	....	1115	....	....	....	....	2020	....	|
	....	|	....	....	....	1045	....	1500	....	....	....		d.Brunswick	d.	....	....	....	0915	....	....	....	....	1830	....	0200
118.00	....	0150	....	....	....	1215	....	1630	....	....	....	*1618*	a.**Jacksonville**	d.	....	....	....	0745	....	....	....	....	1700	....	0030

BRI– Blue Ridge Trailways. Tel.: North Charleston 803 744 0000. *GL*–Greyhound Lines. Tel.: Dallas 214 789 7000. *LFL*–Lake Front Trailways. Tel.: Cleveland 216 267 8810.

Table 541 RICHMOND - NORFOLK

CCC GL

US $	CCC 552		CCC 540	CCC 546	GL 3473	GL 3477 ⑤⑦	GL 3475	CCC 542	CCC 544		CCC 548	km	396 ↓ ↑		CCC 555	CCC 521	CCC 541		CCC 545	GL 543	CCC 549	GL 3476	GL 3474 ⑤⑦	GL 3478	
0.00	0045	....	0645	1000	1245	....	1545	1545	1845	....	2200	*0*	d.**Richmond**	a.	0255	0910	1045	....	1235	1415	1715	2025	....	2305	....
	0145	....	0745	1100	1345	1555	1645	|	1945	....	2300		d.Williamsburg	d.	0155	0810	|	....	1135	1315	1615	1925	2015	2205	....
	s	....	|	|	|	|	|	|	|	....	|		d.Newport News ▶	d.	|	|	|	....	|	|	|	|	|	|	....
	s	....	0850	1210	1450	1700	1750	|	2050	....	2355		d.Hampton	d.	0100	0705	|	....	1030	1210	1510	1815	1915	2100	....
20.00	0300	....	0925	1240	1525	1730	1830	1835	2120	....	0020	*151*	a.**Norfolk**	d.	0030	0630	0800	....	1000	1140	1440	1745	1845	2030	....
20.00	....	....	1015	1320	1605	....	1905		....	....	....		a.Virginia Beach	d.	....	....	0715	....	....	1055	1350	1700	....	1945	....

▶–for Yorktown. *CCC*–Carolina Trailways. Tel.: Raleigh 919 833 3601. *GL*–Greyhound Lines. Tel.: Dallas 214 789 7000.

Table 542 NEW YORK/PHILADELPHIA - WILLIAMSPORT

FMT SHT

US $	SHT 23	SHT 13	FMT 3	FMT 5 ⚒	FMT 61	FMT 15	SHT 21 ⑤⑦	SHT 21	SHT 11	SHT 15 ⑤⑦	SHT 17 ⊔⑤⑥	FMT 39				km	396 ↓ ↑		SHT 16 ⊔⑤⑥	SHT 20	SHT 10	FMT 20	FMT 22	SHT 24 ⑤⑦	SHT 14 ⑤⑦	FMT 60	SHT 22	SHT 12	FMT 40 ex⑦	FMT 44 ⑦			
30.00	....	0730	0830	1100	1320	1515	....	....	1600	1840	1945	2300	....	....	....	*389*	d.**New York**	a.	1030	....	1230	1255	1545	....	1630	1715	....	2100	2120	2355	....	....	....
29.00	....	0800	|	|	1350	|	....	....	|	|	|	|	....	....	....	*373*	d.Newark	a.	|	....	|	|	|	....	|	1636	....	2030s	|	|	....	....	....
23.00	....	0845	|	|	1440	|	....	....	1710	|	|	|	....	....	....	*327*	d.Somerville	d.	|	....	1115s	|	|	....	|	s	....	1945s	|	|	....	....	....
	....	0935	|	|	|	|	....	....	1800	|	|	|	....	....	....		d.Easton	d.	|	....	1045	|	|	....	|	|	....	1900	|	|	....	....	....
20.70	0745	|	|	|	|	|	1300	1630	|	|	|	|	....	....	....	*323*	d. **Philadelphia**	a.	|	1155	|	|	|	1520	|	|	2050	|	|	|	....	....	....
20.70	r	|	|	|	|	|	|	s	|	|	|	|	....	....	....	*310*	d. Quakertown	a.	|	s	|	|	|	|	|	|	1905s	|	|	|	....	....	....
17.50	0945	|	|	|	|	|	|	1810	|	|	|	|	....	....	....	*226*	d. Allentown	d.	|	1025	|	|	|	|	|	|	1850	|	|	|	....	....	....
16.35	1050	1050	|	|	|	|	s	1910	1910	|	|	|	....	....	....	*190*	d.Lehighton	d.	|	0915	0915	|	|	r	|	|	1740	1750	|	|	....	....	....
	|	|	1020	1230	1600	1700	|	|	|	2015	|	0035	....	....	....		d. Stroudsburg	d.	|	|	|	1110	1405	|	1500	1430	|	|	1940	2215	....	....	....
	|	|	1040	1250	1621	1715	|	|	|	|	|	0100	....	....	....		d. Mount Pocono	d.	|	|	|	|	1345	|	|	1405	|	|	1920	2200	....	....	....
	|	|	1120	1325	1655	1755	|	|	|	|	|	0135	....	....	....		d. Scranton	d.	|	|	|	|	1315	|	|	1330	|	|	1850	2135	....	....	....
	|	|	s	|	s	1815a	|	|	|	|	|	|	....	....	....		d. Pittston	d.	|	|	|	|	1230	|	|	1230	|	|	|	|	....	....	....
	|	|	1150	1400	1725	1825	|	|	|	|	|	0200	....	....	....		a. **Wilkes Barre**	d.	|	|	|	1010	....	|	|	1255	|	|	1815	2100	....	....	....
	|	1130	....	....	....	....	1510	|	1945	2115	2215	....	....	....	....		d.Hazleton	d.	0800	|	0840	....	....	1300	1355	....	|	1715	....	....	....	....	....
	|	1225	....	....	....	....	1600	|	2025	2205s	2255s	....	....	....	....		d.Bloomsburg	d.	0715	|	0740	....	....	1215	1250	....	|	1615	....	....	....	....	....
	|	1245	....	....	....	....	s	|	2040	2215s	2300s	....	....	....	....		d.Danville		0700	|	0725	....	....	1201	1235	....	|	1600	....	....	....	....	....
	1150	|	....	....	....	....	|	2010	|	|	|	....	....	....	....		d. Shenandoah	d.	|	0810	|	....	....	|	|	....	1640	|	....	....	....	....	....
	1220	|	....	....	....	....	|	2030	|	|	|	....	....	....	....		d. Mount Carmel	d.	|	0745	|	....	....	|	|	....	1610	|	....	....	....	....	....
	1235	|	....	....	....	....	|	2045	|	|	|	....	....	....	....		d. Shamokin	d.	|	0730	|	....	....	|	|	....	1555	|	....	....	....	....	....
5.90	1305	|	....	....	....	....	|	2105	s	s	|	....	....	....	....	*65*	d. Sunbury	d.	|	0700	|	....	....	|	1205	....	1525	|	....	....	....	....	....
	1325	|	....	....	....	....	s	....	s	s	2335s	....	....	....	....		d. Lewisburg	d.	0635	....	0655	....	....	1125	1155	....	1455	1530	....	....	....	....	....
0.00	1400	1330	....	....	....	....	1655	....	2130	2300	0030	....	....	....	....	*0*	a.**Williamsport**	d.	0610	....	0630	....	....	1100	1125	....	1415	1500	....	....	....	....	....

⊔– Apr. 1-Dec. 31 only. a–⑤ only. *FMT*–Martz Trailways. Tel.: Wilkes Barre 717 821 3838. *SHT*–Susquehanna Trailways. Tel.: Williamsport 717 326 1511.

ble 545 NORFOLK - RALEIGH

CCC

S $	105	303	305	311	km	396	304	104	312	300
.00	....	0800	1230	1830	0	d.**Norfolk Q** ....a.	1400	....	2225	0455
	....	0830	1300	1900		d.Suffolk...............d.	1325	....	2150	0420
.00	....	0925	1355	1955		d.Ahoskie ....d.	1230	....	2100	0330
	....	|	|	|		d.Scotland Neck...d.	|	....	|	|
	....	1040	1455	|		d.Tarboro ....d.	|	....	1945	s
00	....	1120	1530	2135		d.Rocky Mount.....d.	1105	....	1920	0205
00	1110	|	1600	|		d. Wilson ....d.	1030	1725	|	0130
00	1230	1230	1700	2245		a.**Raleigh**.............d.	0930	1615	1800	0030

For Portsmouth. *CCC*–Carolina Trailways. Tel.: Raleigh 919 833 3601.

Table 545a MOREHEAD CITY - RALEIGH

CCC

US $			343		km	396		340		
0.00	....	....	....	....	0	d.Cedar Island......a.	....	....	....	....
	....	....	1650	....		d.**Morehead City** .d.	....	1615	....	....
	....	....	1800	....		d.New Bern ....d.	....	1515	....	....
	....	....	1900	....		d.Kinston ....d.	....	1420	....	....
	....	....	1940	....		d.Goldsboro..........d.	....	1340	....	....
	....	....	2100	....		a.**Raleigh**.............d.	....	1215	....	....

CCC– Carolina Trailways. Tel.: Raleigh 919 833 3601.

ble 546 396 BALTIMORE LOCAL SERVICES

MARC MTA

(C cl. only, 1.435m.), (1.435m.) and services operate in the Baltimore area as follows:

polis (*MTA*) (*31* km, US $: 2.25). From Baltimore: 0543Ⓐ, 0613Ⓐ, 0635†, 0805†, 0935†, 1105†, 1235†, 1405†, 1535†, 603Ⓐ, 1626Ⓐ, 1641Ⓐ, 1703Ⓐ, 1705†, 1746Ⓐ, 1835†, returning at 0620Ⓐ, 0640Ⓐ, 0700Ⓐ, 0720Ⓐ, 0745Ⓐ, 0810†, 0940†, 110†, 1240†, 1410†, 1540†, 1710†, 1716Ⓐ, 1840†, 2010†; from Patapsco: 0532Ⓐ/0610⑥ and frequent (about hourly on ⑥) to 110⑥/2237Ⓐ, returning at 0554Ⓐ/0754⑥ and frequent (about hourly on ⑥) to 2242⑥/2359Ⓐ. Journey: 1¼ hours.

gton ∝ (*MTA*) (❖ km, US $: ❖). From Baltimore Charles Center: 0500Ⓐ/0610⑥ and frequent to 0000②-⑥/0010⑦, returning om Arlington Reisterstown Plaza at 0454Ⓐ/0603⑥ and frequent to 0008ex①. Service on † available by . Journey: 16 ins.

klyn § (*MTA*) (❖ km, US $: ❖). From Baltimore: ❖, returning at ❖. Journey: ❖.

Airport ∝ (*MARC*) (17 km, US $: ❖). From Baltimore Penn. Stn.: 0520Ⓐ, 0550Ⓐ, 0615Ⓐ, 0640Ⓐ, 0650Ⓐ, 0724Ⓐ, 0757Ⓐ, 845Ⓐ, 0940Ⓐ, 1053Ⓐ, 1145Ⓐ, 1253Ⓐ, 1338Ⓐ, 1450Ⓐ, 1555Ⓐ, 1655Ⓐ, 1755Ⓐ, 2030Ⓐ, returning at 0704Ⓐ, 0802Ⓐ, 0905Ⓐ, 014Ⓐ, 1059Ⓐ, 1204Ⓐ, 1259Ⓐ, 1413Ⓐ, 1510Ⓐ, 1618Ⓐ, 1638Ⓐ, 1715Ⓐ, 1740Ⓐ, 1824Ⓐ, 1847Ⓐ, 1925Ⓐ, 2039Ⓐ, 2223Ⓐ. ourney: 20 mins.

nsville § (*MTA*) (❖ km, US $: ❖). From Baltimore: ❖, returning at ❖. Journey: ❖.

dalk § (*MTA*) (❖ km, US $: ❖). From Baltimore: ❖, returning at ❖. Journey: ❖.

ott City § (❖ km, US $: ❖). From Baltimore: ❖, returning at ❖. Journey: ❖.

st Park § (*MTA*) (❖ km, US $: ❖). From Baltimore: ❖, returning at ❖. Journey: ❖.

ord § (*MTA*) (❖ km, US $: ❖). From Baltimore: ❖, returning at ❖. Journey: ❖.

lton § (*MTA*) (❖ km, US $: ❖). From Baltimore: ❖, returning at ❖. Journey: ❖.

landtown § (*MTA*) (❖ km, US $: ❖). From Baltimore: frequent (every 50 mins. on †), returning frequent (every 50 mins. on †). ourney: 26 mins.

downe § (*MTA*) (❖ km, US $: ❖). From Baltimore: ❖, returning at ❖. Journey: ❖.

Laurel ∝ (*MARC*) (*31* km, US $: 3.75). From Baltimore Camden: 0535Ⓐ, 0630Ⓐ, 0705Ⓐ, 0805Ⓐ, 1100Ⓐ, 1545Ⓐ, 1655Ⓐ, 1750Ⓐ, 1835Ⓐ, returning at 0720Ⓐ, 0748Ⓐ, 0858Ⓐ, 1200Ⓐ, 1659Ⓐ, 1742Ⓐ, 1832Ⓐ, 1936Ⓐ, 2029Ⓐ. Journey: 35 mins.

Mount Washington φ (*MTA*) (❖ km, US $: ❖). From Baltimore Lexington Market 0514Ⓐ/0728⑥/1113† and frequent to 1913†/2313⚒, returning at 0600Ⓐ/0812⑥/1112† and frequent to 1912†/2312⚒. Journey: 20 mins.

New Carrollton ∝ (*MARC*) (*46* km, US $: 4.50). From Baltimore Penn. Stn.: 0520Ⓐ, 0550Ⓐ, 0615Ⓐ, 0650Ⓐ, 0757Ⓐ, 0845Ⓐ, 0940Ⓐ, 1053Ⓐ, 1145Ⓐ, 1253Ⓐ, 1338Ⓐ, 1450Ⓐ, 1555Ⓐ, 1655Ⓐ, 1755Ⓐ, 2030Ⓐ, returning at 0640Ⓐ, 0739Ⓐ, 0834Ⓐ, 0949Ⓐ, 1034Ⓐ, 1139Ⓐ, 1234Ⓐ, 1349Ⓐ, 1444Ⓐ, 1554Ⓐ, 1650Ⓐ, 1758Ⓐ, 1820Ⓐ, 1859Ⓐ, 2014Ⓐ, 2157Ⓐ. Journey: 45 mins.

Patapsco φ (*MTA*) (❖ km, US $: ❖). From Baltimore Lexington Market 0418Ⓐ/0533⑥/1018† and frequent to 1933†/2333⚒, returning at 0014ex①, 0029ex①, 0500Ⓐ/0504⑥/1059† and frequent to 2029†/2359⚒. Journey: 15 mins.

Ten Hills § (*MTA*) (❖ km, US $: ❖). From Baltimore: ❖, returning at ❖. Journey: ❖.

Towson § (❖ km, US $: ❖). From Baltimore: ❖, returning at ❖. Journey: ❖.

Turner § (*MTA*) (❖ km, US $: ❖). From Baltimore: ❖, returning at ❖. Journey: ❖.

Washington ∝ (*MARC*) (65 km, US $: 5.75). From Baltimore Penn. Stn.: 0520Ⓐ, 0550Ⓐ, 0615Ⓐ, 0640Ⓐ, 0650Ⓐ, 0724Ⓐ, 0757Ⓐ, 0845Ⓐ, 0940Ⓐ, 1053Ⓐ, 1145Ⓐ, 1253Ⓐ, 1338Ⓐ, 1450Ⓐ, 1555Ⓐ, 1655Ⓐ, 1755Ⓐ, 2030Ⓐ; also from Baltimore Camden: 0535Ⓐ, 0630Ⓐ, 0705Ⓐ, 0805Ⓐ, 1100Ⓐ, 1545Ⓐ, 1655Ⓐ, 1750Ⓐ, 1835Ⓐ. Journey: 1 hour.

Waverly § (*MTA*) (❖ km, US $: ❖). From Baltimore: ❖, returning at ❖. Journey: ❖.

By . §–By . ∝–####.
By between Baltimore and Patapsco on ⚒.

MARC–Maryland Department of Transportation. Tel.: Washington 202 906 3104.
MTA– Maryland Mass Transit Administration. Tel.: Baltimore 301 333 3885.

ble 547 BETHLEHEM/READING - PHILADELPHIA

BI CPB

S $	496	km		*CPB* 42 Ⓐ	*BI* 301 Ⓐ	*BI* 303 Ⓐ	*BI* 401 Ⓒ	*CPB* 30			*BI* 305 Ⓐ			*BI* 307 Ⓐ	*BI* 403 Ⓒ	*CPB* 32			*BI* 405 Ⓒ	*CPB* 34	*BI* 309 Ⓐ			*BI* 407 Ⓒ	
00	Pottsville ....d.	*155*	....	0500	....	....	....	0620	....	....	....	....	....	....	....	1105	....	....	....	1520	....	....	....	....	....
00	**Reading** ◇......d.	*100*	....	0600	....	*0530*	0700	0730	....	....	0730	....	....	1030	1100	1210	....	....	*1500*	1640	....	....	....	*1900*	....
00	Pottstown.........d.	*65*	....	0625	....	|	|	0755	....	....	|	....	....	|	|	1240	....	....	|	1715	....	....	....	|	....
	King of Prussia a.		....	|	....	|	|	0835	....	....	|	....	....	|	|	1320	....	....	|	1750	....	....	....	|	....
00	**Kutztown** ◇ ......d.	*126*	....	|	0500	0600	0730	|	....	....	0800	....	....	1100	1130	|	....	....	1530	|	1655	....	....	1930	....
00	Allentown ....d.	*97*	....	|	0535	0640	0810	|	....	....	0840	....	....	1140	1210	|	....	....	1610	|	1740	....	....	2010	....
00	Bethlehem..........d.	*87*	....	|	0550	0655	0825	|	....	....	0855	....	....	1155	1225	|	....	....	1625	|	1755	....	....	2025	....
50	Quakertown........d.	*68*	....	|	0615	0720	0850	|	....	....	0920	....	....	1220	1250	|	....	....	1650	|	1820	....	....	2050	....
00	**Philadelphia**......a.	*0*	....	0730	0735	0840	1000	0910	....	....	1040	....	....	1340	1400	1400	....	....	1800	1825	1940	....	....	2200	....

↓			*BI* 302 Ⓐ	*CPB* 29	*BI* 402 Ⓒ				*BI* 304 Ⓐ	*BI* 404 Ⓒ		*CPB* 33	*BI* 306 Ⓐ				*CPB* 43 Ⓐ		*BI* 308 Ⓐ		*BI* 406 Ⓒ	*CPB* 37	*BI* 310 Ⓐ		*BI* 408 Ⓒ
ladelphia............d.	....	....	0900	0935	1050	....	....	....	1400	1450	....	1450	1600	....	....	....	1645	....	1730	....	1850	1915	2100	....	2250
kertown.............d.	....	....	1020	|	1210	....	....	....	1520	1610	....	|	1720	....	....	....	|	....	1850	....	2010	|	2220	....	0010
lehem................a.	....	....	1045	|	1235	....	....	....	1545	1635	....	|	1745	....	....	....	|	....	1915	....	2035	|	2245	....	0035
ntown ....a.	....	....	1100	|	1250	....	....	....	1600	1650	....	|	1800	....	....	....	|	....	1930	....	2050	|	2300	....	0050
ztown ◇ ....a.	....	....	1140	|	1330	....	....	....	1655	1730	....	|	1840	....	....	....	|	....	2000	....	2130	|	2340	....	0130
ng of Prussia ......d.	....	....	|	1010	|	....	....	....	....	|	....	1530	|	....	....	....	|	....	|	....	|	1950	|	....	|
ttstown...............d.	....	....	|	1045	|	....	....	....	....	|	....	1610	|	....	....	....	1735	....	|	....	|	2025	|	....	|
ading ◇............a.	....	....	*1230*	1115	*1400*	....	....	....	....	*1800*	....	1640	*1930*	....	....	....	1805	....	*2030*	....	*2200*	2055	*0030*	....	*0200*
ttsville ....a.	....	....	....	1225	....	....	....	....	....	....	....	1755	....	....	....	....	1910	....	....	....	....	2155	....	....	....

BI also operate an express Reading-Kutztown-New York service (*203* km; journey: 3 hours; fare: US $: 6.50) **from Reading** at 0500Ⓐ, 0530Ⓐ, 0630Ⓐ, 0700, 0730Ⓐ, 0900Ⓒ, 0930Ⓐ, 1030Ⓐ, 1100Ⓒ, 1200Ⓐ, 1300Ⓒ, 1330Ⓐ, 1500Ⓒ, 1530Ⓐ, 1700Ⓒ, 1730Ⓐ, 1900; **from New York** at 0830Ⓐ, 0930Ⓐ, 1100Ⓒ, 1200Ⓐ, 1300Ⓒ, 1330Ⓐ, 1500Ⓒ, 1530Ⓐ, 1630Ⓐ, 1700, 1730Ⓐ, 1830Ⓐ, 1900Ⓒ, 1930Ⓐ, 2100Ⓒ, 2130Ⓐ, 2330.

BI– Carl R. Bieber Tourways. Tel.: Kutztown 610 683 7333.
CPB– Capitol Trailways. Tel.: Harrisburg 717 233 7673.

ble 548 NEW YORK - ALLENTOWN

NJT OAE TBR

S$	496 *TBR* ↓	km	102/202 ⚒	204 Ⓒ	104/206 ⚒	208 Ⓒ	106/210	108/212	110/214	114/216	116 Ⓐ	118 Ⓐ	120/218	122 Ⓐ	126/220	128 Ⓐ	130 Ⓐ	132 Ⓐ	134/222	136/224	138/226	140/228	230 ⑦	142/232	234 ⑦
	New York Kennedy Airport .d.		....	....	....	....	....	....	....	....	....	....	1545	....	....	....	....	....	....	1730	1845	....	....	....	....
00	**New York** ★......d.	*0*	0800	0900	1000	1050	1200	1400	1500	1600	1630	1640	1710	1720	1730	1740	1750	1810	1830	1900	2000	2125	2215	2330	2359
15	Newark Intl. Airport ★d.	*17*	0830	0930	1030	|	1230	1430	|	1630	|	|	|	|	|	|	|	|	1855	|	|	2155	|	0000	0040
	Clinton...............d.		0920	1020	1120	1205	1320	1525	1610	1725	1740	|	1820	|	1840	|	1900	1920	1950	2010	2110	2245	2325	0050	0140
	Easton................d.		0940	1040	1140	1220	1345	1545	1635	1745	1805s	|	1845	|	1900b	|	|	1945	2010	2030	2135	2305	2345	0110	0200
55	Bethlehem..........a.	*153*	1000	1100	1200	1240	1405	1605	1655	1805	|	1835	1900s	1910	1920b	1940s	1955s	2005	2030	2050e	2155e	2325e	0005	0130s	0220s
95	**Allentown**.........a.	*161*	1030	1130	1240a	1310	1435	1620	1725	1835	1835	....	1930c	....	1940d	....	....	....	2100	2120	2225	2355	....	0200	s

TBR ↓	101 Ⓐ	103/201 ⚒	105 Ⓐ	109 Ⓐ	113 Ⓐ	111 Ⓐ	115/203	121 Ⓐ	123/205	207 ⑥	125/209	211 ⑥	127/213	129/215	131/217	219 ⑦	133/221	223 ⑦	135/225	227 ⑦	137/229	231 ⑦	233 ⑦	139/235	237 ⑦
ntown...............d.	....	0515	....	0550	....	0605	0600b	....	0715	0745	0800	0830	0915	1030	1210	1315	1330	1445	1515	1630	1715	1800	1900	1925	2130
lehem................d.	0510	0530	0555	|	0615	|	0630	0725	0745	0800	0830	0900	0930	1100	1245	1330	1400	1500	1545	1645	1750	1830	1930	1955	2200
ton......................d.	0525	0550	|	0620	|	|	0650	|	0805	|	0850	0920	0950	1120	1305	1350	1420	1520	1605	1705	1810	1850	1950	2015	2215
ton......................d.	0550	0615	|	0645	|	0705	0715	|	0830	0845	0915	0945	1015	1145	1335	1415	1445	1545	1630	1730	1835	1915	2015	2040	2235
ark Intl. Airport ★..a.	|	0710s	|	|	|	|	0810s	|	0925s	|	|	1040s	|	1240s	|	1510s	|	1640s	1725s	1825s	1930s	|	|	2135s	2325s
York ★..........a.	0710	0740	0755	0805	0815	0825	0840f	0925	0955	1000	1030	1110	1130	1310	1450	1540	1610	1710	1755	1855	2000	2030	2135	2205	2355
York Kennedy Airport a.	....	....	....	....	....	....	....	....	....	....	....	....	1240	....	1600	....	1720	....	....	....	....	....	....	....	....

$	2 Ⓐ	4 Ⓐ	302/6 Ⓒ	6 Ⓐ	8 ⑤	12 Ⓐ	16 Ⓐ	310 Ⓒ	22 Ⓐ	24 Ⓐ	312 Ⓒ	km	495 ↓ *TBR* ↑	7 Ⓐ	301 Ⓒ	13 Ⓐ	303 Ⓒ	15 Ⓐ	17 Ⓐ	309 ⑦	19 Ⓐ	21 Ⓐ	311 Ⓒ	313 ⑦
00	0730	0945	1015	1300	1530	1640	1715	1730	1900	2015	2015	*0*	d.**New York**..................a.	0820	1000	1110	1325	1410	1600	1755	1805	1940	2000	2110
	|	1015	1045	1330	|	|	|	1800	|	2045	2045	*17*	d.Newark International Airport a.	|	0930s	1035s	1255s	1340s	1530s	1725s	|	1910s	1930s	2040s
	0910	1140	1210g	1450	1740	1830	1900	1925	2045	2205	s		d.Lambertville...............d.	0630	0805	0915	1125	1220	1405	1530	1550	1750	1735	1900
	0940	1210	1240g	1525	1810	1900	1930	1955	2115	2235	s		d.Doylestown................d.	0600	0735	0845	1055	1150	1335	1500	1520	1720	1705	1830
	....	....	1305g	1550	1835	1925	1955	2020	2140	s	s		d.Quakertown................d.	0535	0710	0810	1030	....	....	1435	1455	1655	1640	1805
	....	....	1340g	1625	1910	2000	2030	2055	2215	s	s		a.**Bethlehem**................d.	....	0640	0735	1000	....	....	1405	1420	1620	1610	1735

1230 on Ⓐ. b–Ⓒ only. c–1920 on Ⓐ. d–Ⓐ only.
Note s applies on Ⓒ. f–0830 on Ⓐ. g–30 mins. later on †.
Local services (*NJT* **300**) operate New York-Newark International Airport and v.v. every 15 mins (30-90 mins. at night); also by *OAE* at 0500 and frequent to 2359.

NJT– New Jersey Transit. Tel.: Newark 201 762 5100.
OAE– Olympia Airport Express. Tel.: Newark Ø.
TBR– Trans-Bridge Lines. Tel.: Bethlehem 610 868 6001.

Table 549 496 PHILADELPHIA - ATLANTIC CITY — GL NJT

services operate Philadelphia-Atlantic City and v.v. *94* km. Journey: 1½-2 hours. Fare: US $: 12.00

From Philadelphia: *GL* at 0900, 0930, 1130ex②③, 1330, 1415, 1515ex②③, 1730ex①②, 1745, 2030, 2130,2230⑤⑥, 2330⑤⑥; *NJT* **551/5** at 0050, 0250, 0350, 0450, 0550, 0620, 0650, 072 0750, 0820, 0850, 0920, 0950, 1020, 1050, 1120, 1150, 1220, 1250, 1320, 1350, 1420, 1450, 1520, 1550, 1620, 1650, 1750, 1820, 1850, 1920, 1950, 2020, 2050, 2120, 2150, 2220, 225 2350.

From Atlantic City: *GL* at 0130, 0400, 0645⑥⑦, 0715⑥⑦, 0830, 1730, 1745, 1930ex②③, 2145, 2245; *NJT* **551** at 0040, 0140, 0240, 0340, 0410, 0440, 0510, 0540, 0640, 0740, 0810, 084 0910, 0940, 1040, 1110, 1140, 1210, 1240, 1310, 1340, 1410, 1440, 1510, 1540, 1610, 1640, 1710, 1740, 1810, 1840, 1910, 1940, 2010, 2040, 2140, 2240, 2340.

GL–Greyhound Lines. Tel.: Dallas 214 789 7000. *NJT*–New Jersey Transit.

Table 550 NEW YORK - ATLANTIC CITY — NJT

US $						191			192		193	km	396 ↓ ↑		191			192			193			
0.00	....	....	....	....	....	1300	....	....	1800	....	2200	*0*	d.**New York**.................a.	....	1135	....	....	1635	....	....	2035	....	....	....
	....	....	....	....	....	1435	....	....	1935	....	2335	*118*	d.Tom's River...............d.	....	1000	....	....	1500	....	....	1900	....	....	....
23.00	....	....	....	....	....	1545	....	....	2045	....	0045	*206*	d.**Atlantic City**.............d.	....	0900	....	....	1349	....	....	1800	....	....	....
	....	....	....	....	....	1625	....	....	2125	....	0125	*222*	d.Ocean City................d.	....	0809	....	....	1309	....	....	1709	....	....	....
	....	....	....	....	....	1731	....	....	2231	....	0231	*264*	d.Wildwood....................d.	....	0703	....	....	1203	....	....	1603	....	....	....
	....	....	....	....	....	1756	....	....	2256	....	0256	*274*	a.**Cape May**.................d.	....	0638	....	....	1138	....	....	1538	....	....	....

NJT– New Jersey Transit.

Table 552 CLEVELAND - CINCINNATI — GL LFL

US $	396 ↓	km	*GL* 1121	*GL* 1387	*GL* 1171	*GL* 1117	*GL* 1161	*LFL* 11	*GL* 1109	*GL* 1173
0.00	**Cleveland**............d.	*0*	0115	0500	0900	1400	1715	1805	1825	2230
20.00	Mansfield.............d.	*125*	|	|	|	|	|	2015	2035	|
25.00	Columbus.............d.	*219*	0415	0740	1230	1710	2005	2135	2200	0115
40.00	**Cincinnati**............a.	*394*	0605	0930	1420	1920	2155	2315	2340	0305

296 ↓	*GL* 1112	*GL* 1176	*GL* 4818	*LFL* 10	*GL* 1170		*GL* 594		*GL* 1164	*GL* 1166
Cincinnati..................d.	0200	0515	0900	0955	1015	....	1500	....	1950	2130
Columbus..................d.	0420	0745	1105	1205	1245	....	1730	....	2300	2335
Mansfield..................d.	|	|	|	1310	|	....	|	....	|	|
Cleveland..................a.	0645	1010	1350	1535	1530	....	1955	....	0020	0155

GL–Greyhound Lines. *LFL*–Lake Front Trailways.

Table 553 AUGUSTA - SAVANNAH — SES

US $			703		km	396 ↓ ↑		803		
0.00	....	....	1130	....	*0*	d.**Augusta**...........a.	....	1730	....	....
	....	....	1305	....		d.Sylvania ....d.	....	1555	....	....
	....	....	1415	....		a.**Savannah**.........d.	....	1445	....	....

SES– Southeastern Stages.

Table 554 ALBANY - ISLIP — VT

US $			9661		km	396 ↓ ↑		9662		
0.00	....	....	1615	....	*0*	d.**Albany**..............a.	....	1415	....	....
20.00	....	....	1840	....		d.White Plains ......d.	....	1145	....	....
28.00	....	....	1910**s**	....		d.New Rochelle....d.	....	1115	....	....
32.00	....	....	2015	....		a.Hempstead........d.	....	1015	....	....
35.00	....	....	2045**s**	....		a.Huntington.........d.	....	0945	....	....
35.00	....	....	2055	....		a.**Islip**..................d.	....	0925	....	....

VT– Vermont Transit.

Table 555 DULUTH - ST. IGNACE — DTA JJL WPT

US$	*JJL*		*WPT* 1502	*JJL*	km	396 ↓ ↑	*JJL*	*WPT* 1501		*JJL*
0.00	....	....	1915	....	*0*	d.**Duluth** ◇..........a.	....	0710	....	....
⊠4.00	....	....	1925	....	*7*	d.Superior ◇........a.	....	0700	....	....
13.00	....	....	2055	....	*112*	d.Ashland.............d.	....	0540	....	....
22.00	....	....	2215	....	*174*	d.Ironwood ....d.	....	0450	....	....
	....	....	2340	....		d.Iron River ....d.	....	0305	....	....
40.00	....	....	0045	....	*379*	d.Iron Mountain ....d.	....	0205	....	....
50.00	....	....	0315	....	*462*	d.Escanaba ....d.	....	0140	....	....
67.00	2225	....	0600	0700	*462*	a.**St Ignace**..........d.	2200	2245	....	0635
♥25.00	2325	....	....	0750		a.Sault Ste. Marie *MI* ..d.	2115	....	....	0545

◇–Regular local service *(DTA 16)* operates between Duluth and Superior 0536Ⓐ/0610⑥–1825⑥/1848Ⓐ. ⊠–$0.60 by *DTA*. ♥–Fare ex St. Ignace. *DTA*–Duluth Transit Authority. *JJL*–J&J Limo. *WPT*–White Pine Bus Service.

Table 556 LANCASTER/GETTYSBURG — CP

US $	201		203	205	km	396 ↓ ↑	202		204	20
27.00	0845	....	1300	1725		d.**New York**..........a.	1055	....	1555	200
	|	....	|	|		d.Newark Intnl Airport..a.	|	....	|	|
	|	....	|	|	*225*	d. **Philadelphia**...a.	|	....	|	|
12.00	1110	....	1530	1950	*191*	d.King of Prussia..a.	0830	....	1335	174
	1159**s**	....	1620**s**	2040**s**		d.Ephrata ....d.	0740	....	1245	165
5.80	1225	....	1645	2105	*97*	d.Lancaster ....d.	0715	....	1220	162
4.20	1305	....	1725	2140	*58*	d.York ....d.	0635	....	1140	154
	|	....	|	|	*0*	d.Gettysburg.........d.	|	....	|	|
0.00	1340	....	1800	2210		a.**Harrisburg**........d.	0600	....	1100	150

CPB– Capitol Trailways.

Table 557 396 VALLEY FORGE — SE

service 125 Philadelphia-King of Prussia-Valley Forge and v.v. *30* km. Journey hour 10 mins. Fare: US $: 3.20.

From Philadelphia to King of Prussia: 0510Ⓐ, 0530Ⓐ, 0545Ⓐ, 0600, 0615Ⓐ, 0630⚒, 064 and frequent (every 30 mins. on †) to 2100, 2200Ⓐ, 2230Ⓐ, 2300Ⓐ; **Philadelphia** to Val Forge: 0530Ⓐ, 0600, 0630Ⓐ, 0700 and about hourly to 1800, 1900⑥, 2000Ⓒ, 2100Ⓒ.

From King of Prussia: 0010②-⑥, 0020⑦, 0030②-⑥, 0550Ⓐ, 0610Ⓐ, 0630Ⓐ, 0645Ⓐ, 07 and frequent (every 30 mins. †) to 2000, 2030⚒, 2100, 2135⚒, 2205Ⓐ, 2210Ⓒ, 2235 2310Ⓐ, 2335Ⓒ, 2350Ⓐ; **from Valley Forge**◇: 0643Ⓐ, 0654Ⓒ, 0710Ⓐ, 0740Ⓐ, 075 0810Ⓐ, 0854Ⓒ, 0910Ⓐ, 0954Ⓒ and about hourly to 1844Ⓐ, 1854Ⓒ, 1954⑥, 205 2205Ⓒ.

◇– On Ⓒ operates to/from Valley Forge Sheraton, and **not** Valley Forge National Pa

SEP– Southeastern Pennsylvania Transportation Authority.

Table 558 GRAND RAPIDS - DETROIT — G

US $	5095	5089	5091	5093	km	396 ↓ ↑	5088	5090	5092	509
0.00	....	0700	1320	1715	*0*	d.**Muskegon** ....a.	1225	1640	2135	....
8.00	....	0750	|	|	*58*	d. Holland...........d.	|	|	2050	....
10.00	0700	0845	1435	1810	*64*	d.**Grand Rapids** ..d.	1120	1535	2015	213
21.00	0825	1010	1600	1930	*170*	d.Lansing ....d.	1000	1410	1845	201
21.00	0835	1020	1610	1940	*176*	d.East Lansing .....d.	0935	1350	1830	200
33.00	1035	1220	1810	2140	*302*	a.**Detroit** ....d.	0730	1145	1630	180

GL– Greyhound Lines.

⑥–Saturdays **⑦–Sundays** **Ⓒ–Saturdays, Sundays and holidays**

Table 559 ST. LOUIS - NASHVILLE GL

US $	1231	1233	1235	1237	km	396	1236	1230	1232	1234
						↓ ↑				
.00	0045	0615	1330	1930	0	d.**St. Louis**..........a.	1630	2200	0145	0545
.00	|	0650	1405	|	27	d.Belleville...........d.	1555	|	|	0510
.00	|	0840	1545	|	132	d.Mount Vernon....d.	1435	2035	|	|
	0245	|	|	2130		d.Carbondale........d.	|	|	2345	0330
	0335	|	|	2220		d.Vienna..............d.	|	|	2250	|
	0445	|	|	2330		d.Paducah...........d.	|	|	2215	0210
.50	|	1140	1845	|	277	d.Evansville.........d.	1150	1840	|	|
	0600	1330	2035	0040		d.Hopkinsville.......d.	0930	1615	2030	0025
.50	0800	1530	2230	0235		a.**Nashville**.........d.	0730	1415	1830	2230

– Greyhound Lines.

Table 561 RICHMOND - JACKSONVILLE GL

US $		1045	1047	1015	km	396	1046	1014		1044
						↓ ↑				
0.00	....	0415	1000	1000	0	d.**Richmond**........a.	1800	2330	....	0245
8.00	....	|	1035	1035	36	d.Petersburg.........d.	1725	|	....	|
34.00	....	0645	1250	|		d.Rocky Mount.....d.	1525	|	....	0025
	....	|	|	1355		d. **Raleigh**...........a.	|	|	....	|
51.00	....	0805	1400	|	258	d.Goldsboro..........d.	1410	|	....	2315
51.00	....	0925	1515	|		d.Wallace.............d.	1300	|	....	2210
53.50	....	1015	1605	|	409	d.Wilmington........d.	1201	|	....	2115
57.50	....	1300	1845	|	524	d.Myrtle Beach.....d.	0915	|	....	1840
74.00	....	1530	2100	2130	676	d.North Charlestond.	0645	1455	....	1615
89.00	....	1855	....	0045	846	a.Savannah..........d.	0305	1145	....	....
97.00	....	2115	....	0330	1061	a.**Jacksonville**.....d.	0015	0730	....	....

GL– Greyhound Lines.

Table 562 JACKSONVILLE - ST. PETERSBURG GL

US $	3741	3737	5399	5391	517	3709	3733	3745	3731	1097	1007	km	396	5386	5388	1012	3734	1090	3797	3744	1092	506	3750	5384
													↓ ↑											
0.00	0220	0400	0415	0715	0715	....	0930	1300	1330	1715	1930	0	d.**Jacksonville**............a.	0645	1245	1320	1620	1600	....	2115	2320	2325	2330	0230
3.50	|	0535	|	|	|	....	|	|	1510	|	|		d. Gainesville.............d.	|	|	1140	|	|	....	|	|	2150	|	|
9.00	|	|	0610	0905	|	....	1135	1450	|	1915	2130		d.Daytona Beach..........d.	0455	1055	|	1425	|	....	1935	2130	|	2140	|
1.00	|	0640	|	|	|	....	|	|	1615	|	|		d. Ocala......................d.	|	|	1050	|	|	....	|	|	2100	|	|
6.50	0530	|	0815	1010	1045	....	1345	1600	|	2130	2315		d.Orlando *(Disney World)*.d.	0345	0900	|	1230	1315	....	1745	2015	|	2030	0001
9.00	|	|	|	....	1125	....	1425	1640	|	|	|		d.Kissimmee................d.	|	0735	|	1105	|	....	|	|	|	|	|
9.00	0630	|	0915	....	1220	....	|	1730	|	2235	|		d.Winter Haven ....d.	0155	0640	|	1015	|	1240	|	1815	|	|	|
9.00	0700	|	0945	....	1250	....	|	1800	|	2305	|		d.Lakeland...................d.	0120	0610	|	0945	|	1210	|	1745	|	|	|
9.00	0800	1015	1045	....	1350	1415	1540	1915	1900	2359	0055		a.**Tampa**.....................d.	0030	0515	0700	0900	1035	1145	1530	1645	1800	1800	2145
0.00	*0900*	0945	|	....	....	1445	|	|	|	|	|		a.Clearwater................d.	....	....	0730	0815	*0945*	....	|	1600	|	|	|
0.00	*0930*	*1150*	1150	....	....	1515	1705	2030	*2030*	*0140*	0140		a.**St. Petersburg**.........d.	....	....	....	0745	*0945*	....	1440	1530	*1630*	1645	2055

– Greyhound Lines.

Table 564 BALTIMORE - PITTSBURGH CPB GL

US $	GL 4705	GL 4625	GL 4709	CPB 80	km	396	GL 4704	CPB 81	GL 4624	GL 4706
						↓ ↑				
0.50	0620	....	0900	....	0	d.**Baltimore**..........a.	1520	....	....	2125
45.10	|	....	|	1110		d. Harrisburg.....a.	|	1535	....	|
0.75	0825	....	1105	1310	148	d.Hagerstown.......d.	1330	1335	....	1935
8.00	0950	....	1230	....	214	d.Cumberland.......d.	1135	....	....	1740
	1030	....	1310	....		d.Grantsville.........d.	1050	....	....	1655
2.00	|	....	1425	....	306	a.Uniontown.........d.	0950	....	....	|
0.00	|	1115	1530	....	371	a.**Pittsburgh**........d.	0830	....	1645	|
2.00	|	1230	....	....		d. Uniontown.......d.	....	....	1520	|
0.00	1150	1325	....	....		d. Morgantown....d.	....	....	1425	1550
2.25	1245	1430	....	....		a. **Clarksburg**.....d.	....	....	1315	1445

– Fare ex Hagerstown. *CPB*–Capitol Trailways. *GL*–Greyhound Lines.

Table 565 KNOXVILLE - FAYETTEVILLE GL

US $	4844	4842	4840	572	km	396	4841	571	4843	4845
						↓ ↑				
0.00	0300	0645	1315	1505	0	d.**Knoxville**..........a.	1230	1800	2200	0530
24.00	0505	0915	1525	1735	168	d.Asheville............d.	1015	1545	1945	0330
43.00	0845	1240	1930	....	350	d.Charlotte ....d.	0645	....	1615	0040
54.00	r	....	r	....	480	d.Hamlet...............d.	....	....	r	r
68.00	1315	....	2300	....	575	d.**Fayetteville**.......d.	....	....	1145	2010
75.00	1505	....	*0130*	....		d.Wallace ....d.	....	....	0925	1805
75.00	1600	....	*0405*	....		a.Jacksonville.......d.	....	....	0825	1705
80.00	1625	....	*0430*	....		a.Camp LeJeune..d.	....	....	0800	1640

GL– Greyhound Lines.

Table 566 RALEIGH - WINSTON SALEM - ASHEVILLE/CHARLOTTE CCC GL

US $	CCC 21		CCC 571	GL 1053		CCC 25	CCC 579	GL 1057	CCC 15	CCC 39	CCC 525	km	396		CCC 22	CCC 20	GL 1052	CCC 576	CCC 16	CCC 524	CCC 38		GL 572	
													↓ ↑											
0.00	2315	....	0800	....	....	1400	1715	....	1830	2115	....	0	d.**Raleigh**....................a.	....	0935	1545	....	1735	1700	....	2240	....	2359b	....
7.00	2350	....	0840	....	....	1440	1755	....	|	2150	2155	33	d.Durham.....................d.	....	0855	1505	....	1655	|	2040	2200	....	2320b	....
7.00	0120	....	1050	....	....	1645	2000	....	|	....	2320	130	d.Greensboro.................d.	....	0705	1315	1310	1505	|	1920	....	....	2205b	....
2.00	|	....	1220a	1350	....	|	2040	2135	|	....	0010	159	d.Winston Salem...........d.	....	|	|	1230	1400	|	|	....	....	2115b	....
6.00	|	....	1355a	|	....	|	....	|	|	....	|		d.Hickory......................d.	....	|	|	|	....	|	|	....	....	r	....
6.00	|	....	1540a	|	....	|	....	|	|	....	|	389	a.**Asheville**..................d.	....	|	|	|	....	|	|	....	....	1735	....
0.00	s	....	....	|	....	1710	....	|	|	....	|		d. High Point...............d.	....	0630	1230	1135	....	|	1840	....	....	....	....
7.00	s	....	....	|	....	1800	....	|	|	....	|		d. Salisbury.................d.	....	s	1140	1110	....	|	1755	....	....	....	....
0.00	s	....	....	|	....	1825	....	2245	|	....	|		d. Concord ϕ...............d.	....	s	1115	1045	....	|	1730	....	....	....	....
0.00	0320	....	....	1530	....	1855	....	2315	2225	....	0150		a. **Charlotte**................d.	....	0500	1045	1015	....	1305	1700	....	....	....	....

– *GL*. b–*CCC*.
– Kannapolis.
CCC– Carolina Trailways.

GL– Greyhound Lines.

Table 567 NORFOLK - WILMINGTON CCC

US $		387			km	396			382	
						↓ ↑				
0.00	....	0630	....	....	0	d.**Norfolk**............a.	....	....	2200	....
	....	|	....	....	16	d.Portsmouth........a.	....	....	|	....
2.00	....	0720	....	....	84	d.Elizabeth City....d.	....	....	2105	....
0.75	....	0940	....	....		d.Washington.......d.	....	....	1900	....
1.75	....	1025	....	....	280	d.New Bern..........d.	....	....	1800	....
4.75	....	1220	....	....		d.Jacksonville.......d.	....	....	1710	....
5.75	....	|	....	....		a. Camp LeJeuned.	....	....	1630	....
7.25	....	1335	....	....	424	a.**Wilmington**......d.	....	....	1500	....

CCC– Carolina Trailways.

Table 567a RICHMOND - CAMP LEJEUNE CCC

US $	551		559		km	396		550	352	556
						↓ ↑				
0.00	0830	....	1800	....	0	d.**Richmond**........a.	....	1425	....	2340
	0905	....	1835	....		d.Petersburg.........d.	....	1350	....	2305
	1015	....	1945	....		d.Roanoke Rapidsd.	....	1240	....	2155
	1140	....	2105	....		d.Rocky Mount.....d.	....	1140	....	2100
	1235	....	2200	....		d.Greenville..........d.	....	1035	....	1950
	1335	....	2250	....		d.Kinston.............d.	....	0945	....	1900
1.50	1430	....	2345	....		d.Jacksonville.......d.	....	0845	1700	1800
	1500	....	0015	....		a.**Camp LeJeune**.d.	....	0815	1630	....

CCC– Carolina Trailways.

Table 568 ST. IGNACE - DETROIT GL IT

US $	5137	5139	5169	5129	km	396	5130	5128	5166	5140
						↓ ↑				
50.00	....	....	0700a	....	486	d.St. Ignace..........a.	2200a	....	....	....
50.00	....	....	0715a	....	475	d.**Mackinaw City**.a.	2145s	....	....	....
	....	....	0800a	....		d.Petoskey...........d.	2100a	....	....	....
	....	....	|	....		d.Charlevoix.........d.	|	....	....	....
	....	0740	1030	....		d.Traverse City.....d.	1930a	....	2335	....
	....	0845	1135	....		d.Cadillac.............d.	1610	....	2225s	....
	....	1035	1330	....		d.Clare.................d.	1435	....	2040	....
	....	|	1610	....		d. Lansing...........d.	|	....	1830	....
	....	|	1655	....		d. Jackson...........d.	|	....	1740	....
	....	|	1745	....		d. Ann Arbor.......d.	|	....	1645	....
	....	|	1810	....		d. Ypsilanti.........d.	|	....	1615s	....
20.00	0730	1220	|	1640	185	d.Bay City............d.	1240	1605	|	2235
18.00	0755	1245	|	1705	165	d.Saginaw............d.	1205	1540	|	2210s
11.00	0850	1335	|	1755	105	d.Flint..................d.	1130	1455	|	2125
6.00	0940	1425	|	1845	42	d.Pontiac.............d.	1025	1355	|	2025
0.00	1040	1520	1915	1940	0	a.**Detroit**.............d.	0930	1300	1520	1930

a– *IT*
GL– Greyhound Lines.
IT– Indian Trails.

Table 570 STATE COLLEGE

CPB FAB GL

US $	GL 4693	FAB 730	GL 4691	GL 4695	km	396 ↓ ↑	GL 4694	FAB 705	GL 4690	GL 4692
0.00	0730	*0935a*	*1000*	....	*0*	d.**Philadelphia**.....a.	....	*1825a*	*1855*	*2200*
4.00	0805	*1010a*	*1040*	....	*34*	d.King of Prussia..a.	....	*1750a*	*1815*	*2105*
22.00	1015	1345	1415	1945	*179*	d.Harrisburg ....a.	0915	1255	1545	1830
32.00	1125	1500	1530	2100	*244*	d.Lewistown ....d.	0800	1145	1430	1715
36.00	1220	1545	1625	2145	*277*	d.State College.....d.	0715	1100	1345	1630
40.00	1325	|	1725	....	*342*	d.Altoona..............d.	....	....	1235	1515
50.00	1445	|	1845	....	*407*	d.Johnstown.........d.	....	....	1100	1350
50.00	1640	2235	2040	....	*496*	a.**Pittsburgh**........d.	....	....	0900	1201

a–*CPB*. *CPB*–Capitol Trailways. *FAB*–Fullington Trailways. *GL*–Greyhound Lines.

Table 571 DULUTH - THUNDER BAY

LTB

US $			20 ♣		km	396 ↓ ↑		21 ♣		
0.00	....	....	1300	....	*0*	d.**Duluth** ....a.	....	1200	....	....
	....	....	1550	....		d.Grand Marais ....d.	....	0930	....	....
	....	....	1805	....		d.Pigeon River 𝔐.d.	....	0815	....	....
	....	....	1900	....		a.**Thunder Bay** ....d.	....	0800	....	....

𝔐– For Grand Portage.
LTB– HT Leasing Thunder Bay Ltd.

Table 573 DETROIT - TOLEDO - COLUMBUS/CINCINNATI

ABL GL

US $	396 ↓	km	ABL 213	GL 4404	GL 1387		GL 1165	GL 4440		GL 1135		GL 4832	GL 1151	ABL 215	GL 4444	GL 4414		GL 1115	GL 4436	GL 1157	GL 1153	GL 1093	GL 4448		GL 1159
0.00	**Detroit**..............d.	*0*	0445	0630	....	....	0715	1100	....	1115	....	1230	1315	1325	1305	1540	....	1545	2000	1915	2015	2030	2215	....	2200
8.00	Lincoln Park.......d.	*50*	|	0650	....	....	0735	1120	....	|	....	1250	1335	1345	1325	|	....	1605	|	1935	|	|	|	....	|
12.75	**Toledo**..............d.	*99*	0615	0800	....	....	0855	1230	....	1235	....	1410	1445	1500	1435	1700	....	1715	2120	2045	|	2150	2330	....	2315
	North Baltimore ..d.		....	....	....	....	1000	....	....	|	....	1515	1535	....	....	....	....	1820	....	|	|	2255	....	....	|
24.00	Lima...................d.	*237*	....	....	....	....	1050	....	....	|	....	|	1625	....	....	....	....	1910	....	|	|	|	....	....	|
26.00	Marion..............d.	*265*	....	....	....	....	|	....	....	|	....	1620	|	....	....	....	....	|	....	|	|	2359s	....	....	|
	Delaware..........d.		....	....	....	....	|	....	....	|	....	1650	|	....	....	....	....	|	....	|	|	0030s	....	....	|
33.00	**Columbus**.......a.	*330*	....	....	....	....	|	....	....	|	....	1730	|	....	....	....	....	|	....	|	|	00110	....	....	|
34.00	Dayton ....d.	*363*	....	....	0835	....	1250	....	....	1545	....	....	1805	....	....	....	....	2055	....	2340	|	....	....	....	|
	Sharonville ....d.		....	....	|	....	1345	....	....	|	....	....	1900	....	....	....	....	|	....	|	|	....	....	....	|
41.00	**Cincinnati**.........a.	*430*	....	....	0945	....	1415	....	....	1700	....	....	1930	....	....	....	....	2205	....	0050	0105	....	....	....	0310

396 ↓			GL 1622	GL 1148	GL 1605 ⑤	GL 1150		GL 4439		GL 1096	GL 1152		GL 4401			GL 1154	ABL 214		GL 1156		GL 4604	ABL 216	GL 1172		
Cincinnati...............d.	....	....	....	0145	....	0500	....	....	....	....	0915	....	....	....	....	1010	....	....	1430	....	....	....	1815	....	....
Sharonville ....d.	....	....	....	|	....	|	....	....	....	....	|	....	....	....	....	1030	....	....	1450	....	....	....	|	....	....
Dayton ....d.	....	....	....	|	....	0615	....	....	....	....	1040	....	....	....	....	1130	....	....	1605	....	....	....	1950	....	....
Columbus ....d.	....	....	....	|	....	|	....	....	....	0900	|	....	....	....	....	|	....	....	|	....	1730	....	|	....	....
Delaware..................d.	....	....	....	|	....	|	....	....	....	0935	|	....	....	....	....	|	....	....	|	....	1810	....	|	....	....
Marion.....................d.	....	....	....	|	....	|	....	....	....	1005	|	....	....	....	....	|	....	....	|	....	1840	....	|	....	....
Lima.........................d.	....	....	....	|	....	|	....	....	....	|	|	....	....	....	....	1325	....	....	1745	....	|	....	|	....	....
North Baltimore ....d.	....	....	....	|	....	|	....	....	....	1135	|	....	....	....	....	1425	....	....	1845	....	1950	....	|	....	....
Toledo....................d.	....	....	0530	0550	1020	0915	....	1230	....	1235	1340	....	1450	....	....	1530	1505	....	1935	....	2050	2140	2255	....	....
Lincoln Park ....d.	....	....	|	|	|	|	....	1325	....	1345	|	....	1550	....	....	1630	1605s	....	|	....	2150s	2240s	|	....	....
Detroit....................a.	....	....	0640	0700	1130	1025	....	1355	....	1405	1450	....	1610	....	....	1650	1625	....	2045	....	2205	2300	0005	....	....

ABL– American Trailways. *GL*– Greyhound Lines.

Table 574 PITTSBURGH - ST. LOUIS

GL

US $		1355	1377			1379			1369	1371	1367	km	396 ↓ ↑	1368	1360			1346		1380	1374		1376	1366
	....	*1400*	*1700*	....	....	*2100*	....	....	0030	*0645*	*1000*		d.*New York* ....a.	*0335*	*0820*	....	....	*1215*	....	*1245*	*1530*	....	*1940*	*0030*
	....	*1645*	*2020*	....	....	*0001*	....	....	0315	*1000*	*1335*		d.*Philadelphia*.............a.	*0110*	*0525*	....	....	*0930*	....	*1010*	*1210*	....	*1645*	*2140*
0.00	....	0020	0350	....	....	0710	....	....	1220	1800	2145	*0*	d.**Pittsburgh**...............a.	1730	2205	....	....	0200	....	0305	0425	....	0815	1350
	....	|	|	....	....	|	....	....	|	|	|		d.Washington ....d.	|	|	....	....	|	....	|	|	....	|	|
11.00	....	|	|	....	....	0815	....	....	|	1910	|	*70*	d.Steubenville...............d.	|	|	....	....	|	....	|	|	....	|	1245
15.00	....	|	|	....	....	0900	....	....	1345	1950	|	*91*	d. Wheeling.................d.	1550	|	....	....	|	....	|	|	....	|	1205
27.00	....	|	|	....	....	1020	....	....	1455	2100	|	*177*	d.Cambridge..................d.	1445	2000	....	....	|	....	|	|	....	|	1110
35.00	....	|	|	....	....	1050	....	....	1525	2130	|	*219*	d. Zanesville ....d.	1400	|	....	....	2345	....	|	|	....	|	1030
41.00	....	0445	0820	....	....	1255	....	....	1745	2330	0200	*299*	d.**Columbus** ....d.	1300	1820	....	....	2245	....	2350	0115	....	0500	0930
45.00	....	|	0925	....	....	1400	....	....	1850	|	|	*362*	d.Springfield ....d.	1055	|	....	....	2020	....	|	2305	....	|	|
46.00	....	0615	1015	....	....	1455	....	....	1945	0100	|	*406*	d.Dayton.........................d.	1015	1545	....	....	1940	....	|	2225	....	|	0650
53.00	....	|	1115	....	....	1555	....	....	2045	|	|	*474*	d.Richmond....................d.	0905	|	....	....	1830	....	|	|	....	|	|
63.00	....	0910	1325	....	....	1810	....	....	2240	0340	0600	*584*	d.**Indianapolis** ....d.	0735	1330	....	....	1700	....	1850	2010	....	0100	0435
77.00	....	1040	1500	....	....	1955	....	....	0010s	|	|	*694*	d.Terre Haute.................d.	0515	1125	....	....	1335	....	|	1810	....	2210	|
85.00	....	1100	1520	....	....	2010	....	....	|	|	|	*810*	d.Effingham...................d.	|	0915	....	....	1225	....	|	1600	....	2100	|
89.00	....	|	1600	....	....	|	....	....	|	|	|		d.Vandalia ....d.	|	|	....	....	1135	....	|	|	....	|	|
89.00	....	1250	1720	....	....	2200	....	....	0220	0655	0915	*990*	a.**St. Louis**...................a.	0115	0715	....	....	1015	....	1400	1400	....	1900	2230

GL– Greyhound Lines.

Table 575 ST. LOUIS - HOUSTON

GL

US $	1393			1395	km	396 ↓ ↑			1392	1390
0.00	0745	....	....	2230	*0*	d.**St. Louis**...........a.	....	....	2200	0415
30.99	1100	....	....	0130		d.Poplar Bluff ....d.	....	....	1845	0100
44.00	r	....	....	r		d.Walnut Ridge.....d.	....	....	r	r
45.00	1310	....	....	0310		d.Hoxie.................d.	....	....	1645	2320
60.00	1640	....	....	0630		d.**Little Rock**........d.	....	....	1345	2030
64.00	1730	....	....	0720		d.Pine Bluff ....d.	....	....	1225	1910
80.00	2130	....	....	1130		d.Monroe..............d.	....	....	0830	1525
85.00	2335	....	....	1345		d.Alexandria ....d.	....	....	0615	1245
85.00	0230	....	....	1630		d.Lake Charles.....d.	....	....	0400	0930
90.00	0340	....	....	1825		d.Beaumont..........d.	....	....	|	|
100.00	0515	....	....	2000		a.**Houston** ....d.	....	....	0045	0600

GL– Greyhound Lines.

Table 576 TEXARKANA - HOUSTON

GL

US $	7231		7233		km	396 ↓ ↑	7232		7230	
0.00	0715	....	1800	....	*0*	d.**Texarkana** ....a.	1555	....	0600	....
	0900	....	1945	....		d.Marshall ....d.	1410	....	0415	....
	0935	....	2010	....		d.Longview ....d.	1335	....	0340	....
	1050	....	2135	....		d.Tyler...................d.	1235	....	0240	....
	1205	....	2250	....		d.Palestine ....d.	1055	....	0110	....
	1410	....	0055	....		d.Huntsville...........d.	0900	....	2315	....
	1540	....	0225	....		a.**Houston** ....d.	0730	....	2145	....

GL– Greyhound Lines.

Table 577 396 BUFFALO - NIAGARA FALLS

NF

service (**40**) Buffalo-Niagara Falls and v.v. *40* km. Journey: 55 mins. Fare: US $: 1.85.
From Buffalo: 0520Ⓐ, 0600Ⓐ, 0640Ⓐ, 0645⑥, 0731①, 0800⚒, 0805†, 0900, 1005Ⓐ, 1020†, 1022⑥, 1130⚒, 1135†, 1230Ⓐ, 1240⑥, 1300†, 1400Ⓐ, 1415Ⓒ, 1501①, 1530Ⓒ, 1610Ⓐ, 1637Ⓐ, 1640⑤, 1645⑥, 1705Ⓐ, 1720Ⓐ, 1800Ⓒ, 1805Ⓐ, 1930Ⓒ, 1935Ⓐ, 2105⑥, 2110†, 2115Ⓐ, 2207†, 2317⑥, 2322†, 2333Ⓐ.
From Niagara Falls: 0024①, 0538Ⓐ, 0627Ⓐ, 0645Ⓐ, 0655Ⓐ, 0658⑥, 0710Ⓐ, 0745Ⓐ, 0755Ⓒ, 0901①, 0905Ⓒ, 1015Ⓐ, 1025Ⓒ, 1110Ⓐ, 1135Ⓒ, 1230Ⓐ, 1305Ⓒ, 1400Ⓐ, 1415†, 1430⑥, 1530 1535⚒, 1615Ⓐ, 1640Ⓒ, 1719Ⓐ, 1750†, 1805⑥, 1810Ⓐ, 1835Ⓐ, 1930Ⓐ, 1935Ⓒ, 2050⑥, 2100Ⓐ, 2105†, 2215Ⓒ, 2233Ⓐ.

NF– Niagara Frontier Transit Metro.

Table 577a 396 MILWAUKEE - KENOSHA

WSN

service Milwaukee-Racine-Kenosha and v.v. *45* km. Journey: 1 hour. Fare: US $: ❖.
From Milwaukee: 0705Ⓐ, 0905Ⓐ, 1205Ⓐ, 1425, 1625Ⓐ, 1710Ⓐ, 1755Ⓐ, 2145.
From Kenosha: 0530Ⓐ, 0610Ⓐ, 0650Ⓐ, 0845Ⓐ, 1215Ⓐ, 1415Ⓐ, 1620Ⓐ, 1905.

WSN– Wisconsin Coach Lines Inc.

Table 578 COLUMBUS — GL

US $	4371	4363	4373	1109	km	496 ↓ ↑	4362		4350	4352
32.00	0745	1230	1500	1830	0	d.**Cleveland**.........a.	1045	....	1835	2230
22.00	0835	1325	1600	1930		d.Akron ....d.	1000	....	1750	2145
22.00	0915	1400	1640	2005		d.Canton ....d.	0920	....	1710	2105
18.00	1015	1440	1720	2045		d.Wooster..............d.	0830	....	1600	2015
13.00	1050	1525	1805	2130		d.Mansfield.............d.	0750	....	1520	1935
0.00	1210	1650	1920	2245		a.**Columbus** ....d.	0630	....	1345	1800

GL–Greyhound Lines.

Table 580 SHREVEPORT - LAKE CHARLES — GL

US $		6135			km	496 ↓ ↑		6134		
0.00	....	0715	....	....	0	d.**Shreveport**.......a.	....	1645	....	....
24.00	....	1040	....	....		d.De Ridder..........d.	....	1320	....	....
32.00	....	1145	....	....		a.**Lake Charles**....d.	....	1215	....	....

GL– Greyhound Lines.

Table 579 CHARLESTON - COLUMBUS — GL

US $	1096	4600	4606		km	396 ↓ ↑		4601	4832	1093
0.00	0345	1100	1930	....	0	d.**Charleston** ....a.	....	1730	2250	0600
10.00	0440	1201	2030	....	78	d.Huntington..........d.	....	1630	2150	0500
13.00	0520	1245	2110	....	115	d.Ashland..............d.	....	1600	2120	0430
20.00	0610	1135	2200	....	173	d.Portsmouth.........d.	....	1455	2025	0335
	0710	1435	2300	....		d.Chillicothe...........d.	....	1355	1925	|
	0815	1545	2359	....		a.**Columbus** ....d.	....	1245	1815	0145

GL– Greyhound Lines.

Table 582 CHARLESTON - EVANSVILLE — GL

US $		4817	4515		km	496 ↓ ↑	4822	4516		
0.00	....	....	1045	....	0	d.**Charleston** ....a.	....	2115	....	....
10.00	....	....	1145	....	78	d.Huntington..........d.	....	2015	....	....
13.00	....	....	1220	....	115	d.Ashland..............d.	....	*2100*	....	....
	....	....	1505	....		d.Lexington............d.	....	1740	....	....
	....	....	1535	....		d.Frankfort.............d.	....	1650	....	....
	....	1305	1715	....		d.**Louisville** ....d.	1505	1545	....	....
	....	1400	|	....		a.Fort Knox ....d.	1410	|	....	....
	....		|	....		d.Owensboro ....d.	....	|	....	....
	....	....	1815	....		a.**Evansville**..........d.	....	1201	....	....

GL– Greyhound Lines.

Table 583 CINCINNATI - NASHVILLE — GL

US $	496 ↓	km	GL 1161	GL 1155	GL 1157	GL 1159			GL 1123			GL 1387			GL 1107	GL 1165		GL 1171	GL 1163	GL 1135	GL 1151	GL 1103			
	Chicago..............d.		....	1730	....	....	....	....	2300	....	....	....	....	....	0600	*0700*	....	0700	1130	....	....	1500	....	....	....
0.00	**Cincinnati**..........d.	0	2230	|	0135	0350	....	....	|	....	....	1015	....	....	|	1445	....	*1450*	|	1745	2015	|	....	....	....
20.00	Louisville ....d.	165	0040	0035s	|	0610	....	....	0625	....	....	1300	....	....	1345	1715	....	1730	1905	2015	2240	2245	....	....	....
	Fort Knox ....d.	224	|	|	|	|	....	....	|	....	....	|	....	....	|	|	....	1825	|	|	|	|	....	....	....
	Elizabethtown.....d.		|	|	|	|	....	....	0735	....	....	1350	....	....	1435	|	....	1900	|	|	|	|	....	....	....
33.00	Cave City ....d.	295	|	|	|	|	....	....	|	....	....	1335	....	....	|	|	....	1850	|	|	|	|	....	....	....
37.00	Bowling Green....d.	349	|	|	0410	|	....	....	0725	....	....	1405	....	....	|	|	....	1920	|	2110	|	|	....	....	....
44.00	**Nashville** ....a.	436	0245	0245	0525	0815	....	....	0920	....	....	1525	....	....	1555	1920	....	2040	2115	2225	0045	0050	....	....	....

396 ↓			GL 1176	GL 1160		GL 1152	GL 1120		GL 1154	GL 1114			GL 582	GL 1156	GL 5396	GL 1172			GL 598		GL 1166			GL 1148	GL 1168
Nashville ....d.	....	....	2230	2230	....	0200	0200	....	0345	0400	....	....	0630	0625	1030	1045	....	....	1400	....	....	....	....	1815	1815
Bowling Green..........d.	....	....	2340	|	....	|	|	....	|	0510	....	....	|	0740	1145	1155	....	....	1515	....	....	....	....	|	1930
Cave City ....d.	....	....	|	|	....	|	|	....	|	|	....	....	|	0810	|	1230	....	....	|	....	....	....	....	|	2000
Elizabethtown...........d.	....	....	|	|	....	|	|	....	|	0720	....	....	|	1000	1355	|	....	....	1725	....	....	....	....	2140	|
Fort Knox ....d.	....	....	|	|	....	|	|	....	|	|	....	....	|	|	|	|	....	....	|	....	....	....	....	|	|
Louisville ....d.	....	....	|	|	....	0645	0635	....	|	0900	....	....	1120	1201	1525	1545	....	....	1900	....	1900	....	....	2310	2315
Cincinnati................a.	....	....	0420	|	....	0835	|	....	2130	|	....	....	|	1350	|	1735	....	....	|	....	2050	....	....	0100	|
Chicago....................a.	....	....	....	0815	....	....	1130	....	....	1355	....	....	1715	....	2045	....	....	....	2355	....	....	....	....	....	0400

GL– Greyhound Lines.

Table 584 CINCINNATI - KNOXVILLE — ET GL SET

US$	SET 597			GL 1105	ET 17 ④	GL 1121	SET 585	GL 1117		GL 1115		km	496 ↓ ↑	GL 1150	GL 1108		GL 1170	SET 594	GL 1164		ET 18 ④		GL 596	
	1615	....	....	2015	....	....	0700	....	....	....	....		d. *Chicago*....................a.	....	1235	....	....	2100b	....	....	....	....	0515a	....
0.00	0130b	....	....	0350	....	0700	1600	2015	....	2245	....	0	d. **Cincinnati**...............a.	0415	0440	....	0935	1400	1910	....	....	....	0040a	....
17.00	|	....	....	0520	....	0835	1755	2200	....	|	....	135	d. Lexington ....d.	|	|	....	0810	1235	1745	....	....	....	2235	....
	|	....	....	|	....	0930	1850	2300	....	|	....		d. Berea ....d.	|	|	....	0710	1115	1625	....	....	....	2125	....
32.00	|	....	....	|	....	1040	1945	2335	....	|	....	250	d. London......................d.	|	|	....	0630	1035	1545	....	....	....	2045	....
33.00	|	....	....	0635	0930	1100	2005	2350	....	|	....	290	d. Corbin ....d.	|	|	....	0540	1015	1510	....	....	....	2025	....
◇3.00	|	....	....	|	1000	|	|	|	....	|	....		d. Oak Ridge..................d.	|	|	....	|	|	|	....	1530	....	|	....
44.00	0540b	....	....	0815	....	1240	2145	0130	....	0255	....	415	a. **Knoxville**.................d.	0005	0030	....	0400	0835	1330	....	1500	....	1845	....
56.00	....	....	....	....	....	1540	....	....	....	0540	....	600	a. **Chattanooga**............d.	2120	....	....	....	0500	1035	....	....	....	....	....

a–SET. b–GL. ◇–Fare ex Knoxville.. ET–East Tennessee Human Resources Agency. GL–Greyhound Lines. SET–Southeastern Trailways

Table 585 TOLEDO - INDIANAPOLIS — ABL

US $	213	217	215		km	496 ↓ ↑		214	216	220
43.00	0445	....	1325	....		d.*Detroit* ....a.	....	1625	2300	....
36.00	0615	....	1500	....	0	d.**Toledo** ....a.	....	1505	2140	....
22.00	0850	1245	1735	....	138	d.Fort Wayne ....d.	....	1210	1835	2130
	1020	1355	1910	....	211	d.Marion ....d.	....	1045	1742	2030
	1105	1440	1955	....		d.Muncie ....d.	....	0945	1710	1935
13.00	1140	1515	2030	....		d.Anderson.............d.	....	0910	1535	1900
0.00	1240	1625	2130	....	306	a.**Indianapolis**.....d.	....	0810	1435	1800

ABL– American Trailways.

Table 587 RICHMOND - CHARLESTON — GL

US $		3921			km	396 ↓ ↑	3920			
56.00	....	1115	....	....	0	d.**Richmond** ....a.	1415	....	....	....
41.00	....	1255	....	....	127	d.Charlottesville....d.	1220	....	....	....
36.00	....	1350	....	....	176	d.Staunton.............d.	1125	....	....	....
32.00	....	1435	....	....	215	d.Lexington............d.	1040	....	....	....
26.00	....	1510	....	....	271	d.Clifton Forge ....d.	1005	....	....	....
21.00	....	s	....	....	329	d.White Sulphur Springs.d.	s	....	....	....
0.00	....	1850	....	....	490	a.**Charleston** ....d.	0625	....	....	....

GL– Greyhound Lines.

Table 588 WASHINGTON - ROANOKE - KNOXVILLE

GL

US $		1539			1537	1511	1051	1533	1529	3929	1535	km	496 ↓ ↑		3924	1536		1528	1532	1076	1538	1534	1530	
	....	*1300*	....	....	*1800*	*2230*	*0345*	....	*0345*	....	*0900*		d.*New York* a.	....	*0520*	*0520*	....	*0800*	*1120*	*1630*	*1820*	*2130*	....	....
0.00	....	1800	....	....	2330	0300	0930	....	0930	....	1400	*0*	d.**Washington** a.	....	*0005*	2330	....	|	0600	1100	1300	1615	....	....
21.00	....	|	....	....	|	0600	|	1115	|	1545	|	*175*	d. Richmond a.	....	2055	|	....	2359	|	|	|	|	1415	....
11.00	....	|	....	....	|	|	1040	|	|	|	|		d. Fredericksburg d.	....	|	|	....	|	|	|	|	|	|	....
22.00	....	2145	....	....	|	0740	1255	1300	|	|	|	*185*	d. Charlottesville d.	....	|	2020	....	|	|	0805	|	|	1300	....
13.00	....	|	....	....	|	|	|	|	1150	|	|	*106*	d.Winchester d.	....	|	|	....	|	|	|	1040	1355	|	....
25.00	....	|	....	....	|	|	|	|	1340	|	1810	*216*	d.Harrisonburg d.	....	|	|	....	|	|	|	0920	1235	|	....
30.00	....	|	....	....	|	|	|	|	1415	|	1845	*260*	d.Staunton d.	....	|	|	....	|	|	|	0805	1120	|	....
34.00	....	|	....	....	|	|	|	|	1455	|	1925	*314*	d.Lexington d.	....	|	|	....	|	|	|	|	1035	|	....
	....	|	....	....	|	|	|	|	|	1750	|		d. Appomattox d.	....	1950	|	....	2155	|	|	|	|	|	....
33.00	....	2325	....	....	|	0920	1425	1440	|	1825			d. Lynchburg d.	....	1820	1830	....	2125	|	0600	|	|	1055	....
40.00	....	0045	....	....	0430	1050	....	1555	1630	1940	2100	*406*	d.**Roanoke** d.	....	1700	1710	....	2015	0120	....	0630	0935	0935	....
53.00	....	0220	....	....	0645	1300	....	....	1850	....	2300	*486*	d.Wytheville d.	....	....	1455	....	1825	2350	....	0445	0715	....	....
59.00	....	|	....	....	0800	1415	....	....	2005	....	|	*570*	d.Abingdon d.	....	....	1240	....	1635	2200	....	|	|	....	....
61.00	....	|	....	....	0825	1440	....	....	2035	....	|	*591*	d.Bristol d.	....	....	1215	....	1610	2135	....	|	0505	....	....
64.00	....	|	....	....	0935	|	....	....	2120	....	|	*627*	d.Johnson City d.	....	....	1130	....	|	2055	....	|	|	....	....
73.00	....	|	....	....	1100	1645	....	....	|	....	|	*724*	d.Morristown d.	....	....	1000	....	1410	|	....	|	|	....	....
73.00	....	0600	....	....	1159	1745	....	....	2340	....	0240	*800*	a.**Knoxville** d.	....	....	0900	....	1310	1850	....	0035	0250	....	....
	....	0925	....	....	1535	2055	....	....	0230	....	0530		a.*Nashville* d.	....	....	0400	....	0810	1400	....	1900	2215	....	....
	....	1410	....	....	2030	0130	....	....	0700	....	1100		a.*Memphis* d.	....	....	2330	....	0330	....	....	1245	1700	....	....
	....	0130	....	....	....	1130	....	....	1730	....	2145		a.*Dallas* d.	....	....	1220	....	1645	....	....	0230	0540	....	....

GL– Greyhound Lines.

Table 590 KNOXVILLE - COLUMBIA - CHARLESTON

BRI GL SES

US $	*SES* 305	*GL* 4844	*SES* 304		*GL* 4853	*SES* 301	*GL* 1113	*SES* 302	*GL* 572	*GL* 4840	*BRI* 101	km	496 ↓ ↑		*SES* 409	*BRI* 102	*GL* 4856	*SES* 406	*GL* 571	*GL* 4843	*GL* 584	*SES* 402	*GL* 1184	*SES* 403
0.00	....	0240	....	....	0630	....	0900	....	1500	1815	1800	*0*	d.**Knoxville** a.	....	....	1645	1725	....	1800	2215	2359	....	0330	....
21.00	....	0440	....	....	0840	....	1125	....	1715	2020	2055	*168*	d.Asheville d.	....	....	1445	1520	....	1545	2000	2200	....	0125	....
31.00	....	....	....	....	1030	....	1330	....	....	....	|	*262*	d.Greenville d.	....	....	|	1330	....	....	....	2015	....	2345	....
32.00	....	....	....	....	....	....	....	....	....	....	|		d. Spartanburg d.	....	....	|	|	....	....	....	|	....	|	....
	2345	....	*0345*	....	....	*0730*	....	*1215*	....	....	|		d. *Atlanta* a.	....	*1700*	|	|	*2115*	....	....	|	*0045*	|	*0430*
	0220	....	*0645*	....	....	*1145*	....	*1615*	....	....	|		d. *Augusta* a.	....	*1345*	|	1035	*1745*	....	....	|	*2215*	|	*0200*
43.00	0355	....	0845	....	1330	1335	....	1800	....	....	0300	*417*	d.**Columbia** d.	....	1201	0930	....	1600	....	....	1700	2030	2115	0035
	|	....	|	....	....	|	....	|	....	....	|		d. Sumter d.	....	|	|	....	|	....	....	....	|	....	|
53.00	0450	....	0940	....	....	1430	....	1855	....	....	0400	*482*	d.Orangeburg d.	....	1045	0820	....	1435	....	....	....	1915	....	2305
61.00	0615	....	1115	....	....	1600	....	2030	....	....	0530	*596*	a.**Charleston** d.	....	0915	0700	....	1300	....	....	....	1745	....	2130

a– *BRI*. b–*GL*.
BRI– Blue Ridge Trailways.
GL– Greyhound Lines.
SES– Southeastern Stages.

Table 591 CHATTANOOGA - ATLANTA - JACKSONVILLE

GL

US $	1103	1115	1155	1153	1157	5359	1123	1121	1233	1107	1163	km	496 ↓ ↑	5396	1164	5356	1148	1234	1150	1160	1120	1154	582	594
0.00	0130	....	0330	....	0615	0845	1015	....	1615	1700	2200	*0*	d.**Nashville** a.	0930	....	1315	1705	2115	....	2145	0115	0240	0530	....
25.00	|	0600	0700	0930	0945	1345	1415	1600	2015	|	|	*215*	d.**Chattanooga** a.	|	1015	1015	1500	1915	2100	|	|	|	|	0440
35.00	|	|	|	|	|	1530	|	|	|	|	|	*330*	d.Rome d.	|	|	0830	|	|	|	|	|	|	|	|
	0645	0815	0930	1145	1145	1715	1630	1815	2230	2015	0315		a. **Atlanta** d.	0615	0800	0640	1245	1645	1845	1830	2200	2315	0215	0230
	|		|		|	⑤⑥				|	|			|	|						|	|	⑤⑥	
41.00	|	**5383**	|	**1177**	|	**5369**	**5389**	**5399**	**5391**	|	|	*405*	**Atlanta**	|	|	**5384**	**5386**	**5382**	**5398**	**5394**	|	|	**5056**	**582**
	0745	0800	1030	1245	1245	1730	1815	1930	2330	2315	0430		d. **Atlanta** a.	0515	0700	1100	1530	1530	1900	2200	2100	2215	2230	0100
50.00	|	|	|	|	|	|	|	|	|	|	|	*471*	d.Griffin d.	|	|	|	|	|	|	|	|	|	|	|
56.00	0930	1000	1230	1445	|	|	2015	2130	|	|	0605	*540*	d.Macon d.	|	0515	0915	1345	1345	1730	2015	|	2045	2100	2330
67.00	1155	|	|	1715	|	|	|	2340	|	|	0830		d. Tifton d.	|	0305	|	|	1055	1500	|	|	1800	|	|
73.00	|	|	|	|	|	|	|	|	|	|	|		d. Alma d.	|	|	|	|	|	|	|	|	|	|	|
73.00	|	1410	|	|	|	|	0001	|	0430	|	|	*790*	d.Waycross d.	|	|	|	0905	|	|	1535	|	|	|	1855
73.00	1250	|	|	1810	|	2305	|	0035	|	|	0925	*785*	d. Valdosta d.	|	0210	0530	|	1000	1405	|	|	1710	|	|
77.00	1410	|	|	1930	|	|	|	0150	|	|	1045	*831*	d. Lake City d.	|	|	0430	|	0850	1255	|	1545	1600	|	|
	1600	|	|	2150	1930	|	|	|	|	0605	|		d.Ocala a.	2200	|	|	|	|	1025	|	|	1400	|	|
82.00	|	1600	1845	|	|	0115	0145	0300	0615	|	1155	*930*	a.**Jacksonville** d.	|	0001	0315	0730	0730	|	1400	|	|	1400	1715
	|	....	....	2345	|	....	....	....	....	|	....		a. *Tampa* d.	|	....	....	....	....	0645	....	|	1100	....	....
	1745	....	....	....	|	....	....	....	....	|	....		a. *Orlando* d.	|	....	....	....	....	....	....	1245	....	....	....
104.00	2355	....	....	....	0405	....	....	....	....	1620	....	*1505*	a.*Miami* d.	1325	....	....	....	....	....	....	0605	....	....	....

GL– Greyhound Lines.

Table 592 BIRMINGHAM - JACKSONVILLE

GL

US $	5003				km	496 ↓ ↑		5004		
	0200	....	....	....		d.*Memphis* a.	....	*0200*	....	....
0.00	0730	....	....	....	*0*	d.**Birmingham** a.	....	1630	....	....
10.00	0830	....	....	....	*81*	d.Sylacauga d.	....	1525	....	....
22.00	1015	....	....	....	*196*	d.Opelika d.	....	1340	....	....
26.00	1205	....	....	....	*245*	d.Columbus d.	....	1400	....	....
39.00	1430	....	....	....	*360*	d.Albany d.	....	1130	....	....
	1530	....	....	....		d.Tifton d.	....	1025	....	....
64.00	1705	....	....	....	*544*	d.Waycross d.	....	0900	....	....
61.00	|	....	....	....	*515*	d. Valdosta d.	....	|	....	....
64.00	|	....	....	....	*576*	d. Lake City d.	....	|	....	....
73.00	1845	....	....	....	*675*	a.**Jacksonville** d.	....	0715	....	....

GL– Greyhound Lines.

Table 593 ATLANTA - SAVANNAH

GL GTY

US $	*GTY* 8202	*GL* 1155	*GTY* 8204	*GL* 5059	km	496 ↓ ↑	*GL* 5054	*GTY* 8201	*GL* 5056 ⑤⑥	*GTY* 8203
0.00	*0800*b	1030	*1030*b	1815	*0*	d.**Atlanta** a.	1715	*1945*b	2230	*0115*b
19.00	1005	1230	1445	2015	*125*	d.Macon a.	1510	1745	2100	2315
26.00	1100	1330	1545	2115	*209*	d.Dublin d.	1410	1645	1945	2235
33.00	1145	|	1625	|	*320*	d. Vidalia d.	|	1605	|	2130
43.00	1340	1555	1830	2345	*476*	a.**Savannah** d.	1130	1415	1720	1900

b– *GL*.
GL– Greyhound Lines.
GTY– Georgia Trailways.

Table 595 ATLANTA - TALLAHASSEE

CHL GL

US $	496 ↓	km		*CHL* 2100	*GL* 5367 ⑤⑥⑦		*GL* 5365		*GL* 5363	*GL* 585
0.00	**Atlanta** d.	*0*	....	0730	0745	....	1030	....	1730	0430
19.00	Macon d.	*133*	....	|	0940	....	1230	....	1925	0605
	Columbus d.		....	1030	|	....	|	....	|	|
24.00	Americus d.	*220*	....	|	1115	....	1405	....	2100	0740
30.00	Albany d.	*280*	....	|	1215	....	1520	....	2210	0855
36.00	Thomasville d.	*377*	....	|	....	....	1645	....	2335	1020
44.00	**Tallahassee** a.	*426*	....	1430	....	....	1740	....	0020	1130

296 ↑			*GL* 5360	*GL* 5368 ⑤⑥⑦		*GL* 5362	*CHL* 2300	*GL* 594		
Tallahassee d.	....	....	0520	....	....	1230	1515	1845	....	....
Thomasville d.	....	....	0610	....	....	1335	|	1935	....	....
Albany d.	....	....	0740	1245	....	1510	|	2110	....	....
Americus d.	....	....	0845	1345	....	1615	|	|	....	....
Columbus d.	....	....	|	|	....	|	1910	|	....	....
Macon d.	....	....	1030	1530	....	1800	|	2330	....	....
Atlanta a.	....	....	1215	1715	....	1945	2200	0115	....	....

CHL– C & H Bus Lines.
GL– Greyhound Lines.

❖–Information not available ⊡–Supplement payable ●–Alternate days only

able 596 WASHINGTON - ATLANTA

CCC GL

S $	CCC 521	GL 1051	GL 1055	CCC 523	CCC 525	GL 1063	GL 1071	GL 1077	GL 529	GL 1073	GL 1053	km	496 ↓ ↑	GL 1050	GL 520	GL 522	GL 1074	CCC 524	GL 1070	GL 528	GL 1080	GL 1072	GL 1076	GL 1076
0.00	*0200*b	0345	0800	*0800*b	*1000*b	1300	1500	1700	2000	2200	*0015*		d.*New York* ...a.	2340	0240	0520	0215	*0720*b	0630	*1330*	*1120*	1300	*1630*	1800
7.00	*0635*b	0930	1315	1300b	*1530*b	*1825*	*2100*	2215	0100	│	0505	*0*	d.**Washington** ...a.	1600	2120	0005	*2120*	*0305*b	│	│	0630	│	1100	*1245*
	│	1040	│	│	│	│	│	│	│	│	│		d. Fredericksburg ...d.	1450	│	│	│	│	│	│	│	│	│	│
	│	1255	1640	│	│	│	│	│	│	│	│		d. Charlottesville ...d.	1310	│	│	│	│	│	│	│	│	0805	│
	│	1430	1815	│	│	│	│	│	│	│	│		d. Lynchburg ...d.	1105	│	│	│	│	│	│	│	│	0600	│
3.00	1000	│	│	1600	1845	2100	2335	│	0400d	0600	0800		d.**Richmond** ...a.	│	1800d	2100d	1815	2345	2230	0500d	│	0500	│	0930
6.00	│	│	│	│	1920	│	│	│	│	│	│		d.Petersburg ...a.	│	│	│	│	2310	│	│	│	│	│	│
0.00	1325	1605	2000	1935	│	│	│	│	0700d	│	1125		d. Danville ...d.	0935	1515d	1815d	│	│	│	0210d	│	│	0430	0635
3.00	│	│	│	│	2155	│	│	│	│	│	│		d. Durham ...d.	│	│	│	│	2045	│	│	│	│	│	│
3.00	1445	1725	2120	│	2320	│	│	│	0820d	│	1245		d.Greensboro ...d.	0730	1320d	1620d	│	1920	│	0100d	│	│	0300	0445
7.00	1545	│	│	2135	0015	│	│	│	0940d	│	1345		d.Winston Salem ...d.	0655	1230d	1530d	│	1840	│	│	│	0100	│	│
7.00	│	│	│	│	│	│	│	│	1035d	│	│		d.Salisbury ...d.	│	1110d	│	│	1755	│	│	│	│	│	│
5.00	1815b	2000	2345	0001	0245b	0245	0520	0635	1201	1201	1600		d.Charlotte ...d.	0500	1015d	1330d	1300	1700	1715	2300d	2300	2300	0100	0245
	│	2145	│	│	│	│	│	0800	1330	│	1730		d.Spartanburg ...d.	│	0740	1105	│	1420b	│	2050	│	│	│	│
2.00	│	2245	│	│	│	│	│	0900	1420	│	1830		d.Greenville ...d.	│	0700	1025	│	1340b	│	2010	│	│	2230	│
4.00	2230b	0115	0345	0400	0800	0700	0935	1159	1815	1615	2100		a.**Atlanta** ...d.	0015	0415	0715	0800	0930b	1215	1600	1800	1800	1945	2200

GL.
CCC.

CCC– Carolina Trailways.
GL– Greyhound Lines.

able 597 ATLANTA - NEW ORLEANS

CML COT GL

S $	GL 1051	GL 533	COT 61	GL 1079	GL 1563	GL 1169	GL 1565	GL 513	GL 531	COT 67	GL 1553	km	496 ↓ ↑	GL 514	GL 1560	COT 60	GL 1080	GL 1174	GL 3822	GL 3824	COT 62	GL 1050	GL 1052	GL 552
0.00	0145	0500	....	0745	1030	....	1245	1245	1745	....	2145	*0*	d.**Atlanta 766** ...a.	1100	1035	1530b	1700	....	1815	2030	2115b	2315	0315	0615
	│	0615	....	│	1159	....	│	1415	1930	....	│	*105*	d. La Grange ...d.	0915	0905	1400b	│	....	1645	1900	1945b	│	│	│
	│	0725	....	│	│	....	│	1530a	│	....	│	*135*	d.Columbus **766** ...d.	0815	│	1300b	│	....	1545	1730	│	2100	0115	│
	0230	│	....	0830	1201	....	1335	│	│	....	2230	*167*	d. Opelika ...d.	│	0705	│	1415	....	....	....	1745b	│	│	0330
	0415	0810	0920	1030	1400	1435	1545	1645a	2100	2130	0005	*280*	d.**Montgomery 766** ...d.	0415a	0540	1000b	1300	1340	....	....	1615b	1800	2230	0210
	0500	....	1005	│	1450	1525	│	....	....	│	│	*358*	d.Greenville ...d.	....	│	│	│	1250	....	....	1435	1625	2120	│
	0630	....	1140	│	1645	1655	│	....	....	0040	│	*478*	d.Atmore ...d.	....	│	0555	│	1120	....	....	1255	│	│	│
	│	....	│	│	│	1745	│	....	....	│	│	*553*	a. Pensacola ...d.	....	│	│	│	1030	....	....	│	│	│	│
	0815	....	1315	1400	1830	....	1930	....	....	0210	0335	*593*	d.Mobile ...d.	....	0150	0445	0925	....	....	....	1145	1325	1845	2255
	0900	....	1400	│	1915	....	│	....	....	0250	│	*658*	d.Pascagoula ...d.	....	│	0300	│	....	....	....	1015	│	│	│
	0935	....	1430	│	1950	....	│	....	....	0320	│	*793*	d.Biloxi ...d.	....	2355	0230	│	....	....	....	0945	│	│	│
	1005	....	1455	│	2020	....	│	....	....	0345	│	*813*	d.Gulfport ...d.	....	2330	0205	│	....	....	....	0920	│	│	│
	1145	....	1640	1625	2210	....	2155	....	....	0530	0600	*933*	a.**New Orleans** ...d.	....	2210	0015	0615	....	....	....	0730	1015	1530	1945

CML.
GL.

CML– Capital Trailways. *COT–* Colonial Trailways.
GL– Greyhound Lines.

able 598 HOUSTON - NEW ORLEANS

GL

S $	1392	1050	714	1256	1052	1390	1264	5418	522	1560	1246	1248	1262	1080	5414	km	496 ↓ ↑	1247	1243	1261	711	1553	5415	1249	713	1051	1265	1245	1079	1253	5431	1265
00	....	*2030*	....	2345	0145	....	*0315*	....	0515	0845	*1400*	*1400*	*1730*	*1730*	....		d.*San Antonio* ...a.	1515	1655	*1830*	....	*2015*	....	*2230*	....	*0125*	*0125*	*0340*	*0700*	*0700*	....	*0955*
00	0045	0130	....	0400	0600	0600	0740	....	1000	1315	1815	1815	2300	2300	....	*523*	d.**Houston** ...a.	1100	1159	1330	....	1600	....	1730	....	2115	2015	2320	0050	0245	....	0515
00	│	│	....	0535	0740	│	0920	....	1145	1455	│	2000	│	2335	....	*388*	d.Beaumont ...d.	0925	│	│	....	1425	....	1545	....	1940	│	2145	│	│	....	│
	0230	│	....	│	│	0815	0955	....	1240	1530	│	2055	│	│	....		d.Orange ...d.	0815	│	│	....	1315	....	│	....	1900	│	│	│	│	....	│
00	0400	0415	....	│	0915	0930	1100	....	1355	1635	2110	2200	│	0055	....	*297*	d.Lake Charles ...d.	0730	│	│	....	1230	....	1425	....	1815	│	2035	2220	│	....	│
00	....	0545	0750	0755	1100	....	1240	1410	1530	1825	│	2325	0140	0210	0320	*177*	d. Lafayette ...d.	0540	│	│	1030	1030	1220	1245	1550	1605	│	1900	2045	│	2335	0140
00	....	0730	0930	0930	1245	....	1415	│	1710	2000	2330	0045	0330	0345	│	*116*	d.Baton Rouge ...d.	0430	0730	0900	0915	0915	│	1130	1445	1450	1545	1745	1930	2215	│	0030
00	....	│	│	│	│	....	│	1605	│	│	│	│	│	│	0515		d. Morgan City ...d.	│	│	│	│	│	1025	│	│	│	│	│	│	│	2140	│
	....	│	│	│	│	....	│	1735	│	│	│	│	│	│	0645		d. Houma ...d.	│	│	│	│	│	0910	│	│	│	│	│	│	│	2025	│
00	....	0920	1130	│	1445	....	1615	1920	1900	2135	0105	│	│	0520	0830	*0*	a.**New Orleans** ...d.	0225	│	│	0645	0700	0715	0915	1220	1230	│	1500	1700	│	1830	2240
	....	1240	1600	1245	1755	....	2030	....	2210	0100	0400	0400	0645	0840	....		a.*Mobile* **399** ...d.	2340	0330	0500	....	0500	....	0830	....	0825	1201	1201	1400	1830	....	1930

– Greyhound Lines.

able 599 NEW ORLEANS - JACKSONVILLE/MIAMI

COT GL

S $	GL 1246	GL 1248	GL 1262	GL 1080	GL 1252	GL 1161	GL 1256	GL 1258	GL 1264	GL 1254	GL 3689	km	296	GL 1253	GL 1251	GL 1247	GL 1241	GL 1243	GL 1261	GL 598	GL 1249	GL 1265	GL 1245	COT 25
	1815	1815	2200	2130	....	....	0400	0400	....	1315	....		d.*Houston* **398** ...a.	0245	*0515*	1115	....	1159	1330	....	1730	2015	2320	....
0.00	0135	│	│	0615	0600	....	│	1205	1700	│	....	*0*	d.**New Orleans** ...a.	│	2210	0210	....	*0600*	│	....	0840	│	1425	1640
4.00	│	│	│	│	0750	....	│	1405	1840	│	....	*120*	d.Gulfport ...d.	│	2020	│	....	│	│	....	0640	│	│	1455
8.00	│	│	│	│	0815	....	│	1435	1910	│	....	*140*	d.Biloxi ...d.	│	1950	│	....	│	│	....	0610	│	│	1430
1.00	│	│	│	│	0845	....	│	1510	1945	│	....	*275*	d.Pascagoula ...d.	│	1915	│	....	│	│	....	0540	│	│	1400
6.00	0445	0445	0730	0840	1015	....	1345	1645	2115	2240	....	*340*	d.Mobile ...d.	1830	1830	2345	2330	0330	0500	....	0500	1201	1201	1315
5.00	0600	0600	0845	....	1130	....	1500	1800	2230	2350	....	*420*	d.Pensacola ...d.	1640	1640	2155	2135	0140	│	....	│	1010	1010	....
3.00	0845	│	1130	....	1415	*1120*	1745	2045	│	│	....	*595*	d. Panama City ...d.	│	1400	1910	│	│	│	....	│	│	0730	....
6.00	│	0920	│	....	│	1445	1925	│	│	│	....	*660*	d.Marianna ...d.	1320	│	│	1905	2315	│	....	│	0650	│	....
9.00	│	*1055*	│	....	│	1620	2100	│	│	│	....	*740*	d.Chattahoochee ...d.	1330	│	│	│	│	│	....	│	0700	│	....
4.00	1245	1230	1525	....	1815	1810	2245	0045	0330	0445	0800	*800*	d.Tallahassee ...d.	1230	1230	1800	1845	2300	0115	0030	0115	0600	0600	....
3.00	1510	│	│	....	2040	│	│	│	│	│	│	*965*	d.Lake City ...d.	│	0925	1500	│	│	│	│	│	│	│	....
2.00	1630	│	│	....	2200	│	0130	0330	│	│	│	*1064*	a.**Jacksonville** ...d.	│	0800	1330	│	│	│	│	2145	│	0245	....
7.00	....	1510	1835	....	....	2100	....	....	0610	0735	1040	*1040*	a. Gainesville ...d.	0855	....	....	1510	1925	2140	2140	....	0220	│	....
2.00	....	1600	1925	....	....	2150	....	....	0700	0825	1130	*1100*	a. Ocala ...d.	0805	....	....	1420	1835	2050	2050	....	0130	│	....
2.00	....	1745	2100	....	....	*2330*	....	....	0845	│	1400	*1235*	a. Orlando (*Disney World*) d.	0630	....	....	1245	1700	│	1830	....	0001	│	....
2.00	....	│	│	....	....	2345	....	....	....	1015	│	*1240*	a. **Tampa** ...d.	│	....	....	│	│	1900	│	....	│	│	....
2.00	....	│	│	....	....	│	....	....	....	*1150*	│	*1273*	a. St. Petersburg ...d.	│	....	....	│	│	│	│	....	│	│	....
4.00	....	2355	0400	....	....	*0545*	....	....	....	....	2120	*1615*	a.**Miami** ...d.	2325	....	....	0600	0940	1025	1030	....	1715	*1830*	....

COT.
GL.
T– Colonial Trailways.

GL– Greyhound Lines.

able 650 JACKSONVILLE - MIAMI

GL

S $	496 ↓	km	1009	3673	507	1015	1107	1173	1019	5391	1003	3737	3687	5399	3797	505	3689	585	1103	3733	1005	1262	1153	503	3735
0.00	**Jacksonville** ...d.	*0*	0230	....	0415	0430	*0415*	....	0700	0715	1000	....	1000	....	....	1315	....	1315		....	1700	....	1930	2330	....
9.00	St. Augustine ...d.	*39*	│	....	│	....	*0500*	....	│	│	│	....	1045	....	....	│	....	1400		....	│	....	2015	0015	....
9.00	Daytona Beach ...d.	*125*	│	....	│	0610	*0610*	....	│	0900	│	....	1205	....	....	│	....	1520		....	│	....	2130	0125	....
6.00	Orlando (*Disney World*) d.	*214*	│	0540	│		0915	....	│	1100	│	....	│	....	....	│	1430	│	1830	....	│	2130	0015	│	....
3.00	Cocoa ...d.	*250*	│	│	│	0750	1020	....	│	│	│	....	1345	....	....	│	│	1700	│	....	│	2235	│	│	....
2.00	Melbourne ...d.	*286*	│	│	│	0820	1050	....	│	│	│	....	1415	....	....	│	│	1730	│	....	│	2305	│	│	....
6.00	Fort Pierce ...d.	*335*	0700	0830	0830	1015	1235	....	1120	1400	1415	....	1615	....	....	1730	│	1935	│	....	2115	0040	0240	0405	....
4.00	West Palm Beach d.	*419*	0810	0940	│	1145	1345	....	1230	1525	1525	....	1740	....	1745	1840	1850	2100	2155	....	│	0150	0350	0515	....
3.00	Fort Lauderdale ..d.	*490*	0925	1055	1030	1140	1500	1415	1345	1640	1640	1700	1855	1900	2000	1955	2000	2215	2315	2335	2315	0305	0505	0630	0730
6.00	**North Miami Beach** a.	*539*	│		1105	│	│	1450	│	│	│	1735	│	1935	2035	│	│	│	│	│	│	│	│	│	0820
6.00	**Miami** ...a.		1045	1215	1130	1505	1620	1530	1450	1745	1745	1815	2000	2015	2125	2115	2130	2255	2355	0030	0015	0400	0545	0730	0910

Table 650–contd MIAMI - JACKSONVILLE *GL*

296 ↓	5394	5390	1120	3796	3732	1010	1243	3790	3684		598	1261	1024	1164	5396	506	1168	5384		1265	1008	500	1018	1158	1253
Miami d.	....	0605	0605	0730	0800	0840	0940	0945	1040	....	1030	1025	1310	1310	1325	1525	1525	1600	....	1715	1830	1835	2155	2230	2325
North Miami Beach d.	....	|	|		0835	|	|	1020	|	....	|	|	|	|	|	|	1620	|	....	|	|	1910		|	|
Fort Lauderdale d.	0415	0735	0740	0900	0915	1000	1115	1115	1201	....	1201	1201	1445	1430	1445	1700	1655	1720	....	1845	2005	2005	2325	2325	0055
West Palm Beach d.	0520	0840	0850	1100	....	|	1220	....	1305	....	1315	....	|	1535	1550	1805	....	1925	....		|	2110	0030	....	0200
Fort Pierce d.	0715	1035	|	....	....	1230	1355	....	1500	....	|	....	1715	1735	1735	1945	....	2115	....	2115	2230	2245	0205	....	0330
Melbourne d.	0840	1201	|	....	....	|	|	....	1625	....	|	....	|	1900	|	|	....	2230	....	|	|	|	|	....	|
Cocoa d.	0910	1230	|	....	....	|	|	....	1655	....	|	....	|	1930	|	|	....	2300	....	|	|	|	|	....	|
Orlando (*Disney World*) d.	*1030*	*1350*	1230	....	....	|	1615	....	|	....	1730	....	|	|	2010	2130	....	|	....	*1201*	2325	|	0345	....	0545
Daytona Beach d.	1100	1420	1415	....	....	|	....	....	1845	....	....	....	|	2120	*2120*	....	....	0035	...	|	|	|	0420s	....	....
St. Augustine d.	|	|	1530	....	....	|	....	....	1955	....	....	....	|	2230	|	....	....	|	....	|	|	|	0530s	....	....
Jacksonville a.	1300	1600	1615	....	....	1615	....	....	2040	....	....	....	2100	2315	*2315*	....	....	0215	....	*0230*	0215	0230	0615	....	....

GL– Greyhound Lines.

Table 703 SAVANNAH - TALLAHASSEE *GL*

US $		5379			km	296 ↓ ↑			5378	
0.00	....	0615	....	....	*0*	d.**Savannah** a.	....	....	1920	....
21.00	....	0835	....	....	*169*	d.Waycross d.	....	....	1700	....
31.54	....	1010	....	....	*268*	d.Valdosta d.	....	....	1505	....
42.14	....	1110	....	....		d.Thomasville d.	....	....	1405	....
55.75	....	1159	....	....	*378*	a.**Tallahassee** d.	....	....	1315	....

GL– Greyhound Lines.

Table 704 MIAMI - KEY WEST *G*

US $		3713	3711	3715	km	695 ↓ ↑		3712	3714	371
0.00	....	0730	1145	1830	*0*	d.**Miami** a.	....	1300	1730	220
4.00	....	0745	1201	1845	*6*	d.Miami International Apt. a.	....	1245	1715	214
4.00	....	0805	1220	1905	*7*	d.Coral Gables a.	....	1225	1655	212
7.00	....	0855	1310	1955	*49*	d.Homestead d.	....	1135	1630	203
	....	|	|	|		d.Big Pine Key d.	....	|	|	|
28.00	....	1220	1635	2255	*264*	a.**Key West** d.	....	0815	1245	171

GL– Greyhound Lines.

Table 705 TAMPA - NAPLES - MIAMI *GL*

US $	1007	1173			3737	1254	3797	5399	3743	3733	3745	km	695 ↓ ↑		1090		3744	3732	3790	3796	1261	596	1168	501
0.00	0110	0605	....	....	1115	1115	1130	1115	1445	1630	2000	*0*	d.**Tampa** a.	....	1015	....	1515	1700	1710	1715	1750	2115	2345	045
6.00	0145	0715	....	....	|	|	|	1201	|	1715	2045	*33*	d. **St. Petersburg** a.	....	|	....	1430	1550	|	|	|	2030	2300	|
10.00	0245	0830	....	....	|	|	|	1315	1625	1830	2155	*92*	d.Sarasota d.	....	0835	....	1315	1435	|	|	|	1920	2150	|
	|	0950	....	....	|	|	|	1435	1745	1950	2310		d.Port Charlotte d.	....	0715	....	1125	1315	|	|	|	1800	|	|
23.00	0420	1035	....	....	1345	1335	|	1520	1830	2035	2350	*212*	d.Fort Myers d.	....	0630	....	1040	1230	1440	|	1530	1715	2015	023
30.00	0530	1201	....	....	|	|	|	1645	....	2135	0045	*270*	d.Naples d.	....	....	....	0945		1315	|	|	|	1855	012
	|	|	....	....	|	|	1225	|	....	|	....		d. Lakeland d.	....	....	....	....	|	|	1620	|	|	|	|
	|	|	....	....	|	|	1255	|	....	|	....		d. Winter Haven d.	....	....	....	....	|	|	1550	|	|	|	|
	|	|	....	....	|	|	1500	|	....	|	....		d. Sebring d.	....	....	....	....	|	|	1415	|	|	|	|
	|	|	....	....	|	|	1730	|	....	|	....		a. West Palm Beach d.	....	....	....	....	|	|	1115	|	|	|	|
43.00	0730	1400	....	....	1645	1705	....	1845	....	2320	....	*430*	a.Fort Lauderdale d.	....	....	....	....	0930	1115	....	1201	1415	1655	232
44.00	0820	1450	....	....	1735	|	....	1935	....	|	....	*432*	a.**North Miami Beach** d.	....	....	....	....	|	1020	....	|	1320	1600	|
44.00	0910	1530	....	....	1815	1840	....	2015	....	0030	....		a.**Miami** d.	....	....	....	....	0800	0945	....	1025	1245	1525	*215*

GL– Greyhound Lines.

Table 706 CHICAGO - BAY CITY *IT*

US $	62	64	10	14	14	84	66	24		26	28	km	496 ↓ ↑	17	17		21	25	85	27		33	67	69
0.00	....	....	0145	0615	....	....	....	0955	....	1315	1700	*0*	d.**Chicago** a.	....	1310	....	1550	1750	....	1950	....	2325	....	....
6.00	....	....	|	0655	....	....	....	1035	....	1355	1740	*34*	d.Hammond d.	....	|	....	1450	1655	....	|	....	|	....	....
7.00	....	....	0215	0720	....	....	....	1055	....	1420	1805	*49*	d.Gary d.	....	1225	....	1435	1635	....	s	....	|	....	....
19.00	....	....	0435	0945	....	....	....	1325	....	1645	2030	*151*	d.Benton Harbor d.	....	1210	....	1420	1615	....	1850	....	2220	....	....
25.00	....	....	s	1020	....	....	....	|	....	1720	2105s		d.Paw Paw d.	....	1130	....	1335	1535	....	|	....	|	....	....
25.00	....	....	0545	1050	1115	....	....	1455	....	1810	2140	*230*	d.Kalamazoo d.	0935	1100	....	1305	1505	....	1745	....	2120	....	....
30.00	....	....	0630	....	1155	....	....	1530	....	1850	2240	*269*	d.Battle Creek d.	0855	....	....	1155	1405	....	1635	....	2015	....	....
35.00	....	....	0745	....	1310	....	....	1635	....	2000	2345	*342*	d.Lansing d.	0745	....	....	1045	1305	....	1525	....	1915	....	....
35.00	....	....	0755	....	1320	....	....	1650	....	2015	0005	*349*	d.East Lansing d.	0710	....	....	1015	1250	....	1510	....	1900	....	....
39.90	0515	0750	|	....	1355	....	1655	|	....	|	|	*394*	d.Owosso d.	|	....	....	|	|	....	1430	....	|	2210	015
39.90	|	0810	|	....	|	....	|	|	....	|	|	*399*	d.Durand d.	|	....	....	|	|	....	|	....	|	|	|
44.10	0610	0840	0850	....	1445	....	1735	1750	....	2115	0100	*428*	a.**Flint** d.	0615	....	....	0900	1145	....	1335	....	1755	2120	010
50.40	....	....	|	....	|	....	....	|	....	....	....		a. Port Huron d.	....	....	....	....	|	....	|	....	....	....	....
46.20	....	....	0940	....	1535	....	....	1835s	....	....	....	*483*	a. Saginaw d.	....	....	....	....	1055	....	1240	....	....	....	....
50.00	....	....	1005	....	1600	1610	....	1900	....	....	....	*504*	d. **Bay City** d.	....	....	....	....	1030	1210	1215	....	....	....	....
63.00	....	....	....	....	....	1920	....	....	....	....	....		d. Alpena d.	....	....	....	....	....	0920	....	....	....	....	....
	....	....	....	....	....	2130	....	....	....	....	....		d. Mackinaw City d.	....	....	....	....	....	0705	....	....	....	....	....
	....	....	....	....	....	2145	....	....	....	....	....		a. St Ignace d.	....	....	....	....	....	0650	....	....	....	....	....

IT– Indian Trails.

Table 707 CALUMET - GREEN BAY - MILWAUKEE - CHICAGO *GL LAB NST WPT*

US $	*WPT* 1401		*GL* 5787		*WPT* 1201	*NST* 1101	*GL* 5813	*LAB* 211	*WPT* 1404	*NST* 1601	*GL* 5783		*GL* 5725			km	496 ↓ ↑
73.00	2120	....	....	....	....	....	....	....	....	....	....	....	....	....	....	◇*159*	d.**Calumet** a.
73.00	2152	....	....	....	....	....	....	....	....	....	....	....	....	....	....	◇*138*	d.Houghton d.
61.00	r	....	....	....	....	....	....	....	....	....	....	....	....	....	....	*0*	d.Ishpeming d.
61.00	0018	....	....	....	0825	....	....	....	....	....	....	....	....	....	....	*25*	d.Marquette d.
53.00	0145	....	....	....	0950	....	....	....	....	....	....	....	....	....	....	*135*	d.Escanaba d.
49.00	0245	....	....	....	1014	....	....	....	....	....	....	....	....	....	....	*226*	d.Marinette/Menominee d.
	|	....	....	....	|	0630	....	....	....	....	....	....	....	....	....		d. Ironwood a.
	|	....	....	....	|	0830	....	....	....	1201	....	....	....	....	....		d. Rhinelander a.
60.00	|	....	....	....	|	|	....	0910	....	1330	....	....	....	....	....		d. Wausau d.
53.00	|	....	0630	....	|	|	....	|	....	1425	1500	....	....	....	....		d. Stevens Point a.
	|	....	|	....	|	1000	....	0955	....	....	|	....	....	....	....		d. Wittenberg d.
⊗9.00	|	....	|	....	|	|	....	|	....	....	|	....	....	....	....		d. Sturgeon Bay a.
49.00	0405	....	|	....	1120	1130	1140	|	1300	....	|	....	1715	....	....	*310*	d.**Green Bay** d.
49.00	0450	....	|	....	....	....	|	|	1350	....	|	....	|	....	....	*367*	d.Manitowoc d.
	|	....	|	....	....	....	|	|	|	....	|	....	|	....	....	*412*	d. Plymouth d.
48.00	|	....	|	....	....	....	|	1125	|	....	1650	....	1800	....	....	*359*	d. Appleton d.
47.00	|	....	0805	....	....	....	|	1215	|	....	1740	....	1845	....	....	*390*	d. Oshkosh d.
42.00	|	....	0855	....	....	....	|	1250	|	....	1820	....	1925	....	....	*421*	d. Fond du Lac d.
49.00	0535	....	|	....	....	....	|	|	1430	....	|	....	|	....	....	*412*	d.Sheboygan d.
29.00	0640	....	1010	....	....	....	1345	1405	1540	....	1935	....	2040	....	....	*597*	a.**Milwaukee** Ω d.
⊗35.00	....	....	|	....	....	....	*1625*	*1625*a	....	....	|	....	|	....	....	*730*	a.Chicago O'Hare Airport d.
0.00	....	....	1245	....	....	....	1600	*1615*a	....	....	2200	....	*2330*	....	....	*742*	a.Chicago Ω d.

496	*GL* 5784	*WPT* 1403	*GL* 5772	*NST* 1602	*GL* 5810	*WPT* 1202	*NST* 1102			*LAB* 210	*GL* 5790		*WPT* 1402		
d.**Calumet** a.	....	....	....	....	....	....	....	....	....	....	....	....	0710	....	....
d.Houghton d.	....	....	....	....	....	....	....	....	....	....	....	....	0650	....	....
d.Ishpeming d.	....	....	....	....	....	....	....	....	....	....	....	....	0510	....	....
d.Marquette d.	....	....	....	....	....	2150	....	....	....	....	....	....	0450	....	....
d.Escanaba d.	....	....	....	....	....	2030	....	....	....	....	....	....	0315	....	....
d.Marinette/Menominee d.	....	....	....	....	....	1810	....	....	....	....	....	....	0015	....	....
d. Ironwood a.	....	....	....	....	....	|	2150	....	....	....	....	....	|	....	....
d. Rhinelander a.	....	....	....	1645	....	|	1955	....	....	....	....	....	|	....	....
d. Wausau d.	....	....	....	1520	....	|	|	....	....	1945	....	....	|	....	....
d. Stevens Point a.	1310	....	....	1430	....	|	|	....	....	|	2130	....	|	....	....
d. Wittenberg d.	|	....	....	....	....	|	1830	....	....	1905	|	....	|	....	....
d. Sturgeon Bay a.	|	....	....	....	....	|	|	....	....	|	|	....	|	....	....
d.**Green Bay** d.	|	1125	1610	....	1635	1700	1700	....	....	|	|	....	2310	....	....
d.Manitowoc d.	|	1040	|	....	|	....	....	....	....	|	|	....	2135	....	....
d. Plymouth d.	|	|	|	....	|	....	....	....	....	|	|	....	|	....	....
d. Appleton d.	1120	|	1525	....	|	....	....	....	....	1720	2005	....	|	....	....
d. Oshkosh d.	1030	|	1440	....	|	....	....	....	....	1640	1915	....	|	....	....
d. Fond du Lac d.	0955	|	1405	....	|	....	....	....	....	1600	1840	....	|	....	....
d.Sheboygan d.	|	0955	|	....	|	....	....	....	....	|	|	....	2045	....	....
a.**Milwaukee** Ω d.	0835	0845	1245	....	1430	....	....	....	....	1450	1715	....	1935	....	....
a.Chicago O'Hare Airport d.	|	....	|	....	|	....	....	....	....	|	|	....	....	....	....
a.Chicago Ω d.	*0600*	....	*1000*	....	1201	....	....	....	....	*1201*a	1300	....	....	....	....

a– *GL*.
b– † only.
d– ⚒ only.
◇– Km ex Ishpeming.
Ω– Complete *GL* service Milwaukee-Chicago and v.v.; **from Milwaukee**: 0345, 0010, 0700, 0800, 0900, 1100, 1201⑤⑥, 1300, 1400, 1500, 1600, 1700,1800, 1900, 2000, 2145; **from Chicago**: 0115, 0600, 0730, 0900, 1030, 1201, 1300, 1400, 1500, 1600, 1700, 1800, 1900, 2130.
⊗– Fare ex Green Bay.
GL– Greyhound Lines.
LAB– Lamers Bus Lines.
NST– North Star Bus Service. *WPT*–White Pine Bus Service.

able 708 196 DETROIT LOCAL SERVICES

DDT SEMTA WT

:al services operate in the Detroit area as follows:
arborn (SEMTA) (11 km, US $: 1.50). From Detroit: 0050, 0525Ⓐ, 0600Ⓐ, 0610Ⓐ/0815† and frequent to 2000Ⓐ, 2035, 2135Ⓒ, 2136Ⓐ, 2245✕, 2250†, 2346✕, returning at 0023, 0457Ⓐ, 0528Ⓐ, 0546Ⓐ/0901† and frequent to 2107Ⓐ, 2109Ⓒ, 2217✕, 2225†, 2320Ⓐ, 2321Ⓒ. Journey: 40 mins.
st Detroit (DDT) (❖ km, US $: ❖). From Detroit: ❖, returning at ❖. Journey: ❖.
orse (SEMTA) (❖ km, US $: 1.00). From Detroit: 0518Ⓐ, 0550Ⓐ, 0625Ⓐ and about hourly to 1705Ⓐ, 1737Ⓐ, 1812Ⓐ, returning at 0551Ⓐ, 0641Ⓐ, 0712Ⓐ and about hourly to 1832Ⓐ. Journey: 30 mins.
ndale (SEMTA) (❖ km, US $: 1.25). From Detroit: 0000†, 0100ex①⑦, 0449Ⓐ, 0516Ⓐ, 0530Ⓒ, 0539Ⓐ, 0559Ⓐ, 0600†, 0605Ⓒ and frequent (hourly on †) to 2000†, 2020Ⓐ, 22035Ⓒ, 2100†, 2110✕, 2200†, 2220Ⓐ, 2232Ⓒ, 2300†, 2330Ⓐ, returning at 0008①, 0020ex①⑦, 0023⑦, 0500Ⓐ, 0523Ⓐ, 0530Ⓒ, 0550Ⓐ, 0558Ⓐ, 0600Ⓒ, 0622† and frequent (about hourly on †) to 2020†, 2031✕, 2120†, 2142Ⓐ, 2146Ⓒ, 2220†, 2242Ⓐ, 2321Ⓒ. Journey: 40 mins.
oss Pointe Farms (DDT) (❖ km, US $: ❖). From Detroit: ❖, returning at ❖. Journey: ❖.
oss Pointe Park (DDT) (❖ km, US $: ❖). From Detroit: ❖, returning at ❖. Journey: ❖.
oss Pointe Woods (DDT) (❖ km, US $: ❖). From Detroit: ❖, returning at ❖. Journey: ❖.
mtramck (DDT) (❖ km, US $: ❖). From Detroit: ❖, returning at ❖.
zel Park (DDT) (❖ km, US $: ❖). From Detroit: ❖, returning at ❖. Journey: ❖.
ghland Park (DDT) (❖ km, US $: ❖). From Detroit: ❖, returning at ❖. Journey: ❖.
coln Park (SEMTA) (❖ km, US $: 1.25). From Detroit: 0603Ⓐ, 0635Ⓐ/0818Ⓒ/1118† and frequent (hourly on Ⓒ) to 1818Ⓒ, 1825Ⓐ, 2025Ⓐ, returning at 0529Ⓐ, 0559Ⓐ, 0619Ⓐ, 0639Ⓐ/0730Ⓒ/1030† and frequent (hourly on Ⓒ) to 1830Ⓒ, 1840Ⓐ, 1959Ⓐ. Journey: 30 mins.
lvindale (SEMTA) (❖ km, US $: 1.25). From Detroit: 0620Ⓐ, 0716Ⓐ, 0742Ⓐ and about hourly to 1709Ⓐ, 1734Ⓐ, 1808Ⓐ, returning at 0545Ⓐ, 0614Ⓐ, 0644Ⓐ and about hourly to 1759Ⓐ, 1845Ⓐ. Journey: 40 mins.
k Park (SEMTA) (❖ km, US $: 1.50). From Detroit: 0739Ⓐ, 1235Ⓐ, 1445Ⓐ, 1600Ⓐ, 1630Ⓐ, 1703Ⓐ, 1750Ⓐ, returning at 0613Ⓐ, 0643Ⓐ, 0713Ⓐ, 0743Ⓐ, 0848Ⓐ, 0953Ⓐ, 1455Ⓐ. Journey: 50 mins.
River Rouge (SEMTA) (❖ km, US $: 1.00). From Detroit: 0518Ⓐ, 0550Ⓐ, 0625Ⓐ and about hourly to 1737Ⓐ, 1812Ⓐ, returning at 0600Ⓐ, 0652Ⓐ, 0723Ⓐ and about hourly to 1747Ⓐ, 1841Ⓐ. Journey: 25 mins.
Royal Oak (SEMTA) (❖ km, US $: 1.50). From Detroit: 0000⑦, 0100ex①⑦, 0449Ⓐ, 0516Ⓐ, 0530Ⓒ, 0539Ⓐ, 0559Ⓐ, 0600† and frequent (hourly on †) to 2000Ⓒ, 2020Ⓐ, 2035Ⓒ, 2100†, 2110✕, 2200†, 2220Ⓐ, 2232Ⓒ, 2300†, 2330Ⓐ, returning at 0002①, 0015ex①⑦, 0017⑦, 0454Ⓐ, 0517Ⓐ, 0523Ⓒ, 0543Ⓐ, 0553Ⓒ,0616† and frequent (about hourly on †) to 2014†, 2023✕, 2114†, 2134Ⓐ, 2138Ⓒ, 2214†, 2234Ⓐ, 2313Ⓒ. Journey: 50 mins.
St Clair (DDT) (❖ km, US $: ❖). From Detroit: 0700✕ and frequent to 2000✕, returning at 0730✕ and frequent to 2030✕. Journey: ❖.
Warren (DDT) (❖ km, US $: ❖). From Detroit: ❖, returning at ❖. Journey: ❖.
♣ Windsor (WT) (3 km, US $: 2.00). From Detroit: 0550✕/0810† and frequent to 2330†/0050✕, returning at 0540✕/0800† and frequent to 2320†/0040✕.

DT– Detroit Department of Transportation. WT– Transit Windsor (Chartabus).
EMTA–South East Michigan Transportation Authority.

able 709 196 NEW ORLEANS LOCAL SERVICES

NORTA

cal services operate in the New Orleans area as follows:
giers (❖ km, US $: ❖). From New Orleans: ❖, returning at ❖. Journey: ❖.
abi (❖ km, US $: ❖). From New Orleans: ❖, returning at ❖. Journey: ❖.
idge City (❖ km, US $: ❖). From New Orleans: ❖, returning at ❖. Journey: ❖.
ntilly (❖ km, US $: ❖). From New Orleans: ❖, returning at ❖. Journey: ❖.
etna (❖ km, US $: ❖). From New Orleans: ❖, returning at ❖. Journey: ❖.
rvey (❖ km, US $: ❖). From New Orleans: ❖, returning at ❖. Journey: ❖.
nner (❖ km, US $: ❖). From New Orleans: ❖, returning at ❖. Journey: ❖.
Metairie (❖ km, US $: ❖). From New Orleans: ❖, returning at ❖. Journey: ❖.
Shrewsbury (❖ km, US $: ❖). From New Orleans: ❖, returning at ❖. Journey: ❖.
Westwego (❖ km, US $: ❖). From New Orleans: ❖, returning at ❖. Journey: ❖.

ORTA–New Orleans Regional Transportation Authority.

able 712 CHICAGO - MADISON

GL

JS $	5633	5768	1275	5739	5635	5858	5686	1277	5611 ⑤⑦	5613	1273	km	496	1274		5681		5849	5767	1272	5740	5648	1270	5632
0.00	0600	0615	0730	0800	1030	1145	1430	1500	1700	2130	2130	0	d.**Chicago** a.	1000	....	1210	....	1540	1945	1945	1940	2100	2330	0155
8.50	|	0740	|	|	|	1310	1555	|	|	|	|		d.Elgin d.	|	....	1045	....	1415	1820	|	|	|	|	|
8.50	|	0830	|	|	|	1400	1645	|	1845	|	|	145	d.Rockford East d.	|	....	0955	....	1325	1730	|	1810	|	|	|
8.50	|	|	|	1000	|	|	|	|	|	|	|	147	a. Rockford d.	|	....	|	....	|	|	|	....	|	|	|
4.00	|	0900	|	....	|	1430	1715	|	|	|	|	174	d.Beloit d.	|	....	0925	....	1255	1700	|	....	|	|	|
7.00	|	0930	|	....	|	1500	1745	|	|	|	|	195	d.Janesville d.	|	....	0855	....	1225	1630	|	....	|	|	|
4.50	1005	1025	1110	....	1420	1555	1840	1900	2000	0020	0105	260	a.**Madison** d.	0550	....	0800	....	1130	1535	1540	....	1705	2000	2220

L– Greyhound Lines.

able 713 GREEN BAY - MADISON

GL

IS$	5849	5787	5783	5725	km	496 ↓ ↑	5784	5772	5790	5858
0.00	0630	....	....	1715	0	d.**Green Bay** a.	....	1610	....	2050
7.50	0715	....	1655	1800	49	d.Appleton d.	1115	1525	2005	2005
3.00	0800	0805	1740	1845	85	d.Oshkosh d.	1030	1440	1915	1915
4.50	0850	0840	1815	1920	116	d.Fond du Lac d.	0955	1405	1840	1840
0.50	0940	....	....	....	166	d.Beaver Dam d.	....	....	....	1745
2.50	1050	....	....	....	227	a.**Madison** d.	....	....	....	1635

L– Greyhound Lines.

Table 714 LA CROSSE - GREEN BAY

NST RCSB SCE

US$	NST 1101	SCE 532	SCE 603	RCSB	km	496 ↓ ↑	RCSB	SCE 604	SCE 531	NST 1102
42.00	....	0710	....	....	0	d.**La Crosse** a.	....	....	2055	....
42.00	....	0900	0910	....		d.Eau Claire d.	....	1900	1905	....
29.00	....	....	1040	....		d.Abbotsford d.	....	1715	....	....
	....	....	|	1245		d. Marshfield a.	1545	|	....	....
21.50	....	....	1130	1345		d.Wausau d.	1445	1645	....	....
16.00	1000	....	1210	....		d.Wittenberg d.	....	1520	....	1830
0.00	1130	....	1345	....		a.**Green Bay** d.	....	1400	....	1700

NST–North Star Bus Service. RCSB–Radio Cab Bus Shuttle. SCE–Scenic Trailways.

able 715 CHICAGO - INDIANAPOLIS/LOUISVILLE

ABL GL SET

IS$	296 ↓	km		GL 1017	SET 585		ABL 101		SET 0591	GL 4927	GL 1163					ABL 605	SET 597	GL 1155		ABL 107	GL 1105		GL 1123	SET 583	
0.00	**Chicago** d.	0	....	0600	0700	....	....	....	....	1045	1130	....	....	....	....	1500	1615	1730	....	....	2015	....	2300	0245	....
8.00	Hammond d.	35	....	|	0755	....	....	....	....	1135	|	....	....	....	....	1530	1725	|	....	....	|	....	|	|	....
9.00	Gary d.	41	....	|	0815	....	....	....	....	1201	|	....	....	....	....	1550	1745	|	....	....	|	....	|	0325	....
0.00	Lafayette d.		....	|	1055	....	....	....	....	1350	|	....	....	....	....	|	2030	|	....	....	|	....	|	|	....
	Elkhart d.	▼271	....	|	|	....	0740	....	....	|	|	....	....	....	....	|	|	|	....	1700	|	....	|	|	....
	South Bend d.		....	|	|	....	0820	....	....	|	|	....	....	....	....	|	|	|	....	1745	|	....	|	|	....
	Plymouth d.		....	|	|	....	0900	....	....	|	|	....	....	....	....	1830	|	|	....	1830	|	....	|	|	....
	Fort Wayne d.	▼230	....	|	|	....	|	....	....	|	|	....	....	....	....	2020	|	|	....	|	|	....	|	|	....
	Logansport d.	191	....	|	|	....	0955	....	....	|	|	....	....	....	....	....	|	|	....	1925	|	....	|	|	....
	Peru d.	▼125	....	|	|	....	1035	....	....	|	|	....	....	....	....	....	|	|	....	2010	|	....	|	|	....
	Kokomo d.	232	....	|	|	....	1105	....	....	|	|	....	....	....	....	....	|	|	....	2040	|	....	|	|	....
1.50	**Indianapolis** a.	335	....	1025	1215	....	1230	....	....	1610	1555	....	....	....	....	....	2155	2200	....	2200	0040	....	0325	0715	....
	Indianapolis d.		....	1100	1300	....	....	....	1300	1645	1635	....	....	....	....	....	2225	2230	....	....	0100	....	0400	0800	....
5.50	**Louisville** a.	520	....	1300	|	....	....	....	1645	|	1835	....	....	....	....	....	|	0035	....	....	|	....	0610	1025	....
5.50	**Cincinnati** a.	510	....	....	1500	....	....	....	....	1855	....	....	....	....	....	....	0025	....	....	....	0300	....	....	....	....

96 ↓		GL 1160		GL 1120	GL 1108	ABL 102	GL 1114	ABL 604			GL 4928	SET 582		GL 5396		SET 580	ABL 106				SET 598	GL 1168	GL 1124		SET 596
Cincinnati d.	....	....	....	....	0530	....	....	....	....	....	1010	....	....	....	....	1500	....	....	....	....	....	....	....	....	0040
Louisville d.	....	....	....	0635	|	....	0900	....	....	....	|	1120	....	1525	....	|	....	....	....	....	1900	2120	2315	....	|
Indianapolis a.	....	....	....	0845	0750	....	1110	....	....	....	1220	1405	....	1735	....	1710	....	....	....	....	2110	2230	0125	....	0245
Indianapolis d.	....	0515	....	0915	0915	0905	1145	....	....	....	....	1435	....	1815	....	1755b	1800	....	....	....	2130	2300	0150	....	0305
Kokomo d.	....	|	....	|	|	1030	|	....	....	....	....	|	....	|	....	|	1925	....	....	....	|	|	|	....	|
Peru d.	....	|	....	|	|	1055	|	....	....	....	....	|	....	|	....	|	1950	....	....	....	|	|	|	....	|
Logansport d.	....	|	....	|	|	1135	|	....	....	....	....	|	....	|	....	|	2040	....	....	....	|	|	|	....	|
Fort Wayne d.	....	|	....	|	|	|	|	1040	....	....	....	|	....	|	....	|	|	....	....	....	|	|	|	....	|
Plymouth d.	....	|	....	|	|	1235	|	1235	....	....	....	|	....	|	....	|	2135	....	....	....	|	|	|	....	|
South Bend a.	....	|	....	|	|	1320	|	|	....	....	....	|	....	|	....	|	2215	....	....	....	|	|	|	....	|
Elkhart a.	....	|	....	|	|	1350	|	|	....	....	....	|	....	|	....	|	2245	....	....	....	|	|	|	....	|
Lafayette d.	....	|	....	|	1035	....	|	|	....	....	....	1555	....	|	....	1910b	....	....	....	....	|	|	|	....	|
Gary d.	....	0720	....	|	1125	....	|	1315	....	....	....	1635	....	|	....	2000b	....	....	....	....	|	|	|	....	|
Hammond a.	....	0740	....	|	1145	....	|	1330	....	....	....	|	....	|	....	2020b	....	....	....	....	|	|	|	....	|
Chicago a.	....	0830	....	1130	1235	....	1355	1400	....	....	....	1715	....	2045	....	2100b	....	....	....	....	2355	0225	0400	....	0515

-GL. ▼–Km ex Indianapolis. ABL–American Trailways. GL–Greyhound Lines. SET–Southeastern Trailways.

Table 716 CHICAGO - DES MOINES - OMAHA

BTW GL JL

US $		GL 1305	BTW 1302	BTW 1401	GL 1347	GL 5739	GL 1307	GL 5741	GL 1315			GL 5743	GL 1301			km	496 ↓ ↑	GL 1340			GL 1342	GL 5744	GL 5740		GL 1352	JL 405	GL 1348	BTW 1402	GL 5742		GL 1308	
0.00	....	0115	....	0630	0700	0800	1145	1135	1445	....	....	1630	1845	....	....	0	d.**Chicago** a.	1225	....	....	1530	1850	1940	....	2025	....	2210	2330	2355	....	0530	....
10.00	....	|	....	....	0805	|	|	1240	|	....	....	1740	|	....	....	65	d.Aurora d.	1125	....	....	1425	1745	|	....	|	....	|	|	|	....	|	....
	....	|	....	0905	|	|	|	|	|	....	....	|	|	....	....		d. Princeton d.	|	....	....	|	|	|	....	|	....	|	2130	|	....	|	....
	....	|	....	|	|	|	|	|	|	....	....	|	|	....	....		d. Kewanee d.	|	....	....	|	|	|	....	|	....	|	|	|	....	|	....
	....	|	....	|	|	|	|	|	|	....	....	|	|	....	....		d. Galesburg d.	|	....	....	|	|	|	....	|	....	|	|	|	....	|	....
◇30.00	....	|	0930	1245	|	|	|	|	|	....	....	|	|	....	....	415	d. Burlington a.	|	....	....	|	|	|	....	|	1800b	|	1815	|	....	|	....
◇18.00	....	|	|	1445	|	|	|	|	|	....	....	|	|	....	....	535	d. Ottumwa d.	|	....	....	|	|	|	....	|	|	|	1555	|	....	|	....
★12.00	....	|	1030	|	|	|	|	|	|	....	....	|	|	....	....		d. Muscatine d.	|	....	....	|	|	|	....	|	1700b	|	|	|	....	|	....
	....	|	|	|	1125	|	|	1600	|	....	....	2100	|	....	....		d.Moline d.	0805	....	....	|	1430	|	....	|	|	1900	|	2045	....	|	....
31.00	....	|	1130	1030	1155	|	1500	1625	|	....	....	2125	2200	....	....	290	d.Davenport d.	0755	....	....	|	1415	|	....	1725	1615b	1840	|	2030	....	|	....
37.00	....	0535	1240	|	1350	|	1615	1810	1930	....	....	2255	|	....	....	377	d.Iowa City d.	0540	....	....	|	1230	|	....	|	1445b	1645	|	1830	....	0105	....
34.00	....	|	|	|	|	|	|	|	|	....	....	|	|	....	....	220	d. Clinton d.	|	....	....	|	|	|	....	|	|	|	|	|	....	|	....
26.00	....	|	|	|	|	1000	|	|	|	....	....	|	|	....	....	138	d. Rockford East d.	|	....	....	|	|	1810	....	|	|	|	|	|	....	|	....
37.00	....	|	|	|	|	1105	|	|	|	....	....	|	|	....	....	183	d. Freeport d.	|	....	....	|	|	1705	....	|	|	|	|	|	....	|	....
37.00	....	|	|	|	|	1310	|	|	|	....	....	|	|	....	....	293	d. Dubuque d.	|	....	....	|	|	1530	....	|	|	|	|	|	....	|	....
37.00	....	0615	1430a	|	1440	|	|	1900	|	....	....	|	|	....	....	360	d. Cedar Rapids d.	|	....	....	|	1150	|	....	|	1400b	|	|	1750	....	|	....
42.00	....	|	1530a	|	|	1535	|	|	|	....	....	|	|	....	....		d. Waterloo d.	|	....	....	|	|	1245	....	|	1240	|	|	|	....	|	....
43.00	....	0750	....	|	1540	|	|	2000	|	....	....	|	|	....	....	433	d. Tama d.	|	....	....	|	1035	|	....	|	....	|	|	1635	....	|	....
53.00	....	0825	....	|	1615	1715	|	2035	|	....	....	|	|	....	....	470	d. Marshalltown d.	|	....	....	|	1005	1055	....	|	....	|	|	1600	....	|	....
53.00	....	|	....	|	1700	|	|	2120	|	....	....	|	|	....	....	530	d. Ames d.	|	....	....	|	0925	1010	....	|	....	|	|	1520	....	|	....
56.00	....	0930	....	1655	1740	1810	1815	2200	2150	....	....	0100	0050	....	....	572	a. **Des Moines** d.	0335	....	....	0825	0845	0930	....	1420	....	1440	1330	1440	....	2300	....
	....	0945	....	....	1815	....	1845	....	2220	....	....	....	0115	....	....		d. **Des Moines** a.	0315	....	....	0810	....	....	....	1405	....	1425	....	....	....	2215	....
70.00	....	1205	....	....	2030	....	2100	....	0035	....	....	....	0330	....	....	792	a.**Omaha** d.	0100	....	....	0555	....	....	....	1150	....	1201	....	....	....	2000	....

a– *JL*. b–*BTW*. ◇–Fare ex Des Moines. ★–Fare ex Cedar Rapids. *GL*– Greyhound Lines.
BTW– Burlington Trailways. *JL*– Jefferson Lines.

Table 717 CHICAGO - PEORIA

BUA

US $					km	496 ↓ ↑				
0.00	....	....	....	1820	0	d.**Chicago** a.	....	....	1820	....
28.00	....	....	....	2240	253	a.**Peoria** d.	....	....	1430	....

BUA– Blue Star Coaches (Illinois Valley Coaches).

Table 718 INDIANAPOLIS - PEORIA

BUA ISL

US $	BUA	ISL 6	ISL 14	BUA	km	496 ↓ ↑	ISL 5	BUA	ISL 15	ISL 9
0.00	....	0900	1355	....	0	d.**Indianapolis** a.	1250	....	2035	....
4.70	....	1005	1500	....	73	d.Crawfordsville d.	1150	....	1925	....
14.20	....	0955	1500	....	139	d.Danville d.	1000	....	1725	....
20.15	....	1055	1605	....	196	d.Champaign d.	0855	....	1620	....
27.75	0920	1250	1755	2050	278	d.Bloomington d.	0735	0915	1455	....
33.25	1000	1345	1900	2135	345	d.**Peoria** d.	0630	0840	1345	1855
42.25	....	1455	2010	....	426	d.Galesburg d.	....	....	1235	1750
50.25	....	1545	2100	....	510	d.Moline Ω d.	....	....	1140	1655
50.55	....	1610	2125	....	515	a.**Davenport** d.	....	....	1115	1630

Ω– For Rock Island. *BUA*–Blue Star Coaches (Illinois Valley Coaches).
ISL– Illini Swallow Lines.

Table 719 BALTIMORE - OCEAN CITY

CCC

US $	957	955	971 ⑤⑦	953	km	496 ↓ ↑	950	952	970 ⑤⑦	954
36.50	....	....	1815	....	0	d.**Washington** a.	....	....	1600	....
22.00	1115	1805	|	2335		d. **Baltimore** a.	1040	1550	|	2120
20.00	|	|	1855	|	31	d.Annapolis d.	|	|	1510	|
18.00	1225	1915	|	0035		d.Stevensville d.	0940	1450	1450	2020
6.00	1420	2110	2100		167	d.Salisbury d.	0740	|	1255	1820
15.25	|	|	....	0140	122	d. Harrington d.	|	1335	....	|
10.00	|	|	....	r	177	d. Lewes d.	|	r	....	|
9.00	|	|	....	0235	190	d. Rehoboth Beach d.	|	1220	....	|
0.00	1500	2150	....	0320	232	a.**Ocean City** d.	0700	1135	....	1730

CCC– Carolina Trailways.

Table 720 PHILADELPHIA - NORFOLK

CCC GL HCS PPB

US $	496 ↓	km	CCC 931	CCC 903		HCS 15 ex②③④		CCC 925	CCC 901	
	New York d.		....	0830a	....	....	....	*1530*a	2100a	....
0.00	**Philadelphia** d.	0	0530	*1015*	....	....	....	1730	*2250*	....
7.00	Wilmington d.	46	0625	1135	....	....	....	1830	0005	....
	State Road d.		r	r	....	1615	....	r	r	....
17.25	Dover d.	120	0730	1240	....	|	....	1935	0110	....
23.50	Harrington d.	149	0755	1315	....	|	....	2000	0135	....
30.75	Salisbury d.	212	0910	1430	....	1945	....	2110	0245	....
	Crisfield a.		|	|	....	....	....	|	|	....
59.50	**Norfolk** a.	404	1220	1740	....	....	....	0005	0535	....

695 ↓		CCC 930	HCS ex②③④	CCC 904			CCC 924			CCC 902
Norfolk d.	....	0515	....	0900	....	....	1815	....	....	2230
Crisfield d.	....	|	....	|	....	....	|	....	....	|
Salisbury d.	....	0830	1100	1230	....	....	2130	....	....	0130
Harrington d.	....	0930	|	1330	....	....	2230	....	....	|
Dover d.	....	0955	|	1355	....	....	2300	....	....	s
State Road a.	....	r	1425	r	....	....	r	....	....	r
Wilmington a.	....	1100	....	1500	....	....	0015	....	....	0340
Philadelphia a.	....	|	....	*16150*	....	....	0115	....	....	*0450*
New York a.	....	*1320*b	....	1805a	....	....	....	....	....	0645

a– *GL*.
b– *PPB*.
CCC– Carolina Trailways.
GL– Greyhound Lines.
HCS– Handy's Charter Service.
PPB– Peter Pan Trailways.

Table 721 496 ST LOUIS LOCAL SERVICES

BSDA

Local ╫╫ (C cl. only, 1.435m.) and 🚌 services operate in the St. Louis area as follows:

Belleville ∂ (✥ km, US $: 1.00). From East St. Louis 5th and Missouri: 0012, 0514Ⓐ, 0529Ⓐ, 0559Ⓐ, 0629Ⓐ, 0659Ⓐ, 0700Ⓒ, 0722Ⓐ and frequent (about hourly on †) to 1900†, 1920⑥, 1922Ⓐ, 1959Ⓐ, 2000⑥, 2005†, 2039Ⓐ, 2100⑥, 2142Ⓐ, 2200⑥, 2240Ⓐ, 2310⑥, returning at 0437Ⓐ, 0510Ⓐ, 0536Ⓐ, 0541⑥, 0603Ⓐ, 0630Ⓐ, 0641⑥, 0700Ⓐ, 0712†, 0715Ⓐ, 0730Ⓐ, 0738⑥ and frequent (about hourly on †) to 1900⑥, 1904Ⓐ, 1913†, 1949Ⓐ, 2010⑥, 2052Ⓐ, 2105⑥, 2147Ⓐ, 2200⑥, 2249Ⓐ, 2309⑥, 2347Ⓐ. Journey: 45 mins. Also, on Ⓐ only, direct services from St. Louis Jefferson & Market, from 1539Ⓐ until 1740Ⓐ, and from Belleville from 0554Ⓐ until 0629Ⓐ.

Clayton ∂ (✥ km, US $: 1.00). From St. Louis: 0454Ⓐ/0524⑥/0540† and frequent to 2300†/0050⑦/0058②-⑥, returning at 0420Ⓐ/0453⑥/0509† and frequent to 2229†/0011⑥/0021②-⑥. Journey: 35 mins.

East St. Louis π (✥ km, US $: 1.00). From St. Louis 8th and Pine: 0502Ⓐ/0538†/0539⑥ and frequent to 0029②-⑥/0032①⑦, returning from 5th and Missouri at 0514Ⓐ/0603Ⓒ and frequent to 2345⑦/0041②-⑥/0044⑦. Journey: 10 mins.

Fenton ∂ (✥ km, US $: 1.00). From St. Louis: 0508Ⓐ, 0653Ⓐ, returning at 1440Ⓐ, 1640Ⓐ, 1705Ⓐ. Journey: 1 hour.

Granite City ∂ (✥ km, US $: 1.00). From St. Louis: 0552Ⓐ/0720⑥/0845† and frequent (about hourly on †) to 1943†/2348⑥/2359Ⓐ, returning at 0525Ⓐ/0658⑥/0818† and frequent (about hourly on †) to 1920†/2327⑥/2334Ⓐ. Journey: 30 mins.

Madison ∂ (✥ km, US $: 1.00). From St. Louis: 0552Ⓐ/0720⑥/0845† and frequent (about hourly on †) to 1943†/2348⑥/2359Ⓐ, returning at 0530Ⓐ/0703⑥/0823† and frequent (about hourly on †) to 1925†/2332⑥/2339Ⓐ. Journey: 25 mins.

North Hanley π (✥ km, US $: 1.00). From St. Louis 8th and Pine: 0524Ⓐ/0611Ⓒ and frequent to 2341†/0033⑦/0039②-⑥, returning at 0514Ⓐ/0516⑥/0546† and frequent to 2246†/0001⑦/0014②-⑥. Journey: 30 mins.

St. Charles ∂ (✥ km, US $: 1.00). From North Hanley: 0503Ⓐ, 0528Ⓐ, 0610Ⓐ, 1610Ⓐ, 1640Ⓐ, 1709Ⓐ, 1724Ⓐ, 1747Ⓐ, 1810Ⓐ, returning at 0525Ⓐ, 0548Ⓐ, 0602Ⓐ, 0617Ⓐ, 0632Ⓐ, 0647Ⓐ, 0717Ⓐ, 1650Ⓐ, 1720Ⓐ, 1750Ⓐ, 1828Ⓐ. Journey: 35 mins.

University City ∂ (✥ km, US $: 1.00). From St. Louis: 0028②-⑥, 0058②-⑥, 0454Ⓐ/0524⑥/0540† and frequent to 2300†/2355 2359Ⓐ, returning at 0021②-⑥, 0420Ⓐ/0453⑥/0509† and frequent to 2229†/2320⑥/2351Ⓐ. Journey: 35 mins.

Venice ∂ (✥ km, US $: 1.00). From St. Louis: 0552Ⓐ, 0625Ⓐ, 0655Ⓐ, 0720✕, 0750✕, 0820⑥, 0828Ⓐ, 0845†, 0851⑥, 0857Ⓐ a[nd] about every 30 mins. (about hourly on †) to 1900Ⓐ, 1943†, 1950⑥, 2000Ⓐ, 2048⑥, 2100Ⓐ, 2148⑥, 2200Ⓐ, 2248⑥, 2300 2348⑥, 2359Ⓐ, returning at 0525Ⓐ, 0556Ⓐ, 0628Ⓐ, 0658✕, 0713Ⓐ, 0728✕, 0757Ⓐ, 0758⑥, 0818†, 0827✕, 0857✕ and abo[ut] every 30 mins. (about hourly on †) to 1920†, 1926⑥, 1934Ⓐ, 2027⑥, 2034Ⓐ, 2127⑥, 2134Ⓐ, 2227⑥, 2234Ⓐ, 2327⑥, 2334 Journey: 30 mins.

Webster Groves ∂ (✥ km, US $: 1.00). From St. Louis: 0505Ⓐ, 0540Ⓐ, 0625Ⓐ, 0641Ⓒ, 0710Ⓐ, 0721Ⓐ, 0723⑥, 0741†, 0750Ⓐ a[nd] frequent (about hourly on †) to 1947†/2038⑥/2111Ⓐ, 2205Ⓐ, returning at 0516Ⓐ, 0554Ⓐ, 0607⑥, 0613Ⓐ, 0627Ⓐ, 0632 0635Ⓐ, 0647⑥, 0648Ⓐ, 0710Ⓐ, 0728✕, 0747Ⓐ/0817† and frequent (about hourly on †) to 1915†/2038⑥/2111Ⓐ, 2138 2240Ⓐ, 2338Ⓐ. Journey: 1 hour.

π– By ╫╫. ∂–By 🚌. *BSDA*– Bi-State Development Agency.

Table 722 CHICAGO - ST. LOUIS

GL SET

US $	GL 5211		GL 5205		GL 5201		SET 587		GL 5023		GL 5209	km	496 ↓ ↑	GL 5202		GL 5200		SET 586		GL 5204		GL 5206		GL 5208
0.00	0100	....	0600	....	1045	....	1345	....	1630	....	2030	0	d.**Chicago** a.	0930	....	1245	....	1600	....	2045	....	0045	....	0515
8.00	|	....	|	....	1155	....	|	....	|	....	|	70	d.Joliet d.	|	....	1140	....	|	....	1935	....	|	....	|
11.00	|	....	0710	....	|	....	1555	....	|	....	|	90	d. Kankakee d.	0725	....	|	....	1355	....	|	....	|	....	0405
24.00	|	....	0910	....	|	....	1735	....	|	....	|	218	d. Champaign d.	0555	....	|	....	1155	....	|	....	2150	....	0240
32.00	|	....	1015	....	|	....	1840	....	|	....	|	285	d. Decatur d.	0450	....	|	....	1045	....	|	....	2050	....	0145
	|	....	|	....	1245	....	|	....	|	....	|		d.Dwight d.	|	....	1050	....	|	....	1845	....	|	....	|
19.00	|	....	|	....	1310	....	|	....	|	....	|	165	d.Pontiac d.	|	....	1025	....	|	....	1820	....	|	....	|
24.00	0320	....	|	....	1420	....	|	....	1920	....	2310	217	d.Bloomington d.	|	....	0935	....	|	....	1725	....	|	....	|
30.00	|	....	|	....	|	....	|	....	|	....	|	261	d.Lincoln d.	|	....	|	....	|	....	|	....	|	....	|
33.00	|	....	1110	....	1535	....	2005	....	|	....	0025	318	d.Springfield d.	0345	....	0805	....	0950	....	1550	....	1955	....	0045
44.00	|	....	1159	....	|	....	2055	....	|	....	|		d.Litchfield d.	|	....	|	....	|	....	|	....	1900	....	|
50.00	0605	....	1300	....	1720	....	2155	....	2205	....	0210	474	a.**St. Louis** d.	0200	....	0615	....	0800	....	1400	....	1800	....	2300

GL–Greyhound Lines. *SET*–Southeastern Trailways

Table 723 NASHVILLE - TALLAHASSEE/NEW ORLEANS

CML GL

US $	CML 51	GL 1161	GL 1167/9	CML 63	GL 1173	GL 5023	CML 55	GL 1387	GL 1165	GL 1135	GL 5021	km	296 ↓ ↑	GL 5024	GL 1156	GL 598	GL 1168	GL 1174/8	CML 54	CML 62	GL 1176	GL 1158	CML 85	
9.00	....	2230	0135	....	0350	....	....	1015	1445	1745	....	0	d. Cincinnati a.	....	1350	....	0100	....	....	....	0420	0730	....	....
9.00	....	1730	|	....	2300	....	....	0245	0700	1130	....		d. Chicago a.	....	|	2350	0400	0815	....	....	|	1130	....	....
0.00	....	0040	|	....	0610	....	....	1300	1715	2015	....	185	d. Louisville a.	....	1055	1735	2245	|	....	....	|	0605	....	....
9.00	....	0330	0630	....	1000	....	....	1625	2005	2315	....	350	d. **Nashville** a.	....	0525	1245	1730	2145	....	....	2115	0115	....	....
7.00	....	|	|	....	|	....	....	1810	|	|	....	470	d. Pulaski d.	....	|	1100	1615	2030	....	....	|	|	....	....
	....	|	|	....	|	....	....	|	|	|	....		d. Lawrenceburg d.	....	|	|	|	|	....	....	|	|	....	....
	....	|	|	....	|	....	....	|	|	|	....		d. Florence d.	....	|	|	|	|	....	....	|	|	....	....
0.00	....	|	0805	....	|	....	....	1850	2145	0055	....	520	d. Athens d.	....	|	|	|	|	....	....	1945	|	....	....
5.00	....	|	0900	1000	1215	....	....	1940	|	|	....	505	d. Huntsville d.	....	0345	1010	1525	1940	....	2200	|	2315	....	....
0.00	....	0650	1120	|	1435	....	....	2200	2230	0240	....	665	a. **Birmingham** d.	....	0200	0730	1245	1700	....	|	1800	2040	....	....
	2320	0745	1150	|	1515	1545	1815	....	0001	0320	0330		d. **Birmingham** a.	0120	0100	0640	1159	1515	1740	|	1630	1940	2225	....
5.00	0100	1015	1345	1645	1740	|	2015	....	0200	0530	|	820	d. Montgomery d.	|	2320	0500	1005	1415	1540	1630	|	1745	2100	....
1.00	....	1345	....	2015	2035	|	....	....	0420	0810	|	985	d. Dothan d.	|	2025	|	0715	....	....	....	|	1425	1715	....
5.00	....	1445	....	|	2130	|	....	....	|	0920	|	1051	d. Marianna d.	|	1930	|	0620	....	....	....	|	1325	|	....
9.00	....	1725	....	2340	2355	|	....	....	0725	1155	|	1181	a. **Tallahassee** d.	|	1830	0115	0545	....	....	....	|	1240	1545	....
9.00	....	....	....	....	....	|	....	....	....	....	|	2031	a. Miami d.	|	....	....	....	....	....	....	|	....	....	....
1.00	....	....	....	....	....	1705	....	....	....	....	0450		d. Tuscaloosa d.	0005	....	....	....	....	....	....	1500	....	....	....
9.00	....	....	....	....	....	1925	....	....	....	....	0710		d. Meridian d.	2200	....	....	....	....	....	....	1250	....	....	....
8.00	....	....	....	....	....	2035	....	....	....	....	0820		d. Laurel d.	2040	....	....	....	....	....	....	1125	....	....	....
1.00	....	....	....	....	....	2120	....	....	....	....	0915		d. Hattiesburg d.	2000	....	....	....	....	....	....	1045	....	....	....
2.00	....	....	....	....	....	2350	....	....	....	....	1155		a. **New Orleans** d.	1715	....	....	....	....	....	....	0800	....	....	....

ML-Capital Motor Lines. GL–Greyhound Lines.

Table 725 DETROIT - GRAND RAPIDS - MACKINAW CITY/CHICAGO

GL IT

US $	GL 5181	GL 5109	GL 5115	GL 173	GL 5168	GL 5130		GL 5111	IT 80	GL 5175	GL 5177	GL 5166	IT 86	GL 5179	GL 5185	km	396 ↓ ↑	GL 5170	GL 5167	IT 14	GL 5139		IT 81	GL 5110	GL 5169	GL 5176	GL 5112	GL 5178	IT 87	GL 5194	GL 5108	GL 5184
00	0030	....	....	0700	0800	0930	....	....	....	1045	1315	1520	....	1645	1845	238	d. **Detroit** a.	1035	1515	1515b	1520	....	....	....	1915	1930	....	2140	....	0050	....	0620
.00	|	....	....	|	0900s	|	....	....	....	1155s	1415s	1615s	....	1800s	|	229	d. Ypsilanti d.	0925s	1405s	|	|	....	....	....	1810	1835s	....	|	....	|	....	|
.00	|	....	....	0805	0925	|	....	....	....	1220	1440	1645	....	1825	1945	211	d. Ann Arbor d.	0900	1335	1405b	|	....	....	....	1745	1810	....	2030	....	|	....	|
.00	|	....	....	0900	1020	|	....	....	....	1315	1535	1740	....	1920	2040	182	d. Jackson d.	0805	1250	1300b	|	....	....	....	1655	1715	....	1940	....	2305	....	|
.00	|	....	....	|	1105	|	....	....	....	|	|	1820	....	|	|	113	d. Lansing d.	|	1201	|	|	....	....	....	1610	|	....	|	....	|	....	|
.00	|	....	....	|	1120	|	....	....	....	|	|	1840	....	|	|	106	d. East Lansing d.	|	1145	|	|	....	....	....	1540	|	....	|	....	|	....	|
.00	|	....	....	|	....	|	....	....	....	1425	1645	|	....	2030	|		d. Battle Creek d.	0650	....	|	|	....	....	....	|	1600	....	1845	....	|	....	|
.00	|	....	....	1100s	....	|	....	....	1450	1500	1720	|	1900	2110	|		d. Kalamazoo d.	0600	....	1115b	|	....	1445	....	|	1515	....	1810	2120	2145	....	|
00	|	0725	0915	|	....	|	....	1440	1555	....	....	|	2010	....	|	0	d. **Grand Rapids** d.	....	....	|	|	....	1335	1405	|	....	2020	....	2020	|	2235	|
	|	0800	0950	|	....	|	....	1520	|	....	....	|	....	....	|	45	d. Holland d.	....	....	|	|	....	|	1330	|	....	1950	....	....	|	2205	|
	|	0855	1120	1210s	....	|	....	1630	|	....	....	|	....	....	|	129	d. Benton Harbor d.	....	....	0945	|	....	|	1210	|	....	1810	....	....	|	2110	|
	|	|	1150	1225s	....	|	....	1700	|	....	....	|	....	....	|	230	d. Gary d.	....	....	0720	|	....	|	0930	|	....	|	....	....	|	|	|
	|	0940	1210	|	....	|	....	1720	|	....	....	|	....	....	|	236	d. Hammond d.	....	....	0655	|	....	|	0910	|	....	|	....	....	|	|	|
.00	0500	1015	1245	1310s	....	|	....	1815	|	....	....	|	....	....	2330	271	a. **Chicago** a.	....	....	0615	|	....	|	0815	|	....	1500	....	....	1730	1800	0001
.00	....	....	....	....	....	|	....	....	1709	....	....	|	....	....	....	91	d. Big Rapids d.	....	....	....	|	....	1221	....	|	....	....	....	....	....	....	....
.00	....	....	....	....	....	|	....	....	1732	....	....	|	....	....	....	109	d. Reed City d.	....	....	....	|	....	1158	....	|	....	....	....	....	....	....	....
	....	....	....	....	....	1435	....	....	|	....	....	2040	....	....	....		d. Clare d.	....	....	....	1035	....	|	....	1340	....	....	....	....	....	....	....
.00	....	....	....	....	....	1610	....	....	1825	....	....	2225s	....	....	....	157	d. Cadillac d.	....	....	....	0845	....	1105	....	1145	....	....	....	....	....	....	....
.60	....	....	....	....	....	1715	....	....	1930	....	....	2335	....	....	....	238	d. Traverse City d.	....	....	....	0740	....	1005	....	1110	....	....	....	....	....	....	....
10	....	....	....	....	....	....	....	....	|	....	....	....	....	....	....		d. Charlevoix d.	....	....	....	....	....	|	....	....	....	....	....	....	....	....	....
.00	....	....	....	....	....	....	....	....	2112	....	....	....	....	....	....	316	d. Petoskey d.	....	....	....	....	....	0810	....	....	....	....	....	....	....	....	....
.00	....	....	....	....	....	....	....	....	s	....	....	....	....	....	....	379	a. **Mackinaw City** d.	....	....	....	....	....	0725	....	....	....	....	....	....	....	....	....
.00	....	....	....	....	....	....	....	....	2225	....	....	....	....	....	....	390	a. St. Ignace d.	....	....	....	....	....	0710	....	....	....	....	....	....	....	....	....

IT. b–GL. GL–Greyhound Lines. IT–Indian Trails.

Table 726 KNOXVILLE - NASHVILLE - MEMPHIS - DALLAS

BRI GL

US $	296 ↓	km	GL 4843	GL 1151		GL 1529		GL 219		GL 1535				GL 1539			GL 1509		GL 1537	GL 1211	BRI 102		GL 1171	GL 1511	GL 1213
0.00	**Knoxville** d.	0	2245	....	....	0025	....	....	....	0325	....	....	....	0645	....	....	....	....	1310	....	1700	....	....	1830	....
	Cookeville d.		|	....	....	|	....	....	....	|	....	....	....	0755	....	....	....	....	1405	....	1755	....	....	1925	....
	Nashville d.		0050	0130	....	0315	....	....	....	0630	....	....	....	1010	....	....	1400	....	1620	....	1720	....	2130	2145	....
	Jackson d.		....	0340	....	|	....	....	....	0905	....	....	....	1220	....	....	1625	....	1835	....	....	....	2340	|	....
	Memphis a.		....	0530	....	0700	....	....	....	1100	....	....	....	1410	....	....	1810	....	2030	....	....	....	0130	0130	....
	Memphis d.		....	0630	....	0800	....	0800	....	1145	....	....	....	1455	....	....	1930	....	....	2135	....	....	....	0230	0245
	Little Rock d.		....	0915	....	1110	....	|	....	1425	....	....	....	1815	....	....	2230	....	....	0015	....	....	....	|	0525
	Pine Bluff d.		....	|	....	|	....	|	....	|	....	....	....	|	....	....	|	....	....	|	....	....	....	|	|
	Hot Springs d.		....	1035	....	|	....	|	....	|	....	....	....	1935	....	....	|	....	....	|	....	....	....	|	|
	Malvern d.		....	|	....	1155	....	|	....	1520	....	....	....	|	....	....	|	....	....	|	....	....	....	|	|
	Arkadelphia d.		....	1125	....	|	....	|	....	1555	....	....	....	2025	....	....	|	....	....	|	....	....	....	|	|
	Camden d.		....	|	....	|	....	|	....	|	....	....	....	|	....	....	|	....	....	|	....	....	....	|	|
	Texarkana d.		....	1325	....	1415	....	1305	....	1810	....	....	....	2215	....	....	|	....	....	|	....	....	....	0735	0820
	Dallas a.		....	1700	....	1730	....	1615	....	2145	....	....	....	0130	....	....	0400	....	....	0545	....	....	....	1130	1130

6 ↓			GL 6142	GL 1172	GL 1216		GL 1532		BRI 101	GL 1502	GL 1534				GL 1504	GL 1152	GL 4842			GL 1536	GL 1528	GL 1200		GL 1208	
llas d.	....	....	....	....	0030	....	....	....	....	0230	0540	....	....	....	0830	1230	....	....	....	1220	1645	1900	....	2115	....
xarkana d.	....	....	....	....	|	....	....	....	....	0615	0940	....	....	....	1245	1610	....	....	....	1635	2105	2225	....	|	....
Camden d.	....	....	....	....	|	....	....	....	....	|	|	....	....	....	|	|	....	....	....	|	|	|	....	|	....
kadelphia d.	....	....	....	....	|	....	....	....	...	|	|	....	....	....	1415	|	....	....	....	|	2235	|	....	|	....
alvern d.	....	....	....	....	|	....	....	....	....	|	|	....	....	....	1450	|	....	....	....	|	2310	|	....	|	....
Hot Springs d.	....	....	....	....	|	....	....	....	....	|	1210	....	....	....	|	|	....	....	....	1840	|	|	....	|	....
ne Bluff d.	....	....	....	....	|	....	....	....	....	|	|	....	....	....	|	|	....	....	....	|	|	|	....	|	....
Little Rock d.	....	....	0310	....	0615	....	....	....	....	0900	1355	....	....	....	1630	|	....	....	....	2025	0025	|	....	0310	....
emphis a.	....	....	0530	....	0900	....	....	....	....	1159	1615	....	....	....	1930	2045	....	....	....	2245	0245	0300	....	0515	....
emphis d.	....	....	....	0600	....	....	0930	....	....	1245	1700	....	....	....	2030	2130	....	....	....	2330	0330	....	....	....	....
ckson d.	....	....	....	0745	....	....	1115	....	....	1430	1900	....	....	....	2210	|	....	....	....	|	0510	....	....	....	....
ashville d.	....	....	....	1000	....	....	1400	....	1315	1900	2215	....	....	....	0025	0115	0200	....	....	0400	0810	....	....	....	....
ookeville d.	....	....	....	....	....	....	1525	....	1445	2030	|	....	....	....	....	....	|	....	....	|	|	....	....	....	....
noxville a.	....	....	....	....	....	....	1810	....	1740	2340	0220	....	....	....	...	....	0605	....	....	0805	1235	....	....	....	....

RI–Blue Ridge Trailways. GL–Greyhound Lines.

Table 727 COLUMBUS - CLARKSBURG

RSL

US $	100	300 ①④⑤⑦	201	203	km	296 ↓ ↑	200	301 ①④⑤⑦	202	101
0.00	0845	1000a	1230	1730	0	d. **Columbus** a.	1150	1415	1615	2000
	1100	1200	1415	1935		d. Athens d.	0950	1215b	1430	1800
	1215	....	....	s		d. Marietta d.	0835	....	....	1640
	1245	....	....	2035		d. Parkersburg d.	0815	....	....	1600
	1420	....	....	....		a. **Clarksburg** d.	....	....	....	1430

Additional departure at 1430. b– Additional departure at 1645.

SL– Reedy Stage Lines.

Table 728 HUTCHINSON

HSS

US $	6 Ⓐ	2 ⑥		4 Ⓐ	km	695 ↓ ↑	1 ⑥	3 Ⓐ	5 Ⓐ¶	
0.00	....	0645	....	1300	0	d. **Wichita** a.	0645	1125	....	....
	0730	0800	....	1430		d. Hutchinson d.	0515	1000	1700	....
	0830	....	....	1545¶		d. Great Bend d.	....	0830	1545	....
	....	....	....	....		a. **Salina** d.	....	....	....	....

HSS– Hutchinson Bus Line.

Table 730 CHICAGO - MEMPHIS - NEW ORLEANS

ABL COT DEA GL

US $	GL 1215	GL 1211	GL 1279	GL 1203	GL 1225	GL 1213	GL 1221	GL 1207	GL 1217	ABL 215		COT 73	GL 1219	DEA 003	GL 1205	km	496 ↓ ↑	GL 1220	GL 1200	GL 1208		GL 1204	GL 1228	GL 1224	GL 1216	GL 5206	GL 1210	GL 1214	ABL 214	GL 1206	GL 1226	GL 121
0.00	0230	1045	1100	1430	....	1630	1830	2000	2045	....	....	....	2130	....	0001	0	d.**Chicago** a.	1125	1345	1600	....	1800	....	2100	1930	2359	0445	0600	....	0630	....	092
11.00	│	│	1235	│	....	│	2040	│	│	....	....	....	│	....	│	92	d.Kankakee d.	0915	│	│	....	│	....	1930	│	│	│	│	....	0510a	....	│
24.00	0500	│	1415	1730	....	│	2230	│	│	....	....	....	│	....	│	208	d.Champaign d.	0745	│	│	....	1530	....	1800	│	2125	│	│	....	0345a	....	│
35.00	0645	│	1620	1930	....	│	2350	0005	0050	....	....	....	0135	....	0400	323	d.Effingham d.	0600	│	│	....	1345	....	1615	│	....	0110	0215	....	0230	....	054
43.00	0830	1600	1750	2100	....	2130	....	│	0205	....	....	....	│	....	0530	433	d.Mount Vernon d.	....	0900	1115	....	1201	....	1430	1445	....	│	0030	....	│	....	│
61.00	│	│	│	│	....	│	....	│	│	....	....	....	│	....	0725	590	d. Cairo d.	....	│	│	....	│	....	│	│	[illegible]	│	│	....	│	....	│
★53.00	0945	│	1910	│	....	│	....	│	│	....	....	....	│	....	│		d.Carbondale d.	....	│	│	....	1030	....	1300	│	....	│	│	....	│	....	│
64.00	│	│	│	│	....	│	....	│	│	....	....	....	│	....	0825	629	d. Sikeston d.	....	│	│	....	│	....	│	│	....	2135	│	....	2300	....	│
73.00	│	│	│	│	....	│	....	│	│	....	....	....	│	....	0940	739	d. Blytheville d.	....	│	│	....	│	....	│	│	....	2000	│	....	│	....	│
59.00	1201	│	2040	│	....	│	....	│	0445	0450	....	....	│	....	│	613	d.Paducah d.	....	│	│	....	0900	....	1130	│	....	│	2220	2200	│	....	│
61.00	1240a	│	2015a	│	....	│	....	│	0525	0525	....	....	│	....	│	651	d.Mayfield d.	....	│	│	....	0730	....	1030a	│	....	│	2120	2125	│	....	│
70.00	│	│	│	│	....	│	....	│	0755	│	....	....	│	....	│		d. Jackson *TN* d.	....	│	│	....	│	....	│	│	....	│	1910	│	│	....	│
77.00	│	│	│	│	....	│	....	│	0925	│	....	....	│	....	│		d. Corinth d.	....	│	│	....	│	....	│	│	....	│	1710	│	│	....	│
85.00	│	│	│	│	....	│	....	│	1055	│	....	....	│	....	│		d. Tupelo d.	....	│	│	....	│	....	│	│	....	│	1555	│	│	....	│
64.00	1325a	│	2300a	│	....	│	....	│	│	0610	....	....	│	....	│	705	d.Union City d.	....	│	│	....	0640a	....	1000a	│	....	│	│	2040	│	....	│
70.00	1405a	│	2340a	│	....	│	[illegible]	│	│	0650	....	....	│	....	│	762	d.Dyersburg d.	....	│	│	[illegible]	0555a	....	0925a	│	....	│	│	2005	│	....	│
	1610a	2030	0145a	0130	....	0200	....	0530	│	0855	....	....	0715	....	1115		a.	....	0400	0615	....	0400a	....	0700a	0945	....	1830	│	1800	2015	....	234
77.00	DEA 005	GL 1201		│			DEA 001	│	│				GL 1227		│	912	**Memphis**	DEA 004		DEA 006	GL 1172					DEA 002	│	│	[illegible] GL 1212			│
	1645	2115	....	0215	....	....	0515	0700	│	....	....	....	0730	0915	1201		d. a.	1930	....	2245	0255	....	0630	....	....	1600	1715	│	1810	....	....	224
82.00	1830	│	....	│	....	....	0655	│	│	....	....	....	│	1100	1330	1038	d.Clarksdale d.	1755	....	2115	│	....	│	....	....	1420	│	│	1635	....	....	211
92.00	2000	│	....	│	....	....	0845	│	│	....	....	....	│	1250	│	1143	d. Greenville d.	1605	....	1930	│	....	│	....	[illegible]	1230	│	│	│	....	....	│
92.00	....	│	....	│	....	....	│	1010	│	....	....	....	│	1445	│	1283	a. Vicksburg d.	│	....	1720	│	....	│	....	....	....	│	│	│	....	....	│
85.00	....	│	....	│	....	....	│	│	│	....	....	....	│	....	1505	1133	d.Greenwood d.	│	....	....	│	....	│	....	COT	....	│	│	1500	....	....	200
92.00	....	0020	....	│	....	....	│	│	│	....	....	....	1055	....	│	1107	d. Durant d.	│	....	....	2355	....	│	....	70	....	1350	│	│	....	....	│
92.00	....	0100	....	│	....	....	│	│	│	....	....	....	1140	....	│	1164	d. Canton d.	│	....	....	2315	....	│	....	....	....	1305	│	│	....	....	│
	....	│	....	│	....	....	│	│	1315	....	....	....	│	....	│		d. Columbus d.	│	....	....	│	....	│	....	....	....	│	1345	│	....	....	│
92.00	....	0215	....	0700	0700	....	1140	1300	1700	....	....	1750	1300	....	1800	1242	d.Jackson *MS* d.	1250	....	....	2245	....	0230	....	1150	....	1230	0930	1250	....	1800	180
98.00	....	0355	....	│	│	....	....	│	....	....	....	│	│	....	│	1329	d. Columbia d.	....	....	....	2015	....	│	....	│	....	│	....	│	....	│	│
98.00	....	0440	....	│	│	....	....	│	....	....	....	│	│	....	│	1384	d. Bogalusa d.	....	....	....	1930	....	│	....	│	....	│	....	│	....	│	│
104.00	....	0515	....	│	│	....	....	│	....	....	....	│	│	....	│	1433	d. Covington d.	....	....	....	1850	....	│	....	│	....	│	....	│	....	│	│
98.00	....	│	....	0835	│	....	....	1455	....	....	....	│	│	....	1955	1367	d.McComb d.	....	....	....	│	....	0030	....	│	....	0950	....	│	....	│	151
104.00	....	│	....	0950	│	....	....	1615	....	....	....	│	│	....	2110	1453	d.Hammond d.	....	....	....	│	....	2315	....	│	....	0830	....	│	....	│	140
104.00	....	│	....	│	0910	....	....	│	....	....	....	│	1510	....	│		d. Hattiesburg d.		....	....	│	....	│	....	│	....	│	....	0955	....	1520	│
	....	│	....	│	│	....	....	│	....	....	....	1945	│	....	│		d. Laurel d.	....	....	....	│	....	│	....	1000	....	│	....	│	....	│	│
118.00	....	│	....	│	1040	....	....	│	....	....	....	│	1635	....	│		d. Gulfport d.	....	....	....	│	....	│	....	│	....	│	....	0810	....	1340	│
118.00	....	│	....	│	1105	....	....	│	....	....	....	│	1700	....	│		d. Biloxi d.	....	....	....	│	....	│	....	│	....	│	....	0745	....	1315	│
118.00	....	│	....	│	1220	....	....	│	....	....	....	2210	1815	....	│		a. **Mobile** d.	....	....	....	│	....	│	....	0730	....	│	....	0630	....	1201	│
104.00	....	0630	....	1110	....	....	....	1745	....	....	....	....	....	....	2225	1531	a.**New Orleans** d.	....	....	....	1730	....	2200	....	....	....	0715	....	....	....	....	124

★– Fare ex Memphis.
ABL- American Trailways
COT– Colonial Trailways.
DEA– Delta Bus Lines.
GL– Greyhound Lines.

Table 731 MEMPHIS - CHATTANOOGA/ATLANTA

GL

US $		1140	528	1138		1142	1076	1054	1136	520	1074	km	496 ↓ ↑	1055	1143		1137	1561	525		1145	1141	1551	1147
0.00	....	0200	....	0415	....	0600	....	0945	1645	....	2020	0	d.**Memphis** a.	....	1400	....	1745	....	1900	....	2100	0200	....	0630
12.75	....	│	....	0605	....	│	....	1150	│	....	│	145	d.Corinth d.	....	│	....	1535	....	1655	....	│	│	....	│
14.00	....	│	....	│	....	0700	....	│	1745	....	2120		d. Holly Springs d.	....	1300	....	│	....	│	....	1955	0105	....	0530
20.00	....	│	....	│	....	│	....	│	1835	....	2210	120	d. New Albany d.	....	│	....	│	....	│	....	1910	0020	....	0445
	....	0410	....	│	....	0910	....	│	1925	....	2300	160	d. Tupelo d.	....	1105	....	│	....	│	....	1835	2345	....	0410
19.90	....	│	....	0730	....	│	....	1310	│	....	│	236	d.Florence d.	....	│	....	1420	....	1540	....	│	│	....	│
39.00	....	0745	1050	│	....	1315	1500	1710	2235	2320	0300	445	d.**Birmingham** d.	0640	0715	....	│	1205	1225	....	1515	2035	2040	0120
25.85	....	│	│	0925	....	│	│	│	....	│	│	341	d. Huntsville d.	│	....	....	1230	│	│	....	│	│	│	│
34.80	....	│	│	│	....	│	│	│	....	│	│	516	a. **Chattanooga** d.	│	....	....	│	│	│	....	│	│	│	│
	....	0855	1201	1210	....	1425	│	1920	....	│	0410		d.Anniston d.	│	....	....	0905	│	0950	....	1335	1845	│	2340
	....	1145	1445	1500	....	1715	1845	2100	....	0300	0650		a.**Atlanta** d.	0500	....	....	0815	1015	0900	....	1245	1745	1900	2300

GL–Greyhound Lines.

Table 732 ST. LOUIS - MEMPHIS

GL

US $	5237	1205	5231	5235	km	496 ↓ ↑	5234	1210	5236	5232
0.00	0030	....	0830	1930	0	d.**St. Louis** a.	1310	....	0500	0520
25.00	│	....	1040	2125	210	d.Cape Girardeau d.	1055	....	│	0320
31.00	0320	0825	1210	2240	264	d.Sikeston d.	1000	2135	2220	0210
41.00	0435	0940	1345	2355	374	d.Blytheville d.	0830	1000	2035	│
53.00	0615	1115	1520	0125	494	a.**Memphis** d.	0700	1830	1900	2345

GL– Greyhound Lines.

Table 736 BIRMINGHAM - MOBILE

GL

US $	5043	5045			km	496 ↓ ↑	5042		5044	
	....	....	....	....		d.**Chattanooga** a.	....	....	....	....
	....	....	....	....		d.Gadsden d.	....	....	....	....
0.00	0710	1255	....	....	0	d.**Birmingham** d.	1155	....	1925	....
11.00	│	│	....	....	100	d. Tuscaloosa d.	│	....	│	....
	│	│	....	....	155	d. Eutaw d.	│	....	│	....
24.00	│	│	....	....	215	d. Demopolis d.	│	....	│	....
22.00	0940	1525	....	....	140	d.Selma d.	0915	....	1645	....
32.00	1055	1640	....	....	239	d.Thomasville d.	0800	....	1530	....
43.00	1300	1845	....	....	399	a.**Mobile** d.	0600	....	1330	....

GL– Greyhound Lines.

Table 733 INDIANAPOLIS - MEMPHIS

ABL

US $	401	213	215	303	km	496 ↓ ↑	402	402	302	502
70.00	1000	1400	2340	....	0	d.**Indianapolis** a.	1245	1735	....	0645
59.00	1015	1520	2355	....	126	d.Bloomington d.	1130	1620	....	0530
	....	1605	0030	....		d.Bedford d.	....	1535	....	0445
	....	1725	0130	....		d.Washington d.	....	1440	....	0325
59.00	....	1755	│	....	183	d.Vincennes d.	....	1355	....	│
42.00	....	1845	0150	....	313	d.Evansville d.	....	1135	....	0115
41.00	....	1905	0205	....	330	d.Henderson d.	....	1100	....	0040
	....	1945	0245	....		d.Morganfield d.	....	1020	....	2359
	....	2140	0450	1201		d.Paducah d.	....	0845	1110	2220
	....	2300	0610	1325		d.Union City d.	....	0640	0940	2040
	....	2340	0650	1405		d.Dyersburg d.	....	0555	0855	2005
0.00	....	0145	0855	1610		a.**Memphis** d.	....	0400	0700	1800

ABL- American Trailways.

Table 737 OMAHA - MEMPHIS

GL JL

US $	6101 GL	6131 GL	501 JL	5879 GL	km	296 ↓ ↑	5880 GL	502 JL	6100 GL	6132 GL
0.00	....	0720	1345	1925	0	d.**Omaha** a.	0345	1120	....	1820
	....	0830	│	│		d.Nebraska City d.	│	│	....	1715
26.80	....	│	│	2145	192	d. Maryville d.	0125	│	....	│
13.00	....	0857	│	│	100	d. Auburn d.	│	│	....	1640
19.35	....	0940	│	│	157	d. Falls City d.	│	│	....	1605
33.40	....	1120	1610	2240	242	d.St.Joseph d.	0030	0855	....	1425
40.85	....	1230	1725	2340		a.	2330	0740	....	1315
		JL 155	GL 6103		308	**Kansas City**	JL 154	GL 6102		
0.00	0730	1300	1800	....		d. a.	2310	0545	2125	....
15.85	0915	│	1945	....	438	d.Clinton d.	│	0400	1940	....
30.57	1201	1745	2220	....	648	d.Springfield d.	1830	0205	1730	....
	1300	1845	│	....		d. Branson d.	1720	│	1540	....
	1345	1935	│	....		d. Harrison d.	1630	│	1500	....
	│	2035	│	....		a. Little Rock d.	1330	│	│	....
35.20	│	....	r	....	907	d.Walnut Ridge d.	....	r	│	....
67.85	1730	....	0315	....		d.Hoxie d.	....	2055	1115	....
73.15	1755	....	0335	....	948	d.Jonesboro d.	....	2030	1050	....
131.45	1945	....	0530	....	1063	a.**Memphis** d.	....	1840	0900	....

GL–Greyhound Lines. *JL*-Jefferson Lines

Table 735 ▲ ROCHESTER - CEDAR RAPIDS ▲

HKS

US $		18		20	km	595	17			19
0.00	....	0945	....	2000	0	d.**Rochester** a.	0850	....	....	1900
	....	1130	....	2135		d.Decorah d.	0715	....	....	1720
	....	1410	....	....		a.**Cedar Rapids** d.	....	....	....	1430

HKS– Hawkeye Stages Inc.

Table 739 595 CAPE CANAVERAL BRT

Regular local bus services link Cocoa, Rockledge, Melbourne, Cape Canaveral and Port Canaveral.

BRT– Brevard Transportation Authority.

Table 740 MINNEAPOLIS - DULUTH GL

US $	5900	5914	5912		km	296	5913		5907	5909
						↓ ↑				
0.00	0730	1355	1800	....	0	d.**Minneapolis** .....a.	1110	....	1555	2115
11.00	0800	1420	1825	....	16	d.**St. Paul**.............a.	1045	....	1530	2050
18.00	0940	1550	1955	....	150	d.Hinckley ....d.	|	....	1400	1920
30.00	1120	1720	2120	....	270	a.**Duluth** ....d.	0730	....	1230	1750

GL– Greyhound Lines.

Table 741 INTERNATIONAL FALLS TRT

US $	302				km	595		301		
						↓ ↑				
0.00	0800	....	....	....	0	d.**International Falls** a.	....	2135	....	....
9.60	1010	....	....	....		d.Virginia ....d.	....	1955	....	....
16.15	1135	....	....	....		a.**Duluth** ....d.	....	1835	....	....

TRT– Triangle Transportation.

Table 742 DULUTH - GRAND FORKS

US $					km	595				
						↓ ↑				
0.00	....	....	....	....	0	d.**Duluth** ....a.	....	....	....	....
10.75	....	....	....	....		d.Grand Rapids ....d.	....	....	....	....
15.90	....	....	....	....	200	d.Bemidji ....d.	....	....	....	....
24.10	....	....	....	....	340	d.Crookston..........d.	....	....	....	....
32.85	....	....	....	....	384	a.**Grand Forks**.....d.	....	....	....	....

Table 743 595 MINNEAPOLIS - ST. PAUL MTC

Bus service (**16, 94L**) Minneapolis-St. Paul and v.v. *17* km. Journey: 25-45 mins. Fare: US $: 1.00.

From Minneapolis: 0412⑥/0413†/0502Ⓐ and frequent to 0104①/0106⑦/0107②-⑥.

From St. Paul: 0458Ⓐ/0501© and frequent to 0109①/0112ex①.

AMTRAK's Midway rail station is served by route **16**. Bus stop is two blocks south of station on University Avenue.

MTC– Metropolitan Transit Commission. ☎Minneapolis 827 7733.

Table 745 MINNEAPOLIS - KANSAS CITY JL

US $	296	km		405	817		803	905	811	
	↓									
0.00	**Minneapolis** ....d.	0	....	0610	0715	....	1201	1730	1855	....
3.20	**St. Paul** ....d.	16	....	0630	|	....	|	1750	|	....
12.75	Owatonna.............d.	121	....	0815	0835	....	1340	|	2045	....
19.10	Albert Lea ....d.	176	....	0920s	0910	....	1415	2125	2125	....
30.00	Mason City............d.	233	....	1020	1015	....	1520	....	2235	....
40.60	Iowa Falls..............d.	309	....	|	1125	....	|	....	|	....
47.85	Ames.....................d.	376	....	|	1235	....	1700	....	0010	....
52.00	**Des Moines** .... a.	424	....	|	1315	....	1745	....	0050	....
	Des Moines .... d.		....	|	1335	....	1830	....	0125	....
70.75	Eagleville..............d.		....	|	r	....	2025	....	0315	....
70.75	Bethany.................d.	634	....	|	1535	....	2045	....	|	....
91.55	**Kansas City** ...... a.	709	....	|	1715	....	2230	....	0505	....
	Kansas City ...... d.		....	|	1830	....	0020	....	0555	....
42.65	Waterloo ....d.	296	....	1240	|	....	|	....	|	....
54.10	**Cedar Rapids**....a.	406	....	1340	|	....	|	....	|	....
96.75	Lawrence ....d.		....	....	1930	....	|	....	0650	....
106.10	Iola ....d.		....	....	2125	....	|	....	0840	....
	Neodesha ....d.		....	....	|	....	0255	....	|	....
109.20	Coffeyville ....d.	951	....	....	2255	....	|	....	1025	....
113.40	Tulsa ....a.	1167	....	....	0035	....	0515	....	1210	....
123.80	**Oklahoma City**....a.	1470	....	....	0235	....	....	....	1445	....

296	734	812	724		910	730			408	
↓										
Oklahoma City..........d.	0945	....	1215	....	....	2250	....	....	....	....
Tulsa ....d.	1201	....	1430	....	....	0100	....	....	....	....
Coffeyville ....d.	....	....	1625	....	....	|	....	....	....	....
Neodesha ....d.	....	....	|	....	....	|	....	....	....	....
Iola ....d.	....	....	1835	....	....	0410	....	....	....	....
Lawrence ....d.	....	....	2020s	....	....	|	....	....	....	....
Cedar Rapids..........d.	....	....	|	....	....	|	....	....	1430	....
Waterloo ....d.	....	....	|	....	....	|	....	....	1530	....
Kansas City .... a.	....	....	2120	....	....	0630	....	....	|	....
Kansas City .... d.	....	1900	0001	....	....	0730	....	....	|	....
Bethany......................d.	....	2055	|	....	....	0915	....	....	|	....
Eagleville...................d.	....	r	|	....	....	|	....	....	|	....
Des Moines .... a.	....	2245	0315	....	....	1110	....	....	|	....
Des Moines .... d.	....	2330	0350	....	....	1120	....	....	|	....
Ames.........................d.	....	0010	0425	....	....	1205	....	....	|	....
Iowa Falls..................d.	....	|	0525	....	....	|	....	....	|	....
Mason City ....d.	....	|	0645	....	....	1405	....	....	1745	....
Albert Lea ....d.	....	0245	0740	....	0745	1450	....	....	1830	....
Owatonna..................d.	....	0320	0820	....	|	1525	....	....	1935	....
St. Paul ....a.	....	|	|	....	|	|	....	....	2105s	....
Minneapolis ....a.	....	0510	1015	....	1115	1730	....	....	2120	....

JL– Jefferson Lines.

Table 746 MINNEAPOLIS - ASHLAND NLI WNT

US $		NLI 201	WNT 102		km	595	NLI 200	WNT 101		
		▲	▲			↓ ↑	▲	▲		
0.00	....	1300	....	....	0	d.**Minneapolis** .....a.	1140	....	....	....
2.00	....	1325	....	....	16	d.**St. Paul**.............a.	1120	....	....	....
0.00	....	|	1852	....		d. Eau Claire.......a.	|	1110	....	....
◊7.95	....	1605	2003	....	174	d.Rice Lake..........d.	0855	0935	....	....
◊11.20	....	1635	2032	....		d.Spooner ....d.	0810	0850	....	....
◊22.95	....	|	2202	....		a. **Duluth** ....d.	|	0710	....	....
◊22.95	....	|	2212	....		a. Superior ....d.	|	0700	....	....
18.75	....	1710	....	....	257	d.Hayward............d.	0735	....	....	....
26.20	....	1825	....	....	352	a.**Ashland**............d.	0620	....	....	....
31.45	....	1915	....	....	414	a.Ironwood ....d.	0535	....	....	....

◊–Fare ex Eau Claire. NLI–Northfield Lines Inc. WNT–Wisconsin Northern.

Table 747 MINNEAPOLIS - OMAHA GL JRL MLA SQTR

US $	GL 5879	SQTR	MLA 61	MLA 65	km	296	MLA 60	SQTR	GL 5880	MLA 64
				⑤⑦		↓ ↑				⑤⑦
0.00	0805	....	1445	1905	0	d.**Minneapolis** .....a.	1125	....	1505	1850
	|	0800	|	|		d. Winona ....a.	|	1535	|	|
	|	0900	|	|		d. Rochester ......d.	|	1425	|	|
	|	1000	|	|		d. Owatonna ......d.	|	1325	|	|
17.00	1030	1100	1645	2045	131	d.**Mankato** ....d.	0925	1225	1245	1705
25.50	1315	....	....	▬	256	d.Worthington.......d.	....	....	1000	▬
	|	....	....	....		d. Storm Lake......d.	....	....	|	....
	|	....	....	JRL		d. Cherokee.........d.	....	....	|	JRL
74.00	1445	....	....	2120	428	d.Sioux Falls ....d.	....	....	0840	1605
95.00	1655	....	....	2305	525	d.Sioux City..........d.	....	....	0620	1405
98.00	1840	....	....	0045	602	a.**Omaha**..............d.	....	....	0430	1225
US $			22						21	
			⑤		km	↓ MLA ↑			⑤	
0.00	....	....	1645	....	0	d.**Mankato** ....a.	....	....	1915	....
	....	....	1800	....		a.**Fairmont**...........d.	....	....	1810	....

GL–Greyhound Lines. JRL–Jack Rabbit Lines. MLA–Mankato Land to Air Inc. SQTR–Speciality Tours.

Table 748 BURLINGTON - ST. LOUIS BTW

US $				1307	km	695	1302			
						↓ ↑				
0.00	....	....	....	1845	0	d.**Burlington**........a.	0900	....	....	....
8.40	....	....	....	1945	73	d.Keokuk..............d.	0755	....	....	....
16.80	....	....	....	2055	133	d.Quincy...............d.	0650	....	....	....
21.00	....	....	....	2135	182	d.Hannibal............d.	0610	....	....	....
36.75	....	....	....	2345	362	a.**St. Louis**...........d.	0320	....	....	....

BTW– Burlington Trailways.

Table 749 BEMIDJI/HIBBING GL TIQU

US $			GL 5654	TIQU 101	km	296	TIQU 100		GL 5657	
						↓ ↑				
0.00	....	....	1115	1735	0	d.**Minneapolis** .....a.	1348	....	1340	....
11.50	....	....	1310	|		d.St. Cloud ....d.	|	....	1145	....
15.50	....	....	1410	|		d.Little Falls..........d.	|	....	1050	....
18.00	....	....	1445	|		d.Brainerd ....d.	|	....	1000	....
	....	....	|	2235		d.**Hibbing**.............d.	0844	....	|	....
	....	....	|	2310		a.Virginia ....d.	0811	....	|	....
34.50	....	....	1700	....		a. Bemidji............d.	....	....	0745	....

GL–Greyhound Lines. TIQU–Tri-Action Tours Inc.

Table 750 MINNEAPOLIS - ABERDEEN JRL QUC

US $	QUC	QUC	JRL 5613		km	595	QUC		QUC	JRL 5612
	①③⑤	②④				↓ ↑	②④		①③⑤	
0.00	....	....	1530	....	0	d.**Minneapolis** .....a.	....	....	....	1450
28.00	1440	1440	1735	....	150	d.Willmar..............d.	1220	....	1225	1235
43.00	|	|	1915	....	275	d.Ortonville...........d.	|	....	|	1100
	|	|	1930	....		a.Milbank..............a.	|	....	|	1010
	1505	1505	|	....		d. Clara City.........d.	1140	....	1200	|
	1545	|	|	....		d. Granite Falls ...d.	|	....	1130	|
	1800	|	|	....		a. Marshall ....d.	|	....	0900	|
	....	1710	|	....		d. Madison........d.	0950	....	....	|
	....	1800	|	....		a. Ivanhoe.........d.	0900	....	....	|
59.00	....	....	2205	....	440	a.**Aberdeen**..........d.	....	....	....	0815

JRL– Jack Rabbit Lines. QUC–Quality Carriers.

Table 751 SIOUX FALLS - RAPID CITY JRL

US $	11				km	595				10
						↓ ↑				
0.00	0845	....	....	....	0	d.**Sioux Falls**.......a.	....	....	....	2120
21.00	1010	....	....	....	100	d.Mitchell..............d.	....	....	....	2000
	s	....	....	....	150	d.Woonsocket ......d.	....	....	....	1925
33.00	1115	....	....	....	190	d.Huron ....d.	....	....	....	1855
56.00	1415	....	....	....	380	d.**Pierre**.................d.	....	....	....	1550
68.00	1510	....	....	....		d.Wall....................d.	....	....	....	1230
75.00	1630	....	....	....	514	a.**Rapid City** ◊ ...d.	....	....	....	1130

◊– A special 9-hour tour of the Black Hills is operated daily June 15-Sept. 15, dep. Rapid City 0800. JRL–Jack Rabbit Lines.

Table 751a JOPLIN - WICHITA VL

US $		11			km	595			12	
0.00	....	0945	....	....	0	d.**Joplin** ....a.	....	....	2010	....
	....	r	....	....		d.Neodesha..........d.	....	....	1725	....
	....	1435	....	....		a.**Wichita** ....d.	....	....	1515	....

VL– Viking Trailways.

Table 752 395 MILWAUKEE - MADISON — BGC GL

Service Milwaukee-Madison and v.v. *124* km. Journey: 1½-2 hours. Fare: US $: 8.00.
From Milwaukee: *BGC* at 0700, 1000, 1230, 1500, 1730, 1845⑦, 2000, 2230†; *GL* at 0830, 1230, 1740, 2335.
From Madison: *BGC* at 0700, 1000, 1230, 1500, 1615⑤, 1730, 2000, 2230†; *GL* at 0550, 1540, 1935, 2135.
BGC–Badger Coaches. *GL*–Greyhound Lines.

Table 753 ▲ WICHITA FALLS - ABILENE ▲ — SKYK

US $			401 ⚒▲		km	294 ↓ ↑			414 ⚒▲	
0.00	....	....	0845	....	*0*	d.**Wichita Falls**....a.	....	....	1745	....
	....	....	0950	....	*82*	d.Seymour............d.	....	....	1640	....
	....	....	1240	....	*245*	a.**Abilene**............d.	....	....	1400	....

SKYK– Skylark Transportation.

Table 754 ST. LOUIS - MEMPHIS — SOV

US $	1		3	5	km	392 ↓ ↑	2			4
0.00	....	....	1345	1800	*0*	d.**St. Louis**...........a.	1205	....	....	1740
	0800	....	1635	2145		d. Farmington......d.	0800	....	....	1430
25.00	0950	....	....	....	*223*	d.Cape Girardeau.d.	....	....	....	1230
	....	....	....	....	*461*	d.Jonesboro ....d.	....	....	....	....
33.00	....	....	....	....	*579*	a.**Memphis** ....d.	....	....	....	....

SOV– Shumakes Ozark Village.

Table 756 DES MOINES - SPRINGFIELD — SMC

US $	03	01			km	595 ↓ ↑		02	04	
	....	....	....	....	*0*	d.**Des Moines**......a.	....	....	....	....
	....	....	....	....	*162*	d.Ottumwa............d.	....	....	....	....
	....	....	....	....	*265*	d.Kirksville............d.	....	....	....	....
	....	....	....	....	*320*	d.Macon ....d.	....	....	....	....
	....	....	....	....	*356*	d.Moberly ....d.	....	....	....	....
	1020	1630	....	....	*413*	d.Columbia ....d.	....	0925	1540	....
	1100	1720	....	....	*462*	d.Jefferson City ....d.	....	0845	1500	....
	....	1925	....	....	*600*	d.Lebanon ....d.	....	0635	....	....
0.00	....	2020	....	....	*685*	a.**Springfield** ....d.	....	0530	....	....

SMC– Sho-Me Coaches Inc.

Table 757 NORFOLK - CHADRON — KSE

US $			22 ②④		km	494 ↓ ↑	21 ③⑤			
0.00	....	....	1530	....	*0*	d.**Norfolk** ....a.	0730	....	....	....
	....	....	|	....		d.O'Neill ....a.	|	....	....	....
	....	....	|	....		d.Bassett..............d.	|	....	....	....
	....	....	|	....		d.Ainsworth ....d.	|	....	....	....
	....	....	1915	....		d.Valentine ....a.	0330	....	....	....
	....	....	2045	....		d.Gordon ....d.	0030	....	....	....
	....	....	2100	....		d.Rushville............d.	0015	....	....	....
	....	....	2130	....		a.**Chadron** ....d.	2330	....	....	....

KSE– K&S Expressway Inc.

Table 758 ST. LOUIS - OKLAHOMA CITY - DALLAS — CPL GL JL

US $	296 ↓	km	GL 1351	JL 467		GL 6255	GL 473	GL 6207	JL 737		GL 1355		GL 1353		GL 6421	JL 735	GL 6209	GL 6423	GL 6425	GL 475		JL 725			
35.00	*Chicago* **722**.......d.		*2030*	....	....	*0100*	....	....	....	....	0600	....	*1045*	....	....	....	....	....	....	1345	....	....	....	....	....
0.00	**St. Louis**...........d.	*0*	0300	....	....	0745	1015	....	....	....	1345	....	1800	....	....	....	....	....	....	2300	....	....	....	....	....
18.25	Rolla..................d.	*166*	0445	....	....	1045	|	....	....	....	|	....	|	....	....	....	....	....	....	|	....	....	....	....	....
31.00	Lebanon ....d.	*250*	0620	....	....	1210	|	....	....	....	|	....	2140	....	....	....	....	....	....	|	....	....	....	....	....
37.00	Springfield..........d.	*331*	0740	....	....	1320	1430	....	....	....	1750	....	2245	....	....	....	....	....	....	0305	....	....	....	....	....
46.26	Carthage ....d.		0920	....	....	1500	|	....	....	....	|	....	|	....	....	....	....	....	....	|	....	....	....	....	....
50.00	Joplin ....d.	*442*	0950	....	....	1550	|	....	....	....	2010	....	0050	....	....	....	....	....	....	0510	....	....	....	....	....
70.50	Tulsa ....d.	*627*	1340	....	....	1830	1925	....	0045	....	2315	....	0355	....	0530	0615	....	0800	1245	0825	....	1300	....	....	....
88.50	**Oklahoma City** a.	*800*	1530	....	....	....	2115	....	0235	....	0105	....	0545	....	|	0815	....	|	|	1015	....	1445	....	....	....
	Oklahoma City d.		1610	1600	....	....	2145**c**	0015	0315	....	0125	....	0615	....	|	....	1045	|	|	1035**c**	....	....	....	....	....
76.50	Muskogee d.	*665*	|	|	....	....	|	|	|	....	|	....	|	....	|	....	|	0945	1350	|	....	....	....	....	....
88.50	McAlester d.	*752*	|	|	....	....	|	|	|	....	|	....	|	....	0730	....	|	1055	1500	|	....	....	....	....	....
95.00	Ardmore d.	*940*	|	1830**a**	....	....	|	0220	0505**a**	....	|	....	|	....	|	....	1315	|	|	|	....	....	....	....	....
95.00	Durant d.	*882*	|	|	....	....	|	|	|	....	|	....	|	....	0925	....	|	1250	1655	|	....	....	....	....	....
95.00	Sherman d.	*932*	|	|	....	....	|	|	|	....	|	....	|	....	1015	....	|	1340	1745	|	....	....	....	....	....
92.00	Gainesville d.	*1003*	|	1915**a**	....	....	|	0305	0550**a**	....	|	....	|	....	|	....	1355	|	|	|	....	....	....	....	....
94.00	Denton d.	*1050*	|	1955**a**	....	....	|	0345	0630**a**	....	|	....	|	....	|	....	1435	|	|	|	....	....	....	....	....
94.00	**Dallas** a.	*1037*	|	2055**a**	....	....	|	0430	0730**a**	....	|	....	|	....	1159	....	1540	1525	1930	|	....	....	....	....	....
119.00	*Albuquerque* a.	*1700*	0225	....	....	....	0810	....	....	....	1035	....	1650	....	....	....	....	....	....	2200	....	....	....	....	....
139.00	*Los Angeles* a.	*3050*	....	....	....	....	....	....	....	....	1425	....	1015	....	....	....	....	....	....	1725	....	....	....	....	....

296 ↓				GL 1356	GL 6200			JL 734	GL 474			JL 724		GL 6422	GL 468		GL 6424	GL 464	GL 470		GL 6426	JL 730	GL 1346	GL 6208	GL 1352
Los Angeles.........d.	....	....	....	1900	....	....	....	....	....	....	....	....	....	....	....	....	....	....	0925	....	....	....	1415	....	1330
Albuquerque ....d.	....	....	....	1600	....	....	....	....	2045	....	....	....	....	....	....	....	....	....	0610	....	....	....	0940	....	1115
Dallas ....d.	....	....	....	|	0200	....	....	....	|	....	....	....	....	0615	0715	....	1255	1330	|	....	1815	....	|	1900	|
Denton ....d.	....	....	....	|	0250	....	....	....	|	....	....	....	....	|	0815	....	|	1430	|	....	|	....	|	2010	|
Gainesville................d.	....	....	....	|	0325	....	....	....	|	....	....	....	....	|	0905	....	|	1505	|	....	|	....	|	2050	|
Sherman ....d.	....	....	....	|	|	....	....	....	|	....	....	....	....	0800	|	....	1440	|	|	....	2000	....	|	|	|
Durant....................d.	....	....	....	|	|	....	....	....	|	....	....	....	....	0850	|	....	1530	|	|	....	2050	....	|	|	|
Ardmore ....d.	....	....	....	|	0415	....	....	....	|	....	....	....	....	|	0955**b**	....	|	1555**b**	|	....	|	....	|	2140	|
McAlester.................d.	....	....	....	|	|	....	....	....	|	....	....	....	....	1045	|	....	1735	|	|	....	2245	....	|	|	|
Muskogee ....d.	....	....	....	|	|	....	....	....	|	....	....	....	....	1155	|	....	1845	|	|	....	|	....	|	|	|
Oklahoma City a.	....	....	....	0355	0630	....	....	....	0930**c**	....	....	....	....	|	1215**b**	....	|	1820**b**	1850**c**	....	|	....	2115	2345	2355
Oklahoma City d.	....	....	....	0410	....	....	....	0945	1000	....	....	1215	....	|	....	....	|	....	1930	....	|	2250	2135	....	0025
Tulsa ....d.	....	....	....	0700	....	....	....	1145	1250	....	....	1405	....	1430	....	....	2030	....	2220	....	0045	0045	0025	....	0315
Joplin ....d.	....	....	....	0945	....	....	....	....	1505	....	....	....	....	1720	....	....	....	....	0030	....	....	....	0235	....	0525
Carthage ....d.	....	....	....	|	....	....	....	....	|	....	....	....	....	|	....	....	....	....	|	....	....	....	|	....	0555
Springfield ....d.	....	....	....	1210	....	....	....	....	1715	....	....	....	....	1930	....	....	....	....	0215	....	....	....	0420	....	0755
Lebanon ....d.	....	....	....	1310	....	....	....	....	1815	....	....	....	....	2030	....	....	....	....	|	....	....	....	|	....	0900
Rolla..........................d.	....	....	....	|	....	....	....	....	|	....	....	....	....	|	....	....	....	....	|	....	....	....	|	....	1020
St. Louis.................a.	....	....	....	1655	....	....	....	....	2150	....	....	....	....	0045	....	....	....	....	0655	....	....	....	0915	....	1310
Chicago **722**............a.	....	....	....	*0045*	....	....	....	....	*0515*	....	....	....	....	....	....	....	....	....	*1600*	....	....	....	....	....	*2045*

a–*GL*. **b**–*JL*. **c**–*CPL*. *CPL*–Panhandle Trailways. *GL*–Greyhound Lines. *JL*–Jefferson Lines.

Table 759 ABILENE - DEL RIO — KBC SSS

US $	SSS 101	KBC 603	SSS 102		km	695 ↓ ↑	SSS 104		SSS 105	KBS 604
0.00	0615	....	1330	....	*0*	d.**Abilene** ....a.	1215	....	1755	....
	|	0800	|	....		d. **Dallas** ....a.	|	....	|	2035
	|	0845	|	....		d. **Fort Worth** .....a.	|	....	|	1950
	|	1020	|	....		d. Stephenville ....d.	|	....	|	1820
	|	1145	|	....		d. Brownwood .....d.	|	....	|	1655
7.90	0820	1400	1800	....	*150*	d.San Angelo ....d.	1010	....	1550	1455
11.20	1000	1520	1925	....	*255*	d.Sonora ....d.	0855	....	1420	1335
18.00	1200	1710	2125	....	*405*	a.**Del Rio** ....d.	0700	....	1230	1200
	....	1820	....	....		a.Eagle Pass........d.	....	....	....	1045

KBC– Kerrville Bus Co.
SSS– Sun Set Stages.

Table 760 OPELOUSAS — KBC

US $		911			km	196 ↓ ↑		912		
18.00	....	0830	....	....		d.**Lafayette** ....a.	....	2140	....	....
0.00	....	0855	....	....	*0*	d.Opelousas.........d.	....	2115	....	....
7.00	....	1130	....	....	*70*	d.Beaumont.........d.	....	1850	....	....
21.00	....	1325	....	....	*197*	a.**Houston** ....d.	....	1645	....	....

KBC– Kerrville Bus Co.

Table 761 EL DORADO - ALEXANDRIA — SAL

US $	3 ex⑦	5 ex⑤⑦	7 ⑤⑦	9 ⑤⑦	km	196 ↓ ↑	4 ex⑦	6 ⑦	8 ex⑦	10 ⑤⑦
0.00	0905	....	....	....	*0*	d.**El Dorado** ....a.	0855	....	....	....
18.00	1045	1600	1600	2020	*125*	d.Ruston...............a.	0740	1550	1550	2020
23.00	1120	1630	1630	2055	*177*	d.Jonesboro ....d.	0710	1510	1510	1950
40.75	1155	....	1705	....	*282*	d.Winnfield ....d.	....	....	1430	1920
40.75	1305	....	1815	....	*324*	a.**Alexandria**.......d.	....	....	1330	1820

SAL– Salter Bus Lines.

R–Reservation obligatory ♿–Facilities for the disabled ■–Frontier point

ble 762 MONROE - NATCHEZ

RAM

$		22 ⚒			km	694 ↓ ↑				21 ⚒
00	....	0955	....	....	0	d.**Monroe**................a.	....	....	....	1900
	....	1225	....	....	240	a.**Natchez**...............d.	....	....	....	1645

M–Ramsey's Bus Line Inc.

Table 763 VICKSBURG - NEW ORLEANS

DEA GL RAM

US$		RAM 22 ⚒	DEA 003		km	695 ↓ ↑			DEA 006	RAM 21 ⚒
0.00	....	....	1455	....	116	d.**Vicksburg**............a.	....	....	1715	....
13.75	....	1230	1640	....	0	d.Natchez................d.	....	....	1540	1635
24.00	....	1340	1750	....	297	d.St. Francisville......d.	....	....	1410	1520
32.75	....	1415	1825	....	138	d.Baton Rouge........d.	....	....	1330	1445
41.25	....	*1615*a	*2135*a	....	263	a.**New Orleans**........d.	....	....	*0945*a	*1230*a

a–*GL*. *DEA*–Delta Bus Lines. *GL*–Greyhound Lines. *RAM*–Ramsey's Bus Line Inc.

ble 765 SHREVEPORT - NEW ORLEANS

GL KBC

$			GL 1250		GL 710					GL 712	GL 714	km	296 ↓ ↑	GL 1241		GL 711		GL 713					GL 715	
0	....	....	0300	....	0530b	....	....	....	....	1145b	2330b		d.*Dallas*............................a.	1159	....	2230b	....	0140b	....	....	....	....	0730b	....
0	....	....	0645	....	1100	....	....	....	....	1710	0330	0	d.**Shreveport**....................a.	0815	....	1545	....	2045	....	....	....	....	0300	....
0	....	....	0930	....	1355	....	....	....	....	2020	0605	185	d.Alexandria.......................d.	0540	....	1240	....	1805	....	....	....	....	0035	....
0	....	....	1245	....	1700	....	....	....	....	2340	0930	365	d.Baton Rouge...................d.	0325	....	0915	....	1445	....	....	....	....	2210	....
0	....	....	*1445*	....	1915	....	....	....	....	0115	1130	490	a.**New Orleans**..................d.	....	....	0645	....	1220	....	....	....	....	1930	....

TO. *GL*–Greyhound Lines. *KBC*–Kerrville Bus Co.

ble 766 COLUMBIA - MONTGOMERY - DALLAS

CML GL IBL KBC SES

$	296 ↓	km	GL 1561	GL 1545	GL 5023	SES 201	GL 513	KBC 511	SES 208	IBL 32 ⑤	SES 202	CML 73		GL 1551	SES 209			GL 1549	KBC 513	GL 5021		GL 1055	SES 204	SES 205	KBC 515
	Columbia................d.	0	....	....	....	0520	....	....	0845	....	1201	....	....	....	1600	....	....	....	....	....	....	....	2030	0035	....
	Aiken........................d.		....	....	....	0625	....	....	0950	....	1305	....	....	....	1705	....	....	....	....	....	....	....	2135	│	....
0	Augusta....................d.	93	....	....	....	0720	....	....	1045	....	1345	1400	....	....	1745	....	....	....	....	....	....	....	2215	0200	....
	Athens......................d.		....	....	....	0930	....	....	1300	....	│	│	....	....	│	....	....	....	....	....	....	....	│	│	....
	Atlanta.............d.		1015	....	....	1130	1245	....	1500	....	1700	│	....	1900	2100	....	....	2200	....	....	....	0500	0045	0430	....
2	Milledgeville.............d.		│	....	....	....	│	....	....	....	....	1630	....	│	....	....	....	│	....	....	....	│	....	....	....
6	Macon.......................d.	333	│	....	....	....	│	....	....	....	....	1730	....	│	....	....	....	│	....	....	....	│	....	....	....
4	Columbus..................d.	493	│	....	....	....	1530f	....	....	1930	....	1950	....	│	....	....	....	0020	....	....	....	│	....	....	....
0	**Montgomery**............d.	623	│	....	....	....	1715f	....	....	2045	....	2115	....	│	....	....	....	0130	....	....	....	│	....	....	....
	Anniston..................d.		│	....	....	....	│	....	....	....	....	│	....	│	....	....	....	│	....	....	....	│	....	....	....
	Birmingham..........d.		1250	1515	1545	....	│	....	....	....	....	│	....	2115	...	....	....	│	....	0330	....	0710	....	....	....
	Tuscaloosa..........d.		1410	1635	1705	....	│	....	....	....	....	│	....	2230	....	....	....	│	....	0450	....	0820	....	....	....
0	Selma........................d.	725	│	│	│	....	1815f	....	....	....	....	2215	....	│	....	....	....	0230	....	│	....	│	....	....	....
0	Uniontown.................d.		│	│	│	....	1850f	....	....	....	....	2248	....	│	....	....	....	0305r	....	│	....	│	....	....	....
0	Demopolis.................d.	784	│	│	│	....	1915f	....	....	....	....	2310	....	│	....	....	....	0330	....	│	....	│	....	....	....
0	Meridian....................d.	871	1555	│	1925	....	2045	....	....	....	....	0030	....	0015	....	....	....	0445	....	0655	....	1005	....	....	....
	Jackson..................d.	1021	1835	2200	....	....	2330	....	....	....	....	0215g	....	0230	....	....	....	0700	....	....	....	1245	....	....	....
	Vicksburg..................d.	1094	1925	....	....	....	0020	....	....	....	....	....	....	0320	....	....	....	0750	....	....	....	1335	....	....	....
	Tallulah.....................d.	1125	1940	....	....	....	│	....	....	....	....	....	....	│	....	....	....	0815	....	....	....	1400	....	....	....
	Monroe......................d.	1220	2125	....	....	....	│	....	....	....	....	....	....	0440	....	....	....	0945	....	....	....	1515	....	....	....
	Ruston......................d.	1270	2205	....	....	....	│	....	....	....	....	....	....	0520	....	....	....	1025	....	....	....	1555	....	....	....
	Shreveport............a.	1372	2330	....	....	....	0315	....	....	....	....	....	....	0650	....	....	....	1159	....	....	....	1730	....	....	....
0	**Shreveport**............d.		0015	....	....	....	0345	0345	....	....	....	....	....	0725	....	....	....	1230	1730	....	....	1800	....	....	2115
0	Marshall....................d.	1442	0105	....	....	....	│	│	....	....	....	....	....	0815	....	....	....	1320	1825	....	....	1850	....	....	2200
0	Longview...................d.	1484	0140	....	....	....	│	│	....	....	....	....	....	0850	....	....	....	1355	1900	....	....	1925	....	....	2235
0	Tyler.........................d.	1560	0235	....	....	....	│	0535	....	....	....	....	....	0945	....	....	....	1500	2005	....	....	2035	....	....	2335
0	**Dallas**......................a.	1705	0415	....	....	....	0700	0730	....	....	....	....	....	1159	....	....	....	1715	2230	....	....	2230	....	....	0130

↓	IBL 31 ⑤	KBC 516	GL 1076	GL 1176	GL 1544	GL 1548	SES 105		KBC 516		GL 520	SES 101	SES 102	GL 5024	GL 514	KBC 512	SES 108			GL 528	SES 106		CML 2	SES 107	
as.........................d.	....	2330	2330	....	....	0315	....	....	0530	....	0745	....	....	....	1235	1145	....	....	....	1930	....	....	....	....	....
ler.........................d.	....	│	0115	....	....	│	....	....	0800	....	0945	....	....	....	│	1410	....	....	....	2155	....	....	....	....	....
gview.....................d.	....	│	0205	....	....	│	....	....	0900	....	1035	....	....	....	1505	1510	....	....	....	2255	....	....	....	....	....
shall.......................d.	....	│	0240	....	....	│	....	....	0935	....	1110	....	....	....	1540	1545	....	....	....	2330	....	....	....	....	....
eveport..............a.	....	0245	0330	....	....	0630	....	....	1035	....	1159	....	....	....	1630	1640	....	....	....	0020	....	....	....	....	....
eveport..............d.	....	....	0400	....	....	0700	....	....	....	....	1230	....	....	....	1705	....	....	....	....	0050	....	....	....	....	....
ton.........................d.	....	....	0515	....	....	0835	....	....	....	....	1405	....	....	....	1835	....	....	....	....	│	....	....	....	....	....
roe.........................d.	....	....	0600	....	....	0930	....	....	....	....	1455	....	....	....	1930	....	....	....	....	│	....	....	....	....	....
lah.........................d.	....	....	0700	....	....	1050	....	....	....	....	1615	....	....	....	2050	....	....	....	....	│	....	....	....	....	....
sburg......................d.	....	....	0725	....	....	1115	....	....	....	....	1640	....	....	....	2115	....	....	....	....	0340	....	....	....	....	....
kson......................d.	....	....	0905	....	1300	1300	....	....	....	....	1815	....	....	....	2235	....	....	....	....	0515	....	....	0515g	....	....
dian........................d.	....	....	1115	1255	│	1515	....	....	....	....	2010	....	....	2200	0025f	....	....	....	....	0710	....	....	0705	....	....
opolis.....................d.	....	....	│	│	│	1625	....	....	....	....	│	....	....	│	0130f	....	....	....	....	│	....	....	0815	....	....
ntown.....................d.	....	....	│	│	│	1650r	....	....	....	....	│	....	....	│	rf	....	....	....	....	│	....	....	0840	....	....
na..........................d.	....	....	│	│	│	1725	....	....	....	....	│	....	....	│	0230f	....	....	....	....	│	....	....	0915	....	....
uscaloosa...............d.	....	....	1245	1500	1835	│	....	....	....	....	2135	....	....	0005	│	....	....	....	....	0840	....	....	│	....	....
irmingham..............d.	....	....	1500	1630	2000	│	....	....	....	....	2320	....	....	0120	│	....	....	....	....	1050	....	....	│	....	....
nniston...................d.	....	....	│	....	....	│	....	....	....	....	│	....	....	....	│	....	....	....	....	1201	....	....	│	....	....
tgomery...............d.	1600	....	│	....	....	1900	....	....	....	....	│	....	....	....	0445f	....	....	....	....	│	....	....	1245	....	....
mbus.......................d.	1915	....	│	....	....	│	....	....	....	....	│	....	....	....	0815	....	....	....	....	│	....	....	1615	....	....
on...........................d.	....	....	│	....	....	│	....	....	....	....	│	....	....	....	│	....	....	....	....	│	....	....	1845	....	....
dgeville...................d.	....	....	│	....	....	│	....	....	....	....	│	....	....	....	│	....	....	....	....	│	....	....	1935	....	....
Atlanta..................d.	....	....	1845	....	....	2300	2345	....	....	....	0300	0345	0730	....	1100	....	1215	....	....	1445	1600	....	│	1930	....
ns...........................d.	....	....	....	....	....	....	│	....	....	....	....	│	0915	....	....	....	1400	....	....	....	│	....	│	2120	....
usta........................d.	....	....	....	....	....	....	0220	....	....	....	....	0645	1145	....	....	....	1615	....	....	....	1845	....	2200	2330	....
n.............................d.	....	....	....	....	....	....	│	....	....	....	....	0710	1210	....	....	....	1640	....	....	....	1905	....	....	2350	....
mbia....................a.	....	....	....	....	....	....	0340	....	....	....	....	0815	1315	....	....	....	1745	....	....	....	2015	....	....	0050	....

Fare ex Dallas. ≷–Fare ex Shreveport. f–*CML*. g–*GL*. *CML*–Capital Motor Lines. *GL*–Greyhound Lines.
Ingram Bus Lines. *KBC*–Kerrville Bus Co. *SES*–Southeastern Stages.

ble 767 LA CROSSE

GL JL

$	901	903	905	911	km	295 ↓ JL ↑	912	910	904	906
00	0615	1201	1730	1830	0	d.**Minneapolis**........a.	1120	1115	1640	2210
00	0640	1220	1750	1850	17	d.**St. Paul**...............a.	│	│	│	2150s
00	│	│	│	2018	87	d.Red Wing..............d.	0930	│	│	│
00	0855	1425	2010	│	134	d. Rochester...........d.	│	0900	1430	2000
	│	│	2125	│		a. Albert Lea.......d.	│	0745	│	│
00	1005	1530	....	2150	188	d.Winona..................d.	0810	....	1310	1850
00	1045	1610	....	2225	232	d.La Crosse.............d.	0720	....	1230	1815
	│	1705	....	2330		d.Tomah...................d.	0600	....	....	1715
	*1410*a	*1925*a	....	*0210*a		a.**Madison**...............d.	*0355*a	....	....	*1435*a

L. *GL*–Greyhound Lines. *JL*–Jefferson Lines.

Table 768 FARGO - SIOUX FALLS

JRL

US $	30				km	395 ↓ ↑			35	
41.00	0730	....	....	....	0	d.**Fargo**.................a.	....	....	2305	....
	│	....	....	....	8	d.Moorhead..........d.	....	....	│	....
31.20	0830	....	....	....	79	d.Breckenridge.....d.	....	....	2205	....
25.80	0955	....	....	....	194	d.Ortonville...........d.	....	....	2025	....
	1010	....	....	....		a Milbank.............a.	....	....	1945	....
18.60	1140	....	....	....		d.Watertown.........d.	....	....	1845	....
11.40	1250	....	....	....		d.Brookings..........d.	....	....	1755	....
0.00	1430	....	....	....	451	a.**Sioux Falls**.......d.	....	....	1630	....

JRL– Jack Rabbit Lines.

⚒–Daily except Sundays and holidays Ⓐ–Monday to Fridays only, except holidays ⑥–Daily except Saturdays

Table 770 CHICAGO - WINNIPEG/SEATTLE

GL NWL RRS TR

US $	GL 1293	GL 5633		GL 1275	GL 5768	GL 5635	GL 5605 ⑤⑦	GL 5611 ⑤⑦	GL 1277	GL 5613	GL 1273	km	296 ↓ ↑	TRT 321 ♣	GL 1276	GL 5767	GL 1272	GL 1270	GL 5648	GL 5644	GL 1290		GL 5642 ①⑥	G 12
0.00	0115	0600	....	0730	0615	1030	1300	1700	1500	2130	2130	0	d.**Chicago** ....a.	....	1545	1945	1945	2330	2100	0155	0530	....	0815	10
22.50	0320	0830	....	0945	|	1245	|	|	1730	|	2335	140	d. Milwaukee ....a.	....	1335	|	1715	2125	1900	0010	0335	....	|	07
34.50	|	1025	....	1120	1120	1430	1610	2010	1910	0040	0115	260	d.Madison ....a.	....	|	1510	1540	1950	1705	2220	|	....	|	05
43.00	|	1130	....	|	|	1535	|	|	|	|	|	320	d.Baraboo ....d.	....	|	|	1415	|	|	|	|	....	|	|
43.50	|	1150	....	|	|	1555	|	|	2045	|	|	338	d.Wisconsin Dells ....d.	....	|	|	1354	|	|	2105	|	....	|	|
47.50	0650	1325	....	1340	|	1720	1830	2215	2140	0245	0315	406	d.Tomah ....d.	....	1045	|	1245	1800	1455	2010	0045	....	0355	03
51.50	|	|	....	|	1425	|	|	|	|	|	|		d. La Crosse ....d.	....	|	1205	|	|	|	|	|	....	|	|
54.50	0835	1510	....	1515	|	1900	|	|	2310	|	0445	536	d.Eau Claire ....d.	....	|	|	1030	1555	1245	1805	2300	....	|	|
70.00	1025	1655	....	1645	|	2050s	2110s	|	|	0530s	0620	708	d.**St. Paul** ....d.	....	0710	0830	0825	1425	1055	1610	2110	....	|	|
	1045	1720	....	1705	1825	2110	2135	0115	0100	0555	0650		a.	....	0645	0800	0800	1400	1030	1545	2045	....	0030	00
70.00	|			|	▬		▬	TRT 322♣	|		|	725	**Minneapolis**		|	▬		|	▬	▬	|			|
	1201	....	....	1800	....	....	....	0130	0145	....	0730		d. a.	0445	0550	....	....	1245	....	....	1840	....	....	23
80.00	1320	....	....	1955	....	....	....	0245	0305	....	0855	830	d.St. Cloud ....d.	0325	0435	....	....	1145	....	....	1700	....	....	21
80.00	|	....	....	2050	....	....	....	|	|	....	1015		d.Little Falls ....d.	|	|	....	....	|	....	....	|	....	....	21
85.00	|	....	....	2125	....	....	....	|	|	....	1050		d.Brainerd ....d.	|	|	....	....	|	....	....	|	....	....	20
85.00	|	....	....	2200	....	....	....	|	|	....	1125	912	d.Motley ....d.	|	|	....	....	|	....	....	|	....	....	19
91.00	1730	....	....	0040	....	....	....	|	|	....	1415	1092	d.Moorhead ....d.	|	0120	....	....	|	....	....	1225	....	....	16
91.00	1815	....	....	0115	....	....	....	0800	0730	....	1450	1100	d.Fargo ....d.	2330	0115	....	....	0700	....	....	1220	....	....	16
94.00	1945	....	....	|	....	....	....	1025	|	....	|	1235	d. Grand Forks ....d.	2145	|	....	....	|	....	....	1015	....	....	|
Δ58.00	....	....	....	|	....	....	....	1240	|	....	|	1360	d. Emerson ....d.	1800	|	....	....	|	....	....	....	....	....	|
Δ69.00	....	....	....	|	....	....	....	1315	|	....	|	1402	d. Morris ....d.	1730	|	....	....	|	....	....	....	....	....	
Δ69.00	....	....	....	|	....	....	....	1410	|	....	|	1470	a. **Winnipeg** ....d.	1630	|	....	....	|	....	....	....	....	....	
94.00	....	....	....	0220	....	....	....	▬	0845	....	1605	1197	d.Valley City ....d.	....	2325	....	....	0445	....	....	....	....	....	15
94.00	....	....	....	0300	....	....	....	....	0930	....	1650	1265	d.Jamestown ....d.	....	2245	....	....	0400	....	....	....	....	....	14
99.00	....	....	....	0500	....	....	....	....	1210	....	1935	1430	d.Bismarck ....d.	....	2030	....	....	0155	....	....	....	....	....	11
	....	....	....	|	....	....	....	....	1145	....	1910	1438	d.New Salem ....d.	....	1845	....	....	0010	....	....	....	....	....	09
105.00	....	....	....	0615	....	....	....	....	1355	....	2100	1583	d.Dickinson ....d.	....	1710	....	....	2235	....	....	....	....	....	08
105.00	....	....	....	|	....	....	....	....	1420	....	2125		d.Belfield ....d.	....	1605	....	....	2155	....	....	....	....	....	07
118.00	....	....	....	0815	....	....	....	....	1605	....	2310	1738	d.Glendive ....d.	....	1425	....	....	2015	....	....	....	....	....	05
118.00	....	....	RRS	0955	....	....	....	....	1810	....	0100s	1868	d.Miles City ....d.	....	1220	....	....	1845	....	....	....	RRS	....	03
118.00	....	....	3	1155	....	....	....	....	|	....	0235s	2008	d.Custer ....d.	....	|	....	....	1615	....	....	....	6	....	02
131.00	....	....	1345	1400	....	....	....	....	2145	....	0430	2118	d.Billings ....d.	....	0930	....	....	1510	....	....	....	0010	....	01
143.00	....	....	1610	1630	....	....	....	....	2355	....	0650	2308	d.Livingston ....d.	....	0605	....	....	1145	....	....	....	2140	....	22
143.00	....	....	1645	1720	....	....	....	....	0055	....	0815	2355	d.Bozeman ....d.	....	0510	....	....	1050	....	....	....	2105	....	21
≤26.00	....	....	1915	|	....	....	....	....	|	....	|		d. Helena ....d.	....	|	....	....	|	....	....	....	1910	....	
143.00	....	....	|	1945	....	....	....	....	0320	....	1100	2500	d.Butte ....d.	....	0320	....	....	0900	....	....	....	|	....	19
155.00	....	....	|	2035	....	....	....	....	|	....	1150	2566	d.Deer Lodge ....d.	....	0200	....	....	0735	....	....	....	|	....	16
155.00	....	....	2130	2220	....	....	....	....	0545	....	1340	2696	d.Missoula ....d.	....	0025	....	....	0615	....	....	....	1600	....	15
164.00	....	....	....	0050	....	....	NWL	GL	0855	....	1630	2981	d.Coeur d'Alene ....d.	....	1945	GL	....	0125	NWL	....	....	....	....	09
164.00	....	....	....	0130	GL	....	736	5599	0940	....	1715	3035	a. **Spokane** ....d.	....	1850	5596	....	0045	737	GL	....	....	....	09
	....	....	....	0215	5597	....	1030	1115	1020	....	1815		d. **Spokane** ....a.	....	1740	1745	....	2345	1835	5598	....	....	....	08
164.00	....	....	....	|	0630	....	|	1550	|	....	|	3310	d. Wenatchee ....d.	....	|	1350	....	|	|	2000	....	....	....	
164.00	....	....	....	0535	0800	....	1415	|	1405	....	2210	3315	d.Ellensburg ....d.	....	1420	|	....	1955	1525	1830	....	....	....	04
164.00	....	....	....	|	|	....	|	1900	|	....	|	3510	d. Everett ....d.	....	|	1015	....	|	|	|	....	....	....	
164.00	....	....	....	0735	1010	....	1640	1940	1645	....	0025	3475	a.**Seattle** ....d.	....	1201	0930	....	1745	1240	1745	....	....	....	02

Δ–Fare ex Minneapolis. ≤–Fare ex Billings. *GL*–Greyhound Lines. *NWL*–Northwestern Trailways. *RRS*–Rimrock Trailways. *TRT*–Triangle Trailways.

Table 772 AUSTIN - VICTORIA

VTC

US$					km	396				
0.00	....	1145	....	....	0	d. **Austin** ....a.	....	1830	....	....
	....	1245	....	....		d. Luling ....d.	....	1740	....	....
	....	1445	....	....		a. **Victoria** ....d.	....	1530	....	....

VTC– Valley Transit Co.

Table 774 OSOYOOS - YAKIMA

US $					km	595				
	....	....	....	....	0	d.**Osoyoos** ....a.	....	....	....	....
0.00	....	....	....	....		d.Brewster ....d.	....	....	....	....
	....	....	....	....		d. Grand Coulee .d.	....	....	....	....
	....	....	....	....		a. **Spokane** ....d.	....	....	....	....
	....	....	....	....		d.Wenatchee ....d.	....	....	....	....
	....	....	....	....		d.Ellensburg ....d.	....	....	....	....
	....	....	....	....		a.**Yakima** ....d.	....	....	....	....

Table 775 LIBERAL - AMARILLO

C

US $			121		km	296 ↓ ↑	120			
	....	....	1400	....		d.**Liberal** ....a.	1325	....	....	....
	....	....	1500	....		d.Perryton ....d.	1215	....	....	....
	....	....	1540	....		d.Spearman ....a.	1145	....	....	....
	....	....	1625	....		d.Stinnett ....d.	1055	....	....	....
	....	....	1650	....		d.Borger ....d.	1035	....	....	....
	....	....	1720	....		d.Panhandle ....d.	|	....	....	....
	....	....	|	....		d. Fritch ....d.	1015	....	....	....
0.00	....	....	1800	....	0	a.**Amarillo** ....d.	0930	....	....	....

CPL– Panhandle Trailways.

Table 773 OMAHA - NORFOLK ♿

BHL

US $				41 Ⓐ	km	495 ↓ ↑	42 Ⓐ			
0.00	....	....	....	1245	0	d.**Omaha** ....a.	1110	....	....	....
10.00	....	....	....	1340	54	d.Fremont ....d.	1005	....	....	....
16.90	....	....	....	1450		d.Columbus ....d.	0900	....	....	....
	....	....	....	|	◇143	d. Sioux City ....a.	|	....	....	....
26.15	....	....	....	1555	174	a.**Norfolk** ....d.	0800	....	....	....

◇– Km ex Norfolk. *BHL*–Black Hills Trailways.

Table 776 DALLAS - LAREDO

ARO CTX GL VT

US $	GL 7255	GL 7265	GL 1211	GL 7271	CTX 561	GL 6415	GL 6469	GL 1213	CTX 563	GL 6471	GL 1219	CTX 565	GL 7251	GL 6459	GL 7907	km	296 ↓ ↑	GL 6466	GL 6410	GL 7252	GL 7254	GL 560	GL 1200	GL 562	GL 1208	GL 7904	GL 564	GL 1216	GL 6464	GL 7280	GL 6462	7
	....	....	1045	....	....		....	1630	....	....	2130	....	....	....	....		d.*Chicago* 716 ....a.	....	....	....	....	....	1345	....	1600	....	....	1930	....	....	....	
0.00	....	....	|	....	....		....	|	....	....	|	....	....	....	....	0	d.*St. Louis* ....a.	....	....	....	....	....	|	....	|	....	....	|	....	....	....	
0.00	0230	0515	0700	0800	0800	....	1250	1305	1315	1630	1800	1800	2030	2200	2300		d.**Dallas** ....d.	1130	....	1615	1600	1830c	1745	2045c	2000	2115	2345c	2315	0130	0430	0500	0
	|	|	|	|	0920	....	|	|	1435	|	|	1920	|	|	|		d.Hillsboro ....d.	1010	....	|	|	1710c	|	1925c	|	|	|	|	|	|	|	
19.00	|	0700	|	|	1015a	....	|	|	1530a	1825	|	2015a	|	2350	|		d.Waco ....d.	0930	....	1435	|	1630c	|	1845c	|	|	2200c	|	2350	|	|	0
24.00	|	0745	|	|	1100a	....	|	|	1615a	1910	|	2100a	|	|	|		d.Temple ....d.	0830	....	1335	|	1530a	|	1755a	|	|	|	|	|	|	|	
	0515	|	|	|	1150a	....	|	|	1710a	|	|	2150a	|	|	|		d.Killeen ....d.	|	....	1250	|	1445a	|	1710a	|	|	2035a	|	|	0145	|	
	|	|	|	|	1300a	....	|	|	1815a	|	|	2250a	|	|	|		d.Round Rock ....d.	|	....	|	|	|	|	1550a	|	|	|	|	|	|	|	
34.00	0645	0915	|	1135	1335	1445	1630	1645	1850b	2035	|	2325b	0005	0155	|		d.Austin ◇ ....d.	0720	0935	1130	1235	1325a	1420	1530a	1635	1750	1915a	1950	2150	0030	0140	0
37.00	0725	0955	|	1215	|	1525	1715	1730	1930b	2115	|	0005b	|	|	|		d.San Marcos ◇ ....d.	0615	|	1030	1130	1220	|	1415	|	|	1815	|	|	2330	|	
	0750	|	|	1240	|	1550	|	|	1955b	|	|	0030b	|	|	|		d.New Braunfels ◇ ....d.	0545	|	1000	1100	|	|	1345	|	|	1745	|	|	2310	|	
	|	|	|	|	|	1630	|	|	|	2145	|	|	|	|	|		d.Seguin ....d.	|	|	|	|	1150	|	|	|	|	|	|	|	|	|	
42.00	0830	1100	1145	1320	1510b	....	1815	1830	2035b	2230	2245	0110b	0140	0330	0345		a.San Antonio ◇ ....d.	0505	0800	0915	1020	1105	1230	1300	1445	1600	1705	1800	2000	2230	2350	(
64.00	1140	1425	1515	1640	1840b	....	2110	2200	2340b	0210	0210	0425b	0510	0655	0655		a.Laredo ....d.	0145	....	0600	0715	0715	0915	0915	1130	1230	1330	1430	1600	1915	2030	2

a- *ARO*. b–*GL*. c–*CTX*. ◇-*VTC* service from Austin 0840, 1000, 1600, 1830, 2000. *VTC*– Valley Transit Co.
from San Antonin 0900, 1215, 1700.

ARO– Arrow Trailways of Texas.
CTX– Central Texas Trailways.
GL– Greyhound Lines.

①–Mondays ②–Tuesdays ③–Wednesdays

Table 777 WICHITA

GL

US $	6209	467	6207		km	395 ↓ ↑	6208	6200	468	
0.00	0015	0730	1330	....	0	d.**Kansas City** .....a.	0915	1740	2235	....
10.00	0105	0830	1435	....	50	d.Lawrence..........d.	0810	1635	2140	....
14.00	0140	0905	1510	....	92	d.Topeka ....d.	0735	1600	2105	....
	|	|	|	....		d. Salina ....d.	|	|	|	....
	|	|	|	....		d. Newton ....d.	|	|	|	....
✤	0515	1240	1855	....	✤	d.Wichita ....d.	0350	1225	1750	....
✤	0740	|	2105	....	✤	d.Ponca City.........d.	|	0945	1535	....
	|	1353	|	....		d. Blackwell.........d.	0222	|	|	....
	0835	|	2200	....		d.Stillwater ....d.	|	0850	1440	....
✤	1015	1555	2325	....	✤	a.**Oklahoma City** .d.	0030	0710	1250	....

GL– Greyhound Lines.

Table 778 ST. LOUIS - DENVER

GL

US $	695 ↓	km		1331	6201		6230 ⑤⑦	1333		1335
	St. Louis.............d.	414	....	0245	0730	....	1330	1330	....	1800
	Kingdom City........d.		....	|	0940	....	|	1550	....	2015
	Columbia.............d.	210	....	|	1010	....	1550	1620	....	2045
0.00	**Kansas City** ......a.	0	....	0650	1240	....	1755	1840	....	2255
	Kansas City ......d.		....	0815	....	....	....	1935	....	0010
10.00	Lawrence ....d.	50	....	0915	....	....	....	2035	....	0100
14.00	Topeka.................d.	92	....	0950	....	....	....	2115	....	0135
23.00	Manhattan............d.	170	....	1105	....	....	....	|	....	|
33.00	Salina ....d.	285	....	1325	....	....	....	0001	....	0425
50.00	Hays.....................d.	435	....	1505	....	....	....	0135	....	0600
	WaKeeney ....d.		....	1555	....	....	....	0225	....	0655
	Oakley..................d.		....	1700	....	....	....	|	....	0800
77.00	Limon ....d.	845	....	1950	....	....	....	0535	....	1100
85.00	**Denver**................d.	1010	....	2140	....	....	....	0715	....	1250

695 ↓		1330		1332				6202 ⑤⑦	1334	6204
enver.....................d.	....	0810	....	1500	....	....	....	....	2230	....
imon ....d.	....	1005	....	1705	....	....	....	....	0001	....
akley.......................d.	....	1455	....	2155	....	....	....	....	|	....
VaKeeney ....d.	....	1600	....	2300	....	....	....	....	0455	....
lays..........................d.	....	1650	....	2345	....	....	....	....	0545	....
alina ....d.	....	1835	....	0125	....	....	....	....	0730	....
lanhattan ....d.	....	|	....	|	....	....	....	....	0945	....
opeka ....d.	....	2135	....	0410	....	....	....	....	1100	....
awrence ....d.	....	2210	....	0445	....	....	....	....	1140	....
ansas City ....a.	....	2300	....	0535	....	....	....	....	1240	....
ansas City ....d.	....	0010	....	0700	....	....	....	1330	1330	1845
olumbia ....d.	....	0225	....	0930	....	....	....	1550	1550	2125
ingdom City.............d.	....	|	....	1005	....	....	....	|	1625	2155
t. Louis....................a.	....	0440	....	1210	....	....	....	1805	1830	2359

GL– Greyhound Lines.

Table 779 DENVER - CHEYENNE

PDR TNO

US $	396 ↓	km	PDR	TNO 436		PDR 102	TNO 422	PDR 120	TNO 420	
0.00	**Denver**.................d.	0	0700	0800	....	1400	1805	2130	2225	....
7.00	Greeley ....d.		|	0955	....	|	1955	|	2335	....
14.25	Fort Collins...........d.		0855	1030	....	1545	2030	2325	0010	....
7.00	Greeley ....d.		0930	|	....	1615	|	0005	|	....
21.00	**Cheyenne**............a.		1030	1120	....	1720	2130	0100	0100	....

96 ↓		PDR 121/41	TNO 425	PDR 125/45	TNO 437		PDR 101		TNO 421	
heyenne..................d.	....	0340	0630	1100	1135	....	1745	....	1930	....
reeley ....d.	....	0430	|	1200	|	....	1845	....	|	....
ort Collins.................d.	....	0500	0725	1235	1225	....	1920	....	2020	....
reeley ....d.	....	|	0805	|	1300	....	|	....	2100	....
enver.......................a.	....	0645	1005	1440	1450	....	2050	....	2205	....

PDR– Powder River Trailways. TNO– TNM&0 Coaches.

Table 780 HOUSTON - ABILENE

ARO KBC

US $	ARO 101	KBC 202	ARO 107	ARO 105	km	396 ↓ ↑	ARO 100	KBC 207	ARO 104	ARO 106
0.00	0615	0715a	1900	2350	0	d.**Houston** ....a.	1730	1825	2130	0315
15.00	0835	|	|	|		d. Bryan............d.	1450	|	|	|
17.00	0905	|	|	|		d. Hearne..........d.	1415	|	|	|
12.00	|	0835	|	|		d.Brenham ....d.	|	1640	|	|
30.00	|	1010	2200	0250	264	d.Austin................d.	|	1445a	1830	0030
37.00	1030	....	....	....	291	d. Temple............d.	1305	....	....	....
40.00	1135	....	....	....	325	d.Killeen ....d.	1215	....	....	....
44.00	1350	....	....	....	380	d.Lampasas..........d.	0955	....	....	....
59.00	1550	....	....	....	492	d.Brownwood ....d.	0805	....	....	....
59.00	1640	....	....	....		d. Coleman.....d.	0720	....	....	....
67.00	1740	....	....	....	570	a.**Abilene**............d.	0615	....	....	....

a– Local trips also operate Houston-Austin and v.v.; from Houston *(KBC)* at 0900, 1130, 1430, 1730 ; from Austin *(KBC)* at 0900, 1155, 1315, 1700.
ARO– Arrow Trailways of Texas. KBC–Kerrville Bus Co.

Table 781 OMAHA - SALT LAKE CITY

GL STS

US $	296 ↓	km	GL 1315	GL 1301	GL 1357	GL 1305	GL 1341	STS 7 ④	GL 1347	GL 1307
	Chicago **716**.........d.	0	1445	1845	....	0035	....	....	1130	1145
0.00	**Omaha**................d.	0	0145	0445	....	1210	....	....	2130	2200
11.00	Lincoln..................d.	87	0250	0605	....	1315	....	....	2235	2305
26.00	Grand Island ....d.	232	|	0830	....	1520	....	....	|	|
33.00	Kearney................d.	305	|	0935	....	1615	....	1600	|	|
43.00	North Plate ....d.	460	0705	1155	....	1805	....	|	|	|
28.00	Hastings ....d.	247	|	|	....	|	....	|	|	|
	Minden ....d.	299	|	|	....	|	....	1700	|	|
50.00	McCook.........d.	452	|	|	....	|	....	....	|	|
	Sterling ....d.		|	1440	....	2020	....	....	|	0450
70.00	Fort Morgan.....d.	722	|	1535	....	2115	....	....	|	0545
77.00	**Denver**..............a.	852	|	1700	....	2240	....	....	|	0710
	Denver..............d.		|	1830	1915	0001	0001	....	|	0840
	Kimball ....d.		1005	|	|	|	|	....	|	|
73.00	**Cheyenne**............d.	820	1245	|	|	|	|	....	0640	|
	Laramie ....d.	907	1350	|	2155	|	0240	....	0735	|
85.00	Rawlins ....d.	1069	1535	|	|	|	0425	....	0934	|
	Rock Springs........d.	1244	1755	|	0150	|	0645	....	1155	|
104.00	**Salt Lake City** .....a.	1595	2125	|	0505	|	1020	....	1540	|
142.00	*Los Angeles* **843** ..a.	2795	|	1635	|	2055	....	....	|	0625
142.00	*San Francisco* **842** ..a.	2845	1330	....	2230	....	....	....	0840	....

296 ↓	STS 8 ④	GL 1340	GL 1312	GL 1314	GL 6244	GL 1342	GL 1348		GL 1306	GL 1308
San Francisco **842** .....d.	....	....	....	1300	....	....	....	....	1815	0030
Los Angeles **842** ......d.	....	0900	1400	|	....	....	2315	....	|	|
Salt Lake City ....d.	....	|	|	0800	0800	....	|	....	1145	1900
Rock Springs.............d.	....	|	|	1220	1201	....	|	....	1540	2305
Rawlins ....d.	....	|	|	1410	1350	....	|	....	1730	0050
Laramie ....d.	....	|	|	1545	1535	....	|	....	1915	0235
Cheyenne ....d.	....	|	|	1715	|	....	|	....	|	0335
Kimball ....d.	....	|	|	|	|	....	|	....	|	0550
Denver......................a.	....	1020	1325	|	1810	....	2225	....	2145	|
Denver......................d.	....	1100	1445	|	....	1820	2340	....	....	|
Fort Morgan...........d.	....	1220	1605	|	....	|	0055	....	....	|
Stirling ....d.	....	1320	1705	|	....	|	0155	....	....	|
McCook..............d.	1300	|	|	|	....	|	|	....	....	|
Minden ....d.	|	|	|	|	....	|	|	....	....	|
Hastings............d.	|	|	|	|	....	|	|	....	....	|
North Platte..............d.	|	1750	2130	|	....	|	0550	....	....	1140
Kearney.....................d.	1400	1945	|	|	....	|	0735	....	....	1350
Grand Island ....d.	....	2040	0005	|	....	|	0825	....	....	1545
Lincoln......................d.	....	2305	|	|	....	|	1045	....	....	1735
Omaha.......................a.	....	0005	0245	0335	....	0510	1145	....	....	1835
Chicago **716**..............a.	....	1230	1315	1350	....	1850	2230	....	....	0530

GL– Greyhound Lines.
STS– Senlow Transportation

Table 783 DALLAS/FORT WORTH - HOUSTON

ARO CTX GL

US $	296 ↓	km	GL 7219	GL 7265	GL 7205	CTX 30	GL 7207	GL 1254	GL 6481 ⑤	ARO 100	GL 7231	CTX 17A	GL 7209	GL 1248	CTX 32	CTX 5	GL 6489	GL 6487	GL 1262	CTX 19A	CTX 34	GL 7233	GL 7227	CTX 18A	GL 6459
	Fort Worth....d.	★120	....	....	....	....	....	....	....	....	....	1245	....	....	....	....	....	....	....	1745	....	....	....	2100	....
0.00	**Dallas** ....d.	0	0115	0515	0530	0800	0700	0800	1030	....	....	|	1210	1310	1315	....	1500a	1615	1700	|	1800	....	2030	|	2200
19.00	Waco..................d.	150	|	0655	0745	1000	|	|	1215	....	....	1510	|	|	1515	1630	1645	|	|	1950	2000	....	|	2325	2340
30.00	Hearne ....d.	270	|	....	0905	....	|	|	1335	1415	....	....	|	|	....	|	1805	|	|	....	....	....	|	....	....
32.00	Bryan ....d.	303	|	....	0940	....	|	|	1410	1450	....	....	|	|	....	|	1840	|	|	....	....	....	|	....	....
11.00	Corsicana.........d.	91	|	....	|	....	0810	|	|	|	....	....	1320	|	....	1750	|	1725	|	....	....	....	|	....	....
	Buffalo ....d.		|	....	|	....	0915	|	|	|	....	....	|	|	....	....	|	1830	|	....	....	....	|	....	....
31.00	Huntsville ....d.	276	|	....	|	....	1045	|	|	|	1410	....	1530	|	....	....	|	2005	|	....	....	2155	|	....	....
39.00	**Houston** ....a.	463	0515	....	1215	....	1215	1215	1645	1730	1540	....	1700	1725	....	....	2115	2130	2115	....	....	2325	0045	....	....

96 ↓		GL 7288	GL 1253	CTX 17	GL 7250	ARO 101	GL 6484	GL 7232	GL 6486	GL 7252	GL 6490	GL 6488	CTX 18	CTX 31	GL 1261	CTX 33	GL 6494	GL 6492	GL 6480	CTX 19	CTX 35	CTX 5A	GL 7212	GL 7230	GL 6464
ouston ....d.	....	....	0330	....	....	0615	0615	0730	0800	....	1145	1245	....	....	1430	....	1600	1700	1830	....	....	....	2100	2145	....
Huntsville ....d.	....	....	|	....	....	|	0750	0900	|	....	|	1415	....	....	|	....	|	1845	|	....	....	....	|	2315	....
Buffalo ....d.	....	....	|	....	....	|	0925	....	|	....	|	|	....	....	|	....	|	2015	|	....	....	....	|	....	....
Corsicana................d.	....	....	|	....	....	|	1030	....	|	....	|	1630	....	....	|	....	|	2120	|	....	....	2215	|	....	....
ryan ....d.	....	....	|	....	....	0840	|	....	|	....	1410	|	....	....	|	....	1845	|	|	....	....	|	|	....	....
earne ....d.	....	....	|	....	....	0905	|	....	|	....	1440	|	....	....	|	....	1910	|	|	....	....	|	|	....	....
/aco..........................d.	....	0545	|	0930	0930	....	|	....	|	1415	1605	|	1630	1630	|	1845	2045	|	|	2200	2200	2330	|	....	2350
allas ....a.	....	0725	0730	|	1130	....	1145	....	1215	1600	1745a	1745	|	1830	1845	2045	2230	2230	2245	|	2345	....	0115	....	0130
Fort Worth..........a.	....	....	....	1201	....	....	....	....	....	....	....	....	1850	....	....	....	....	....	....	2340	....	....	....	....	....

– ⑤⑦ only b–*GL*. c–*CTX*.
– Km ex Waco.

ARO– Arrow Trailways of Texas. CTX–Central Texas Trailways.
GL– Greyhound Lines.

Table 785 DALLAS - FORT WORTH - ABILENE - EL PASO

GL

US$		1415	1419	1409		1407		1241	1413		1435	km	296 ↓ ↑		1418		1416		1250	1412	1408	1404	1414	
0.00	....	0001	0245	0530	....	0830	....	1320	1815	....	1930	*0*	d.**Dallas** a.	....	1730	....	2245	....	0145	0440	0700	0725	1025	....
7.00	....	0050	|	0620	....	0920	....	1420	|	....	2020	*50*	d.**Fort Worth** a.	....	1640	....	2200	....	0100	|	|	0615	0935	....
17.00	....	|	|	0725	....	|	....	1525	|	....	|	*126*	d.Mineral Wells d.	....	1525	....	|	....	|	|	|	|	0830	....
	....	|	|	0857	....	|	....	|	|	....	|		d.Albany a.	....	|	....	|	....	|	|	|	|	0657	....
25.00	....	|	|	|	....	1122	....	1637	|	....	|	*215*	d. Eastland d.	....	|	....	1958	....	|	|	|	0448	|	....
34.00	....	0345	0645	1010	....	1305	....	1845	2145	....	2330	*321*	d.**Abilene** d.	....	1325	....	1850	....	2220	0130	0350	0340	0615	....
39.00	....	|	0735	1105	....	1355	....	1940	|	....	|	*389*	d.Sweetwater d.	....	1201	....	1715	....	**as**	|	|	|	0445	....
50.00	....	0550	0855	1230	....	1515	....	2110	|	....	0130	*471*	d.Big Spring d.	....	1045	....	1555	....	2000	2305	|	0125	0335	....
56.00	....	0640	0945	1320	....	1610	....	2200	|	....	0220	*534*	d.Midland d.	....	0950	....	1500	....	1905	2200	0135	0020	0235	....
56.00	....	0800	1035	1405	....	1655	....	2245	0050	....	0255	*567*	d.Odessa d.	....	0920	....	1430	....	1835	2130	|	2350	0205	....
64.00	....	0930	1205	1535	....	1825	....	0015	|	....	|	*687*	d.Pecos d.	....	|	....	1240	....	1700	1940	|	2225	0020	....
73.00	....	1115	1410	1740	....	2045	....	|	|	....	|	*827*	d.Van Horn d.	....	0615	....	1105	....	1530	1810	2125	2055	2255	....
85.00	....	1220	1540	1845	....	2150	....	0250	0505	....	0645	*1027*	a.**El Paso** d.	....	0235	....	0725	....	1140	1430	1800	1735	1930	....
118.00	....	2215	0100	0315	....	0630	....	1230	1440	....	1615	*1677*	a.*Phoenix* d.	....	1725	....	2140	....	0245	0500	0845	0800	0930	....
142.00	....	0505	0825	1050	....	1625	....	2015	2115	....	2300	*2327*	a.*Los Angeles* d.	....	0700	....	1120	....	1800	2000	2345	2140	0040	....

a– Calls on ⑦ only. *GL*–Greyhound Lines.

Table 786 DALLAS - DENVER

TNO

US$	396 ↓	km	458	438			436	434	430	
0.00	**Dallas** d.	*0*	....	0220	....	....	1300	1830	2300	....
4.45	**Fort Worth** d.	*50*	....	|	....	....	1400	1930	2345	....
16.85	Wichita Falls d.	*225*	....	0540	....	....	1630	2215	0200	....
	Vernon d.		....	0630	....	....	1735	2320	0250	....
	Quanah d.		....	0710	....	....	1815	0001	0320	....
41.10	**Amarillo** d.	*585*	....	1205	....	....	2235	0400	0730	....
	Wichita d.	*◇490*	0515	|	....	....	|	|	|	....
	Pratt d.		0657	|	....	....	|	|	|	....
	Dodge City d.	*◇240*	0845	|	....	....	|	|	|	....
	Garden City d.	*◇157*	1000	|	....	....	|	|	|	....
65.60	Lamar d.	*944*	1110	1520	....	....	0215	0715	|	....
72.50	La Junta d.	*1035*	1240	1700	....	....	0330	0855	|	....
79.40	**Pueblo** a.	*1145*	1405	1825	....	....	0440	1025	1345	....
82.85	*Denver* a.	*1294*	....	2200	....	....	0730	1330	1700	....

396 ↓	459	439			435			437		431
Denver d.	....	0715	....	....	1045	....	....	1600	....	2300
Pueblo d.	0135	1015	....	....	1410	....	....	1920	....	0135
La Junta d.	0300	1135	....	....	1535	....	....	2045	....	|
Lamar d.	0410	1305	....	....	1700	....	....	2155	....	|
Garden City d.	0705	|	....	....	|	....	....	|	....	|
Dodge City d.	0830	|	....	....	|	....	....	|	....	|
Pratt d.	1000	|	....	....	|	....	....	|	....	|
Wichita a.	1140	|	....	....	|	....	....	|	....	|
Amarillo d.	....	1920	....	....	2315	....	....	0355	....	1015
Quanah d.	....	2205	....	....	**s**	....	....	0640	....	1305
Vernon d.	....	2245	....	....	**s**	....	....	0715	....	1340
Wichita Falls d.	....	2359	....	....	0345	....	....	0840	....	1500
Fort Worth a.	....	|	....	....	0605	....	....	1045	....	1715
Dallas a.	....	0245	....	....	0700	....	....	1145	....	1815

◇–Km ex Lamar. *TNO*–TNM&O Coaches.

Table 787 DALLAS - FORT WORTH

396 COMPLETE SERVICE *GL KBC TNO*

service Dallas-Fort Worth and v.v. *50* km. Journey: ¾-1¼ hours. Fare: US$: 7.00.
From Dallas: *GL* at 0001, 0530, 0800**a**, 0830, 1245**a**, 1300, 1320, 1815, 1930; *KBC* at 0800; *TNO* at 1300, 1830, 2300.
From Fort Worth: *GL* at 0105, 0630, 0945, 1020**a**, 1430**a**, 1645, 1835**a**, 1930, 2205; *KBC* at 1950; *TNO* at 0610, 1050, 1720.

a– Stops at Irving and Arlington.
GL– Greyhound Lines. *KBC*–Kerrville Bus Co. *TNO*–TNM&O Coaches.

Table 789 195 HOUSTON - GALVESTON

TXB

service Houston-Galveston and v.v. *81* km. Journey: 1¼-1¾ hours. Fare: US$: 4.50.
From Houston: 0645, 1000, 1330, 1700.
From Galveston: 0830, 1130, 1515, 1845.

TXB– Texas Bus Lines.

Table 790 TUCSON - DOUGLAS

BWTS

US$	2	4		6	km	695 ↓ ↑	5	3	1	
0.00	0700	1300	....	1800	*0*	d.**Tucson** a.	1230	1830	2245	....
14.00	0830	1430	....	1930	*122*	d.Sierra Vista d.	1100	1700	|	....
19.00	0930	1530	....	2030	*227*	a.**Douglas** d.	1000	1600	2045	....

BWTS–Bridgewater Transport.

Table 794 AMARILLO - SAN ANTONIO

KBC TNO

US$	*TNO* 441	*TNO* 443		*TNO* 447	km	396 ↓ ↑		*KBC* 703	*KBC* 705	*KBC* 707
0.00	0400	0930	....	1900	*0*	d.**Amarillo** a.	....	2140**b**	0230**b**	0700**b**
	0550	1110	....	2055		d.Plainview d.	....	1940**b**	0050**b**	0515**b**
	0745	1240	....	2305		d.Lubbock d.	....	1835**b**	2359**b**	0425**b**
	0915	1405	....	0025		d.Lamesa d.	....	1645**b**	2215**b**	0230**b**
	1050**a**	1605**a**	....	0140**a**		d.Big Spring d.	....	1555**b**	2115**b**	0145**b**
	1240**a**	1750**a**	....	0320**a**		d.San Angelo d.	....	1305	1905	2335
	1415**a**	1915**a**	....	0455**a**		d.Brady d.	....	1125	1725	2155
	1725**a**	2205**a**	....	0800**a**		a.**San Antonio** d.	....	0815	1420	1830

a–*KBC*. b–*TNO*. *KBC*–Kerrville Bus Co. *TNO*–TNM&O Coaches.

Table 791 MEMPHIS - OKLAHOMA CITY

GL JL

US$	296 ↓	km		*GL* 6141	*JL* 714		*JL* 702	*GL* 6143		
0.00	**Memphis** d.	*0*	....	*0245*	....	....	....	2140	....	....
24.00	Little Rock d.	*220*	....	0615	1110	....	1800	0030	....	....
44.00	Fort Smith d.	*456*	....	1015	1530	....	2100	0345	....	....
56.00	Muskogee d.	*551*	....	1150	|	....	|	0515	....	....
	McAlester d.	*590*	....	|	1800	....	|	|	....	....
	Shawnee d.		....	1420	2000	....	2330	0730	....	....
73.00	**Oklahoma City** a.	*766*	....	1500	2045	....	0015	0810	....	....

296 ↓	*JL* 120		*GL* 6140					*GL* 6142		*JL* 124
Oklahoma City d.	0415	....	1100	....	....	....	....	1915	....	0010
McAlester d.	0700	....	|	....	....	....	....	|	....	|
Shawnee d.	0500	....	1140	....	....	....	....	1955	....	0050
Muskogee d.	|	....	1415	....	....	....	....	2210	....	|
Fort Smith d.	1000	....	1615	....	....	....	....	2350	....	0320
Little Rock a.	1330	....	1955	....	....	....	....	0250	....	0600
Memphis a.	....	....	*2245*	....	....	....	....	0530	....	....

GL–Greyhound Lines.
JL–Jefferson Lines.

Table 792 SHREVEPORT - HOUSTON

KBC

US$	196 ↓	km		810	814	806	802	818		804
0.00	Texarkana d.		....	....	0730	....	....	1415	....	....
	Shreveport d.	*0*	....	0630	0915	1015	1315	1600	....	1800
	Nacogdoches d.	*145*	....	0850	....	1245	1525	....	....	2020
	Houston a.	*342*	....	1150	....	1555	1945	....	....	2325

196 ↓			803	815	805		807	809	811	
Houston d.	....	....	0945	....	1415	....	2030	0115	....	....
Nacogdoches d.	....	....	1320	....	1745	....	2340	0415	....	....
Shreveport d.	....	....	1600	1700	2005	....	0200	0640	0745	....
Texarkana a.	....	....	....	1830	....	....	....	....	0930	....

KBC– Kerrville Bus Co.

Table 793 NORTON - DODGE CITY

BLB

US $	101 ex⑦				km	195 ↓ ↑		102 ex⑦		
0.00	0800	....	....	....	*0*	d.**Norton** a.	....	1620	....	....
10.90	0910	....	....	....		d.WaKeeney d.	....	1500	....	....
29.05	1105	....	....	....		a.**Dodge City** d.	....	1230	....	....

BLB– Bickel Bus Line.

Table 796 KANSAS CITY - TEXARKANA

JL KBC

US$	*JL* 103	*KBC* 817	*JL* 117	*KBC* 813	km	196 ↓ ↑	*KBC* 816	*JL* 302	*JL* 312	*JL* 314
0.00	0020	....	1830	....	*0*	d.**Kansas City** a.	....	0700	1815	2310
	0310	....	2120	....		d.Fort Scott d.	....	0410	|	2035
	0535	....	2255	....	*242*	d.Joplin d.	....	0250	1435	1920
	0945	1000	0305	0315	*458*	d.Fort Smith d.	2220	2230	0945	1500
	....	1400	....	0715	*761*	a.**Texarkana** d.	1835	....	....	*0940*

a–*KBC*. b–*JL*. *JL*–Jefferson Lines. *KBC*–Kerrville Bus Co.

Table 797 EAGLE PASS

KBC

US$	107	109	111	113	km	196 ↓ ↑	108	110	112	114
0.00	0850	1230	1830	2300	*0*	d.**San Antonio** d.	1000	1620	2000	0115
10.40	1015	|	|	0050	*125*	d.Uvalde d.	0815	|	|	2325
	1150	1530	2130	0215	*225*	a.**Eagle Pass** d.	0700	1320	1700	2200

KBC–Kerrville Bus Co.

⑦–Sundays ©–Saturdays, Sundays and holidays †–Sundays and holidays

Table 798 HOUSTON - BROWNSVILLE GL VTC

US $	GL 7227	VTC 201	GL 7219	VTC 202	VTC 63	VTC 203	GL 7217	VTC 204	GL 7229	VTC 205	VTC 206	GL 7221	VTC 207	GL 1265	VTC 208	km	296 ↓
0.00	0125	0400	0600	0600	....	1220	1245	1340	1400	1625	1745	1800	2015	2145	2145	0	d.Houston
15.30	|	|	0845	0850	....	1500	1510	|	1645	1935	|	2030	2315	0005	0020	115	d.Victoria
	|	0720	|	|	....	|	|	1630	|	|	|	|	|	|	|		d. Port Lavaca
25.85	|	0915	1100	1115	1300	1715	1710	1900	1900	2140	2220	2230	0130	|	0230	320	d.Corpus Christi
	|	|	|	|	1400	|	1815	|	|	|	|	2325	|	|	|		d. Alice
	|	|	|	|	1620	|	|	|	|	|	|	0140	|	|	|	550	a. Laredo
32.95	|	1010	1201	1215	....	1810	|	2000	2000	|	|	....	0215s	|	0315s	383	d.Kingsville
	|	1210	1355	1410	....	2015	|	2200	2155	0040	0040	....	0405	|	0510	538	d. Harlingen
	0845	1345	*1530*	1540	....	2130	2050	0210	*2340*	0210	|	....	0515	0515	0730	587	a. McAllen ◇
43.70	1045	1310	1435	*1510*	....	*2110*	2200	2310	2230	*0120*	0120	....	*0510*	0715	*0555*	608	a.Brownsville

296 ↑	GL 7210	VTC 51	VTC 101	GL 6480	VTC 103	VTC 102	VTC 104	GL 7214	VTC 105	VTC 53	VTC 106	GL 7218	VTC 107	GL 1264	VTC 108
Houston a.	1245	....	1515	1745	1745	1845	2000	2110	2135	....	0015	0515	0300	0700	0545
Victoria d.	0955	....	1215	1500	|	|	1715	1840		....	|	0245	0010	|	0345
Port Lavaca d.	|	....	|	|	1415	|	|	|	|	....	|	|	|	|	|
Corpus Christi d.	0800	1105	1020	1315	1230	1430	1515	|	1710	1700	2000	0100	2220	|	0130
Alice d.	0645	1005	|	1155	|	|	|	|	|	1555	|	2340	|	|	|
Laredo d.	0430	....	|	|	|	|	|	|	|	1345	|	|	|	|	|
Kingsville d.	....	....	0910	*1201*	|	1320	1400	|	1600	....	|	|	2115	|	|
Harlingen d.	....	....	0715	0800	0915	1115	1215	1215	1415	....	1715	1945	1915	*2230*	2215
McAllen ◇ d.	....	....	0600	0930	0745	0945	1045	1345	1245	....	1545	2110	1745	0001	2030
Brownsville d.	....	....	0615	0715	0815	*1015*	*1115*	1130	*1315*	....	*1615*	1900	*1815*	2240	*2115*

◇– Regular service (*VTC*) McAllen-Reynosa 0530 and every 15 mins to 2230; Reynosa-McAllen 0545 and every 15 mins to 2300.
GL– Greyhound Lines.
VTC– Valley Transit Co.

Table 800 MIDLAND - PRESIDIO/SAN ANGELO CCI IBU

US $	CCI 4 ◇	CCI 6 ◇	IBU 2	CCI 8 Ⓐ	km	195 ↓ ↑	CCI 3 ◇	IBU 1	CCI 5 ◇	CCI 7 Ⓐ
	0745	1245	....	1800		d.San Angelo ....a.	1550	....	1940	0030
0.00	0945	1445	1740	2000	0	d.**Midland** ....d.	1345	1510	1730	|
2.30	1020	1520	1840	2040	33	d.Odessa...........d.	1310	1430	1700	2100
8.75	....	....	2055	....	173	d.Fort Stockton.....d.	....	1235	....	....
13.70	....	....	2225	....	278	d.Alpine..............d.	....	1105	....	....
15.60	....	....	2300	....	333	d.Marfa...............d.	....	1030	....	....
19.90	....	....	0015	....	428	a.**Presidio** ....d.	....	0915	....	....

◇–Daily except holidays. *CCI*–Concho Coaches. *IBU*–All American Travels.

Table 801 DEL RIO - BROWNSVILLE GL VTC

US $	VTC 1D	GL 1474	VTC 63	GL 1476	km	296 ↓ ↑	GL 1475	VTC 1L	GL 1477	VTC 55
51.00	....	0545	....	1300	0	d.**Del Rio** ....a.	1810	....	2305	....
43.00	....	0700	....	1415		d.Eagle Pass........d.	1655	....	2155	....
29.00	0800	1000	1700	1715		d.**Laredo**.............d.	1425	1305	1925	2105
23.50	0900	1105	1800	1820		d.Zapata..............d.	1300	1205	1800	2005
8.00	1145	1340	2020	2050		d.McAllen ★........d.	1045	0925	1545	1745
8.00	1210	r	2105	s		d.Alamo ★...........d.	r	0900	s	1715
4.00	1315	1500	2200	2300		d.Harlingen ★......d.	0915	0800	1415	1615
0.00	1410	1540	2310	2240		a.**Brownsville** ★ .d.	0830	0700	1330	1515

★–Regular service (*VTC*), 0545, 0645, 0735ex⑦, 0845 and hourly to1745, 2020, 2355 McAllen-Brownsville, returning 0015, 0515, 0600, 0700, 0815 and hourly to 1715, 1945.
GL–Greyhound Lines. *VTC*–Valley Transit Co.

Table 802 DENVER - SALT LAKE CITY GL

US $		6241		6243	km	695 ↓ ↑	6240			6242
0.00	....	0830	....	2200	0	d.**Denver**.............a.	2000	....	....	0655
10.00	....	1025	....	2340	120	d.Winter Park ....d.	1805	....	....	0505
13.00	....	1050	....	0020	150	d.Granby ....d.	1745	....	....	0445
27.50	....	1340	....	0235	280	d.Steamboat Springs...d.	1545	....	....	0250
35.25	....	1445	....	0340	348	d.Craig ....d.	1410	....	....	0120
45.75	....	1625	....	0520	493	d.Dinosaur............d.	1225	....	....	2335
45.75	....	1705	....	0600	548	d.Vernal................d.	1145	....	....	2300
65.00	....	2020	....	0915	822	d.Heber City.........d.	0830	....	....	2000
65.00	....	2120	....	1015	888	a.**Salt Lake City** ..d.	0730	....	....	1900

GL– Greyhound Lines.

Table 803 GRAND FORKS - BISMARCK TRT

US $		501			km	695 ↓ ↑		500		
25.15	....	1025	....	....		d.**Grand Forks**.....a.	....	2130	....	....
14.90	....	1245	....	....		d.Devil's Lake.......d.	....	1925	....	....
0.00	....	1530	....	....	0	d.**Minot** ....d.	....	1630	....	....
6.10	....	....	....	....	82	d.Coleharbor Ω.....d.	....	....	....	....
14.30	....	....	....	....	185	a.**Bismarck**..........d.	....	....	....	....
	....	....	....	....	275	a. Jamestown......d.	....	....	....	....

Ω– For Audobon Wildlife Refuge and Lake Sakakawea.
TRT– Triangle Transportation.

Table 804 AMARILLO - EL PASO TNO

US$		451	453	455	km	396 ↓ ↑	450	452	426	454
0.00	....	0330	1150	1835	0	d.**Amarillo**...........a.	1815	2210	....	0330
	....	0420	1245	1925	76	d.Hereford ....d.	1725	2115	....	0240
14.65	....	0445	1320	1950	170	d.Clovis ....d.	1505	1855	....	0035
	....	0510	1345	2015	201	d.Portales.............d.	1430	1820	....	0005
27.35	....	0710	1545	2230	350	d.Roswell ....d.	1245	1640	....	2225
44.00	....	0940	1830	0055	535	d.Alamogordo.......d.	0930	1355	1355	1945
52.40	....	1100	2000	|	645	a.Las Cruces........d.	|	1215	|	1810
	....	|	|	f		a.Orogrande.........d.	|	|	f	|
52.40	....	1150	2055	0245	703	a.**El Paso**.............d.	0730	1110	1215	1715

TNO– TNM&O Coaches.

Table 805 196 BOISE - SUN VALLEY SVS

Local service Boise Airport-Sun Valley and v.v. ❖ km. Journey: 3 hours. Fare: US $: 35.00.
From Sun Valley: 0800R, returning at 1415R.

R– Dec. 15-end of ski season only. *SVS*–Sun Valley Stages.

Table 806 DEL RIO KBC

US $	101	103	105		km	495 ↓ ↑	102	104		106
0.00	0815	1300	1820	....	0	d.**San Antonio**.....a.	1050	1645	....	2115
10.40	1030	1505	2020	....	128	d.Uvalde..............d.	0840	1435	....	1905
14.35	1155	1635	2150	....	244	a.**Del Rio** ....d.	0700	1300	....	1730

KBC– Kerrville Bus Co.

Table 807 DENVER - GRAND JUNCTION GL

US $	196 ↓	km	1307					5915	1301	1303
0.00	**Denver**.................d.	0	0840	....	....	....	....	1530	1900	0001
	Idaho Springs.......d.		|	....	....	....	....	1615	1945	|
24.00	Vail......................d.	179	1035	....	....	....	....	1735	2140	0150
37.00	Glenwood Springs d.	256	1215	....	....	....	....	1910	2315	0325
43.00	Rifle......................d.		1250	....	....	....	....	1945	|	|
	Aspen ....a.	324	|	....	....	....	....	|	|	|
52.00	**Grand Junction** ..a.	395	1400	....	....	....	....	2100	0030	0410

196 ↓			1310		1312	1302	5912			
Grand Junction ....d.	....	....	0445	....	0745	1210	1600	....	....	....
Aspen ....d.	....	....	|	....	|	|	|	....	....	....
Rifle.........................d.	....	....	|	....	0858	1320	1710	....	....	....
Glenwood Springs ......d.	....	....	0625	....	0935	1355	1745	....	....	....
Vail...........................d.	....	....	0755	....	1115	1525	1915	....	....	....
Idaho Springs............d.	....	....	0935	....	1240	|	|	....	....	....
Denver......................a.	....	....	1020	....	1325	1740	2210	....	....	....

GL– Greyhound Lines.

Table 808 OKLAHOMA CITY - EL PASO CAR JL SWT TNO

US $	JL 329		JL 335	JL 325	km	396 ↓ ↑	JL 330	JL 334	JL 326	
0.00	2155	....	1030	1630	0	d.**Oklahoma City** .a.	2130	0805	1159	....
	2255	....	1135	1730	78	d.Chickasha ....d.	2030	0705	1100	....
	|	....	|	1800	107	d.Anadarko...........d.	|	0635	|	....
	0010	....	1320	1905	144	d.Lawton *(Fort Sill)* d.	1930	0535	1000	....
	0115	....	1420	2110		a. Wichita Falls d.	1715	0315	0855	....
	TNO 351		TNO 353		228	Wichita Falls ..		TNO 352	TNO 354	
	0155	....	1700	....		d. Wichita Falls a.	....	0130	0815	....
	0255	....	1800	....	311	d.Seymour............d.	....	0020	0715	....
	r	....	1920	....	413	d.Guthrie ....d.	....	2305	r	....
	r	....	2000	....		d.Dickens ....d.	....	2230	0530	....
	0700	....	2230	....	563	d.Lubbock ....d.	....	2100	0415	....
	0745	....	0001	....		d.Brownfield ....d.	....	1845	0245	....
	0830	....	|	....	687	d.Seminole ....d.	....	|	0200	....
	0805	....	0100	....	734	d.Hobbs.................d.	....	1555	0035	....
	0945	....	0230	....	845	d.Carlsbad.............d.	....	1430	2315	....
	r	....	r	....	874	d.Whites City ....d.	....	r	r	....
	1305	....	0545	....	1138	a.**El Paso**.............d.	....	1100	1930	....
US $		①③⑤		①③⑤	km	195 *SWT* ↓ ↑	①③⑤		①③⑤	
0.00	....	1010	....	2010	0	d.Lawton ....a.	1000	....	1815	....
	....	1115	....	2125		a.**Altus**...................d.	0830	....	1645	....
R.T. US $					km	395 *CAR* ↓ ↑				
0.00	1050	....	....	....	0	d.Whites City........a.	1120	....	....	....
5.00	1105	....	....	....	10	a.**Carlsbad Caverns** .d.	1110	....	....	....

CAR– Carlsbad Caverns Coaches.
JL– Jefferson Lines.
SWT– Southwest Transit.
TNO– TNM&O Coaches.

Table 810 CARLSBAD TNO

US $		203 ex⑥⑦		201	km	695 ↓ ↑	204 ex①⑦		202	
0.00	....	0845	....	1715	0	d.**Albuquerque** ....a.	1115	....	1615	....
	....	1045	....	1940	170	d.Vaughn.............d.	0905	....	1415	....
	....	1245	....	2135	320	d.Roswell ....d.	0715	....	1215	....
	....	1345	....	2230	391	d.Artesia...............d.	0535	....	1050	....
	....	1430	....	2315	449	d.**Carlsbad**...........d.	0445	....	1000	....
	....	....	....	....	588	d.Pecos.................d.	....	....	....	....
	....	....	....	....	672	a.**Fort Stockton**...d.	....	....	....	....

TNO– TNM&O Coaches.

Table 811 ALBUQUERQUE - ABILENE TNO

US $				379	km	396 ↓ ↑				378
0.00	....	....	....	1530	0	d.**Albuquerque** ....a.	....	....	....	0030
8.75	....	....	....	1715	170	d.Santa Rosa ....d.	....	....	....	2230
	....	....	....	1800		d.Ft Sumner ....d.	....	....	....	2140
	....	....	....	|		d.Portales.............d.	....	....	....	2020
18.00	....	....	....	1940	355	d.Clovis ....d.	....	....	....	1955
50.35	....	....	....	2345	515	d.Lubbock ....d.	....	....	....	1810
	....	....	....	0225	699	d.Sweetwater ....d.	....	....	....	1400
74.90	....	....	....	0315	765	a.**Abilene**.............d.	....	....	....	1315

TNO– TNM&O Coaches.

Table 812 195 DENVER - BOULDER ♿ — RTD

Bus service Denver-Boulder and v.v. *49* km. Journey: 50 mins. Fare: US$: 2.50.
From Denver 16th & Market ◇: 0007ex①, 0008⑦, 0107ex①, 0108⑦, 0538Ⓐ, 0608Ⓐ, 0623Ⓐ, 0638Ⓐ, 0640Ⓐ, 0653Ⓐ, 0655Ⓐ, 0708⚒, 0710Ⓐ, 0723Ⓐ, 0730Ⓐ, 0738Ⓐ, 0753Ⓐ, 0800Ⓐ, 0808, 0823Ⓐ, 0830Ⓐ and frequent to 2107⑤, 2108⑥, 2137Ⓐ, 2207⑤, 2208⑥, 2307⑤, 2308⑥.
From Boulder ◇: 0440Ⓐ, 0500⚒, 0515Ⓐ, 0530Ⓐ, 0543Ⓐ, 0552Ⓐ, 0600, 0603Ⓐ, 0613Ⓐ, 0622Ⓐ, 0630Ⓐ, 0635Ⓐ, 0643Ⓐ, 0650Ⓐ, 0658Ⓐ, 0700, 0706Ⓐ, 0714Ⓐ, 0718Ⓐ, 0726Ⓐ, 0730Ⓐ, 0734Ⓐ, 0742Ⓐ, 0750Ⓐ, 0758Ⓐ, 0800 and frequent to 2000, 2030Ⓐ, 2105, 2205, 2305.
RTD operates frequent bus services throughout the Denver Metropolitan area.

◇–Most trips are extended to serve Stapleton Airport.
RTD–Regional Transportation District.

Table 813 DENVER - ALBUQUERQUE — TNO

US$	396 ↓	km	439	427	435	425	437	423	431	421
0.00	**Denver** d.	*0*	0715	0715	1045	1045	1600	1815	2300	2300
	Aurora d.		0740	|	1110	|	1625	|	|	|
14.00	Colorado Springs d.	*115*	0910	0915	1240	1245	1805	1955	0030	0030
22.00	Pueblo d.	*185*	1000	1025	1335	1405	1855	2100	0135	0135
	Walsenburg d.		....	1110	....	1455	....	s	0225	|
	Alamosa d.		....	|	....	1635	....	|	|	|
	Antonito d.		....	|	....	1705	....	|	|	|
34.00	Trinidad d.	*320*	....	1155	....	|	....	2215	|	0300
37.99	Raton d.	*353*	....	1245	....	|	....	2250	0335	0335
	Capulin d.	*400*	....	|	....	|	....	|	r	|
	Dalhart d.	*553*	....	|	....	|	....	|	0705	|
	Amarillo d.	*715*	....	|	....	|	....	|	0915	|
	Springer d.	*423*	....	1330	....	|	....	|	....	|
53.00	Las Vegas d.	*535*	....	1440	....	|	....	0040	....	|
	Cimarron d.		....	|	....	|	....	|	....	0430
47.30	Taos d.	*467*	....	|	....	1830	....	|	....	0600
61.00	Santa Fe d.	*633*	....	1550	....	2005	....	0145	....	0735
70.00	**Albuquerque** a.	*733*	....	1700	....	2120	....	0300	....	0845

396 ↓	426	436	428		434	422	430	438	420	
Albuquerque d.	2000	....	0045	....	....	0630	....	....	1130	....
Santa Fe d.	2135	....	0155	....	....	0740	....	....	1305	....
Taos d.	|	....	|	....	....	0910	....	....	1445	....
Cimarron d.	|	....	|	....	....	1040	....	....	|	....
Las Vegas d.	2245	....	0305	....	....	|	....	....	|	....
Springer d.	0001	....	s	....	....	|	....	....	|	....
Amarillo d.	|	....	|	....	....	|	0730	....	|	....
Dalhart d.	|	....	|	....	....	|	0915	....	|	....
Capulin d.	|	....	|	....	....	|	r	....	|	....
Raton d.	0110	....	0510	....	....	1155	1135	....	|	....
Trinidad d.	0140	....	0540	....	....	1220	1205	....	|	....
Antonito d.	|	....	|	....	....	|	|	....	1600	....
Alamosa d.	|	....	|	....	....	|	|	....	1650	....
Walsenburg d.	0220	....	0625	....	....	|	1250	....	1825	....
Pueblo d.	0330	0450	0745	....	1040	1410	1410	1900	1930	....
Colorado Springs d.	0430	0545	0845	....	1140	1505	1505	2010	2025	....
Aurora d.	|	|	|	....	|	|	1630	|	|	....
Denver a.	0605	0720	1035	....	1330	1700	1700	2200	2200	....

TNO–TNM&O Coaches.

Table 816 BILLINGS - CHEYENNE — PDR

US$	695 ↓	km	125/45	10	303	101	304	13		121/41
61.00	**Billings** d.	*780*	0100	....	....	1300	....	....	....	1345
	Crow AgencyΘ d.		|	....	....	|	....	....	....	|
46.00	Sheridan d.	*555*	0325	....	....	|	....	....	....	1600
44.00	Buffalo d.	*502*	0400	....	....	|	....	....	....	1650
	Cody d.		|	....	1325	|	....	....	....	|
	Powell d.		|	....	1355	|	....	....	....	|
	Deaver d.		|	....	1430	1430	1435	....	....	|
	Powell a.		|	....	....	|	1505	....	....	|
	Cody a.		|	....	....	|	1535	....	....	|
46.00	Worland d.	*551*	|	....	....	1620	....	....	....	|
42.00	Shoshoni d.	*466*	|	....	....	1800	....	....	....	|
53.00	Rapid City Φ d.	*676*	|	....	....	|	....	1630	....	|
	Deadwood d.		|	....	....	|	....	|	....	|
	Spearfish d.	595	|	....	....	|	....	1730	....	|
44.00	Sundance d.	*487*	|	....	....	|	....	1810	....	|
39.00	Gillette ★ d.	*389*	0615	0800	....	|	....	1930	....	1930
	New Castle a.		|	|	....	|	....	....	....	|
40.00	Moorcroft d.	*434*	|	0830	....	|	....	....	....	|
44.00	Sundance d.	*487*	|	0905	....	|	....	....	....	|
48.00	Spearfish d.	*595*	|	0945	....	|	....	....	....	|
	Deadwood d.		|	|	....	|	....	....	....	|
53.00	Rapid CityΦ a.	*676*	|	1035	....	|	....	....	....	|
35.00	Casper d.	*309*	|	....	....	1955	....	....	....	|
	Rawlins a.		|	....	....	|	....	....	....	|
27.00	Douglas d.	*209*	0820	....	....	2035	....	....	....	2140
0.00	**Cheyenne** a.	*0*	1030	....	....	....	....	....	....	2359

296 ↓		120	10	301	102	302			13	122
Cheyenne d.	....	0105	....	....	....	....	....	....	....	1215
Douglas d.	....	0325	....	....	0505	....	....	....	....	1435
Rawlins d.	....	|	....	....	|	....	....	....	....	|
Casper d.	....	|	....	....	0715	....	....	....	....	1630
Rapid CityΦ d.	....	|	....	....	|	....	....	....	1630	|
Deadwood d.	....	|	....	....	|	....	....	....	|	|
Spearfish d.	....	|	....	....	|	....	....	....	1730	|
Sundance d.	....	|	....	....	|	....	....	....	1810	|
Moorcroft d.	....	|	....	....	|	....	....	....	1840	|
New Castle d.	....	|	....	....	|	....	....	....	|	|
Gillette ★ d.	....	0730	0820	....	|	....	....	....	1910	1930
Sundance d.	....	|	0925	....	|	....	....	....	....	|
Spearfish d.	....	|	1010	....	|	....	....	....	....	|
Deadwood a.	....	|	|	....	|	....	....	....	....	|
Rapid City Φ a.	....	|	1100	....	|	....	....	....	....	|
Shoshoni d.	....	|	....	....	0900	....	....	....	....	|
Worland d.	....	|	....	....	1025	....	....	....	....	|
Cody a.	....	|	....	1100	|	....	....	....	....	|
Powell a.	....	|	....	1130	|	....	....	....	....	|
Deaver d.	....	|	....	1205	1205	1210	....	....	....	|
Powell d.	....	|	....	....	|	1240	....	....	....	|
Cody d.	....	|	....	....	|	1310	....	....	....	|
Buffalo d.	....	0835	....	....	|	....	....	....	....	2035
Sheridan d.	....	0925	....	....	|	....	....	....	....	2130
Crow AgencyΘ d.	....	|	....	....	|	....	....	....	....	|
Billings a.	....	1140	....	....	1340	....	....	....	....	2345

★– For Devils Tower. Θ– For Custer Battlefield National Monument.
Φ– For Mt. Rushmore. *PDR*–Powder River Transportation.

Table 815 ALAMOGORDO — TNO

US$	423	421			km	396 ↓ ↑		426	428	
0.00	0345	0930	....	....	*0*	d.**Albuquerque** a.	....	1830	0001	....
12.16	0635	1235	....	....	*280*	d.Carrizozo d.	....	1520	2050	....
16.66	0750	1350	....	....	*375*	d.Alamogordo d.	....	1400	1940	....
	|	1510	....	....		a.Las Cruces d.	....	|	|	....
38.75	0945	1625	....	....	*515*	a.**El Paso** d.	....	1201	1730	....

TNO–TNM&O Coaches.

Table 818 HOBBS - ODESSA — TNO

US$		207 ex⑦	211		km	396 ↓ ↑		206 ex⑦		210
19.00	....	0700	....	....	*0*	d.**Hobbs** a.	....	1310	....	....
23.00	....	|	1240	....		d. Lubbock a.	....	|	....	2140
18.00	....	|	1415	....		d. Brownfield d.	....	|	....	2055
11.00	....	0850	1515	....	*47*	d.Seminole d.	....	|	....	2000
0.00	....	1005	1645	....		a.**Odessa** d.	....	1130	....	1845

TNO–TNM&O Coaches.

Table 820 SALT LAKE CITY - ALBUQUERQUE — GL TNO UTA

US$	*GL* 1302	*TNO* 381 ex⑤⑦		*GL* 1348			*GL* 5910	*GL* 1310	*TNO* 457	*GL* 1312		km	396 ↓ ↑		*TNO* 378			*GL* 1307	*GL* 1317	*TNO* 382 ex⑤⑦	*TNO* 456	*GL* 1301	*GL* 1305	
99.00	....	....	....	....	....	....	2145	....	....	....	....	*0*	d.**Salt Lake City Ω** a.	....	2020c	....	....	....	....	....	....	....	....	....
	....	....	....	....	....	....	2240	....	....	....	....	*65*	d.Provo Ω d.	....	1925c	....	....	....	....	....	....	....	....	....
	....	....	....	....	....	....	0015	....	....	....	....		d.Price d.	....	1750c	....	....	....	....	....	....	....	....	....
	1005	....	....	1440	....	....	0135	0240	....	0530	....	*289*	d.Green River d.	....	1630c	....	....	1625	2340	....	....	0240	0705	....
66.00	1200	....	....	1655	....	....	0500a	0500	0645	0755	....	*469*	d. Grand Junction d.	....	1445c	....	....	1445	2200	....	2130	0100	0525	....
	1740	....	....	2210	....	....	|	1020	|	1325	....	*889*	a. *Denver* d.	....	|	....	....	0840	1530	....	|	1900	0001	....
60.50	....	....	....	....	....	....	0615a	....	0810	....	....	*569*	d. Montrose d.	....	1205	....	....	....	....	....	2005	....	....	....
∂20.00	....	....	....	....	....	....	|	....	0930	....	....	*679*	d. Gunnison d.	....	|	....	....	....	....	....	1845	....	....	....
∂29.00	....	....	....	....	....	....	|	....	1130	....	....	*829*	d. Salida d.	....	|	....	....	....	....	....	1645	....	....	....
∂36.00	....	....	....	....	....	....	|	....	1245	....	....	*931*	d. Canon City d.	....	|	....	....	....	....	....	1530	....	....	....
∂39.00	....	....	....	....	....	....	|	....	1330	....	....	*989*	a. **Pueblo** d.	....	|	....	....	....	....	....	1445	....	....	....
59.00	....	....	....	....	....	....	ra	....	....	....	....	*629*	d.Ouray d.	....	r	....	....	....	....	....	....	....	....	....
54.00	....	....	....	....	....	....	0825a	....	....	....	....	*666*	d.Silverton d.	....	1015	....	....	....	....	....	....	....	....	....
	....	....	....	....	....	....	|	....	....	....	....		d. Mesa Verde a.	....	|	....	....	....	....	....	....	....	....	....
	....	....	....	....	....	....	|	....	....	....	....		d. Dove Creek a.	....	|	....	....	....	....	....	....	....	....	....
	....	....	....	....	....	....	|	....	....	....	....	*528*	d. Cortez d.	....	|	....	....	....	....	....	....	....	....	....
45.00	....	1645	....	....	....	....	1000a	....	....	....	....	*747*	d.**Durango** d.	....	0805	....	....	....	....	1620	....	....	....	....
29.00	....	s	....	....	....	....	sa	....	....	....	....	*805*	d.Aztec d.	....	s	....	....	....	....	s	....	....	....	....
24.50	....	1805	....	....	....	....	1115a	....	....	....	....	*828*	d.Farmington d.	....	0635	....	....	....	....	1505	....	....	....	....
13.00	....	2010	....	....	....	....	1320a	....	....	....	....	*983*	d.Cuba d.	....	0405	....	....	....	....	1255	....	....	....	....
0.00	....	2145	....	....	....	....	1455a	....	....	....	....	*1118*	a.**Albuquerque** d.	....	0240	....	....	....	....	1130	....	....	....	....

a– *TNO*. c–*GL*. ∂–Fare ex Grand Junction. Ω–Frequent local service (*UTA* routes **1/801**) Salt Lake City-Provo and v.v.
GL– Greyhound Lines. *TNO*–TNM&O Coaches. *UTA*–Utah Transit Authority.

Table 826 ALBUQUERQUE - EL PASO (TNO)

US$			419	425	km	396	422		424	
0.00	....	....	1515	2200	0	d.**Albuquerque** ....a.	0530	....	1430	....
13.00	....	....	1655	2325	105	d.Socorro ....d.	0355	....	1255	....
25.00	....	....	1815	0040	225	d.Truth or Consequences d.	0240	....	1115	....
38.75	....	....	1945	0210	350	a.Las Cruces ....d.	0110	....	0945	....
38.75	....	....	2050	0305	408	a.**El Paso** ....d.	0015	....	0845	....

TNO–TNM&O Coaches.

Table 827 SALMON (BSG SBL)

US $	BSG 4▲	SBL ▲ ①②④⑤	BSG 8▲ ⑦	BSG 6▲ ex⑦	km	694 ↓ ↑	BSG 3▲		SBL ▲ ①④	SBL ▲ ②⑤
	....	....	1500	1630	0	d.**Missoula** ....a.	1230	....	....	....
	0530	....	1615	1815		d.Hamilton ....d.	1100	....	....	....
0.00	0800	0800	....	....		d.Salmon ....d.	0815	....	1830	1930
	....	0930a	....	....	98	d.Challis ....d.	....	....	|	1800
	....	1045a	....	....	181	d.Mackay ....d.	....	....	|	1700
	....	1130a	....	....	223	d.Arco ◇ ....d.	....	....	|	1620
	....	|	....	....	324	d.Blackfoot ....d.	....	....	|	|
15.90	....	|	....	....	352	a.**Pocatello** ....d.	....	....	|	|
14.10	....	1300b	....	....	264	a. Idaho Falls ....d.	....	....	1500	1500

a–②⑤ only. b–1130 on ①④. ◇–For Craters of the Moon. *BSG*–Bitterroot Stages. *SBL*–Salmon Bus Lines Inc.

Table 828 IDAHO FALLS - SWEETGRASS (RRS)

US$	296 ↓	km	16	7		2	9		14	
49.00	**Idaho Falls** ....d.	0	2330	....	....	....	....	....	1500	....
28.00	Dillon ....d.	225	0145	....	....	....	....	....	1740	....
20.00	Butte ....d.	0	0330	....	....	....	....	....	1930	....
13.00	Helena ....d.	110	0500	....	....	....	....	....	2115	....
0.00	Great Falls ....a.	260	0645	....	....	....	....	....	2305	....
	Great Falls ....d.		....	0800	....	1845	1845	....	....	....
15.00	Lewistown ....d.	175♀	....	|	....	2115	|	....	....	....
24.00	Roundup ....d.	304♀	....	|	....	2240	|	....	....	....
28.00	Billings ....d.	391♀	....	|	....	2345	|	....	....	....
15.00	Havre ....a.	445	....	|	....	....	2115	....	....	....
13.00	Shelby ....d.	410	....	1045	0945	....	....	....	....	....
15.00	Cut Bank ....d.	447	....	|	1015	....	....	....	....	....
17.00	**Sweetgrass** 🛃 ....d.	467	....	1125	....	....	....	....	....	....
18.00	Coutts 🛃 ....a.		....	1130	....	....	....	....	....	....

695 ↓			15		10		1		8	13
Coutts 🛃 ....d.	....	....	....	....	....	....	....	....	1150	....
Sweetgrass 🛃 ....d.	....	....	....	....	....	....	....	....	1200	....
Cut Bank ....d.	....	....	....	....	....	....	....	1015	|	....
Shelby ....d.	....	....	....	....	....	....	....	1045	1240	....
Havre ....d.	....	....	....	....	1245	....	....	....	|	....
Billings ....d.	....	....	....	....	|	....	1300	....	|	....
Roundup ....d.	....	....	....	....	|	....	1400	....	|	....
Lewistown ....d.	....	....	....	....	|	....	1545	....	|	....
Great Falls ....a.	....	....	....	....	1515	....	1800	....	1430	....
Great Falls ....d.	....	....	0715	....	....	....	....	....	....	1545
Helena ....d.	....	....	0900	....	....	....	....	....	....	1745
Butte ....d.	....	....	1045	....	....	....	....	....	....	1930
Dillon ....d.	....	....	1155	....	....	....	....	....	....	2035
Idaho Falls ....a.	....	....	1430	....	....	....	....	....	....	2300

♀– from Great Falls
RRS– Rimrock Trailways.

Table 830 IDAHO FALLS - SALT LAKE CITY (GL PUT)

US$	PUT	GL 5919		GL 5923	km	196 ↓ ↑	GL 5922		PUT	GL 5918
69.00	....	0910a	....	....	631	d. Bozeman ....a.	1945a	....	....	....
56.00	....	1201a	....	....	486	d. West Yellowstone d.	1840a	....	....	....
70.00	....	1335a	....	....	363	d. St. Anthony ....d.	1520a	....	....	....
38.00	1030b	1455	....	0015	312	d.**Idaho Falls** ....d.	1430	....	1730	2310
35.00	1245	1615	....	0130	250	d.Pocatello ....d.	1305	....	1630	2200
12.00	....	1935	....	0350	85	d.Brigham City ....d.	0935	....	....	1920
8.49	....	2010	....	0425	48	d.Ogden ....d.	0905	....	....	1850
0.00	....	2055	....	0515	0	a.**Salt Lake City** ....d.	0815	....	....	1800

a– Summer only Ends Oct 3 . b– Check in time, departs at 1145
GL– Greyhound Lines.
PUT- Pocatello Urban Transit.

Table 831 PRESCOTT (NHT PTA)

US$		PTA	NHT	NHT	km	396 ↓ ↑	NHT	PTA	NHT	
0.00	....	....	1135	1750	0	d.**Phoenix** ....a.	1035	....	1545	....
	....	0915	|	|		d. Prescott ....a.	|	1215	|	....
10.00	....	1015	1400	2000		d.Camp Verde ....d.	0830	1115	1340	....
	....	....	|	|		a.**Williams** ....d.	|	....	|	....
21.50	....	....	1510	2110		a.Flagstaff ....d.	0710	....	1220	....
34.00	....	....	*1735*	....		a.Grand Canyon ....d.	....	....	*1000*	....

NHT– Nava Hopi Tours. *PTA*–Prescott Transit Authority.

Table 832 AJO - TUCSON (PP)

US$	①③⑤				km	694 ↓ ↑			①③⑤	
0.00	0600	....	....	....	0	d.**Ajo** ....a.	....	....	1845	....
7.50	0900	....	....	....	225	a.**Tucson** ....d.	....	....	1520	....

PP– La Tortuga Transit.

Table 833 DEL RIO - EL PASO (GL)

US $	1477		1475		km	296 ↓ ↑	1476		1474	
0.00	2305	....	1825	....	0	d.**Del Rio** ....a.	1300	....	0545	....
	0350	....	2310	....	283	d.Alpine ....d.	0815	....	0100	....
	0425	....	2345	....	325	d.Marfa ....d.	0740	....	0025	....
	0615	....	0110	....	442	a.Van Horn ....d.	0615	....	2300	....
	0715	....	0230	....	635	a.**El Paso** ....d.	0245	....	1930	....

GL– Greyhound Lines.

Table 835 GREAT FALLS - WHITEFISH (RRS)

US$		17	11		km	695 ↓ ↑		12	18	
0.00	....	....	1815	....	0	d.**Great Falls** ....a.	....	1835	....	....
	....	....	1945	....		d.Lincoln ....d.	....	1650	....	....
	....	1515	2225	....		d.Missoula ....d.	....	1515	2200	....
	....	1715	2350	....		d.Polson ....d.	....	1135	2025	....
	....	1825	0055	....		d.Kalispell ....d.	....	1035	1925	....
	....	1845	0120	....		a. **Whitefish** ....d.	....	1000	1855	....

RRS– Rimrock Trailways.

Table 836 395 YELLOWSTONE PARK (GL PDR TSL YP)

🚌 *(YP)* services operate on all major routes within the park. They link the main resort areas and principal monuments within the park with the main gateways at West Yellowstone (*GL* to Idaho Falls), Jackson Lake (*TSL* to Idaho Falls), Grand Teton National Park, Cody (*PDR* to Billings), Bozeman (*GL* to Billings/Butte), Livingston (*GL* to Billings/Butte), Billings (*GL* to Fargo).

GL–Greyhound Lines. *PDR*–Powder River Trailways. *TSL*–Teton Stage Line. *YP*–Yellowstone Park Co.

Table 837 694 PARK CITY/SNOWBIRD (LB UTA)

🚌 *(LB)* service Salt Lake City-Park City and v.v. *48* km. Journey: 1 hour. Fare: US$: 6.00 ($14.00 to Airport) Ⓡ.

From Park City to Salt Lake City: 1000, 1700.
From Park City to Salt Lake City Airport: 0600 and every 30 mins. to 2100.
From Salt Lake City to Park City: 0820, 1515, 2245.
From Salt Lake City Airport to Park City: 0930 and every 30 mins. to 2330, 2359.

🚌 *(LB)* service Park City-Snowbird-Alta and v.v. 72 km. Journey: 1½ hours. Fare: US$: 10.00 Ⓡ.

From Park City: 0800. **From Alta**: 1700.

🚌 *(UTA)* service Salt Lake City-Alta and v.v. *30* km. Journey: 1 hour. Fare: US$: 3.00 ($6.00 from Airport) (routes **92/93/94/98**).

From Salt Lake City: 0545, 0715, 0725, 0734, 0752©, 0754, 0814, 0834, 0854, 0945, 1045, 1059, 1145©, 1200, 1515, 1545, 1630.
From Alta: 0900©, 0917, 0930, 1000, 1015, 1047, 1145, 1200, 1230, 1310, 1400, 1430, 1515, 1600©, 1615, 1620©, 1630, 1645, 1650, 1700, 1710, 1715, 1730, 1800.
From Salt Lake City Airport: 1100, 1200, 1500.
From Alta (to Airport): 0900, 1315.

LB–Lewis Bros. Stages. *UTA*–Utah Transit Authority.

Table 838 AUSTIN (TNS)

US$		①③⑤		②④	km	694 ↓ ↑	②④		①③⑤	
0.00	....	....	....	0900	0	d.**Reno** ....a.	1645	....	....	....
	....	....	....	1315		d.Austin ....d.	1315	....	....	....
	....	0800	....	1615		d.Ely ....d.	0915	....	2200	....
	....	1230	....	....		a.**Las Vegas** ....d.	....	....	1730	....

TNS– TransNevada Stages.

Table 840 GRAND CANYON (NHT)

US$		✕		✕	km	396 ↓ ↑	✕			✕
12.50	....	1000	1700	1830	0	d.**Grand Canyon** ....a.	0940	1035	....	1735
9.00	....	|	1815a	|	92	a. Williams ....d.	0825	0920a	....	|
0.00	....	1145	1900	2020	130	a.**Flagstaff** ⊠ ....d.	0730	0830	....	1545

a–In Winter, calls only if Grand Canyon Railway is operating. ⊠–*NHT* operates a day tour in summer on ①③⑤ (subject to a minimum of 4 passengers) from Flagstaff at 0730 to Kayenta and Monument Valley (return to Flagstaff at 1900). ✕–Summer service only (April 2-end October). *NHT*–Nava Hopi Tours.

Table 841 SEATTLE - WALLA WALLA (GL)

US$	5560	1421	5594		km	695 ↓ ↑	5559	1422	5561	
0.00	0645	1135	1645	....	0	d.**Seattle** ....a.	1130	1905	1945	....
22.00	0925	1410	1920	....	160	d.Ellensburg ....d.	0910	1635	1715	....
28.00	1020	1515	2015	....	223	d.Yakima ....d.	0810	1540	1620	....
31.00	1130	1550	2110	....	254	d.Toppenish ....d.	0720	1450	1540	....
37.00	1310	....	2230	....	349	d.Richland ....d.	0520	....	1350	....
39.00	1345	....	2250	....	362	d.Pasco ....d.	0500	....	1330	....
44.00	1455	....	0001	....	438	a.**Walla Walla** ....d.	0335	....	1215	....
	1600	....	0105	....		a.Pendleton ....d.	0230	....	1110	....

GL– Greyhound Lines.

Table 842 SALT LAKE CITY - SAN FRANCISCO

AM GL ST

US $	*GL* 8301	*AM/ST* 35	*GL* 1347	*AM/ST* 34	*GL* 8305	*GL* 1315	*GL* 8313	*GL* 8307	*GL* 8333	*AM/ST* 37	*GL* 8319	*GL* 1357	*AM/ST* 31	*GL* 8309	*GL* 8325	km	296 ↓ ↑	*GL* 1308	*GL* 8310	*GL* 8316	*AM/ST* 35	*GL* 8318	*AM/ST* 32	*GL* 8312	*GL* 1314	*GL* 8324	*AM/ST* 34	*GL* 8328	*GL* 1306	*AM/ST* 37	*GL* 8344 ⑤⑥	*GL* 8338
0.00	....	....	1700	....	....	2230	....	....	....	....	....	0615	....	....	....	*0*	d.**Salt Lake City** ..... a.	1740	....	....	....	....	....	....	0630	....	....	....	1035	....	....	....
	....	....	1905	....	....	0035	....	....	....	....	....	0820	....	....	....		d.Wendover .... d.	1540	....	....	....	....	....	....	0430	....	....	....	0840	....	....	....
32.00	....	....	1930	....	....	0040	....	....	....	....	....	0845	....	....	....	*290*	d.Wells .. .. d.	1320	....	....	....	....	....	....	|	....	....	....	0635	....	....	....
37.00	....	....	2030	....	....	0150	....	....	....	....	....	0945	....	....	....	*364*	d.Elko.... .... d.	1155	....	....	....	....	....	....	0125	....	....	....	0525	....	....	....
56.00	....	....	2345	....	....	0435	....	....	....	....	....	1255	....	....	....	*504*	d.Winnemucca........ d.	0920	....	....	....	....	....	....	2240	....	....	....	0255	....	....	....
64.00	....	....	0100	....	....	|	....	....	....	....	....	1410	....	....	....	*659*	d.Lovelock .... d.	0750	....	....	....	....	....	....	2105	....	....	....	|	....	....	....
73.00	0035	0200	0315	0630	0615	0810	0735	1000	1130	1130	1310	1630	1430	1520	1840	*814*	d.**Reno** .. .. d.	0615	1255	1425	1515	1900	1815	1845	1930	2125	2115	2345	0005	2315	0030	0240
77.00	0125s	|	|	|	0705	|	0825	|	|	|	1400	|	|	|	|	*870*	d.Truckee .... d.	|	|	1325	|	1750	|	|	|	|	|	2235	|	|	|	|
82.00	0230s	|	|	|	0820	|	0955	|	|	|	1515	|	|	|	2030	*975*	d.Colfax . ... d.	|	|	1220	|	1645	|	|	|	|	|	2130	|	|	|	|
	0255s	0420s	|	0820	0845	|	1020	|	|	1345	1540	|	1700	|	|		d.Auburn .... d.	|	|	1150	1245	1610	1545	|	|	|	1845	2055	|	|	|	|
85.00	0425	0450s	0630	0850	1030	1130	1230	1330	1430	1430	1730	2030	1730	1830	2215	*1034*	d.**Sacramento**........ d.	0250	0940	1030	1215	1450	1515	1530	1540	1740	1815	1935	2055	2025	2150	2320
92.00	0600	0620s	|	1045	|	|	1410	1620	1530	1600s	|	|	1900	|	2325s	*1155*	a.Vallejo. .... d.	|	|	|	1040	1215	1340	|	|	|	1625	|	|	1920	|	|
	|	|	|	|	|	|	|	|	|	|	|	|	|	|	|		a.Richmond........... d.	|	|	|	|	|	|	|	|	|	|	|	|	|	|	|
92.00	0700	0705	0820	|	1210	1300	1510	1710	1625	|	1910	2200	1940	2000	0005	*1168*	a.**Oakland** .... d.	0100	0730	0830	1000	1230	1300	1330	1330	1530	1535	1735	1855	1830	2000	2130
92.00	0730	0720	0840	1125	1230	1330	1530	1535	1655	1700	1930	2230	1955	2030	0025	*1179*	a.**San Francisco** .... d.	0030	0700	0800	0940	1201	1240	1300	1300	1500	1515	1700	1815	1800	1930	2100

a– ⑤⑦ only.
AM– Amador Stage Lines.
GL– Greyhound Lines.
ST– Sierra Trailways.

Table 843 SALT LAKE CITY - LAS VEGAS

GL

US $		1305		6027		1307		1317	5910	6051	1301	km	296 ↓ ↑		1302		1348	6022	5911	1310			1312	6050
0.00	....	....	....	0845	....	....	....	....	2145	2200	....	*0*	d.**Salt Lake City** ....a.	....	....	....	....	1650	2020	....	....	....	....	0640
9.00	....	....	....	0940	....	....	....	....	2240	2300	....	*65*	d.Provo ....d.	....	....	....	....	1545	1925	....	....	....	....	0545
◇118.00	....	0001	....	|	....	0840	....	1530	|	|	1830	★*892*	d. *Denver* **820** ....a.	....	1740	....	2225	|	|	1020	....	....	1325	|
◇59.00	....	0720	....	|	....	1640	....	2355	0135	|	0225	★*292*	d. **Green River** ....a.	....	0950	....	1500	|	0425	0225	....	....	0515	|
◇42.00	....	0945	....	|	....	1905	....	0215	....	|	|	★*94*	d. Richfield....................d.	....	0725	....	1225	|	....	0005	....	....	0255	|
34.00	....	1110	....	1305	....	2030	....	0340	....	0225	0615	*309*	d.Beaver........................d.	....	0615	....	1115	1230	....	2255	....	....	0145	0250
41.00	....	1210	....	1410	....	2130	....	0440	....	0330	0715	*392*	d.Cedar City...................d.	....	|	....	0945	1125	....	2140	....	....	0030	0135
	....	1310	....	1520	....	2230	....	0550	....	0420	0825		d.St. George...................d.	....	|	....	0850	1030	....	2045	....	....	2335	0045
64.00	....	1415	....	1635	....	2335	....	0655	....	0535	0935	*687*	a.**Las Vegas** ....d.	....	0050	....	0535	0630	....	1720	....	....	2035	2120
92.00	....	2055	....	0015	....	0630	....	1340	....	1355	1635	*1147*	a.*Los Angeles* **870** ....d.	....	1800	....	2315	0001	....	0900	....	....	1400	1315

◇–Fare ex Las Vegas. ★–Km ex Beaver. *GL*–Greyhound Lines.

Table 844 EL PASO - PHOENIX

GL

US $	296	km	GL 241	*GL* 6371	*GL* 1241		*GL* 1413	*GL* 407	*GL* 1435	*GL* 6379	*GL* 6373		*GL* 243	*GL* 401		*GL* 1415	*GL* 1419		*GL* 403	*GL* 1409		*GL* 1407		*GL* 405	
	Dallas **785**.d. ↓		....	....	1320	....	1815	....	1930	....	....	....	....	....	....	0001	0245	....	....	0530	....	0830	....	....	....
0.00	*Houston* **888**.......d.	*0*	....	....	|	....	|	....	|	....	....	....	....	2200	....	|	|	....	*0330*	|	....	|	....	0815	....
92.00	Van Horn............d.	*960*	....	....	|	....	0355	....	|	....	....	....	....	1100	....	1115	1410	....	1725	1740	....	2040	....	2200	....
104.00	**El Paso**............a.	*1160*	....	....	0250	....	0505	....	0645	....	....	....	....	1159	....	1220	1540	....	1830	1845	....	2145	....	2300	....
	El Paso............d.		....	....	0350	....	0630	0650	0745	....	....	....	....	1300	....	1330	1645	....	1920	1945	....	2300	....	0001	....
104.00	Las Cruces.........d.	*1238*	....	....	0445	....	|	0745	|	....	....	....	....	1350	....	1425	1745	....	2015	|	....	|	....	|	....
118.00	Lordsburg...........d.	*1418*	....	....	0725	....	0930	1005	1030	....	....	....	....	1615	....	1640	2005	....	2235	2245	....	0200	....	0305	....
	Benson Ω...........d.		....	....	0925	....	|	|	1240	....	....	....	....	|	....	1845	|	....	|	|	....	|	....	|	....
131.00	Tucson ....d.	*1678*	0845	0930	1030	....	1240	|	1400	1445	1545	....	1700	|	....	2005	2300	....	0130	|	....	|	....	|	....
	Casa Grande .d.		|	1045	|	....	|	|	1515	1600	|	....	1815	|	....	|	|	....	|	|	....	|	....	|	....
131.00	Globe ....d.	*1663*	|	|	|	....	|	1335	|	|	|	....	|	1950	....	|	|	....	|	|	....	|	....	0620	....
131.00	**Phoenix**.............a.	*1863*	1045	1220	1230	....	1440	1600	1615	1745	1745	....	1915	2215	....	2205	0100	....	0330	0315	....	0630	....	0855	....
142.00	*Los Angeles* **845** d.	*2488*	....	....	2015	....	2115	0010	2300	....	....	....	....	*0505*	....	....	0815	....	....	1045	....	1625	....	1715	....

296 ↓	*GL* 1250	*GL* 408	*GL* 1412	*GL* 240	*GL* 1404	*GL* 6372	*GL* 1408	*GL* 1414		*GL* 402	*GL* 6370		*GL* 242	*GL* 6378		*GL* 404		*GL* 1418			*GL* 1416			*GL* 406
Los Angeles **845** d.	1800	1800	2000	....	2140	....	2345	0040	....	....	....	....	....	....	....	0700	....	0700	....	....	1120	....	....	1330
Phoenix..................d.	0245	0430	0400	0645	0800	0730	0845	0930	....	0930	1201	....	1430	1615	....	1710	....	1725	....	....	2230	....	....	0001
Globe ....d.	|	0655	|	|	|	|	|	|	....	1225	|	....	|	|	....	2000	....	|	....	....	|	....	....	|
Casa Grande d.	|	|	|	|	|	0915	|	|	....	|	1300	....	1630	1815	....	|	....	|	....	....	|	....	....	|
Tucson ....d.	|	|	0640	0845	1015	1030	1100	1201	....	|	1415	....	....	1940	....	|	....	1940	....	....	0045	....	....	0215
Benson Ω ....d.	|	|	|	....	1105	....	|	1250	....	|	....	....	....	....	....	|	....	2025	....	....	|	....	....	|
Lordsburg.................d.	0755	1045	1035	....	1335	....	1410	1530	....	1545	....	....	....	....	....	2315	....	2245	....	....	0335	....	....	0515
Las Cruces................d.	0950	1255	|	....	1545	....	|	1735	....	1755	....	....	....	....	....	0115	....	|	....	....	0540	....	....	0730
El Paso...................a.	1040	1345	1320	....	1635	....	1700	1825	....	1845	....	....	....	....	....	0205	....	0130	....	....	0630	....	....	0820
El Paso...................d.	1140	1445	1430	....	1735	....	1800	1930	....	1940	....	....	....	....	....	0300	....	0235	....	....	0730	....	....	0935
Van Horn..................d.	1530	1830	1810	....	2055	....	2125	2255	....	2250	....	....	....	....	....	0630	....	0615	....	....	1105	....	....	1310
Houston **888**............a.	|	0645	|	....	|	....	|	|	....	1215	....	....	....	....	....	2030	....	|	....	....	|	....	....	0315
Dallas **785**.......a.	0145	....	0440	....	0725	....	0700	1025	....	....	....	....	....	....	....	....	....	1730	....	....	2245	....	....	....

Ω– For Tombstone.
GL– Greyhound Lines.

Table 845 PHOENIX - LOS ANGELES

GL

US $	196 ↓	km	1435		6363	407	6364	1415		6349	1419	6991		403	6337	1409	6343	6341	1407	405	6353	6351	1241	6375 ⑤⑦	
0.00	**Phoenix**.............d.	*0*	1600	....	....	1600	....	2120	....	....	0045	....	....	0320	....	0320	....	....	0645	0845	....	....	1300	....	....
	Wickenburg ....d.		|	....	....	|	....	|	....	....	|	....	....	|	....	|	....	....	0825	|	....	....	|	....	....
	Blythe..................d.		1900	....	....	1905	....	2250	....	....	0330	....	....	0620	....	0620	....	....	1105	1210	....	....	1545	....	....
	Indio ....d.		|	....	1930	2100	2115	|	....	0235	0520	0530	....	|	0810	0815	0900	1220	1300	1405	1530	1710	1740	1740	....
	Palm Springs......d.		|	....	2005	|	2250	|	....	|	|	0605	....	|	0845	|	0935	1255	1335	1440	1605	1745	|	1815	....
	San Bernardino ..d.		|	....	|	2225	|	|	....	|	|	0720	....	|	1000	|	1130	1405	1455	1550	1735	|	1905	|	....
	Riverside ....d.		|	....	2115	2245	|	|	....	|	|	0740	....	|	1020	|	|	1425	1515	|	1800	1900	|	1925	....
	Claremont *(Pomona)* .d.		|	....	|	2330	|	|	....	|	|	0815	....	|	1055	|	|	|	|	|	1835	1920	|	|	....
	El Monte *(Alhambra)*..d.		2230	....	|	|	|	|	....	|	|	|	....	|	1125	1020	1225	1525	|	|	1910	|	|	|	....
	Los Angeles......a.		2300	....	2025	0010	2359	0505	....	0505	0815	0925	....	1020	1155	1050	1255	1555	1625	1715	1940	2050	2015	2040	....

196 ↓	6339	1414			6346	404	1418			6348	1416		6994		406			6352	1250	408	6354		1412	1404	1408
Los Angeles............d.	0030	0040	....	....	0530	0700	0700	....	....	1045	1120	....	1201	....	1330	....	....	1515	1800	1800	1930	....	2000	2140	2345
El Monte *(Alhambra)* d.	|	|	....	....	0600	0730	0730	....	....	1115	|	....	1225	....	|	....	....	1550	|	1830	|	....	|	|	|
Claremont *(Pomona)* d.	|	|	....	....	0635	|	0805	....	....	1150	|	....	1305	....	|	....	....	1625	|	1905	|	....	|	|	|
Riverside ....d.	|	|	....	....	0720	|	0845	....	....	1235	1235	....	1350	....	|	....	....	1710	|	1950	|	....	|	|	|
San Bernardino ....d.	|	|	....	....	0745	0840	0910	....	....	1300	1300	....	1415	....	1510	....	....	1740	|	2025	2100	....	|	2300	|
Palm Springs............d.	|	|	....	....	0915	|	|	....	....	1425	1400	....	1540	....	|	....	....	1845	|	|	2220	....	|	|	|
Indio ....d.	0300	|	....	....	0950	1015	1045	....	....	1530	1450	....	1615	....	1700	....	....	1955	|	2200	2310	....	|	0035	0220
Blythe ....d.	....	0505	....	....	....	1235	1300	....	....	....	1700	....	....	....	1910	....	....	....	2215	0005	....	....	0015	0245	0415
Wickenburg ....d.	....	|	....	....	....	|	|	....	....	....	1905	....	....	....	|	....	....	....	|	|	....	....	|	|	|
Phoenix..................a.	....	0735	....	....	....	1510	1630	....	....	....	2040	....	....	....	2200	....	....	....	0045	0240	....	....	0245	0515	0645

GL–Greyhound Lines.

Table 845a OKLAHOMA CITY - PHOENIX
🚌 *CPL GL*

US $	*GL* 473	*GL* 1353	*GL* 475	*GL* 1351	km	296 ↓ ↑	*GL* 474	*GL* 470	*GL* 1352	*GL* 1356
	0745	1800	2300	0300		d.*St. Louis* **758**.....a.	2150	0620	1255	1620
0.00	2145a	0545	1035a	1610	*0*	d.**Oklahoma City**.d.	1000a	1930a	0025	0410
	|	0840	1310a	1855		d.Sayre ....d.	|	1615a	2115	|
	0155a	|	1510a	|		d.Pampa...............d.	0525a	1435a	|	|
41.00	0405	1215	1720	2200	*420*	d.Amarillo ....d.	0415a	1325a	1855	2330
	|		|	|		d.Vega ....d.	|	|	|	|
59.00	|	1340	1850	2325	*605*	d.Tucumcari ....d.	0020	0930	1455	1940
	0610	1450	2000	|	*704*	d.Santa Rosa ....d.	2240	|	1159	1800s
77.00	0915	1805	2300	0315	*890*	d.**Albuquerque**....d.	2045	0610	1115	1600
82.00	1045	1935	0030	0445	*1015*	d.Grants ....d.	1820	|	0845	1345
98.00	1155	2045	0140	0555	*1114*	d.Gallup................d.	1715	0300	0740	1240
	1210	2040	|	0610		d.Houck................d.	1550	|	0555	1035
98.00	1320	2150	0245s	0720	*1269*	d.Holbrook............d.	1405	2350	|	0925
98.00	1405	2235	0330	0815	*1356*	d.Winslow.............d.	1320	2304	0330	0845
98.00	1550	0010	0510	0930	*1437*	d.Flagstaff ....d.	1215	2205	0225	0835
	....	0250	....	1230	*1777*	a.**Phoenix**............d.	0825	....	2300	....

– *CPL*. *CPL*–Panhandle Trailways.
GL– Greyhound Lines.

Table 845b FLAGSTAFF - LOS ANGELES
🚌 *GL*

US $	475	1351	473		km	296 ↓ ↑		470	1346	1356
	0610	1030	1800	....	*0*	d.**Flagstaff**...........a.	....	2235	0150	0755
	0655	1115	|	....	*45*	d.Williams.............d.	....	|	|	0710
	0945	1325	2045	....	*270*	d.Kingman............d.	....	1955	2320	0500
	1025	1505	2125	....	*375*	d.Needles.............d.	....	1625	|	0155
	1310	1805	0005	....	*605*	d.Barstow.............d.	....	1350	1825	2325
	1535	1930	|	....		d.San Bernardino .d.	....	1125	1615	2120
	1550	|	|	....		d. Riverside.........d.	....	|	|	2050
	|	|	|	....		d.Claremont *(Pomona)*.d.	....	1035	1525	2015
	|	|	|	....		d.El Monte *(Alhambra)*.d.	....	|	1445	1930
0.00	1725	2040	0225	....		a.**Los Angeles**.....d.	....	0925	1415	1900

GL– Greyhound Lines.

Table 847 FLAGSTAFF - PHOENIX
🚌 *GL NHT*

US $	296 ↓	km	*GL* 1353	*GL* 6361	*NHT*	*GL* 1351	*NHT*	*GL* 6307		
0.00	**Flagstaff**..............d.	*0*	0010	0730	0710	0930	1220	1600	....	....
21.50	**Phoenix**...............a.		0250	1030	1035	1230	1545	1920	....	....

296 ↓	*GL* 1352			*GL* 474	*NHT*	*GL* 6362		*NHT*	*GL* 6308	
Phoenix.....................d.	2300	....	....	0825	1135	1150	....	1750	1815	....
Flagstaff....................a.	0155	....	....	1140	1510	1500	....	2110	2125	....

GL– Greyhound Lines.
NHT– Nava Hopi Tours.

Table 846 296 TUCSON - NOGALES
🚌 *CAS*

🚌 service Tucson-Nogales and v.v. *105* km. Journey: 1¾ hours. Fare: US $: 5.60.
From Tucson: 0700, 0900, 1100, 1300, 1500, 1700, 1900, 2100.
From Nogales: 0700, 0900, 1100, 1300, 1500, 1700, 1900, 2100.
CAS– Citizen Auto Stage Co.

Table 852 LOS ANGELES - SAN DIEGO
🚌 *GL*

US $	7099			6867	7071	7095	7077		7059	6366	7093	7091	7097	7089	7087	km	296
0.00	0045	....	....	0300	0645	0800	0945	....	1130	1201	1400	1615	1745	1815	2130	*0*	d.**Los Angeles** ♣ ... a.
	|	....	....	|	|	0905	|	....	1225	|	1455	|	1845	|	2205		d. Long Beach....... d.
	0110	....	....	|	0720	|	|	....	|	1235	|	1650	|	1850	|		d. Norwalk.......... d.
	|	....	....	|	0740	|	1030	....	|	1255	|	1715	|	1920	|	*50*	d.Anaheim *(Disneyland)* d.
	0140	....	....	0340	0805	0945	1050	....	|	1315	|	1740	|	1945	2250	*60*	d.Santa Ana........... d.
	|	....	....	|	0830	|	|	....	|	|	|	1805	|	|	|		d.Irvine .... d.
	|	....	....	|	0845	|	|	....	|	|	|	|	|	|	|		d.San Juan Capistrand.
	|	....	....	|	0855	|	1130	....	1330	|	1610	1840	2000	|	2330		d.San Clemente...... d.
	0245	....	....	0445	0935	1050	1205	....	1400	1420	1655	1910	2030	2050	2359	*140*	d.Oceanside........... d.
	0305	....	....	0520	1025	1140	1255	....	1450	1510	1745	2000	2120	2145	0050	*205*	a.**San Diego** ♣ ...... d.

296	7084	7078	7094	7074	7050	7052	7070	7080	7088	7072	7024	7076	7082		
d.**Los Angeles** ♣ ... a.	0925	0935	1225	1305	1345	1620	1725	1905	1935	2055	2215	0040	0240	....	....
d. Long Beach....... d.	0815	|	|	1215	|	1520	|	1805	|	|	2140	|	|	....	....
d. Norwalk.......... d.	|	0855	1150	|	1315	|	1630	|	1905	2025	|	|	|	....	....
d.Anaheim *(Disneyland)* d.	|	0835	1130	|	1255	|	1600	|	1840	2000	|	|	0150	....	....
d.Santa Ana........... d.	|	0815	1110	|	1235	|	1540	|	1820	1945	|	|	|	....	....
d.Irvine .... d.	|	|	1045	|	|	|	|	|	|	|	|	|	|	....	....
d.San Juan Capistrand.	|	|	|	|	|	|	|	|	|	|	|	|	|	....	....
d.San Clemente...... d.	0700	0720	|	1120	|	|	1450	1635	|	1900	|	|	|	....	....
d.Oceanside........... d.	0630	0700	0950	1050	1130	1350	1420	1605	1710	1835	2025	2240	0045	....	....
a.**San Diego** ♣ ...... d.	0500	0600	0900	1000	1040	1300	1330	1515	1615	1735	1930	2150	2350	....	....

♣– Additional express services operate from Los Angeles at 0600, 0700, 0800, 0900, 1000, 1100, 1201, 1300, 1400, 1500, 1600, 1700, 1800, 1940, 2240 returning from San Diego at 0700, 0800, 0900, 1000, 1100, 1201, 1300, 1400, 1500, 1600, 1700, 1800, 1900, 2030.
GL– Greyhound Lines.

Table 857 296 HOUSTON LOCAL SERVICES
🚌 *HCT*

Local 🚌 services operate in the Houston area as follows:
Bellaire (❖ km, US $: ❖). From Houston: ❖, returning at ❖. Journey: ❖.
Galena Park (❖ km, US $: ❖). From Houston: ❖, returning at ❖. Journey: ❖.
Jacinto City (❖ km, US $: ❖). From Houston: ❖, returning at ❖. Journey: ❖.
Park Place (❖ km, US $: ❖). From Houston: ❖, returning at ❖. Journey: ❖.
Pasadena (❖ km, US $: ❖). From Houston: ❖, returning at ❖. Journey: ❖.
South Houston (❖ km, US $: ❖). From Houston: ❖, returning at ❖. Journey: ❖.

HCT– Metropolitan Transit Authority of Harris County.

Table 858 296 MIAMI LOCAL SERVICES
🚌 *DCT GL TR*

Local #### (C cl. only, 1.435m.) and 🚌 services operate in the Miami area as follows:

Boca Raton ° *(TR)* (❖ km, US $: 4.50). From Miami Metrorail: 0452Ⓐ, 0552Ⓐ, 0557Ⓒ, 0652Ⓐ, 0752Ⓐ, 0757Ⓒ, 0812†, 0907Ⓒ, 0912Ⓐ, 1009†, 1126Ⓒ, 1207Ⓐ, 1212Ⓒ, 1307Ⓒ, 1422Ⓒ, 1424Ⓐ, 1542Ⓐ, 1602†, 1626Ⓒ, 1642Ⓐ, 1742Ⓐ, 1822Ⓒ, 1842Ⓒ, 1942Ⓐ, 2037Ⓒ, 2042Ⓐ, 2237Ⓐ, 2337Ⓒ, returning at 0516Ⓐ, 0617Ⓐ, 0620Ⓒ, 0717Ⓐ, 0815Ⓒ, 0817Ⓐ, 0837†, 0933Ⓒ, 0938Ⓐ, 1033Ⓐ, 1034†, 1047Ⓒ, 1229Ⓐ, 1231Ⓒ, 1332†, 1445Ⓒ, 1448Ⓐ, 1605Ⓐ, 1627†, 1646Ⓒ, 1704Ⓐ, 1804Ⓐ, 1850Ⓒ, 1904Ⓐ, 1907†, 2004Ⓐ, 2100Ⓒ, 2103Ⓐ, 2300⚒. Journey: 1 hour.

Boynton Beach ° *(TR)* (❖ km, US $: 5.50). From Miami Metrorail: 0452Ⓐ, 0552Ⓐ, 0557Ⓒ, 0652Ⓐ, 0752Ⓐ, 0757Ⓒ, 0812†, 0907Ⓒ, 0912Ⓐ, 1009†, 1126Ⓒ, 1207Ⓐ, 1212Ⓒ, 1307Ⓒ, 1422Ⓒ, 1424Ⓐ, 1542Ⓐ, 1602†, 1626Ⓒ, 1642Ⓐ, 1742Ⓐ, 1822Ⓒ, 1842Ⓒ, 1942Ⓐ, 2037Ⓒ, 2042Ⓐ, 2237Ⓐ, 2337Ⓒ, returning at 0502Ⓐ, 0602Ⓐ, 0607Ⓒ, 0702Ⓐ, 0802⚒, 0824†, 0920Ⓒ, 0925Ⓐ, 1017Ⓐ, 1018†, 1034Ⓒ, 1216Ⓐ, 1218Ⓒ, 1316†, 1432Ⓒ, 1435Ⓐ, 1552Ⓐ, 1611†, 1632Ⓒ, 1649Ⓐ, 1749Ⓐ, 1837Ⓒ, 1849Ⓐ, 1851†, 1949Ⓐ, 2047Ⓒ, 2049Ⓐ, 2247⚒. Journey: 1¼ hours. Also ◨ *(GL)* from Miami at 0730, 1600, returning at 1015, 1815.

Coconut Grove ° *(MTD)* (❖ km, US $: ❖). From Miami Government Center: 0555Ⓐ/0600Ⓒ and frequent to 0024, returning 0520Ⓐ/0533Ⓒ and frequent to 0008. Journey: 15 mins.

Coral Gables ◨ *(DCT)* (❖ km, US $: ❖). From Miami: ❖, returning at ❖. Journey: ❖. Also *GH* from Miami at 0730, 1145, 1830, returning at 1225, 1655, 2125.

Dadeland South ° *(MTD)* (❖ km, US $: 1.25). From Miami Government Center: 0555Ⓐ/0600Ⓒ and frequent to 0024, returning 0512Ⓐ/0525Ⓒ and frequent to 0000. Journey: 20 mins.

Delray Beach ° *(TR)* (❖ km, US $: 5.00). From Miami Metrorail: 0452Ⓐ, 0552Ⓐ, 0557Ⓒ, 0652Ⓐ, 0752Ⓐ, 0757Ⓒ, 0812†, 0907Ⓒ, 0912Ⓐ, 1009†, 1126Ⓒ, 1207Ⓐ, 1212Ⓒ, 1307Ⓒ, 1422Ⓒ, 1424Ⓐ, 1542Ⓐ, 1602†, 1626Ⓒ, 1642Ⓐ, 1742Ⓐ, 1822Ⓒ, 1842Ⓒ, 1942Ⓐ, 2037Ⓒ, 2042Ⓐ, 2237Ⓐ, 2337Ⓒ, returning at 0511Ⓐ, 0612Ⓐ, 0615Ⓒ, 0712Ⓐ, 0810Ⓒ, 0812Ⓐ, 0832†, 0928Ⓒ, 0933Ⓐ, 1027†, 1028Ⓐ, 1042Ⓒ, 1224Ⓐ, 1226Ⓒ, 1325†, 1440Ⓒ, 1443Ⓐ, 1600Ⓐ, 1620†, 1641Ⓒ, 1659Ⓐ, 1759Ⓐ, 1845Ⓒ, 1859Ⓐ, 1900†, 1959Ⓐ, 2055Ⓒ, 2058Ⓐ, 2255⚒. Journey: 1¼ hours. Also ◨ *(GL)* from Miami at 0730, 1600, returning at 1235, 1835.

Fort Lauderdale ° *(TR)* (*49* km, US $: 4.00). From Miami Metrorail: 0452Ⓐ, 0552Ⓐ, 0557Ⓒ, 0652Ⓐ, 0752Ⓐ, 0757Ⓒ, 0812†, 0907Ⓒ, 0912Ⓐ, 1009†, 1126Ⓒ, 1207Ⓐ, 1212Ⓒ, 1307Ⓒ, 1422Ⓒ, 1424Ⓐ, 1542Ⓐ, 1602†, 1626Ⓒ, 1642Ⓐ, 1742Ⓐ, 1822Ⓒ, 1842Ⓒ, 1942Ⓐ, 2037Ⓒ, 2042Ⓐ, 2237Ⓐ, 2337Ⓒ, returning at 0546Ⓐ, 0647Ⓐ, 0651Ⓒ, 0747Ⓐ, 0848Ⓒ, 0849Ⓐ, 0907†, 1002Ⓒ, 1007Ⓐ, 1102Ⓐ, 1116Ⓒ, 1302⚒, 1400†, 1515Ⓒ, 1518Ⓐ, 1636Ⓐ, 1655†, 1717Ⓒ, 1734Ⓐ, 1835Ⓐ, 1919Ⓒ, 1935Ⓒ, 2035Ⓐ, 2130Ⓒ, 2134Ⓐ, 2329Ⓒ, 2231Ⓐ. Journey: 1¼ hours. Also ◨ *(GL)* from Miami at 0330, 0600, 0605, 0730, 0800, 0840, 0940, 0945, 1025, 1030, 1040, 1245, 1310, 1325, 1525, 1600, 1715, 1830, 1835, 2155, 2230, 2325, returning at 0305, 0505, 0630, 0745, 0925, 1030, 1055, 1345, 1400, 1415, 1500, 1640, 1700, 1720, 1855, 1900, 1955, 2000, 2015, 2215, 2315, 2335.

Goulds ◨ *(DCT)* (❖ km, US $: ❖). From Miami: ❖, returning at ❖. Journey: ❖.

Lake Worth ° *(TR)* (❖ km, US $: 6.00). From Miami Metrorail: 0452Ⓐ, 0552Ⓐ, 0557Ⓒ, 0652Ⓐ, 0752Ⓐ, 0757Ⓒ, 0812†, 0907Ⓒ, 0912Ⓐ, 1009†, 1126Ⓒ, 1207Ⓐ, 1212Ⓒ, 1307Ⓒ, 1422Ⓒ, 1424Ⓐ, 1542Ⓐ, 1602†, 1626Ⓒ, 1642Ⓐ, 1742Ⓐ, 1822Ⓒ, 1842Ⓒ, 1942Ⓐ, 2037Ⓒ, 2042Ⓐ, 2237Ⓐ, 2337Ⓒ, returning at 0456Ⓐ, 0556Ⓐ, 0601Ⓒ, 0656Ⓐ, 0756⚒, 0818†, 0914Ⓒ, 0919Ⓐ, 1011Ⓐ, 1013†, 1028Ⓒ, 1210Ⓐ, 1212Ⓒ, 1311†, 1426Ⓒ, 1429Ⓐ, 1546Ⓐ, 1606†, 1626Ⓒ, 1643Ⓐ, 1743Ⓐ, 1831Ⓒ, 1843Ⓐ, 1846†, 1943Ⓐ, 2041Ⓒ, 2043Ⓐ, 2241⚒. Journey: 1½ hours.

Metrorail ° *(MTD)* (❖ km, US $: ❖). From Miami Government Center: 0529Ⓐ/0543Ⓒ and frequent to 0017, returning at 0536Ⓐ/0541Ⓒ and frequent to 0005. Journey: 20 mins.

Miami Airport ° *(TR)* (❖ km, US $: 2.00). From Miami Metrorail: 00001ex①, 0618Ⓐ, 0720Ⓐ, 0721Ⓒ, 0820Ⓐ, 0918Ⓒ, 0922Ⓐ, 0938†, 1032Ⓒ, 1036Ⓐ, 1131Ⓐ, 1134†, 1146Ⓒ, 1332Ⓒ, 1333Ⓐ, 1432†, 1545Ⓒ, 1549Ⓐ, 1708Ⓐ, 1727†, 1747Ⓒ, 1806Ⓐ, 1907Ⓐ, 1949Ⓒ, 2006Ⓐ, 2007†, 2105Ⓐ, 2200Ⓒ, 2204Ⓐ, returning at 0445Ⓐ, 0545Ⓐ, 0550Ⓒ, 0645Ⓐ, 0745Ⓐ, 0750Ⓒ, 0805†, 0900Ⓒ, 0905Ⓐ, 1002†, 1119Ⓒ, 1200Ⓐ, 1205Ⓒ, 1300Ⓒ, 1415Ⓒ, 1417Ⓐ, 1535Ⓐ, 1555†, 1619Ⓒ, 1635Ⓐ, 1735Ⓐ, 1815Ⓒ, 1835Ⓒ, 1935Ⓐ, 2030Ⓒ, 2035Ⓐ, 2230Ⓐ, 2330Ⓒ. Journey: 9 mins.

Miami Beach ◨ *(DCT)* (❖ km, US $: ❖). From Miami: ❖, returning at ❖. Journey: ❖.

Okeechobee ° *(MTD)* (❖ km, US $: ❖). From Miami Government Center: 0529Ⓐ/0543Ⓒ and frequent to 0017, returning 0531Ⓐ/0536Ⓒ and frequent to 0000. Journey: 25 mins.

Palm Beach ° *(TR)* (❖ km, US $: 6.00). From Miami Metrorail: 0452Ⓐ, 0552Ⓐ, 0557Ⓒ, 0652Ⓐ, 0752Ⓐ, 0757Ⓒ, 0812†, 0907Ⓒ, 0912Ⓐ, 1009†, 1126Ⓒ, 1207Ⓐ, 1212Ⓒ, 1307Ⓒ, 1422Ⓒ, 1424Ⓐ, 1542Ⓐ, 1602†, 1626Ⓒ, 1642Ⓐ, 1742Ⓐ, 1822Ⓒ, 1842Ⓒ, 1942Ⓐ, 2037Ⓒ, 2042Ⓐ, 2237Ⓐ, 2337Ⓒ, returning at 0449Ⓐ, 0549Ⓐ, 0554Ⓒ, 0649Ⓐ, 0749⚒, 0809†, 0907Ⓒ, 0909Ⓐ, 1004Ⓐ, 1006†, 1020Ⓒ, 1203Ⓐ, 1205Ⓒ, 1304†, 1419Ⓒ, 1422Ⓐ, 1536Ⓐ, 1559†, 1619Ⓒ, 1636Ⓐ, 1736Ⓐ, 1824Ⓒ, 1836Ⓐ, 1839†, 1936Ⓐ, 2034Ⓒ, 2036Ⓐ, 2234⚒. Journey: 1½ hours.

Pompano Beach ° *(TR)* (❖ km, US $: 4.50). From Miami Metrorail: 0452Ⓐ, 0552Ⓐ, 0557Ⓒ, 0652Ⓐ, 0752Ⓐ, 0757Ⓒ, 0812†, 0907Ⓒ, 0912Ⓐ, 1009†, 1126Ⓒ, 1207Ⓐ, 1212Ⓒ, 1307Ⓒ, 1422Ⓒ, 1424Ⓐ, 1542Ⓐ, 1602†, 1626Ⓒ, 1642Ⓐ, 1742Ⓐ, 1822Ⓒ, 1842Ⓒ, 1942Ⓐ, 2037Ⓒ, 2042Ⓐ, 2237Ⓐ, 2337Ⓒ, returning at 0528Ⓐ, 0629Ⓐ, 0632Ⓒ, 0729Ⓐ, 0829Ⓒ, 0831Ⓐ, 0840†, 0945Ⓒ, 0950Ⓐ, 1046†, 1045Ⓐ, 1059Ⓒ, 1244Ⓐ, 1246Ⓒ, 1344†, 1457Ⓒ, 1500Ⓐ, 1617Ⓐ, 1639†, 1658Ⓒ, 1716Ⓐ, 1816Ⓐ, 1902Ⓒ, 1916Ⓐ, 1919†, 2016Ⓐ, 2112Ⓒ, 2115Ⓐ, 2312⚒. Journey: 1¼ hours. Also ◨ *(GL)* from Miami at 0730, 1600, returning at 1320, 1920.

West Palm Beach ° *(TR)* (*69* km, US $: 6.00). From Miami Metrorail: 0452Ⓐ, 0552Ⓐ, 0557Ⓒ, 0652Ⓐ, 0752Ⓐ, 0757Ⓒ, 0812†, 0907Ⓒ, 0912Ⓐ, 1009†, 1126Ⓒ, 1207Ⓐ, 1212Ⓒ, 1307Ⓒ, 1422Ⓒ, 1424Ⓐ, 1542Ⓐ, 1602†, 1626Ⓒ, 1642Ⓐ, 1742Ⓐ, 1822Ⓒ, 1842Ⓒ, 1942Ⓐ, 2037Ⓒ, 2042Ⓐ, 2237Ⓐ, 2337Ⓒ, returning at 0445Ⓐ, 0545Ⓐ, 0550Ⓒ, 0645Ⓐ, 0745⚒, 0805†, 0900Ⓒ, 0903Ⓐ, 1000Ⓐ, 1002†, 1016Ⓒ, 1159Ⓐ, 1201Ⓒ, 1300†, 1415Ⓒ, 1418Ⓐ, 1532Ⓐ, 1555†, 1615Ⓒ, 1632Ⓐ, 1732Ⓐ, 1820Ⓒ, 1832Ⓐ, 1835†, 1932Ⓐ, 2030Ⓒ, 2032Ⓐ, 2232⚒. Journey: 1½ hours. Also ◨ *(GL)* from Miami at 0100, 0610, 0740, 1025, 1145, 1310, 1600, 1725, 1900, 2155, returning at 0150, 0350, 0515, 0940, 0945, 1315, 1525, 1740, 1840, 1900, 2130.

°– By ####. ◨–By 🚌.
DCT– Dade County Transit.
GL– Greyhound Lines.
MTD– MetroDade.
TR– Tri-Rail.

Table 860 BISMARCK - RAPID CITY
🚌 *BSI*

US $		1 ▲			km	594 ↓ ↑	2 ▲			
0.00	....	1200	....	....	*0*	d.**Bismarck**..........a.	1730	....	....	....
	....	1420	....	....		d.Hettinger ....d.	1345	....	....	....
	....	1600	....	....		d.Buffalo...............d.	1110	....	....	....
	....	1745	....	....		d.Belle Fourche....d.	0950	....	....	....
	....	1800	....	....		d.Spearfish ....d.	0930	....	....	....
	....	1845	....	....		d.Deadwood.........d.	0905	....	....	....
	....	2000	....	....		a.**Rapid City**........d.	0800	....	....	....

BSI– Bus Services Inc.

Table 861 BARSTOW - BAKERSFIELD
🚌 *ORB*

US $	703	709	1ATC	201	km	296 ↓ ↑	200	2ATC	708	704
0.00	....	....	1150	1410	*0*	d.**Barstow**...........a.	1230	1635	....	....
10.15	0655	1025	1335	1550	*100*	d.Mojave ....d.	1055	1445	1720	2100
10.15	0825	1155	1515	1720	*213*	a.**Bakersfield**.......d.	0915	1330	1605	1935

ORB– Orange Belt Trailways.

Table 862 SPOKANE - RENO

BW NWL STM

US$	NWL 730	STM 6 ®▲		NWL 734	km	395 ↓ ↑		NWL 735	STM 5 Ⓐ▲	BW 2
19.00	0945	1600	....	1900	172	d.**Spokane** ....a.	....	1020	1015	1745n
	|	1700	....	|		d. Coeur d'Alene ....a.	....	|	0935	|
	1135	1900	....	2055		d.Moscow ....d.	....	0815	0740	1600n
◇0.00	1215	2000	....	2145	0	a. Lewiston ....d.	....	0725	0630	1510n
	1225	....	....	....		d. Lewiston ....a.	....	....	....	1500n
17.00	|	....	....	....	160	a. Walla Walla .....d.	....	....	....	|
	|	....	....	....	233	a. Pendleton ....d.	....	....	....	|
6.70	1400	....	....	....	130	d.Grangeville ....d.	....	....	....	1330n
17.20	1745	....	....	....	285	d.McCall ....d.	....	....	....	1145n
25.60	2145b	....	....	....	460	d.**Boise** ....d.	....	....	....	0915n
◇1.90	2210b	....	....	....	488	d.Nampa ....d.	....	....	....	0635
◇2.40	2230b	....	....	....	522	d.Caldwell ....d.	....	....	....	0610
◇22.50	0230b	....	....	....	942	d.Winnemucca ....d.	....	....	....	0040
	0345b	....	....	....		d.Lovelock ....d.	....	....	....	2300
	0500b	....	....	....		a.Sparks ....d.	....	....	....	2145
	0530b	....	....	....		a.**Reno** ....d.	....	....	....	2115

b–*BW*. n–*NWL*. ◇–Fare ex Boise. *BW*–Boise-Winnemucca Trailways.
NWL–Northwestern Trailways.
STM–St. Maries Bus Lines.

Table 863 YOSEMITE PARK ♿

CYT YTS

US$	YTS	CYT	YTS	CYT	km	395 ↓ ↑	CYT	YTS	CYT	YTS
0.00	0800	....	1445	....	125	d.**Merced** ....a.	....	1310	....	1940
	|	0830	|	1450	130	d. Fresno ....a.	1315	|	2010	|
13.00	1030	1240	1715	1840	0	a.**Yosemite Lodge** d.	0855	1100	1615	1720
US $					km	↓ YTS ↑				
0.00	....	0825	1450	....	0	d.**Fresno** ....a.	1300	1925	....	....
	....	0950	1555	....		d.Squaw Valley ....d.	1115	1805	....	....
	....	1355	1750	....		a.**Sequoia NP** ∧ ..d.	0850	1440	....	....

∧–Sequoia National Park, Giant Forest Lodge.
CYT–California Yosemite Tours. *YTS*–Yosemite VIA.

Table 864 PORTLAND - ASTORIA

RAZ

US$		16	18		km	694 ↓ ↑		17	19	
0.00	....	0630	1630	....	0	d.**Portland** ....d.	....	1225	2215	....
	....	|	|	....	43	d. Glenwood........d.	....	|	|	....
14.00	....	|	|	....	105	d. Tillamook ....d.	....	|	|	....
14.00	....	0845	|	....	125	d. Seaside...........d.	....	|	2000	....
7.00	....	|	1715	....	49	d.St. Helens ....d.	....	1135	|	....
20.00	....	0915	1915	....	165	a.**Astoria**.............d.	....	0930	1930	....

RAZ–Raz Transportation Co.

Table 865 RENO - PHOENIX

GL KTS

US$		KTS 411	GL 6365	GL 6361	KTS 509	KTS 507		GL 6369				km	296 ↓ ↑	KTS 506	GL 6358		GL 6362			GL 6390	KTS 510	KTS 410		
	....	....	....	....	....	....	....	....	....	....	....	445	d.Klamath Falls ....a.	....	....	....	....	....	....	....	....	....	....	....
	....	....	....	....	....	....	....	....	....	....	....		d.Alturas.......................d.	....	....	....	....	....	....	....	....	....	....	....
0.00	....	0730	....	....	....	....	....	....	....	....	....	0	d.**Reno**.........................a.	....	....	....	....	....	....	....	....	1745	....	....
	....	0810	....	....	....	....	....	....	....	....	....		d.Carson City ....d.	....	....	....	....	....	....	....	....	1705	....	....
6.95	....	1015	....	....	....	....	....	....	....	....	....	150	d.Schurz.......................d.	....	....	....	....	....	....	....	....	1445	....	....
14.75	....	1325	....	....	....	....	....	....	....	....	....	370	d.Tonopah ....d.	....	....	....	....	....	....	....	....	1200	....	....
16.30	....	1400	....	....	....	....	....	....	....	....	....	412	d.Goldfield ....d.	....	....	....	....	....	....	....	....	1055	....	....
20.15	....	1525	....	....	....	....	....	....	....	....	....	520	d.Beatty..........................d.	....	....	....	....	....	....	....	....	0945	....	....
26.40	....	1800	....	....	....	....	....	....	....	....	....	705	a. **Las Vegas** ....d.	....	....	....	....	....	....	....	....	0715	....	....
	....	....	1800	0001	0630	1100	....	1500	....	....	....		d. **Las Vegas** ....a.	1530	1645	....	2210	....	....	0020	0530	....	....	....
26.60	....	....	|	|	|	|	....	|	....	....	....	742	d.Boulder City ....d.	|	|	....	|	....	....	|	|	....	....	....
	....	....	|	|	|	1425	....	|	....	....	....		d. Needles.....................d.	1205	|	....	|	....	....	|	|	....	....	....
	....	....	|	|	|	1640	....	|	....	....	....		d. Lake Havasu City....d.	1220	|	....	|	....	....	|	|	....	....	....
80.10	....	....	2230	0500	1145	|	....	1945	....	....	....	863	d.Kingman ....d.	|	1420	....	1945	....	....	2220	0305	....	....	....
	....	....	0055	|	1400	1925	....	2210	....	....	....		d.Wickenburg ....d.	0905	1105	....	|	....	....	1940	0005	....	....	....
97.20	....	....	0215	1130	1515	2045	....	2330	....	....	....	1168	a.**Phoenix** ....d.	0745	0930	....	1300	....	....	1800	2245	....	....	....

GL–Greyhound Lines. *KTS*–K-T Services.

Table 870 LAS VEGAS - LOS ANGELES

GL GLSN

US$	296 GL ↓	km	1307	6049			6025	6051	1317	6037 ⑤⑥⑦	6031				1301	7015		6029	6047	1035		6035 ⑤⑦	6027	6053 ⑦	
0.00	**Las Vegas** ★ ....d.	0	0030	0030	....	....	0610	0640	0800	0900	1000	....	....	....	1100	1130	....	1300	1445	1515	....	1735	1735	1945	....
28.00	Barstow ....d.	255	|	0340	....	....	|	1010	1110	|	1350	....	....	....	1415	1515	....	|	1815	1835	....	2115	2055	|	....
37.00	San Bernardino ....d.	380	|	|	....	....	1030	1150	|	1410	1525	....	....	....	|	1655	....	1720	1950	|	....	|	2235	|	....
39.00	Riverside ....d.	395	|	0505	....	....	|	1210	|	|	|	....	....	....	|	1720	....	|	|	|	....	|	|	|	....
41.00	Claremont *(Pomona)* .d.	431	|	0540	....	....	|	1245	|	|	1600	....	....	....	|	....	....	|	2025	|	....	|	2310	|	....
47.75	Anaheim *(Disneyland)*.d.	439	|	|	....	....	|	|	|	1520	|	....	....	....	|	....	....	1830	|	|	....	|	|	|	....
43.00	El Monte *(Alhambra)* .d.	476	|	0615	....	....	|	|	|	|	1635	....	....	....	|	....	....	|	2100	|	....	|	2345	|	....
43.00	Pasadena ....d.	461	|	|	....	....	|	1325	|	|	|	....	....	....	|	....	....	|	|	|	....	|	|	|	....
50.00	**Los Angeles**............a.	501	0625	0645	....	....	1140	1355	1340	1605	1705	....	....	....	1635	....	....	1915	2130	2055	....	2335	0015	0115	....

296 GL ↓		6022			6024		1310		6040	6042	7000	6050	1312		6056 ⑤⑥⑦		6044 ⑤	1302	6048				6068		1340
Los Angeles...............d.	....	0001	....	....	0600	....	0900	....	1000	1100	....	1315	1400	....	1545	....	1700	1800	1800	....	....	....	2000	....	2315
Pasadena ....d.	....	|	....	....	|	....	|	....	|	|	....	|	|	....	|	....	|	|	|	....	....	....	|	....	|
El Monte *(Alhambra)* ...d.	....	|	....	....	|	....	0930	....	|	|	....	1345	|	....	|	....	|	|	1830	....	....	....	|	....	|
Anaheim *(Disneyland)*d.	....	|	....	....	0645	....	|	....	|	|	....	|	|	....	1635	....	|	|	|	....	....	....	|	....	|
Claremont *(Pomona)*...d.	....	|	....	....	|	....	1005	....	|	|	....	1420	|	....	|	....	|	|	1905	....	....	....	|	....	|
Riverside ....d.	....	|	....	....	0745	....	1050	....	|	|	1425	|	|	....	1735	....	|	|	1945	....	....	....	|	....	|
San Bernardino ....d.	....	|	....	....	0815	....	1115	....	1130	|	1510	1510	|	....	1810	....	1850	|	2025	....	....	....	2125	....	0040
Barstow ....d.	....	|	....	....	1010	....	1305	....	|	1350	|	1705	1635	....	|	....	|	2035	2215	....	....	....	|	....	|
Las Vegas ★ ....a.	....	0520	....	....	1325	....	1610	....	1550	1705	1925	2005	1930	....	2010	....	2050	2350	0130	....	....	....	0130	....	0430

★–Charter (GLSN) service Las Vegas-Death Valley Junction-Furnace Creek Ranch-Scotty's Castle and v.v. *GL*–Greyhound Lines. *GLSN*–Gray Line of Southern Nevada.

Table 875 PORTLAND - SALT LAKE CITY

GL PUT RAZ UTA

US$	GL 5544		GL 5530		CAC ★	PSL 201	GL 1421	GL 5534		GL 5532	PUT 102	km	396 ↓ ↑	CAC ★	GL 1422	GL 5533	GL 5537	GL 5549			PSL 202	PUT 101	GL 5543	GL 5547
0.00	1030	....	1300	....	1330	....	....	1615	....	2230	....	0	d.**Portland** ....a.	1100	....	1430	1615	1950	....	....	....	....	0510	1015
19.00	1230	....	1445	....	|	....	....	|	....	0010	....	136	d.The Dalles.......................d.	|	....	|	1420	1805	....	....	....	....	|	0830
	1255	....	1515	....	|	....	1800	|	....	|	....	172	d.Biggs...............................d.	|	1250	|	1350	1735	....	....	....	....	|	0800
37.00	....	....	1740	....	|	....	|	|	....	0230	....	340	d.Pendleton.........................d.	|	|	|	1100	....	....	....	....	....	0125	....
44.00	....	....	1845	....	|	....	|	|	....	0335	....	425	d.La Grande ....d.	|	|	|	0925	....	....	....	....	....	2350	....
53.00	....	....	2005	....	|	....	|	|	....	0505	....	488	d.Baker ....d.	|	|	|	0835	....	....	....	....	....	2300	....
11.00	....	....	|	....	r	....	|	1800	....	|	....	91	d. Government Camp........d.	0930	|	1255	|	....	....	....	....	....	|	....
Ω22.00	....	....	|	....	|	1535	|	|	....	|	....	▼205	d. Eugene ....a.	|	|	|	|	....	....	....	2115	....	|	....
33.00	....	....	|	....	1730	1805	2100	2100	....	|	....	276	d.Bend ....d.	0700	0955	0955	|	....	....	....	1815	....	|	....
	....	....	|	....	....	....	....	....	....	|	....	470	d.Burns ....d.	....	....	....	|	....	....	....	....	....	|	....
	....	....	2230	....	....	....	....	....	....	0735	....	⌧600	d.Ontario ....d.	....	....	....	0735	....	....	....	....	....	2205	....
67.00	....	....	2305	....	....	....	....	....	....	0810	....	⌧766	d.Caldwell ....d.	....	....	....	0700	....	....	....	....	....	2130	....
70.00	....	....	2325	....	....	....	....	....	....	0830	....	⌧800	d.Nampa ....d.	....	....	....	0640	....	....	....	....	....	2110	....
70.00	....	....	0015	....	....	....	....	....	....	0940	....	⌧828	d.**Boise** ....d.	....	....	....	0610	....	....	....	....	....	2040	....
82.00	....	....	0240	....	....	....	....	....	....	1305	....	⌧1013	d.Twin Falls.........................d.	....	....	....	0240	....	....	....	....	....	1630	....
85.00	....	....	|	....	....	....	....	....	....	1355	1435	⌧1114	d.Burley...............................d.	....	....	....	0130	....	....	....	....	1430	1530	....
92.00	....	....	|	....	....	....	....	....	....	|	1615	⌧1244	a. Pocatello.........................d.	....	....	....	|	....	....	....	....	1300	|	....
98.00	....	....	0615	....	....	....	....	....	....	1650	....	⌧1279	d.Brigham City ....d.	....	....	....	2330	....	....	....	....	....	1230	....
98.00	....	....	0650	....	....	....	....	....	....	1725	....	⌧1316	d.Ogden ▶ ....d.	....	....	....	2300	....	....	....	....	....	1201	....
98.00	....	....	0740	....	....	....	....	....	....	1820	....	⌧1374	a.**Salt Lake City** ▶ ....d.	....	....	....	2205	....	....	....	....	....	1100	....

Ω–Fare ex Bend. ⌧–Km via Bend. ▼–Km ex Bend. ★- ex Holidays. ▶–Local (*UTA* **55/70/71/170**) operates Salt Lake City-Ogden and v.v. 0600⚒ and frequent (hourly after 1800) to 2307⑥/2337Ⓐ. *CAC*–CAC Transportation Inc. *GL*–Greyhound Lines. *PUT*–Pocatello Urban Transit. *PSL*–Porter Stage Lines. *UTA*–Utah Transit Authority.

Table 880 VANCOUVER - SEATTLE

APS GL NWL QUS TNW

US $	695	km	TNW 8011	APS	QUS	GL 6529	QUS	TNW 8013	APS	NWL 733	QUS	APS	QUS	GL 6505	QUS	APS	QUS	GL 6577	TNW 8508	APS	QUS	APS	GL 6527	APS	QUS
	↓		♣	R	♣		♣	♣	R		♣		♣		♣	R	♣		♣	R	♣	R		⑥R	♣
28.00	**Vancouver**.........d.	0	0400	....	0600	....	0730	0830	....	....	0930	....	1030	....	1115	....	1245	....	1230	....	1530	....	....	....	1830
25.00	New Westminster (u)d.	19	|	....	|	....	|	|	....	....	|	....	|	....	|	....	1325	....	|	....	|	....	....	....	|
21.00	Blaine ◇........d.	58	|	0610	|	....	|	|	0810	....	|	1010	|	....	|	1210	|	....	|	1410	|	1610	....	1810	|
18.00	Bellingham ....d.	93	|	0710	|	0805	|	|	0910	1000	|	1110	|	1225	|	1310	|	1415	|	1510	|	1710	1800	1910	|
	Mount Vernon ....d.		|	0750	|	0840	|	|	0950	1030	|	1150	|	1300	|	1350	|	1450	1500	1550	|	1750	1835	1950	|
7.00	Everett ....d.	198	|	|	|	0925	|	|	|	1115	|	|	|	1350	|	|	|	1545	|	|	|	|	1915	|	|
0.00	**Seattle** ....a.	250	0740	|	0915	1010	1045	1130	|	1201	1245	|	1345	1430	1430	|	1600	1630	1700	|	1845	|	2000	|	2145
	Seattle/Tacoma Airport.a.		....	0940	0945	....	1115	....	1140	....	1315	1340	1415	....	1500	1540	1630	....	....	1740	1915	1940	....	2140	2215

695	TNW 8012	APS	QUS	APS	QUS	APS	GL 6526	QUS	TNW 8907	QUS	QUS	APS	QUS 110	APS	GL 6532	NWL 732	GLC 188	QUS	APS	APS	QUS	GL 6540	APS	TNW 8014	APS
↓	♣	R	♣	R	♣	R		♣	♣	♣	♣	R	♣	R			♣	♣	R	R	♣		R	♣	⑥R
Seattle/Tacoma Airport.d.	....	0700	0745	0900	1000	1100	....	1115	....	1200	1245	1300	1445	1500	....	....	1630	1700	1700	1900	1930	....	2100	....	2300
Seattle ....d.	0800	|	0820	|	1035	|	1130	1150	1230	1235	|	|	1520	|	1530	1700	1715	1735	|	|	2000	2045	|	2115	|
Everett ....d.	|	|	|	|	|	|	1215	|	|	|	|	|	|	|	1615	1755	|	|	|	|	|	2130	|	|	|
Mount Vernon ....d.	|	0850	|	1050	|	1250	1305	|	1415	|	|	1450	|	1650	1705	1840	|	|	1850	2050	|	2220	2250	|	0050
Bellingham ....d.	|	0930	|	1130	|	1330	1340	|	|	|	|	1530	|	1730	1740	1910	1855	|	1930	2130	|	2255	2330	|	0130
Blaine ◇.............a.	|	1020	|	1220	|	1420	....	|	|	|	|	1620	|	1820	....	....	|	|	2020	2220	|	....	0020	|	0220
New Westminster (s)a.	|	....	|	....	|	....	....	|	|	|	|	....	|	....	....	....	2020	|	....	....	|	....	....	|	....
Vancouver..............a.	1215	....	1135	....	1350	....	....	1505	1645	1550	1615	....	1835	....	....	....	2045	2050	....	....	2315	....	....	0015	....

◇–For Semi-Ah-Moo. *APS*–Airporter Shuttle. *GL*–Greyhound Lines. *NWL*–Northwestern Trailways. *QUS*–Quick Shuttle. *TNW*–Trailways Northwest.

Table 881 PORT ANGELES

US $					km	295				
						↓ ↑				
0.00	....	....	....	....	0	d.**Seattle** ....a.	....	....	....	....
7.00	....	....	....	....	65	d.Port Ludlow ....d.	....	....	....	....
	....	....	....	....	90	a. Port Townsend ★d.	....	....	....	....
10.00	....	....	....	....	115	d.Sequim..............d.	....	....	....	....
12.00	....	....	....	....	145	a.**Port Angeles**....d.	....	....	....	....

★– Connecting Port Ludlow-Port Townsend and v.v.

Table 882 HOQUIAM - OLYMPIA

GHT

US $	1	3	5	7	km	296	12	4	8	10
			Ⓐ			↓ ↑	Ⓐ			
0.00	0555	1105	1310	1510	0	d.**Hoquiam**...........a.	1145	1500	1905	....
0.75	0610	1130	1330	1530	7	d.Aberdeen...........d.	1130	1445	1850	2200
0.75	0740	1300	1505	1700	84	a.**Olympia**...........d.	1000	1310	1715	2035

GHT– Grays Harbor Transportation Authority.

Table 883 SEATTLE - PORTLAND

GL NWL

US $	GL 1439	GL 6501	GL 6543	GL 1447	GL 1423		GL 6549	NWL 738	GL 6545	GL 1429	GL 1429	km	296 ↓
0.00	0045	0805	1045	1201	1340	....	1500	1700	1735	1800	2015	0	d.**Seattle**
	|	|	|	|	1405	....	|	|	1800	|	|		d.Seattle/Tacoma Airport
	0135	0855	1135	|	1440	....	1555	1805	1835	|	2105	52	d.Tacoma
	0205	0925	|	|	1510	....	1625	|	1905	|	|		d.Fort Lewis
	0240	0955	1225	|	1540	....	1655	1900	1935	|	2145	93	d.Olympia
	|	1030	1300	|	|	....	1730	1925	2010	|	|	131	d.Centralia *(Chehalis)*
	|	1120	1340	|	1655	....	1820	2005	2100	|	|	201	d.Longview
	|	1210	1440	|	|	....	1910	2050	|	|	|	266	d.Vancouver
	0455	1230	1500	1515	1755	....	1930	2110	2200	2115	2359	278	a.**Portland**

km	296 ↑	GL 6526	GL 1436	NWL 739	GL 6528	GL 1440	GL 6514	GL 1420	GL 6588		GL 6542	GL 1424
0	d.**Seattle** ....a.	1100	1025	1230	1500	1425	1710	1625	2015	....	2315	0130
	d.Seattle/Tacoma Airport..a.	1035	1015	|	|	1405	|	1600	1950	....	|	|
52	d.Tacoma ....d.	1005	0945	1150	1415	|	1625	|	1920	....	2230	0045
	d.Fort Lewis ....d.	0930	|	1120	1335	|	1550	|	1845	....	|	|
93	d.Olympia....................d.	0905	|	1040	1310	|	1525	|	1820	....	2140	0001
131	d.Centralia *(Chehalis)*...d.	0825	|	1000	1230	|	1445	|	1740	....	2100	|
201	d.Longview.................d.	0735	|	0910	1140	|	1355	|	1650	....	2010	2230
266	d.Vancouver................d.	0645	|	0820	1050	|	1305	|	1555	....	1920	|
278	a.**Portland** ....d.	0625	0700	0800	1030	1100	1245	1300	1535	....	1900	2130

GL– Greyhound Lines. *NWL*– Northwestern Trailways.

Table 856 296 SAN DIEGO - TIJUANA ♣

GL MC

service San Diego-San Ysidro -Tijuana and v.v. *20* km. Journey: 45 mins.-1 hour. Fare: US $: 5.25.

From San Diego Greyhound Terminal *(GL)*: 0120, 0420, 0730, 0840, 0955, 1045, 1140, 1240, 1355, 1440, 1540, 1700, 1750, 1905, 2010, 2040, 2225.

From San Diego Amtrak *(MC)*: 0900, 1100, 1400, 1600, 1800.

From Tijuana (to San Diego Greyhound Terminal) *(GL)*: 0215, 0515, 0610, 0715, 0815, 0910, 1010, 1125, 1210, 1310, 1410, 1515, 1630, 1715, 1915, 2030, 2130, 2200, 2345.

From Tijuana (to San Diego Amtrak) *(MC)*: 0800, 1000, 1200, 1500, 1700, 1845, 2100©.

GL–Greyhound Lines. *MC*–Mexicoach.

Table 887 PORTLAND - SACRAMENTO

GL

US $	1429	1439	6521	1443	6559	6557	1447	1421	6531	1423	6545	km	296 ↓
0.00	0045	0540	1040	1300	....	1545	1630	....	1730	1845	2230	674	d.**Portland**
❖	|	0645	1201	1415	....	1715	1740	....	1850	1950	2335	598	d.Salem
	|	0720	1235	|	....	1750	|	....	1925	|	0010	565	d.Albany
❖	0305	0900	1430	1550	1600	1915	1920	....	2050	2125	0135	500	d.Eugene
	|	1035	1625	|	|	....	2055	....	....	2240	....	390	d.Roseburg
❖	|	|	|	|	|	....	|	1515	....	|	....		d. **Yakima**
❖	|	|	|	|	|	....	|	1800	....	|	....		d. Biggs
❖	|	|	|	|	|	....	|	|	....	|	....		d. The Dalles
❖	|	|	|	|	|	....	|	2115	....	|	....		d. Bend
❖	0530	1225	1800	|	|	....	2215	|	....	|	....	284	d.Grants Pass
❖	0625	1320	1845	1935	|	....	2315	|	....	0050	....	238	d.Medford
❖	|	|	▬	|	1940	....	|	0035	....	|	....		d. Klamath Falls Ω
	0850	1510	**1441**	2125	....	....	|	|	....	|	....		d.Weed
❖	0920	1540	....	|	....	....	|	|	....	|	....		d.Dunsmuir
❖	1100	1725	1320	2320	....	....	0230	0430	....	0415	....	0	d.Redding
❖	1140	1815	1410	|	....	....	|	0520	....	0455	....		d.Red Bluff
❖	1250	1925	1530	|	....	....	|	0630	....	|	....		d.Chico
❖	1415	2050	1710	|	....	....	|	0815	....	|	....		d.Marysville
❖	1505	2140	1800	0205	....	....	0510	0905	....	0735	....		a.**Sacramento**

km	296 ↑	6536	6538 ⑤	6546	1424	1428	1450	1436	1440	1420	6554	1422
674	d.**Portland** ....a.	1805	1815	2015	2100	2350	....	0555	1010	1215	1405	....
598	d.Salem.........................d.	1635	|	1915	2000	2250	....	|	0910	|	1235	....
565	d.Albany.......................d.	1600	|	1840	|	|	....	|	0835	|	1201	....
500	d.Eugene.......................d.	1430	1545	1715	1835	2130	....	0340	0705	1000	1030	....
390	d.Roseburg....................d.	1230	....	....	1655	1945	....	|	|	0825	|	....
	d. **Yakima** ....a.	|	....	....	|	|	....	|	|	|	|	1530
	d. Biggs.......................d.	|	....	....	|	|	....	|	|	|	|	1330
	d. The Dalles ....d.	|	....	....	|	|	....	|	|	|	|	|
	d. Bend........................d.	|	....	....	|	|	....	|	|	|	|	0955
284	d.Grants Pass ....d.	1055	....	....	1540	1825	....	|	|	0635	|	|
238	d.Medford.....................d.	1015	....	....	1500	1745	....	0035	0350	0555	|	|
	d. Klamath Falls Ω....d.	....	....	....	|	|	....	|	|	|	0615	0630
	d.Weed ....d.	....	....	....	1220	1455	....	|	0150	|	....	0420
	d.Dunsmuir....................d.	....	....	....	1150	1425	....	|	0125	|	....	0355
0	d.Redding.....................d.	....	....	....	1040	1315	1900	2115	0015	0245	....	0245
	d.Red Bluff ....d.	....	....	....	|	1205	1820	|	2315	0150	....	0200
	d.Chico.........................d.	....	....	....	|	1105	1730	|	2225	|	....	0110
	d.Marysville ....d.	....	....	....	|	0930	1555	|	2055	|	....	2355
	a.**Sacramento**.............d.	....	....	....	0700	0830	1500	1815	2000	2300	....	2300

Ω– For Crater Lake. *GL*– Greyhound Lines.

Table 888 HOUSTON - EL PASO

GL KBC

US $	GL 1245	GL 7341	KBC 403	GL 7263	GL 405	GL 7275	GL 1243	GL 7279	GL 7283	GL 7339	GL 7281	km	296 ↓
0.00	0015	0330	....	0600	0815	1145	1300	1430	1645	1830	2200	0	d.**Houston**
	|	0615	....	0910	1100	|	1620	|	|	2145	|		d.Seguin
34.00	0340	0700	0800	0955	1300a	1515	1655	1800	2045a	2230	0215a	305	d.San Antonio
	....	....	0935	....	1440a	....	....	....	2205a	....	0330a	417	d.Kerrville
59.00	....	....	1140	....	1640a	....	....	....	2359a	....	0526a	585	d.Sonora
73.00	....	....	1445b	....	1935	....	....	....	0250	....	0830	875	d.Fort Stockton
92.00	....	....	1655b	....	2145	....	....	....	|	....	1025	960	d.Van Horn
104.00	....	....	1830b	....	2300	....	....	....	0545	....	1159	1160	a.**El Paso**

km	296 ↑	GL 1052	GL 408	GL 552	GL 402	GL 1560	GL 7258	GL 404	GL 7270	GL 7276	GL 406	GL 1256
0	d.**Houston** ....a.	0515	0645	0915	....	1230	1600	2015	2045	2359	....	0315
	d.Seguin.........................d.	|	|	0600	....	|	1245	1700	|	|	....	|
305	d.San Antonio ....d.	0145	0315	0515	0700a	0900	1201	1615	1715	2030	2140a	2345
417	d.Kerrville ....d.	....	0130a	....	0545a	....	....	1345a	....	....	2010a	....
585	d.Sonora ....d.	....	2330a	....	0342a	....	....	1140a	....	....	1810a	....
875	d.Fort Stockton.............d.	....	2100a	....	0115a	....	....	0900a	....	....	1540a	....
960	d.Van Horn.....................d.	....	1830	....	2250	....	....	0630	....	....	1310	....
1160	a.**El Paso**....................d.	....	1445	....	1940	....	....	0300	....	....	0935	....

a– *KBC*. b–*GL*. *GL*–Greyhound Lines. *KBC*–Kerrville Bus Co.

Table 891 PORTLAND - SAN FRANCISCO (FAL GL)

US $	GL 1489	FAL 1	GL 6642	GL 1483	km	296 ↓ ↑	GL 1490	GL 6643	GL 1482	FAL 2
92.00	0845	a	....	2130	0	d.**Portland** ....a.	1815	....	0915	b
82.00	1300	....	....	0115	190	d.Newport..........d.	1455	....	0500	....
	1445	....	....	|		d.Reedsport..........d.	1255	....	|	....
73.00	1545	....	....	0405	365	d.Coos Bay ....d.	1201	....	0230	....
59.00	2000	....	....	0755	585	d.Crescent City ....d.	0815	....	2300	....
43.00	2220	....	....	1005	720	d.Eureka..............d.	0605	....	2040	....
35.00	0001	....	....	1150	820	d.Garberville.........d.	0340	....	1835	....
25.00	0140	....	....	1330	970	d.Willits ....d.	0200	....	1655	....
22.00	0230	....	....	1440	1007	d.Ukiah.................d.	0110	....	1550	....
	|	0730	....	|		d. Fort Bragg ....a.	|	....	|	2030
	0335	1020	....	1545		d.Healdsburg.........d.	2359	....	1435	1750
11.00	0405	1040	1620	1615	1099	d.Santa Rosa ....d.	2340	1400	1415	1730
8.00	0430	1100	|	1640	1125	d.Petaluma...........d.	2305	|	1335	1655
4.00	0500	1140	|	1705	1167	d.San Rafael ....d.	2240	|	1310	1620
	|	|	1905	|		a. **Sacramento** ...d.	|	1030	|	|
0.00	0540	1215	....	1745	1195	a.**San Francisco**..d.	2200	....	1230	1540

a– 4½ hours later on †. b–1¼ hours later on †.
FAL– Falcon Bus Lines.
GL– Greyhound Lines.

Table 892 RENO - LOS ANGELES (GL)

US $			6005		km	595 ↓ ↑				6008
0.00	....	....	0730	....	0	d.**Reno**..................a.	....	....	....	0545
7.00	....	....	0820	....	49	d.Carson City ....d.	....	....	....	0455
33.00	....	....	1335	....	329	d.Bishop...............d.	....	....	....	0030
59.00	....	....	1800	....	679	d.Mojave ....d.	....	....	....	2040
67.00	....	....	2030	....	821	d.Hollywood..........d.	....	....	....	1705
73.00	....	....	2055	....	845	a.**Los Angeles**.....d.	....	....	....	1635

GL– Greyhound Lines.

Table 893 AUSTIN - KERRVILLE (KBC)

US $				208	km	595 ↓ ↑		203		
0.00	....	....	....	1835	0	d.**Austin**...............a.	....	1045	....	....
❖	....	....	....	2010	❖	d.Fredericksburg ..d.	....	0900	....	....
❖	....	....	....	2055	❖	a.**Kerrville**............d.	....	0830	....	....

KBC– Kerrville Bus Co.

Table 897 SEATTLE - VICTORIA (GLS WIC)

US $	GLS 114 ♣				km	196 ↓ ↑			GLS 114 ♣	
0.00	0555	....	....	....	0	d.**Seattle** ....a.	....	....	1735	....
	|	....	....	....	52	d.Everett...............d.	....	....	|	....
	|	....	....	....	❖	d.Mount Vernon....d.	....	....	|	....
10.75	0800	....	....	....	157	d.Anacortes..........d.	....	....	1515	....
17.60	1130	....	....	....	250	d.Sidney...............a.	....	....	1200	....
21.00	1500	....	....	....	280	a.**Victoria**.............d.	....	....	1000	....

GLS– Gray Line of Seattle (Evergreen Trails Inc).
WIC– Whidbey Island Coach.

Table 895 SACRAMENTO - SAN JOSE (GL)

US $	296 ↓	km	8393	8361	6908 ⑤⑥⑦	8369	6809	8375		
	South Lake Tahoe.d.	◇299	0335	0830	....	1201	....	1835	....	....
	Sacramento.......a.		0630	1159	....	1440	....	2135	....	....
26.00	**Sacramento**.......d.	0	0650	....	1230	1530	....	*2215*	....	....
14.00	Stockton..............d.	79	0810	....	1350	|	1725	|	....	....
	Tracy...................d.		0840	....	1425	|	1820	|	....	....
	Oakland.........a.		|	....	|	1720	|	*2355*	....	....
	San Francisco a.		|	....	|	1750	|	*0025*	....	....
	Palo Alto *(Mountain View)*..d.		|	....	|	....	|	....	....	....
0.00	**San Jose**............a.	209	1010	....	1545	....	1930	....	....	....

296 ↓	8356	8350	6806	8372	8324	8392		6909 ⑤⑥⑦		
San Jose...................d.	....	....	0850	....	....	1445	....	1815	....	....
Palo Alto *(Mountain View)*.d.	....	....	|	....	....	|	....	|	....	....
San Francisco....d.	....	*0800*	|	1201	1500	|	....	|	....	....
Oakland..............d.	....	*0830*	|	1230	1530	|	....	|	....	....
Tracy.........................d.	....	|	1025	|	|	1630	....	1945	....	....
Stockton.....................d.	....	|	1100	|	|	1720	....	2020	....	....
Sacramento.............a.	....	*1000*	1215	1400	1710	1835	....	2115	....	....
Sacramento.............d.	0800	1030	....	1430	....	1915	....	....	....	....
South Lake Tahoe ...a.	1045	1340	....	1710	....	2150	....	....	....	....

◇–Km ex Stockton. *GL*–Greyhound Lines.

Table 905 OAKLAND - SANTA CRUZ (PLS)

US $		441			km	394 ↓ ↑		432		
0.00	....	1215	....	....	0	d.**Oakland**............a.	....	1240	....	....
	....	1345	....	....		d.San Jose...........d.	....	1135	....	....
	....	1455	....	....		a.**Santa Cruz**.......d.	....	1030	....	....

PLS– Peerless Stages.

Table 906 TACOMA - BREMERTON

US $					km	↓ ↑				
0.00	....	....	....	....	0	d.**Tacoma**............a.	....	....	....	....
	....	....	....	....		a.**Bremerton**........d.	....	....	....	....

Table 908 295 SALINAS - MONTEREY ♿ (MST)

service Salinas-Monterey and v.v. *30* km. Journey: 50 mins. Fare: US $: 2.50.
From Monterey: 0700Ⓐ, 0745Ⓐ, 0815⚒, 0845⚒, 0915⚒, 0945, 1015⚒, 1045, 1115⚒, 1145, 1215⚒, 1245, 1315⚒, 1345, 1415⚒, 1445, 1515⚒, 1545, 1615⚒, 1645, 1715⚒, 1745, 1815⚒, 1915⚒, 2015⚒, 2115⚒, 2215⚒.
From Salinas: 0520Ⓐ, 0542Ⓐ, 0642Ⓐ, 0712Ⓐ, 0715Ⓐ, 0742⚒, 0815⚒, 0842⚒, 0915⚒, 0942, 1015⚒, 1042, 1115⚒, 1142, 1215⚒, 1242, 1315⚒, 1342, 1415⚒, 1440⚒, 1442†, 1515⚒, 1542, 1615⚒, 1642, 1705Ⓐ, 1715⚒, 1742, 1815⚒, 1915⚒, 2015⚒, 2115⚒, 2215⚒.
MST– Monterey Salinas Transit.

Table 909 296 SAN FRANCISCO LOCAL SERVICES ♿ (ACT BART BG GGF GGT GL RW)

Local #### (C cl. only, 1.676m.), ferry and bus services operate in the San Francisco area as follows:

Alameda ∃ *(ACT)* (❖ km, US $: ❖). From San Francisco: 0500 and frequent to 0200, returning at 0500 and frequent to 0100. Journey: ❖. Also △ *(BG)* from San Francisco at 0630Ⓐ, 0735Ⓐ, 0840Ⓐ, 0925©, 1030Ⓐ, 1050©, 1215Ⓐ, 1310©, 1400Ⓐ, 1545©, 1615Ⓐ, 1710Ⓐ, 1715©, 1800Ⓐ, 1840©, 1910Ⓐ, 2020Ⓐ, returning at 0610Ⓐ, 0715Ⓐ, 0820Ⓐ, 0925Ⓐ, 1010©, 1050Ⓐ, 1120©, 1235Ⓐ, 1330©, 1420Ⓐ, 1605©, 1635Ⓐ, 1735©, 1740Ⓐ, 1820Ⓐ, 1900©, 1930Ⓐ, 2040Ⓐ.

Alcatraz △ *(RW)*. Regular tour/cruise sailings 0930-1615. Round-trip fares only (US $: 10.00).

Angel Island △ *(RW)* (❖ km, US $: 9.00L). From San Francisco: 1000, 1200©, 1400©, 1600©, returning at 1025Ⓐ, 1100©, 1300©, 1410Ⓐ, 1500©, 1640©. Journey: 20 mins.

Berkeley µ *(BART)* (❖ km, US $: 1.80). From San Francisco Embarcadero: 0418Ⓐ/0618⑥/0819† and frequent to 0019②-⑥/0020①⑦, returning at 0422Ⓐ/0608⑥/0756† and frequent to 0024. Journey: 25 mins.

Larkspur △ *(GGF)* (❖ km, US $: ❖). From San Francisco: 0840Ⓐ, 1045Ⓐ, 1245Ⓐ, 1445Ⓐ, 1545Ⓐ, 1645Ⓐ, 1725Ⓐ, 1835Ⓐ, returning at 0700Ⓐ, 0730Ⓐ, 0945Ⓐ, 1145Ⓐ, 1345Ⓐ, 1545Ⓐ, 1630Ⓐ, 1730Ⓐ. Journey: 1 hour.

Oakland µ *(BART)* (❖ km, US $: 1.55). From San Francisco Embarcadero: 0418Ⓐ/0618⑥/0819† and frequent to 0019②-⑥/0020①⑦, returning from Oakland 12th Street at 0439Ⓐ/0645⑥/0841† and frequent to 0041. Journey: 5 mins. Also ∃ *(ACT)* from San Francisco Transbay and Oakland, frequent service 24 hours each day.

Piedmont ∃ *(ACT)* (❖ km, US $: ❖). From Oakland: 0530⚒/0630† and frequent to 2359, returning at 0600⚒/0700† and frequent to 0030. Journey: ❖.

Richmond µ *(BART)* (❖ km, US $: 2.10). From San Francisco Embarcadero: 0418Ⓐ/0618⑥/0819† and frequent to 0019②-⑥/0020①⑦, returning at 0409Ⓐ/0615⑥/0811† and frequent to 0011. Journey: 35 mins.

San Leandro µ *(BART)* (❖ km, US $: 2.35). From San Francisco Embarcadero: 0607Ⓐ/0637⑥/*0819*† and frequent to *0019②-⑥/0020①⑦*, returning at 0415Ⓐ/0610⑥/*0816*† and frequent to 0020②-⑥/*0020①⑦*. Journey: 25 mins.

San Rafael ∃ *(GGT)* (❖ km, US $: ❖). From San Francisco: 0500 and frequent to 0203, returning at 0008, 0508 and frequent to 2238. Journey: 1½ hours.

Sausalito ∃ *(GGT)* (❖ km, US $: ❖). From San Francisco: 0409 and frequent to 0203, returning at 0458 and frequent to 2258. Journey: 40 mins. Also △ *(GGF)* from San Francisco: 0750Ⓐ, 1025Ⓐ, 1130©, 1145Ⓐ, 1300©, 1310Ⓐ, 1430©, 1435Ⓐ, 1600©, 1610Ⓐ, 1730, 1840Ⓐ, 1855©, 2000Ⓐ, returning at 0715Ⓐ, 0825Ⓐ, 1050©, 1105Ⓐ, 1215©, 1225Ⓐ, 1345©, 1355Ⓐ, 1515©, 1520Ⓐ, 1645, 1805Ⓐ, 1810©, 1920Ⓐ, and *RW* at 1040©, 1100Ⓐ, 1215Ⓐ, 1225©, 1335Ⓐ, 1350©, 1500Ⓐ, 1515©, 1645©, 1650Ⓐ, 1830©, 2025F, returning at 1120©, 1150Ⓐ, 1305, 1430, 1540Ⓐ, 1555©, 1725©, 1745Ⓐ, 1910©, 2000Ⓐ, 2050G, 2100H.

Tiburon ∃ *(GGT)* (❖ km, US $: ❖). From San Francisco: ❖, returning at ❖. Journey: ❖. Also △ *(RW)* from San Francisco: 0715Ⓐ, 0815Ⓐ, 1000©, 1100Ⓐ, 1200©, 1215Ⓐ, 1335Ⓐ, 1400©, 1500Ⓐ, 1600©, 1605Ⓐ, 1625Ⓐ, 1645©, 1650Ⓐ, 1725Ⓐ, 1815Ⓐ, 1830©, 1915Ⓐ, 2025F, returning at 0600Ⓐ, 0650Ⓐ, 0750Ⓐ, 0845Ⓐ, 1035©, 1125Ⓐ, 1235©, 1240Ⓐ, 1355Ⓐ, 1435©, 1520Ⓐ, 1705©, 1700Ⓐ, 1725Ⓐ, 1750, 1840Ⓐ, 1930©, 1945Ⓐ, 2110G, 2120H.

Vallejo △ *(BG)* (❖ km, US $: 7.50). From San Francisco: 0845, 1140©, 1415Ⓐ, 1430©, 1650©, 1655Ⓐ, 1940, returning at 0630Ⓐ, 1010, 1315©, 1545, 1830©, 1835Ⓐ. Journey: 1¼ hours.

Other services operate:

service *(ACT)* San Francisco-Berkeley-San Pablo and v.v. ❖ km. Journey: 1½ hours. Fare: US $: 1.75. ♿.
From San Francisco: 0600⚒/0800† and frequent to 2300.
From San Pablo: 0600⚒/0800† and frequent to 2300.

service *(GL)* San Francisco-Vallejo-Calistoga/Sacramento and v.v. *145* km. Journey: 2¼ hours. Fare: US $: 17.50.
From San Francisco: 0030, 0600, 0700, 0800, 1000, 1100, 1201, 1300, 1400, 1500, 1550**a**, 1600, 1645, 1700, 1730, 1800⑤⑥, 1815, 1930⑤⑥, 2000, 2100.
From Sacramento: 0200⑥, 0630, 0730, 0830, 0905**a**, 0930, 1030, 1130, 1230, 1330, 1430, 1530, 1630, 1700⑥⑦, 1730, 1830⑥⑦, 2030, 2215.

service *(GGT)* San Francisco-Petaluma-Santa Rosa and v.v. ❖ km. Journey: 1½ hours. Fare: US $: 1.50. ♿.
From San Francisco: 0500 and frequent (about hourly on ©) to 0203.
From Santa Rosa: 0406 and frequent (about hourly on ©) to 0100.

F– ⑤⑥ May 28-Sept. 4. G–⑤ May 28-Sept. 4.
H– ⑥ May 28-Sept. 4. L–Round trip fare.
a– To/from Calistoga, **not** Sacramento.
µ– By ####. ∃–By bus. △–By ferry.
ACT– AC Transit.
BART– Bay Area Rapid Transit.
BG– Blue & Gold Fleet.
GGF– Golden Gate Ferries.
GGT– Golden Gate Transit.
GL– Greyhound Lines.
RW– Red & White Fleet.

Table 910 PHOENIX - SAN DIEGO (GL)

US $	6343	6325	6341	6315	6353	6351	6363	6331	6364	6313	6349	km	296	6339	6841	6312	6326	6346	6366	6348	6314	6352	6332	6354
0.00	....	....	....	0930	....	....	....	1400	....	2245	....	0	d.**Phoenix**..............a.	....	....	1640	....	....	....	....	0210	....	0730	....
	....	....	....	1100	....	....	....	1535	....	0005	....	105	d.Gila Bend.............d.	....	....	1455	....	....	....	....	0050	....	0545	....
	....	....	....	1340	....	....	....	1825	....	0225	....	305	d.Yuma ....d.	....	....	1245	....	....	....	....	2245	....	0340	....
	0600	0900	0920	1400	1220	1420	1635	1845	1845	0245	0005	388	d.Calexico ....d.	0535	0850	0955	1440	1320	1835	1805	2120	0025	0110	0505
	0640	0925	1005	1430	1300	1500	1715	1910	1925	0310	0045	406	d.El Centro...............d.	0510	0820	0925	1420	1255	1815	1745	1950	0005	0040	0445
	0845	|	1150	|	1500	1645	1915	|	2240	|	0220		a. Indio....................d.	0305	0615	|	|	1040	|	1530	|	2215	|	0240
	1255	|	1555	|	1940	2050	2225	|	2359	|	0505		a. *Los Angeles*..........d.	0030	....	|	|	0530	|	1045	|	1800	|	2240
	....	1220	....	1700	....	....	....	2135	....	0540	....	611	a.**San Diego** ....d.	....	....	0645	1115	....	1535	....	1715	....	2210	....

GL– Greyhound Lines.

Table 915 SAN FRANCISCO - LOS ANGELES

GL IC ST

US $	296	km	GL 6747	GL 6863	GL 6753	GL 6869	GL 6843	GL 6741	GL 1447	GL 6837	GL 6729	GL 6751	GL 1423	GL 6725	GL 6771	GL 6733	GL 6779	GL 6881	GL 6879 ⑤⑥⑦	GL 6845	ST 103 ✉	IC ✉	GL 6806	GL 6833	GL 6705	GL 6777	GL 1421	GL 6731	GL 6759 ⑤⑦	GL 6899 ⑤⑦	GL 6897	GL 6887	GL 6885 ⑤⑦	GL 6889
0.00	San Francisco d.	0									0515			0700	0800					1000				0745	0830	1030		1030	1230	1130	1245	1040		
4.00	S Francisco Intl Apt d.	40																							0855	1055								
7.00	P Alto (Mtn View) d.	49																							0940	1135								
	Santa Cruz d.																								1105									
10.00	San Jose d.	76									0625			0820	0930								0850			1215		1145	1340					
	Gilroy d.										0710			0905	1015											1305		1230						
	Los Banos d.																									1415								
	Watsonville d.																								1130									
21.00	Salinas d.	170									0805			1000											1255			1325	1500					
23.00	Monterey d.	196																							1225									
37.00	San Luis Obispo d.	380						0730			1135			1335														1615	1750					
53.00	Santa Barbara d.	585	0545		0745			1045			1410	1410		1620		1620												1845						
	Ventura d.		0625		0825			1125				1450				1700																		
4.00	Oakland d.	11																		1035				0815						1201	1315	1110		
	Tracy d.																						1025	0950						1335		1250		
◇14.00	Sacramento d.	⊠130		0240a					0630				0855					0845	1040		0945		1215∫				1040						1535	1535
18.00	Stockton d.	⊠47		0345					0735				1015					0950			1045		1100				1159			1405			1635	1640
19.00	Modesto d.	166		0430					0820									1035			1130			1055			1255				1515	1350		1725
24.00	Merced d.	231		0515					0920									1130			1230			1150			1350					1445		
33.00	Fresno d.	310		0655		0515	0640		1100	1035							1145	1310	1415		1330	1330		1340		1600	1540				1740	1645		1930
	Visalia d.						0740																	1450										
44.00	Bakersfield d.	505				0750	0930			1315							1420	1520	1630					1700			1750				1950	1855		2135
59.00	Oxnard d.	640	0655		0850			1150				1515				1725												1930						
61.00	Glendale ★ d.	695													1625		1650																	
61.00	Malibu Beach d.	714																																
61.00	Santa Monica a.	734			1020							1645																						
61.00	Hollywood a.	730	0910			1020		1320		1600			1650			1855				1745				1930				2050	2145			2135		
61.00	Los Angeles a.	750	0940	1105	1045	1045	1215	1340	1510	1625	1610	1520	1725	1840	1700	1915	1720	1755	1905	1820		1730		1955			2015	2110	2205		2215	2205	2305	0005

296	GL 6871	GL 6703	GL 8392	GL 6870 n⑤⑦	GL 6867	GL 6735	GL 6781	GL 6841	GL 6909 ⑤⑥⑦	GL 6839	GL 6709	GL 6875	GL 6891	GL 6847	GL 6877	GL 1439	GL 6849	GL 6739	GL 6743
San Francisco d.		1330		1515	1425	1500	1720			1645	1810		1810	2130			2200	2000	2200
San Francisco Intl. Apt. d.		1356									1835								
Palo Alto (Mountain View) d.		1445									1920								
Santa Cruz d.											2050								
San Jose d.		1510	1445			1615	1900		1815									2120	2315
Gilroy d.						1700	1950											2205	0001
Los Banos d.							21000												
Watsonville d.											2115								
Salinas d.						1805					2230							2305	
Monterey a.											2200								
San Luis Obispo d.						2135												0155	
Santa Barbara d.						0010												0415	
Ventura d.																			
Oakland d.				1530	1455					1730			1835	2200			2230		
Tracy d.			1630		1625				1940	1915			2015						
Sacramento d.	1305		1825∫					1730	2115∫			1830			2015	2250			
Stockton d.	1415		1700					1850	2020			1930	2045		2135	2350			
Modesto d.	1520				1735			1950		2010		2020			2220				
Merced d.	1620				1835			2115		2105		2110			2320				
Fresno d.	1805				2015		2230	2245		2245		2245			0045				
Visalia d.					2115														
Bakersfield d.	2055				2315			0055		0115		0115			0320				
Oxnard d.																			
Glendale ★ d.	2320																		0550
Malibu Beach d.																			
Santa Monica a.																			
Hollywood a.				2240	0135										0555		0540s		
Los Angeles a.	2359			2300	0200	0200				0405				0520	0620	0615	0600	0610	0620

296	GL 6894	GL 8393	GL 8372	GL 6704	GL 6838	GL 6850	GL 6774	GL 6840	GL 6742	GL 6908 ⑤⑥⑦	GL 6726	GL 1436	GL 6896 ex②③④	GL 6858	IC ✉	GL 6770	GL 6809	ST 102 ✉	GL 6886	GL 6724	GL 6766	GL 6892	GL 1440	GL 6844
Los Angeles d.					0115	0115		0330	0330		0625	0700		0700	0930	0830			0830	1000	1020	1030	1015	1100
Hollywood d.											0650			0725					0855		1045			1120
Santa Monica d.																				1030				
Malibu Beach d.																								
Glendale ★ d.												0725				0855								
Oxnard d.											0835									1201	1210			
Bakersfield d.					0410	0410		0610				1010		1040					1220			1310	1255	
Visalia d.						0540		0745																
Fresno d.					0700	0720	0915	0930				1240		1345	1330			1400	1450			1535	1520	
Merced d.					0825	0830		1055				1400		1500				1505	1600					
Modesto d.					0930	0930		1201				1455		1610				1600	1700			1725		
Stockton d.	0700	0810			1025			1300		1350		1535	1615				1725	1640	1740					
Sacramento a.		0650∫			1120			1410		1230∫		1645					1600∫	1745	1845				1840	
Tracy d.	0730	0840				1020				1420			1645				1755					1805		
Oakland a.	0905					1205							1830	1830								1935		1835
Ventura d.											0855													
Santa Barbara d.									0540		0955									1300	1330			
San Luis Obispo d.									0840		1325										1610			
Monterey d.				0830																				
Salinas d.				0755					1210		1640										1900			
Watsonville d.				0925																				
Los Banos d.							1045																	
Gilroy d.							1150		1250		1720										1940			
San Jose d.		1010	1030				1250		1345	1545	1815					1610	1930				2030			
Santa Cruz d.				1000																				
Palo Alto (Mountain View) a.				1125			1310																	
San Francisco Intl. Apt. a.				1210					1435		1905													
San Francisco a.	0930		1130	1225		1225	1415		1500		1930		1850	1850		1720					2130	1955		1905

296	GL 6710	GL 6820	GL 6780	GL 6842	GL 6734	GL 6730	GL 1420	GL 6874 ⑤⑦	GL 6866	GL 6888 ⑤⑦	GL 6754	GL 6740	GL 6852	GL 6732	GL 6822	GL 1442	GL 6872	GL 1424	GL 6834	GL 6756	GL 6868	GL 6740	GL 6848	GL 6876	GL 1428	GL 6752
Los Angeles d.		1230		1230	1245	1410	1330	1430	1430	1715	1630	1740	1700	1945	1805	1900	2055	2130	2010	2115	2210	2210	2300	2300	2315	0045
Hollywood d.		1255			1310				1450		1700		1730	2010	1835		2120				2235	2235	2325			
Santa Monica d.																										
Malibu Beach d.																										
Glendale ★ d.				1245			1355																		0140	
Oxnard d.					1455						1850			2155								2355				
Bakersfield d.		1555		1555				1710	1750	2010			2045		2135	2140	0005	0025			0115					
Visalia d.													2220													
Fresno d.		1825	1830	1850				1905	2010	2220			2325		2350	0001	0220	0235	0235		0345					
Merced d.		1940		2005						2325											0500					
Modesto d.		2035		2100						0020						0150			0425		0600					
Stockton d.		2120					2045			0100						0230					0645				0605	
Sacramento a.		2225					2140			0155						0325		0540			0740				0715	
Tracy d.				2140																						
Oakland a.				2315															0605				0640			
Ventura d.											1910															
Santa Barbara d.					1555	1625					1950	2020		2255						2325		0035				
San Luis Obispo d.						1920						2235								0210						
Monterey d.	1715																									
Salinas d.	1635					2220														0500						0715
Watsonville d.	1800																									
Los Banos d.			2030																							
Gilroy d.			2140																	0540				0515s		
San Jose d.			2225			2345														0615				0610		0840
Santa Cruz d.	1840																									
Palo Alto (Mountain View) a.	1950																									
San Francisco Intl. Apt. a.	2035																			0730						
San Francisco a.	2100			2335		0045													0625	0800			0710	0720		0950

★– Burbank. ✉–Apr. 1-Jan. 6. ◇–Fare ex Modesto. ⊠–Km ex Modesto. GL–Greyhound Lines. IC–Intercalifornias. ST–Sierra Trailways.
∫– Via Stockton a– Non stop on⑤ arrives 1000

Table 920 ALASKA — ADL AYM HBL SEW VAB

US $			ADL	ADL		196			ADL	ADL
			002A	002					001	001A
			T	U	km	↓ ↑			U	T
99.00	....	....	....	0900	0	d.**Fairbanks** ....a.	....	....	1730	....
75.00	....	....	....	1430	195	d.Denali Park ....d.	....	....	1330	....
25.00	....	....	1730	│	392	d. Talkeetna ....a.	....	....	│	1030
0.00	....	....	2000	2000	572	a.**Anchorage** ....d.	....	....	0800	0800
US $	R	R				396 AYM	R	R		
	①③⑤	②⑤⑦			km	↓ ↑	①③⑤	②⑤⑦		
0.00	....	0800	....	....	0	d.**Fairbanks** ....a.	1900	....	....	....
49.00	....	1100	....	....	158	d.Delta ....d.	1645	....	....	....
62.00	1100	1330	....	....		a. **Tok** ....d.	1400	1530	....	....
	1430	....	....	....		d.Glenallen ....d.	....	1230	....	....
140.00	1800	....	....	....	586	a.**Valdez**...............d.	....	0800	....	....
US $		AYM	HBL	SEW		695	SEW		HBL	AYM
		W	✡		km	↓ ↑			✡	W
0.00	....	0730	1245	1430	0	d.**Anchorage** ....a.	1200	....	1910	2300
55.00	....	0915	│	│	80	d.Portage ◇.........d.	│	....	│	2100
55.00	....	│	│	│		a. Whittier ◇.......d.	│	....	│	│
59.00	....	1115	│	1730	212	a.**Seward** ....d.	0900	....	│	1900
38.00	....	....	1840	....	365	a. Homer...........d.	....	....	1320	....
US $	BCK		VAB	AYM		396	VAB	AYM		BCK
	V▣			2				1		V▣
	ex⑦		ex①	V	km	↓ ↑	ex①	Q		ex⑦
0.00	....	....	0900	0800	0	d.**Valdez**...............a.	1715	1800	....	....
A49.00	1700	....	│	│		a. McCarthy....d.	│	│	....	1130
A14.00	1930	....	│	│		d. Chitina ....d.	│	│	....	0830
	│	....	│	│	169	d.Copper Center...d.	│	│	....	│
49.00	2045	....	1330	│	184	d.Glenallen ....d.	1330	│	....	0715
89.00	....	....	1700	1800	412	a.**Anchorage** ....d.	0930	0800	....	....
R.T.			007			495 ADL		007		
US $					km	↓ ↑				
495.00	....	....	★	....	0	d.**Prudhoe Bay**....a.	....	★	....	....
	....	....	★	....		d.Wiseman ....d.	....	★	....	....
	....	....	★	....		d.Fairbanks ....d.	....	★	....	....
0.00	....	....	★	....		a.**Anchorage** ....d.	....	★	....	....

A–Fare ex Glenallen. **Q**–May 21-Sept. 16. **R**–May 15-Sept. 19. **T**–May 1-31. **U**–June 1-Sept. 21. **V**–May 23-Sept. 17. **W**–May 15-Sept. 20, also ⑥⑦ Sept. 10-25. ◇–#### service only (see Table **272**). ✡–May 1-Sept. 30. ★–Special 7-day excursion service; from Anchorage on June 18, July 18, Aug. 15. *ADL*–Alaska-Denali Transit. *AYM*–Alaskon Express. *BCK*–Backcountry Connection. *HBL*–Homer Bus Line (Kenai Peninsula Bus Lines) *SEW*–Seward Bus Line. *VAB*–Valdez-Anchorage Bus Line.

Table 921 WHITEHORSE - SKAGWAY — ADB AYM SD

US $	ADB	SD		AYM		195	AYM	SD	ADB	ADB
		Q						Q		
	♣Π	♣		P♣	km	↓ ↑	P♣	♣	♣Π	♣ℵ
0.00	1200	1400	....	1630	0	d.**Whitehorse**.......a.	1130	1230	1930	....
21.00	1430	1500	....	1730r	69	d.Carcross............d.	1030r	1130	1620	1750
53.00	1530	1600	....	1830	179	a.**Skagway**...........d.	0730	0830	1400	1530

P–May 15-Sept. 17. **Q**–Runs daily May 1-Sept. 30; daily subject to a minimum of 3 passengers and road conditions Oct. 1-Apr. 30. Π–Daily in summer; ①② only in winter, subject to road conditions. ℵ–Runs on ①② only, in winter only, subject to road conditions, and only if previous 1400 trip unable to operate because of weather conditions. *ADB*–Alaska Direct Bus Line Inc. *AYM*–Alaskon Express. *SD*–Sourdough Co.

Table 922 ANCHORAGE - HAINES — ADB AYM NWS

US $	AYM	NWS	NWS	ADB		296	NWS	ADB		AYM
	6									7
	♣	R	R	♣			R	♣		♣
	S	⑤	①③	ϱ	km	↓ ↑	①③⑤	ϒ		Q
0.00	0730	....	....	0600	0	d.**Anchorage** ....a.	....	2300	....	1930
57.00	1230	....	....	1100	301	d.Glenallen...........d.	....	1845	....	1500r
0.00	│	....	....	│	⊠409	d. Valdez.............a.	....	│	....	│
	│	....	....	│	⊠247	d. Copper Center d.	....	│	....	│
	0800	....	....	*0900*		d. **Fairbanks** ..a.	....	*1900*	....	*1900*
	1100	....	....	*1200*		d. Delta...........d.	....	*1700*	....	*1645*
102.00	1530	....	....	1430	528	a. Tok ....d.	....	1500	....	1100
	1600	....	....	1430		d. Tok ....d.	....	1500	....	1100
▼126.00	1930	....	....	1830	708	a. Beaver Creek ■ d.	....	1245	....	0845
	0900	1415	1615	1830		d. Beaver Creek ■ a.	1400	1245	....	1930
◇35.00	│	1715	1845	2100	884	d.Burwash Landing d.	1120	1045	....	│
◇33.00	1230	1800	1900	│		d.Destruction Bay.d.	1100	│	....	1700
◇30.00	│	1830	1930	│		d.Kluane Park ▶..d.	1030	│	....	│
165.00	1430	1930	2030	2215	1018	d.Haines Junction.d.	0930	0845	....	1500
200.00	*1830*	│	│	│	1250	a. **Haines**..........d.	│	│	....	*0815*
190.00	1630	2130	2245	2400		a.**Whitehorse**.......d.	0700	0700	....	1200

Q– ②④⑦ May 17-Sept. 18.
R– May 1-Aug. 30. **S**–②⑤⑦ May 14-Sept. 16.
ϱ– Runs on ③⑤⑦ in summer, ⑦ in winter.
⊠– Km ex Tok. ▼–Fare ex Valdez. ◇–Fare ex Whitehorse in CA $.
▶– Sheep Mountain. ϒ–Runs on ③⑤⑦ in summer, ③ in winter.
ADB– Alaska Direct Bus Line Inc. *AYM*–Alaskon Express.
NWS– North West Stage Lines.

Table 930 SELECTED HAWAIIAN BUS SERVICES

HILO 296
Hilo-Keaukaha and v.v. ❖ km. Journey: ❖. Fare: US $: ❖.
Hilo dep.: ❖. Keaukaha dep.: ❖.
Hilo-Volcano House and v.v. ❖ km. Journey: ❖. Fare: US $: ❖.
Hilo dep.: ❖. Volcano House dep.: ❖.

HONOLULU 495
Honolulu-Aiea and v.v. *8* km. Journey: ❖. Fare: US $: ❖.
Honolulu dep.: *MTL* ❖. Aiea dep.: *MTL* ❖.
Honolulu-Ewa and v.v. ❖ km. Journey: ❖. Fre: US $: ❖.
Honolulu dep.: *MTL* ❖. Ewa dep.: *MTL* ❖.
Honolulu-Kailua and v.v. ❖ km. Journey: ❖. Fare: US $: ❖.
Honolulu dep.: *MTL* ❖. Kailua dep.: *MTL* ❖.
Honolulu-Kaneohe and v.v. ❖ km. Journey: ❖. Fare: US $: ❖.
Honolulu dep.: *MTL* ❖. Kaneohe dep.: *MTL* ❖.
Honolulu-Lanikai and v.v. ❖ km. Journey: ❖. Fare: US $: ❖.
Honolulu dep.: *MTL* ❖. Lanikai dep.: *MTL* ❖.
Honolulu-Pearl City and v.v. ❖ km. Journey: ❖. Fare: US $: ❖.
Honolulu dep.: *MTL* ❖. Pearl City dep.: *MTL* ❖.
Honolulu-Wahiawa and v.v. ❖ km. Journey: ❖. Fare: US $: ❖.
Honolulu dep.: *MTL* ❖. Wahiawa dep.: *MTL* ❖.
Honolulu-Waialua and v.v. ❖ km. Journey: ❖. Fare: US $: ❖.
Honolulu dep.: *MTL* ❖. Waialua dep.: *MTL* ❖.
Honolulu-Waipahu and v.v. ❖ km. Journey: ❖. Fare: US $: ❖.
Honolulu dep.: *MTL* ❖. Waipahu dep.: *MTL* ❖.

WAILUKU 296
Wailuku-Kahului and v.v. ❖ km. Journey: ❖. Fare: US $: ❖.
Wailuku dep.: ❖. Kahului dep.: ❖.
Wailuku-Lahaina and v.v. ❖ km. Journey: ❖. Fare: US $: ❖.
Wailuku dep.: ❖. Lahaina dep.: ❖.
Wailuku-Paia and v.v. ❖ km. Journey: ❖. Fare: US $: ❖.
Wailuku dep.: ❖. Paia dep.: ❖.

MTL– MTL Inc (The Bus).

INDEX

READER SURVEY

If you enjoyed using this book, or even if you didn't, please help us improve future editions by taking part in our reader survey. Every returned form will be acknowledged, and to show our appreciation we will give you £1 off your next purchase of a Thomas Cook guidebook. Just take a few minutes to complete and return this form to us.

When did you buy this book?

Where did you buy it? (Please give town/city and if possible name of retailer)

When did you/do you intend to travel in North America?

Did you/ Will you travel mainly . . . ❑ by train? ❑ by bus?
For how long (approx.)?
How many people in your party?

Which cities, national parks and other locations did you/do you intend mainly to visit?

Did you/will you travel on:
❑ An Amtrak Pass? ❑ A VIA Rail Pass? ❑ A Greyhound Pass?
❑ Other passes or tickets (please specify)?

Did you/do you intend to use this book:
❑ For planning your trip? ❑ During the trip itself? ❑ Both?
Did you/do you intend also to purchase any other guidebooks/maps for your trip? If so, which?

Have you used any other Thomas Cook guidebooks in the past? If so, which?

Please rate the following features of *North American Rail and Bus Guide 1996* for their value to you (Circle VU for 'very useful', U for 'useful', NU for 'little or no use'):

Travelling North America by rail on pages 4–9	VU	U	NU
Travelling North America by bus on pages 11–12	VU	U	NU
Flights and air passes on pages 13–14	VU	U	NU
Major cities on pages 15–60	VU	U	NU
The timetables on pages 65–138	VU	U	NU

Please use this space to tell us about any features that in your opinion could be changed, improved, or added in future editions of the book, or any other comments you would like to make concerning the book:

Your age category: ❑ 21-30 ❑ 31-40 ❑ 41–50 ❑ over 50

Your name:

Mr/Mrs/Miss/Ms: First name or initials:

Last name:

Your full address (please include postal or zip code):

Your daytime telephone number:

Please detach this page and send it to: The Project Editor, *North American Rail and Bus Guide 1996*, Thomas Cook Publishing, PO Box 227, Peterborough PE3 8BQ, United Kingdom.

We will be pleased to send you details of how to claim your discount upon receipt of this questionnaire.